CREATING CHANGE™

CREATING CHANGE™

SEXUALITY, PUBLIC POLICY, AND CIVIL RIGHTS

EDITED BY

John D'Emilio

William B. Turner

Urvashi Vaid

ST. MARTIN'S PRESS   NEW YORK

Design by Richard Oriolo

www.stmartins.com

Library of Congress Cataloging-in-Publication Data

Creating change : sexuality, public policy, and civil rights / [edited
by] John D'Emilio, William B. Turner, Urvashi Vaid.—1st ed.
    p.   cm.
Includes bibliographical references.
ISBN 0-312-24375-8
    1. Gay liberation movement—United States—History.
2. Gay rights— United States— History.   3. Gays—Govern-
ment policy—United States—History.   I. D'Emilio, John.
II. Turner, William B. (William Benjamin), 1964–   III. Vaid,
Urvashi.

HQ76.8.U5 C74   2000
305.9'0664'0973—dc21   00-031718

First Edition: October 2000

10   9   8   7   6   5   4   3   2   1

CONTENTS

A MERE GENERATION AGO, IN 1966, A *TIME* MAGAZINE essay described homosexuality as "a pathetic little second-rate substitute for reality, a pitiable flight from life." Among that era's more notable representations of gay life were Mart Crowley's play *The Boys in the Band,* in which a group of gay men cry in their cocktails and wound each other with lacerating wit, and the Hollywood version of Lillian Hellman's *The Children's Hour,* which ended with an unhappy lesbian hanging from the rafters.

Today, three decades later, Asheville, North Carolina, has a gay men's chorus. Oklahoma City, Oklahoma, boasts its own gay newspaper. Smiling lesbians and their babies appear on the cover of *People.* The Amoco Corporation and Chevron Oil, along with scores of other corporations, offer domestic partnership benefits to same-sex couples, while *The New York Times* editorializes in favor of gay marriage. The United States Senate has come within a single vote of passing a measure that would outlaw, not gay sex, but antigay discrimination. Both President Clinton and Vice President Gore have been the featured speaker at black-tie fund-raising dinners of gay rights organizations. And, in March 1999, residents in every state in the union plus Puerto Rico organized in their capitals for lesbian, gay, bisexual, and transgender civil rights in a series of events called "Equality Begins at Home."

Over the last generation the change in the texture of gay and lesbian life and in its relationship to American society has been extraordinary. The shift has been both dramatic and unexpected, and at least as extensive as the change witnessed, over comparable periods of time, in race or gender relations. Remarkably, it has occurred at the same time as an apparently deepening conservative hold upon national and state politics.

Think for a minute about some signal moments in the life of queer America. The Stonewall riots in New York City, the event most often used to mark the birth of a gay liberation movement, occurred only a few months after the inauguration of Richard Nixon. Twelve years later, Ronald Reagan entered the White House and a Republican Senate considered the overtly antigay Family Protection Act, just as the first cluster of AIDS cases among gay men was discovered. In 1995 a national debate over same-sex marriage erupted even as conservative ideologues in the Republican Party assumed control over both houses of Congress. Somehow lesbians and gay men have managed to effect a social transformation of gargantuan scope in the face of dauntingly unfavorable political conditions.

How has this happened? Changes in law, public policy, and institutions are provoked in many different ways. Big events, such as war, economic depression, or natural disasters, can so destabilize the normal workings of society that avenues for change are opened. Strong leaders can arouse public sentiment and forge a political consensus that supports innovation. Sometimes ordinary individuals, by their courage and determination, can inspire others to act as well, creating a swell of human energy that pushes relentlessly for change. New ideas can sweep through a society, provoking reappraisals of how things should be done. In a democracy, rivalries between political parties, the clash of ideologies, or competing interest groups can incite pressures that modify policies or revise the law. Bureaucracies themselves produce change, although usually in ways that are slow and deliberate enough that change comes incrementally and is not readily apparent.

The changes in this book deal primarily with the public-policy arena of civil rights—the basic proposition in the United States that all citizens are equal before the law, and that we enjoy certain immunities from the power of potentially tyrannical majoritarian government. The exact meaning of civil rights has varied depending on the minority in question. The group that gave us the definitive civil rights movement, African-Americans, fought for over a century for the right to vote, the right to equal education, the right to sit unmolested in a restaurant and eat a meal. They used the federal courts to battle segregation, but won their greatest victories by engaging in nonviolent civil disobedience—the simple, but dangerous, refusal to abide by unjust laws requiring segregation of the races. Often at great personal cost, large numbers of African-Americans created changes in public policy in order to live their lives as full citizens of our new republic. Lesbian, gay, bisexual, and transgender activists have borrowed from their arsenal, using sit-ins, lawsuits, and marches on Washington, D.C.

But the content of civil rights struggles has looked very different around matters of race and sexual identity. Among the changes that lesbian, gay, bisexual, and transgender civil rights activists of whatever color have wrought is a change in the very meaning of the term *civil rights*. For sexual minorities, while the immorality and injustice of invidious discrimination remain the same, its specific manifestations, and therefore the most effective means of resistance, are different. Few lesbian, gay, bisexual, or transgender persons face serious impediments to their right to vote, or to receive service in a restaurant, on the basis of their sexual or gender identity. Most of us can hide. But this advantage for avoiding the daily humiliations of overt prejudice and discrimination exacts other costs. We do face threats to our right to education, although not from segregated schools. Rather, Jamie Nabozny of Wisconsin sued his school after suffering harassment and attacks to the point of physical injury requiring surgery—all while school administrators did nothing. We do face denial of basic public services that others take for granted. In Washington, D.C., one transgender person died recently when emergency medical technicians refused to treat her after an accident.

How do we organize invisible persons? Especially since the 1960s, social movements have emerged as critical agents of change. Sometimes based on identity (the black freedom struggle, the women's movement, the rights of the disabled), and sometimes focused on an urgent issue (environmentalism, the antiwar movement), they mobilize masses of people to act collectively. One could make a compelling argument that since 1960, social movements of the left or the right have been the key levers of change in the realm of politics and social policy in the United States.

Creating Change traces the work and gauges the impact of the gay and lesbian movement in the generation since Stonewall. It explores a particular, though critically significant, arena in which change has occurred—the world of public policy making, especially at the level of the federal government—and scrutinizes the who, how, why, and what of it. Our contributors look at presidential action (and inaction); judicial decisions about the civil rights of sexual minorities; the operations of the federal bureaucracy; and the receptivity (or not) of the two political parties to the queer agitators within them. They examine a broad range of issues that have roused gay, lesbian, bisexual, and transgender Americans to action and assess the extent of change. And they survey some of the contexts that have shaped an environment in which activism can succeed—international feminism, movement organizations, and mass marches in the nation's capital.

A number of important themes emerge. Perhaps first and foremost is the power of citizens to propel change forward. Accounts written by participants in the struggles they describe—Frank Kameny's discussion of federal employment and security clearances; Jean O'Leary's and Rich Tafel's respective chapters on the Democratic and Republican Parties—suggest that even in the face of strong resistance, determined activists can find allies, exploit openings, recover from defeats, and return for the next fight. In the space of a decade, AIDS activists were able to move from a position of helpless outsiders with barely a clue as to what to do into the role of major players in the shaping of national policy. Lesbian health advocates were able to build on the experience they had accumulated in a grassroots self-help movement and prod government bureaucrats to take small, but nonetheless groundbreaking, steps to address the medical needs of lesbian and bisexual women.

One key to success seems to be the recognition that change often comes incrementally, sometimes involving two steps forward and one step back, so that success becomes a matter of staying power. In her treatment of parenting issues, Nancy Polikoff discusses small but subtle alterations in the overall prospects for lesbian and gay parents. Even as judges continue to hand down hostile decisions, some states have seen significant movement away from the homophobic assumptions of a generation ago. Over time, the arguments that have led to legislative repeal or judicial scrutiny of sodomy laws have shifted, and the process has continued, even in the face of the unfavorable Supreme Court decision *Bowers v. Hardwick* that Arthur Leonard describes. Chai Feldblum discusses more than two decades of lobbying work for a federal anti-discrimination bill. In the mid-1970s, there were barely a handful of cosponsors and supporters; by the mid-1990s, the Employment Non-Discrimination Act (ENDA) received 49 votes in the Senate. In between were many congressional hearings, many meetings between elected officials and their constituents, and many years of patient work creating coalition partners within the civil rights community. And more hearings, meetings, and partners will be needed before ENDA becomes law.

The flip side of the notion of incremental change is the relatively long history of agitation that the essays in this volume reveal. For most Americans, perhaps even for most lesbian and gay Americans, issues of sexual identity seemed to spring suddenly into public view in the 1990s, in the wake of the 1992 election, the "gays in the military" debate of 1993, and the media fascination with "gay marriage." But William Turner lets us see how the gay politics of the Clinton presidency had a precedent of sorts in the administration of Jimmy Carter in the 1970s, while O'Leary reminds us that the first discussion of gay issues at a national political convention happened in 1972. David Chambers tells us that some activists were agitating for the right to marry in the early 1970s, and Nancy Polikoff describes a whole generation of court battles over the right to parent. Long before the brutal killing of Matthew Shepard in Wyoming, queer activists were forming local organizations to protect themselves against homophobic violence. David Wertheimer describes the activities, local and national, that have brought homophobic hate-violence into the realm of public policy debates.

"Coalition" is a concept that recurs frequently in *Creating Change*. It figures prominently in Feldblum's analysis of the history of the civil rights bill. It makes its way into David Wertheimer's account of the building of an antiviolence movement, and the chapter by Tom Burrows describing the family politics of the 1970s. As John-Manuel Andriote suggests, the AIDS movement of the 1980s needed to mobilize a broad range of coalition partners in order to win substantial funding to fight the epidemic. Within Congress, Barney Frank was able to win the elimination of exclusion provisions in U.S. immigration law because he was a respected member of a broad coalition intent on a major reformation of immigration policy. Yet coalitions are not simple matters. The Congressional Black Caucus has been the most consistent supporter of gay and lesbian issues on Capitol Hill, yet as Cathy Cohen reveals, mobilization of African-American communities and leadership around AIDS has proven difficult. The experience of fighting for the Children of the Rainbow Curriculum in New York City (see chapter 12) suggests that while coalitions can and have formed across lines of race, class, and sexuality, holding those coalitions together after a particular crisis passes remains an elusive goal.

Creating Change also, we think, gives some sense of the complexity and variety of strategies required to rewrite law and remake public policy. Barney Frank argues passionately for the proposition that change demands an active engagement with the political process and requires having individuals well positioned on the inside to shepherd proposals along.

At the same time, friends in high places are not enough. Rimmerman's analysis of Clinton's policies is highly critical of the president, and Plumb describes how, even with a more open federal bureaucracy in the 1990s, lesbian health advocates had to push hard. Frank himself acknowledges that the legislative work he was able to do on the inside was dependent on the broader cultural and social changes that the lesbian and gay movement had provoked. Nancy Polikoff demonstrates effectively that unfavorable decisions from the courts can coexist with a social climate in which many gay, lesbian, bisexual, and transgender parents feel less beleaguered.

Although not the major focus of this book, the issue of climate, of the context in which policy gets debated and laws get made, is the place where we have chosen to end. For underlying all of the changes described by our contributors is the work of a broad mass of activists willing to commit some of their time and energy toward remaking the world in which they live. Some of this effort occurs transnationally, in the kind of work that Charlotte Bunch and Claudia Hinojosa describe in their chapter on lesbians and international feminism.

Sometimes it occurs in the streets, in marches on Washington where the massing of individuals from across the country sparks a sense of collective power that, later, has profound effects on community mobilization. And sometimes it occurs within the world that a social movement creates—such as the organizational environment that John D'Emilio describes in his analysis of the history of the National Gay and Lesbian Task Force, or the intramovement debates about transgender inclusion that Phyllis Frye recounts.

Finally, if the stories in this collection reveal anything to us, they alert us to the unpredictability of the future. The readers of *Time* magazine in 1966 could hardly have expected that, three decades later, the rights of sexual minorities would be debated and discussed in national, state, and local politics. Nor can we know with any confidence which of the many issues discussed in this book will continue to agitate the body politic, and which newer ones will come to dominate public discourse. Will gender identity come to replace sexual orientation as the lens through which these issues of inequality and oppression get debated? Will a civil rights framework within the United States come to seem less compelling than a framework of international human rights? Will a single court decision suddenly end the long history of sodomy laws? Will a favorable court decision put to rest the tumultuous politics of same-sex marriage?

What we can predict is that the question of creating change will continue to resonate long after any of the particular issues discussed in this volume have been resolved. Hence, the experiences that are chronicled in these pages and the insights that can be extracted from them should compel our attention.

Putting together a volume like this is a labor of love—and requires lots of labor. We want to thank all of our contributors for responding so graciously to our harassing E-mails and telephone calls, as we prodded them to make their meaning clearer or their argument stronger. Jed Mattes, our agent, has been encouraging of this project from start to finish. Keith Kahla, our editor at St. Martin's, maintained his patience when we failed to meet his deadlines. Sally Kohn has provided a huge amount of editorial assistance and, unlike the rest of us, has met every deadline we set for her. Without her, we might still be assembling this collection.

Finally, we take inspiration from the women and men, past and present, of the National Gay and Lesbian Task Force, many of whom we have worked with closely for a number of years. Out title comes from NGLTF's annual conference, an event that has created more change than any of us can keep track of. May it—and all of us—continue to make change for many years to come.

PART I

VIEWS OF THE TOP

MIRROR IMAGES: LESBIAN/GAY CIVIL RIGHTS IN THE CARTER AND REAGAN ADMINISTRATIONS

WILLIAM B. TURNER

O N MARCH 3, 1980, ROBERT STRAUSS, CHAIR OF THE Carter/Mondale Presidential Committee, wrote to Charles Brydon and Lucia Valeska of the National Gay Task Force in response to a questionnaire from the Task Force asking about Carter's record on lesbian and gay civil rights issues. Strauss closed his letter with the statement that "the President's record shows that he has taken steps, in his first three years in office, to address most of the public issues articulated historically within the gay community. I believe this record warrants your continued support."[1] One might be tempted to dismiss this statement as election-year hyperbole, especially given that for the Carter administration to have addressed most of the gay community's issues between 1977 and 1980 would mean the political equivalent of going from zero to sixty in three seconds flat.

Work on lesbian/gay civil rights during Jimmy Carter's administration reflected both the impressive gains of the civil rights revolution during the 1950s and 1960s, and the peculiar relationship between lesbian/gay civil rights claims and the tradition of civil rights activism and policy that emerged in response to discrimination against African-Americans. On one hand, the fledgling lesbian/gay civil rights movement would not have enjoyed substantial access to the White House had their African-American and feminist predecessors not paved the way by articulating the logic of civil rights such that lesbian/gay activists could invoke it for their own issues. Carter was the first Democratic president elected after 1969—the year in which the Stonewall riots precipitated a burst of militant lesbian/gay activism and organizing, resulting, among other things, in the founding of the National Gay Task Force in 1973; and the year in which Richard Nixon, having won election by promising law and order on behalf of the "silent majority" of Americans who had grown suspicious of the various protests, including civil rights protests, was first inaugurated. Any Democrat elected in 1976 would have governed under the shadow of the expectations that Lyndon Johnson had created by signing the 1964 Civil Rights Act and the 1965 Voting Rights Act, and Carter was personally sympathetic to the basic goals of the civil rights revolution.

On the other hand, discrimination against lesbians and gay men remained a relatively abstract proposition to most people, including President Carter. That the logic of prohibiting discrimination against African-Americans and women should also entail prohibiting discrimination against lesbians and gay men was by no means obvious to him. It was obvious to several members of his White House staff, however, and in the name of nondiscrimination Carter allowed members of his staff, and of executive branch agencies, to work hard in cooperation with lesbian/gay activists. For all their dedication and hard work, the leaders of the NGTF in the late 1970s did not command the political clout necessary for the kind of access that they enjoyed to the Carter White House. Their extraordinary success depended on intelligent effort, but it also depended on historical circumstance in the form of Carter's commitment not only to the basic logic of the civil rights revolution, but to an open and honest federal government in the wake of the Watergate scandal.

So there is a substantial element of truth to Strauss's claim. Clearly, Carter did not single-handedly solve the problems of America's lesbians and gay men in the space of three years. Nor did most lesbians and gay men seem to appreciate what Carter's administration did for them. But the point remains that, even as Carter himself rarely mentioned lesbian/gay rights issues, members of his White House staff poured a remarkable amount of energy into addressing complaints of discrimination from representatives of the National Gay Task Force and other lesbian/gay civil rights activists.

This is the point on which the administration of Jimmy Carter (1977–81) and that of his successor, Ronald Reagan (1981–89), differed most sharply for lesbians and gay men. Neither president spoke much about lesbian/gay issues. In contrast to Carter's mostly sympathetic staff, however, White House aides under Reagan were indifferent at best, and in some cases actively hostile, to the claims of lesbian/gay civil rights activists. In this respect, the Carter and Reagan administrations were mirror images of each other: two presidents remaining largely silent on the issue while their two staffs ranged in opposite directions behind them. Reagan's attack on "big government" focused heavily on economic regulations, but in practice he also significantly reduced enforcement of existing civil rights laws. But because those laws did not include sexual orientation as a protected category, official White House indifference, even hostility, might have had little concrete effect on lesbian/gay civil rights activism. Reagan actually served as something of a moderating influence on the conservative extremists who supported him, often paying lip service to their positions on social issues while doing little or nothing to bring their policy preferences about.

But lesbians and gay men will always remember the Reagan administration primarily for its response, or lack of response, to acquired immune deficiency syndrome (AIDS), which doctors in the United States began to recognize in the form of unusual infections in otherwise healthy gay men during 1981. AIDS provides an interesting test case of Ronald Reagan's conservatism. To the end of his second term, Reagan and his White House aides apparently remained convinced that they really had done all that they should have done in responding to the new epidemic. Overwhelming evidence indicates that, in the name of smaller, cheaper government, the Reagan administration persistently and willfully obstructed the efforts of members of Congress to provide, and of public health officials to use, adequate resources for research on and treatment of AIDS. White House staffers, however, repeatedly emphasized the claim that they intended to deal with AIDS as a public health issue, thus removing it from the realm of politics.

The consistently ideological tone of the administration's AIDS policies, and the leadership that conservative activists such as Secretary of Education William Bennett and his protégé Gary Bauer exercised on the issue, gave a distinctly politicized character to those policies from the perspective of most lesbians and gay men, activists or not. The civil rights revolution had made the language of discrimination and equal opportunity commonplace in American life, but never before had that language applied either to a minority defined in terms of sexuality or to persons who suffered from a disease. AIDS and the Reagan administration's response thoroughly reoriented the lesbian/gay civil rights movement, galvanized that movement and the individuals who supported and worked within it, and provided unexpected opportunities for individuals inside and outside of government to decide against perpetuating discrimination based on sexual orientation, even if they had no intention of supporting activists who strove to eliminate such discrimination.

The 1976 presidential campaign was the first in the nation's history in which lesbian/gay civil rights became a significant topic for debate. While

President Ford was at best equivocal, Jimmy Carter campaigned actively for lesbian and gay votes. He expressed his principled opposition to all forms of discrimination on the basis of sexual preference or orientation and called for an end to harassment at all levels of government. That principled position led to his support for New York representative Bella Abzug's bill that would have amended the 1964 Civil Rights Act to include "sexual or affectional preference" as a protected category. Carter appointed three known lesbians, including Jean O'Leary, co–executive director of the National Gay Task Force, to his 51.3% committee, which was designed to ensure that women had ample opportunity to express their opinions on policy decisions and to channel qualified women applicants into administration jobs.[2] The Democratic Presidential Campaign Committee funded the group California Gay People for Carter-Mondale, which issued a press release shortly after the Democratic National Convention announcing support for Carter's campaign from such nationally known lesbian/gay rights activists as the Reverend Troy Perry, founder of the nation's only Christian denomination for lesbians and gay men, and Del Martin and Phyllis Lyon, a lesbian couple famous for founding the Daughters of Bilitis, a lesbian rights organization, and for writing the book *Lesbian/Woman*.[3]

Carter did not support lesbian/gay rights unequivocally. In response to specific queries, campaign aides acknowledged his "personal discomfort with homosexuality," and his reservations about potential threats to national security should lesbians or gay men with security clearances become involved in scandals.[4] But his willingness to take a public position opposing discrimination and harassment on the basis of sexual orientation made him the candidate of choice for lesbian/gay activists and precipitated calls from Jean O'Leary and Bruce Voeller, co–executive directors of the National Gay Task Force (NGTF), for him to continue speaking out on behalf of lesbian/gay rights as part of his broader support for civil rights and human rights generally.[5]

Carter seemed to confirm the high expectations that lesbian/gay rights activists had developed during the campaign when he appointed Margaret Costanza as director of the Office of Public Liaison and Marilyn Haft as one of Costanza's assistants. Haft had extensive experience with lesbian/gay civil rights issues, having worked as a staff attorney in the national office of the American Civil Liberties Union and written the ACLU pamphlet *The Rights of Gay People,* as well as serving on the board of the Gay Rights National Lobby.[6] During her tenure in the Office of Public Liaison, Haft would serve as the primary contact in the administration for the NGTF and other lesbian/gay rights activists, setting up meetings with federal agencies, speaking to lesbian/gay political groups, and keeping Costanza informed of any developments on those issues.

Keeping Midge Costanza informed on developments in the federal government with respect to lesbian/gay rights proved a simple task because

Costanza herself had a keen interest in the topic. In her capacity as vice mayor of Rochester, New York, Costanza had worked extensively on a Human Rights Municipal Code for the city that would include information about and protections for lesbians and gay men.[7] Similarly, during the summer of 1976, while working on the platform committee for the Democratic National Committee, she received recommendations from NGTF's O'Leary and Voeller and specifically committed herself to work on a "limited group of issues," including lesbian/gay rights. Her proposed plank on the subject endorsed the Abzug bill.[8]

But Costanza's significant and unprecedented work on behalf of lesbian/gay rights at the federal level began in earnest with her appointment as director of the Office of Public Liaison. The Office of Public Liaison had a peculiar function under President Carter. In previous administrations, much the same office under various different names had primarily served as the vehicle through which the White House staff drummed up support among interest groups for the president's chosen policies. The focus of the office was outward, spreading from the president via his aides to his constituents. In contrast, Carter wanted the Office of Public Liaison to provide the window through which "organized America" could bring their concerns to the White House staff, with the hope that the staff or the president himself would address their grievances. Although in theory all groups would have equal access, Costanza put far more energy into some issues than others.[9]

The National Gay Task Force clearly benefited from Costanza's distribution of administrative energy. She replied quickly to a request from NGTF co–executive directors O'Leary and Voeller for a meeting at the White House.[10] The meeting took place on March 26, 1977. The final roster for the meeting included fifteen representatives from the NGTF covering a wide range of issues. They described discriminatory treatment of lesbians and gay men at the Internal Revenue Service; the Department of Defense; the Department of Housing and Urban Development; the Department of Health, Education, and Welfare; the Federal Communications Commission; the Bureau of Prisons; and the Immigration and Naturalization Service. They asked for the administration's support in persuading the United States Civil Rights Commission to add "sexual preference" to the categories of discrimination and prejudice that it dealt with, and in passing federal legislation prohibiting discrimination on the basis of sexual preference in hiring, education, and public accommodations. And they included presentations on religious issues and parents of lesbians and gay men.[11]

Public response to the meeting seemed fairly evenly balanced across a continuum of approval, disinterest, and outrage. Presidential press secretary Jody Powell, appearing on *Face the Nation* the next day, fielded questions about the NGTF meeting at the White House. He said he did not know if the president had received notice of the meeting in advance and pointed out that

Costanza was only doing her job when she used the Office of Public Liaison to allow groups to present issues that they would like the administration to address. He foreshadowed the argument that Costanza herself would consistently offer in response to criticisms of the meeting: a basic tenet of American government is the right of citizens to petition that government. But perhaps the most important aspect of the issue as Powell and reporters addressed it on national television was its apparent unimportance. Two mild-mannered questions about the NGTF meeting came near the end of the broadcast, with the host closing the show immediately after Powell finished answering the second question.[12]

Costanza did have to answer some sharp criticism from vehement opponents of lesbian/gay civil rights as a result of the meeting. She drafted a standard letter that she sent out in response to the letters and telegrams that came to the White House expressing opposition to her decision to meet with the NGTF.[13] She also provided a statement defending the meeting to the weekly tabloid *National Enquirer*, which conducted a poll asking their readers if Costanza should have met with a lesbian/gay rights group. The format of the poll called for prefatory statements from persons on both sides of the issue. Costanza offered the argument that everyone has a right to petition the government, and that President Carter especially had committed himself to preserving openness in government. The Reverend L. Duane Browne, president of the American Council of Christian Churches, provided the opposing message, asking, "If the White House is going to meet with homosexuals, why not meet with exhibitionists, prostitutes, and panderers?" In the first reported results of the poll, 80 percent of readers opposed the meeting.[14]

In sharp contrast, Costanza also received a report of phone calls to the White House during the period from June 9 to June 16, 1977, not quite three months after the initial meeting with the NGTF. According to this report, 1,438 calls came in on the general topic of "gay rights." All of these calls expressed support, which strongly suggests that the NGTF or some other group was deliberately encouraging its members to call. During the weeks just before and after the meeting the White House also received letters of support from members of the House of Representatives who had large lesbian/gay constituencies, including Ed Koch and Elizabeth Holtzman of New York, and John Burton of California.[15]

Lesbian and gay activists could hardly have encouraged Costanza to greater efforts on their behalf, however. At the end of the March 26 meeting, she agreed to arrange subsequent meetings between NGTF representatives and all of the agencies against which the activists had lodged complaints, with the exception of the Internal Revenue Service.[16] Carter appointees seemed concerned about the appearance of political interference with the IRS. As it happened, in June of 1977 the IRS changed its policy anyway, dropping its requirement that lesbian/gay groups applying for tax-exempt status agree not to publicize the idea that homosexuality is the equal of heterosexuality nor to hold public meetings at which homosexuals might congregate and violate state sodomy laws.[17]

But the IRS was the only federal agency or department that gave Costanza and the Office of Public Liaison any hesitation. After the meeting, Haft worked with Bob Malson in the Civil Rights cluster of the Domestic Policy Staff to distribute information about and assignments of lesbian/gay rights issues among the other aides on the Civil Rights staff.[18] Thus, although Haft and Costanza continued to take the lead in arranging meetings for NGTF representatives with agencies and departments, they also distributed responsibility for the issue to other appropriate aides in the White House. By February 1978, eleven months after the initial meeting at the White House, NGTF representatives had met with representatives from the Department of Justice, the Immigration and Naturalization Service, the Civil Rights Commission, the Public Health Service, and the Federal Communications Commission.[19]

In some cases the NGTF met with almost immediate success. Where the administration had the power to set policy, executive branch agencies typically responded quickly to direction from the White House, acting to address claims of discrimination on the basis of sexual orientation. The Civil Rights Commission agreed, albeit "under much pressure," to include lesbians and gay men under its jurisdiction via statutory authority to investigate the unequal administration of justice.[20] The Federal Communications Commission began to include lesbians and gay men in its process for determining community standards for broadcasting.[21]

But perhaps the best indication of the role that White House staff and political appointees in executive agencies played in helping NGTF activists came from the Bureau of Prisons. At the initial White House meeting, NGTF representatives presented an extensive list of complaints, including information challenging claims that administrators at the Bureau of Prisons used to justify their discriminatory treatment of gay prisoners. Roughly a year elapsed before representatives of NGTF and the Universal Fellowship of Metropolitan Community Churches (MCC), a Christian denomination of and for lesbians and gay men, met with Norman Carlson, director of the Bureau of Prisons. Before the meeting, Robert Keuch, a deputy assistant attorney general in the Criminal Division, objected to the meeting in a memo to Patricia Wald, assistant attorney general in the Office of Legislative Affairs, in whose conference room the meeting would take place.

Keuch explained that both NGTF and MCC had filed suit against the Bureau to change policies governing the admission of gay literature, and MCC ministers, into federal prisons. He worried that those topics would inevitably come up during the meeting, and that the resulting discussions might prejudice ongoing litigation. Better to postpone the meeting until after the lawsuits had been resolved, he argued. Wald replied that representatives of the Justice Department and the Bureau of Prisons could simply announce at the outset either that the issues currently involved in litigation would not be discussed or that any debate of those issues would have no impact on the court proceedings. Her response to the suggestion that no meeting take place until after the resolution of the lawsuits is notable:

> If . . . your recommendation is that no meetings be held with these groups on any aspect of homosexuality in the prisons until the pending litigation is completed, I must respectfully disagree. Completion of that litigation could conceivably take years, and the policy questions presented are of sufficient importance to make cutting off contact with these groups for any substantial period of time unwise.[22]

Wald's position reflects the attitudes of several White House staffers, such as Costanza, Haft, and Malson, that some urgency was attached to questions of lesbian/gay civil rights, and that executive branch personnel should go out of their way to address these issues. Haft did so on June 6, 1977, by writing a memo on behalf of Calvin Keach, a named plaintiff in the NGTF's lawsuit against the Bureau of Prisons and an inmate in the federal prison at El Reno, Oklahoma. Keach's mother reported that prison authorities had threatened to transfer him to Leavenworth unless he withdrew from the suit. Haft asked an unidentified official to look into the matter.[23]

In other areas, the NGTF was less successful. They presented evidence of, and the case against, discriminatory policies on the part of the armed forces against lesbians and gay men. Such policies included not simply the practice of discharging known lesbian/gay personnel, but doing so with less than honorable discharges, which routinely created problems for former soldiers in finding civilian jobs. Activists also complained about the practice of armed forces Disciplinary Control Boards declaring bars in the vicinity of military bases off-limits to military personnel if the bars included lesbians and gay men, or "sexual deviates" in the phrase of a sample letter presented at the March 26 meeting, among their customers.[24] This challenge to military policy took place in the context of the recent, high-profile case of Leonard Matlovich. A Republican who had served two tours of duty in Vietnam, Matlovich filed suit to prevent the air force from discharging him for being gay, appearing on the cover of *Time* magazine in the process.[25] As a result of the Matlovich and other cases, the Department of Defense revised its policy during the Carter administration, but the changes were a mixed blessing. So long as no misconduct had occurred, lesbian/gay soldiers could receive honorable discharges, but for the first time the policy contained the statement that "homosexuality is incompatible with military service."[26]

The case of immigration proved more complicated. Immigration and Naturalization Service commissioner Leonel Castillo and his chief counsel, David Crosland, insisted that they could not administratively change the policy prohibiting lesbian and gay aliens from entering the country. Congress first enacted legislation that had the effect of excluding lesbian/gay aliens from the United States in 1917. Changes in terminology in 1952 and 1965 tightened the exclusionary category, which survived Supreme Court review in 1967. The immigration reform of 1965 illustrates vividly how far the lesbian/gay civil rights movement had advanced in twelve years. The Johnson administration designed the bill to eliminate the explicitly racist national-origins quota system, which the civil rights revolution had rendered unacceptable. Questions of sexuality remained so firmly entrenched in the logic of psychopathology a mere four years before the Stonewall riots, however, that no one in Congress even thought to challenge the antigay exclusion.

Costanza arranged for Castillo and Crosland to meet with NGTF representatives shortly after the initial White House meeting in 1977. Castillo and Crosland insisted that they could not change INS policy on lesbian/gay aliens administratively because the policy reflected a statutory requirement. Activists who were organizing the first March on Washington for Lesbian/Gay Civil Rights in 1979 brought up the issue again, pointing to the case of Zenaida Rebultan, a Filipino woman who could not join the rest of her family in immigrating to the United States because she was a lesbian.

The activists' case centered on the point that the statutory language, and therefore INS policy, rested on the clear presumption that lesbian/gay identity necessarily indicated some mental illness, thus making the exclusion of such aliens desirable. In keeping with the APA's removal of "homosexuality" from the *Diagnostic and Statistical Manual,* Carter's surgeon general directed in 1978 that Public Health Service doctors would no longer conduct medical examinations of incoming aliens whom INS officials suspected of being lesbian or gay because no medical diagnosis of "homosexuality" was possible. Given that the statute prohibited admission of aliens who displayed "psychopathic personality disorder," but nowhere used more specific terms such as *lesbian, gay,* or *homosexual,* and given that the INS had administratively changed its definition of moral turpitude in response to federal court decisions, activists insisted that the INS could now change its definition of "psychopathic personality disorder" in light of changing medical definitions.

INS officials continued to demur, however, in the process giving themselves the difficult task of deciding how ordinary immigration officers would enforce a medical exclusion without the help of Public Health Service doctors.

From August 1979 until September 1980, the INS simply allowed all suspected lesbian/gay aliens into the country under administrative waivers with the expectation that their cases would be reviewed on settlement of the policy question. In September 1980, Crosland, in his capacity as acting commissioner, directed that officers should exclude only those persons who made an "unambiguous, unsolicited declaration" that they were gay. INS officers should not ask nor should they take any apparel with gay rights statements as evidence. They applied this policy even with the sudden influx of Cuban refugees during 1980, despite clear evidence that many of those whom Castro expelled were gay. The INS even worked with gay organizations to resettle gay refugees.[27]

Crosland received no useful guidance from the judiciary in setting policy for lesbian/gay aliens. The Supreme Court refused to hear either of two directly conflicting federal court decisions, one holding that the INS could not enforce medical exclusions without a doctor's examination, while the other held that they could. This confusion remained until the passage in 1990 of a comprehensive reform of exclusionary categories that eliminated the antigay exclusion. Representative Barney Frank, the Democrat from Massachusetts who disclosed his own gay identity as part of a scandal in 1986, played a central role in writing and passing the 1990 reform.[28] This legislative change on behalf of lesbian/gay civil rights depended not only on the fortuitous presence of an openly gay member of Congress, but also on the presence of broad political support for comprehensive immigration reform. Senator Alan Cranston had introduced a bill in 1980 to remove the antigay exclusion in response to the Rebultan case, but that bill made no progress. It seems unlikely that, even ten years later, Representative Frank would have been able to remove the antigay exclusion as a freestanding bill. Instead, it became one part of a larger proposal, and a relatively unimportant part for most nongay persons.

Even as NGTF activists met with numerous federal agencies and departments, a peculiar relationship developed between President Carter and lesbians and gay men around the nation. As early as December 1976, the NGTF had encouraged its constituents' high expectations of the Carter administration, telling members to write letters to Carter asking him to support repeal of state sodomy laws, among other things. And the NGTF dutifully reported on its first meeting at the White House in its newsletter.[29] Not content with agency meetings, however, lesbian/gay activists outside Washington expected Carter to use the presidential bully pulpit to speak out on behalf of lesbian/gay civil rights. In part, Carter invited this demand from lesbians and gay men with his denunciations of human rights abuses abroad. With remarkable consistency, letters to the White House on this subject draw a sharp contrast between the president's oft-stated expectation that other nations should improve their human rights records and his failure to enunciate such an expectation of his fellow Americans with respect to lesbian/gay civil rights.[30]

In part, lesbian and gay demands on the president for public statements resulted from specific fights over lesbian/gay rights in Florida and California. After Dade County commissioners enacted a civil rights ordinance that prohibited discrimination on the basis of sexual preference, singer and former beauty queen Anita Bryant began a campaign with the title "Save Our Children" to repeal the ordinance. Bryant's campaign reached its peak when Dade County residents repealed the gay rights ordinance by a two-to-one margin in June 1977. Bryant's campaign achieved not just national but international attention. On January 9, 1978, an advertisement appeared in *Time* magazine under the large heading "What's Going on in America?" The main point of the ad consisted of the argument that "President Carter's human rights policy can gain credibility only if the rights of homosexuals in the United States of America are bound inseparably to human rights for all people." The ad specifically mentions that "we are alarmed by the campaign of Anita Bryant, who preaches discrimination in the name of God." "We" refers to the signatories to the statement, who included Simone de Beauvoir, Jean-Paul Sartre, Günter Grass, Sir John Gielgud, and numerous political leaders from the Netherlands, Belgium, Germany, England, France, Italy, and Spain.[31]

During the summer of 1978, Californians debated the merits of the Briggs initiative, which would have required school districts to fire all "notorious homosexuals" from positions in which they would have contact with children. At San Francisco's annual gay pride march in June 1978, city supervisor Harvey Milk, probably the most famous gay political leader in the nation at the time, pointedly addressed Carter on the issue in his speech. "Jimmy Carter," Milk said, "you talk about human rights a lot, in fact, you want to be the world's leader for human rights. Well, damn it, lead! . . . It is up to you. And now, before it becomes too late, come to California and speak out against Briggs." With his speech in June 1978, Milk was only perpetuating a year-old practice of chiding the Carter administration publicly for the president's failure to speak out on lesbian/gay civil rights issues.[32]

In a minor incident on June 23, 1977, lesbian/gay activists protested at the Waldorf-Astoria Hotel in New York when the president appeared there for a Democratic Party fund-raiser. It is perhaps indicative of Jimmy Carter's political luck that he attracted both lesbian/gay rights and antiabortion protesters at the same event. Four days earlier, a more serious incident occurred in San Francisco. Appearing on a stage at Golden Gate Park with Mayor George Moscone, Vice President Mondale faced protesters chanting "Gay rights now" during his speech. Moscone managed to quiet the crowd, but when Mondale began to extol the administration's human rights campaign, the protesters responded with "Gay rights are human rights," at which point the vice president simply abandoned his speech and left the stage.[33] The problem stemmed at least in part from the fact that the publisher of the only lesbian/gay publication with national distribution at the time, *The Advocate*, was feuding with NGTF co–executive director Voeller and so refused to publish any information about NGTF meetings at the White House or with executive agencies. According to Jean O'Leary, Voeller's co–executive director, the NGTF got some of the best publicity for its White House meetings from Anita Bryant's denunciations of them.[34]

Thus, events in the summer of 1977 foreshadowed persistent misunderstandings during the rest of the Carter administration with respect to lesbian/gay rights issues. The pace of contacts between the NGTF and the White House slowed appreciably during 1978, after Haft left the Office of Public Liaison to serve as deputy counsel to Vice President Mondale and Costanza's dissent from administration policy on federal funding for abortions led to her resignation from the administration.[35] Sarah Weddington and Jane Wales continued to arrange meetings for the NGTF with federal agencies and otherwise addressed lesbian/gay rights issues under their responsibilities for women's issues. Also, aides in the Civil Rights cluster of the Domestic Policy Staff, especially Bob Malson, continued to monitor lesbian/gay rights issues. Costanza and Haft seem to have been primarily responsible for the concentrated burst of attention that lesbian/gay rights issues received in the early days of Carter's presidency, but others in the White House sustained that attention, albeit less intensely, after Costanza and Haft had left.[36] Still, it is clear that, at this early date, the successes of the lesbian/gay civil rights movement depended heavily on a particular combination of individuals. In 1978, the lesbian/gay civil rights movement had developed neither an established political constituency and logic that the White House would automatically understand, nor a set of well-established advocacy organizations.

With the approach of the 1980 election, White House aides viewed lesbian/gay rights with some trepidation because of the potential political volatility of the issue, but they seemed confident that the administration's record would impress lesbian and gay voters.[37] Briefing Stuart Eizenstat for an interview on April 19, 1980, with gay reporter Larry Bush, Bob Malson listed the administration's accomplishments. He disputed Bush's contention that work in the White House on lesbian/gay rights had stopped when Costanza left, pointing to his own responsibility for the issues, along with that of Allison Thomas. Malson also pointed to new FCC requirements for inclusion of lesbians and gay men in determining community standards for purposes of broadcasting, and to the change in IRS policy with respect to tax exemptions for lesbian/gay groups. The Bureau of Prisons was revising regulations to permit gay ministers and nonpornographic gay literature into federal prisons. And with respect to immigration, the administration expected soon to announce its support for the Cranston bill that would remove the prohibition on lesbian/gay aliens from federal immigration law.[38]

Malson also referred in his memo to new civil service rules that included protections for lesbians and gay men. On the issue of civil service reform, Malson's description of the administration's accomplishment seemed a bit disingenuous. As drafts of the civil service reform bill circulated within the administration in early 1978, Costanza sent a memo to the president pointing out that it did not include sexual or affectional preference among the categories protected from discrimination.[39] This omission would probably precipitate a fresh round of criticism from lesbian/gay activists, but inclusion of such language would almost inevitably embroil an otherwise popular piece of legislation in political controversy. Richard Pettigrew, speaking from his recent experience with the issue in Dade County, Florida, went so far as to predict that an explicit proposal to protect lesbians and gay men would prompt members of Congress explicitly to exclude sexual or affectional preference from the list of protected categories. Militating further against inclusion was the Civil Service Commission's revision in 1975 of its policy of excluding or firing lesbians and gay men. Counsel for the Commission was willing to put in writing the expectation that this rule would continue under the savings provisions of the proposed act. With all of his advisers, save the officially neutral Costanza, strongly urging him not to add "sexual or affectional preference" to the list of protected categories, and recognizing a significant political threat to an otherwise successful major domestic-policy initiative, Carter chose not to include the new language.[40]

In his memo for Eizenstat, however, Malson pointed to language in the act requiring that federal employers refrain from considering aspects of a potential or actual employee's personal life that had no bearing on the employee's work life. He attached supporting documentation to demonstrate that civil service rules explicitly included "sexual orientation" among the factors that employers should not take into account. Malson thus represented the administration as having contributed directly to a specific advance for lesbian/gay rights when actually its role had been more that of allowing existing practice to continue.

Carter's decision to leave "sexual orientation" out of the protected categories in his Civil Service Reform Act suggests a slight modification of his reputation for disregarding political considerations in favor of doing the right thing.[41] Carter's decision also illustrates the peculiar position of lesbian/gay rights in debates over civil rights during the late 1970s. They seldom used the word, but the criticisms that lesbians and gay men lodged when they wrote to the White House clearly imply that they considered the president something of a hypocrite. They could not understand how a president who openly campaigned for lesbian and gay votes, and who took considerable political risks in pursuing the cause of human rights abroad, could possibly justify his failure to speak up loudly and often on behalf of lesbian/gay civil rights.[42]

But even a president who became notorious for pursuing a large number of highly complex and highly controversial policy initiatives from the very beginning of his presidency had priorities arranged according to limited presidential time and attention. Briefing Pettigrew in November 1977 for a speech in San Francisco, Marilyn Haft warned him that he might have to explain why the president had stated in June "that he was too busy to deal with gay rights problems."[43] Perhaps *Washington Post* columnist William Raspberry was right when he wrote, in June 1977, that most people wanted both sides of the lesbian/gay rights debate to "shut up about it." The broad middle, Raspberry suggested, found both Anita Bryant's crusade against lesbian/gay rights, and lesbian/gay activists' crusade for those rights, equally extreme and indefensible. People at the conservative end of the broad middle might wish to exclude openly lesbian or gay persons from certain types of employment, while people at the liberal end might insist on equal treatment. But Raspberry's political continuum carried the suggestion that most people in the middle considered the issue relatively unimportant and wished to devote little time and attention, if any at all, to it.[44]

For most people, including President Carter, lesbian/gay rights presented a relatively abstract issue. Carter was quite sincere in his opposition to discrimination and in his belief that no one should suffer harassment at the hands of their own government. But the social movement had not dramatized for the general public what exactly Anita Bryant's Save Our Children campaign or the Briggs initiative would mean in the lives of ordinary lesbians and gay men if they succeeded. The social movement had its stirring beginnings in the Stonewall riots, but it had not yet had a Birmingham, in which the nation could see firsthand the effects of prejudice.

Indeed, although lesbian and gay civil rights leaders consciously evoked the African-American civil rights movement as a model for their own, the analogy proved in some respects difficult to make.[45] Stereotypes of African-Americans relied heavily on assumptions of sexual immorality, but sexual excess was an effect, not a cause, in the minds of segregationists. Opponents of lesbian/gay rights, in contrast, could focus much more directly on their claim that alleged discrimination against lesbians and gay men served only to prohibit immoral conduct. The notion of lesbian/gay civil rights, on this view, is a category error, because definitionally one cannot claim civil rights protections from legitimate expressions of a community's moral standards.

Here, perhaps, is the central difficulty for the lesbian/gay civil rights movement. This difficulty, in turn, may help us understand both President Carter's approach to lesbian/gay civil rights issues during his administration, and the role of lesbian/gay civil rights claims in the nation's changing understanding of and approach to civil rights generally during the late 1970s and 1980s. Carter believed in nondiscrimination as a basic principle, but perhaps he had difficulty understanding how lesbians and gay men as a group could claim a need for redress of present injustice and past wrongs similar to those of African-Americans or women. Thus, he was perfectly happy to win the votes of lesbians and gay men, and to allow members of his White House staff to work closely with lesbian/gay rights activists, but he did not see in the issue the same sort of moral immediacy that he saw in the plight of Soviet dissidents or Central American peasants.

Carter lent support to this interpretation of his actions by writing an opinion piece in 1996 condemning the efforts of Christian conservatives to use lesbian/gay rights issues in that year's presidential campaign. Carter wrote:

> The driving issues in the early Republican primary contests have made a strange and disturbing shift from economic and budget items to divisive social issues, notably abortion and homosexuality. In the early caucus contests, pressures from the more extreme religious activists have pushed almost every candidate to demagoguery, emphasizing vicious attacks on gay men and women ostensibly based on the teachings of Jesus Christ. An even more disquieting claim is that AIDS is God's punishment on someone who has sinned and that the sufferers should be treated accordingly. Jesus had similar encounters with lepers, who were also looked upon as condemned by God and capable of contaminating their neighbors. Christ set an example for us by reaching out to them, loving and healing them.[46]

As the baleful effects of efforts to scapegoat lesbians and gay men became more evident, Carter chose to speak out on the subject when he might easily have ignored it. In doing so, he noted that Christians no longer call for legislation restricting the options of divorced persons or adulterers, even though the Bible condemns both practices. In effect, Carter agreed with opponents of lesbian/gay civil rights on the moral status of lesbians and gay men. The difference lay in his more scrupulous adherence to the principle of church-state separation, and his decision to emphasize the redemptive aspects of Christian doctrine over its moralizing aspects.

While Carter was president, lesbian/gay rights occupied a peculiar position in his administration. In the White House, it stood somewhat alone, vaguely attached to women's issues, but not firmly entrenched within the logic of the civil rights revolution. Conservative activists, by contrast, seem to have had good luck using lesbian/gay rights as political tar. In June of 1977, 93 percent of callers to the White House on the subject of the International Women's

Year conference in Houston associated that conference with the Equal Rights Amendment, abortion, and lesbians, all of which they disapproved of. Some gay activists in Dade County claimed that Anita Bryant was really using her opposition to the gay rights ordinance there as a ruse to stop ratification of the ERA, and at least one Florida state senator switched from supporting to opposing the ERA because he feared that it would require legalization of same-sex marriages.[47]

The growing political power of New Right activists, especially their ability to influence the 1980 elections, was by no means obvious, however. *The Advocate,* published in 1980 a general call for political involvement among its readers, suggesting that lesbians and gay men work on the campaign of their favored candidate, whoever that might be—including the favored candidate of the New Right, Ronald Reagan. *The Advocate's* editors predicated their willingness to encourage Reagan's lesbian/gay supporters on the candidate's denunciation in 1978 of the Briggs initiative.[48] For those lesbians and gay men who wanted public statements opposing discrimination from their elected leaders, Reagan might actually have looked better than Carter from the vantage point of the 1980 election season.

Even so, it was not clear how lesbian/gay civil rights activists should have reacted to the new Republican administration. Lucia Valeska and Charles Brydon served as co–executive directors of the National Gay Task Force at the time of Ronald Reagan's election. Brydon would later criticize Valeska and many other lesbian/gay rights activists for their automatic assumption, as good leftists, that there was little point in trying to work with the new Republican conservative administration. Brydon stated that Reagan had more gay people on his White House staff than Carter did, and that ideological rigidity at the NGTF caused activists there to miss an excellent opportunity to work with the Reagan administration.[49]

But the Reagan campaign seems to have ignored entirely efforts by the Gay Vote 1980 National Convention Project to reverse official antigay stands by the Republican Party. Under the direction of the NGTF, the Gay Rights National Lobby (GRNL), the Lesbian Caucus of the National Women's Political Caucus, and the National Coalition of Black Gays, the Convention Project tried two different tactics. Shortly after the Republican convention, two gay delegates wrote to Reagan, objecting to elements of the Family Protection Act (FPA), then pending in Congress, which the GOP had pledged to support in the "Family Protection" plank of their platform. The gay delegates pointed to language in the FPA that would have amended the 1964 Civil Rights Act so that actions against lesbian/gay employees would never be unlawful.

The Convention Project also issued a press release pointing to three areas of concern. In addition to the FPA, this release noted that the Platform Committee had added a list of specific categories to a general statement condemning discrimination. It quoted the sponsor of the list, Guy Farley Jr., to the effect that his list would serve "to make clear that equal rights 'doesn't include homosexual rights.'" The release also expressed concern about language in the plank on immigration and refugee policy that might inhibit efforts to repeal the statutory prohibition on lesbian/gay aliens and to expand refugee policy to include persons who suffered persecution because of their sexual orientation.[50]

Further, it was far from clear that the presence of lesbians and gay men in the Reagan administration would automatically translate into support for lesbian/gay civil rights activists. Journalist Taylor Branch seemed to confirm Brydon's opinion about Reagan's White House staff, and the implicit corollary that the right wing harbored at least as many lesbians and gay men as the left wing, with his 1982 article on the world of closeted Washington in *Harper's* magazine. But Branch also described the book *God's Bullies,* referring to "anti-homosexual homosexuals" in order to explain the peculiarities of life in the closet for lesbians and gay men at the seat of national power. Well before gay journalist Michelangelo Signorile made "outing" a national controversy, *God's Bullies* named names of closeted gay men among the conservative activists then asserting themselves in national policy and politics.[51]

At the head of the list appeared the name of Terry Dolan, chief fund-raiser for the National Conservative Political Action Committee (NCPAC), a leading organization in the Republicans' electoral successes of the 1980s. As Branch put it, "If there were a war of outage . . . its victims would include members of the elected Republican leadership in Congress, some of the leaders who pushed the McDonald Amendment [which would have prohibited the Legal Services Corporation from assisting lesbians and gay men], and also some of the principal supporters of the Hyde Amendment, which prohibits federally funded abortions."[52] Dolan himself would go on to die of AIDS after incurring denunciations, and at least one drink thrown in his face, by AIDS activists who accused him of contributing to the electoral successes of the very conservative Republicans who consistently resisted increased funding for AIDS research and services.[53]

Thus, Brydon was mistaken in his sanguine assessment of the opportunities lesbian/gay civil rights activists faced in working with the Reagan administration. He did not know of attempts by his successor at NGTF, Jeff Levi, to continue the practice of meeting with White House staff members. Levi had one unavailing meeting with Aram Bakshian of Reagan's Office of Public Liaison early in 1981. In September of that year, New York congressman Bill Green wrote to Director of Public Liaison Elizabeth Dole asking that she meet with Levi and other NGTF representatives.

Dole's assistant, Diana Lozano, attached a note to the letter, suggesting to Office of Public Liaison staffer William Triplett that he "just hold onto this. We can't really agree to meet—Aram already did. Any further contact is pointless. Can you think of a polite way to say the above?" A letter from Lozano to Green on October 7 explained, "As you are aware, the Gay Task Force has already been involved in informal discussions with Aram Bakshian, a member of this staff. Due to limitations upon Mrs. Dole's schedule during October, it is unlikely that she would be able to attend an additional meeting in the near future. As you have noted, however, the group includes people with a broad range of interests, and they may well be included in other meetings or briefings pertinent to other individual interests."[54] In other words, lesbian/gay identity per se would constitute no bar to meetings in the White House, but Reagan aides had no intention of pursuing action on lesbian/gay civil rights claims.

Brydon failed to appreciate the role of gender and sexuality as issues that motivated social conservatives during the late 1970s, and the role of social conservatives in electing Ronald Reagan to the presidency. For social conservatives, many of whom remained dubious about the means, if not the ends, of the civil rights revolution, the efforts of lesbians and gay men to climb aboard the civil rights bandwagon offered the clear signal that the movement had gone too far. During Carter's administration, conservative organizers and theorists extended their powerful critique of activist government to include federal policies designed to eliminate discrimination on the basis of gender and sexuality. Such policies, whether currently in place or only proposed, posed a grave threat to the nation as a whole according to the conservative activists who supported Reagan's nomination as the Republican standard-bearer in 1980. A centerpiece of this New Right program became the Family Protection Act, first introduced in Congress in 1979 by longtime Reagan associate Paul Laxalt, and reintroduced in 1980 and 1981. The Family Protection Act took as its major goal to "strengthen the American family and to remove those Federal government policies which inhibit its strength and prosperity."[55]

Among various relatively technical provisions of the act dealing with school prayer, tax credits for housewives who volunteer their time, and similar conservative desiderata, lay a sweeping provision aimed at lesbian/gay civil rights advocacy. The bill would have denied federal funds "to any public or private individual, group, foundation, commission, corporation, association, or other entity which presents homosexuality, male or female, as an acceptable alternative life style or suggests that it can be an acceptable life style."[56] As gay literary critic Lee Edelman has recently suggested, conservative activists often seem more concerned with representations of lesbian and gay persons, or of their sodomitical sin, than with any actual acts.[57] The New Right chose not to attempt any new federal sanctions directed at lesbian or gay sexual activity, but at any representation of such activity or its supposed "lifestyle" implications in a positive light. Conservatives aimed not to extirpate lesbians and gay men, but to prevent public discussion of them, especially insofar as they might control or contribute significantly to that discussion themselves and thereby challenge the conservative tenet that lesbian and gay lives exhibited irresponsibility at best, unalloyed tragedy at worst.

The attitude that Diana Lozano revealed in her response from the Office of Public Liaison to Jeff Levi's request for further meetings between White House staff and NGTF activists, along with the presence of leading antigay conservatives such as Pat Buchanan, William Bennett, and Gary Bauer on Reagan's staff, illustrates the primary difference that the Republican victory in 1980 made for lesbian/gay civil rights activists. Rather than having highly sympathetic White House and executive-agency staffers serving under a largely indifferent president who supported the basic logic of civil rights, suddenly activists faced hostile staffers serving under a largely indifferent president who opposed the basic logic of civil rights. Whereas Midge Costanza and Marilyn Haft routinely corresponded and met with representatives of the NGTF and other lesbian/gay groups, Judi Buckalew and Faith Whittlesey of Ronald Reagan's staff met with Howard Phillips of the Conservative Caucus and Ron Godwin of the Moral Majority to discuss AIDS issues. Interestingly, the meeting with Phillips took place roughly two weeks after Buckalew met with Jeff Levi and Ginny Apuzzo of the NGTF, but Buckalew consistently misidentified the organization as the Gay Alliance Task Force and ended her memo to Whittlesey with a reference to Representative Ted Weiss (D-NY) as trying "hard to discredit the Administration's response to the AIDS outbreak" as part of "the Democrats [sic] attempt to politicize the issue."[58]

As Lozano made clear, the change in administration meant the end of NGTF activists' access to White House staff, at least on lesbian/gay civil rights issues. The emergence of AIDS gave the NGTF a renewed entrée to the White House, but Levi and Apuzzo still met with aides who were more sympathetic to the Conservative Caucus and the Moral Majority than to the NGTF. The files of Reagan's White House aides contain letters and flyers from the American Legislative Exchange Council, which claimed that lesbians and gay men must recruit children because they cannot reproduce; Exodus International, an organization dedicated to the proposition that lesbians and gay men can change with God's help; and Paul Cameron, a psychologist whom the American Psychological Association expelled for misusing the results of other researchers in his efforts to paint gay men in the worst possible light.[59] It is difficult to trace specific policy outcomes to the impact of these sources for ideas about lesbians and gay men, if only because the Reagan administration rarely addressed lesbian/gay civil rights directly, but the disparity between the Carter administration and the Reagan administration in terms of basic attitudes toward the topic is clear.

And, whatever the ambiguity of specific policy outcomes in the area of lesbian/gay civil rights, the implications of opinions in the White House for the federal response to the emerging AIDS epidemic quickly became clear. This brief chapter can add little substance to Randy Shilts's massive study of politics and policy during the first six years of the AIDS epidemic, 1981 to 1987. It can, however, refine Shilts's interpretation in light of previously unavailable documents from within the Reagan administration. Shilts's book *And the Band Played On* offered solid, damning empirical evidence in support of the perception, already firmly entrenched among lesbians, gay men, and medical professionals on the front lines of the epidemic when the book appeared in 1987, that the Reagan administration had consistently failed to provide national leadership in response to a public health crisis because the president and his staff cared little for the well-being of the gay men who comprised the vast majority of those who suffered from the disease in the United States.[60] In an odd sense, from the perspective of lesbians and gay men, Reagan was guilty of the same sin as Carter: out of indifference to prejudice and discrimination, he failed to use the presidential bully pulpit to call on the nation to live up to its better nature.

But, if the effects of prejudice and discrimination based on sexual orientation remained relatively abstract during Carter's presidency, they became terrifyingly concrete with the advent of AIDS, first identified at the Centers for Disease Control in the same year as Reagan's inauguration, 1981. Not only did hundreds, then thousands, of young persons die rapidly from a bewildering array of nasty diseases, but they increasingly suffered discrimination and harassment from a fearful population in the process. Reagan came to office with a well-developed and clearly articulated political philosophy calling for significant reductions in the size, cost, and responsibilities of the federal government. This ideological position of the president and his most politically loyal assistants had a profound impact on the course of the epidemic, and on lesbian/gay politics and activism.

As Shilts has described, Reagan refused to speak publicly about AIDS for the first five years of the epidemic while members of Congress routinely forced increased appropriations for research and treatment on the Department of Health and Human Services (DHHS), where staffers found themselves caught between their commitment to public health and their loyalty to the administration. Various DHHS officials, especially Secretary Margaret Heckler, came under fire for repeating the administration's official line that the federal response reflected a commitment to AIDS as the nation's number one health problem and that researchers had all the funds they needed in the face of repeated congressional inquiries indicating otherwise.[61] In an important sense, however, Heckler steered a middle course between members of Congress who demonstrated the inadequacies of the DHHS response to the epidemic and the conservative activists who enjoyed significant access to the administration. On August 22, 1983, Howard Phillips wrote to Heckler, "Dear Peggy, I must say I am shocked at the extent of your pandering to win votes from the homosexual community even at the risk of jeopardizing the health of the public at large. . . . A little less research and a little more quarantine might discourage homosexuals from further infecting themselves and polluting millions of innocent victims."[62]

By August 1983, just over two years into the epidemic, the number of persons diagnosed with AIDS stood at 1,922. The overall mortality rate was 39 percent, but for those who had been diagnosed before July 1982, some 66 percent had died.[63] Even as the federal health bureaucracy struggled to respond, the president remained silent. Only in December 1985 did the president decide within the administration to "deal with AIDS as a major public health problem."[64] Jeff Levi, who worked for the NGTF at the time and played a key role in developing the lesbian/gay civil rights movement's response to the epidemic, has suggested that the president's silence was perhaps beneficial from the perspective of lesbians and gay men. Had he addressed the issue, his statements would probably not have conveyed much sympathy for the largely gay male population suffering from the disease. More importantly, Levi and other activists strove to increase the federal response to AIDS while operating below the conservative radar, where sympathetic bureaucrats could provide them with information—often in plain brown envelopes—and respond to their requests without attracting the attention of White House ideologues.[65]

Reagan's private statements about the epidemic confirm Levi's fears. During a meeting of the Domestic and Economic Policy Councils in December 1985, roughly two months before AIDS first appeared in the president's annual legislative message to Congress, "A general discussion about AIDS followed, with the President noting that several eminent medical scientists suggested that individual responsibility for one's behavior is a key factor in the struggle against AIDS."[66] While it was certainly true, as administration staff routinely pointed out, that in the absence of a cure one could avoid dying from AIDS only by not catching it, it was equally true that individuals needed reliable information on transmission of HIV, the virus that causes AIDS, in order to take responsibility for themselves.

But the president only approved basic principles to guide federal education policy on AIDS on February 11, 1987. Those principles may serve as the Reagan administration's manifesto on the proper role of the federal government, and on ideals of sexual conduct. "The scope and content of the school portion of this AIDS education effort should be locally determined, and should be consistent with parental values," while the federal government should "not mandate a specific school curriculum on this subject." And, of course, "Any health information developed by the Federal Government that will be used for education should encourage responsible sexual behavior—based on fidelity, commitment, and maturity, placing sexuality within the context of marriage."[67]

One clear implication of these principles was the assumption on the part of Reagan's staff that only married—meaning heterosexual—couples were capable of "fidelity, commitment, and maturity," or of sexual responsibility.

President Reagan's principles for AIDS education reflected much more the preferences of his secretary of education, William Bennett, and Bennett's aide Gary Bauer, than they did the conclusions of Surgeon General C. Everett Koop, as detailed in the 1986 "Surgeon General's Report on Acquired Immune Deficiency Syndrome." That the secretary of education should have input into principles for education may seem unsurprising. What indicates the extent to which Secretary Bennett served as the administration's guarantor of ideological purity in debates over AIDS policy was the Department of Education's proposal "Preventing the Spread of AIDS Through Routine and Voluntary Testing."[68] Only in the particular conservative logic of the Reagan administration did it make sense to ignore the surgeon general's recommendations in favor of the secretary of education's recommendations for HIV testing.

On one hand, the tone of the proposal indicates a dispassionate, practical approach to HIV testing. It gave highest priority to those geographical areas where the prevalence of AIDS was already highest, noting that the cities with the highest prevalence accounted for 70 percent of AIDS cases but only 27 percent of the total population. It called for federal legislation expanding assistance to states and municipalities for testing, but also for counseling, and the "establishment of procedural safeguards to ensure the protection of AIDS victims and those not infected."[69] On the other hand, despite its neutral tone, the report contained proposals that terrified those lesbians and gay men, activist or not, who had been following the Reagan administration's attitudes toward AIDS for nearly seven years. The two most controversial provisions advocated "cost-effective contact tracing and notification," and "report [of] summary test results . . . on a monthly basis to the state health department and to the Centers for Disease Control . . . , with the following information: age, sex, race, zip code of residence, HIV risk factor, HIV infection status, prior testing results."

Despite repeated insistence from Secretary Bennett himself that the administration was committed to protecting the confidentiality of HIV test results, and the civil rights of persons with AIDS, most lesbians and gay men remained suspicious. In part, Bennett's lack of credibility among lesbians and gay men stemmed from his willingness to contradict the surgeon general. Koop's report called for "education concerning AIDS . . . at the lowest grade possible," including "information on heterosexual and homosexual relationships." He also wrote that "compulsory blood testing of individuals is not necessary."[70] Bennett carefully used the word *routine,* rather than *compulsory,* but the point remained clear when he wrote, "While there is general agreement on the need for more widespread AIDS testing, some balk at going about this in the most effective way. They call for more testing, but only voluntary testing.

They reject out of hand proposals for routine testing of individuals upon certain occasions."[71] "Routine" testing, Bennett acknowledged, is the opposite of "voluntary" testing.

But the Department of Education's recommendations for HIV testing, reasonable as they sound on their face, simply reconfirmed to lesbians and gay men the suspicion that the Reagan administration hoped to find out if HIV and AIDS were spreading beyond the gay men and intravenous drug users who were first identified with the disease in the United States so that they could decide whether they cared to respond effectively. The Secretary of Education's role in setting administration policy on AIDS was consistent with the perception that William Bennett, Gary Bauer, and Ronald Reagan saw in the epidemic primarily a morality play that neatly suited the administration's desire to lecture the nation on the personal preferences of the conservative elite. By 1987, when Bennett wrote publicly on HIV testing, lesbians and gay men inevitably interpreted his statements in light of the consistent disparity between the administration's words and its actions with respect to AIDS. The administration's own internal discussions reflect both the disparity and the apparent inability of executive branch officials to recognize that disparity. On March 30, 1987, the Working Group on Health Policy reported to the Domestic Policy Council (DPC) that they had first received a briefing from DHHS Secretary Heckler about AIDS on September 11, 1985. In the intervening two years, the DPC had addressed AIDS on five different occasions, belying the administration's claim to have made AIDS a major priority.[72]

The process of creating and appointing members to the Presidential Commission on the Human Immunodeficiency Virus Epidemic demonstrated this problem. Bauer took primary responsibility for choosing the members of the commission, which the president created only after proposals appeared in Congress to mandate the commission legislatively. The roster of commissioners included no lesbian or gay man until public outcry over so obvious an omission led Nancy Reagan to intervene personally. Less widely publicized was that Assistant Secretary of Health Robert Windom proposed, along with the Presidential Commission, the creation of an AIDS Policy Board consisting of cabinet-level officials who would receive advice from the commission and expedite the implementation of policy recommendations that would cut across existing divisions within the executive branch. Windom's proposal apparently fell victim to the administration's ideological preferences in much the same way as Koop's recommendations for AIDS education and HIV testing. According to the March 30, 1987, memo, "Other members of the Working Group have said that they would prefer not to separate AIDS policy matters from the [Domestic Policy Council] process."[73] In other words, even as they insisted that they wished to deal with AIDS as a public health issue rather than a political issue, Reagan's aides continued to exert control over AIDS policy from the White House at the expense of the Department of Health and Human Services and the public health experts who worked there.

The nakedly and disingenuously political approach to AIDS that Reagan and his staff revealed helped propel growing numbers of lesbians and gay men into activism during the 1980s. Initially, the efforts of Ginny Apuzzo and Jeff Levi to respond to the crisis nearly bankrupted the NGTF. AIDS required a fundamental reorientation of the whole movement. Organized lesbians and gay men had mostly directed their efforts at minimizing government's involvement in their lives—Frank Kameny and Barbara Gittings picketed the White House and the Civil Service Commission because of systematic employment discrimination in the federal government; the Stonewall riots resulted from a police raid on a gay bar; a major priority for the movement at the state and federal level was the repeal of sodomy laws. Now, suddenly, lesbian/gay civil rights activists had to learn the arcana of the federal budget process and communicate with the far-flung federal health bureaucracy. At the same time, however, legislation to provide funding, and to direct its use, for AIDS gave members of Congress the opportunity to vote indirectly on behalf of lesbian/gay civil rights, often in the form of votes against the most homophobic proposals from Senator Jesse Helms (R-NC) and Representative William Dannemeyer (R-CA), among others. Such legislation also motivated an increasing number of lesbian and gay constituents to contact members of Congress who did not know that they had lesbian and gay constituents.

Ironically, then, the Reagan administration's thunderous silence helped to galvanize the still fledgling lesbian/gay civil rights movement. Because of AIDS, many individuals faced difficult choices. Overall, their decisions redounded to the long-term strength of the movement. Closeted lesbians and gay men working for the federal government, but also public health officials with some political loyalties to the Reagan administration, walked a fine line in adhering publicly to the administration's official position that they had made AIDS a top priority while quietly helping activists and members of Congress demonstrate otherwise.

Overall, historical circumstance worked to the advantage of lesbian/gay civil rights activists between 1977 and 1989. As latecomers to the civil rights revolution, they had to operate within a political and policy logic that others had created for their own purposes. Despite their best efforts, lesbian/gay civil rights activists could not simply plug "sexual preference" or "sexual orientation" into a receptacle built for "race" and "sex." Although the fit was far from perfect, what mattered most for activists such as Jean O'Leary, Ginny Apuzzo, and Jeff Levi was not so much the details as the commitment, or lack of commitment, to the broad concept of active government concern for equal opportunity and equal treatment that elected and appointed officials brought to their offices.

Jimmy Carter hardly fit the mold of a traditional New Deal Democrat, but he possessed a profound, sincere commitment to the basic concept of nondiscrimination. As president, he did not always act on that commitment in ways that lesbian/gay activists wanted him to, but he also disappointed many other traditional Democratic constituencies, especially African-Americans, women, and organized labor.[74] There is more than mere symbolism in the fact that the self-identified defender of traditional liberal groups in the Carter White House, Midge Costanza, was at once the leader on lesbian/gay civil rights in the administration, and the aide who left the White House after fifteen months under a cloud of controversy over her public disagreements with the president.[75] With Carter's connections to established civil rights constituencies strained, it should come as no surprise that lesbians and gay men received little of his attention. Still, his administration stands clearly as the first in the history of the republic during which White House aides deliberately—even eagerly—used the enormous leverage of the presidency to change specific policies that discriminated on the basis of sexual orientation.

The biggest challenge lesbian/gay civil rights activists faced in 1980 was the resurgence of overall hostility to civil rights claims in general, as embodied in the small-government philosophy of Ronald Reagan and his New Right followers. But New Right activists seem to have overplayed their hand. Americans had grown suspicious of affirmative action and other apparent attempts to achieve equality of results, but they remained firmly committed to the basic logic of equal opportunity, however narrowly defined, even for persons whom they disapproved of. We cannot know what would have happened in the absence of AIDS, but it seems highly unlikely that the indifference, and in some cases the overt hostility, of Reagan's White House staff could have completely prevented the social movement for lesbian/gay civil rights from advancing its cause during the 1980s. If the White House was closed, there were other avenues—Congress, the courts, state and local governments.

AIDS appeared, however, and fundamentally altered the context for lesbian/gay civil rights activism. And it appeared in the same year as the inauguration of a president who apparently harbored no ill will toward individual lesbians and gay men, but who clearly cared not a whit for the goals of the lesbian/gay civil rights movement, in part because he doubted the very logic of civil rights policy and politics as they had developed since World War II, in part because, whatever the legitimacy of protections against discrimination on the basis of race and sex, for Reagan and the New Right, sexual orientation was a different matter altogether. Pat Buchanan only articulated what many others in the Reagan White House apparently believed: "The poor homosexuals; they have declared war upon nature, and now nature is exacting an awful retribution."[76] The conservative true believers in the White House could not acknowledge what even the Presidential Commission on HIV stated clearly in its preliminary report—lesbians and gay men had demonstrated the chief Republican virtues of personal responsibility and self-sufficiency in their response to the AIDS epidemic.[77]

They did so in part by developing the San Francisco model of community-based care for persons with AIDS who could not adequately care for themselves, but who did not require hospitalization. They did so in part by developing innovative approaches to education, teaching gay men how to minimize their exposure to HIV. And they did so in part by successfully learning to lobby Congress, by persuading even many Republican members that the administration's response to the epidemic was grossly inadequate. Ginny Apuzzo and Jeff Levi at NGTF formed the core, along with other concerned individuals, who demanded attention to the AIDS epidemic, in the name of the gay men who were the chief sufferers in the early years, but also in the name of good public health.

But AIDS and lesbian/gay civil rights are not the same things. Lesbian/gay civil rights activists, along with certain public health officials and members of Congress, were the first to demand an adequate response to AIDS because it was clear to them that indifference to the epidemic was a function of indifference to the lives of gay men. Responding to the AIDS crisis at first imposed significant burdens on NGTF, but both NGTF and the movement as a whole dramatically increased their political capacity in the process. Gay men who had remained closeted suddenly had no choice but to come out—they could no longer hide their disease. Members of Congress who thought they had no lesbian or gay constituents learned otherwise when they received demands from within their districts for increased federal funding for research, treatment, and education. Most parents whose children suffered from AIDS exhibited more concern for adequate treatments and research into possible cures than for the details of how their children came to have the syndrome in the first place. Apuzzo, Levi, and other activists, with the help of congressional staffers such as Tim Westmoreland, learned to lobby Congress effectively.

Lesbian/gay civil rights and AIDS would eventually go their separate ways. An industry of impressive dimensions has grown up around AIDS research and treatment such that, in terms of institutions and dollars, activity around AIDS now dwarfs lesbian/gay civil rights activity. In the long run, however, we may see the Carter and Reagan administrations, and the emergence of AIDS during the 1980s, as the period in which the seeds for future institutional growth, political experience, and policy successes in the lesbian/gay civil rights movement were sown.

CHAPTER 2

Beating Around Bush: Gay Rights and America's 41st President

Joe Rollins

Introduction

Writing the story of gay rights and the Bush administration is a bit like telling the story of the hole in a doughnut; the hole itself is defined only in relation to what surrounds it. Digging through sources of historical material, gay and mainstream presses, and scholarly analysis, one is left with the feeling that George Bush had relatively little to say about gay rights and was generally out of touch with issues of importance to the gay and lesbian community. Criticized for his inaction on the AIDS battlefront, Bush could not be characterized as an ally (as some might characterize Clinton), but neither can he be vilified like many other figures in the Republican Party (Strom Thurmond, Jesse Helms, Patrick Buchanan, or Robert Dornan to name a few). Although many important advances were made during Bush's watch, most of the truly momentous events and noteworthy historical moments between January of 1989 and January of 1993 took place entirely outside the Oval Office.

The following pages jump through the hole in the doughnut and attempt to characterize how America's forty-first president grappled with some of the most contentious political issues of the twentieth century. The discussion proceeds along several dimensions, beginning with a brief biographical introduction. Next, the chapter turns to an examination of the 1988 election cycle, emphasizing the Republican Party platform. While gay rights and AIDS politics are clearly separate issues, the distinction was blurred during the 1988 election as HIV was taking a serious toll on the gay community. The third section of the chapter is organized under three headings intended to characterize the major events in gay rights that occurred on Bush's watch. Despite the president's relative silence on the issue of gay rights, many important events occurred during this period, setting the stage for what happened in the administration and in the election of 1992. Probably the most memorable event during the Bush presidency was Desert Storm; the most memorable idea propounded during the administration was undoubtedly "family values." These two constructs help organize the major issues in gay rights between 1989 and 1992. Finally, the chapter takes a look at why Bush lost the 1992 election. Attributing his loss to the absence of a gay rights plank in the GOP platform would be an overstatement, but there was clearly a shift in political discourse during his administration, and gay rights may ultimately serve as a symbol of the GOP's inability to represent mainstream America. By 1992, twenty-three years after Stonewall, the gay and lesbian movement in the United States had come of political age. Organized and motivated by AIDS, we emerged into the presidential campaign as a visible presence, and our rights, issues, and pride ultimately became central features of the year's political debates.

A BRIEF BIOGRAPHY

George Herbert Walker Bush was born on June 12, 1924, in Milton, Massachusetts. A child of privilege, his father was a wealthy Wall Street banker who represented Connecticut in the U.S. Senate from 1952 until 1963. Bush was raised in Connecticut, received his early education at the prestigious Phillips Academy in Massachusetts, and joined the navy after graduation in 1942, where he became the youngest bomber pilot in that branch of the armed services. Upon leaving the service, Bush attended Yale University, where he was captain of the baseball team and graduated Phi Beta Kappa with a degree in economics. After graduation, Bush returned to the family oil business in Texas and started his political career. In 1964, he unsuccessfully ran for a Senate seat against Democrat Ralph Yarborough, but when reapportionment gave Houston an additional House seat two years later, Bush ran for that seat and won. Serving on the House Ways and Means Committee, he developed a strong relationship with Richard Nixon. In 1968, when Nixon was elected president, Bush was reelected to the House. In 1970 he left his House seat to make a run for the Senate, but lost to Democrat Lloyd Bentsen.

Between 1970 and 1979 Bush further developed his conservative political associations through a number of different positions in and out of the federal government. He was appointed ambassador to the United Nations by President Nixon in 1970, but left that post in 1972 to chair the Republican National Committee. When Ford moved into the White House, Bush appeared to be the front-runner for the vice-presidential position, but Nelson Rockefeller, governor of New York, was selected instead. Bush bypassed the opportunity to serve as ambassador to Britain or France, instead opting to serve as chief of the U.S. Liaison Office in the People's Republic of China. In 1975, Ford recalled Bush from China and asked him to take over as director of the Central Intelligence Agency. The CIA had been shaken by allegations of illegal activity, mismanagement, and assassination plots against foreign officials and was badly in need of restructuring. During the next two years, Bush earned praise from Republicans and Democrats alike for his role in repairing the agency's morale and public image. In 1979, he announced his candidacy for president and, after losing to Ronald Reagan in the primary, was selected as the vice-presidential running mate. When Reagan's second term ended, Bush ran for president on his own, defeating Michael S. Dukakis.[1] Throughout his life Bush cultivated ties to the more conservative elements of the Republican Party. His privileged upbringing, his close ties to conservative icons Nixon and Reagan, as well as his stewardship of the CIA, suggest that his administration might have been more actively homophobic than it actually was.

THE 1988 ELECTION

Gay rights issues took very different forms in the two Bush presidential campaigns. Throughout the 1988 election cycle, the Bush camp worked hard to distinguish itself from the policies of the Reagan administration. Gay rights per se were relatively absent from general political discourse, but AIDS policy issues appeared prominently and were often conflated with gay rights in public debate. Some within the Republican Party suggested that Bush should use AIDS as a wedge issue to move out of the shadow of the Reagan administration, a suggestion that Bush rejected.[2] AIDS discourse overshadowed gay rights issues in 1988 as public health measures and research funding dominated that year's political agenda. Struggling under the devastation of HIV, much of the gay community was more committed to saving lives and caring for the ill than pursuing other political demands. Moreover, gay and lesbian rights issues had never yet played a substantial role in presidential politics.

The 1988 Republican Party platform claimed that the "Reagan-Bush Administration launched the nation's fight against AIDS, committing more than $5 billion in the last five years. For 1989, the President's budget recommends

a 42% increase in current funding."[3] Such hyperbolic self-congratulation—
seemingly ignorant that AIDS had taken a substantial toll on the gay community for several years before the Reagan administration reluctantly acted, and
then only after mounting protests and political activism—reflected the Republican Party's general uneasiness with AIDS. The GOP's philosophy about gay
rights is more aptly characterized in the following excerpt from the party's 1988
platform:

> We must not only marshall our scientific resources against AIDS, but
> must also protect those who do not have the disease. In this regard, edu-
> cation plays a critical role. AIDS education should emphasize that absti-
> nence from drug abuse and sexual activity outside of marriage is the
> safest way to avoid infection with the AIDS virus.[4]

At first glance this passage suggests a proactive approach to curbing new HIV
infections. On closer inspection, however, it reflects the heteronormative policies of the political right. Explicit limitation of sexual activity to marriage—a
social and legal status denied to gay men and lesbians—makes it clear that
their relationships were not to be recognized or respected by the GOP. Without any explicit reference to gays and lesbians, the platform expressed a commitment to continued suppression of same-sex sexuality and avoidance of the
gay community's political goals. Ironically, the platform further stated a commitment to recognizing the ability of "families, communities, places of work
and voluntary associations" to cope with problems more effectively than government; the statement accurately describes the gay community's responses to
AIDS.[5] Moreover, the GOP also claimed that their party "has stood for the
worth of every person."[6] In the weeks just prior to the 1988 election, AIDS was
notably absent from all major speeches. In his 1989 inaugural address Bush
made no reference to AIDS.[7]

Against this background, it was difficult to predict how President-elect
Bush would position his administration vis-à-vis gay rights. Since the Republican Party was officially committed to maintaining an idealized notion of the
American family (i.e., heterosexual marriage in its most patriarchal, heterosex-
ist, monogamous, and procreative guise), it would have surprised no one if
Bush had adopted an ardently antigay posture. Indeed, one would probably expect a former military, athlete, Republican Texan who came of age in the rabidly homophobic 1950s to stand staunchly opposed to the rights claims of the
gay and lesbian community. Other members of the GOP strongly encouraged
Bush to adopt a rabidly homophobic posture, most notably Representative
William E. Dannemeyer (R-CA). During Bush's first year in office, Dannemeyer was particularly alarmed by reports that a Washington-based male
prostitution ring had been catering to officials high in the administration. Dan-

nemeyer cautioned the president that homosexuals in the administration had moved White House policy away from "traditional family values" to promote the "homosexual movement."[8] Thomas Stoddard, executive director at the time of the Lambda Legal Defense and Education Fund, responded by thanking Mr. Dannemeyer: "Th[e] letter is so extreme in tone [it] will greatly enhance our fund-raising efforts and demonstrates more concretely than any other document I have ever seen that gay people are still the object of irrational hatred in this country."[9] The White House had no immediate reaction to the letter, and by the time Bush left office in January of 1993 significant advances had been made on a number of fronts. While radical antigay forces in the Republican far right may have pulled the administration in their direction, their most homophobic elements were never fully embraced or given a voice from the White House.

The gay and lesbian community won several important victories in Congress during the Bush years. Funding for AIDS care, prevention, and research grew significantly; legislation intended to protect people with AIDS was successfully steered through Congress; several distinguished appointees supported by the gay community were posted to key positions within the administration. While some of these events say little about the president himself, they establish a context and highlight some of the most visible moments in a history of gay rights between 1989 and 1993.

AIDS AND THE BUSH ADMINISTRATION

Early in his administration, Bush won praise from the AIDS community for his appointment of David Rogers and Belinda Madison to the National Commission on AIDS. Rogers, a professor at Cornell University, and Madison, president of the National Association of People with AIDS, were called "strong, credible, and important additions to the commission" by Representative Henry Waxman, Democrat from Los Angeles, California.[10] Although Reagan's appointments to the panel were new to AIDS work and had strongly conservative credentials, these two Bush appointments had expertise in the area of AIDS work and their appointments appeared less politically motivated.

For the most part, however, George Bush was criticized for his lack of leadership regarding AIDS. June E. Osborn, chair of the National Commission on AIDS during the Bush years, described the administration as "woefully inadequate" in its response to the crisis. In response, Louis Sullivan, director of Health and Human Services, asserted that he felt politically "ambushed" by the criticism, but the White House maintained its silence. Magic Johnson, one of the most visible members of the commission, resigned to protest the Bush administration's reticent approach to the problem. Moreover, the head of the

CDC during this period, William Roper, opposed sexually explicit AIDS education materials, allowing official homophobia to hamper educational programs.[11]

Bush attempted to use appointment powers to gain political ground in the gay and AIDS communities. Among his more highly regarded attempts was Anthony Fauci, whom he asked to head the National Institutes of Health, an offer Fauci declined in order to maintain his focus on AIDS research. David Kessler, another notable appointment initially welcomed by the gay community, was praised for expediting the FDA's clinical trials process and attempting to move potentially beneficial AIDS drugs onto the market.[12] Many industry leaders criticized Kessler for his seemingly antibusiness position, but he earned praise from many AIDS activists.

By the end of his administration, reviews of Bush's response to AIDS ran the gamut. In 1992 *The Advocate* conducted an interview with four notable players in the administration's fight against HIV: Dr. James Mason, assistant secretary of Health and Human Services and director of the U.S. Public Health Service; Dr. Antonia Novello, surgeon general; Dr. June E. Osborn, chairwoman of the National Commission on AIDS; and Dr. Donald Francis, virologist and epidemiologist with the CDC. When asked "How do you think Bush is handling the AIDS crisis?" responses ranged between criticism and praise. Mason was quoted as saying that "President Bush has done a wonderful job—he has done more for AIDS than any president, any government leader." Furthermore, he continued by asserting that "Bush has been instrumental against AIDS discrimination," noting that the president frequently visited people with AIDS.[13] Novello was relatively measured in her response, offering a hopeful plea intended to increase both research and public understanding. Osborn, on the other hand, was quoted as saying, "There is really nothing too harsh that can be said about the lack of leadership of this administration to this epidemic," a sentiment underscored by Francis.[14] In the final analysis, Bush's response to AIDS was minimal, lacked focus, and was the cause of considerable protest.[15] His public appearances were frequently interrupted by protesters expressing their frustration with his policies.[16]

STATUTORY SUCCESSES

Several gay-friendly laws were passed by Congress between 1989 and 1993, giving Bush the chance to sign laws that congressional allies had worked hard to see enacted. In April of 1990, George Bush signed into law the Hate Crimes Statistics Act, sponsored by Senator Paul Simon (D-IL). The act directs the attorney general to collect statistics on hate crimes committed against individuals on the basis of religion, race, ethnicity, or sexual orientation. The bill marked two significant milestones for the gay community. First, it marked the first time that sexual orientation had been written into a federal law, and second, the signing ceremony marked the first time that gay activists received a formal invitation to the White House for the signing of a bill. Twelve invitations were sent to the Human Rights Campaign Fund, seven to the National Gay and Lesbian Task Force, and three to Parents and Friends of Lesbians and Gays (PFLAG). Notably absent from the guest list was Urvashi Vaid, as Bush was ostensibly still stinging from her public critique of his AIDS policy agenda.[17]

Reactions within the gay community were generally positive, with the *Washington Blade* referring to the event as a "landmark development." Conservative commentators, meanwhile, worried that the event would signal tolerance of gays and lesbians, potentially threatening relations with the Middle American power base of the Republican Party.[18] Although the attempt to collect statistics on hate crimes bodes well for furthering our understanding of crime in America, it's still impossible to paint an accurate picture of crimes based on sexual orientation. The confines of the closet and the disinclination of law enforcement to see such crimes as motivated by homophobia make it difficult to tell exactly how much the act has improved the accuracy of hate-crime-statistics reporting.

In addition to the Hate Crimes Statistics Act, Bush signed two other pieces of legislation that were hailed by the gay and lesbian community. The Americans with Disabilities Act, providing protection for people with AIDS, became law in 1990 and, for the most part, has protected people with HIV from discrimination. When lower courts disagreed on whether the act applied to asymptomatic HIV infection, that issue was settled by the U.S. Supreme Court in 1998. Eight years after its original signing, the act has finally become broadly applicable to people with HIV even if they have no symptoms.[19]

The Ryan White Comprehensive AIDS Resources Emergency (CARE) Act, one of the most important pieces of legislation enacted since the AIDS crisis began, was signed into law in August of 1990. The act, named for an Indiana teenager who fought discrimination in school and died of AIDS-related complications in 1993, funded medical care in the nation's hardest-hit cities. In the Senate, Edward Kennedy, Democrat of Massachusetts, sponsored the bill, with strong support on the Republican side of the aisle from Orrin Hatch, Republican of Utah. Henry Waxman was the bill's chief proponent in the House. Although Kennedy and Waxman had been strong supporters of progressive AIDS policy throughout the crisis, the support of Hatch, a conservative Mormon from Utah, was more surprising but not inconsistent with his positions throughout the epidemic.

By year's end, 1990 had turned out to be relatively successful for the gay and lesbian community. The Ryan White CARE Act, the Hate Crimes

Statistics Act, and the Americans with Disabilities Act were major legislative accomplishments. Congress also voted to reauthorize the budget for the National Endowment for the Arts, despite homophobic attacks by Jesse Helms, and to remove homosexuality from a list of reasons to exclude travelers or immigrants from the United States. Surprisingly, a record number of twelve senators and seventy-nine representatives signed on to a comprehensive gay and lesbian civil rights bill that has been a source of controversy since the seventies.[20] Despite moments of strong resistance on the far right, gay rights advocates made modest advances through the early years of the Bush presidency.

APPOINTMENTS TO THE SUPREME COURT

Supreme Court appointments are one of the most enduring means by which a president can insure the longevity of his political ideals since most justices remain on the nation's high court for decades after a president leaves office. Bush had the opportunity to appoint two justices to the Supreme Court during his time in office: David Hackett Souter in 1990 and Clarence Thomas in 1991. The story of these justices and gay rights will not be conclusively written for generations to come, but a few recent cases suggest that Bush's gay rights track record on the Supreme Court may be mixed.

Justices Souter and Thomas have participated in a few cases of importance to the gay and lesbian community, and despite the ominous portents of the Court's decision in *Hurley v. Irish-American Gay, Lesbian and Bisexual Group of Boston, Inc.*,[21] their voting records suggest that Justice Souter may be more amenable to claims of gay litigants. In *Hurley*, the Court allowed the exclusion of gay Irish-Americans from Boston's St. Patrick's Day parade. The Supreme Judicial Court of Massachusetts had ruled in favor of the gay group, asserting that the state's public accommodation law prohibited exclusion because it explicitly named sexual orientation as a protected class. Justice Souter, writing for a unanimous Court, recast the issue squarely within the confines of the First Amendment. Distinguishing between public accommodations and the expression of a political viewpoint, Souter's opinion for the Court was less an assault on gay rights than it was the enforcement of a heterosexual status quo in a tricky First Amendment case. In short, the rights of the gay Irish group were not recognized because the Court would not force parade organizers to express a political point of view with which they disagreed. For this moment in constitutional history the lesbian and gay community appeared to be simply an idea and not a group of individuals seeking inclusion in society.

The Court's ruling in *Romer v. Evans* was more encouraging and may more accurately foreshadow how Justices Souter and Thomas will deal with gay rights issues.[22] A majority of the justices, including Justice Souter, voted to overturn Colorado's Amendment 2, which prohibited protections against discrimination on the basis of sexual orientation. The *Romer* decision is, to date, the most encouraging sign from the Supreme Court that gays and lesbians may be moving into the constitutional fold. Justice Souter's vote to overturn Amendment 2, and Justice Thomas's vote to uphold it, indicates that George Bush's Supreme Court legacy may be a double-edged sword for gay and lesbian rights.

MAKE WAR NOT LOVE

Perhaps the most memorable event of the Bush administration was the 1991 war in the Persian Gulf. When the war began, gays and lesbians were being routinely purged from the military, and the debate about "don't ask, don't tell" was still well in the future, yet the military opted to suspend antigay witch-hunts to assure combat readiness in the Gulf. Under the Pentagon's "Stop Loss Policy," administrative separations of lesbian and gay service personnel were temporarily halted, reflecting the same duplicitous policy change that gay and lesbian service members had seen in earlier conflicts.[23] In January of 1991, Randy Shilts of the *San Francisco Chronicle* reported that several gay and lesbian service members had outed themselves to commanding officers and were told that they had to serve in the Gulf War regardless of their sexual orientation. Furthermore, they were also informed that they would most likely be discharged when they returned home.[24]

When the war was over and the troops returned home, the military resumed purging gay and lesbian service members from its ranks. In August of 1991, Shilts reported that discharges were resuming apace to the disappointment of many in the gay and lesbian community. Despite the initial impression that policies had changed and discharges would stop, Department of Defense officials insisted that the policy had never been altered; Pentagon policy remained as homophobic as ever.[25]

THE ROTC AND FBI

In keeping with military policy to exclude gays and lesbians from service, the ROTC also continued expelling service members because of their sexual orientation. During 1989 and 1990, the ROTC not only expelled gays and lesbians from their programs, denying them scholarships and access to an education, but subsequently sought repayment for tuition and expenses already invested in the educational project. In some instances, expelled students were prosecuted by the U.S. attorney's office in attempts to recoup more than $25,000 in educational expenses.[26]

In addition to excluding gays and lesbians from the military, the FBI pursued similarly vigorous expulsion projects throughout the Bush administration. In one of the most notable cases, Frank Buttino was fired from his job as an FBI agent in June of 1990 after the government received an anonymous letter stating that Buttino was gay. Buttino's suit against the FBI turned on issues that have been central to government employment for decades, namely, that gays and lesbians are security risks because they are vulnerable to blackmail or coercion. The FBI denied having an explicit antigay policy and argued that Buttino was fired because he had repeatedly lied about his sexual orientation while FBI investigators were trying to determine if he posed a security risk to the agency.[27]

Buttino pursued legal action against the FBI until the Clinton administration reversed course and added sexual orientation to the list of prohibited forms of discrimination in federal employment. The day after the federal government opened its defense in the case in 1993, Attorney General Janet Reno publicly announced the change in policy. Three months later the case settlement was approved in San Francisco's federal district court. Buttino won almost $100,000 in cash, legal fees of approximately $53,000, and the reinstatement of his pension at age sixty-two.[28]

FAMILY VALUES

Late in the Reagan administration, the Department of Health and Human Services undertook a detailed analysis of teenage suicide. In the summer of 1989 the results were made public and curiously repudiated by Secretary Louis W. Sullivan.[29] Researchers had concluded that one of the primary risk factors for suicide among teenagers was sexual identity. In short, gay and lesbian youth were significantly more likely to attempt suicide than their heterosexual counterparts. As noted literary theorist Eve Kosofsky Sedgwick observes, these conclusions were sharply at odds with official Republican policy. Sullivan wanted not only to repudiate the report, but to deny its very existence. In a written response to the researchers' findings, Sullivan asserted that "the views expressed in the paper entitled 'Gay Male and Lesbian Youth Suicide' do not in any way represent my personal beliefs or the policy of this Department. I am strongly committed to advancing traditional family values. . . . In my opinion, the views expressed in the paper run contrary to that aim."[30] As a result of its unwelcome reception in the administration, the report has been largely ignored throughout the country, and teenage sexuality continues to be controversial.

Sullivan's harkening to family values echoed a theme that was prominent throughout the Bush administration, especially in the rhetoric of Vice President Dan Quayle. Quayle often served as the administration's contact with the religious right, which gained considerable power through the Reagan administration and became a formidable force during the Bush years. Barbara Bush stirred controversy on the Republican right in 1990 when, in a letter to Paulette Goodman, president of PFLAG, she stated, "I firmly believe that we cannot tolerate discrimination against any individuals or groups in our country."[31] Barbara Bush's maternal agreement with Paulette Goodman was condemned by religious fundamentalists, who portrayed such parental acceptance as antithetical to family values. George Bush, meanwhile, remained moderate, stating in an interview with the *New York Times* that he did not consider homosexuality to be normal, but acknowledged that he would continue to support and embrace a gay grandchild.[32] During the 1992 election Bush stated publicly that his administration had no "litmus test" that might automatically exclude gays and lesbians from staff positions.[33] Dan Quayle, on the other hand, took a more conservative position, stating at the 1992 GOP convention that it was wrong to treat "alternative lifestyles [as] morally equivalent to more traditional ones."[34]

THE 1992 ELECTION

George Bush's defeat by William Jefferson Clinton has been analyzed and examined from numerous perspectives. What were the factors that contributed to his unexpected loss of the White House? At the start of the 1992 electoral season all indicators suggested that Bush had the election in his back pocket. As presidential scholar Richard Waterman writes:

> In March 1991 George Bush's approval rating was measured at 89 percent, making him the most popular president since the Gallup organization began polling perceptions of presidential performance in the mid-1930s. Based on these exalted approval ratings, administration insiders, political pundits, and even many Democrats believed that Bush would easily win reelection to a second term as president of the United States in 1992.[35]

Although it is tempting to assert that gay rights issues bore sufficient weight to tip the electoral scales, gay rights can probably be best understood as a barometer for some other larger political storm. Standing in relief against the Republican trope of family values, Bill Clinton's support of the gay and lesbian community seemed particularly risky, yet William Schneider, a political analyst with the American Enterprise Institute, observed that it was also risky for the Republicans. "They can't appear repressive," the *New York Times* quoted him as saying, "[b]ut polls show people are uncomfortable with it. They don't approve of it. The Democrats can't be perceived as promoting it. It's not clear how it's going to play out, because we've never had it in a Presidential race like this before."[36] By most accounts, both sides took a gamble and used the rights of gays and lesbians as a chip in their game.

In stark contrast to the silence of the 1988 GOP platform, the 1992 platform engaged gay and lesbian issues with an oppressive stance. No representatives of gay rights groups were allowed to speak to the Republican platform committee, and no openly lesbian or gay delegates attended the GOP convention. Whereas the 1988 GOP platform contained no explicit references to gay rights, the 1992 platform specifically denounced them: "We oppose efforts by the Democratic Party to include sexual preference as a protected minority receiving preferential status under civil rights statutes at the Federal, state and local level."[37] Not only did the 1992 platform specifically state opposition to civil rights protections, but the platform also denounced same-sex marriages, adoption and foster care by gays and lesbians, and called for continued support of policies excluding gays and lesbians from military service.[38] What had been almost a nonissue four years earlier emerged as a point of distinction between the two parties.

Antigay sentiments rang out from the podium at the GOP convention as Patrick Buchanan insisted that Bill Clinton would impose gay rights on the nation, along with a list of other ostensible horribles such as abortion on demand and women in combat. Bowing to these pressures, the Bush campaign planned to hit the issue hard in the final months before the election. Radio spots considered for broadcast in the South described a Clinton victory as a way to assure more gay and lesbian teachers in schools.[39] While the more acerbic elements in the Republican Party named gays and lesbians as a serious political danger, campaign officials close to the president tried to moderate his image, asserting that Bush was not antihomosexual but anti–special rights.

On the same weekend as the GOP convention, Log Cabin Republicans met to determine the direction of their electoral support. The group, representing over six thousand gay and lesbian Republicans, could not endorse Bill Clinton due to the organization's bylaws, but they also voted not to endorse Bush. As reported by the *New York Times*, "Group members couldn't help smiling as they cited what they called the hypocrisy of the party leaders. 'There are plenty of gay people working for George Bush and around him,' said Tony Zampella of San Diego. 'We know it. He knows it. Who's kidding who?'"[40] Paul

Cellupica, legal adviser to federal "drug czar" William Bennett and lifelong Republican, stated in the *New York Times* that he had voted for Clinton because "the litany of the White House's attacks on lesbians and gay men was simply too long and too painful."[41] In the end, the rhetoric of oppression that alienated Log Cabin Republicans may have helped alienate other voters as well and likely contributed to Bush's defeat in the 1992 election.

Clinton, meanwhile, was receptive to gay and lesbian support but simultaneously sought to moderate his image against attacks from the Republican right. While asserting that he did not advocate gay marriage, Clinton reiterated that he was opposed to discrimination in employment and in the military.[42] Advocates within the gay and lesbian community were encouraged by the increased visibility of gay rights issues within the larger political arena, announcing that "gay and lesbian civil rights issues . . . have broken through the glass ceiling at last."[43] Moving out of the shadow of AIDS, the voices of the gay and lesbian community found a receptive ear in 1992. Clearly, the community had earned a place at the political table and has become a palpable presence in American politics.

CONCLUSION

Analysts have offered several reasons for the Republicans' failure to retain the White House in 1992. Richard W. Waterman attributes Bush's loss partly to his inflated sense of popularity after the Gulf War.[44] Many in the campaign expected high public approval ratings to carry the president through the election. Consequently, Bush was slow to begin his campaign in earnest, and by the time he did, his opponents had established the terms of debate. Furthermore, Waterman argues, Bush did not perceive himself to be a strong campaigner and, consequently, failed to coordinate the White House with his campaign. "By the time James Baker was finally brought in to provide a sense of order and coordination between the two organizations, the president's reelection prospects were all but doomed. In other words, by that time, the proverbial barn door had been closed too late."[45]

It is tempting to assert that the 1992 Bush campaign failed in part because the Republican Party's staunchly homophobic platform contrasted with the Democratic Party's embrace. It would also stretch the credible estimation of our community's political clout. It is equally tempting to suggest that George Bush was hoist by his own homophobic petard, but that would also be too much of a stretch. In retrospect, however, it seems that gay rights received more positive media coverage and that the lesbian and gay community fostered more direct links to the Clinton White House than to any previous administration.

The relationship between Bush and the gay rights movement was tenuous but may ultimately have been a symptom of his disinclination to steer the ship of state with intent and direction. As presidential scholar Dean Hammer observes:

> Speculation by political strategists, Democrat and Republican alike, almost demanded that Bush provide a vision of the future to save his candidacy. What Bush demonstrated was a rather unpragmatic inability to articulate such a vision. And this inability, by Bush's own admission as well as the testimony of his closest advisors, seems more a matter of character than design.[46]

CHAPTER 3

A "Friend" in the White House? Reflections on the Clinton Presidency

Craig A. Rimmerman

Clinton has done more for the gay and lesbian community than has any other president.

—A NATIONAL LESBIAN AND GAY ORGANIZATION LEADER

The fault partly resides with a president whose prodigious capacity to display empathy has never been matched by a willingness to risk anything in order to translate kindly feelings into effective action.

—DAVID L. KIRP, "POLITICS OUT OF THE CLOSET," THE NATION, SEPTEMBER 9/16, 1996

Finally, let me say again, this is not an election, or it should not be, about race or gender or being gay or straight or religion or age or region or income. What kills the country is not the problems it faces. . . . What kills the country is to proceed day in and day out with no vision, with no sense that tomorrow can be better than today, with no sense of shared community. What I came here today to tell you in simple terms is: I have a vision and you are part of it.

—BILL CLINTON, MAY 18, 1992

ON MAY 18, 1992, THEN PRESIDENTIAL CANDIDATE Bill Clinton gave a speech to the Los Angeles–based organization ANGLE (Access Now for Gay and Lesbian Equality). The idea was to have a million-dollar fund-raising event for Clinton in the lesbian and gay community. Six hundred and fifty lesbians and gays spent at least $100 each to hear Clinton's speech. As the above words suggest, Clinton spoke with eloquence and passion about the need for a more inclusive America, one that included lesbians and gays. He outlined his commitment to support a "Manhattan Project on AIDS," which would mean a sharp increase in funds for AIDS research and would be coordinated by one individual, an AIDS czar, someone "who can cut across all the departments and agencies, who has the president's ear and the president's arm."[1] Videotaped copies of Clinton's speech were distributed throughout the country and played all fall at lesbian and gay fund-raisers. Many perceived that Clinton's words signaled a serious, sincere commitment to the concerns of the lesbian and gay community. As a result, Clinton received the support and endorsement of an array of lesbian and gay individuals and financial contributions from lesbians and gays throughout the country.

And what did Clinton promise during the 1992 presidential campaign? He pledged that he would not forget the interests of his lesbian and gay constituents if he was elected. At various points during the campaign, Clinton said that he would recognize lesbians and gays in ways unheard of during previous presidencies. He also promised that he would provide lesbians and gays greater access to his administration than previous presidents had done. One way that he pledged to accomplish this latter goal was to appoint openly lesbian and gay officials to his administration. He also promised to overturn the ban on lesbians and gays in the United States military and escalate the federal governmental response to AIDS by creating an AIDS czar and increasing funding for AIDS research. Clinton made additional promises as well: to support a gay civil rights bill and to issue an executive order barring discrimination on the basis of sexual orientation in all federal agencies. Compared to previous occupants of the Oval Office, Clinton's presidency would be different, as he promised to do much more substantively and symbolically on behalf of lesbians and gays. The promise began to take shape at the 1992 Democratic National Convention when Roberta Achtenberg, a California lesbian, and Bob Hattoy, a gay man with AIDS, were both given speaking opportunities. Eventually, both Achtenberg and Hattoy received appointments in the Clinton administration.

This essay examines how Clinton attempted to translate his campaign promises into concrete public policy. It also explores to what extent Clinton attempted to follow through on his campaign promises, the opposition to those promises, and what he and his administration did in the face of that opposition. The response of the lesbian and gay community to having a so-called friend in the White House is also explored. The chapter ends by discussing the lessons that the lesbian and gay movement might learn from the Clinton experience and how these lessons might be applied to dealing with future residents of the Oval Office. While the Clinton presidency has meant greater visibility for lesbians and gays, as well as greater access to political power at the national level, the overall Clinton substantive record has been decidedly mixed and, on balance, disappointing.

As governor of Arkansas, Bill Clinton had no record of supporting lesbian and gay rights. Indeed, he never even offered a public utterance in support of a lesbian or gay cause. But in an October 1992 interview with Jeffrey Schmalz, Clinton admitted that his Los Angeles fund-raising event forced him to realize that "running for president would require me to think about things that I just didn't have to deal with as governor."[2] Rahm Emanuel, one of Clinton's political advisers and the finance director for the campaign, put the issue more bluntly: "The gay community is the new Jewish community. It's highly politicized, with fundamental health and civil rights concerns. And it contributes money. All that makes for a potent political force, indeed."[3]

There was tremendous jubilation in the lesbian and gay community on the night of Clinton's election. Pollsters estimate that Clinton received some 75 percent of the lesbian and gay vote, and that the community had contributed some $3 million to his campaign war chest.[4] Indeed, there was tremendous hope and excitement because for the first time a presidential candidate had courted the lesbian and gay vote, had been elected with the support of the community, and would now have to govern with that reality in mind.

But for presidents at the end of the twentieth century, what does governance really mean in our political system? At one level, a lasting legacy of the constitutional framers is that individual presidents have the freedom to choose among the opportunities and the constraints facing them as they exercise presidential power. Yet in their efforts to promote liberty and impede majority tyranny, the architects of the Constitution may have performed their task too well. Nowhere is this more evident than when a president attempts to sustain the momentum of his honeymoon period by building the governing coalition that he needs in Congress and in the electorate to translate his domestic and foreign policy campaign promises into concrete public policy.[5] All presidents soon learn that our fragmented political system makes it increasingly difficult for presidents to accomplish their domestic policy goals in a timely manner. This was especially true as Clinton attempted to carry out his campaign promise of overturning the military ban on lesbians and gays through an executive order.

For Bill Clinton, there was virtually no governing coalition as he won with merely 43 percent of the popular vote. He was in a particularly vulnerable position, despite the fact that Democrats controlled both the House and the Senate. As the political scientist David Rayside points out, "It was easy enough for other politicians and observers to conclude that Clinton's victory had been a negative vote—a rejection of President Bush."[6] In addition, Ross Perot's strong showing as a third-party candidate had denied Clinton the important symbolic power of winning more than half of the vote.

While the Democrats had control of both the House and the Senate, they were hardly united on how or even whether to address lesbian and gay concerns. Indeed, most congressional members of the Democratic Party had other more "important" domestic policy concerns on their minds—the economy, health care, social security, trade, welfare reform, the budget—that were central elements of Clinton's own successful campaign strategy.

THE MILITARY BAN

Clinton's honeymoon period was very short indeed. One reason for this was the furor caused by his attempt to overturn the military ban on lesbians and gays through an executive order. At a Harvard University forum in the fall of 1991, then presidential candidate Bill Clinton was asked whether he would issue an executive order to rescind the ban on lesbians and gays in the military. Clinton responded, "Yes," and explained further: "I think people who are gay should be expected to work, and should be given the opportunity to serve the country." He continued with this pledge as a presidential candidate and as president-elect.[7]

But once he took office, President Clinton failed in performing his important leadership role in educating the public regarding why he believed that the military ban should be overturned. In a previous study of this issue, I outlined several reasons for his failure to do so.[8] First, Clinton clearly recognized that he did not have the required votes in Congress to sustain his promise of issuing an executive order to overturn the ban. In addition, compromise comes easily to Clinton, as building consensus characterizes his approach to governance. This is what he attempted to do with his Don't Ask, Don't Tell, Don't Pursue compromise proposal. A third explanation is that Clinton has embraced policy positions associated with the New Democrats,[9] those who believe that it is important for the Democratic Party to move in a more moderate direction. From this vantage point, then, it made good sense for Clinton and his advisers to distance themselves from so-called modern liberal special-interest groups such as lesbian and gay organizations. Finally, Clinton was worried about squandering valuable political capital early in his first term on overturning the ban, capital that he would surely need in his budget and health-care fights with Congress.

During the campaign, Clinton's promise had provoked little response from George Bush or Dan Quayle. Indeed, the August 1992 Republican National Convention was characterized by considerable antigay vitriol, which public opinion polls indicated alienated much of mainstream America. Bush and Quayle, then, tried to avoid using antigay rhetoric during their general-election campaign. In doing so, they perhaps gave Clinton and his lesbian and gay supporters a false sense of confidence and security regarding the possibility of overturning the military ban. Soon after Clinton confirmed his intention to follow through on his campaign promise (at his first news conference following his election), the religious right began mobilizing and organizing. They had the strong support of Senator Sam Nunn (D-GA), then chair of the Senate Armed Services Committee, veterans' groups, and antigay personnel in the military hierarchy. Clinton's perceived weakness on military issues gave further ammunition to those opposed to lifting the ban, as did his determination to focus "like a laser beam" on the economy immediately upon taking office. As it became increasingly clear that overturning the ban would be fraught with considerable political peril and erosion of political capital, Clinton and his advisers distanced themselves from the issue.

The result was a compromise proposal, one that shattered the hopes of his lesbian and gay supporters, who were convinced that he would at least have the political courage to follow through with his original plan. On April 16, 1993, Clinton had even met with six lesbian and gay representatives—the first publicly announced session of gay representatives with any president in the Oval Office—to discuss the military ban. Tom Stoddard, the head of the Campaign for Military Service,[10] attended the session and reported that the president was "completely sympathetic" and "understood all the points that were raised."[11] Stoddard and several of his colleagues mistook access to the president for substantive support, a mistake that many in the lesbian and gay movement were to make during the Clinton presidency.

There were, however, signals along the way that Clinton was quickly retreating from his original promise. On May 27, 1993, Clinton appeared on a live broadcast of *CBS This Morning,* where a Virginia minister asked him about the issue. The president responded:

> Most Americans believe that the gay lifestyle should not be promoted by the military or anybody else in this country. . . . We are trying to work this out so that our country does not appear to be endorsing a gay lifestyle. . . . I think most Americans will agree when it works out that people are treated properly if they behave properly without the government appearing to endorse a lifestyle.

In answering the question, Clinton used the worst form of language— "lifestyle," "endorse," "approve," "promote"—from the antigay lexicon. Members of the lesbian and gay community quickly responded. David Mixner,

Clinton's longtime friend and a leading openly gay member of the Democratic Party, announced that he was physically sickened by Clinton's response. Those supporting overturning the ban had good reason to be disturbed. Bill Clinton had clearly begun to retreat in public from his promise to overturn the ban through an executive order. It is clear in retrospect that for political reasons Clinton was trying to distance himself from lesbian and gay groups. What better way to accomplish this than to embrace some of the language of the radical-right groups who were so feverishly working to uphold the ban?

But Clinton was also clearly signaling to lesbian and gay groups as well as their supporters that he would likely compromise on his original promise. That compromise took the form of his July 1993 Don't Ask, Don't Tell, Don't Pursue proposal. Sam Nunn toughened Clinton's proposal so that those lesbians and gays serving in the military were punished even more harshly than in the Clinton compromise. Ultimately, Nunn's changes were codified into law by Congress, thus making it much more difficult for opponents of the ban to offer serious structural reforms in the future. Any future changes to Nunn's congressional policy would require congressional consent. This also signaled a major defeat for opponents of the ban since the previous ban had been enforced through an executive order, which could at least be changed through a presidential missive.

How did Clinton defend his compromise proposal? The president called the plan an "honest compromise" and acknowledged that the plan's specifics were not necessarily in agreement with his own goals. Almost all interviewees informed me that in the face of intense congressional and military opposition to lifting the ban, Clinton believed that the policy was the closest he could actually come to meeting his campaign promise. As one administration official stated: "The president believes that it is a solid advance forward in terms of extending rights to gays and lesbians in the military."[12]

As one would expect, lesbian and gay activists and their supporters were furious with Clinton's compromise plan. Torie Osborn, executive director of the National Gay and Lesbian Task Force, argued that the plan is "simply a repackaging of discrimination." Tom Stoddard, the coordinator of the Campaign for Military Service said, "The president could have lifted up the conscience of the country. Instead, he acceded without a fight to the stereotypes of prejudices he himself had disparaged." But perhaps a *New Republic* editorial best captured the anger of those who expected so much more from the president:

> And the most demeaning assumption about the new provisions is that they single out the deepest moment of emotional intimacy—the private sexual act—as that which is most repugnant. Its assumption about the

dignity and humanity of gay people, in and out of the military, in public and in private, is sickening.[13]

The implementation of the plan over the past four years has done nothing to assuage the concerns of the president's most serious critics. The Servicemembers Legal Defense Network has conducted yearly studies of the military's implementation of the Don't Ask, Don't Tell policy and has repeatedly found a pattern of violations that often render the policy little more than Ask, Pursue, and Harass.[14]

One study of the entire debate revealed that Clinton's leadership on the issue did have positive consequences for public opinion regarding allowing lesbians and gays to serve openly. Political scientists Clyde Wilcox and Robin Wolpert found that "Clinton's stand may have mobilized increased support for lifting the ban among those who liked him."[15]

But most of what came out of the experience was quite negative. A president who had campaigned for lesbian and gay support by promising to overturn the ban had broken his promise within six months of taking office. Empirical studies of the plan's implementation over the past four years indicate that the policy has been a dismal failure. And the lesbian and gay movement learned that it could not trust a so-called friend in the White House. Unfortunately, this conclusion would be reinforced in a variety of ways during the Clinton presidency's following six years.

AIDS

In his infamous Los Angeles campaign speech, Clinton said, "If I could wave my arm for those of you that are HIV-positive and make it go away tomorrow, I would do it—so help me God, I would. If I gave up my race for the White House and everything else, I would do that."[16] During that same speech, he promised to sharply increase AIDS research funds.

But soon after taking office, Clinton was under fire from AIDS activists for failing to provide the necessary leadership on the HIV immigration issue. During the campaign, Clinton had promised to rescind the Bush administration's rule that barred HIV-infected immigrants from entering the United States, even for a visit. In early 1993, Republicans approved an amendment to a Department of Health and Human Services authorization bill that converted the rule into a law. The Clinton administration spoke out against the amendment, but AIDS activists believed that the response was far too halfhearted. In the end, Clinton antagonized lesbian, gay, and AIDS activists by refusing to veto the HHS bill that contained the HIV immigrant ban.[17]

The Clinton administration deserves credit for significantly increasing overall funding for AIDS prevention, services, and research programs. In addition, he brought much needed visibility to AIDS by convening and attending the first White House conference on the issue. AIDS activists also give him credit for strongly opposing Republican proposals to cut Medicaid, which helps finance care for as many as 40 percent who have been diagnosed with HIV or who are living with AIDS,[18] and for supporting full funding of the Ryan White Act.

As promised, Clinton created the position of AIDS czar (sometimes known as the White House director of national AIDS policy), though many believe that Kristine Gebbie and Sandra Thurman have played more symbolic than substantive roles in addressing AIDS, perhaps because neither of them has had the power or visibility that Clinton suggested in the campaign. AIDS activists also point out that the administration has failed to establish the promised "Manhattan Project" to address AIDS in a meaningful way.

The Clinton administration has been justifiably criticized, as well, for failing to "lift a nine-year-old ban on federal financing for programs to distribute clean needles to drug addicts, even as the government's top scientists certified that such programs did not encourage drug abuse and could save lives by reducing the spread of AIDS."[19] AIDS activists faulted the president for ignoring an array of available evidence that suggests that lifting the ban is morally right and wise policy.

Finally, the Clinton administration's failure to overhaul the health care system has meant that increasing numbers of Americans, many of whom are HIV-positive or who have been diagnosed with AIDS, lack affordable health care. That Clinton never even seriously considered embracing comprehensive medical care has been a particular disappointment to progressive members of the lesbian and gay community and AIDS activists.

Reflecting on Clinton's overall record, one leading AIDS activist said, "Clinton is at risk of missing an opportunity in history." He pointed out that the Clinton administration could do much more in terms of increasing the access of HIV-positive people and those diagnosed with AIDS to drugs. Yet he also gives the president high marks for using the presidency as a bully pulpit for addressing AIDS symbolically.[20] One example of this symbolism is Clinton's attendance at the AIDS Quilt display in Washington, D.C. That a leading gay AIDS activist would identify this as a central strength of the Clinton approach is an indication of how little Presidents Reagan and Bush accomplished in addressing AIDS, as well as how a limited symbolic response from Clinton can evoke public approval and sympathy. As this and other examples suggest, President Clinton has been the recipient of enormous generosity from leading members of the lesbian and gay movement during his presidency.

THE DEFENSE OF MARRIAGE ACT

Clinton received strong criticism from some members of the lesbian and gay movement when he signed the antigay Defense of Marriage Act (DOMA) on September 21, 1996. The law is designed to accomplish two goals: "(1) prevent states from being forced by the Full Faith and Credit Clause to recognize same-sex marriages validly celebrated in other states, and (2) define marriages for federal purposes as the union of one man and one woman."[21] Unlike the military ban issue, however, Clinton was at least consistent on lesbian and gay marriage, as he announced his opposition in the 1992 campaign. But those most critical of the president argued that DOMA was both unnecessary and highly discriminatory, and that Clinton could have vetoed DOMA while still being opposed to the principle of lesbian and gay marriage.[22] Others understood, however, that Clinton was forced to sign DOMA to avoid attacks by the religious right during the 1996 presidential campaign. Indeed, the Dole campaign had run a radio ad that criticized Clinton for supporting overturning the military ban. The Clinton forces responded by releasing their own ad celebrating the president's signing of DOMA. This ad was run on Christian radio stations across the United States, despite the president's criticism of the authors of DOMA for attempting to inject such a difficult issue into presidential politics during an election year. In fact, Clinton actually signed the bill after midnight so that there would be as little attention drawn to his decision as possible. Understandably, lesbian and gay movement members protested loudly when the Clinton campaign advertisement was broadcast on Christian radio. In response, the Clinton campaign pulled the ad in two days.[23]

Could the movement have done more to force the Clinton administration to support same-sex marriage? In answering this question, it is important to remember that same-sex marriage is not a crucial issue for many movement members. Those who think it should be a key goal of movement organizing efforts—individuals such as Andrew Sullivan and Bruce Bawer—generally represent the more moderate to conservative element of the movement. But as we have already learned from the military-ban debate, the movement cannot pick and choose when specific issues will come to the fore. And in some ways, same-sex marriage could not have come at a worse possible time. The Republicans controlled both houses of Congress, it was a presidential election year, and the movement simply did not have the time, organizational skills, or resources to mount an effective organizing and educational campaign on an issue that appeared to be unpopular with the American public, especially given the Christian right's vast organizational resources. Indeed, the Republicans were searching for a popular election-year wedge issue when they introduced the Defense of Marriage Act on May 8, 1996. Rich Tafel, executive director of the

Log Cabin Republicans, supported several of these points when he said, "Marriage is so visceral, such a negative in the polls. My experience in debating this issue is that if I have an hour or two hours, I can win, but if I have five minutes, I can't. This is all being done in five minutes."[24] As a campaign issue, opposition to same-sex marriage served several purposes. It was an opportunity for some politicians to reach out to both the center and the right, given the larger public's apparent lack of support for the issue. And it forced President Clinton to tackle a difficult issue at a time when he did not want to relive the military fiasco of several years before. Clinton had no choice, then, but to alienate some members of his voting base.

How might Clinton have handled the situation differently? He could certainly have forbidden his campaign team from broadcasting a radio ad supporting DOMA on Christian radio. That the campaign ran such an ad suggests how badly Clinton and his campaign advisers wanted to straddle all sides of the issue, especially given his public statements that Republicans were putting him in a difficult situation by introducing DOMA in the middle of an election campaign. He might also have vetoed DOMA, while expressing his opposition to same-sex marriage, by suggesting that such legislation was inappropriate at the time and was being used as a mere political weapon, without the kind of lengthy public education and discussion that the issue deserves. We should not be surprised that Clinton did not follow this latter strategy, given his previous record on the military ban. For him to take a bold and creative position, one rooted in educational leadership, would have been out of keeping with his political character.

How else has the Clinton administration disappointed lesbian and gay activists? In the legal battle over Colorado's Amendment 2, the Clinton administration's Justice Department received considerable and justifiable criticism when it failed even to file a "friend of the court" brief on behalf of lesbian and gay groups that were seeking to have Colorado's antigay ballot initiative declared unconstitutional.[25] In 1992, Colorado voted by a 53 percent majority to prevent the passage of equal-rights laws for lesbians and gays, a referendum that led to the striking down of existing city ordinances. What made the subsequent Supreme Court case particularly noteworthy is that it is perhaps the most important civil liberties Supreme Court case of the past five years. Clinton justified his decision by arguing that he acted upon the advice of Attorney General Janet Reno, who opposed the government's taking a legal stance on the case. When the Supreme Court issued its 1996 *Romer v. Evans* decision, which ruled Colorado's antigay ballot initiative unconstitutional, many lesbian and gay activists tempered their anger at Clinton.[26]

THE CLINTON ADMINISTRATION'S
ACCOMPLISHMENTS

While Clinton disappointed lesbian and gay activists by failing to issue an executive order to overturn the military ban on lesbians and gays, he did issue executive orders in two different cases that extended lesbian and gay civil rights. The first, signed into law on August 3, 1995, "prohibits government agencies from denying security clearances to applicants solely on the basis of their sexual orientation." Clinton's action was the first time a president had included a pro-lesbian-and-gay clause as a part of an official presidential order.[27]

Perhaps the most substantive lesbian and gay rights accomplishment of the Clinton era was his May 1998 executive order that banned antigay discrimination against federal civilian employees. The front-page headline of the *Washington Blade*—"President's Order Protects Workers"—lent testimony to the importance of Clinton's decision. Capping a forty-one-year effort to end federal workforce bias, Clinton's "action formally adds sexual orientation to Executive Order 11478, which banned job discrimination against federal workers based on race, color, religion, sex, national origin, handicap, and age."[28] Frank Kameny, a longtime gay activist who was fired from his federal job in 1957 on grounds of homosexuality, hailed the decision: "It doesn't do anything new, but it ties up loose ends and, therefore, brings closure to what has been a twenty-five-year . . . improvement process. . . . The deed is done, it is over, we can move on to other battles. It is a total victory, which could not have been conceived when I was fired."[29]

Clinton also deserves credit for endorsing and lobbying the U.S. Senate for passage of the Employment Non-Discrimination Act (ENDA), a lesbian and gay civil rights bill, which was narrowly defeated. In doing so, he became the first president to back lesbian and gay civil rights legislation and he did so enthusiastically and publicly. The president has also consistently opposed antigay ballot initiatives that have increasingly appeared throughout the United States. He has urged voters to reject such initiatives because they seek to deny civil rights to lesbians and gays.[30] Finally, when Senate majority leader Trent Lott compared homosexuality to alcoholism, kleptomania, and sex addiction, the White House joined lesbian and gay civil rights leaders in publicly repudiating him.[31]

The Clinton administration has also deservedly earned high marks for appointing openly lesbian and gay officials at all levels of government. Clinton created the White House liaison to the gay community in June 1995, the first time any president had established an official White House position to work with the lesbian and gay community. But his first appointment, Marsha Scott, immediately encountered criticism for being a heterosexual political aide, rather than someone who was a part of the lesbian and gay community.[32] However,

Clinton assuaged his critics when he chose an openly gay official at the Department of Labor as the new White House liaison in June 1996.[33]

Clinton's other accomplishments have been to use his presidential bully pulpit—giving speeches in which he supported lesbian and gay rights, and issuing gay pride statements, acts that would have been unheard of from any other previous president of the United States. For example, Clinton's November 1997 speech to a $300,000 fund-raiser sponsored by the Human Rights Campaign (HRC) was noteworthy because it was the first speech delivered by a sitting president to a lesbian and gay rights organization. In that speech, the president renewed his support for ENDA in the following way: "Being gay, the last time I thought about it, seemed to have nothing to do with the ability to read a balance book, fix a broken bone, or change a spark plug. Firing or refusing to hire people because they are gay is akin to discrimination based on race, religion, or gender. It is wrong and it should be illegal."[34] Clinton's speech is also noteworthy for the publicity it received not only in the lesbian and gay press, but in dailies throughout the United States. In this way, he helped to bring further attention to the concerns of the lesbian and gay civil rights movement.

IMPLICATIONS FOR THE LESBIAN AND GAY MOVEMENT

What are the lessons that the lesbian and gay movement might learn from dealing with a so-called friend in the White House? How might these lessons be applied to dealing with future occupants of the Oval Office? And how might the experiences in dealing with Clinton inform the future direction of the movement?

Before these questions can even be addressed, it is first important to recognize that to speak of "the lesbian and gay movement" may suggest a level of cohesion and consensus that hardly exists. There are many different aspects of the larger movement, only some of which have been addressed in this essay. And there continue to be debates over movement strategy. In the words of the historian John D'Emilio, "We are in a period now characterized by fractiousness to the debate about homosexuality that highlighted the lack of social consensus and that often produced political stalemate, contradiction, or both."[35]

The years of the Clinton presidency have borne witness to this heightened fractiousness both within the lesbian and gay movement and in the larger society around lesbian and gay issues. One movement leader complained bitterly to me that "our national organizations, such as the National Gay and Lesbian Task Force (NGLTF) and Human Rights Campaign (HRC), wasted the first four years of the Clinton administration. We still don't have a comprehensive agenda."[36] A comprehensive agenda has not yet emerged because of fundamental disagreements within the movement itself over strategy.

If anything, the attention given to national-level policymaking, which is the central focus of this essay, ignores the rich tapestry of grassroots organizing and mobilizing that is currently being done in communities throughout the United States. This much-needed work at the state and local level can proceed regardless of who occupies the White House. This is one important lesson of the Clinton years. Indeed, I have argued elsewhere that perhaps our nationally based organizations would be better off devoting some of their resources to grassroots political work to fight the vast organizational network of the religious right at the state and local level.[37] After all, most people do not live in Washington, D.C. One example of such a grassroots effort is the National Gay and Lesbian Task Force's "Celebrating Our Families" campaign, which was launched in spring 1998, an organizational initiative rooted in addressing community concerns about family issues and building support for families that celebrate sexual difference. A second example of grassroots political work is the "Equality Begins at Home" campaign, a series of coordinated actions on behalf of lesbian, gay, bisexual, and transgendered civil rights, which occurred during March 1999 in the capital cities of all fifty states and U.S. territories. The goal of this organizing initiative was to draw national attention to battles in statehouses as well as to highlight state organizing challenges. This sort of organizing is crucial to create the much-needed political, cultural, and educational changes at all levels of society.

In the end, what is needed is a coherent strategy that pushes national political officials, including the president, to exercise meaningful policy leadership on substantive issues concerning lesbians, gays, and bisexuals, and other groups who are at the margins of American society. Undoubtedly, future historians will likely record that the Clinton presidency has made some progress in exercising this leadership. But it is also clear that that progress would not have been made without the organizing efforts of the lesbian and gay movement, which forced the Clinton administration to respond. Ultimately, several additional lessons grow out of how the movement has interacted with the Clinton presidency. One is that the lesbian and gay movement cannot merely trust a so-called friend to follow through on campaign promises and to do what is right once he assumes the presidency. A second is that the movement must do even more organizing to create a political and cultural climate that allows future presidents to support various movement goals. This is hard, but essential, work. Finally, the movement needs to expect more from presidents than mere access to the White House and the appointment of openly lesbian, gay, and bisexual people. Policy results are far more important than access to power. Perhaps one of the greatest contributions of the Clinton presidency has been to force the movement to reassess its strategy for political and social change at all levels of society, so that we can do a better job as we interact with future occupants of the Oval Office. When all is said and done, this may well be Bill Clinton's lasting legacy.

The author wishes to thank an array of national movement leaders who gave quality time in the form of personal interviews and thus provided invaluable material for this chapter.

CHAPTER 4

From *Bowers v. Hardwick* to *Romer v. Evans:* Lesbian and Gay Rights in the U.S. Supreme Court

ARTHUR S. LEONARD

O N JUNE 30, 1986, THE U.S. SUPREME COURT AN-nounced its decision in *Bowers v. Hardwick,* holding that the Constitution's protection for personal liberty does not include the right of adult lesbians and gay men to have consensual sex in private. On May 20, 1996, just ten years later, the Court announced its decision in *Romer v. Evans,* holding that the Constitution's guarantee of equal protection of the laws includes the right of lesbians and gay men to seek legislation banning discrimination on the basis of sexual orientation.

The *Hardwick* decision was widely denounced by lesbian and gay Americans as a profound insult to our status as equal citizens of this country, while the *Romer* decision was widely hailed as vindicating our entitlement to equal rights of citizenship. In the former case, Supreme Court justice Byron R. White had characterized our claim to protection under the constitutional right of privacy as "facetious." In the latter case, Supreme Court justice Anthony M. Kennedy Jr. scorned the challenged Colorado Amendment 2 (which declared that no state policy could treat homosexuals as a protected class of persons) as an unconstitutional attempt to "deem a class of persons a stranger to its laws."

Why did the Supreme Court change its tune, or did it? Is the path from

Hardwick to *Romer* the result of a change of heart by the Court, or are the two cases so different that no valid comparison can be made?

Understanding the path from *Hardwick* to *Romer* requires understanding the constitutional claims and arguments raised by each of these landmark cases. This chapter will discuss each of these cases in turn, setting out the background for the cases, explaining the relevant constitutional arguments, and showing the role that each has played or might play in the future of the struggle for lesbian and gay rights in the courts.

Both the lesbian and gay community and the public at large were caught relatively unaware by the *Hardwick* decision, to judge by the immediate reaction of the media and of gay people. This is not all that surprising, since public awareness of the Supreme Court's ongoing business is not particularly high, and most people have only the most generalized notion of their legal rights. Just as today some nongay people mistakenly think that same-sex couples have the right to marry, having seen such marriages performed in television sitcoms and movies, most people, both gay and nongay, probably assumed in 1986 that private sexual activity between consenting adults of the same sex was no longer a concern of the criminal law. By 1986, openly lesbian and gay people were depicted in movies and novels, on television, and in the press without any reference to criminal law, and most people in the United States lived in jurisdictions where sodomy laws had either been repealed or were rarely, if ever, enforced. Furthermore, press reports on the oral argument in *Hardwick* reflected an optimism that the Court would act to strike down Georgia's sodomy law, which would have been consistent with the trends in U.S. constitutional jurisprudence of the preceding twenty years.

In the 1950s, the reforming American Law Institute (ALI) proposed a Model Penal Code, which, if adopted by the states, would repeal all laws against private sexual acts by consenting adults. The ALI proceeded on the supposition, then widely believed, that homosexuality was a mental illness, and as such should be dealt with by the medical profession rather than through law enforcement. By the end of the 1950s, the illness consensus was being challenged by Evelyn Hooker's pioneering research, and the emergence of an increasingly articulate "homosexual rights" movement was pushing the learned professions to reconsider their views on the issue. By the early 1970s, professional associations were abandoning the illness model and calling for decriminalization of homosexual acts on the grounds of respect for individual privacy and toleration of difference. During the 1970s, about half of the states followed that suggestion, legislating the old sodomy laws out of existence, largely by adopting the Model Penal Code's provisions on sex crimes. (Under these provisions, criminal sanctions would still be imposed for sexual conduct that took place in public, between adults and minors, or under other circumstances where consent was lacking.)

Where the state legislatures had failed to act, a few state high courts struck down the laws as violating either the federal constitutional right of privacy or, in some cases, the right of equal protection of the laws. These lawsuits built on a small but influential group of U.S. Supreme Court decisions, beginning in the mid-1960s, that had discovered in the Bill of Rights and the Due Process Clause of the Fourteenth Amendment a right of sexual privacy under which laws against the sale or distribution of contraceptives and laws criminalizing abortion had been declared unconstitutional. The key cases were *Griswold v. Connecticut* (1965), invalidating a ban on contraceptive use by married couples, and *Eisenstadt v. Baird* (1972), invalidating a similar ban applied to unmarried heterosexual couples, and *Roe v. Wade* (1973), which announced a constitutional right for a woman to obtain an abortion.

Perhaps the most prominent of the state court cases striking down sodomy laws was *People v. Onofre*. This 1980 New York decision combined several cases, one stemming from the breakup of an affair between two men living in central New York State, the others from prosecutions of female prostitutes for engaging in oral sex with male customers in the city of Buffalo. The New York sodomy law prohibited anal or oral sex between persons who were not married to each other. The prohibition of particular sex acts between unmarried consenting adults of the opposite sex no longer appeared viable under the U.S. Supreme Court's *Eisenstadt* decision, and New York's highest court, the Court of Appeals, could find no rational basis for striking down the law as it applied to the heterosexual prostitutes but not as it applied to the homosexual couple.

However, attempts to challenge the constitutionality of sodomy laws were notably unsuccessful in the U.S. Supreme Court. In *Wainwright v. Stone* (Florida, 1973) and *Rose v. Locke* (Tennessee, 1975), the Court rejected the argument that the ancient verbiage of "crime against nature" used in these statutes was unconstitutionally vague, and the Court affirmed without even writing an opinion the decision by a federal district court panel in Virginia in *Doe v. Commonwealth's Attorney for City of Richmond*, rejecting a privacy-based challenge to Virginia's sodomy law, in 1976.

Despite the wave of state law repeals and some favorable state court decisions, two regions of the country solidly persisted in refusing to repeal their sodomy laws: the states of the old Confederacy in the Southeast and the Rocky Mountain states. Resistance to gay rights was particularly strong in the South, as shown by the vigorous defenses mounted by the attorneys general of Florida, Tennessee, and Virginia in the failed Supreme Court challenges to sodomy laws. In 1976, the unusual action of the Dade County, Florida, commissioners in adopting an ordinance banning sexual orientation discrimination brought an immediate backlash in the form of a petition campaign and referendum, putting gay rights on the front pages of America's newspapers for the first time. So it is not surprising that Southern states provided the setting for the two most important legal challenges to sodomy laws during the 1980s, in Texas and Georgia.

The Texas sodomy law had been challenged before, in *Buchanan v. Batchelor* (1971), resulting in a political compromise that reduced the penalty from a felony mandating significant prison time to a misdemeanor subject to a $200 fine. But so long as the law was on the books, it served to stigmatize lesbian and gay Texans, to bar them from various forms of employment, to encourage police harassment against gay meeting places and organizations, and to justify discrimination against their rights as parents. A group of gay Texans under the leadership of Donald Baker, a public school teacher, organized as the Texas Human Rights Foundation to bring a test case challenging the law in the federal district court in Dallas.

They were lucky to have their case assigned to Judge Jerry Buchmeyer, a liberal maverick who was disinclined to credit the old-style "experts" the state produced in support of the sodomy law. In a historic ruling in *Baker v. Wade* in 1982, Buchmeyer found that the Texas sodomy law, which prohibited anal or oral sex between consenting adults of the same sex, violated both the liberty and equal-protection interests of gay Texans. Reasoning directly from the Supreme Court's privacy cases, Buchmeyer found that the constitutional right of privacy encompasses an individual's ability to define his or her sexual identity and to act on that identity, and that the state's arguments that removing the stigma of the criminal law from gay sexuality would harm society were totally unsupported. Buchmeyer also concluded that there was no rational justification for prohibiting gay people from engaging in the same sex acts that were permitted for nongay people. Unfortunately, the U.S. Court of Appeals for the Fifth Circuit reversed Buchmeyer's decision, relying on *Doe v. Commonwealth's Attorney for Richmond*, the Supreme Court's 1976 action upholding the Virginia sodomy law.

Meanwhile, in Atlanta, in the same month when Buchmeyer issued his Texas decision, a gay man was arrested for having oral sex with another man in his bedroom, setting the stage for the next Supreme Court decision on sodomy laws. Michael Hardwick was outraged after spending a night in the Atlanta jail and agreed to be the lead plaintiff in a test case against the Georgia sodomy law brought by an American Civil Liberties Union volunteer attorney in Atlanta. Unlike the rather mild Texas law, the Georgia sodomy law outlawed all anal or oral sex between consenting adults and authorized a prison term of up to twenty years for a violation.

Not surprisingly, a federal district judge in Atlanta quickly dismissed Hardwick's case, ruling that the Supreme Court's 1976 Virginia decision was binding and ended the matter. However, Hardwick scored a surprise victory on appeal to the U.S. Court of Appeals for the Eleventh Circuit, which ruled 2–1 that the earlier Virginia case was not necessarily binding, that subsequent Supreme Court decisions had expanded the concept of privacy, and that the state of Georgia should be required to provide an objective justification for its sodomy law. According to the appeals court judges, Hardwick's right to choose his sexual partners came within the fundamental right of privacy under the Due Process Clause of the Fourteenth Amendment. Georgia attorney general Michael Bowers promptly petitioned the Supreme Court for review.

Although the Texas case was started first, the Georgia case was first to reach the Supreme Court for two simple reasons. Judge Buchmeyer held a lengthy trial, unlike the Atlanta judge, who tossed the case out quickly. And the Texas case had a lengthy history before the Fifth Circuit as well, due to the reluctance of the Texas attorney general to appeal Buchmeyer's strongly worded opinion. A local prosecutor in the Texas hill country filed a separate appeal, which ultimately provided the vehicle for the Fifth Circuit to overrule Buchmeyer's opinion, but not before much time-consuming procedural wrangling had taken place. Thus, it was not until after the Supreme Court announced that it would hear Georgia's appeal of the Eleventh Circuit decision that the Fifth Circuit issued its final decision and Don Baker filed his petition for review with the Supreme Court. The Court put the Texas petition "on hold" while it dealt with the Georgia case.

In retrospect, the Supreme Court's handling of *Bowers v. Hardwick* seems quite peculiar. The Court was split 5–4. Justice Lewis F. Powell Jr. issued a separate opinion agreeing that the Georgia sodomy law did not violate the right of privacy, but suggesting that anyone sentenced to prison under the law might have a valid claim under the Eighth Amendment, which forbids cruel and unusual punishment. (In light of the difficulties of enforcing a sodomy law against consenting adults who conduct their activities in private, a prison term for consensual sodomy would be highly unusual and wildly disproportionate to the penalties imposed for more serious offenses.)

Furthermore, Justice White's opinion for the Court disclaimed any view about whether the sodomy law might violate any constitutional rights apart from the right of privacy. This narrow focus stemmed from the peculiar history of the case. Although Michael Hardwick's lawyers had argued before the Eleventh Circuit that the law violated a host of constitutional provisions, including the Equal Protection Clause, the Eleventh Circuit grounded its ruling solely on the right of privacy, and the state's appeal focused narrowly on whether its law violated that particular constitutional right.

But the opinion for the Court by Justice White was also peculiar in its formulation of the question for decision and its handling of the Court's previous decisions about the right to privacy. Justice White began by stating that the case raised the question whether the Constitution confers upon "homosexuals" a "fundamental right to engage in sodomy," rather than whether the right of all persons, regardless of sexual orientation, to engage in the conduct covered by the Georgia statute was at stake. By so narrowly formulating the question, White was trying to make the Court's developed privacy jurisprudence irrelevant to the outcome.

In the first contraception case, *Griswold v. Connecticut,* Justice William O. Douglas's opinion for the Court had spoken broadly of a right of privacy derived from various aspects of the Bill of Rights and the whole constitutional scheme of respect for individual liberty. In the second major contraception case, *Eisenstadt v. Baird,* Justice William J. Brennan Jr.'s opinion for a plurality of the Court had spoken of the privacy right in terms suggesting that the state would be broadly excluded from interfering in a person's fundamental decisions about how to live his or her life. In the landmark abortion case, *Roe v. Wade,* Justice Harry Blackmun's opinion for the Court stated that the outer limits of the right of privacy had not yet been marked by the Court, but that the right of an individual woman to terminate a pregnancy during its early stages clearly came within those limits. Taken together, these cases suggested a sphere of personal autonomy large enough to include the sexual activities of consenting adults. When such activities took place in private, especially in somebody's home, they arguably came within the broad privacy umbrella of another important case, *Stanley v. Georgia* (1969), in which Justice Thurgood Marshall wrote for the Court that a person's right of privacy in his home shielded him from prosecution for possession and use of obscene matter, even though obscene matter does not have any First Amendment protection under the Supreme Court's precedents.

In his *Hardwick* opinion, Justice White swept aside the seemingly broader significance of these prior decisions, asserting that each of them related only to the particular situation before the Court in each case, and that they had not served to mark out a broader concept of privacy. Some might criticize White's decision as an example of "gay exceptionalism," of twisting and distorting constitutional law in order to reach the result he and four of his colleagues wished to reach, but this would be to overlook White's consistent past hostility to the type of judicial reasoning exemplified by the opinions of Douglas, Brennan, Blackmun, and Marshall. White was a member of the Court on those prior cases, but he could usually be found writing concurring opinions resting his result on different theories, or dissenting. Indeed, the key language of White's opinion in *Hardwick,* about the dubious validity of purported constitutional rights not explicitly based on the text of the Constitution, is found verbatim in White's dissenting opinion issued just a month earlier in *Thornburgh v. American College of Obstetricians and Gynecologists,* a case in which the Court struck down a variety of restrictions on abortion that had been enacted by the state of Pennsylvania.

To White, if there was a "constitutional right for homosexuals to engage in sodomy," it would have to stand on its own, without reference to the rights of individuals to use contraceptives to prevent pregnancy or the right of women to abort their pregnancies. Reaching back to verbal formulas the Court had used in earlier cases to try to identify "fundamental rights" protected by the Due Process Clause, White asked whether "the right of homosexuals to engage in sodomy" was "deeply rooted in this Nation's history and tradition" or might be characterized as "implicit in the concept of ordered liberty." Without any further explanation, he concluded that the "claimed right" in this case failed to qualify under either of those tests, characterizing the claim as "facetious."

It would be difficult to argue that the "right of homosexuals to engage in sodomy" was "deeply rooted" in American history, inasmuch as sodomy was a crime under the English common law governing the colonies and remained either a common-law or statutory crime in every state until Illinois adopted the Model Penal Code in 1960. Of course, White oversimplified this part of the analysis by failing to note that until relatively recently, all sodomy laws were concerned solely with the acts performed, without any regard for the gender of the participants, and thus were not focused on "homosexual sodomy" as such. Thus, most of the history White cited was irrelevant to the question whether "homosexuals" could be singled out and denied the right to engage in sodomy while others were allowed to do so.

White's failure to discuss why the "claimed right" here was not "implicit in the concept of ordered liberty" was a serious flaw in his opinion. As Justice Blackmun argued in his passionate dissenting opinion, White had prejudged the conclusion by his selection of the question to be answered and, in so doing, had placed in question the constitutional validity of the contraception and abortion decisions as well. Blackmun criticized the "obsession" with homosexuality that marked the Court's opinion. The case was not about "the right of homosexuals to engage in sodomy," he argued; rather, it was about the right of individuals to be let alone to lead their lives without undue interference by their government. If it is "implicit in the concept of ordered liberty" that a man and a woman have a right to obtain and use contraceptives to be able to have sex without risking pregnancy or the transmission of venereal diseases, or "implicit in the concept of ordered liberty" that a woman who is pregnant has the right, at least during the early part of her pregnancy, to terminate the pregnancy, then how is it not "implicit in the concept of ordered liberty" for any individual to decide with whom to engage in the intimacies of sexual contact free from government interference? White never expressly addressed this question, but Blackmun apparently found these situations relevantly analogous. The puzzle was why Powell, who had agreed with the contraception and abortion decisions, including a controversial abortion decision issued just a month prior to the *Hardwick* ruling, had not.

Soon after the *Hardwick* decision was issued, reports surfaced in the press that Justice Powell had initially voted in favor of Michael Hardwick's challenge to the Georgia sodomy law, that Justice Blackmun had been assigned by Justice Brennan (the senior justice in the majority) to write an opinion that would have declared all laws against consensual sodomy between adults unconstitutional, and that Justice White would be writing a dissent. However, Powell, who was not firm in his views on this issue, wavered and ultimately changed his mind, thus giving White the fifth vote to uphold the Georgia law and converting Blackmun's role from opinion writer to dissenter. The details were later revealed in a biography of Powell written by Professor John C. Jeffries Jr., published in 1994, after Powell had retired from the Court. In 1990, while answering questions from law students at New York University after delivering a lecture, Powell responded to a question about the *Hardwick* case by publicly stating that he had made a "mistake" in that case, and that after reading over the opinions again, he found he agreed with Blackmun's dissent.

What this story shows is that the defeat for gay rights in *Hardwick* was not the pronouncement of a monolithic Supreme Court overwhelmingly set against equal rights for lesbians and gay men. Rather, it was a narrow 5–4 decision, in which the fifth vote for upholding the sodomy law was tentative at best and provided by a man who later admitted he had made a mistake. Not only did Blackmun argue, with the concurrence of Justices Brennan, Marshall, and John Paul Stevens, that the Georgia law violated the fundamental right of privacy, but Justice Stevens, in a separate concurrence joined by Brennan and Marshall (and with the apparent agreement of Blackmun, according to a footnote reference in his opinion), argued that the statute also violated Hardwick's right to equal protection of the laws. Stevens pointed out that under the Court's existing sexual privacy cases, Georgia could not constitutionally apply its sodomy law to heterosexuals, thus raising the inevitable question why the state should be able to draw a distinction between heterosexuals and homosexuals when it came to private, consensual adult sex. Stevens saw no rational basis for making such a distinction.

Nonetheless, *Hardwick* carried a heavy sting, both because it marked a major setback in the campaign to invalidate the remaining U.S. sodomy laws, and because of the language of Justice White's opinion, characterizing the privacy claim as "facetious"—a figurative slap in the face to millions of Americans, and the even more offensive tone of a short concurring opinion by Chief Justice Warren Burger, which quoted a passage from a colonial-era English treatise, Blackstone's *Commentaries on the Laws of England,* to the effect that sodomy was a worse crime than rape.

The *Hardwick* decision was not always popular with state court judges. In a serious of decisions over the following decade, appellate courts in Kentucky (*Commonwealth v. Wasson*), Tennessee (*Campbell v. Sundquist*), Texas

(*State v. Morales*), and Montana (*Gryczan v. State*) all stated their disagreement with Justice White's analysis in declaring sodomy laws unconstitutional under their state constitutions. (The Texas decision, from an intermediate appellate court, was reversed on other grounds by the Texas Supreme Court.) The decision also provoked a storm of disapproval from legal scholars, beginning with a highly critical commentary published in the *Harvard Law Review* in November 1986 (100 *Harv. L. Rev.* 210), the first in a steady stream of law journal articles that has continued to the present.

On the other hand, some state court judges in jurisdictions that still have sodomy laws continue to use them to justify depriving lesbian or gay parents of child custody or to sharply restrict their visitation rights. (For a recent example, see *Weigand v. Houghton*, a 1999 decision by the Mississippi Supreme Court that characterizes a gay father as a criminal, even though he lives in California, where the state legislature repealed the sodomy law during the 1970s.) And the army of federal appellate judges appointed during the administrations of Ronald Reagan and George Bush have seized upon the *Hardwick* opinion for a justification to deny claims of equal protection of the laws brought by gay litigants in cases challenging discriminatory government policies. Their argument, first articulated in *Padula v. Webster*, a 1987 decision denying a discrimination claim by a lesbian applicant for employment by the Federal Bureau of Investigation, went as follows: outlawing gay sex is the ultimate antigay discrimination by government; if the Supreme Court rules that a state may outlaw gay sex, then surely the government can take the less drastic step of disfavoring gays under its other policies without offending the constitutional requirement of equal protection of the laws.

However, one case decided in the years between *Hardwick* and *Romer* did give a hint of changes in the air. In *Hurley v. Irish-American Gay, Lesbian and Bisexual Group of Boston*, the Court had to decide whether Massachusetts violated the First Amendment's protection of freedom of speech by requiring the South Boston Allied War Veterans Council to include a gay and lesbian Irish group in their annual St. Patrick's Day parade. The Massachusetts Supreme Judicial Court had rejected the parade organizers' free speech claim and enforced the state's public accommodations law against them. The Supreme Court ruled unanimously, in an opinion by Justice David Souter, that the parade organizers had a constitutionally protected right to determine the "message" of their parade and to exclude groups based on the organizers' view that their inclusion would dilute or change that message.

Although the lesbian and gay Irish organization lost the case, readers of the opinion were struck by Justice Souter's language, which appeared to reflect a sea change from the terminology Justice White used in *Hardwick*. Instead of White's repeated references to "homosexuals," Souter referred to the respondents as "gay, lesbian, and bisexual individuals." And Souter's opinion made

clear that the Court's unanimous approach to the case sprang not from any belief that gay, lesbian, and bisexual individuals do not have a right to proclaim
their message publicly, and certainly not from any view that the Massachusetts
Law Against Discrimination (which forbids sexual orientation discrimination)
is unconstitutional, but rather from the view that parades are a quintessential
exercise of the First Amendment speech rights of their organizers, and thus the
state would be overstepping the bounds of freedom of speech to require a private parade organizer to include a group with whose views the organizer disagreed. As the *Romer* case was well on its way to the Court by the time the
Hurley decision was announced, gay legal observers eagerly looked to the language of the opinion for intimations that the Court might have become more
enlightened on lesbian and gay issues with the passage of time and the changes
of membership. (Souter, by the way, was appointed by President Bush to replace a *Hardwick* dissenting voter, Justice Brennan, and Anthony M. Kennedy,
who would ultimately author the *Romer* decision, was appointed by President
Reagan to replace Justice Powell.)

The Supreme Court's decision in *Romer v. Evans* was much less of a surprise to lesbian and gay Court observers than the decision in *Hardwick.* Most
who attended the oral argument in the *Hardwick* case emerged with the hopeful view that *Hardwick* might have won the five votes necessary to uphold the
Eleventh Circuit's ruling, and their impressions based on the demeanor and
questioning of the justices would not have been far off, in light of subsequent
revelations about the initial vote among the justices, so the ultimate ruling of
the Court was something of a surprise. At the oral argument in *Romer,* it was
clear from the questioning that Justices Kennedy, Souter, Ruth Bader Gins-
burg, Stephen Breyer, Stevens, and possibly even Sandra Day O'Connor, all
had grave concerns about Colorado Amendment 2. And well they might, considering the unusual nature of the measure whose constitutionality they were
considering. Among those justices whose questions suggested doubts about
Amendment 2, only two—Stevens and O'Connor—had been on the Court
when *Hardwick* was decided ten years previously.

Amendment 2 was the brainchild of the right-wing Christian fundamentalist movement that had taken root in Colorado Springs, although its wording
was based on a similar proposition that was put to a vote in Oregon at the same
time. Amendment 2 was intended to add to the Colorado state constitution a
provision banning state and local governments from adopting any measure that
would treat "homosexuality" as a protected class or as the basis for a discrimination claim. Amendment 2 passed after a fervent media campaign in which
the proponents argued that they were trying to block the powerful homosexual
community from obtaining "special rights" at the expense of ordinary Col-

oradans. It had the immediate effect of rendering unenforceable, at least to the extent that they could be used to redress discrimination claims brought by lesbian, gay, or bisexual people, local ordinances banning sexual orientation discrimination in several Colorado cities, an executive order by Governor Roy Romer banning sexual orientation discrimination by the state government, and some antidiscrimination policies adopted by state agencies and the state judicial system. It also barred all state entities from adopting policies on sexual orientation discrimination in the future.

Immediately after the measure passed, a coalition of plaintiffs filed suit in the state district court in Denver to challenge its constitutionality and prevent it from taking effect. They were able to persuade trial judge Jeffrey Bayless to issue a preliminary injunction on January 14, 1993, which would stop Amendment 2 from becoming effective until the lawsuit was finally concluded. Bayless adopted the theory that Amendment 2 probably violated the federal constitution by placing an endorsement of discrimination into the state constitution. He asserted that individuals have a fundamental right not to have the state "endorse and give effect to private biases." Since a fundamental right was at stake, Amendment 2 would only survive judicial review if the state could show that its enactment was necessary to achieve a compelling state interest and that it was narrowly tailored to achieve that interest without unduly burdening constitutional rights. Bayless opined that the plaintiffs were likely to succeed in having Amendment 2 invalidated, and that letting it take effect in the meantime would cause irreparable injury.

The state immediately appealed. By a vote of 6–1, the Colorado Supreme Court upheld Bayless's decision to issue the preliminary injunction, but adopted a different theory as to why Amendment 2 might be unconstitutional. According to the Colorado Supreme Court, identifiable groups of people have a fundamental right to equal participation in the political process. This right means more than just the right to vote or run for office, according to the Court; it also includes the right to propose legislation and have it considered. By taking away from the state government at all levels the authority to legislate concerning protection for or discrimination against lesbians, gay men, and bisexuals, Amendment 2 rendered those people "unequal" participants in the state's polity, thus abridging a fundamental right. The state may only abridge a fundamental right of an identifiable group for a compelling reason, thus subjecting Amendment 2 to "strict scrutiny," the most demanding level of judicial review.

The state attempted to get the U.S. Supreme Court to review this ruling, but was quickly rebuffed, and the parties returned to the Denver district court for a trial.

At the trial, which began on October 12, 1993, the state faced the difficult task of showing that it was necessary to strip the government of any power to protect or assist gay people in order to accomplish a compelling, legitimate

goal of state government, and that Amendment 2 went no further than necessary to achieve such a goal. The plaintiffs decided to use the trial to persuade
Bayless of an alternative theory: that legislation classifying people for differen-
tial treatment according to their sexual orientation creates a "suspect classification" that is also subject to "strict scrutiny" judicial review. They hoped to
achieve a victory that would be more likely to stand up on appeal, especially if
it was ultimately appealed to the U.S. Supreme Court, by persuading the Colorado courts that Amendment 2 was doubly unconstitutional: first as a violation of fundamental rights, and second as the improper use of a suspect
classification. Under either theory, Amendment 2 could only survive if it met
the strict-scrutiny test.

The Supreme Court has ruled that most classifications the government
uses in statutes should be presumed to be constitutional, but that certain classifications are inherently "suspect" because they are probably due to prejudice
rather than unbiased lawmaking. If a government policy uses a "suspect classification," the presumption of constitutionality is reversed, and the burden falls
on the state to show that the policy is necessary to achieve a compelling state
interest.

Race was the first suspect classification identified by the Court and has
served as the paradigm for deciding whether other classifications are suspect.
The Court has ruled that sex is not a suspect classification, because there are
various circumstances in which it may be reasonable for the government to
treat men and women differently due to inherent differences between the
sexes, but that enough stereotyping and prejudice exist around the issue of sex
to justify the courts' applying "heightened scrutiny" to sex classifications by the
government, which could be called quasi-suspect classifications.

A few courts have suggested that sexual orientation might be either a suspect or quasi-suspect classification, but most courts that have considered the issue have disagreed. Among the many factors the Supreme Court has articulated
in various decisions as relevant to this determination are whether a group seeking judicial protection from discrimination has suffered a history of prejudice
and discrimination based on the classification, whether the relevant characteristic is basic, fundamental, or immutable as an aspect of the identity of those
suffering the prejudice and discrimination such that they should not or could
not be expected to change it, whether the group suffering discrimination is so
lacking in political power that it cannot protect its interests in the give and take
of representative government, and whether the characteristic is relevant to the
ability of members of the group to participate in and contribute to society.

This area of constitutional law lends itself to analytical confusion because courts, including the Supreme Court, have been imprecise in their language and in dealing with the equal-protection concept, referring sometimes to
"suspect classes" rather than "suspect classifications" and focusing on the at-

tributes of particular groups as if the classifications involved did not apply to everybody. The Supreme Court's approach to equal protection has seemed to shift from time to time as it changes its terminology, sometimes discussing whether discrimination against particular groups of people, such as women, for example, is "suspect," while at other times speaking more generally in terms of suspect classifications (e.g., discrimination on the basis of sex, which can affect men as well as women, depending upon the circumstance).

The Court's race-discrimination jurisprudence illustrates the conceptual problems. In finding racial classifications inherently suspect, the Court has focused on the history of discrimination against people of color, noting, for example, that Africans were forcibly brought to this country as slaves, that Africans, Asians, and Native Americans have suffered through various degrees of enforced segregation and discrimination, and that people of color have had difficulty until recent times in amassing sufficient political power to gain legislative redress; the Court has also treated racial categories as being founded on essential or immutable characteristics (in the sense that an individual cannot change his or her skin color). This reasoning could justify treating as inherently suspect government classifications that disadvantage people of color; however, it is hard to understand how this history would justify subjecting to strict scrutiny government classifications that disadvantage white people, who have suffered no disadvantages in the United States based on their race. Nonetheless, in recent years, under the slogan "Our Constitution is colorblind," the Court has struck down affirmative action programs intended to assist people of color in achieving equal participation in the nation's economic life, by treating as "inherently suspect" any racial classification, even one that was adopted for benign or remedial purposes.

Thus, in cases brought by people of color to challenge racial segregation, the Court has analyzed their claims as involving discrimination against a "suspect class," established the presumption that discrimination against members of "suspect classes" is inherently unconstitutional, and proceeded from there to generalize race, the characteristic defining the class, as a "suspect classification." Then, when white people came along to protest affirmative action policies, the Court used the concept of "suspect classification" to subject those policies to the same strict scrutiny that had been used to declare racial segregation unconstitutional, even though one could plausibly argue that because there was no history of purposeful discrimination against white people, and because white people, as a group, constitute a powerful political majority, strict scrutiny should not be used to evaluate the constitutionality of those racial classifications adopted to assist people of color that may have an incidental effect of appearing to disadvantage particular white people. If the Supreme Court's approach to equal protection and discrimination is to be analytically coherent, the Court should either abandon the notion of "suspect classes" and concentrate on "suspect classifications," or the reverse. If the Court is serious about the contention that the Constitution is color-blind and the government is required to be neutral in matters of race, then the notion of a "suspect class" should be banished from its equal-protection analysis.

Some of the same logical confusion attends the arguments about sexual orientation discrimination, as the Amendment 2 trial revealed. Amendment 2 described a particular group of people—lesbians, gay men, and bisexuals—and held that they could not be afforded protection from discrimination by the state, without expressly explaining why this particular group should be thus deprived. In analyzing the equal-protection claim brought by this group, the question should be whether the characteristic by which Amendment 2 defines this group, their sexual orientation, can legitimately be the basis for establishing a government policy. The question should not be how much gay people are like people of color, but rather how is sexual orientation like or unlike race, as these concepts are defined and affect human behavior. If U.S. courts would seriously undertake such an analysis, they would likely find that sexual orientation is "analogous" to race, as the Canadian Supreme Court concluded in *Egan v. Canada,* its decision that the equal-protection provision of the Canadian Charter of Rights must be interpreted to include "sexual orientation" as an "analogous ground" to the specified grounds of race and sex, because race and sexual orientation as socially constructed human characteristics bear similar roles today in constructing personal identity and are similarly employed by many people in deciding how they will relate to other people.

At the trial before Judge Bayless, the state specified six "compelling interests" to justify Amendment 2. It argued that sexual orientation discrimination should be dealt with solely on a statewide level, to avoid factionalism in city-by-city and county-by-county arguments over whether such discrimination should be outlawed. It argued that Amendment 2 must be upheld to vindicate the right of the people to make fundamental policy decisions for their state. It argued that Amendment 2 was necessary to preserve the ability of the state to enforce civil rights protection on behalf of members of already recognized protected classes by preventing diversion of resources to enforcement of gay rights laws. It argued that Amendment 2 was necessary to prevent the government from interfering with the privacy rights of Coloradans who might want to avoid interacting with gay people for religious, familial, or other personal reasons. It argued that Amendment 2 was necessary to prevent the state from endorsing or assisting a particular special interest group. Finally, the state argued that Amendment 2 was necessary to advance the state's interest in promoting the physical and psychological well-being of children by supporting "traditional family values," which had come to be a code phrase for opposition to any public recognition of gay people as healthy, normal, or deserving of civic equality. Thus, the state's case at trial was devoted to supporting these arguments, as well as opposing the plaintiffs' contention that sexual orientation is a suspect classification.

Although the Colorado Supreme Court had framed the case as an Equal Protection "fundamental rights" case rather than a "suspect classification" case, the plaintiffs nonetheless had to show at trial, at minimum, that Amendment 2 created a cognizable classification on the basis of which it discriminated with regard to a fundamental right, and then to rebut the defendants' arguments that the state's purported justifications for Amendment 2 actually amounted to compelling interests that could only be achieved by stripping the government of any power to protect gay people from discrimination. The plaintiffs voluntarily took on the additional task of persuading the court that sexual orientation is a suspect classification to provide an alternative theory for imposing on the state the burden of showing a "compelling interest" to support Amendment 2.

Interestingly, most of the trial time was devoted to the suspect-classification issue, an issue that the Colorado Supreme Court had avoided, and as to which ultimately the U.S. Supreme Court took no position in its disposition of the case. The plaintiffs presented a string of experts, some live, some on tape, and some by written deposition testimony, on the nature of homosexuality, the history of anti-gay discrimination, philosophical views of homosexuality from ancient Greece and Rome, and political science evaluations of the political power gays might wield. The state then took on the task of rebutting this evidence by presenting its own experts on many of the same points. Although this entire battle of the experts ultimately proved irrelevant to the final determination of the case (and failed to persuade Bayless that homosexuals are a "suspect class"), it provided a useful exercise in public education as the national media reported summaries of the testimony to the public.

Judge Bayless did not have much trouble in concluding that the state's purported justifications for Amendment 2 fell far short of meeting the strict-scrutiny test. Indeed, reading about the testimony in the definitive account of the trial, *Strangers to the Law: Gay People on Trial* (University of Michigan Press, 1998), by gay rights attorney Suzanne Goldberg and journalist Lisa Keen, one is struck by the state's inability to relate the testimony it was presenting to the logical question of whether a measure as absolute as Amendment 2 was essential to accomplish any of these goals. The state's argument boiled down, at its core, to the proposition that the majority of Colorado's voters had a compelling interest in driving homosexuals underground or out of the state to ensure the survival of heterosexuality, and its proof of this proposition appeared founded on sloganeering, pseudoscience, and superstition.

Even though Bayless was not called upon to do so by the Colorado Supreme Court's direction for the trial, the plaintiff's insistence on pushing the "suspect classification" question and the enormous proportion of trial time devoted to it caused him to issue a ruling on this question as well. Observing that a group constituting a small percentage of the population (trial testimony suggested around 4 percent) had been able to persuade 46 percent of the electorate to vote against Amendment 2, Bayless concluded that gay people did not lack political power to the degree that they would need special assistance from the courts and thus could not be considered a "suspect class." (This analysis conveniently overlooked the continuing status of sex and race as "suspect classifications," even though women and people of color have gained the enactment of laws banning sex and race discrimination from the federal government and almost all the state governments.) However, Bayless refused to rule on the next inevitable question: If this was not a fundamental-rights case, could Amendment 2 still be held unconstitutional based on a conclusion that there was no rational basis for Colorado's citizens to single out lesbians, gay men, and bisexuals as the only distinct group in Colorado that would be disqualified from seeking legal protection against discrimination? The plaintiffs sought such a ruling to bolster their victory on the fundamental-rights claim, just in case the Colorado Supreme Court changed its mind about this claim or the U.S. Supreme Court rejected it entirely. (In the end, the U.S. Supreme Court did not treat this as a fundamental-rights case.) But Bayless was not willing to oblige, merely concluding that Amendment 2 failed strict scrutiny and was thus unconstitutional in light of the Colorado Supreme Court's opinion.

The state appealed again. The Colorado Supreme Court, again voting 6–1, reaffirmed its earlier holding that Amendment 2 potentially violated gay peoples' fundamental right of equal participation in the political process and approved Bayless's conclusion that Amendment 2 flunked the strict-scrutiny test. However, the court took the next step that Bayless had avoided, commenting that Amendment 2 might survive the less demanding rational-basis test that courts apply in Equal Protection cases where no fundamental right is at stake and the classification in question is neither suspect nor quasi-suspect. All legislation must at least relate rationally to a legitimate concern of the state, but it is rare for a court to conclude that a legislative body (or the electorate in a referendum or initiative) has so abandoned reason as to adopt a measure from sheer prejudice, so laws subjected to rational-basis review almost always survive that review.

The state appealed to the U.S. Supreme Court a second time, the Court granted review, and Bayless's decision declaring Amendment 2 unconstitutional was affirmed again, by a vote of 6–3. However, the Supreme Court announced that it was not deciding this as a fundamental-rights case or a suspect-classification case, and Justice Kennedy, in his opinion for the Court, never discussed either the Colorado Supreme Court's theory about equal rights to participate in the political process or the plaintiffs' claim that sexual orientation is a suspect classification. Instead, the Court proceeded to treat Amendment 2 as that extremely rare thing: a measure that adopted a classification solely for the purpose of discrimination against an unpopular group.

In retrospect, it appeared that the Supreme Court majority had a clearer view of what was going on in Colorado when Amendment 2 was passed than the Colorado courts had. Even while rejecting the state's arguments that its proffered justifications for Amendment 2 were compelling enough or tailored narrowly enough to uphold the measure, Bayless had accorded those arguments some degree of credibility. But it was abundantly clear that those arguments were manufactured after the initiative vote, for the purpose of defending Amendment 2 in court. If one looked at the election campaign, one saw virtually no articulation by proponents of Amendment 2 of any of the arguments that were subsequently made at trial, and so the scant attention Kennedy paid to those arguments in his opinion seems abundantly justified.

Kennedy cut right to the heart of the matter in his opening paragraph. Quoting the historic dissent by Justice John M. Harlan in the infamous case of *Plessy v. Ferguson* (1896), in which the Supreme Court had officially adopted the "separate but equal" policy in support of racial segregation of public facilities, Kennedy asserted that the Constitution requires "a commitment to the law's neutrality where the rights of persons are at stake." Amendment 2 was not neutral. It violated Justice Harlan's admonition that the Constitution "neither knows nor tolerates classes among citizens" by making a classification for no apparent reason other than the desire by a majority of Coloradans to declare themselves superior to the homosexuals among them.

After discussing the sheer breadth of Amendment 2's disqualification of gay people from equal treatment by the state government and its subdivisions, Kennedy expressly rejected the state's argument that Amendment 2 was intended to prevent homosexuals from obtaining "special rights" from the state and local governments in Colorado. "We find nothing special in the protections Amendment 2 withholds [from lesbians, gay men, and bisexuals]," Kennedy wrote. "These are protections taken for granted by most people either because they already have them or do not need them; these are protections against exclusion from an almost limitless number of transactions and endeavors that constitute ordinary civil life in a free society."

Proceeding to evaluate Amendment 2's standing under the Equal Protection Clause, Kennedy asserted that the measure actually "confounds" the "normal process of judicial review," under which the Court would customarily ask what legitimate state interests a government-adopted classification was supposed to achieve. Kennedy characterized as "unprecedented in our jurisprudence" a statute that disqualifies a whole class of citizens from "the right to seek specific protection from the law" and called it "not within our constitutional tradition."

A law declaring that in general it shall be more difficult for one group of citizens than for all others to seek aid from the government is itself a denial of equal protection of the laws in the most literal sense. In light of Amendment 2's sweeping nature, and the almost irrelevant justifications the state offered at trial, Kennedy concluded that Amendment 2 raised "the inevitable inference that the disadvantage imposed is born of animosity toward the class of persons affected." Citing *U.S. Department of Agriculture v. Moreno*, a 1973 case in which the Court had struck down a provision of the food stamp law that was expressly intended by Congress to prevent "hippie communes" from qualifying for food stamps, Kennedy stated the Court's conclusion that Amendment 2 offends the bedrock constitutional principle that "a law must bear a rational relationship to a legitimate governmental purpose."

The only apparent purpose of Amendment 2, however, was to exclude gays as a class from being able to seek protective measures from their government, apparently solely due to animus against gays as a group. Or, as Kennedy eloquently stated in concluding his opinion:

> We must conclude that Amendment 2 classifies homosexuals not to further a proper legislative end but to make them unequal to everyone else. This Colorado cannot do. A State cannot so deem a class of persons a stranger to its laws. Amendment 2 violates the Equal Protection Clause, and the judgment of the Supreme Court of Colorado is affirmed.

The Court's opinion drew an impassioned dissent from Justice Antonin Scalia, joined by Chief Justice William H. Rehnquist (a member of the *Hardwick* majority) and Justice Clarence Thomas. Although Scalia went on at length about the lack of evidence that a majority of Coloradans were motivated by animus against gay people when they voted for Amendment 2, his argument boiled down to three principal points. First, he asserted that the Court's ruling was totally inconsistent with *Bowers v. Hardwick*, a case that Kennedy never mentioned in his opinion for the Court. Scalia picked up the argument that had been accepted by many federal appeals courts that so long as it was constitutional for a state to outlaw gay sex, lesser forms of antigay discrimination must be constitutional as well. Scalia emphasized that Amendment 2 had been adopted by a majority of the voters in a democratic process that, he contended, should not be invalidated by the elitist federal judges; for Scalia, the question of gay rights was the kind of political question that should be left wholly to the voters. Finally, Scalia, an economic and political conservative, firmly believed that all laws banning discrimination confer special rights on those groups who most benefit from them, and so he saw nothing inaccurate or prejudicial about the campaign themes that Amendment 2's proponents had used in Colorado.

The *Romer v. Evans* decision was hailed in some quarters as a virtual

"Magna Carta" for gay rights. For the first time in its history, the Supreme Court had struck down as unconstitutional a statute that explicitly singled out gay people for disparate treatment. (The only previous victories gay rights litigants had ever achieved in the Supreme Court were a pair of rulings issued in 1958 and 1962, *One, Inc. v. Olesen* and *Manual Enterprises, Inc. v. Day*, establishing that gay literature was not automatically obscene and thus could be transmitted through the U.S. mails. These decisions focused on rulings by administrators, not explicitly antigay statutes or regulations.) Furthermore, the victory came with a decisive 6–3 vote, including in the majority the conservative "swing voters" on the Court, Kennedy and O'Connor. (O'Connor had voted with the majority in *Hardwick*.)

Shortly after the *Romer* decision was announced, the U.S. Court of Appeals for the Seventh Circuit suggested in *Nabozny v. Podlesny* that the continuing citation of *Bowers v. Hardwick* against gay litigants in Equal Protection cases should be a thing of the past. Building on the perceived conflict between the two cases, gay rights groups for the first time since *Hardwick* brought forward new sodomy law challenges using federal constitutional theories in Maryland and Arkansas, setting up the possibility for a direct assault on the *Hardwick* ruling in the Supreme Court. (The Maryland case was soon settled, with the government agreeing that the sodomy law could not be enforced against participants in private, consensual adult sex, after a trial judge ruled that it should be narrowly interpreted to avoid confronting the serious constitutional question of privacy.)

And with perhaps the deepest sense of poetic justice, in 1998 the Georgia Supreme Court announced in *Powell v. State* that the Georgia sodomy law, the same law that had been upheld in *Hardwick*, violated the state constitution's right of privacy. The Georgia court airily dismissed the *Hardwick* decision as "irrelevant" in a footnote, as did the Louisiana Court of Appeals in ruling that state's sodomy law unconstitutional early in 1999 in *State v. Smith*.

On the other hand, by failing to address the suspect-classification issue and by striking down Amendment 2 as an irrational, totally animus-driven measure, the Court had avoided the question of what level of scrutiny should be given to antigay governmental policies in future Equal Protection cases. Indeed, some courts have interpreted *Romer v. Evans* as holding that antigay discrimination should be subject to the normally deferential rational-basis test, even though Justice Kennedy's opinion never explicitly discussed what level of scrutiny should be used in sexual orientation discrimination cases. (On the other hand, *Romer* itself suggested that it is possible to reject an antigay enactment using the language of rational-basis review, when the only apparent motivation for adopting the enactment is dislike or disapproval of homosexuality.) The persistence of one federal appeals court in upholding a virtual clone of Amendment 2 that was passed as an amendment to the Cincinnati City

Charter in 1993, in *Equality Foundation of Greater Cincinnati v. City of Cincinnati,* suggests that the *Romer* victory will not be complete until the Supreme Court has itself taken up another sexual orientation discrimination case. The Court's puzzling refusal to review the lower court's decision in *Equality Foundation* contributes to continued uncertainty about how gay litigants will fare when they present future Equal Protection challenges to the Supreme Court.

Taking a long view of the judicial treatment of lesbian and gay litigants over the forty years during which such claims have been presented to U.S. courts, the Supreme Court's decision in *Bowers v. Hardwick* looks less like a momentous defeat than a temporary, and perhaps aberrational, setback. The four dissenting votes in *Hardwick* actually marked an advance, as the Court's prior decisions rejecting challenges to sodomy laws had either been unanimous or had drawn fewer dissenting votes, and the "inside" history of how *Hardwick* was decided shows that, at least briefly, there was even a majority of the Court prepared to reject the statute. The subsequent reaction of state supreme courts, rejecting Justice White's reasoning as they invalidated sodomy laws based on state constitutional-privacy theories, dramatically showed how out of step the Supreme Court was with evolving understandings of individual privacy rights, at least within the legal community.

Furthermore, the Court's opinion in *Hardwick* had a galvanizing effect in the lesbian and gay community, stimulating demonstrations (including a colorful protest at the Supreme Court building itself during the National March on Washington in October 1987) and increased membership in state and national organizations working to change public opinion. The opinion also generated extensive discussion in the legal community. Prior to *Hardwick,* a handful of journal articles and books discussed the constitutional status of sodomy laws. After *Hardwick,* this trickle grew to a veritable river, and the near unanimity of opposition to the Court's decision expressed by legal commentators certainly contributed to a climate for change in the courts. Increased visibility by openly lesbian and gay people in the media and in politics during the decade after *Hardwick,* accelerating a trend already under way when that decision was issued, also helped to create a climate in which discrimination against gay people became less and less socially acceptable.

Thus, the Supreme Court's implicit rejection of *Hardwick* in *Romer v. Evans* (made explicit by the outraged protest in Justice Scalia's dissenting opinion) can be seen as more of a natural evolutionary step than as a sharp move in a new direction. On the other hand, the *Romer* opinion is a slender reed on which to proclaim anything as fundamental as a "Magna Carta" for gay rights. Kennedy's opinion for the Court treated this as an unusual case that "defied" the normal process of constitutional analysis, and the Court made no direct statement on how courts should deal with sexual orientation discrimination issues in future cases. Further doubt is cast on the precedential weight of *Romer* by the Court's refusal to review the subsequent decision of the U.S. Court of Appeals for the Sixth Circuit, upholding the constitutionality of the Cincinnati city charter amendment that adopted the policy of Amendment 2 on a municipal scale.

Nonetheless, where *Hardwick* was a defeat, *Romer* was a victory, and in light of the trend of decisions in lower federal and state courts and the language the Supreme Court has come to use in cases raising gay concerns, it is clear that progress has been made. The decision in *Romer v. Evans* suggests that lesbian, gay, and bisexual litigants may now attack antigay government policies under the Equal Protection Clause and receive at least a respectful hearing in most courts, which is an important step forward in light of the way some lower courts were using *Bowers v. Hardwick* to block such lawsuits at their inception.

Shortly after the *Romer* decision was announced, the U.S. Court of Appeals for the Seventh Circuit, sustaining an Equal Protection claim by Jamie Nabozny, a gay high school student challenging harassment, commented that "*Bowers* will soon be eclipsed in the area of equal protection by the Supreme Court's holding in *Romer*." On a less technical, more symbolic level, *Romer v. Evans* signaled lower courts, legislators, and society at large that antigay government policies raise constitutional questions and should not be lightly adopted.

Finally, *Romer v. Evans* gave lesbian and gay people a glimmer of hope that the long-term battle for social, political, and legal equality is not a hopeless task, that progress is being made, and that persistent struggle may actually bring us to the ultimate goal of full equality someday.

CASE REFERENCES

A list of case references appears in the Notes, pages 495–96.

PART II

ACCESSING INSTITUTIONS

CHAPTER 5

FROM AGITATOR TO INSIDER: FIGHTING FOR INCLUSION IN THE DEMOCRATIC PARTY

JEAN O'LEARY

INTRODUCTION

It was another weekly Monday-night meeting in the early 1970s of the Lesbian Liberation Committee—a subcommittee of the Human Rights Committee of the Gay Activists Alliance. For quite some time, and for many reasons, I had been convinced that the lesbians of the gay movement should have more stature than this. I had just returned from the West Coast Lesbian Conference and was more determined than ever to split from GAA and form our own lesbian separatist organization. We were invisible to the general society, patronized by the men, and ignored or feared by the feminist organizations.

The problem was that in those days, in a feminist environment, the popular way for women to make decisions was by consensus; and we had been discussing the issues of separating for weeks without coming to a unanimous consensus, which I, as chair, had promised we would do. Finally we had to bite the bullet and take a vote. It was a scary thing for a lot of the women. We had few resources, and it was hard for some to give up the male-dominated but financially secure resources of the GAA and the Firehouse where we had our meetings. But we did, and Lesbian Feminist Liberation, a lesbian separatist organization, was born. We defined a new radicalism, beyond the political and theoretical limits of the existing gay and feminist movements.

It's 1999. I sit on the Executive Committee of the Democratic National Committee, and we have just taken a vote to define caucuses—effectively reinstating the Gay and Lesbian Caucus to the DNC. Recently we passed a motion to change the delegate selection rules to include strong outreach to the gay and lesbian community, which will increase our number of delegates to the 2000 convention significantly. I'm counting the money raised by our community and the votes and measuring the impact we will have on the upcoming presidential elections.

In the past thirty years I've moved from a lesbian separatist group that went beyond the politics of the New Left and second-wave feminism, to the Executive Committee of the nation's oldest political party. I believe my personal changes and growth correspond closely to the movement of lesbian/gay civil rights issues from beyond the pale of Democratic Party concerns to solid inclusion in the mainstream of the party.

As we look at the progress we have made as measured from national convention to national convention (and corresponding four-year periods), we see fairly clearly the struggle and the triumphs we have experienced in our fight to be mainstream—in our fight to make lesbian/gay civil rights a solid plank in the Democratic Party platform and Democratic Party structure.

Just telling it from my point of view, it's been a long and exciting journey with my values and focus changing yearly as I fought for our equality and freedom. I was a lesbian separatist for only a short time. The separation had given us the strength and the power to demand equality—equal time at the microphones, at the news conferences—equal recognition of issues important to women. But I couldn't reconcile the theories expounded at the time with the reality of the world we lived in. Men did exist and men had the power, and instead of running the other way we had to come back in to integrate and make equality the norm.

I left Lesbian Feminist Liberation with mixed feelings. Unless you were a purist, there was always the question of "selling out"—a theme that ran through many movements and certainly through the seventies. All I knew was that we were on the back burner of both the gay and feminist movements—yet we were the backbone for both in largely invisible strength. As far as the world at large, lesbians were nonexistent except perhaps in sex videos. I wanted to change that, but in a larger context than weekly meetings and a few specific lesbian demonstrations.

I started to make the trip to Albany, New York, once a month to educate specific legislators on gay and lesbian issues. Soon I had a small group join me, and we caravanned in our cars, stopping overnight and making it fun as well as educational. But I needed something else. I wanted a structure I could work through.

I went to Bruce Voeller, who was president of GAA at the time we split and was now executive director of the National Gay Task Force. We agreed we had both grown and changed and were ready to work together again, and that I should become the legislative director for NGTF. I had always liked Bruce and we made a great team for the next few years, as I moved from the legislative position to becoming co–executive director with Bruce. We made a lot of breakthroughs for our community during this time. Bruce took on the bulk of the structural and financial responsibilities of NGTF, and I became more mainstream political. During this time I ran for delegate to the 1976 Democratic National Convention, organized the first meeting with gays and lesbians in the White House, and became the first G/L to be appointed to a presidential commission (The Presidential Commission on the Observance of International Women's Year).

We acted as a clearinghouse for gay civil rights legislation that was being introduced around the country. We traveled extensively, and I found the gay and lesbian community beginning to take a real interest in mainstream politics and understanding that we had to pass laws to protect us. That meant we had to influence politicians to vote for us, which meant that we had to get involved on all levels of government. There was a great distrust of politicians and a great fear of coming out of the closet to lobby them or even write checks to them.

Anita Bryant and the Dade County referendum in Florida changed all that. The blatant homophobia displayed in that campaign compelled thousands of people to come out of the closet, and to get actively involved. Money poured into the campaign and later to NGTF. I learned two valuable lessons from that experience. First, no matter how hard our enemies hit us, or if we won or lost, the mobilizing effect it had on the G/L community was incredible—and we just grew stronger after each attack. Second, there was nothing more powerful individuals could do for themselves and for the movement than to come out. This is a truth that motivates much of what I do politically and is the main reason Rob Eichberg and I founded National Coming Out Day in 1988.

AIDS has had an enormous impact on our community and has taken its toll in thousands of productive lives. Despite AIDS, not because of it, we have become stronger. Our community fought, nurtured, gave money, cared for our sick, and became actively involved on all levels in trying to get government to respond to the disease and to us. We found some powerful allies, and we've had incredible disappointments. A large number of activists pulled back from the "mainstream" and fought from outside. During the early years of AIDS I was executive director of the National Gay Rights Advocates.

We fought through the courts and won many victories for the G/L community. We increased our power politically because politicians didn't have to deal directly with the gay and lesbian issue. Years later when we refocused on these issues, we had a support base and hundreds of thousands more "out" people—all of whom had friends and relatives, which strengthened our cause politically.

Now we not only want fair representation from politicians—we not only want a "place at the table"—we want full and equal representation and full participation in society. The cutting issue is not civil rights now—it is marriage, with another go-round at our political friends to come one step further with us in our fight for equality.

The Democratic Party has recognized that we are at least 5 percent of the voting electorate, and this represents only the people who will attest to being gay or lesbian in surveys at the polls. We are being courted like any other important base-vote constituency, and we can only expect greater and deeper gains in the near future despite our constant right-wing opposition.

THE 1972 DEMOCRATIC NATIONAL CONVENTION

In 1972 a lesbian and a gay man addressed the Democratic National Convention for the first time. They spoke at 2 A.M., presumably because the McGovern campaign wished to minimize exposure of our issue. McGovern's people also scheduled a speaker who opposed lesbian/gay civil rights. But following the infamous 1968 Chicago convention, party reforms, especially in the area of delegate selection, had already initiated changes that would help lesbian/gay activists eventually make lesbian/gay civil rights a solid plank in the Democratic Party platform. Still, at this convention, despite heavy lobbying of the McGovern campaign by the gay community, we were definitely shut out.

In 1972 the post-Stonewall gay and lesbian movement was just beginning to get organized, and our main goal was simply to get our agenda on the map—to be noticed. Invisibility had been our greatest problem, and we were happy and felt victorious if any mention of us was made—at least it gave people something to talk about at the office the next day. "Coming out" was a priority we in the movement could all agree upon. Beyond that, we were divided between those who believed we should integrate gays and lesbians into the mainstream, and those who wanted to revolutionize society. We had long discussions about which ism—racism, classism, or sexism—was the most all-encompassing, and lesbian feminists were examining separatism and our relationship to the gay and the feminist movements.

Few gay people had ventured into the realm of electoral politics. I was busy leading the women of the Gay Activists Alliance out of the organization to form a separate group called Lesbian Feminist Liberation. Bella Abzug had not yet introduced the early version of ENDA into Congress, and our legislative priorities focused on the repeal of sodomy laws.

The Democratic Party was trying to pull itself back together after the 1968 Chicago convention fiasco. Massive reforms in convention rules and delegate-selection procedures dramatically influenced the 1972 Democratic National Convention. Gay and lesbian issues were not a priority. They were looked upon as a joke or an albatross. However, the Commission on Party Structure and Delegate Selection made one change that opened up the party enormously and served as the precursor for gay and lesbian inclusion in the future. They required that women, youth, and minority groups be included in delegations "in reasonable relationship" to their presence in a state's population. As a consequence, at the 1972 convention, 40 percent of the delegates were challenged, and more than four-fifths of the challenges were filed on the basis of inadequate representation.

Meanwhile delegates Jim Foster and Madeline Davis and three alternates represented us at the convention. Jim was a political organizer who traveled up and down the West Coast organizing the first gay and lesbian Democratic clubs. He was also heavily involved in the San Francisco political scene. Madeline was the librarian for the Matachine Society in Buffalo, New York, and knowing she would be speaking at the convention, she had to come out to her family and her coworkers before coming to Florida. Both Jim and Madeline spoke to the convention delegates. No gay man or lesbian had ever before addressed a Democratic National Convention. The speeches were broadcast nationally, and even though they played at 2 A.M., this was a historic moment. Many believe, as do I, that the McGovern operatives scheduled the speeches at this time to minimize exposure of our issue. McGovern had been saddled with the "Three A's"—abortion, amnesty, and acid—by his opposition, and he didn't want to deal with another potentially "embarrassing" issue.

Walter Cronkite introduced Jim Foster by saying that a few years ago Americans thought the civil rights movement was radical, but now we take it for granted. In time to come Americans might feel that way about this issue as well. Jim's speech was powerful and self-righteous. He impressed upon the delegates that we weren't pleading for understanding or asking for affirmation of our lifestyle. We were protesting the discrimination and harassment of our community that brings shame to the concept of justice in this country.

When Madeline got up to speak, Cronkite introduced her as a communications worker from Buffalo, New York, who has just announced that she is a lesbian: "Let's listen in . . ." Madeline gave the politically effective lines for that time and called for the support of our basic civil rights: "Our rights don't infringe upon the rights of others." She called for the passage of the gay plank in the platform and said that a vote in favor would influence the potential 20 million gay and lesbian American voters who could help put a Democrat in the White House. "I am your neighbor, your sister, and your daughter. Everyone in this room knows someone gay. Pass this plank and you will enable all homosexual men and women across the country to live their lives in peace."

Unfortunately, as well as scheduling the gay and lesbian speakers at such an ungodly hour, the McGovern operatives also scheduled an opposition speaker by the name of Kathleen Wilch from Ohio. She linked the gay movement to child molestation, white slavery, and pandering. This was to make sure that any wavering delegates got the message that the plank was to be voted down.

Much organizing went on at and before the '72 convention to introduce pro-gay language into the party platform. The Gay Activists Alliance on the East Coast did much of it. We had been disillusioned by McGovern, who was the paragon of progressive values—a moral leader and a liberal who had been in the forefront of the antiwar movement. We were the only group in the "liberal left coalition" that was not a full partner in that ideological movement. So we put on pressure to get the campaign to issue statements supporting gay rights in New York and other places around the country.

Attorney General Bob Abrams chaired McGovern's primary campaign in New York and gave his chief of staff, Ethan Geto, a year off to work as McGovern's director of press and communications in New York State. Ethan was a gay activist and a skilled political operative. He had always kept his professional life and personal opinions separate—but he made an exception with the McGovern campaign. By day he would manage the candidate's image and platform positions for the campaign, and by night he would huddle with Gay Activists Alliance allies—plotting strategy to get the attention of the campaign.

Ethan came up with the idea to take over the McGovern campaign headquarters and have the gay activists chain themselves to the furniture and take over the phones. The campaign would then be forced to respond to the "zap," and Ethan, as the official spokesperson, would deliver the response. The zap went on for hours as Ethan consulted with senior advisers, many of whom were sympathetic, but anxious and afraid because of the way the Republicans were manipulating other liberal social issues of the day. Ethan insisted that they respond or risk losing many of their liberal coalition allies, especially in New York. He was finally authorized to make a positive statement from the campaign. It was a major victory for us early in the campaign. And because of the much sought after media attention, it was a victory for gay rights in general. It was also another step toward inclusion of our issue in the broader human rights and civil liberties dialogue.

The fight for inclusion continued around the country and finally into the convention. Attempts to include us in the official platform of the Democratic Party failed. The 1972 Democratic platform, probably the most liberal ever offered by a major political party, was more a collection of independent reform proposals than a unified plan of action. Twenty separate minority amendments to the proposed platform planks were considered by the convention, but only two were adopted. The right of women to control their reproductive lives lost on a roll-call vote.

Throughout the days and nights of the convention, gay and lesbian activists fought to get our plank included. They held endless meetings at the Fontainebleau and Doral Hotels. Once again Ethan provided gay activists with the inside track and who was making the decisions. The delegates discussed whom to lobby, where to pass out leaflets, what special interest groups to approach, and which state delegations to concentrate on.

Ron Gold, who later became National Gay and Lesbian Task Force media director, and who at the time wrote for *Variety* magazine, went to speak to the South Dakota delegation. He was bodily removed from the state's meeting and carried to the hotel lobby. Luckily for him, Shirley MacLaine was passing by and intervened on his behalf. Ron was freed, but was unable to return to the delegation to make his case.

According to Madeline Davis, the gay and lesbian delegates knew in their minds they would not get the plank passed; but in their hearts there were moments of belief, and some encouraging moments occurred as they advanced the agenda and raised consciousness throughout the convention.

One of the problems with the minority plank might have been its wording. Instead of focusing on civil rights, it endorsed the repeal of all laws regarding voluntary sex acts performed by adults in private. Delegates might have been more sympathetic to civil rights language than to sodomy law repeal. But in the early stages of the movement there was no national gay civil rights bill, and much of the movement's focus was directed toward repealing those sodomy laws.

The gay and lesbian plank went down to defeat by a voice vote. But we had made our first inroads toward influencing Democratic Party policy at a national convention.

THE 1976 DEMOCRATIC NATIONAL CONVENTION

At the 1976 convention gay/lesbian civil rights were still considered beyond the pale of the Democratic Party. We used the convention to raise consciousness, make contacts, and advance our issues. There was a growing political movement taking root in scattered places, especially metropolitan areas, but few took it seriously. When they did, politicians considered it more of a liability than anything else. However, we made solid contacts with some of the Carter forces. With some we battled fiercely; with others, such as Midge Costanza, we found our way to the White House and government appointments.

Between the 1972 and 1976 conventions the gay and lesbian community did not advance much in the realm of electoral politics. Many new organizations were founded, we were growing internally, some new gay and lesbian political clubs had been started, but most of our gains were made in the cultural arena. We still strove for media attention, and education of the general public and of our own community were important goals. Nineteen seventy-six was pre–Anita Bryant, and there was no major public sense of our community as a movement. I was co–executive director of NGTF (with Bruce Voeller) at the time. I made it onto the *Today* show, thanks to the efforts of Ron Gold, NGTF's media director. During my interview, I tried to show there was a growing cultural and political movement in the country, which was best illustrated by tracing the efforts of several municipalities to pass gay civil rights ordinances.

The Democratic Party had tightened up dramatically after the platform and delegate-selection battles of the two prior conventions. The party abolished the implicit quota systems of the 1972 delegate-selection rules and raised the signature requirement for convention minority reports from 10 percent to 25 percent of Standing Committee members. With Richard Nixon resigning in disgrace over the Watergate affair, and Gerald Ford, the man who pardoned him, leading the country, the time seemed right to take back the White House. Democrats all over the country were serious about doing just that.

For myself, I had one major goal—to make the gay and lesbian agenda part of the Democratic consciousness, if not part of the formal agenda. Bruce Voeller and I searched through the list of platform committee members from around the country to try to identify gay-friendly or at least liberal members. Then Bella Abzug and I spoke at a function during her primary campaign for the U.S. Senate. She told me that a member who was also the cochair of the New York State platform committee, Midge Costanza from Rochester, could probably be helpful. I was excited and immediately wrote to Midge saying that we wanted the 1976 platform to include gay rights; the time was now, and could she help us get that message back to the Carter campaign and Stu Eisenstat? She sent me back a handwritten letter over four legal-size sheets explaining how much she'd like to help and mentioned things she'd already done for our cause. I was impressed, and thinking we'd really hit the jackpot, I arranged to meet her during an upcoming visit to New York City. We met at the old Americana Hotel and solidified our mission. She agreed to support our issue and speak for us at the upcoming platform hearings in Washington, D.C.

The weekend of the platform hearings I also had an NGTF board meeting in New York, so I was still in New York when I got a call during the meeting from Lee Novick of Bella's staff. She told me that the abortion issue was in trouble and we would probably have problems with the gay rights issue. I called Midge, who was in Rochester, and she agreed to fly to Washington immediately. I then called my friend Ginny Apuzzo and asked her if she'd like to drive to Washington since we had been discussing the gay and lesbian political platform. We plotted strategy on the way to Washington in her yellow Volkswagen.

We tried to introduce sexual orientation language in three different platform subcommittees, with no success at all. When we arrived at the Civil Rights and Liberties Subcommittee, they were just getting ready to take a crucial vote on a section in which we should have been included. We had little hope of being included, but we weren't going out without a fight. Midge delivered the message with our prompting that "the gay community has waited long enough . . . our patience has run out . . . we can no longer tolerate discrimination from a party that has always been against social injustice." That's about as far as we got. When the final vote on the proposed platform was taken, we were nowhere in the document.

Later Ginny and I tried to garner support for a minority report, but there was none; in fact, Stu Eisenstat threw us out of the room, calling us an embarrassment to the party.

Meanwhile, back in New York, I had decided to run for delegate to the Democratic National Convention. In New York you had to run on a slate committed to a candidate and run district-wide. This meant getting a slate to accept me and then convincing people to vote for me, just as in any election. I picked Birch Bayh because he seemed the best on gay issues and we had the best connections to his campaign. We had a fund-raiser for him at Uncle Charlie's bar, and I believe that was the first time a presidential candidate ever made a speech to a gay group. Ethan Geto was Birch Bayh's New York campaign manager and helped get Allen Roscoff and me onto Bayh's slate in our districts. We opened up a joint banking account and started raising money for the race.

Unfortunately, Bayh's campaign collapsed in Massachusetts, before the New York primary, and he dropped out of the race. New York has a two-part primary, and as long as someone qualifies as a candidate for president, he/she can create an official slate. Since we were still legally on the ballot, we were therefore potential delegates looking for a candidate. Bella Abzug had put together an independent slate, and there was a Mo Udall slate as well. The party naturally wanted to collapse the three slates into one official slate. With six nominees on each of these slates, eighteen people were vying for only six delegate positions that would eventually became the Udall slate. An incredible political battle ensued for these positions. I managed to get on the Udall slate with Bella opposing me all the way, even to the point of trying to physically keep me out of negotiating meetings. I actually had to push the door open with her trying to keep it closed from the other side. After that we made our peace (one of many times) and campaigned together. Ethan Geto designed a campaign for me based on the theme of "someone special." We had to present the campaign in a way that we would attract, not alienate voters—a real feat in those days, since being gay or lesbian was more of a liability than a plus. Even liberal Democrats were accusing me of being a "spoiler" and said that my presence on the ticket would ensure a conservative Scoop Jackson victory in my district. Eventually we overcame the odds and I was on my way to the convention.

Allen Roscoff, in the other district, fared worse. Like the rest of the Bayh delegates he had a legal right to remain on the ballot. That would get messy for the party, of course, because they wanted one official slate, so many promises and deals were made to make this happen. Paul Kirk (future chair of the DNC) promised Allen he would make him a Udall delegate if he would remove his name. Allen did, but he wasn't made a delegate. This was the first of several promises to the gay community that Kirk made and broke.

Bruce Voeller and I were determined to make as significant a presence as we could for our issues at the convention. The NGTF had a combination media and hospitality room across the street from Madison Square Garden where the convention was held. We held press conferences announcing the number of openly gay and lesbian delegates (there were three of us), and about our issues, which never made it into the platform. Since we were a novelty, we got several stories written about our presence. We tried our best to pass out educational material to the delegates, and generally to make as great an impact on the convention as we could. We networked and made friends with people who would later be of political value for our issues in other parts of the country. NGTF's main role was to foster gay and lesbian grassroots organizing at the local, state, and national levels.

One crucial moment at the convention challenged and helped shape my political future and the access we would have to the new president of the United States.

When it came time for the balloting for president, I was being lobbied heavily by elected officials who were Carter delegates to switch my vote from Udall to Carter. (There was no binding vote on the first ballot as there was in 1980.) At the same time I was being enormously pressured by my peers (many of whom had lobbied heavily to get me on the Udall ballot), who wanted to make a symbolic gesture of loyalty to Mo Udall. I was tremendously torn between the thought of alienating political allies, many of them good friends, and casting my vote with the clear winner of the nomination.

I finally decided to go with Carter. To be able to say I had made that critical decision, should Carter become president, would be valuable in creating opportunities for our community later. I was looking to the future and realized that I was the only gay or lesbian person at that time connected enough, through Midge Costanza and others, to make the switch in my vote count for something for our community. Udall had already thrown his support to Carter *before* the balloting, so voting for Udall seemed like a useless gesture. It turned out that I had made the right decision, as Carter went on to become the next president. For the first time in gay and lesbian history we began to have access to the White House and make real inroads on the federal level.

Shortly after the inauguration Midge was appointed assistant to the president—the highest level in the White House and the highest appointment ever for a woman. We asked for and she set up a meeting in the White House for NGTF and fourteen people we picked to cover the major issues for our community. It was a historic first for us and was by no means just symbolic. Moreover, the boost in the press that we got went a long way toward legitimizing our issues at that time. For two years after we presented our issues at the meeting with Midge and her staff, we systematically worked those issues through each federal agency that had jurisdiction over them. We worked with the Civil Rights Commission, the Justice Department, the Federal Trade Commission, and the Federal Bureau of Prisons, to name a few. A call from Midge Costanza to Carter's surgeon general, and follow-up by NGTF, resulted in his decision that Public Health Service doctors would no longer examine aliens suspected of being gay because it was not a medical issue. It was amazing how a call from the White House brought the heads of these departments to the same table with gay and lesbian community members whom they would never have taken seriously otherwise.

Carter established the Presidential Commission on the Observance of International Women's Year and named me to it as the first open gay or lesbian person appointed to a presidential commission. When Midge talked to him about it, she reminded him how I had switched my vote at the Democratic National Convention to vote for him. That made an impact on him, but he asked, "Well, all right, but does she have to use her title?" (co-executive director of the National Gay Task Force). Midge replied, "Do you have to use yours, sir?"

I used my position as a commissioner to organize lesbians in all fifty states to get our lesbian agenda accepted at each state's convention. The other forty-two women commissioners (with the exception of NOW president Elli Smeal) rejected our lesbian agenda as a legitimate issue. As a result, we had to organize at each state convention leading up to the national convention in Houston, Texas. We needed thirty-five states and we got more than that. The commissioners then tried to bury our issue at the end of the agenda. They decided to make the agenda alphabetical and defeated our attempts to call the issue "alternative lifestyle" or "lesbianism." Instead they used "sexual orientation"—relegating it to the end of the agenda and almost guaranteeing that our issue would not be heard at the national convention. For the convention, we had buttons made that said, "Keep the agenda moving—let every issue be heard," and convinced hundreds of delegates to wear them. As part of our lobbying efforts, Dolores Alexander, Charlotte Bunch, and I got Betty Friedan to apologize for the role she played in keeping lesbians from participating in the National Organization of Women. In the end, we made it through the agenda and our issue passed, but not before two Southern state delegations stood up and turned their backs on us and one delegation walked out. When the vote came, we released yellow balloons and cheered, "Thank you, sisters." The lesbian agenda was officially part of the feminist agenda for the first time ever and was touted as such shortly thereafter in *Ms.* magazine.

THE 1980 DEMOCRATIC NATIONAL CONVENTION

By the time of the 1980 convention we had made enormous political progress. This was reflected in the number of delegates (77) to the convention, our inclusion in the official platform for the first time, and our permanent incorporation through the Rules Committee in the Charter of the Party. One of the delegates, an African-American man, was chosen by the Gay and Lesbian Caucus to be our vice-presidential nominee, so we had visibility at the podium. The Anita Bryant campaign and other initiatives around the country, though painful and hard fought, had served to mobilize and strengthen the movement as never before.

By 1980 a major sea change had taken place within the gay and lesbian community. In 1977 we suffered through Anita Bryant and her Save Our Children campaign. Although it took place in Florida, gay men and lesbians across the country rallied around the effort to defeat her referendum to repeal the gay civil rights ordinance. Prior to that, Bruce Voeller and I had helped with the passage of the ordinance in our NGTF clearinghouse capacity. We had considered it a major victory as we counted up the cities that were beginning to pass these gay civil rights ordinances. We were disgusted that one person could make us pour so much money and human resources into fighting a battle for basic human rights. Jack Campbell formed the Dade County Coalition for Human Rights and was the chair of the campaign, with Ethan Geto and Jim Foster as the campaign managers. I spent a lot of time at the campaign headquarters working with them, and we soon began to realize even in the middle of the daily wars that this was probably the single most unifying event ever at the national level for the gay and lesbian community. Ethan especially used this opportunity to pitch the national media, and in a short time Florida was in the national spotlight. We were desperate for money in the beginning of the campaign, but toward the end hundreds of letters came pouring in with small checks along with exciting and moving coming-out stories. Instead of hiding ashamed in the closet, gay people everywhere began to think of themselves as members of society with a political agenda. It spearheaded mobilizing efforts everywhere as we sought out our gay-identified peers.

Shortly after our defeat in Florida we were faced with referenda in Wichita, Kansas; St. Paul, Minnesota; and Eugene, Oregon. In California we soundly defeated the infamous Briggs initiative, which would have prohibited gay men and lesbians from teaching in the classroom. These battles mobilized our community more effectively than anything we could have come up with on our own. I still don't believe our enemies realize how much these events energize and unite us, as painful as they may be at the time.

In 1979, a decade after the Stonewall riots, we had the first national march on Washington and celebrated ten years of liberation with gay pride celebrations around the country. Harvey Milk was assassinated, and there was rioting in the streets of San Francisco after the Dan White trial. But many had also realized it was time to take our battles from the streets to the corridors of power, and this was reflected in the record number of seventy-seven delegates to the 1980 Democratic National Convention.

The Democrats were engaged in a major power struggle between Kennedy and Carter for the Democratic presidential nomination. This served our community well, as we had good connections with both camps. In California, gay and lesbian delegates were organizing under the "Destination New York" banner, a project of the Stonewall Democratic Club in the south, and Harvey Milk and Alice B. Toklas Clubs in the north. California alone sent thirty-three gay and lesbian delegates to the convention. In the East, the National Gay Task Force and Gay Rights National Lobby formed the National Convention Project with Tom Bastow and Mary Spotswood Peu as co–executive directors, and steered by Tom Chorlton as the sole staff member. From the fall of 1979 through the convention they established as many contacts as possible and really worked the Platform and Rules Committees.

Garry Shay and Steve Weltman from the Stonewall Democratic Club came up with a huge proposal for many rules changes, which was later broken into three targeted parts by Tom Chorlton with emphasis on "affording full participation and prohibiting discrimination in all party affairs on the basis of sexual orientation." Tom and others had lined up speakers and orchestrated a production to include this language in the rules changes to be offered by the Rules Committee in its report to the convention. The key to the whole operation was getting a commitment from the Kennedy people to sign a petition to introduce our language as a minority plank if the Rules Committee (somewhat controlled by the Carter forces) did not accept it.

Tom Chorlton prepared the petition and got a solid commitment from Pete Edelman and the Kennedy people, who then positioned themselves with the petitions in the four corners of the room. Tom went to Tom Donilon of the

Carter camp and asked for his support. Donilon responded, "No, we can't let that go." Chorlton then pointed to the positioned Kennedy people and said, "See those guys with the clipboards? We have the support to make this go. You can give it to us now in the basement of the Mayflower Hotel without the TV cameras, or you can watch us fight it out on the floor of the convention in New York." Chorlton walked away, and when it came up for a vote, Pete Edelman gave the thumbs-up sign for the Kennedy votes, and Donilon slowly put his thumb up—the rest of the hands in the room went up and we had a solid vote for inclusion. This was an extremely important victory because, whereas the platform changes every four years, these rules changes permanently amended the party's charter and bylaws. This new rule was the crowbar that opened up the whole process, and Tom Chorlton used it four years later to make sure state delegations complied with this policy.

We were constantly amazed at the successes we had at the 1980 convention. It was such a change from the past. We had gone from being an albatross to a defined constituency, with all the benefits of money, power, and votes attached to that definition. We had six members on the platform committee, including Bill Kraus and Ginny Apuzzo, who made speeches and lobbied with many others to include sexual orientation in the platform for the first time. We were also included in the immigration issue. We went into the convention with major victories under our belts.

By this time I had left the Task Force and moved to California, where I got appointed as a Kennedy delegate. We had a larger gay and lesbian caucus than at any prior convention.

Ginny Apuzzo and Bill Kraus were elected cochairs of the Gay and Lesbian Caucus. The National Convention Project's leadership role was set to self-destruct after the election of the cochairs. Tom Chorlton had gone out to a disco with Bill Kraus the night of the chairs vote and asked him what the next plans were. Bill responded that he hadn't yet thought about it. So the next morning Jack Campbell, Tom Chorlton, and Tom Bastow met for breakfast and decided to explore Jack's idea of running a gay or lesbian candidate for vice president. When Jack had originally broached the subject before the convention, it only took fifty delegates who hadn't signed any other vice-presidential candidate's petition to nominate a candidate at the convention. The Carter forces thought they had effectively cut off this avenue of protest, and therefore our means of visibility at the convention, by changing the rule to require over three hundred signatures. We were not daunted in the least. We set out to collect signatures from anywhere we could find them. Another issue group turned over their names to us because they had been given time on the podium as a trade-off for dropping their vice-presidential bid. We still had to solicit their signatories to sign our petition, but at least we knew they were available. Of five other issue groups, only the antidraft movement was also able to secure enough signatures to nominate a VP candidate.

After a great lobbying effort, which raised a lot of consciousness, we came up with more than enough signatures on our vice-presidential petitions. We selected Mel Boozer, an African-American man from Washington, D.C., as our candidate. Bill nominated and Ginny seconded him on the convention floor, and Mel gave a speech that was incredibly moving. A line that most people remember was "Would you ask me how I dare to compare the civil rights struggle with the struggle for lesbian and gay rights? I can compare and I do compare them. I know what it means to be called a nigger. I know what it means to be called a faggot. I can sum up the difference in one word. None!"

The 1980 convention was an enormous success. We were in the platform for the first time and permanently included in the Charter of the Party. We had gotten national visibility and increased our respect from within the party. All in all, the gains reflected the ones we had made in the larger culture. We were definitely making progress.

Unfortunately, Carter lost the election and we were faced with Ronald Reagan and what would evolve into twelve long years under Republican White House leadership.

THE 1984 DEMOCRATIC NATIONAL CONVENTION

By 1984, the gay and lesbian movement had advanced and matured internally. The wording for inclusion in the official party platform was created by the consensus of five national organizations. Tough new delegate selection rules limited our numbers to sixty-five, but years of education and internal organizing made the platform stronger than ever. Nondiscrimination clauses were stronger and much more specific. Funding for AIDS research, education, and patient care reflected the devastating impact the disease was having on our community. The Rules Committee included a requirement for outreach to the gay/lesbian community. However, we had virtually no official visibility within the convention—perhaps reflecting the reluctance of some Democratic leaders to associate with a still-contested constituency that now had the added burden of the controversial AIDS issue.

The years between the 1980 and 1984 Democratic conventions were sometimes heady, but perplexing. We were definitely advancing in our struggle for civil rights and in our visibility in the general culture. Many new organizations were formed, including the Human Rights Campaign Fund (HRCF) in 1982. In 1981, I became the executive director of the National Gay Rights

Advocates (NGRA). During this time NGRA became the largest membership organization in the country. Sean Strub (now the president of *Poz* magazine) and I were finding new ways to reach our community through direct mail and telemarketing, and we knew we were only scratching the surface of the millions of lesbians and gay men in various stages of coming out.

Books and movies were being made about us. We had our own radio shows, pride celebrations were taking place in dozens of cities, and we were winning important court cases such as *Board of Education of Oklahoma City v. National Gay Task Force,* a case the National Gay Rights Advocates had been working on for years. The U.S. Supreme Court struck down the Oklahoma law on First Amendment grounds because it would have prohibited teachers from discussing homosexuality in the classroom.

At the same time, AIDS was emerging as the most gargantuan problem we had ever faced and threatened to put an end to our progress and our lives. It also shifted the focus from civil rights to issues involving the epidemic. NGRA and Lambda Legal Defense Fund fought dozens of AIDS-related cases, winning many of them in the courts. NGTF and HRCF were lobbying successfully for increased AIDS funding. Politicians and others had a way to support the gay and lesbian community indirectly. This much-needed support later translated into endorsements for gay civil rights issues.

Gay and lesbian politicos mobilized within our community and within the Democratic Party structure to further the civil rights and AIDS agendas. After the 1980 election, the delegates and others realized the need for a permanent organization that would target Democrats and increase our role within the party. Tom Chorlton became the steering-committee coordinator for this effort, and about twelve people met several times in Washington, D.C., to form the organization. The National Association of Gay and Lesbian Democratic Clubs was formalized in 1982, with Frank Kameny making the final motion to name the organization. Peter Vogel and Gwen Craig were the first cochairs, and Tom became the first executive director. NAGLDC got a warm reception from the DNC. At the time, Ann Lewis was the political director of the party.

In 1982 the Democrats held their third and last midterm convention. Garry Shay was a delegate from southern California. When he received his convention packet, there was nothing in the proposed party position statements about gay and lesbian rights. Garry drew up some nondiscrimination language reflecting the 1980 platform, and the delegates agreed to include us in the midterm document. That same year HRCF held its first banquet at the Waldorf-Astoria. Walter Mondale attended as their guest of honor and reiterated his support for what the 1980 convention had approved. (Tony Randall was the MC, and Ted Koppel used the banquet as the lead-in for the first appearance of gays and lesbians on *Nightline*).

In February 1983 the first official Gay and Lesbian Caucus of the DNC was created. Democratic National Chairman Charles Manatt had established a policy by which the DNC formally recognized member caucuses. Don Fowler, who later became DNC chair, was serving as the chair of the Rules and Bylaws Committee. He was a good friend and strong supporter of our efforts to form a caucus within the DNC. Signatures representing 10 percent of the DNC membership were required to establish a new caucus. The DNC member signatures were collected at the state level by lesbian and gay Democratic clubs and political organizations and coordinated by NAGLDC. Over 20 percent of DNC members from twenty-three states, including twenty-one state chairs, signed the petitions. Recognition of our caucus was subsequently approved unanimously by the DNC Executive Committee. Dick Hanson of Minnesota was selected as chair of our caucus. Stephen Smith of California served as its secretary-treasurer. At that time we had only two openly gay members on the DNC, so this recognition was a great step for our official inclusion within the party.

The lesbian and gay agenda presented to the Democratic Platform Committee for the 1984 convention was created through consensus by five national organizations: the National Gay Task Force, the Human Rights Campaign Fund, the Gay Rights National Lobby, the National Coalition of Black Gays, and the National Association of Gay and Lesbian Democratic Clubs. Besides demanding an end to discrimination based on sexual orientation, we wanted wording that called for an end to antigay violence, discrimination against gays in the military, security agencies, and other federal agencies, removal of archaic provisions of the Immigration and Naturalization Act, and support for adequate funding for AIDS research, education, and patient care. All of these provisions were included in the 1984 Democratic platform.

These five national lesbian and gay organizations also organized the "'84 and Counting" effort to register 1 million new lesbian and gay voters by election day. NAGLDC sent out a voter-registration handbook as their part in this effort. The Democratic National Committee helped to pay for the printing of this document, underscoring their commitment to our constituency.

Years of education and behind-the-scenes organizing contributed to the success of the platform effort. For the 1984 convention, we had six gay and lesbian members of the two hundred total (including temporary and permanent) Platform Committee members, but we were better organized than anyone else was. The party did not send out a list of members to anyone, but it was public record, so Tom Chorlton copied all the names and contact information and sent it to local organizers. They lobbied the members and added information that would be helpful in swaying votes. Congresswoman Geraldine Ferraro, who was later tapped as Mondale's running mate, chaired the committee and wanted a platform of broad themes and few specifics. However, other groups and we won the day; the platform was specific and gave our community something to get excited about.

We also made great gains within the Rules Committee. We had four openly gay and lesbian members out of one hundred eighty-four. The Rules Committee members voted that all committees of the National Committee include at least one member of each recognized caucus. Since we had been officially recognized in 1983, we were now assured of having lesbian and gay representation on each committee. Rules members also approved an amendment to ban discrimination on the basis of "sexual orientation" and continued the requirement for "outreach" in state delegate-selection plans. To make sure that this provision didn't slip through the cracks in the implementation, our delegates called for the inclusion of one gay man and one lesbian on the Compliance Assistance Commission, which oversaw the state delegate-selection plan.

NAGLDC had played the "overseeing role" during the 1984 selection of delegates and found six states not in compliance. All eventually revised their selection plans to comply with the rules. NAGLDC also sent out a delegate-selection handbook on how to run for delegate with information specific to each state to help gay and lesbian candidates. There were tough new 1980 delegate-selection rules that made it more difficult for grassroots activists to win seats to the convention. In fact, we had only sixty-five delegates in 1984 compared to seventy-seven in 1980.

I did not attend the 1984 convention as a delegate because my attention was almost entirely focused on the National Gay Rights Advocates. But I was at the convention for many of the speeches and the march the day before the convention of several hundred thousand lesbians and gay men. Some party officials feared that we would have massive demonstrations in the streets, evoking memories of 1968 and Chicago, but these fears never materialized.

Inside the convention hall, we had basically no visibility. We were not invited to speak from the podium. None of our supporters or presidential candidates with the exception of Jesse Jackson made direct reference to us, although each of them recited the litany of other Democratic constituencies. Eight people representing various constituencies introduced Jackson, but there was no gay representation. So while much progress had been made within the party, we could only hope that the written words of the platform would soon become the spoken words of the party standard-bearers.

THE 1988 DEMOCRATIC NATIONAL CONVENTION

The 1988 convention was generally one of unity and reflected the tightening up that was going on everywhere in the party. We sent Dukakis off from the convention with a twelve-point lead against George Bush. We were definitely looking forward to Democratic control of the White House once again.

However, the Gay and Lesbian Caucus at the convention was split between Dukakis and Jesse Jackson. Jackson had wholeheartedly invited us into his rainbow coalition, and his platform was better than Dukakis's stance on our issues. Dukakis was great on issues concerning AIDS, but horrible on gay and lesbian foster parents. Jesse Jackson gave a tremendously moving speech at the convention that will always be remembered for his emphasis on gay and lesbian rights and inclusion of our community in the Rainbow Coalition.

Between the 1984 and 1988 conventions, the gay and lesbian movement was dominated by the issue of AIDS, and it was often used as a thinly veiled excuse for homophobia.

Conversely, it forced many people out of the closet and broadened our support base. During this time Rock Hudson died, Elizabeth Taylor became the chair of the American Foundation for AIDS Research (AMFAR), and gay and lesbian leaders met for the first time regarding AIDS issues with a surgeon general, Everett Koop.

AIDS officially became the leading killer of young men and women in New York City. At the National Gay Rights Advocates we were pursuing numerous AIDS-related lawsuits. We sued a California insurance company for $11 million when they tried to redline applicants who had AIDS. It was later settled out of court.

In 1986, Lyndon LaRouche tried to use California's initiative process to play on people's fears and homophobia. He got a proposition (No. 64) on the ballot that was designed to quarantine people with AIDS. Fortunately, it was soundly rejected at the polls.

We continued to make gains in the area of civil rights. Some of our gains were probably a result of the widespread attention on AIDS issues our community received and created. The 1987 National March on Washington was the most well attended gay and lesbian event we had ever held. The National Gay Rights Advocates hosted a post-march party that drew over three thousand people.

Following the march, a large number of gay and lesbian leaders met in Virginia for a "war conference." There, Rob Eichberg and I decided we would personally take on "coming out," one of the four major issues at the conference. We founded National Coming Out Day (NCOD), and NGRA supported it financially that year. NCOD was launched in 1989 with a nationally televised show on *Oprah*. Gerry Studds was reelected as the first openly gay member of Congress, and Congressman Barney Frank also came out. There were growing numbers of openly gay Democrats who held local and state elective office.

Within the Democratic Party we were having a pretty mixed reception. In congressional campaigns, the Human Rights Campaign Fund contributed heavily to Democratic candidates; among the seventy-four congressional cosponsors of the House Gay Rights Bill who sought reelection, all, except the delegate from Guam, were victorious. However, politicians remained skeptical of claims by activists that gays represented a large voting block. There was much strategizing about what could be used to convince party officials and the press of the true size of the gay vote in many areas of the country.

Following Ronald Reagan's horrible defeat of Mondale in 1984, many Democratic leaders thought the party had become balkanized and torn apart by special interest groups. In 1985, DNC member Richard Koster, then chair of the Latin American Democrats, proposed a resolution that would have abolished the DNC's existing system for recognizing caucuses. This would have impacted our two-year-old caucus, as well as caucuses devoted to blacks, women, Hispanics, Asians, and others (liberal/progressive, business and professional, etc.).

DNC member Rick Stafford of Minneapolis, chair of the Lesbian and Gay Caucus, in conjunction with NAGLDC, led the effort to defeat Koster's resolution. A week before the committee meeting, Stafford sent a two-page letter to all DNC members urging them to reject Koster's resolution and to support an alternative proposal from Kathy Vick, a member from New Orleans. Vick's proposal suggested withdrawing the new rule, passed by the Rules Committee at the 1984 Convention, that mandated that representatives of each caucus be members of most party committees. Stafford was adamant that the Koster resolution proposed retribution against those very members of our Democratic family who worked hardest for the national ticket in the general election, and that the approach was unjust and politically counterproductive. Our efforts were successful and Koster's resolution died for lack of a second on the first day of the National Committee meeting.

Paul Kirk was elected the new chair of the DNC, replacing outgoing Charles Manatt. At first, Kirk seemed as though he would support us. During his campaign he promised Rick Stafford he would keep the caucuses intact. Brian Lunde, whom Kirk named as the new executive director of the party, also promised Tom Chorlton the same. But shortly after Kirk's election, he presided over an Executive Committee meeting of the DNC where a resolution was introduced to abolish the caucuses. No one had any advance notice of this or time to prepare a defense. At that time, the Black, Hispanic, and Women's Caucuses had seats for their respective caucuses on the Executive Committee. The Executive Committee decided the chairs of these caucuses would keep their seats, but the party would no longer recognize caucuses. Brian Lunde told Chorlton that this was probably the best thing that could have happened to the party.

The 1988 convention reflected the increased control that party leaders strove to exercise in all areas. Determined to win back the White House, Democrats staged a show of unity in Atlanta, Georgia. For the most part, issue-oriented activists were focused on party victory, and the convention sent Dukakis off with a twelve-point lead over Bush. Elaine Noble, Vincent McCarthy, and I were whips at the convention, since we had been early Dukakis supporters. Early on, Hilary Rosen, then chair of HRCF, had arranged a breakfast with Congressman Barney Frank and me to discuss my involvement in the campaign. He hooked me up with other Massachusetts operatives and I started working on Dukakis's election.

It was difficult in some ways to support Dukakis because he had a terrible stand on gay and lesbian foster parents. But he had a wonderful record on all the issues that affected our AIDS agenda, which was paramount at the time. I also knew that he was close to Bob Farmer (his finance chair) and Bob's lover, Tim McNeil, who played a major role in the campaign. They had adopted two Vietnamese children whom the governor and his wife visited regularly. I thought Dukakis could be educated on our issues and that our best bet was to get him elected first. (In fact, several years later, he vetoed a bill in Massachusetts that would have prohibited gay adoptions or foster parenting.) Elaine Noble and Vincent McCarthy had a harder time of it because they both lived in Massachusetts, where Dukakis had ordered the removal of two children from the care of gay foster parents. But he looked at that time like the candidate who could beat Bush, and we desperately needed someone in the White House who would show serious governmental commitment to halting the spread of AIDS and providing medical support services for those who were already HIV-positive.

I organized a press conference for Dukakis in Los Angeles to take place when the California Gay and Lesbian Democratic Clubs were having their statewide meeting. It was his first and only national press conference with the community. He was challenged on the foster parents issue after he had given excellent responses about AIDS issues. Of course, the foster parent response got played up in our community. Even though, as Lew Wilson said to Vincent McCarthy after a meeting in San Francisco, many party activists had "no interest in winning—only in being right," Dukakis still managed to get considerable support.

However, it was hard to resist the appeal of Jesse Jackson and his Rainbow Coalition. We felt totally comfortable as an accepted community there, and he gave a remarkable speech at the convention that included us in his coalition. Elaine Noble commented that it sure looked like a lot more fun over in that camp. The Jackson delegates had better parties, a more substantial platform, and interesting people.

I worked closely with Tim McNeil throughout the campaign. He was working full-time for Dukakis. Together, we managed to orchestrate a few events, such as the gay and lesbian press conference in California. He was the one on the inside who was drafting the position papers in response to questionnaires from gay organizations and developing policy for the platform on AIDS issues and lesbian and gay rights.

After Tim arranged Dukakis's visit to Bailey House, a hospice for people with AIDS in New York City, the governor's political operatives started pulling Dukakis back from gay and lesbian events. Tim then worked on Kitty Dukakis and had her show up at various functions such as the National AIDS Conference in San Francisco in 1988.

During this time Tim and I became fairly close. We had a lot of the same goals and ideas, and we had been through a tough primary season together. At the convention we celebrated. We thought we were on our way to presidential victory. The last night of the convention, Tim spent the whole night meeting with the campaign and negotiating with Jesse Jackson's campaign for seats on the Democratic National Committee. In the end, they agreed that Jackson would get twelve DNC seats and Dukakis would receive eight. Tim called me at four in the morning and asked me if I would accept one of the Dukakis DNC appointments. I had had no hint of this until the phone call, but I gladly said yes. It made all the long months seem a little less strenuous, and I felt happy that I could continue my efforts with the party in an enhanced capacity.

THE 1992 DEMOCRATIC NATIONAL CONVENTION

The 1992 convention was the most euphoric and heady convention we as a community had ever experienced. We had over one hundred delegates and caucus members, and most of us were convinced that we would have a change in the White House. We finally had a candidate we were excited about—who was going to make a difference for us. He was a candidate we had campaigned for, had raised money for, and in whom we believed. Although the platform as a whole was heavily influenced by the centrist ideas of the Democratic Leadership Council (DLC), our issues were solidly included. There were some tense moments concerning Clinton's acceptance speech, but we worked through them and celebrated exuberantly afterward. We had gay and lesbian speakers at the podium inside the convention, and outside the convention the United for AIDS Action Rally was taking place. It was one of the largest AIDS protests ever in the country.

In the years leading up to the convention, the gay and lesbian movement had become much more diversified, militant, and sophisticated. ACT UP was created and Silence = Death became the slogan that engaged thousands of activists as we fought for funding, care, and a cure for AIDS. Their Presidential Project challenged candidates throughout the primary season.

We were on the news constantly for one issue or another, and we had truly broken through the barriers of invisibility. The fight to lift the military's ban on gay men and lesbians was raging, although there was some conflict between those who wanted to end discrimination and those who were antimilitary.

Outing came into vogue, although it was controversial within the community, and queer politics became Queer Nation and Year of the Queer. Domestic partnership laws were being passed in San Francisco and other places, and corporations were starting to look seriously at partnership benefits for gay men and lesbians.

Ron Brown became the chair of the DNC in 1989 after a hard-fought battle against five other candidates. I was an early supporter of his, and he reappointed me to the DNC. Ron was supportive of our issues, and for the first time a DNC chair gave an interview to *The Advocate* magazine, which became a major article on the importance of the lesbian and gay community to the Democratic Party. During this period I resigned from National Gay Rights Advocates and became involved in campaign fund-raising for Dianne Feinstein's gubernatorial race in 1990 and the Clinton/Gore campaign in 1992, raising over $2 million in small-donor contributions through house parties.

Our community had a vital interest in the presidential election of 1992. We were more powerful than ever before, and increasingly candidates courted our votes and money. We were no longer being rejected as too controversial to associate with. The gay and lesbian community was divided on which candidate to support. Many leaned toward Tsongas because of his outstanding record on gay and lesbian civil rights issues. Clinton was an unknown entity to most of us at that time.

Then David Mixner, an old friend of Bill Clinton's, became involved in his campaign. He set up meetings with Clinton and AIDS activists on the East Coast and with ANGLE (Access Now for Gay and Lesbian Equality) on the West Coast. At the ANGLE meeting with Clinton we discussed Governor Pete Wilson's veto of a gay civil rights bill, which had caused nonstop demonstrations by the community for the previous two weeks. After Clinton left our meeting, he made it a point to tell the *Los Angeles Times* that he would have signed the legislation. We were impressed by this and by other signs over the next few weeks that Clinton might be the man to get behind.

Mixner approached the campaign with the possibility of doing a million-dollar national fund-raiser with satellite hookups. It got scaled back to a $100,000 fund-raiser on the West Coast, due to prohibitive costs and perhaps a touch of homophobia at such a public gay and lesbian event. Nevertheless, David and ANGLE went ahead and organized a spectacular event at the Hollywood Palace Theater. Clinton was moving, promising us that "we didn't have a person to waste," that he would address the military issue, and reaffirming his commitment to battle AIDS.

The community was impressed. Videotapes of the event were sent out everywhere around the country, and during the campaign we raised well over $3 million for the Clinton/Gore ticket.

Roberta Achtenberg, a well-known San Francisco supervisor, was introduced to the Clinton campaign by David Mixner, and after negotiations with the campaign she became the second significant endorsement, after AN-GLE, of Clinton from our community. Prior to the convention she served on the drafting committee for the Democratic platform and, with total support of the Clinton forces, drafted language that included gay and lesbian civil rights as well as AIDS issues, in spite of the fact that the '92 platform as a whole was much more conservative than in recent years. The Democrats were determined to win back the presidency in 1992 and adopted a platform heavily influenced by the centrist ideas of the Democratic Leadership Council (DLC). It clearly reflected the Clinton view of how the Democratic Party should present itself to voters.

So did the convention itself. Clinton clearly controlled the focus and direction of the convention. There were many attempts to show that the Democratic Party had been unified and redefined in Clinton's centrist image. And there was a sense of optimism and determination to end twelve years of Republican control of the White House.

By virtue of being on the DNC, I was automatically a delegate—a "superdelegate"—which meant I didn't have to endorse a presidential candidate. Of course, I had endorsed Clinton early in the campaign and raised a lot of money for him. I believed we would make tremendous gains under his administration if he was elected president. I was again a whip at the convention, and this time it came in handy because I had access to the press area and the operations trailer.

We had all worked so hard for Clinton's nomination, and we were pretty confident that he would include us in his acceptance speech, but I wanted to make sure we were in there. I kept checking the press operation and finally they released the "final copy" of the speech. I hurriedly scanned through it until I found the usual litany of Democratic constituencies—and then slowed down. We were not there! I had to read it a couple of times before it totally sank in. I immediately got copies to Ann Northrop and David Mixner, who started organizing efforts on the floor to get us included at the last minute. They organized calls to the campaign's trailer from the chairs of various delegations at the request of the gay and lesbian delegates from the states. I kept checking back with operations, and finally John Emerson reported to us that Clinton had been reached and the speech would be changed to include us. Sure enough, he did, and we all were exuberant again. But those moments had been tense, and I felt as if I'd been on an emotional roller coaster. Minor shades of things to come! But this was then, and when Clinton finished his address, we all formed a conga line and worked our way through the packed convention as best we could to strains of "Can't Stop Thinking about Tomorrow."

There were many highlights at that convention. We had 104 caucus members from twenty-two states, and the Gay and Lesbian Caucus had been meeting all week. I only dropped in on a couple of meetings, because at this point I was caught up in the convention strategy sessions and, quite frankly, having a lot of fun with the California delegates. But to me the highlight of the caucus sessions was when Ted Kennedy addressed us. The convention organizers finally moved us out of the cramped room they had assigned the caucus for the week and into a major ballroom so we could accommodate the crowd who wanted to hear him.

Urvashi Vaid and Robert Bray of NGLTF and Vic Basile of HRCF organized the pressroom and main office space again and provided visibility for the community and delegates. Along with other national groups they organized the United for AIDS Action Rally outside the convention.

Inside the convention, we finally had substantial gay and lesbian representation on the podium. Roberta Achtenberg addressed the delegates and asked them to adopt the platform. She spoke about our progressive side of the party and how the issues in the platform affected her as a woman, as a Jew, as a lesbian, and as a mother.

Probably the most moving moment of the entire convention for me was when Bob Hattoy spoke as a gay man with AIDS. He talked from his heart about his feelings and how the gay and lesbian community had so courageously battled this disease on so many different fronts. Elizabeth Glaser followed him as a woman with AIDS, and the two of them provided the most dramatic event of the convention.

We left the convention ready to pour all our energies into the general election and the defeat of George Bush. For the first time much of the community was genuinely excited about our candidate, and not feeling the way we usually did: "Oh, well, it's the best we've got and better than the alternative."

We won the election, and clearly we had not only raised significant sums of money for Clinton, we had also turned out the gay vote in force. We now had access to power and someone whom we thought would change the gay and lesbian world as we knew it. We needed to get down to the business of the transition team—lining up support for our appointees, and anticipating an executive order that would ban discrimination in the military. But not before we partied!

The 1993 inauguration was probably the most fun series of parties I have ever experienced. And it was all because of the mood. Expectations were high, and even though there had been some early signs of trouble with the military issue, it just seemed that the transition staff was going through the usual jockeying for power and position, and that they would get around to our issue soon. We now know there was a vacuum of leadership on the issue. After Clinton announced at his first press conference that he would keep his promise on the military issue, the right wing had a field day. Unfortunately there was no leadership coming from our community or from the Clinton team, and yet the White House was urging us to keep a low profile.

I think most of us were still confident that Clinton would do the right thing. We proceeded to fan out to the various balls at the inauguration in Washington, winding up at the HRCF Ball at the National Press Club. Melissa Etheridge and k.d. lang were there kissing and coming out from the balcony. Kate Clinton emceed the event, and we danced, socialized, and celebrated all night with gay men and lesbians from all over the country.

THE 1996 DEMOCRATIC NATIONAL CONVENTION

This convention reflected the many advances we had made within the party. We had an official gay/lesbian constituency desk. Our numbers had increased within the DNC, and I had been appointed to the Executive Committee. We were recognized as at least 5 percent of the voting electorate and were considered an official base constituency. The Gay and Lesbian Caucus of the convention was showered with official attention, and elected officials were vying for time to address the caucus. The DNC chair, Don Fowler, held an official breakfast welcoming our delegates. We had one hundred forty caucus members, five speakers from the podium, and practically no politician failed to mention us if he or she addressed constituencies in any manner. Unlike the euphoria of the 1992 convention, we were a more somber group. The president had dampened our expectations with the military fiasco and the probable signing of DOMA, but we had also made considerable gains. We were gaining strength and maturing as a movement.

After the election of President Clinton in 1992, it seemed all gay and lesbian politics had something to do with the White House—mostly concerning civil rights matters and adequate AIDS funding, care, and treatment. The military issue became the focus for quite a while. During this time, Clinton became the first sitting president ever to hold a meeting with gay and lesbian leaders in the White House. At that meeting he again reassured the community that the military ban would be lifted. The saga went on. We organized heavily within the community, but it was not enough to counter the right-wing efforts and opposition by the Joint Chiefs of Staff, including the well-respected General Colin Powell. Eventually, "don't ask, don't tell" was instituted, and we were bitterly disappointed that the president had not kept his word. A lot of Monday-morning quarterbacking has gone on since then—was this the right issue, the right timing, the right political orchestration? At the time it didn't matter. We were handed a serious defeat, one we still live with today. However,

Clinton has made over one hundred gay and lesbian appointments to his administration, endorsed ENDA, and generally done more *by far* on civil rights
and AIDS issues than any of his predecessors.

After the 1992 election the DNC brought on openly gay Rocco Claps to
head up the newly formed Gay and Lesbian Constituency desk. Desks were
created for all constituencies for the purpose of paralleling the constituencies
represented in the White House. Unfortunately, at the time Rocco had no
counterpart at the White House. It would have made it much easier for him to
respond to the community if we had had a Richard Socarides, who later became the first openly gay presidential liaison to the gay/lesbian community, in
the White House. Rocco did set up meetings between DNC chair David Wilhelm, who was supportive, and a number of gay and lesbian leaders. Working
with Alexis Herman and Mario Cooper, he helped set up the historic meeting
at the White House before the 1993 march on Washington.

It was also at this time that David Wilhelm appointed me to the Executive Committee of the DNC, making me the highest-ranking gay or lesbian
party official. This was a first for our community and was meant to show the
greater integration of gays and lesbians into the Democratic Party. Wilhelm
also increased our numbers of at-large DNC members, and with newly elected
state members, we now had a caucus of seven. We started to have meetings
regularly and introduced several civil rights and AIDS-related resolutions
through the DNC body.

Rocco eventually left the G/L desk to work with planners for the 1996
convention, and the position remained unfilled for some time. Following the
disastrous 1994 midterm elections, Don Fowler, who had been an effective
supporter of the community, became the new DNC chair. Brian Bond, another
openly gay staff member, volunteered to take over the desk part-time in conjunction with his other responsibilities and was eventually promoted full-
time to the Gay and Lesbian Constituency desk. Brian worked with Fowler and
then DNC political director Minyon Moore in concentrated coalition politics
meant to strengthen our constituencies for the 1996 elections. Brian and I
strategized on ways to make the caucus more effective, and to communicate to
the community those positive advances that were being made in this administration.

Brian put together an extensive plan for field-driven activities such as
voter registration and GOTV (Get Out the Vote) efforts, and to assure major
donors that their contributions were being afforded credit in the campaign. He
had to mitigate lingering damage from the military issue and get out the president's and the party's message of inclusion on ENDA, and on health issues,
both AIDS funding and women's health care. He also reminded the community about the large number of gay and lesbian appointees in the administration. This included Roberta Achtenberg, appointed assistant secretary for fair

housing at HUD, the first openly G/L nominated by a president and confirmed by the U.S. Senate.

At this time the president appointed Marsha Scott, a heterosexual woman, as the liaison to the gay and lesbian community. Her appointment coincided with a White House shift to more access for people at the DNC and others to the White House, which allowed better communication and resulted in more accomplishments. She made sure that gay and lesbian people were included in any discussions, planning, or forums at the White House. Unfortunately she started the same week the "glove" incident occurred. The Victory Fund, an organization that helps gay and lesbian candidates win elective office, had organized a meeting of openly gay and lesbian elected officials to visit the White House. Guards who wore gloves because of their fear of catching AIDS searched purses, bags, and briefcases. Once the White House found out about this incident, Marsha had to make sure it never happened again, mitigate the damage done, apologize to the community, and educate the Secret Service that there is no way on earth that you could contract AIDS like that.

Chairman Fowler was one of the most supportive chairs we have had at the DNC. He and the executive director, B. J. Thornberry, urged the White House to approve the extension of domestic-partner benefits at the DNC. Initially, the White House put the proposal on the back burner, so as not to reescalate the discussion around DOMA, the antigay Defense of Marriage Act. Finally in 1997, the DNC included domestic partner benefits in its employee coverage.

The day the White House announced that Clinton would sign DOMA, B. J. Thornberry called a meeting of the DNC gay and lesbian staff and commiserated with them. The next day, at a full staff meeting, both she and Fowler addressed the issue. They said there were issues in the campaign that were making some of the staff who had worked so hard for this party and this president feel less than complete and whole, and they were sorry this was happening. Each person in this room deserved to be treated with respect.

Fowler went on the road and had meetings with the gay and lesbian community everywhere he went, before, during, and after DOMA. He would talk about the issues and the campaign. I attended one of those meetings that Eric Bauman and the Stonewall Democratic Club set up in southern California and was impressed by Fowler's sincerity and caring. He obviously took a lot of heat for the administration's position on DOMA.

Fowler went to a constituency meeting in New Mexico and took Brian and the state chair with him. Up to this time, the New Mexico party had just mouthed support for the community. Fowler asked Brian Bond how much he had raised for the Get out the Vote effort in New Mexico. He answered, "Five thousand dollars." "How much do you need?" Fowler asked the gay and lesbian leaders. They responded, "Ten thousand dollars." Fowler then looked at the state chair and said, "Can you raise the next five?" The chair responded affirmatively, and another bond was formed. Don Fowler was really in our corner and was always trying to build coalitions. He also brought all the gay and lesbian Democratic clubs to Washington, D.C., for a full two days of meetings, organized by the DNC.

On another front, Jeff Forbes from the Clinton/Gore campaign worked closely with Brian Bond during the 1996 delegate-selection process to make sure that gays and lesbians around the country would be included in larger numbers. Harold Ickes, working with Jeff Soref, cochair of the Empire State Pride Agenda, raised the number of delegates from New York City from one in 1992 to twenty delegates and committee members in 1996. Outstanding fundraising efforts on the part of Soref and others helped quite a bit, as delegates from our community often had to be chosen at the at-large level, where the campaign would weigh in heavily.

The 1996 convention was a great one for the gay and lesbian community. We had over 140 members of our caucus; and Democratic Party leaders and the Clinton presidential campaign showered us with attention.

Don Fowler had appointed me the temporary chair of the Gay and Lesbian Caucus, responsible for the initial organizing before the caucus met. At the first meeting of the caucus, Fred Hochberg nominated me to be permanent chair, which the body approved by acclamation. A motion was then made to elect five vice chairs, which we did, to help highlight the diversity of the caucus.

The DNC and the White House lined up an impressive array of speakers to appear before the daily meetings of the Gay and Lesbian Caucus. Many who wanted to speak had to be turned away for lack of time. Among the speakers who addressed either the Gay Caucus or one of the numerous gay and lesbian receptions held by HRC and others were Tipper Gore; George Stephanopoulos, senior White House adviser to President Clinton; Donna Shalala, secretary of Health and Human Services; Judith Light, actress; Alan Wheat, deputy campaign manager in the Clinton-Gore '96 election campaign; Alexis Herman, assistant to the president and director for public liaison; Senators Kennedy, Dodd, and Boxer; and Congresspersons Barney Frank, Gerry Studds, and Maxine Waters. As I introduced many of these officials, I couldn't help but think back to twenty years ago—to 1976, when we were a caucus of three, and the only attention that we could get was perhaps a little press for this novelty gay issue.

Richard Socarides and I worked hard to keep the caucus moving and to try to fit in the dozens of elected officials and community leaders who wanted to address the caucus in some way or at least be acknowledged. I loved working with Richard on the convention. He was professional and fun and made a sometimes tension-filled job enjoyable. Vicki Johnson, whom Brian Bond hired as deputy director of the Office of Lesbian and Gay Outreach, and Paul Yandura, director of the Lesbian and Gay Outreach desk for the Clinton/Gore '96 reelection effort, were also a great help. While Brian Bond had done all the organizing leading up to the convention, he was assigned to other areas during the convention. I missed having him around, but he had done a wonderful job in laying the groundwork for this impressive showing.

Some of the gay and lesbian delegates were worried about our visibility, but needlessly so. From the president's speech, which included us (the first time an incumbent president ever uttered the word *gay* to a prime-time televised audience), to the official gay and lesbian delegate breakfast hosted by Don Fowler, to the orchestrated floor demonstrations with GAY AND LESBIAN EQUALITY signs provided by HRC, we were visible.

Five openly gay men or lesbians addressed the Convention: Phill Wilson, Assemblywoman Sheila Kuehl, Congressman Barney Frank, congressional candidate Rick Zbur, and Emily's List president Ellen Malcolm. Frank spoke at length about the need for civil rights for gays and lesbians. Senator Kennedy accused the Republican Party of gay bashing. Every time someone mentioned any of our issues in any way, the signs would wave and the cheering would start. This was all picked up on national television many times.

Once again the platform opposed antigay discrimination, supported a gay civil rights bill pending in Congress (ENDA), and called for the "full inclusion" of gay people in the "life of the nation." The full-inclusion language was meant to counter the negative effect of President Clinton's intention to sign DOMA.

BEYOND THE 1996 CONVENTION

Gay and lesbian participation in the election of 1996 was organized from the DNC staff by Brian Bond, who raised a lot of money from major donors and spent most of it on field operations for the gay and lesbian community. We distributed printed cards at gay pride and other events around the country with all the major accomplishments of the Clinton administration, which were many, despite the military fiasco and the DOMA issue. In 1996 the gay and lesbian community represented 5 percent of the electorate and 7 percent of the vote for Clinton, as much as many other major constituencies, and equal to the Hispanic turnout.

During the campaign, Clinton announced that he would sign DOMA into law if Congress passed it. That did not necessarily surprise us, although we were not happy about it. What really upset the community was that an ad ran during the campaign on Christian radio touting the fact that he had signed it. I heard about it and immediately brought it to Brian's attention. He talked to Harold Ickes, deputy chief of staff at the White House, and the ad was pulled almost immediately. We wanted an apology from the campaign, but never got it. They basically just dropped the issue.

Peter Knight, the campaign manager for Clinton/Gore, wanted to use money Brian and others had raised to go into the general advertising fund as opposed to funding an active gay presence in the campaign. Many of our supporters, including Ickes, Fowler, B. J. Thornberry, and Minyon Moore got involved in the issue, and the money was directed back to the gay and lesbian community. B. J. told Brian to go ahead and start sending out checks to the gay and lesbian Democratic clubs, and Harold Ickes made it official.

Of course we won the '96 election, and there was cause for celebration in the community, but nothing like the excitement we had felt in 1992. This president had truly done more than any other president for us, but we had fought hard fights during the past four years, and things were not changing as fast as we would have liked. But we celebrated again at the inaugural. The Victory Fund, the National Gay and Lesbian Task Force, and the Human Rights Campaign held an inaugural ball at the Omni Shoreham Hotel.

The important milestone of this particular inaugural was the establishment for the first time of a gay and lesbian inaugural desk. We joined the other constituencies formally in making sure people who were involved in the election received top tickets and memorabilia, and that we were included in the parade and other official functions. This may seem to some like superficial trappings, but these changes all represented the growing respect for the power of the gay and lesbian constituency.

Through 1998 we made many gains as a community in many diverse ways. We lost ENDA by one vote in the Senate, at the same time that they passed DOMA. The ENDA vote was much closer than anyone had expected and was probably due, in my opinion, to the fact that the two bills were in front of them at the same time, and many senators did not want to be seen as voting against us on both issues. DOMA also had a positive impact in raising the level of discussion on domestic partner rights, and pushing the envelope of gay rights and AIDS issues to one of full inclusion in American life.

Reports show that one to three companies add domestic partner policies every week. The DNC announced its DP benefits plan in 1997. Many major corporations joined other Fortune 500 companies in extending benefits, and many cities followed suit. Republican mayor Rudolph Giuliani signed his sweeping domestic partnership proposal into law in New York City. Over two hundred polities now have laws banning antigay discrimination covering one-third of the U.S. population.

In other arenas, *Ellen* became the first prime-time TV show with a gay lead, received five Emmy nominations, and brought thousands of people together for HRC house parties, probably bringing as many out of the closet, or at least to their next stage of coming out—before being canceled by ABC.

Clinton issued a gay pride proclamation and addressed HRC's nationally televised banquet in Washington, D.C. Richard Socarides, gay/lesbian liaison to the president, got a status boost to special assistant to the president. Later Fred Hochberg was appointed deputy administrator of the Small Business Association, and Ginny Apuzzo became the highest G/L appointee ever as assistant to the president for management and budget. Clinton had another high-level meeting with gay activists, and Vice President Gore is presently holding meetings with us throughout the United States.

At the DNC, we are also advancing. Steve Grossman, former chair of the Massachusetts State party, and Governor Roy Romer of Colorado have become the new chairs of the party. They have been wonderfully responsive to our community in numerous ways. They have spoken out time and again against gay bashing in the 1998 elections. They reappointed me to the Executive Committee and increased the number of at-large G/L members of the DNC, so we now number thirteen with elected members.

The increase of our numbers, the acknowledgment of our community as a powerful constituency, and the considerable fund-raising efforts of Jeff Soref, newly appointed at-large DNC member, and others have enabled the G/L caucus of the DNC to make some important gains in 1999. We lobbied for, and with strong support of Chairs Steve Grossman, Roy Romer, and Harold Ickes, obtained a major delegate-selection rules change. Introduced in the DNC Rules Committee by Garry Shay and passed by the full DNC, the rule stipulates that state Democratic parties must develop and submit to the DNC outreach plans for selecting delegates to the 2000 Democratic National Convention. These plans must include those "historically underrepresented" in the Democratic Party due to their "race/ethnicity, age, sexual orientation, or disability." The rule calls for state Democratic parties to give "priority of consideration" to such underrepresented groups "in order to assist in the achievement of full participation by these groups." This really means that state parties must be proactive in their outreach to groups such as the G/L community—and it was intended to ensure that their awareness about the participation of these groups is heightened. This rule change was initiated by Jeff Soref at the DNC Gay and Lesbian Caucus and in conversations with Steve Grossman, because of the mechanisms Soref had to go through to have fair gay delegate representation in New York for the 1996 convention. Rick Boylan, director of party affairs and delegate selection, and the longest-serving openly gay staff member (since 1982) was, as always, enormously helpful with the wording. Tony Winnicker, who was serving as the DNC's G/L desk staff, also worked closely with Rick, Garry, Jeff, and me on the language to be incorporated.

This is a permanent change that has been added to the delegate selection rules and increases our negotiating strength at the at-large appointment level, which accounts for about one-third of the delegates to the Democratic National Convention. As chair of the G/L DNC caucus, I am working with Mark Spengler, who is assigned to the G/L constituency desk, to make sure gay and lesbian Democratic clubs and organizations use this powerful tool to increase our numbers to the convention in the year 2000.

On another front, Chairman Grossman has established an ad hoc committee to review the status of all caucuses of the DNC. The caucus issue has a long and mixed history, especially for the Gay and Lesbian Caucus. In 1985, Paul Kirk introduced a resolution at the Executive Committee ending formal DNC recognition of caucuses, and the practice of adding seats to the Executive Committee for caucus chairs (except that the Black, Hispanic, and Women's Caucus chairs were "grandfathered" in). Since that time the Asian Pacific American Islanders Caucus has been reinstated, mainly because of all the fund-raising flap in the Asian community and the DNC. At the time of their reinstatement, in May 1998, we supported them and everyone acknowledged that we would proceed forward with our own reinstatement. Carol Migden, assemblywoman from San Francisco, and I approached Steve Grossman with this request. His response was to establish the ad hoc committee to study the entire caucus issue. This committee included two of our recommended representatives, Jeff Soref and Alice Huffman. DNC vice chair Lottie Shackelford, who chairs the ad hoc committee, asked Jeff to chair a committee to draft a proposal that would be considered by the ad hoc committee and ultimately presented to the Executive Committee. He was unable to do so because of time pressures, but that offer, and the inclusion of me on monthly conference calls with the chairs, officers of the party, chairs of caucus and constituency groups, and standing committees, sent a strong signal that the Gay and Lesbian Caucus would be reinstated. The ad hoc committee reported to the Executive Committee in September 1998, delineating the criteria for constituting a caucus. We met the criteria, drew up bylaws, and became an official caucus at the next meeting in March 1999. One of the criteria was that caucuses could not be issued-based, but had to be determined only by inherent and immutable traits. Our being a caucus strengthens our case within the party when we deal with such issues as representation and delegate selection.

As we approached the 1998 midterm elections, the GOP was making a concerted effort at gay bashing, the purpose of which was to galvanize part of their voting base in a low-turnout election year. They were being so virulent that it backfired on them. It began with the deliberate holding up of President Clinton's nominee for ambassador to Luxembourg, gay philanthropist Jim Hormel of San Francisco, by Senate majority leader Trent Lott of Mississippi. Then Lott and others engaged in inflammatory antigay rhetoric, likening us to alcoholics, sex addicts, and kleptomaniacs. We beat back an attempt to overturn an executive order signed by President Clinton in May outlawing discrimination in federal hiring on the basis of sexual orientation. However, legislation passed that would cut federal housing funds to San Francisco and other cities as long as firms doing business with the city are required to provide domestic partnership benefits to employees. This could cost the city of San Francisco alone an estimated $21 million in federal housing money this year. Two antigay amendments dealing with adoption and needle exchange were attached to the District of Columbia appropriations bill. They both passed the House. Some say all this activity is a mere coincidence, but our community recognizes it as an orchestrated attempt to energize religious activists in the Republican Party.

Whether this attempt at gay-bashing backfires or just raises the debate within the Republican Party, this kind of activity broadens our base of support as many Republican legislators are leery of the forced roll-call votes and of appearing intolerant. It also gave the chairs of the DNC the opportunity to issue a press release denouncing GOP gay bashing and intolerance. Every time something like this causes our friends to speak out, it strengthens support for our issues. They also recognize that we have to galvanize our base in the Democratic Party for the midterm elections, and that the G/L community is a strong part of that base.

CONCLUSION

It has become clear to me over the years that politics is incremental, and those who have the patience and stamina to move our agenda forward will eventually prevail. It is incredible to me how far we have come over the past three decades from where we were before Stonewall. Having lived through this movement in various roles from firebrand to insider, and sometimes both at the same time when there were too few of us to play all the roles that were needed, I truly believe that for every step backward that we are forced to take, we move two steps forward. I have believed from the very beginning that our biggest oppression was invisibility, which enabled people to tell lies about us, in turn keeping us in our closets of shame. Most of us have long passed that time—but coming out is a political process and we are at the stage of educating our friends so they will have the ammunition to defend us when homophobes challenge us. We have an army of supporters now, and it is growing every day. Our community is also getting stronger as more and more people get involved in obtaining our full participation in American life, in whatever way is most natural for them. We can never turn our back on the political process, no matter how slow it seems, and how discouraging at times. If we put it into context we can see the progress that has been made, but if we take ourselves out of the process, the right wing—our enemies—whoever they may be, will rush in to fill the vacuum.

CHAPTER 6

Caught Between Worlds: Gay Republicans Step Out, and into the Political Fray

RICHARD TAFEL

WHILE MOST GAY HISTORIANS FOCUS ON REPORTING the political debate within the gay community as between the assimilationist Democrats who want acceptance and liberationist Democrats who seek a dramatic overhaul of society, they often ignore libertarian gay Republicans, who believe in individual rights, individual responsibility, less government, and free markets. These differ from the liberationists in that they believe in the American system and believe that success for the individual can be reached through the current system. They agree with liberationists on the issue of civil liberties. The libertarians are more like the assimilationists in style. They tend to look and behave like assimilationists, but they do not share the belief that we need to be just like heterosexuals to move forward. They are individualists, instead.

While many activists today claim gay Republicans are new to the movement, they have played an important role all along. The most notable of the early gay Republican leaders was publisher Dorr Legg, who was a member of the first pre-Stonewall organization, the Mattachine Society. Legg went on to run the first gay magazine, called *ONE,* and made gay history by winning a

1958 Supreme Court case that upheld his right to publish *ONE* despite Post Office attempts to shut it down.

Dorr Legg was not the only famous gay Republican to play a pivotal role in early gay politics. Long before gays in the military became a national issue, a gay Republican, Leonard Matlovich, decided to challenge discrimination against gays who wanted to serve openly in the armed services. His protest of the military's exclusion eventually landed him on the cover of *Time* magazine. It marked the first time that an openly gay person made it onto the cover of a national magazine, and he was a gay Republican.

Following the Stonewall riots, and in the spirit of the late 1960s, the gay movement moved away from the Mattachine Society and began forming new groups with a more liberationist agenda, such as the Gay Liberation Front, which advocated a more aggressive approach to gay rights. Chapters formed around the country and were soon followed by a more assimilationist organization, called the Gay Activists Alliance. Both organizations modeled themselves after the feminist and black power coalition movements developing in the Democratic Party. Neither of the two organizations left much ideological room for gays who were libertarian.

Throughout the eighties, gay Republicans began forming their own groups. In Washington, they called themselves Gay Republicans of Washington (GROW). In southern California they called themselves, first, Lincoln clubs, then, Log Cabin clubs. In northern California they were Concerned Americans for Individual Rights (CAIR); in Dallas, Metroplex Republicans; in Chicago, Chicago Area Republican Gay Organization (CARGO); in the District of Columbia, The Walt Whitman Club; and in New York, the Stonewall Republicans. These organizations, in many ways, existed more as a support group for gays who didn't want to abandon their Republican politics as they came out of the closet than as a vehicle for political action.

COMING TOGETHER

The California gay Republican clubs were the only ones with any track record of success. In 1980, the Los Angeles club ran Frank Ricchiazzi for state assembly, despite the fact that he had no chance of winning. While his campaign was certain to fail, Ricchiazzi's race did help galvanize the club's growth in California. In San Francisco, the CAIR organization was successful in working within a moderate-Republican local county party.

The local gay Republican clubs decided in 1984 to form an umbrella organization named United Republicans for Equality and Privacy. By electing officers and producing a national newsletter, UREP hoped to promote a sense of unity that would lead clubs to support one another in meeting common goals.

However, soon, both the president and the treasurer of the organization died of AIDS, necessitating new leadership. Continuing efforts to organize a national organization failed.

In 1987, some gay Republicans tried to revitalize UREP. Like many other organizations, gay Republican clubs held a national strategy meeting during the march on Washington. At this meeting, they elected new officers and left with new hopes of getting UREP up and going. Unfortunately, the recently elected leadership again died of AIDS, and UREP's efforts were again derailed.

The gay Republicans set yet another meeting date for December 1990 in Tampa, Florida. Two important publicity events had helped the local clubs. First, in 1990, Frank Ricchiazzi, a leader in the California Log Cabin organization, published a point of view on the last page of *The Advocate,* the nation's largest gay publication. References to gay Republicans in the gay press were few and far between, and those references were typically attacks on gay Republicans. Further publicity came when Marvin Liebman, a famous conservative, came out to his friend Bill Buckley in the pages of the *National Review,* also in 1990. Liebman was a conservative pioneer, having created the Young Americans for Freedom and a number of other anticommunist organizations. He followed up his letter to Buckley with a book called *Coming Out Conservative.* The gay Republicans had their first celebrity, and Liebman agreed to give the keynote speech at the UREP meeting in Tampa.

There were also positive developments on the political front. In California, the gay vote played a key role in electing Pete Wilson governor. During the campaign, Wilson committed verbally to Log Cabin's leadership to signing a nondiscrimination bill as he held fund-raising events at the homes of prominent gay Republicans. He also committed to hiring openly gay Log Cabin members in his administration. This was a vast improvement over his predecessor's indifference to California's gay community.

Also in 1990, in Massachusetts, a gay Republican named Mike Duffy ran for state representative. Duffy, who had worked for the state GOP, organized a campaign composed primarily of gay Republicans who also organized on behalf of GOP gubernatorial candidate William Weld. These new activists found themselves in the unusual position of supporting and educating an open-minded Republican candidate who was running against a Democrat, John Silber, the former president of Boston University who was adamantly antigay. Much of the gay establishment leadership, including Democratic congressional members Barney Frank and Gerry Studds, endorsed Silber. Governor Weld went on to win with commitments to place gays in key leadership positions within his administration.

FINDING COMMON GROUND

At the organizational meeting in December of 1990, gay Republicans tried once again to create a new formal umbrella federation to share ideas and strategies. Clubs from New York City, Washington, D.C., Tampa, Chicago, San Francisco, Los Angeles, Orange County, Palm Springs, and San Diego, and the fledgling Boston club, attended.

The major issue to be discussed was what to name the new entity. The clubs from the East Coast primarily supported a continuation of UREP, but the California clubs were pushing for their name—Log Cabin. Only recently had all of the California clubs organized under that name, overcoming rivalries and mistrust between northern and southern regions of the state. Now the mistrust and rivalry lay between the East and West Coast. The California clubs had gained some visibility and were riding high on the election of Pete Wilson, but the Eastern clubs felt that the name only had importance in California and nowhere else. California won the day, and the group called itself the Log Cabin National Federation. Following interviews with the local gay press, the leaders realized that the name was too difficult to say, and the simpler Log Cabin Federation was chosen. The only new business conducted was to choose Chicago as the location for the next year's convention.

Later that year, when the United States went to war against Iraq, the National Gay and Lesbian Task Force wrote a policy paper condemning the United States for attacking Iraq, claiming that the war was blood for oil, and that those funds could be better spent on AIDS funding.

LCF wrote its own op-ed stressing that this wasn't a gay issue and that the Task Force didn't speak for all gays. This was the first time the Log Cabin Federation ever did a nationally released op-ed. The response was interesting. Many gays seemed to agree with our perspective, and our members were thrilled finally to have someone speaking for them. Log Cabin's entry into any debate seemed to strike a nerve with longtime activists and some gay journalists. First, it appeared that there was the presumption that gay Republicans might be tolerated, but only if they kept their mouths shut. Second, it seemed as if the far left groups felt they had to crush this voice of gay conservatives before it grew into anything.

The Chicago convention of 1991 went well with a turnout of just forty people. Marvin Liebman, the highest-profile gay conservative, was the keynote speaker, which helped draw attendees. Vice Chair Marti Goodson gave her presentation on grassroots organizing. Mike Duffy, who was now an appointee of Governor Weld of Massachusetts, gave a speech about running for office. At that meeting, the California and Massachusetts clubs gave encouraging reports that Governors Wilson and Weld were both appointing high-profile Log Cabin members to their administrations.

Slowly but surely, Log Cabin clubs started to spring up around the country. New clubs started in California, Texas, Florida, Ohio, and Oregon. In two years, the original nine chapters had grown to twenty-six. The Log Cabin Federation looked forward to continuing a fairly positive relationship with President Bush and decided to hold its convention at the site of the much anticipated Houston Republican National Convention in 1992. Log Cabin didn't have a Houston club per se, but we did have one member there who agreed to organize Log Cabin's presence in Houston.

Then came the storm clouds that would dominate the political landscape for all Republicans, especially gay Republicans, for the rest of the decade. In the spring of 1992, Urvashi Vaid, executive director of the National Gay and Lesbian Task Force, used her friendship with Dee Mosbacher, a lesbian and the daughter of the Bush-Quayle '92 campaign chairman, Robert Mosbacher, to obtain a meeting with him. Vaid formally requested that the campaign promise not to gay-bash. The meeting went well, and Mosbacher committed to avoid gay bashing. Vaid took a picture of the meeting and released the story to the *Washington Blade*. When the social conservatives, who already distrusted Bush, heard about this, they went on the warpath against the campaign.

Some gay Republicans were furious that we had not held the meeting ourselves and criticized Vaid. The truth was that LCF didn't have the wherewithal to mount this most basic effort for a meeting, and anger by gay Republicans toward Vaid more vividly demonstrated our own lack of presence in Washington. Gay Democrats and those in the gay left also criticized Vaid for daring to even speak with Republicans. And the religious right began a phone campaign to the Bush-Quayle campaign. I received a call from a campaign staffer named Tyler Franz, who asked me to coordinate a call-in campaign to the Bush offices.

Franz met with Mosbacher, who confided that there was a serious negative reaction among social conservatives. Bush, who had already alienated the fiscal-conservative base of the Republican Party, had never effectively handled the social conservatives. The campaign decided to make an all-out effort to reach out to social conservatives and decided that gay rights would be an effective wedge issue to accomplish it. Social conservatives were obsessed with the issue, and gays were perceived to be completely in the pocket of the Democratic Party.

Those within the Bush campaign who opposed gay bashing were losing ground. To assuage the far right, Mosbacher now claimed he'd met with Vaid as a favor to his daughter. Tory Clarke, who had agreed to speak to the Capital Area Log Cabin Club, canceled. Mosbacher, who previous to the Vaid meeting had agreed in principle to meet with me on behalf of Log Cabin, wouldn't even respond to Log Cabin Federation's correspondence.

Tyler Franz, who was working within the campaign as an openly gay man, called me weekly to report on the growing prominence and influence of the religious right on the campaign staff. The campaign, for the first time in GOP history, even hired a liaison to the Christian right.

Franz's updates grew more depressing. Log Cabin, which imagined itself as the libertarian voice in the gay community and supportive of the Republican Party, was coming to realize that its role in the GOP would be more adversarial than cooperative. Franz's reports moved from his personal observations of what was happening within the campaign to what slowly began to happen to him personally. The strategy of using gays as a wedge issue in the new culture war intensified. The growth of this crusade began with the ferreting out of gays within the campaign staff, and Tyler became a target.

Franz's boss met with him to tell him that the social conservatives found him to be rude to them, so he was being relocated to a floor in the campaign where he would be the only person, and his pay would be cut. Franz was being pushed off the campaign. After talking to some legal advisers, he decided to file a discrimination suit against the campaign since the District of Columbia prohibited firing someone based on sexual orientation.

Franz asked me to fly down to D.C. to offer him moral support throughout this difficult period, and I agreed. Kevin Ivers, the press officer for the local Log Cabin Club in Washington, coordinated a press strategy. He spoke with the staff of the *Wall Street Journal*, offering an exclusive on this gay Republican staffer who was suing the Bush presidential campaign and on the bigger story that Bush had given over control of his campaign to the far right.

The night before the story appeared, *Nightline* invited Franz and me to be on the show. At that time, I was an openly gay appointee of Republican governor William Weld of Massachusetts. In Washington, D.C., a Log Cabin media team had developed with Kevin Ivers coordinating these TV appearances and print interviews. Marvin Liebman made available to us his Dupont Circle apartment to use as a media center. Meanwhile, Franz was preparing for the TV appearance and talking to his attorney. *Nightline* marked the first time most Americans had ever heard of the Log Cabin Federation or gay Republicans.

The *Nightline* program went well, and Larry King was impressed enough to invite us to appear on *Larry King Live*. *Fox News* then had us on, and most major newspapers covered the story. When I returned to Boston, my answering machine was flooded with calls from gay Republicans wanting to start clubs. The one act by Tyler Franz did more for Log Cabin's organizing than anything that had come before. He eventually gave up his lawsuit and left Washington.

Long before the GOP convention of 1992, Log Cabin was acutely aware that our earlier hopes of a supportive relationship with the Bush campaign had evaporated. As we made plans to set up our LCF convention at the Woodlands, their security team informed us that they were getting harassing calls and recommended we have a police presence. When we asked if the hostile calls were coming from the left or the right, the hotel spokesperson laughed and said both. ACT UP had threatened to zap us for being Republicans, while religious right groups were threatening their own protests.

When Log Cabin's twenty-six clubs congregated in Houston, we voted not to endorse Bush for president. We met before the GOP convention, but what was coming was no surprise for us. I left the convention disgusted by the entire tone of intolerance that the Bush campaign had allowed and took my protest to the national media. I spoke on *Good Morning America* and the *Today* show, further building our organization's size and demonstrating to the Bush campaign that the Log Cabin Federation would not sit quietly by while the GOP seemed hijacked by the far right.

It became a national story that the Bush campaign had a clear strategy, for the first time in presidential politics, explicitly to use gays as a wedge issue of attack. It never materialized. Mary Matalin, the campaign manager, later said that the campaign had to spend the months following the Houston convention trying to tell the country that Bush was not a homophobic bigot. On election day, two-thirds of gay Republicans who had voted for Bush in 1988 voted for Clinton or Perot instead.

In the final weeks of the campaign, the writing was on the wall. A gay Republican named Marvin Collins, who had been the chairman of the Texas Republican Party years earlier, called me and invited me to dinner in Boston to discuss his vision. Collins was politically astute and knew people with money. He concluded that gay Republicans could not remain in the party if we faced another Houston. He believed that only a full-time national office could even hope to challenge effectively the rise of the far right in the GOP. Log Cabin Federation members had long dreamed of such, but they were mostly lower-income individuals who had trouble funding a quarterly newsletter. The hope of a national office seemed unrealistic.

Collins agreed to provide the start-up funds for me to travel and raise money for an office, and he agreed to fund a business plan. We began traveling for funds and interviewing potential executive directors. Potential donors all had the same message: they wouldn't fund anything until they knew whom the executive director was going to be. Some had encouraged me to take the position, but I was now happily serving as an appointee of Governor Weld, and I didn't want to give up that security.

Our efforts to hire an executive director were not going well. Finally, we had one candidate, who was actually a regional coordinator for the Bush campaign. We agreed on salary and a start date. He was a genuine GOP insider and very telegenic. Then he explained that he did not want to have to come out— that ended the hire. I knew a national office would be a great step in the right direction, and I began to realize that unless I was willing to put myself on the line, no one would take the risks in investing in it. We had given up on hiring someone as an executive director. The candidates rightfully asked what assurances there were that they would be paid through the long term. Setting what seemed an ambitious goal for us of raising $100,000, and hiring one additional staff person, I prepared to move to Washington. Kevin Ivers, the media guru of the Tyler Franz episode, agreed to join me on staff.

Through a generous challenge grant from one donor we were able to achieve $100,000 in pledges by the summer of 1993. That spring, many gays believed that with Democrats in control of the White House and Congress, there was no need for gay political groups anymore, and especially not gay Republicans. When I arrived in Washington in the fall of 1993, the response from the gay community and the press was a mix of hostility and a collective yawn.

CREATING THE LOG CABIN REPUBLICANS

The grassroots clubs of the Log Cabin Federation agreed in principle to the creation of a Washington office, but they were unwilling to finance it. Serving as both president of the Federation and executive director for Log Cabin Republicans would create a conflict, so I stepped down from LCF. The clubs would elect their own president and I would serve as national or executive director of the new Washington-based entity. At the 1993 Log Cabin convention in Philadelphia, Abner Mason, from Boston, was elected to head up the Log Cabin Federation.

The new donors to the national office were, for the most part, not involved in Log Cabin clubs. They wanted to create a new legal entity with its own board and its own name. The only debate for these donors was whether to choose a name that showed a connection to the Log Cabin Federation. There was a large chasm between the gay Republican donor type and the grassroots activists. The donors felt that the clubs were, in many cases, made up of geeks. The clubs resented the check-writing activists and feared being taken over by them.

Ironically, Pat Buchanan played a role in naming the new organization and in raising money to open. In the weeks before the new board met, he blasted the Log Cabin Federation. Those who wanted to keep Log Cabin in the name used Buchanan's quote as proof that the name held meaning in the media. The debate was so divisive that after the board voted to call itself Log Cabin Republicans, one member of the donor board actually resigned over the choice.

The new board hired Vic Basile as a consultant to draw up a start-up business plan. Vic had built up the Human Rights Campaign Fund and the Victory Fund with great success. Though a liberal Democrat, Basile saw the importance of Log Cabin, and no one had more expertise in the gay world for getting organizations off the ground.

The national office was opened in October 1993. We leased a tiny two-hundred-square-foot space from PFLAG, sharing the use of their copy machine. In lieu of a desk, we sat on pillows, working until late at night to get the office off the ground.

The attitudes we encountered from fellow gay activists varied, but none were very pleased. The leader of the Human Rights Campaign Fund conceded to me that he didn't want a Republican version of HRC to compete with them for funds. Most other gay groups simply asked why I had come to D.C. With Democrats safely in control of the House and Senate and White House, the concept of a gay Republican lobby seemed silly to them. Gay and AIDS organizations were downright hostile to lobbying Republicans.

We chose to sublease from PFLAG for a number of reasons. The Human Rights Campaign Fund and the Victory Fund were also housed in that same building. We were trying to send a message that we could all work together. Yet, for our first few months, our door sign, written on paper, became the target of graffiti from our fellow organizational members in the building. Each week we needed a new sign as questions were scribbled on our door, such as "Where are your women?" and "Why?" to remind us we were on unwelcome terrain.

The political director of the Human Rights Campaign Fund invited LCR to take part in weekly drafting sessions for a new federal gay rights bill, which came to be known as ENDA. As became the pattern at every meeting I attended, the question of my being there was addressed. An HRCF staffer came to our defense: "HRCF is bipartisan, but LCR rounds out our Republican side." At every meeting, a strange alliance developed. I made the case that explicit anti-affirmative-action language be instituted and clear religious exemptions be listed. This made the majority of the more liberal groups there upset, but Congressman Frank's emissary at the meeting agreed with us. No one has been more critical of LCR than Frank, so the fact that we both agreed on the content of the bill did get everyone's attention.

HRCF also came up with the idea of getting members of Congress to sign on to a nondiscrimination policy concerning their own gay staff. Others in the community saw little importance to this symbolic gesture, but I saw it as an important step forward. We were asked to take the Republicans, while HRCF would gather Democrats. It turned out to be very important as key Republican leaders, such as Senator Dole and Congressman Kasich, signed the documents.

LCR began the lonely job of knocking on doors on Capitol Hill. Almost every staffer and member I met had never been lobbied by anyone in the gay community, and many had bitter stories of how they were protested or opposed by gay organizations. Most had never heard of gay Republicans or Log Cabin. Some even scheduled me with their environmental staffer or business staffer to discuss home building or syrup. We learned to be explicit in setting up our meetings.

Throughout the spring of 1994, the prospect of a Republican takeover of the Senate was growing. The rhetoric within the gay press about such a takeover verged on hysteria. But nowhere did that hysteria reign more than among AIDS organizations. The omnibus AIDS-care bill, Ryan White CARE Act, would be up for reauthorization in 1995. If Republicans took over the Senate in 1995, AIDS activists were sure that the program would not be renewed, and worse, all AIDS funds would be cut out of the budget.

For AIDS organizations, the solution was an intense dedication to passing the Ryan White CARE Act before the GOP took over the Senate. They organized an aggressive campaign to "hot-wire" the multimillion-dollar bill, which would mean bypassing hearings and allowing the bill to be renewed exactly as it was now. Senator Kennedy (D-MA) led the effort to get sixty senators to approve the hot-wire concept and thus reauthorize the bill a year early.

Democratic AIDS activists who were hostile or indifferent to Log Cabin's presence in Washington only months earlier now called to seek our support of the early reauthorization. At the first meetings I attended, my presence was questioned by some of the organizations in attendance, just as it had been in the ENDA meetings.

We began to make appointments with key Republican senators and representatives whose committees handled AIDS funding. We discovered a few things. First, while most Republicans were not enthusiastic about my coming to visit on gay-specific legislation, they were much more interested in talking about AIDS. It was a health-care issue that involved constituent concerns and dollars to their states. As much as the AIDS community distrusted GOP Hill members, the members distrusted AIDS activists. So, for many Hill members, they saw Log Cabin as someone they could trust. Also, most of those lobbying had a direct financial stake in the bill, which directly impacted their lobby pitch. But Log Cabin received no federal funds. Finally, Log Cabin created a PAC that supported Republicans. Every other lobby group would make strong demands on the GOP members, but at the end of the day, these members knew that the liberal AIDS activist would have nothing positive to say about them on election day.

LCR had a pronounced ignorance of the details of the bill when I joined other AIDS lobbyist on the Hill. Their message focusing on reauthorizing the bill early to avoid the risk presented by a potential GOP takeover did not fly with Republicans. Particularly, this lobbying effort met resistance from moderate Kansas senator Nancy Kassebaum, chairwoman of the Health and Human Services Committee.

Kassebaum responded to the activists' concerns with a simple point. The Ryan White CARE Act was five years old. It needed to be revamped to meet the new needs of the current epidemic. Because she was from Kansas she was particularly concerned that current formulas disproportionately favored urban programs with little money getting to rural states. She wanted hearings and formula changes. To many AIDS lobbyists whose programs benefited from the current urban favoritism, Kassebaum's words were anathema to their strategy. Senator Kennedy (D-MA), who led the effort to hot-wire Ryan White, had an excellent relationship with Kassebaum, but she felt the principle was too important to forfeit hearings.

The AIDS lobbyists moved to plan B—demonization. They brought hundreds of people with AIDS to D.C. to lobby for reauthorization. These patients, who made effective lobbyists, had been advised that if Ryan White wasn't reauthorized early, they'd lose their benefits the following year. This misinformation turned these patient activists into angry, frightened activists.

A group of these activists encircled the now demonized Senator Kassebaum and began chanting murderer. Another group staged a sit-in at her office. The same was happening at Congressman Bliley's office on the House side. Log Cabin made it our mission to apologize to these key elected officials. We also became much more independent in our thinking when it came to AIDS lobbying.

November 1994 brought the historic GOP takeover of the House and Senate. Fortunately, Log Cabin could return to the friends we had made in the 103rd Congress. LCR's work with Republicans in the 103rd paid off. LCR became the only gay group to be asked to testify before the House on AIDS issues, and we were able to make some clear progress on the Ryan White CARE Act's movement and eventual passage in the House with Representative Gunderson's (R-WI) help.

In the Senate, we needed to get Senator Dole on board, as Senator Helms (R-NC) put a hold on the bill. We met with Majority Leader Dole's staff. We were also meeting with his nascent presidential campaign. When LCR was asked by the Dole campaign to give $1,000 to his presidential campaign, we saw a double opportunity: get to know his presidential campaign and help get access on Ryan White. At the D.C. fund-raiser we attended with our PAC check, Senator Dole thanked me for our gift and acknowledged that he was well aware of my concern about Ryan White and that he'd see that it got through.

The biggest fear LCR had after the GOP takeover of Congress was AIDS funding. Over the next four years, our efforts paid off. The GOP Congress actually passed the Ryan White CARE Act and dramatically increased funding. In fact, they surprised the AIDS community by increasing funding well above the president's requests, something that Republicans never got credit for.

PASSING THE BUCK

Meanwhile, in 1995, the organization reached a significant milestone when, for the first time in history, a Republican presidential campaign sought the endorsement of a gay organization. It was calculated that Dole had to raise over $25 million to clinch the nomination, and people like John Moran, Bob Dole's finance director, spent little time with individual donors. Instead, he was looking for networks of people who could give the maximum dollar amount in short order. Gays already had a serious reputation for generosity in politics. Moran invited me to the Dole campaign headquarters to discuss what stood in the way of Log Cabin supporting Bob Dole. Dole was interested in reaching out to Log Cabin.

I went to that meeting skeptical about the whole thing. Working on political campaigns had taught me to be cautious. During the meeting, I was frank about my chief concern—that Dole would pander to the antigay movement during the primaries.

"Do you want Phil Gramm to be our nominee?" Moran asked. "Bob Dole is an honorable man with many gay friends. He isn't a bigot. I'll be with him this week and share with him your concerns, but you have nothing to worry about with Bob Dole."

I explained that in addition to the assurance of no antigay moves, we would need something to energize our members in favor of Dole. The Ryan White CARE Act was scheduled for reauthorization in Congress in 1995. Senator Jesse Helms promised to stop it dead in its tracks on the Senate floor. Dole would have to take on Helms and make sure the bill passed. CARE was Log Cabin's top legislative priority. Moran assured me that he would see what he could do.

After some follow-up correspondence and calls, we had clear assurances that the campaign would not do anything antigay. Because they put our conversations and the follow-up in writing, it seemed that the Dole people were serious. Their support would be a monumental accomplishment in our party and would send an important message to the radical right.

Word came to me from his office that Dole was preparing to join as cosponsor of the Ryan White CARE Act reauthorization bill—a public announcement to Jesse Helms that if he were to raise a finger against the bill, Dole was ready to fight. There was much elation in the Ryan White coalition when we let them know. The pressure was now on for us to deliver on our end of the bargain.

In the following weeks I had to make sure that other Log Cabin members were turning up at fund-raisers in other cities. Then, in June, an elaborate $1,000-per-person Dole fund-raiser was scheduled for Washington. I explained to the campaign that I would be coming on an LCR Political Action Committee check, which meant our support would be public. They assured me it was no problem.

The event was chock-full of Republican House and Senate members, and I spoke to many of them with my LOG CABIN REPUBLICANS name tag prominently visible. When I finally got a chance to talk with Dole, he nonchalantly read my name off the tag, thanked me for coming, and assured me that the Ryan White CARE Act would be voted out of the Senate in the next month. "I know of your concerns with one of the members," Dole told me. "But we're going to work it out." I was impressed with his knowledge of our concern, and this was the first indication that the leadership was ready to schedule a vote.

And, indeed, Bob Dole delivered. The bill came onto the floor despite Senator Helms's attempts to put a procedural hold on it. Helms reacted by throwing five separate amendments at the bill, each designed to gut or disable it. Through the leadership's use of several maneuvering tactics in tandem with Senator Nancy Kassebaum, the bill's chief sponsor, Helms's amendments were disabled. So only months after AIDS groups had predicted the destruction of AIDS legislation as we knew it, Bob Dole supplanted Jesse Helms and ushered through a huge AIDS bill on the Senate floor. The gay press gave credit to Dole for his accomplishment.

In the months since I had given Dole the PAC check, things weren't looking good for the presumed front-runner. Phil Gramm had just pulled dead even with Dole in the Iowa straw poll, which sent pundits reeling. Every major voice in the Republican Party was criticizing Dole for being too moderate and for having a staff that was too open to centrist views. In particular, they were attacking his Senate chief of staff, Sheila Burke, who had opened the lines of communication with Log Cabin back in 1993 when Kevin Ivers and I had met with her in the Capitol on the issue of gays in the military. Moran called campaign manager Scott Reed, the former executive director of the Republican National Committee. The finance side of the campaign, made up largely of moderate Republicans, had not felt Log Cabin's involvement with the campaign was worthy of telling Reed. Now it was going to be a story and Moran thought Reed should know about it. Reed went into a full-scale panic. Without contacting Dole, who was in New Hampshire, Reed released a written statement to Deb Price, a lesbian columnist for the *Detroit News*, claiming that the campaign would return the $1,000 check to the LCR, as the Dole campaign was in "one hundred percent disagreement with the agenda of the Log Cabin Republicans."

When Price called me and read their statement, it was very clear to me what was going on. I was shocked. I knew they were pandering to the religious right and using us to do it. For better or worse, I felt I had no choice but to fire back. I called my friends on the finance committee and was surprised when each of them tried to talk me into remaining silent. "Be a statesman. Don't say anything," they said.

I soon learned that Dole had been totally out of the loop and had heard about Reed's action through a wire-service piece in New Hampshire. I learned also that he was angry at his campaign manager, but was not going to second-guess his staff at a moment of crisis. To my disappointment, Dole defended Reed's actions when the press cornered him into commenting on the matter. Reed and campaign spokesman Nelson Warfield were telling reporters that our check had made it through their screening process by mistake—"a screwup." Warfield went so far as to say that we had set up the Dole campaign because we were "struggling for credibility." So I released all the personal correspondence with the campaign showing their requests for funds and follow-up letters from our meetings. I was not going to let the lies stand.

Reed's attempts to spin began to crumble, and the campaign was left looking craven and self-serving. Nearly every major English-language newspaper in the world, from *The New York Times* and *The Washington Post* to the *Atlanta Constitution* and the *Times* of London, ran an editorial or opinion piece blasting Bob Dole and defending our integrity. Even gay staffers inside the Dole campaign, most of whom had never done a thing for the gay community previously, personally lobbied Dole to reverse his position.

The unrelenting criticism in the press and from his own supporters on the road—public words of reproach from Governor George Pataki of New York; Governor Christie Whitman of New Jersey; Senator Alfonse D'Amato, Dole's national cochairman; and others—was too much for Dole, particularly since it was an action with which he disagreed and would never have allowed had he known of it. Finally, in an impromptu meeting in the Capitol in October 1995, Sabrina Eaton, a lesbian reporter for the *Cleveland Plain Dealer,* asked Dole if he regretted the decision to return the Log Cabin check. The true story slipped out—he said he wasn't consulted, didn't approve of it, and would not have done it if he had known about it. ABC-TV's *World News Tonight,* only hours later, reported Dole's turnabout. "It seems that one-thousand-dollar check from the Log Cabin Republicans has been everywhere and back again," Peter Jennings mused sarcastically.

The check debate placed gay issues firmly into Republican politics. The failure of the effort to pander to the far right taught the lesson that gay bashing didn't work in GOP politics. The incident showed the power of ideas and integrity. The press made Bob Dole apologize for something that he had never approved of but had refused to fix.

Dole's coalitions organizer came to meet with us to seek our endorsement. I was still angry about the check, but put that behind me, as this was another unique historic opportunity to make some headway for the gay community.

We told the campaign that to receive our endorsement it would have to make several commitments. These included maintaining nondiscrimination policies for gay federal appointees, full funding for federal AIDS programs, a serious discussion with Log Cabin about employment nondiscrimination laws, a Republican convention free of gay bashing, the chance for an openly gay person to speak at the convention, and a public request for our endorsement. One by one, over time, each of our demands was met. The openly gay speaker was Steve Fong, president of our San Francisco club, who talked about the importance of education for young people during one of the many nontelevised speeches.

CONFRONTING IGNORANCE: THE HEFLEY AMENDMENT

Following the reelection of the perceived gay-supportive Bill Clinton combined with the failure of Republicans to get much of their agenda through Congress, the far right of the GOP grew angry. That antigay legislation had not been passed made them even angrier. In the spring of 1998, Congressman Hefley (R-CO), in whose district sits James Dobson's antigay Focus on the Family, saw his chance to pass an antigay bill. A few months earlier, the president had extended the nondiscrimination protection for federal employees to gays and lesbians. Hefley set forth an amendment that would reverse the president.

Early predictions were that Hefley's effort would roll through Congress much like the Defense of Marriage Act and Don't Ask, Don't Tell. This time President Clinton didn't buckle and announced he'd oppose the repeal. We in Log Cabin knew that this would be the true test of all of our House visits and local efforts. We would need to get about twenty-five Republicans to oppose the effort and hope that no more than twelve Democrats supported Hefley.

A powerful team developed. First, openly gay Jim Kolbe (R-AZ) took the lead in opposing the bill, holding our strategy meetings in his office. Then a group of gay Democratic and Republican staffers joined the cause. Some were openly gay and others were not. In addition, we were joined by key Republican and Democratic hill staffers who were not gay.

As the Hefley amendment came to the floor, our lobby efforts were paying off. The Speaker's office saw clearly that the GOP faced certain defeat on this bill, and the Speaker now tried to pull the bill. Messengers were sent to ask our support of a watered-down version of the bill, but we refused and insisted on its being voted up or down on its merits. In the vote, sixty-three Republicans opposed it. Representative Frank, LCR's chief critic, had worked successfully with the Republican manager, Jim Kolbe. It was wonderful to watch two openly gay members lead the charge against the mean-spirited far right.

Log Cabin's success on AIDS funding and other legislative efforts like the Hefley bill turned us from the pariah in the D.C. community to a key player on legislative issues. We actually had to find ways to turn away requests and be selective about the legislation we would involve ourselves in. At least among the D.C. organizations, LCR became an important player in efforts to support gay rights in Washington.

Today, Log Cabin is on the front lines of the GOP's civil war between centrists and the right wing. While it is uncertain what the political landscape will yield for gay Republicans in the next century, the Log Cabin Republicans will continue to be uncompromising against the far right's theocratic politics and rhetoric of intolerance. At the same time, Log Cabin has challenged a gay community that prides itself on expressions of diversity, but has failed to make room for ideological differences. The ultimate contribution of Log Cabin may be to expose the dangers of stereotypes and remind both the Republicans and gay activists that all of us are complex individuals, and America is a better place when it embraces true diversity, instead of pigeonholing people.

CHAPTER 7

A Wheel Within a Wheel: Sexual Orientation and the Federal Workforce

LEONARD P. HIRSCH

THE COUNTDOWN

3. June 30, 1999: Office of Personnel Management director Janice Lachance releases a guide for federal employees that outlines their rights to grievance procedures if they believe that they have been discriminated against due to sexual orientation.[1] This is a milestone. Is this a mountain or a molehill or a sandpit?

2. May 28, 1998: President William Jefferson Clinton signs executive order 13087, which, while it "does not and cannot create any new enforcement rights," for the first time in history includes sexual orientation in the official list of categories protected from discrimination in the federal workplace.[2] This is a milestone. The June 30 guide mentioned above is the first official executive branch response to the executive order (it took well over a year!), though the right wing in Congress responded before, trying unsuccessfully to overturn it.

1. December 1957: Frank Kameny is fired from the federal workforce when an arrest for lewd conduct was uncovered and brought to the

attention of his agency. While he was one of many people whose livelihoods were undermined by legal discrimination, this is a milestone.

The story of the increasing application of the words of the Declaration of Independence and the Constitution to treat *all* people equally is a history of milestones, large and small. These events have shown the foresight of the founders and the perspicacity of later individuals and organizations to reach for that grail. This article will look at a small piece of that historical machinery— the recent work of federal employees, through Federal GLOBE (Gay, Lesbian, Bisexual Employees of the Federal Government), to move the federal workplace to one free from discrimination and harassment. It is a work in progress, a history unfolding, processes continual.[3]

THE PAST AS PROLOGUE

While the June 1969 Stonewall Inn riots are commonly seen as the beginning of the modern gay rights movement,[4] they, of course, occurred in a time and place that made this particular noncompliance with authority stand out from the others that were occurring. It was a time of questioning authority, as epitomized in the antiwar movement, the civil rights movement, the women's rights movement, and the antinuclear movement. However, this particular moment followed many years of lesbian and gay organizing and agitation. As is now being chronicled by a growing host of scholars, the post–World War II period was one of change and development of an incipient homophile movement stemming from demobilization and a swelling homosexual presence in the big cities, through the truly offensive McCarthy years into the turbulent 1960s.

During the 1950s and 1960s, not only was it legal, but it was frequently portrayed as patriotic to fire homosexuals from government jobs and to purge them from the military. President Dwight D. Eisenhower issued an executive order in 1953 barring gay men and lesbians from all federal jobs. Many state and local governments and private corporations followed suit. The U.S. Civil Service Commission, which oversaw the hiring, work conditions, and firing of government workers, allowed the denial of jobs or removal from position of anyone for "criminal, infamous, dishonest, immoral, or notoriously disgraceful conduct," under which they included homosexuality.[5] However, lesbians and gays did join the military and take federal jobs. One such person, a Harvard Ph.D. in astronomy, Franklin Kameny, started to work for the U.S. Army Map Service in early 1957. Later that year, Kameny was fired when an FBI check uncovered a 1956 arrest for lewd conduct. This legal injustice started an active and vocal lifetime response from Kameny, who in the decades since has been at the forefront of activism to make the federal workforce, and the America it works for, free from discrimination and harassment. Kameny, at first naively, and later simply with the conviction of the wronged, pressed his case against wrongful dismissal as far as it could go and, when he did not prevail, took on other cases and pressed on until he did win.[6]

Kameny cofounded and was the first president of the Washington chapter of the Mattachine Society, which, with the Daughters of Bilitis, was among the leading U.S.-based homophile organizations in the 1950s and 1960s. The D.C. chapter quickly became the more radical arm, with (very, very well behaved) pickets of the White House and campaigns to end the government-sanctioned witch-hunts and purges of federal employees. Kameny used this base to campaign to change the premier wrong he saw—the legal discrimination by the U.S. government against its homosexual citizens. He broke with the more timid members of the homophile movement by being unwilling to apologize for being gay or to accept anything less than full civil rights. His argumentation (frequent and loud) and leadership created the base for the articulation of equal rights that undergirds the current lesbian/gay/bisexual/transgender (LGBT) movement. His 1968 speech and subsequent article "Gay Is Good," while shortly overtaken by Gay Power as a slogan, still reverberates and remains an important milestone.

Kameny's experience in his own lawsuits prepared him well for the long-term process. Mattachine Society members became active in the D.C. chapter of the ACLU and convinced them to fight the Civil Service Commission policy to fire known homosexuals. In 1965, they won their first case, a U.S. Court of Appeals decision that linked the purported activity (homosexuality) to occupational competence, thereby creating an irreparable crack in the foundation of legal discrimination. A meeting between Mattachine and Civil Service Commission representatives did not move equality forward, but forced the commission to outline their rationale for exclusion (the repugnance of the behavior),[7] which gave ammunition for later cases. By 1973, the commission was backtracking from its policy that homosexuality, sensu stricto, was cause for dismissal. They now said that there had to be a nexus with fitness, and in 1975, finally, the policy was changed to apply the same standard for evaluating sexual conduct whether heterosexual or homosexual.

This policy change was great, and important, but the battle for the hearts and minds of employers and colleagues was just beginning.

IN THE BEGINNING

For the 1990 National Coming Out Day,[8] two Smithsonian employees posted signs for a brown-bag luncheon for Smithsonian lesbian and gay employees to meet one another and celebrate NCOD. Signs were put up, and quickly torn down, but not before eighteen employees saw or heard about it and attended the gathering. From that luncheon discussion can be traced the genesis of Federal GLOBE. The attendees at that event were less diverse than the queer Smithsonian world, but reflected the "out" world—mostly white, mostly male, mostly professional. The discussions that took place there, it turns out, also reflected queer workplace organizing—strongly polarized between those who wanted to organize for policy reasons and those who wanted to create a social group.

Over the next year both social brown-bags and organizing meetings occurred, leading to the creation of SILGIC, the Smithsonian Institution Lesbian and Gay Issues Committee, in 1991. SILGIC's mission was "to ensure adequate and appropriate representation of lesbians, gay men, and bisexuals, their history, rights, and concerns, in Smithsonian policies and programs." In the early 1990s, ensuring appropriate workplace behavior was on the national agenda. The social changes emerging from the rights movements of the 1960s were now being addressed in the mundane minutiae of workplace rules and expectations. Organizations such as BIG (Blacks in Government) and FEW (Federally Employed Women) were active, and at the Smithsonian, many groups were working to make the organization more representative of the workers and America. The secretary of the Smithsonian, Robert McC. Adams, strongly encouraged this (at least verbally), and the groups blossomed in the early nineties. The queer group[9] was part of the more general workplace discourse and quickly became integrated within the larger structure, working to get both antidiscrimination policies and programs of interest to the broader lesbian and gay constituency of the Smithsonian. It was not an easy road.

In the fall of 1991, a like-minded group formed at the U.S. General Accounting Office (Gay and Lesbian Employee Association: GLEA). A chance meeting of members of the two groups in early 1992 led to the idea of developing a contingent for the 1992 Washington, D.C., gay pride parade. A small announcement in the *Washington Blade* brought over twenty people to a meeting at the Smithsonian. Within minutes, there was a call for the creation of a government-wide employee organization to work for the improvement of conditions for lesbians and gays across the federal workforce. The next meeting, announcing the creation of a federal employees group, brought out over one hundred people. And so, Federal GLOBE (Gay, Lesbian, Bisexual Employees of the Federal Government) began.[10] We marched in the parade, and we started collecting our histories and creating our strategies.

The mission statement of Federal GLOBE is "to eliminate prejudice and discrimination in the federal government based on sexual orientation by (1) developing and providing educational programs, materials, and assistance mechanisms which address the distinctive concerns and problems of lesbians, gay men, and bisexuals in the federal government and (2) educating the general public and policymakers about issues of concern to lesbians, gay men, and bisexuals and to federal government employees." While the goals of Federal GLOBE are simple and straightforward, getting there is a lot of work.

The first few months were a busy time, with meetings every month, and attendance not below fifty. Clearly there was a need and desire for such an organization. Early on, it was decided to create an umbrella organization for networking and exchanging ideas, while forming individual groups for different federal agencies. Organizations quickly sprouted in many agencies, most of which remain extant today, such as Commerce GLOBE and GLIFAA (Gays and Lesbians in Foreign Affairs Agencies). We participated in the pride march and festival, AIDSWALK, the presentation of the AIDS Memorial Quilt on the National Mall, and increased programming on World AIDS Day. Programs were held on issues of security clearances,[11] AIDS awareness, and employment protection.

Quickly, information was brought together and core principles of nondiscrimination, freedom from harassment, and rights to organize were developed. To quote the first newsletter: "What the group will evolve into down the road is anybody's guess. But now one thing is clear—it's an important first step toward the goal of full equality for lesbian and gay federal employees." That quote shows how little of our history we knew during those days not very long ago. Few people there knew of Frank Kameny. Fewer knew of any of the history during the eighties. However, one employee of the Department of Labor, Craig Howell, knew of a document from 1980 that was to prove extraordinarily important in the early days of Federal GLOBE.[12] This was a memo from Alan Campbell, the Office of Personnel Management director, interpreting the 1978 Civil Service Reform Act (CSRA, also known as the whistle-blower law).

The 1980 Campbell memo and policy statement was issued on May 12, 1980. In it, OPM interprets the CSRA in light of "discrimination on the basis of conduct which does not adversely affect the performance of employees or applicants for employment," effectively codifying the changes that Kameny and others had wrought. In the explanatory attachment, sexual orientation is explicitly mentioned:

> The privacy and constitutional rights of applicants and employees are to be protected. Thus the applicants and employees are to be protected against inquiries into, or actions based upon, non-job-related conduct, such as religious, community or social affiliations, or sexual orientation.

While the Campbell memo is clear, it was also basically without immediate consequences. Shortly after its promulgation, the 1980 election brought forward a very different leadership at OPM, one that, while not negating the interpretation, quietly put out word simply to shelve the memo.[13] It stayed in purgatory for twelve years until Howell brought it to one of the Federal GLOBE meetings and asked if anyone knew about it. Members of Federal GLOBE from OPM, led by Ron Patterson (a Federal GLOBE founding Board of Directors member), researched the memo and developed the language we would need to start bringing it to light. It is one thing to have a policy and a very different thing to implement it. As we are still seeing with the 1998 presidential executive order, implementation is the long-haul effort.

During that first year, other information came to light. In San Francisco, there had been a group of lesbian and gay federal employees who had been organized for years, Federally Employed Lesbians and Gays (FLAG). In the more hospitable climate of San Francisco and through hard and persistent work spearheaded by Don Henry and Jim Shevock, they had managed to get the Western Region of the Park Service to issue a nondiscrimination statement including sexual orientation. They were working on issues of decreasing harassment, increasing visibility, and AIDS awareness. We also found that a statement including nondiscrimination based on sexual orientation had already been signed at the Government Printing Office.[14]

The work of Henry, Shevock, and their colleagues was invaluable to Federal GLOBE in two ways. Substantively, they had done much of the homework on policy and regulation. As important, the simple existence of the nondiscrimination statement set into play one of the major strategies that Federal GLOBE has used since—using the leaders to convince the cautious to move and to show up the laggards. It is important to realize that the government is not monolithic and that internal politics, internal relationships, and internal processes are important and variable across and within the agencies. Just as in business, federal departments and agencies have reference groups—the different enforcement agencies with one another, the science agencies, the foreign affairs agencies, etc. Additionally, employees of each department consider their department politics to be unique, and while each is, in some ways, each is the same. U.S. federal departments are large, multifaceted, and generally contain units that have internal cultures different from the dominant one (such as the Agricultural Research Service within Agriculture, or Customs within Treasury) or have units that do not integrate, such as in the Department of Commerce, where NOAA, NIST, the Census, and PTO might as well be on different continents (the National Oceanographic and Atmospheric Administration, the National Institute of Standards and Technology, the Bureau of the Census, and the Patent and Trademark Office respectively, for those not living in D.C.'s alphabet soup). Using that diversity, competition, and referencing became a major tool for moving forward, ever so slowly, in making the workplace more hospitable. In each agency, work was needed, because each agency, even the "liberal" ones, were a reflection of American society with all of the homophobic baggage that entails.

Just as the 1980 presidential election impacted the move toward equality negatively, the 1992 election had a major salubrious effect. Suddenly, rather than planning for continuous rearguard actions, we were contacted by the transition team, asked for materials and ideas, and kept in the loop on a series of discussions. When the gays-in-the-military issue surfaced, we were among the only ones (perhaps because we understood Washington) who expected the disaster that resulted. There were discussions of having an executive order eliminating discrimination in the federal workforce, but the imbroglio over the military killed the enthusiasm in the new White House, and after consultation with Congressman Frank, the board of Federal GLOBE agreed to drop the demand in favor of continuing our strategy of ratcheting up the platform by using the leaders/cautious/laggards methodology. Of course, given the large number of openly lesbian and gay appointments by President Clinton in addition to the closeted ones that every administration has, we had the luxury of having many more leaders in place.[15]

The following is from the letter the Board of Directors of Federal GLOBE sent to President-elect Clinton in late 1992:

Specifically we hope that during the transition period and in the first 100 days you will:

- Meet with leaders of the gay and lesbian community to further address the issues of concern to our community. We feel that communication and leadership are the necessary conditions for increasing tolerance and eliminating discrimination in our society.

- Appoint and support openly lesbian and gay people to high level positions, based solely on their professional accomplishments.

- Authorize workplace guidelines barring discrimination based on sexual orientation in the military and other federal agencies; rescind DOD Directive 1332.14; issue an Executive Branch nondiscrimination statement (we include language for a possible directive—one issued by the Peace Corps last year).

- Announce and promote your "Manhattan Project on AIDS." AIDS education in the United States has been so controlled by the radical right that many Americans—who are now infected or dead—could have been spared the agony of this virus had our government possessed the guts and humanity to deal openly and honestly with the multiple pathways of AIDS transmission. For example, public signs in France and Great Britain openly advocate the use of condoms—

without a breakdown in public morality. We hope that your government will assertively lead the way in this discussion and explore the many research and educational needs of this complex issue.

- Direct the Office of Personnel Management to develop programs and policies that eliminate the current discrimination against lesbian and gay federal employees. This includes developing options in health and insurance programs that provide coverage for domestic partners. City governments and private industry are offering such options with increasing frequency. As you so clearly understand, we do form families and are asking simply for a level playing field and the ability to nurture ourselves and our loved ones.

The meetings and the appointments occurred and have continued throughout the Clinton presidency. The gays-in-the-military blowup put off the civilian executive order for six years and led to the disastrous Don't Ask, Don't Tell, Don't Pursue policy. On AIDS, there are and will be many more books dissecting the mix of policies and pronouncements of this administration. Clearly it was more supportive than the prior two presidencies, both symbolically and in reality, with increased funding and service. But, the difficult decisions of direct and honest education have been more frequently sidestepped and are a continuous issue for Federal GLOBE. We still have to monitor training and World AIDS Day events to make certain that they are not offensive or evasive. There has been a decrease in security-clearance problems but continued inequality in benefits structures.

For the first few years, issues of security clearances and investigations were common topics. We had programs with Frank Kameny and local attorney Harvey Friedman, both of whom have strong track records on representing and litigating for changes in procedures and reinstatements from illegal dismissals. Our issues committee, chaired by Ed Horvath, developed information packets on how to deal with a security clearance—what to say, what not to say, how to handle yourself, and what was and was not appropriate for the investigators to ask. The work we did, building on that of Kameny, Friedman, and many others, paid off when President Clinton signed an executive order in August 1995 finally stating that sexual orientation would not be a factor in granting security clearances. Many played a role in the formulation and promulgation of the executive order, but none more so than Congressman Barney Frank.

It is worth a digression to highlight the extraordinary role that Barney Frank has played over the last ten years in Washington, and in particular, in moving lesbian and gay policy issues forward in the Congress and the administration.[16] American politics is very much interest group politics. Frank is the foremost representative for lesbian and gay issues in Washington, and his office does queer constituency service for the nation.[17] He has had some of the most effective staff in Robert Raben and Marcia Kuntz, who have responded to individual needs and provided the grease and/or the muscle to resolve individual cases of harassment or discrimination, to ask administration officials who may not understand policy what the hell they are doing, and to be a voice at the White House when the walk ain't being walked. There has been no time since the founding of Federal GLOBE that Congressman Frank has not been there for assistance or advice.

The particular meeting where a strategy on security clearance was discussed occurred just after the massive 1993 March on Washington for Lesbian and Gay Rights. At that meeting, Frank fulminated on the paucity of congressional visits by those participating in the march and its associated parties and what he considered the inappropriate behavior by some on and off of the stage. As he put it, Redd Foxx did not entertain at the seminal 1963 civil rights rally at the Lincoln Memorial to lead up to the Reverend Martin Luther King Jr's "I Have a Dream" speech. The 1993 march was important for community building and empowerment, but it was a bust when it came to direct impact in Washington (other than in helping the D.C.-based advocacy groups raise money and membership). Its timing at the height of the gays in the military debate and early in the Clinton administration probably minimized the negative impact it could have had and maximized the benefit from empowering people necessary to do work in the next few years.

In our discussion, we outlined our strategy and set a goal of getting nondiscrimination statements across the government, to be followed up by policies implementing those statements. We discussed the boring and time-consuming, but necessary, day-in and day-out activities such as organizing, writing letters and memos, and setting up meetings with administration appointees. Working with leaders such as Assistant Secretary of Commerce and Commissioner of Patents and Trademarks Bruce Lehman, Secretary of Commerce Ron Brown,[18] Secretary of Transportation Federico Peña, and Secretary of Agriculture Mike Espy (the latter being the only person I know of who added sexual orientation to his nondiscrimination letter without being asked to do so by gay employees), Federal GLOBE was able to move forward.

We planned to work with the lesbian and gay political appointees of the Clinton administration, who, in reality did not live up to their potential. The political appointees never organized effectively. Each had his or her own job, often time-consuming and complex, and many simply assumed that everyone was on the same wavelength and good things would just happen. They don't.

Prior to the 1996 elections, the White House appointed a liaison to the lesbian and gay community, Marsha Scott, replaced later on by Richard Socarides. Their jobs were not always easy, for they had to juggle the demands of the White House master with those of the thousands of self-appointed masters (of which Federal GLOBE was certainly one). Scott had strong political connections and was able to remove blockages, such as when the Veterans Administration GLOBE, working through channels, developed a nondiscrimination policy. They worked hard and had it vetted throughout the agency only to have it sit on the desk of the secretary of veterans affairs. He did not want to sign it. It was signed within a week of a meeting between GLOBE's Board of Directors and Scott. Socarides was less effective in removing blocks and was sometimes perceived as being one of the blocks himself.

Some other political appointees were influential in moving forward policies within their offices, such as Romulo Diaz at Energy and John Berry at Interior, but on the whole, the place at the table has not been what it was expected to be. In addition to the lack of organization of the politicals, they and Federal GLOBE had no staff to dedicate to working the issue. All of the GLOBE activities have been voluntary. With no paid staff, no office space, and as an organization that I refer to as most people's fourth outside interest (social, political, and health concerns coming before employment-related), GLOBE frequently found itself short-volunteered.

Due to this voluntary nature, we have seen a consistent pattern in Federal GLOBE and in the agency GLOBEs—the quick flowering and early successes followed by a quick drop-off in participation and constant problems with getting enough people interested in doing the work. In each agency, a handful of hardworking individuals are carrying the rest. We have tried to structure Federal GLOBE to be able to withstand such vicissitudes and provide a home for agency GLOBEs that falter and for individuals in small agencies without the critical mass for an organization.

THE WICKED DO NOT REST

While continual progress has been made over the years in implementing process and procedures of equality across the administration, it has been neither easy nor simple. The right wing has spent substantial time watching the activities of Federal GLOBE and has shown a great facility in finding friends in Congress to try to stop progress. Whether it is Helms in the Senate or Hefley in the House, many of the good deeds of the administration have not gone unpunished.

The *Washington Times,* a right-wing newspaper, reports on GLOBE activities more than Federal GLOBE does itself. Luckily for Federal GLOBE, one of the board members, Kitti Durham of the Department of Transportation, reads the *Times* daily and flags controversies for us as they are being started. Most of the board members have spent substantial time talking with reporters—often working to keep things out of the press, which has also generally kept them out of congressional hearings. One of the most effective tools became linking with the private-sector GLOBEs, such as those at AT&T, Xerox, and Kodak, and using the experience of workplace programs on nondiscrimination and diversity in the Fortune 500 companies to make the new programs in the federal government "not news."

But it is new to most people. The vast majority believe that there should not be discrimination in the workplace, but other than the most blatant examples, most people do not see it when it happens. This lack of sensitivity is one of the major issues we have to face daily. We try to deal with situations by figuring out where they come from—is it active, intentional homophobia? Or is it due to ignorance?[19] We have found that more often it is the latter. Ignorance can be dealt with through education, and Federal GLOBE has tried to make that a major part of its mission and activities.

In 1993, NOAA invited Federal GLOBE to participate in a forum on sexual orientation in the workplace. The materials for the forum created the package that over the years has been developed and honed (with the great assistance of Hollywood Supports and HRC) into the training module *Sexual Orientation in the Workplace*. In it, we try to sensitize individuals to what the issues are and how they can be dealt with. Training becomes an important tool for addressing both individual cases of discrimination or harassment (we try to make it a part of any settlement) and for the broader systemic ignorance of the issues. But getting people to the sessions is not easy. To most people, this is not their issue, and as busy individuals, they have little incentive to participate. Additionally, the Republicans in Congress have mandated that sensitivity (and AIDS-awareness) training cannot be compulsory and, in some agencies, cannot be supported with federal dollars. One of the projects of Federal GLOBE yearly is to watch the appropriations bills for language that will make it difficult or impossible for agencies to create a nonhostile work environment.

One of the right-wing strategies is quite brilliant—if you keep the populace ignorant and scared, they won't organize and complain. If you continue to attack on basics, you can drain capacity. Much of the right-wing attack on GLOBE specifically, and on diversity and AIDS-awareness training in general, attempts to minimize the empowerment that knowledge brings and to take up resources that could otherwise be used for positive action in fighting rearguard actions instead.

We have constantly found that one of the biggest hurdles we face in getting our queer sisters and brothers involved is their own understanding of the issues.[20] Many of us either do not see the problems ("No one has harassed *me*") or have bought into the social mores of accepting some harassment or discrimination ("it happens," or in a self-hating fashion, we bring it on ourselves—"the cost of being out"). There is a systemic ignorance of the issues, which our mission is to eradicate. But this takes lots of time and effort.

142 | Leonard P. Hirsch

Given the relative anomie of the lesbian and gay employees, we cannot expect most heterosexuals to understand the issues immediately. In the Clinton administration, luckily, the most senior-level appointees need little educating to *see* the problem. Most of them understand the issues and accept their importance. However, the pressure or fear of a congressional hearing does tamp down their enthusiasm for positive action.

We have found more resistance in the middle-management sectors. Just where you think the understanding should be most prevalent, in the civil rights and human resources offices, we find the greatest gaps. There are a number of reasons for this. First, these offices are frequently understaffed and under attack for inefficiency. The last thing they want is to add another issue, especially one with such high potential for failure.[21] There is an enormous amount of misinformation about the rules and regulations in the federal government, and even without that, there is still great uncertainty on how far the authority to eliminate harassment and discrimination actually goes. There has not yet been a court case that affirms the Campbell interpretation or the presidential executive order.

Additionally, federal Civil Rights and EEO offices were set up to improve the condition of certain classes of traditionally discriminated-against people. Some of the leaders in these offices see the world in zero-sum terms—if they help lesbians and gays, they take away from blacks and Hispanics. Since so often the face of the movement is white (and male), it rubs these people wrong. We work with them to understand that discrimination is discrimination and that what we are attempting to do is increase the size of the pie, not take from others.

GLOBE has tried to develop strong coalitions with other groups, be they employee groups in the agencies or labor unions. In some agencies, such as Commerce and Labor, the GLOBE groups have become integrally intertwined in the department's employee relations and development programs. As one of the pillars for workplace security are the negotiated grievance procedures, we also try to work closely with labor unions. Here, we have been only marginally successful. The fragmentation of the union structure in the federal workforce has made it difficult to know where to go, and the overwhelmingly white-collar participation in GLOBE activities also limits our entrée to the unions. We have also found that organized labor's acceptance of sexual orientation issues very much reflects the government's—at the senior policy level, there is great buy-in, but at the lower, implementation levels, it is frequently seen as suspect or something to bargain away. There is great opportunity to strengthen the relationship with organized labor, and hopefully Federal GLOBE will do this in the coming years.

FEDERAL GLOBE: THE GAY AGENDA

When President Clinton signed the 1998 executive order on discrimination, the board of Federal GLOBE set up an appointment with Richard Socarides for the following day and a follow-up with a larger group of influential people within a week. We created a checklist for implementing executive order 13087 that has thirty-two elements under the broader categories of policy articulation, administrative redress procedures, union/negotiated redress procedures, training, diversity programs, hiring and outreach, and benefits.[22] A theory of organizational growth stipulates that there is an order to these—getting the policy basics in place, setting the stage with process and staff, and then recruitment and retention. Each on its own is done somewhere in the government and in many places in the private sector.

In the follow-up meeting, which included Virginia Apuzzo and Richard Socarides (White House), Mark Hunker (Office of Personnel Management), Paul Richard (Equal Employment Opportunities Commission), Elaine Kaplan (Office of Special Counsel), Robert Raben (Congressman Frank's staff), and Rob Sadler and myself (Federal GLOBE Board of Directors), Federal GLOBE asked the administration to put out a guidance on the executive order that would outline the thirty-two elements and request a report back to OPM within six months on implementation. (We crafted the letter and worksheet.) We also shared with them the work that was done by Commerce GLOBE in creating a booklet on redress procedures for lesbian and gay employees.

While the meeting was historic—this was the first time a president had issued an executive order that barred discrimination based on sexual orientation in the federal workforce—it was not celebratory. There were strong differences on approach and coverage. We heard a go-slow message, which as it turns out was understated, and a strong fear of backlash. The Commerce booklet mentioned above has a large pink triangle on the front cover, which led to a discussion on the appropriateness of a government publication using such a symbol!

During the meeting, we were increasingly frustrated at the apparent lack of direction in putting out a directive. We asked for simple justice in implementing the EO. In a prophetic statement, Ginny Apuzzo stated that the response should be no less (and no more) than other executive orders on workplace concerns, and that anything less would be discrimination. She asked Hunker and Socarides to research and report back on such practices. We never heard back. We have gotten much less than is normal. The irony is that the executive order barring discrimination has been implemented (such as it is) in a discriminatory fashion.

During the year following the signing of the executive order, Federal GLOBE waited for the direction from OPM and the White House. Clearly, they were concerned that our thirty-two points were too long and inclusive.

Kitti Durham of the Board of Directors worked with them on streamlining and shortening the statement, so that a single-page letter could go out. Midway through the year, the OPM GLOBE group contacted Federal GLOBE with alarm over a purported draft of an advisory booklet on discrimination based on sexual orientation in the federal workplace that they had heard was about to be released. They asked if we had seen and/or approved it. It was the first we had heard of it, and after repeated phone calls and some months, a draft was seen by one of the board members. It was basically a watered-down version of the Commerce booklet, with no cover memo or implementation guidelines. It stated that this was interpretation, not law. Both OPM GLOBE and Federal GLOBE wrote strongly worded letters to get a little more teeth into the booklet and asking for the rest of the needed directives. While some wording was strengthened, the words read that agencies *should* develop policies, not *must*.

The executive order is to create a "uniform policy" across the federal government. Our approach of leaders/cautious/laggards had created an inequality in the standards being applied throughout the government. The June 30, 1999, OPM guidance references the four avenues for federal employees seeking help and brings useful information together in one easily accessible document. However, it does little to further the intent of the executive order and does not address the harder issues of preventing sexual orientation discrimination in the federal workplace.

Since the issuance of EO 13087, departments and agencies have responded neither uniformly nor quickly to bring consistency to a complex process. The goal is to arrive at a consistent set of published procedures in every department and agency according to which complaints of discrimination on the basis of sexual orientation will be addressed within the agency in a manner equivalent to those using EEO procedures, even though they will not have the recourse of final appeal to the EEOC that traditional EEO cases have. As of February 2000, twenty-one months after the order, only six departments or agencies (out of at least eighty-two that have independent processes) have announced uniform procedures. OPM's action fails to give appropriate guidance to the agencies and does not address the continuing inconsistency of treatment of such discrimination.

So, it looks like Federal GLOBE, all of the agency GLOBEs, and the many labor and advocacy groups will still have lots to do in the coming years.

THE MILLENNIUM APPROACHES

JUNE 1999 *The thirtieth anniversary of Stonewall; speech by Congresswoman Tammy Baldwin to the Department of Interior GLOBE group; speech by Congressman Barney Frank to the Small Business Administration*

GLOBE group; the swearing in of (openly gay) James Hormel as the ambassador to Luxembourg; reintroduction of the Employment Non-Discrimination Act in Congress; the federal designation of the Stonewall Inn on the National Registry of Historic Places; presidential proclamation honoring lesbian and gay pride month; first roundtable on sexual orientation in the federal workforce at the EEOC, with participation of (openly gay) John Berry, assistant secretary of interior; (openly gay) Elaine Kaplan, special counsel and director of the Office of Special Counsel; (openly gay) Mark Hunker, special assistant to the director of OPM; (openly gay) Rob Sadler, member of the Board of Directors of Federal GLOBE and member of the Vice President's National Performance Review Taskforce on Diversity; chaired by (openly gay) Paul Richards, of the EEOC; and so much more.

These milestones created a historic moment. They are representative of the cumulative successes that the homophile/gay power/gay liberation/lesbian, gay, bisexual, transgender rights movement and communities have brought in the last fifty years in concert with progressive movements in gender, race, labor, and human rights across the globe. While they need to be celebrated, we are not celebrating victory. Many individuals still do not feel secure in the protections they do have, and many rights and privileges are still not accorded to queer Americans. What has been learned from Federal GLOBE's experiences in this history?

Federal GLOBE and the agency GLOBEs show that collective action is possible, doable, and can lead to enormous success. But they also show that bringing together individuals to form the necessary organization for this action is not easy or simple. Some impediments within our communities make workplace organizing more difficult than usual, such as the closet and the higher ranking of other concerns (health concerns, for example). Our experience also shows that the problem of free riders is serious.[23] The federal workforce numbers about 2.8 million. There is no census, so we do not know how many of these are lesbian, gay, bisexual, or transgender, but if they are a reflection of the voting public, we can assume that about 112,000 would self-identify as such.[24] It would be wonderful if Federal GLOBE and the agency GLOBEs had such membership! My "rule of 10s" is that in any group, about 10 percent will be interested in any particular subject (11,200), 10 percent of those will do something about it (1,120), and 10 percent of those will become active on the issue (112). There are more than 112 active individuals in the GLOBE movement in the federal government, and more than 1,120 members within the GLOBEs. How to get the rest involved and move them from free-ridership is a perpetual agenda item. We are working on increasing our outreach and communications, through the development of our Web site (www.fedglobe.org) by Annie Rivera of the Department of Labor GLOBE (GLOBAL) and a newly refashioned newsletter, *Globalview* by board member Jeff Brooks of IRS. But we need to get more visibility within the departments and agencies in internal publications and in the community through the lesbian and gay press.

Building on the efforts of giants such as Frank Kameny and Barney Frank, we have been able to use the historical opportunities provided by the Clinton administration to expand the rights of protection from harassment and discrimination based on sexual orientation in the federal workplace and influence their implementation. While not yet fully implemented, all of the necessary components are in place to move this forward at an even greater speed than we have so far. While the support may not always continue to exist at the top of the administration, we hope that the principles of nondiscrimination are so fully embedded in law and procedure that weak support will not roll back the gains. Clearly, this will need constant monitoring regardless of who is president. To do so, we must continue and strengthen the agency GLOBEs. Without effective on-the-ground organizing, activities, and monitoring, progress cannot be made and backsliding will occur.

Using the leader/cautious/laggard methodology has allowed us to build a solid platform of successes and advances. Now, with the executive order, for the government to institutionalize these, we need to work more closely with nonqueer individuals and groups. We have to mainstream the issues and concerns in the larger civil rights and human-resources communities. We need all managers and labor organizers to understand the issues and to press for changed working conditions.

Federal GLOBE's position as a not-for-profit 501.C.3 organization makes it different from the agency GLOBEs, which are internal employee groups. The synergies of working together form a powerful base where Federal GLOBE can do things that the agency units might be restricted from doing and can have the single voice that the administration wants to deal with, while the agency GLOBEs can move the activities within their many units. Both as a voice and as an actor, our job is to create the situations and tools to make the implementation easier for the federal government. To do this, we will need to get more people active, educated, and involved. We need to look into getting grant monies and an endowment so as to have some full-time paid staff to keep continuity. We are looking into these options, but are in the catch-22 of not having full-time staff to do the work and organizing.

Progress in human rights is always slow. Too many people see the world as zero-sum and resent forward movement by others. Too many people are threatened by success. But we will work around these people and try to get them to understand that increasing rights and freedoms benefits all and empowers all. As part of the larger civil rights movement and as part of the larger federal government reinvention, Federal GLOBE will continue to press these points and work to make the federal workforce, the country, and the world free from harassment and discrimination of all sorts.

PART III

GAY AGENDAS

CHAPTER 8

THE FEDERAL GAY RIGHTS BILL: FROM BELLA TO ENDA

CHAI R. FELDBLUM

O N MAY 14, 1974, CONGRESSWOMAN BELLA ABZUG, an outspoken feminist congresswoman from New York, introduced a sweeping and comprehensive antidiscrimination bill that aimed to change dramatically the face of federal civil rights law. The bill prohibited private employers, some private businesses, state governments, and educational facilities from discriminating on the basis of sex, marital status, or sexual orientation. The only public notation of the bill was a brief sentence at the back of the *Congressional Record,* in the list of public bills and resolutions introduced that day. Apart from some coverage in the gay press, nobody in America noticed.[1]

Twenty years later, on June 23, 1994, the Employment Non-Discrimination Act (ENDA), a significantly more modest bill prohibiting private employers from discriminating on the basis of sexual orientation, was introduced on the same day in both the United States Senate and House of Representatives.[2] The introduction came replete with a major news conference attended by Democratic and Republican members of Congress and the leading luminaries of the civil rights movement. This time, America noticed. Over 180 mainstream news outlets carried stories covering introduction of the bill or later activities surrounding the bill.[3] Two years later, in September 1996, the United

States Senate voted on ENDA and failed to pass it by just one vote.[4] And in January 1999, for the first time ever, endorsement of a gay civil rights bill was part of the President's State of the Union message.[5]

The effort to pass a federal gay civil rights bill has come a long way in the past twenty-five years. The saga is rich with stories about the gay rights movement and with lessons for the future of the movement. It is a story of increasing political activism and political savvy on the part of both national and local gay rights groups. It is a story of making slow, but steady, headway against the public's discomfort with homosexuality and with politicians' fears of allying themselves with gay civil rights. And it is a story of the impact the AIDS epidemic has had on reshaping the priorities of the gay rights movement on the national level.

While the story of the federal gay civil rights bill is one of remarkable political change and growth, it is also a story of remarkably static rhetoric and analysis. The basic concern raised by those opposing passage of a gay civil rights bill has remained the same over the past twenty-five years: passage of such a law would result in the government's legislating a moral view of homosexuality at odds with the majority's. The official response of gay leaders and nongay allies has also remained remarkably the same: passage of such a law says nothing about the moral goodness of homosexuality, but simply legislates equal rights for gay people.

Over the years, a greater number of politicians have accepted this response of gay rights leaders as sufficient to justify their vote and calm their fears. Indeed, we may be poised for passage of a gay employment civil rights bill in the next few years based on the tried-and-true answers of the past quarter century. But the question remains: Are those answers correct? Does passage of a gay civil rights law really not say *anything* about whether "gay is good"? At the very least, should we be arguing that it does? As the wheels of time so often demonstrate, our answers to those questions may simply return the gay rights movement to where it began twenty-five years earlier.

I. 1965–74: FIRST A REVOLUTION, THEN REFORM

The latter half of the 1960s and the early 1970s witnessed the establishment of a range of new gay rights organizations. Some, such as the Gay Liberation Front (GLF), patterned directly after antiwar and black nationalist organizations, were concerned with system-wide oppression and were fiercely democratic and consensus-based. Others, such as the Gay Activists Alliance, focused primarily on gay oppression, but were still run by nonhierarchical consensus. Finally others, such as the National Gay Task Force, were explicitly reformist and mainstream. For the reform-oriented organizations, a federal gay civil rights bill epitomized their hopes and dreams for a gay civil rights movement.

In 1966, three years before the famous riot at Stonewall, fifteen gay (they were often then called homophile) organizations joined together to form the North American Conference of Homophile Organizations (NACHO).[6] NACHO published studies on homosexual law reform and employment discrimination, supported court cases that challenged antigay policies in immigration law and the military, and helped form local homophile groups. In 1968, inspired by the Black Is Beautiful motto of the burgeoning radical black civil rights movement, NACHO adopted Gay Is Good as its motto and distributed buttons with that proud and defiant message.[7]

On June 27, 1969, the rhetoric of defiance came to life with a riot against police raiding the Stonewall bar. Shortly thereafter, in July 1969, the Gay Liberation Front (GLF) was founded in New York City. The group's mission was explicitly radical. GLF's first statement announced: "Gay Liberation Front is a revolutionary group of homosexual women and men formed with the realization that complete sexual liberation for all people cannot come about unless existing social institutions are abolished." Part of the group's political theory was that the sexist and racist capitalist system had to be undermined if gay liberation were truly to be achieved.[8]

Some activists, unhappy with GLF's radical agenda and often chaotic decision-making process, left to form the Gay Activists Alliance (GAA), an organization explicitly devoted exclusively to gay issues. The agenda of GAA was intentionally more reformist than radical, with a strong emphasis on law reform and heavy involvement in electoral politics. For example, in 1971, GAA started the struggle for passage of a gay rights bill in New York City. But the tactics of the group still borrowed significantly from the confrontational, passionate politics of the era, with direct-action tactics known as zaps intended to embarrass and shake up political officials.[9]

In 1973, the National Gay Task Force (NGTF) was established in New York by several members of GAA. The founders of NGTF wanted a more structured organization that would work to advance gay rights on a national level. They wanted a board of directors, a paid staff, and membership, and they actively sought to establish the mainstream respectability of the group by recruiting prominent openly lesbian and gay professionals to NGTF's board.[10]

The reform-oriented approach of gay groups came to dominate the movement in the early 1970s. Energy and focus was devoted more to the struggle to achieve gay civil rights rather than to the struggle to liberate all human sexuality from the oppression of societal structures. As historian John D'Emilio has pointed out, the movement "returned to the reform-oriented perspective of the pre-Stonewall homophile movement. Rather than a struggle for liberation, the movement had become, once again, a quest for 'rights.'" Nevertheless, as D'Emilio also points out, the movement had absorbed the lessons of pride and self-acceptance taught by the lesbian and gay liberation movement. As D'Emilio observes, "Many gay activists remained as bold and brazen as their GLF predecessors had been. They expected and demanded acceptance for who they were, without apology."[11]

Congresswoman Bella Abzug's introduction of a gay civil rights bill on the federal level in 1974 fit right in with the reformist political agenda of groups such as NGTF. Abzug introduced the bill six months before her November 1974 reelection bid and campaigned on a promise to fight for such legislation. But political support for such a bill was clearly lacking on Capitol Hill. Indeed, the capacity even to *speak* about gay rights in the U. S. Congress was minimal. The next eight years would bring an increased role and visibility of reformist gay political groups in Washington, D.C., and a slowly, but steadily, heightened capacity on the part of politicians to address the need for a gay rights bill on the federal level. It would also bring to the fore the focused opposition of a reinvigorated conservative and religious right.

II. 1974–82: THE EARLY YEARS OF THE FEDERAL GAY CIVIL RIGHTS BILL

A. Speaking about Gay Civil Rights

Members of Congress ordinarily love to talk about the bills they introduce. Indeed, introducing bills and talking about them consumes a significant amount of time in Congress. But in the area of gay civil rights, the challenge was simply to find members of Congress willing to speak about the issue. From 1974, when Congresswoman Abzug first introduced a gay civil rights bill, until 1978, the primary goal for a group such as NGTF—the single national group lobbying on behalf of the bill—was to raise the visibility of the gay rights issue and to encourage members of Congress to take up airspace on the issue.

The bill Abzug introduced in May 1974, entitled the Equality Act of 1974, reflected her commitment to feminism, as well as to lesbian and gay equality. Federal law at the time prohibited discrimination based on race, color, religion, and national origin in employment, private housing, in a few selected areas of private commerce known as public accommodations (places of lodging, eating, and recreation), by any business that received federal financial assistance, and by public schools and facilities.[12] The only protection for women, at the time, was in employment and education.[13] Abzug's bill thus aimed to expand the scope of civil rights laws for women, as well as for gay men, lesbians, and unmarried people. First, Abzug's bill made it illegal to discriminate on the basis of "sex" in public accommodations, federally assisted programs, public facilities, and the sale and rental of private housing. Second, the bill made it illegal to discriminate in those same areas on the basis of "marital status" or "sexual orientation," and also prohibited discrimination on those bases in private employment and education.[14]

Congresswoman Abzug's broad equality bill never made it past the House Judiciary Committee (where it was referred for consideration), and when Abzug returned to Congress in 1975, she bifurcated the bill—one dealing with sexual orientation and one dealing with sex and marital status. There is no indication whether Abzug did this because she felt a bill with only sex and marital status as prohibited grounds of discrimination would be more politically palatable than a bill that also included sexual orientation, or whether she did it because groups like NGTF wanted a more targeted, narrow approach to sexual orientation. In any event, in January 1975, Abzug introduced a gay civil rights bill on behalf of herself and four other members of Congress. The bill, entitled Civil Rights Amendments of 1975, added "affectional or sexual preference" to the same sections of civil rights law that the broad equality bill had covered.[15]

Much of the activity on the gay civil rights bill would consist, over the years, in slowly convincing additional members of Congress to cosponsor the bill. The only way to officially demonstrate the existence of additional cosponsors on a bill, however, was to reintroduce the bill, with a new bill number and a new list of cosponsors. Hence, much of the activity around the gay civil rights bill in early years consisted simply of frequent reintroductions of the bill, with a slowly increasing number of cosponsors.

While Abzug's bill ultimately garnered twenty-seven cosponsors by the end of 1976, there was minimal coverage or movement on the gay civil rights bill. But 1976 did witness the beginning of an important organization in the life of the federal gay rights bill and the end of Abzug's congressional career. In 1976, the Gay Rights National Lobby (GRNL) was created at a private conference called by David Goodstein, a wealthy gay businessman and owner of *The Advocate,* a national gay newsmagazine.[16] The mission of GRNL was to lobby on the federal level. Although GRNL's efforts during its first two years were less than impressive, it was to become an important organization in advancing the gay civil rights bill from 1978 to 1982 under the leadership of Steve Endean. But 1976 also saw Abzug's defeat in a four-way primary for a New York U.S. Senate seat. Thus, in January 1977, Congress began with Ted Weiss in Abzug's former congressional seat, and with Congressman Ed Koch of New York taking up leadership of the gay civil rights bill.

Koch followed the pattern of introducing a gay civil rights bill early on in the congressional session and then frequently reintroducing the bill with additional cosponsors. Koch's bills were initially referred solely to the House Judiciary Committee, as had been Abzug's bills. This made sense, given that the bills amended existing civil rights bills that were under the jurisdiction of the Judiciary Committee. But the gay civil rights bill was clearly going nowhere fast in that committee. Neither Peter Rodino (D-NJ), chair of the Judiciary Committee, nor Don Edwards (D-CA), chair of the Judiciary's Subcommittee on Civil and Constitutional Rights, were cosponsors of the gay civil rights bill, and neither seemed inclined to move the bill forward.

By contrast, the House Education and Labor Committee seemed a much more attractive location for the bill. Augustus (Gus) Hawkins, a Democrat from California, was chair of that committee's Subcommittee on Employment Opportunities. A case could certainly be made that the gay civil rights bill (which covered employment, as well as a host of other areas) could legitimately be considered by the Education and Labor Committee.

Members of Congress who chair committees ordinarily guard their jurisdictional turf jealously. The only exception is when they would rather not deal with a bill ordinarily under their control. In such a case, the member may be more than willing to share the bill with another committee. This seems to have been the situation with regard to the gay civil rights bill. In March 1977, Congressman Rodino, chair of the House Judiciary Committee, asked for and received the unanimous consent of the House of Representatives for the gay civil rights bill to be jointly referred to the Judiciary Committee and the Education and Labor Committee.[17]

The gay newspaper in Washington, the *Blade,* viewed all this activity with enthusiasm. In the April 1977 issue of the paper, in a story titled "Gay Civil Rights Bill Gathers Momentum," the paper reported the bill now had thirty-nine cosponsors, including two Republicans. The story, which carried no byline, asked readers to urge their congresspeople to cosponsor the bill, and to send copies of those letters to the "Congressional File" c/o the UFMCC (Universal Fellowship of Metropolitan Community Churches) Washington office.[18]

Despite the enthusiasm of the *Blade,* Koch's bill had little momentum behind it, and there was no active and sophisticated gay rights group organizing the lobbying activity in Washington. The very fact that the current state of lobbying consisted primarily of sending copies of letters of support to a "Congressional File" at the Washington office of the UFMCC should itself have been a bit disheartening. Presumably, the letters were sent there because NGTF used the Washington offices of the MCC when it did its federal lobbying.

State and local events, however, soon catapulted the issue of gay rights into the national consciousness, resulting in both a focus on, and a heightened opposition to, the federal gay civil rights bill. On January 18, 1977, the Dade County Commission, in Dade County, Florida, voted 5–3 to prohibit discrimination based on sexual orientation in housing, public accommodations, and employment. In doing so, Dade County was following the lead of a number of localities and municipalities that had recently passed such ordinances.[19] But

Dade County's action triggered a backlash. An effort to repeal the gay rights ordinance, led by Anita Bryant, succeeded on June 7, 1977, by a 69 percent vote.
The campaign to repeal the ordinance triggered broad national attention and
galvanized both supporters and opponents of gay rights.

The Dade County controversy led Gallup to run its first poll on the public's attitudes to homosexuality in July 1977. The results were intriguing, as
would be the relative stability of polling results on identical questions over the
next twenty years. Gallup reported that 56 percent of respondents believed gay
people should have equal job rights. Only 43 percent of respondents, however,
felt homosexual relations should be legal.[20] In explaining this disparity,
Michael Kagay, a polling consultant for *The New York Times,* observed that it
reflected a familiar pattern of attitudes toward nonconforming groups. As Kagay explained, "Americans may tolerate the abstract idea of equal rights for homosexuals, but do not want to sanction their behavior legally."[21]

A similar view was articulated by William Safire, a former speechwriter
for Richard Nixon, in an op-ed column, "Now Ease Up, Anita," which appeared two days after the successful Dade County repeal effort. Safire cautioned Bryant that she had not been given a mandate "to put the gays on the
run," since no "bluenose moralizer should have the power to tell consenting
adults of the same sex" what they can do in private. But the private/public distinction was key to Safire. He chastised the "militant leaders of the gay rights
movement" for framing the issue as "civil rights versus outright bigotry," when
the overwhelming majority "did not see it that way." As Safire explained:

> Most of the voters framed the issue, as I did, between tacit toleration and
> outright approval of homosexuality. Most Americans are inclined to let
> consenting adults do what they like, short of injury, in private; but the gay
> activists want more: the basic "right" they sought was the assertion by so-
> ciety that what they were doing was right.
>
> But they are wrong. In the eyes of the vast majority, homosexuality is
> an abnormality, a mental illness, even—to use an old-fashioned word—a
> sin. Homosexuality is not the "alternative lifestyle" the gay activists pro-
> fess; it may be tolerable, even acceptable—but not approvable.

Thus, according to Safire, when gay people seek ordinances stating they
may not be discriminated against on the basis of their sexual orientation, they
essentially want "the seal on their housekeeping to say good." But while that is
a moral judgment gay people are free to make, Safire explained, it is not a moral
judgment gay people have the right "to insist upon from the rest of society,
which has the right to make its own contrary judgment and to persuade its children of its value."[22]

In the meantime, on Capitol Hill, supporters and opponents of gay rights were responding in different ways to the heightened focus on gay rights engendered by the local gay rights ordinances and repeal efforts. In June 1977, Koch reintroduced his gay rights bill with a new section, titled "To Prevent Misinterpretation." This section provided that gay people could not claim their rights had been violated simply because of a statistical disparity between the number of gay people in the general population and the number of gay people in a particular workplace.[23] The provision also provided that if discrimination on the basis of sexual preference was proven, a court could not fashion a remedy that required a quota of hiring a set number of people of a particular sexual preference.[24]

In introducing his new version of the bill, Koch explained that one of the scare tactics successfully used by opponents of the Dade County ordinance was to argue that the law "required employers to engage in affirmative action which would result in the compulsory hiring of homosexuals in order to make up for the prior years of discrimination."[25] The same false allegation, Koch noted, was being made against his gay civil rights bill. While the bill would have no such result, Koch explained he was introducing a new version of the bill that explicitly prohibited affirmative action and quotas.

Koch did not respond to the question of whether passage of a gay civil rights law would send the message that gay relations were morally good, the complaint raised by Safire in his column. Rather, in what would become a time-honored tradition of avoiding such questions and focusing instead on the moral correctness of "equality," Koch observed he had taken up the cause of human rights his whole life, beginning with fighting in World War II against the Nazis, and "[homosexuals] are sons and daughters of people we all know and it is simply wrong to turn our back upon them and deprive them of equality before the law."[26]

Koch also invoked the maxim that "the state has no business in the bedrooms of this nation."[27] To Koch, what people did in the privacy of their homes was not government's business, and as a logical corollary, if such activity became the basis for discriminatory action, government should legitimately intervene to prohibit such discrimination. To opponents of gay rights, however, this corollary was neither logical nor correct. Many of them were more than willing to let gay people do what they wished to do in the privacy of their own homes. But when such individuals decided to be *open* and *honest* about what they were doing in the privacy of their own homes, and *then* subsequently demanded protection against the understandable moral outrage that followed (including adverse, discriminatory actions), then gay rights advocates were going too far. In response to such demands by militant gay activists, opponents believed it was imperative for the government, at all levels, to make clear its *condemnation,* and *nonsupport,* of homosexuality.

While the latter view may not have been the actually held majority view among members of Congress in 1977, it was certainly the view the majority would take if pushed to a public vote. For example, in June 1977, Congressman Larry McDonald (R-GA) offered an antigay amendment to the bill that funded the Legal Services Corporation. The amendment provided that no money in the bill could be used "to provide legal assistance with respect to any proceeding or litigation arising out of disputes or controversies on the issue of homosexuality or so-called gay rights."[28] A voice vote on the amendment was called as a "no" vote by the presiding Speaker, and McDonald asked for a division vote, in which members stand and are counted. (A division vote includes only those members who are on the House floor at the time.) On that vote, McDonald's amendment again lost, 39–80. McDonald then called for a recorded vote. A recorded vote summons all members of the House to the chambers for the vote and is taken by electronic device. On that vote, the McDonald amendment passed 230 to 133, with seventy members not voting.[29]

One of the most striking elements of the vote on the McDonald amendment was the lack of *any* debate on the amendment—either pro or con. McDonald and other supporters of the amendment were apparently supremely confident their amendment would pass, with no need for persuasive debate, as long as members were subjected to a public, recorded vote. For their part, opponents of the amendment seemed to have no stomach to engage in a discussion of the provision. Indeed, it is unclear what the provision was even intended to do—would a gay person be precluded from using a Legal Services attorney in a landlord-tenant dispute, or were Legal Services attorneys simply precluded from bringing "so-called gay rights" cases? Whatever the effect of the provision, while 133 members were willing to vote no, none was willing to engage the issue in public debate.

In July 1977, Bruce Voeller and Jean O'Leary, codirectors of NGTF, met in Senator Alan Cranston's office to discuss common strategy with representatives from the ACLU, the League of Women Voters, the National Organization of Women (NOW), the National Women's Political Caucus, and the Women's Action League. O'Leary observed that NGTF and other groups were "facing common enemies," as a "new right" had formed to challenge the Equal Rights Amendment, abortion, and gay rights.[30] But the truth was that the general civil rights community did not view "gay rights" as part of its mandate. Indeed, in 1977, when NGTF applied to become a member of the leading civil rights coalition in Washington, the Leadership Conference on Civil Rights (LCCR), its membership application was rejected.[31]

Gay rights groups would have a long road ahead of them in building bridges and connections to the general civil rights community. But it would be next to impossible for gay rights groups to do that without lobbyists in D.C. who could become team players and contributors to the general civil rights struggles taking place on the federal level. A visit from NGTF's codirectors was a fine start, but a New York–based organization, without a Washington office, would be inherently limited in its capacity to form a real partnership with the civil rights community.

B. Building Political Savvy and Collecting Votes

In 1978, the gay civil rights bill received a significant jumpstart when Steve Endean came to town as executive director of the Gay Rights National Lobby (GRNL). Under Endean's persistent lobbying, the bill would garner sixty cosponsors in the House of Representatives by 1982, a companion Senate bill would be introduced, and the House bill would be the subject of two congressional hearings. Over four years, a bill—and an issue—that had been greeted with relative silence and obscurity would become a legitimate topic of political discourse. Indeed, in 1982, it would seem as if passage of the bill was actually possible.

Endean had been a leader in the successful lobbying effort to pass gay civil rights ordinances in Minneapolis and St. Paul and had worked on a statewide gay rights bill that had come within two votes of passage in the Minnesota state legislature in 1977.[32] When Endean joined GRNL, the organization was on its last legs. The organization's phone was disconnected, the mail unopened, and the treasury depleted. The group's executive committee conceded that, while the group had provided information on gay rights to members of Congress, it had done no direct lobbying in the previous two years.[33]

Endean's stated priority, when he joined GRNL, was to contact and work "with all progressive elements" of Congress and the Washington establishment. Endean presumably knew from his successful work in Minnesota the importance of engaging in coalition work, strategic thinking, building grassroots support, and persistent vote gathering to create a successful legislative result. In 1978, Endean embarked on just those activities in pursuit of passage of a federal gay rights bill.

By 1978, Congressman Weiss had decided he should be the leader on the gay civil rights bill because Ed Koch had left Congress to successfully run as mayor of New York City. So, following the usual pattern, in February 1979, Weiss introduced essentially the same version of the gay civil rights bill with no additional cosponsors. But Endean had clearly been planning to break from the usual pattern and had been having discussions with the office of Congressman Henry Waxman (D-CA) about introducing a separate gay rights bill that might be more limited in scope. As Bruce Wolpe, a Waxman staff person at the time, recalls, "Tip O'Neill was Speaker and liberalism was at an apogee, so of course you could talk about two gay rights bills, in an effort to get more support for the more centrist bill."[34] Ultimately, however, Waxman chose not to introduce a separate piece of legislation, but instead became a lead sponsor of Weiss's bill and worked with GRNL to add cosponsors to that legislation.

Endean proceeded one step at a time on the bill, lining up cosponsors and getting to know other civil rights lobbyists in town. He also clearly wanted to shape a specific political message for the bill: that passage of a gay civil rights bill need not be equated with an endorsement of homosexuality. For example, Congressmen Paul McCloskey (CA) and William Green (NY), two of only three Republican cosponsors of the bill, wrote their Republican colleagues in November 1979 to urge them to sponsor the bill. The two congressmen stressed for their colleagues that endorsement of civil rights for gays did not necessarily mean an endorsement of homosexuality.[35] While there is no official record indicating that Endean worked with the offices of McCloskey and Green to pen this letter, it would be surprising if Endean had not been a major player in having this "Dear Colleague" letter drafted and circulated.

Another of Endean's efforts came to fruition in December 1979 when Senator Paul Tsongas (D-MA) introduced a gay rights bill, with Senators Lowell Weicker (R-CT) and Daniel Moynihan (D-NY) as cosponsors. The Senate bill was quite different from the House bill, in that it covered private employment and no other area. From a strategic perspective, having a gay rights bill with a more limited scope presumably made sense. While the more limited scope of the Senate bill could have been controversial, this aspect was neither commented upon nor criticized in any of the gay media coverage.

During 1980, Endean focused on building GRNL's political, lobbying, and grassroots capacities.[36] He worked with NGTF to help start the National Convention Project, which worked successfully with local gay Democratic groups to help elect openly gay delegates to the Democratic convention and ultimately resulted in the inclusion of support for a federal gay civil rights bill in the Democratic Party's national platform.[37] Endean also commissioned a research study on the political fate of state and local legislators who had supported gay rights. The study concluded that "gay rights is not the 'kiss of death' which some politicians still believe it to be."[38] Finally, together with the offices of Congressmen Waxman and Weiss, Endean helped organize the first House briefing on the gay civil rights bill in the spring of 1980. Virginia Apuzzo, a member of GRNL's board of directors, spoke at the briefing, as did John Spiegel, former president of the American Psychiatric Association, and Eleanor Smeal, president of NOW.[39]

Early in 1980, Weiss asked Hawkins, chair of the Subcommittee on Employment Opportunities, for a hearing on the gay rights bill, and in September 1980, Hawkins announced that a hearing would be held in San Francisco the following month.[40] Held on October 10, this first congressional hearing on a federal gay civil rights bill was an event. Even the dry pages of the transcript

seem charged with the electricity of the moment. While no congressional opponents attended the hearing, the subcommittee's Republican counsel, Jim
Stephens, peppered witnesses throughout the hearing with questions that reflected the key legal and political concerns of those opposed to the bill.

The hearing opened with testimony from Art Agnos, a member of the
California State Assembly who had been active in the successful effort to pass
a nondiscrimination law based on sexual orientation in San Francisco in 1977.
Agnos pointed out that "the reason we have worked so hard on this issue . . . is
because we believe no request is more legitimate in our society than the freedom to live and work in peace and dignity, free from discrimination." He also
emphasized that empirical research indicated no candidate had ever been defeated because of a vote in favor of gay rights and concluded, "So I think it is a
political myth that this can hurt you in your reelection, and I hope this is carried through to your colleagues in the Congress." Finally, Agnos pointed to the
experience in San Francisco, in which a total of 584 cases had been filed under its ordinance from 1977 to 1979, to conclude that discrimination based on
sexual orientation was indeed live and well.[41]

While these aspects of Agnos's testimony followed the usual line of support for a gay civil rights bill, Agnos's testimony was unusual and refreshing in
its straightforward engagement with issues of character and sin. Agnos noted
that, in light of the separation of church and state, "what we must do as legislators is differentiate between crime and sin." As Agnos explained, "Some religions claim it is a sin to drive a car; still others say it is sinful to eat pork; still
others say it is sinful to drink Coca-Cola, tea, or milk. Yet despite that, no one
is denied the right to work because of that activity." Agnos also challenged the
assertion that being gay comprised a morally fatal flaw as a secular matter. As
Agnos put it, "Sexual orientation does not comprise one's character, it only
states one's sexual relationships with members of one sex or another."[42]

Perhaps given Agnos's candor, it is not surprising that the first question
directed to him by minority counsel Jim Stephens focused on the issue of homosexual marriage. Stephens noted he was concerned about the overall "political agenda" of the gay community, and he quoted from a booklet from the
Libertarian Party that called for the legalization of gay marriage. Stephens
asked whether Agnos could "make a distinction between prohibiting discrimination in the workplace, on the one hand, and continuing, on the other hand,
the historic prohibition against homosexual marriage," and whether Agnos
himself would support a bill that authorized homosexual marriage.

While Stephens's questions were not surprising, Agnos's responses
were. To the latter question, regarding support of legislation to allow gay marriage, Agnos's answer was a simple yes. Moreover, his response indicated his
understanding that the distinction between an antidiscrimination law with regard to employment and housing (for example), and an antidiscrimination law

with regard to marriage, is really more of degree than of kind. As Agnos explained:

> I think that [passing a law authorizing gay marriage] will take the same kind of educational process we are having to deal with now about the mythology that involves gay people in employment. I think that extends into other areas. What gay marriages really mean, as I understand it, is an expression of affection—that is what homosexuality is all about—for someone of the same sex. It is a kind of predetermined, in my judgment, natural preference. I think that marriage is merely the ultimate expression of that kind of love.[43]

How refreshing! And how utterly unusual to hear such a response in a congressional hearing on an employment, housing, and public accommodations antidiscrimination bill. But, of course, how utterly frightening to the politically savvy lobbyists sitting in the audience who wished to present the civil rights bill as a matter of "simple equality," manifesting no view on the moral goodness of this particular "expression of love" and certainly no view on gay marriage. Indeed, as soon as Congressman Ted Weiss could get control of the microphone, he was quick to point out that he was "concerned that when the record is complete, that we will have lost some loose ends which will then become part of the myth considered by some who have not been present." Weiss emphasized that "regardless of one's view of the issue of marriage among gays, it has nothing at all to do with this specific piece of legislation."[44]

Stephens's other principal question to Agnos was one that would continue to be raised by opponents to the bill over the next twenty years: whether it was legitimate to consider discrimination based on homosexuality as analogous to discrimination based on race, since gay people seemed to have clear economic advantages over the general public—in striking contrast to the economic disadvantages that had been suffered by black people. To support his proposition, Stephens quoted a survey from *The Advocate,* a gay magazine, indicating that the average income of a gay person was $23,000, about 50 percent above the national average; that 70 percent of gay people were college graduates; and that projections suggested gays controlled 19 percent of the spendable income in the United States.[45]

Agnos was not prepared, at that moment, to rebut Stephens's statistics—and thus, while evidencing some doubt about the figures, Agnos's basic response was that they were irrelevant to the issue posed by the legislation. As Agnos explained, "Those same people are vulnerable to the kinds of discrimination this legislation would wipe out. My analogy to blacks is not to create the historical comparisons, but the legal comparisons." A short time later, having received a note from David Goodstein, the editor of *The Advocate,* Agnos also clarified that Stephens's statistics came from a survey that had been done *solely* of *Advocate* subscribers. As Agnos explained, "magazine subscribers tend to be more affluent," and hence the statistics are "really reflective of [*The Advocate's*] readership and subscribers rather than the entire gay community."[46]

What is fascinating about this exchange is the durability of this line of questioning during the twenty-five years that Congress has struggled with a gay civil rights bill. The validity of such statistics, developed to encourage companies to market to the gay community, have been rebutted in almost every hearing held on a gay civil rights bill—by Agnos in 1980, and three times by this author in 1994, 1996, and 1997. Economists, such as Lee Badgett, have undertaken studies that directly contradict these survey results with regard to the gay community overall, and a more statistically valid survey done by Yankelovich Partners in 1994 also rebuts these statistics.[47] Moreover, as a matter of common sense, it seems intuitively obvious that gay people will occupy all strata of society—from poor to low income to middle income (these are probably the bulk of the magazine buyers) to wealthy to superwealthy.

Finally, as Agnos's answer clarified (and the answers of advocates throughout the coming years would continue to clarify), even for those gay people who are middle income or affluent, the prospect of discrimination remains terrifying. Indeed, it is often precisely because such individuals have hidden their sexual orientation that they have been permitted to remain in high-paying jobs. As long as the ability to remain in a job—whether a low-paying one or a high-paying one—remains at the whim of an employer who can fire anyone for allegedly being gay, the *legal* need for an antidiscrimination law seems intuitively obvious.

But the key objection to a gay civil rights bill has always been that it endorses immorality, and such objections came to the fore forcefully during the 1980 hearing. The Reverend Charles A. McIlhenny, whose First Orthodox Presbyterian Church in San Francisco had recently enjoyed some prominence because it had fired an organist who was gay,[48] testified that homosexuals were not a "bona fide minority," because while minorities cannot change their color, national origin, or sex, "homosexual behavior can be changed if the individual really desires such change." Thus, according to McIlhenny, not only would gay rights legislation set a "new and dangerous precedent—the protection of a form of behavior as a civil right," it would do so for behavior that is *immoral*. As McIlhenny exclaimed:

> Homosexuality poses a substantial threat to the real meaning of civil rights. It places an unfair burden on those who endeavor to be moral by forcing them to accept such immoral behavior. . . . It is unjust to impose on the citizenship of our country a law which discriminates against morality. The government will now decide what is relevant morality.[49]

The members of Congress listening to McIlhenny chose not to engage this issue directly. Rather, they focused primarily on McIlhenny's comments about the ability of homosexuals to change their behavior. Both Congressman Phillip Burton (D-CA) and Congressman Weiss asked McIlhenny whether it was not equally true that people could change their religion. But McIlhenny brought the moral question to the fore once again by challenging his questioners as to whether they were "equating religion with homosexuality." Neither congressman chose to answer that question.[50]

The remainder of the hearing consisted largely of witnesses testifying in support of the legislation, and Stephens throwing questions at them about morality, various kinds of sexual behavior, and cross-dressing. The hearing closed with an eloquent statement from Gwen Craig, representing the Harvey Milk Gay Democratic Club. Craig reported on a series of compelling instances of employment discrimination against gay people. Craig was also direct about the unique oppression of "the closet," with some echoes of the Gay Is Good motto of the late 1960s:

> We know at times that behind the protestations of disbelief [about the fact of discrimination] that come from those that oppose gay rights is sincere confusion, confusion that results from the issue of the closet. . . . Yes, the closet allows you to hide. But hiding isn't non-discrimination, it is merely a more invidious form of discrimination. . . . Must gay people hide from discrimination? Must we treat our personal lives as if they were dirty little secrets to be cloistered in secrecy, as if our greatest prizes, our personal relationships, were our greatest vices?[51]

The 1980 hearing provided the gay civil rights bill with the type of visibility that provokes response. In late October 1980, Jerry Falwell pronounced his opposition to the gay civil rights bill at a speech at the National Press Club on the grounds that "if it were to pass—and it will not—it would establish homosexuality as a legitimate minority such as Hispanics and blacks." Falwell explained that "one does not choose to be a black or Hispanic, but homosexuality is a lifestyle choice." Steve Endean's response to Falwell, as noted in the *Washington Blade,* was not to argue that gay people *were* a "legitimate minority," but simply to observe that "the reality is that civil rights laws are not designed as a Good Housekeeping seal of approval."[52]

If it seemed essential in October 1980 to people like Endean to downplay any potential radical aspects of the gay civil rights bill (beyond the radical aspect of its very existence), the elections of November 1980 served only to reinforce such concerns. Ronald Reagan won the presidency, and the Republican Party won a majority of the U.S. Senate. There was a perceived rightward turn in the country, with negative campaigns having been waged against several liberals in 1980, and that was taking its toll on gay rights support.[53]

Prospects for either a House or Senate bill in 1981 and 1982 were not particularly promising. Just a week before the Senate bill was introduced in October 1981, the House had voted overwhelmingly to overturn the D.C. Sex Law Reform Act, which would have decriminalized sodomy in the District of Columbia. In the Senate, the gay rights bill was referred to the Senate Labor and Human Resources Committee, chaired by Senator Orrin Hatch, a Republican Mormon senator from Utah. Hatch's committee was also due to take up consideration of the Family Protection Act, a bill that, among other provisions, denied federal funds "to any public or private individual, group, foundation, commission, corporation, association, or other entity for the purpose of advocating, promoting, or suggesting homosexuality, male or female, as a lifestyle."

Gay rights advocates were thus forced to play mostly on the defensive during 1981, as they attempted to counter conservative efforts to condemn homosexuality through governmental action. But Democratic control of the House of the Representatives meant that, in January 1982, another hearing could be held on the bill—this time in an ordinary hearing room in Washington, not at a field hearing in San Francisco.

The hearing was again convened by a sympathetic Gus Hawkins. Unlike in 1980, the Republican counsel did not participate in questioning the witnesses. But tension and drama nevertheless ran high throughout the hearing. The testimony was led off by Jean O'Leary, executive director of Gay Rights Advocates, a board member of GRNL, a former coexecutive director of NGTF, and a former Catholic nun. O'Leary was quick to tell the members what the legislation would do "and more importantly, what it would not do."[54] What the legislation would do, according to O'Leary, was provide individuals the right to work secure in the knowledge that an irrelevant criterion—sexual orientation—would not be used against them. What it would *not* do was impose a quota system or affirmative action, affect the marriage laws in any way, or condone homosexuality. As O'Leary put it:

> H.R. 1454 will not condone homosexuality. Legislation to protect gay people from discrimination will not endorse or approve homosexuality, any more than the inclusion of religion in civil rights legislation indicates support for any particular religion, religion in general, or even an absence of religion. The overwhelming support of religious leaders and organizations, many of whom continue to hold reservations on the lifestyle, speaks clearly to this point.[55]

O'Leary was correct that several religious denominations had endorsed a gay civil rights bill while maintaining reservations about the moral correctness of homosexuality itself. Moreover, GRNL had clearly decided this premise should be a prominent part of its choreographed message on the bill. But O'Leary's analogy to civil rights coverage of religion had some logical flaws. It is true that the prohibition on taking religion into account in employment, as set forth in Title VII of the Civil Rights Act of 1964, does not indicate support for any *particular* religion. But, contrary to O'Leary's assertion, such inclusion could well be seen as indicating support for "religion in general, or even an absence of religion." For example, with Title VII as part of the law, an individual can be proudly religious, or proudly nonreligious, and the law will protect that individual from being fired for either. The same cannot be said for someone who proudly insists he beats his wife. Such people can be fired with impunity by most employers in this country. The absence of a law protecting individuals who beat their spouses certainly seems to indicate a governmental policy of *not* affirmatively supporting such an activity. Thus, while passage of Title VII does not indicate support for any *particular* religion, it *does* indicate governmental support in favor of people who are either religious or not religious.

The logical flaw in O'Leary's analogy was exposed during an exchange between O'Leary and Congresswoman Millicent Fenwick, a feisty Republican from New Jersey with a longtime record of supporting civil rights. O'Leary had directly addressed the issue of gay teachers in her testimony and had asserted that the issue of concern to parents was "teacher misconduct, not sexual orientation." And, as O'Leary explained, "teachers can be fired for misconduct, whether heterosexual or homosexual, with or without this law." Moreover, O'Leary had pointed out, over 90 percent of child molestation occurs between adult males and young girls.[56]

But Congresswoman Fenwick had a different concern about teachers. Fenwick noted she had struggled for years to ensure children had black role models in schools, as teachers and as superintendents. These role models were important "to show children what they could become." Fenwick worried, therefore, about the "proclaimed homosexual." As she put it, "If we could somehow frame this legislation so that this would be an impossibility, that nobody could parade in a small town on Sunday for homosexual rights and expect to teach in the classroom on Monday."

O'Leary was adamant that the legislation could not be modified in the manner Fenwick suggested, but was reduced to the sole argument that she could not believe that what someone did outside the classroom for political reasons should have an impact inside the classroom. To that, Fenwick had a clear and adamant response of her own:

> We were brought up on the Bible. . . . You cannot expect to proclaim something that is called an abomination in the Book we live by, proclaim it, and then expect to be guaranteed your right to teach the children of

that town. . . . It seems that one can in privacy keep one's private life to oneself, and that is what I think the community has a right to ask. This cannot be proclaimed.[57]

Thus, Fenwick did understand that passage of a gay civil rights law would allow gay people to be proud and open about their sexual orientation, just as Title VII allows people to be proud and open about their religion or lack of religion. And yet, because Fenwick could not—as a moral matter—bring herself to equate religion and homosexuality (indeed, it was *because* of religion that she could not make this equation), the logical implications of a gay civil rights law were too much for Fenwick to accept.

Apart from this exchange between Fenwick and O'Leary, and the testimony of Connie Marshner of the National Profamily Coalition that would come later in the hearing, there was little talk during the hearing about the morality or immorality of proclaiming one's homosexuality. The hearing consisted primarily of a solid lineup of support for the bill. Senator Paul Tsongas testified that it made "good economic and business sense not to discriminate," and that the issue was simply one of "equal rights and privacy." Jane Wells-Schooley, representing the National Organization of Women, focused on the diatribes and misrepresentations about the bill emanating from the Christian Voice and Jerry Falwell. Dr. Martin Weinberg, director of the Sex Research Center, testified that "gay people are just as likely as heterosexuals are to be productive, constructive, and well-adjusted members of American society." Dr. Avery Post, president of the United Church of Christ (UCC), repeated the oft-stated view that "one did not need to make an ethical judgment about same-gender relationships" in order to support the bill. And Craig Christensen, a law school dean, attacked the two premises he saw as underlying opposition to the bill: that there is a monolithic gay lifestyle, and that the goal of antidiscrimination law is to "provide a statutory imprimatur for the conduct chosen by the practitioners of that lifestyle."[58]

Opponents of the bill, at least as represented at the hearing by Connie Marshner from the National Profamily Coalition, seemed most frightened by the prospect of out-of-the-closet gays. Marshner noted her organization's members were simply advocating that their "right of privacy be respected: that the homosexual lifestyle not be flaunted in [their] neighborhoods." As Marshner put it, "The public has a right to be protected from the promotion and glamorization of something that is by its nature antithetical to the social order."

According to Marshner, the claim by homosexuals that they are not at fault for their orientation (just as people are not at fault for their ethnic origin or skin color), while "in doubt scientifically," was also "irrelevant to the present debate." Mere orientation was not the issue, Marshner explained, "overt sexual behavior is the issue." And that overt sexual behavior was an issue because it is *immoral*. As Marshner explained:

> Mere homosexual orientation, without overt behavior, has never caused discrimination or disadvantage. . . . Discovered homosexual behavior has caused disadvantage because we in the Judeo-Christian tradition regard such behavior as immoral. . . . Therefore, to ask us to regard militant and practicing homosexuals as a minority is to ask us, the majority, to abandon our morality. It is to ask us to consider "unfairly disadvantaged" a group which our morality commands us to regard as fairly and justly disadvantaged. For the same reason, we will refuse to consider those prone to wife beating [or racism] a legitimate minority. . . . Do not say these comparisons fail, because wife beating and racism are immoral activities, while homosexuality is not. For whether homosexuality is moral is precisely the issue.[59]

As polls had indicated, while a majority of Americans agreed with Marshner that homosexuality was not an activity to be condoned, they disagreed with Marshner by simultaneously believing gay people should not be punished for their conduct through the loss of jobs or housing.[60] To the extent that logic could be discerned in this dual position, it seemed to be that while a majority of the public believed homosexuality to be "immoral," a majority did not concomitantly believe it to be *such* an evil that the government needed actively to repress it, or that gay people needed to be punished through loss of jobs or other discrimination. The divergence between the presumed majority view and Marshner's view was illuminated during the hearing. For example, responding to questions, Marshner compared homosexuality to child slaughter.[61] Polls certainly did not indicate that a majority of the public similarly viewed homosexuality in this extreme manner.

The key challenge for gay rights groups, therefore, was to translate public support of *some* protection for gay people into tangible antidiscrimination legislation. To do so, the gay rights movement would need to forge bonds with the mainstream civil rights community and would need to become more sophisticated in electoral politics. Initial steps toward both these goals were taken in 1982. During that year, Endean formed the Human Rights Campaign Fund, a political action committee (with Endean as its head) operated out of the GRNL office to raise money for candidates sympathetic to gay rights. In addition, in July 1982, GRNL and NGTF applied for admission into the Leadership Conference on Civil Rights (LCCR) and were accepted.[62]

GRNL's and NGTF's admission into LCCR in 1982 marked a significant moment in the effort to establish a solid relationship with the civil rights community. Several factors distinguished this successful effort from NGTF's failed effort to gain admission into LCCR several years earlier. As noted above, the civil rights community had not initially viewed gay civil rights as part of its mandate. Moreover, some of the leading organizations in LCCR either had strong institutional objections to homosexuality (such as the U.S. Catholic Conference) or had leaders who were unsympathetic to gay rights (such as George Meany of the AFL-CIO). To overcome the expected opposition from such groups, and to enlist the support of other groups on LCCR's Executive Committee, would require a lengthy period of working with those other groups on a range of civil rights issues. That "bonding period" had clearly not happened by 1977 when NGTF first applied for admission to LCCR.

By 1982, by contrast, the necessary groundwork had been laid through Endean's coalition work with LCCR on various non-gay-related civil rights issues, such as the campaign to extend the Voting Rights Act and the effort to block approval of one of President Reagan's nominations to the U.S. Civil Rights Commission.[63] Moreover, the leadership of some of the influential groups that had blocked NGTF's earlier admission had changed; of particular importance, George Meany had been replaced by Lane Kirkland as head of the AFL-CIO, and the labor organization was beginning to move toward a pro-gay-rights position. Finally, Ralph Neas, the relatively new executive director of LCCR, was ready to be helpful to GRNL and NGTF in navigating the political mazes of LCCR. Neas helped contrive a strategy that placed some restrictions on GRNL and NGTF as conditions of their admission. As Neas recalled over ten years later:

> When gays first joined, we had to discuss strategy and work out a compromise. We agreed they would not ask LCCR to take a position in regards to a gay civil rights bill. The reasoning was to get the gay organization in first, then build bridges of understanding, give the other organizations a chance to see that gays were talking about fundamental civil rights. They had to compromise in the short term to get long-term support.[64]

By the end of 1982, things were looking good for the gay civil rights bill. A record number of sixty members in the House of Representatives had cosponsored the bill, HRCF had raised $500,000 and had contributed $150,000 directly to candidates in the 1982 elections, and the results of those elections were positive for continuing work on a gay rights bill. All House and Senate cosponsors of the gay civil rights bill who ran for reelection were successful, and the records of some of the newly elected members indicated that as many as seventy-five cosponsors could be enlisted for the bill in the upcoming Congress.[65]

But by the end of 1983, everything looked different. GRNL was in chaos,

Endean had resigned as executive director, and work on the gay civil rights bill had taken a backseat to the emerging, intense fight against AIDS led by a reinvigorated and politically sophisticated Washington office of NGTF. The next ten years would see an explosion of activity on the AIDS front, with fights against anti-AIDS amendments being waged alongside affirmative efforts to fight the epidemic with both money and positive policies. New AIDS organizations and coalitions would form, GRNL would merge with HRCF, and NGTF (soon to become NGLTF) would continue to be a leading voice on AIDS until 1989. Not until 1991 would serious efforts once again be taken to move a gay civil rights bill forward in the U.S. Congress.

III. 1983–90: THE WANE OF GAY CIVIL RIGHTS AND THE RISE OF THE FIGHT AGAINST AIDS

The year 1983 started much as any other year for the gay civil rights bill. First in January, and then again in April, Weiss introduced the gay civil rights bill—the second time with fifty-nine cosponsors. The Senate bill, again limited solely to employment, was introduced by Senator Tsongas with four Senate cosponsors in February 1983. In a *Washington Blade* story on the House and Senate bills, Endean was optimistic about obtaining a record number of supporters for both bills.[66] Life seemed to be proceeding on track.

But by early 1983, reports had begun to surface that GRNL had accumulated a mounting debt and that HRCF had virtually no funds with which to start working on the 1984 election cycle. Endean came under increasing attack for his financial and management capacities and was forced to resign as executive director of HRCF.[67] But the deeper conflict concerning Endean revolved around his lobbying efforts on the emerging AIDS epidemic. By 1982, Virginia Apuzzo had become executive director of NGTF, and in 1983 she hired Jeff Levi to be the director of its Washington office. Together with Tim Westmoreland, a staff person for Congressman Henry Waxman, Levi and Apuzzo began to put together a detailed and sophisticated response to the problem of underfunding for AIDS research and treatment. This response included creating relationships with key individuals in the Reagan administration and on the Hill, developing a sophisticated knowledge of what was necessary to advance research and treatment in the AIDS arena, and establishing NGTF as a credible and respected source for information on AIDS policy.[68]

Gay press reports at the time began to fault Endean and GRNL for not being similarly focused on and sophisticated about the lobbying required for combating the AIDS epidemic. As a *Washington Blade* story several years later noted:

Critics accused Endean of failing to grasp the importance of the worsening AIDS epidemic. The critics noted that GRNL's lobbying operation, while geared for promoting a gay rights bill, failed to set up a mechanism for monitoring and influencing Congress's highly complex appropriations process, which was involved in approving funds for AIDS programs.[69]

Larry Bush, a writer for *The Advocate,* was a careful observer and reporter of the strategic battles surrounding AIDS funding.[70] He reported, in some detail, on the differences in approach and strategy with regard to AIDS lobbying that were apparent between GRNL and NGTF. For example, at a June 1983 meeting of the U.S. Conference of Mayors, GRNL testified before the mayors and asked them to endorse a proposal for a $50-million AIDS budget for 1984. This was significantly lower than the $100-million figure NGTF was lobbying for on the Hill and with the administration. GRNL's deputy director noted in his testimony that "while more than this [$50 million] is clearly needed, and some groups may ask for $100 or $200 million, GRNL feels that in terms of political realities on Capitol Hill, $50 million is a reasonable, winnable figure."[71]

While it is always important to be politically reasonable, what might have been politically reasonable for the substance of a gay civil rights bill might not necessarily have been politically reasonable in an appropriations fight over AIDS funding. Moreover, GRNL had declined a request from NGTF for an advance strategy discussion on the presentation (Jeff Levi from NGTF had testified before the mayors as well), had not discussed its budget target figure with other gay groups, and had arrived at its proposed figure by simply doubling the existing federal budget amount, rather than consulting with AIDS groups and medical researchers.[72] In fights over appropriation figures, a united front from affected interest groups is often critical to success on Capitol Hill. Hence, Endean's and GRNL's independent and sometimes ill-informed positions on AIDS were beginning to rankle observers of the federal legislative scene.

In June 1983, David Goodstein, publisher of *The Advocate,* printed an editorial calling for Endean to resign from GRNL. Goodstein noted that he had "lost confidence" in Endean's capacity to manage the organization professionally, to plan a political agenda for the 1984 elections, and to address effectively current problems regarding AIDS. As Goodstein put it, "Events have moved faster than [Endean's] ability to handle them," and "what sufficed in 1981 will not do now."[73]

Following four months of controversy, including public criticism and mounting private criticism by influential gay activists, Endean announced in October 1983 that he would resign as executive director of GRNL.[74] Up until his last days at GRNL, however, Endean continued to focus primarily on gathering support for the gay civil rights bill. Indeed, Endean noted to the press that his priorities during the transition period before his departure were to get GRNL back in shape financially, continue its programs on Capitol Hill, and seek additional cosponsors for the gay civil rights bill. For example, during his last week on the job in January 1984, Endean traveled to Atlanta to lobby a congressman to cosponsor the gay civil rights bill and helped draft a "Dear Colleague" letter seeking support for the bill.[75]

While presidential primary politics in 1983 and 1984 gave the gay civil rights bill its customary preelection boost, with Democratic nominee contenders Senator Fritz Hollings, former vice president Walter Mondale, and Senator Gary Hart all endorsing the bill,[76] the focus of gay groups such as NGTF was not primarily on passage of a gay civil rights bill. Throughout 1984 and 1985, NGTF (which became NGLTF in 1986) was the premier gay rights group engaged in Washington lobbying, and under Jeff Levi's leadership, it focused its energies primarily on getting increased funding for AIDS research and treatment—not on seeking passage of a gay civil rights bill. Starting in 1986, both NGTF and HRCF (which had absorbed GRNL in 1985 as its lobbying arm) focused their collective energies on defeating the spate of anti-AIDS amendments that were beginning to be offered regularly in both the Senate and the House of Representatives. Moreover, both NGLTF and HRCF continued to spend energy and resources seeking increased funding for AIDS research, treatment, and prevention, and the passage of legislation that would provide confidentiality and antidiscrimination protection for people with HIV/AIDS.

I entered this political scene in September 1987, as the legislative research director for AIDS Action Council, one of the new groups that had sprung up to address the challenges of the AIDS epidemic.[77] Two weeks into the job, I got my first taste of how anti-AIDS and antigay amendments were intertwined on Capitol Hill in the late 1980s. Senator Jesse Helms offered an amendment to an appropriations bill for the Department of Health and Human Services (HHS) (which included millions of dollars for AIDS testing and counseling) providing that none of the funds could be used for AIDS educational materials if they "directly or indirectly promoted or encouraged homosexuality." The amendment passed by a vote of 94–2, with only Senators Moynihan and Weicker voting against the provision.[78] The best my colleagues and I could do that year was to get the word *indirectly* dropped from the provision when the House and Senate met in conference on the bill.

The next year, we were better prepared for the HHS appropriations bill. In one of my first forays into the arena I would come to call "legislative lawyering,"[79] I drafted an amendment to be offered *before* Senator Helms offered his amendment again. This amendment provided that no federal funds could be used for AIDS educational materials that were *designed* to promote or encourage homosexuality *or* heterosexuality.[80] This provision gave members of

Congress the political cover they needed to vote for a provision that sounded tough on homosexuality, but was, in practice, an evenhanded provision designed to have a less detrimental effect on the development of AIDS educational materials.

While there was little activity on passage of a gay civil rights bill through the late 1980s, the years from 1987 to 1990 did see a significant rise in legislative activity focused on establishing antidiscrimination protection for people with disabilities, including people with HIV/AIDS. These efforts gave those opposed to antidiscrimination protection on the basis of HIV status (and/or on the basis of sexual orientation) a ready catalyst for advancing amendments that would exclude protection for such individuals. AIDS and gay rights advocates were thus kept busy fighting off such amendments, as well as helping to pass the underlying legislation.

Antidiscrimination protection for people with HIV/AIDS in the 1980s was derived from laws that protected people with disabilities generally. In February 1987, the Supreme Court had ruled that a teacher with tuberculosis was protected from discrimination under Section 504 of the Rehabilitation Act, a law that prohibited discrimination based on handicap by recipients of federal financial assistance.[81] Although the case concerned tuberculosis, the media trumpeted the fact that people with AIDS would similarly be protected under the law. Two days after the Supreme Court handed down its decision, Senators Robert Dole (R-KS) and William Armstrong (R-CO) introduced a bill to exclude individuals with "contagious diseases" from the protection of Section 504.[82]

At around the same time, the Senate was considering legislation to amend Section 504 and three other civil rights laws that applied to recipients of federal funds. This bill, the Civil Rights Restoration Act of 1987 (CRRA), was designed to overturn a restrictive Supreme Court ruling on the scope of such laws,[83] and was a high priority for the mainstream civil rights community, led by LCCR. When the Civil Rights Restoration Act was considered by the Senate Labor and Human Resources Committee, Senator Gordon Humphrey (R-NH) offered an amendment designed to exclude people with AIDS from the protection of Section 504.[84] Although that provision failed easily in committee, it was not clear to gay rights and AIDS advocates (including me) that it would similarly fail easily on the Senate floor. Hence, in another foray into legislative lawyering, we drafted a provision excluding only those individuals with contagious diseases or infections who posed a "direct threat" to others.[85] Again, we managed to provide political cover for members of Congress, while drafting a provision that ensured no legal harm to people with HIV/AIDS, who would not meet the required legal standard of posing a "direct threat."

While it was important, of course, to achieve the successful outcome of maintaining protection for people with HIV/AIDS in a civil rights law, the coalition effort involved in winning that fight was itself of significant, long-term importance. Three coalitions converged in the fight on the Civil Rights Restoration Act: the National Organizations Responding to AIDS (NORA), a coalition of consumer and provider groups devoted to AIDS policy issues;[86] the Civil Rights Task Force of the Consortium for Citizens with Disabilities (CCD), a coalition of disability groups; and the Leadership Conference of Civil Rights (LCCR), the lead coalition in Washington on civil rights issues. All three coalitions participated in the lobbying effort to defeat an exclusion of people with HIV/AIDS from the law. This joint effort helped solidify political connections between the primary AIDS and gay rights groups of the time (AIDS Action Council, NGLTF, HRCF, and the ACLU's AIDS and Lesbian and Gay Rights Projects) and the mainstream disability and civil rights organizations—CCD and LCCR.

This joint effort of AIDS and gay rights groups with disability and civil rights groups occurred as well during the following two years, during passage of the Fair Housing Amendments Act of 1988 and the Americans with Disabilities Act of 1990. The Fair Housing Amendments Act prohibited discrimination on the basis of disability in the sale or rental of private housing. Again, attempts were made to exclude people with HIV and AIDS from the protection of the new law, and again, those attempts were defeated through joint coalition efforts.[87] By the time disability and civil rights groups began working for passage of the Americans with Disabilities Act, a bill that would prohibit discrimination in private employment and private businesses on the basis of disability, the mainstream civil rights and disability coalitions were firmly in support of covering people with HIV/AIDS under a disability civil rights law. Indeed, I served as the chief legislative lawyer on the ADA for the overall CCD coalition, while working as a legislative counsel for the ACLU's AIDS Project. A difficult challenge on the ADA arose when an amendment passed on the House floor that excluded people with contagious diseases (including people with HIV/AIDS) solely from food handling jobs.[88] Yet, even with that more targeted amendment, the disability and civil rights groups remained firmly in support of people with HIV/AIDS, even when that position threatened passage of the ADA itself. Through another legislative-lawyering maneuver, we neutralized that amendment, and the ADA became law in 1990.[89]

The latter half of the 1980s was thus a busy time for gay rights groups. Their energy and resources, however, were not directed at advancing a gay civil rights bill. Rather, they were devoted to seeking affirmative responses to the AIDS epidemic, through passage of laws such as the Ryan White CARE Act and the ADA, and to warding off challenges and attacks arising from the AIDS epidemic. The gay civil rights bill itself continued to be introduced in each new congressional session from 1985 to 1990, with the House bill continuing to be an omnibus bill covering many areas, and the Senate bill a more targeted bill focused on employment. While HRCF and NGLTF continued to seek and obtain additional cosponsors of the bill during this time, no hearings were held on the bill and there were no significant increases in the number of cosponsors.[90] But the fact that HRCF and NGLTF fought anti-AIDS and antigay attacks together with the civil rights and disability communities during this period helped the gay rights groups solidify their political relationship with the mainstream civil rights community. These relationships would play an essential role in convincing that community to finally embrace the goal of civil rights for gay men and lesbians.

IV. 1991–99: THE CIVIL RIGHTS COMMUNITY ENGAGES: THE FINAL PUSH?

By 1991, federal legislative activity on AIDS and disability rights had settled into a relatively manageable routine. The Americans with Disabilities Act had become law, and efforts in that area shifted to enforcement. The Ryan White CARE Act had passed as well, and those efforts also shifted to funding and implementation. While anti-AIDS amendments periodically surfaced on annual funding bills, responses to such amendments now followed a more predictable pattern. We had developed the content of those responses through legislative lawyering, and we had established lobbying mechanisms for carrying out those responses through the staffs of HRCF and NGLTF.

The time was ripe, therefore, for the focus to shift back to gay rights. The election of President Bill Clinton in 1992 gave that focus particular momentum and energy. Clinton had explicitly stated his strong support for gay and lesbian rights during the campaign, and the gay community was energized and exhilarated by his victory. But instead of a forceful push on a federal gay civil rights bill in 1993, the focus came to rest on lifting the ban on the service of gay men and lesbians in the military.

In a sense, the focus on the military ban in 1993 was a fluke. While campaigning, Clinton had promised to lift the ban, and shortly after his election, he reaffirmed that promise. Although the powerful chair of the Senate Armed Services Committee, Senator Sam Nunn (D-GA), had immediately announced his opposition to lifting the ban, both gay rights organizations and individual gay friends of Clinton's encouraged him to move forward. The fight to lift the military ban would not only consume time and resources that would otherwise have been devoted to work on the gay civil rights bill, but the defeat of that effort in July 1993 would ultimately affect the substance of the gay civil rights bill itself.

A. The Gay Military Ban Campaign and a New Beginning at LCCR

In the fall of 1992, I was beginning my second year as a visiting professor at the Georgetown University Law Center in Washington, D.C. With passage of the ADA in 1990, I had come to Georgetown to coauthor a book on disability law and to teach classes on gay rights, disability rights, and legislation. But in the spring of 1993, I found myself in the midst of the campaign to lift the military ban on gay men and lesbians.

I had been part of Clinton's transition team for the Department of Justice in December 1992 and had written an internal memo counseling that Clinton not immediately move forward on lifting the military ban. Given Senator Nunn's opposition, I had suggested that Clinton instead establish a one-year interagency task force to explore the issue. That would allow the administration to get through its first year without a congressional vote on the military ban and would allow the relevant political organizations time to develop a coherent lobbying strategy.

Events were moving too fast for any memo buried in the bowels of a transition plan to change, however, and work moved forward on helping the president in his stated desire to lift the ban. A new short-term organization, the Campaign for Military Service (CMS), was created in January 1993 solely to assist the president in his effort. Tom Stoddard became the volunteer executive director of the group, and I became the consultant legal director.

During the following six months, gay rights activists in Washington were consumed with research, drafting, lobbying, and negotiating on the gay military ban. Most of the cards were stacked against our effort from the beginning. With the key Democratic congressional player, Senator Sam Nunn, orchestrating the opposition, with a White House never fully engaged in pushing a truly acceptable compromise on the issue, and with limited lobbying capacity on the part of the gay rights organizations (exacerbated by tensions between CMS, an upstart new organization, and the long-term organizations of HRCF and NGLTF), it is no wonder that the effort finally failed. In my vision of an effective legislative advocacy effort, a campaign needs a visionary strategist, persistent lobbyists, a creative legislative lawyer, a talented media director, and grounded grassroots organizers.[91] CMS and the other gay rights organizations had some of these components in 1993, but not all. And one needs all of them to win.

The effort to lift the gay military ban came to a dismal end in July 1993 when President Clinton announced the Don't Ask, Don't Tell, Don't Pursue policy. Although presented as a compromise, the policy was actually a reaffirmation of the current ban. Matters took an even worse turn when the ban, which had always been solely an administrative policy, was codified by Congress in a defense bill in the summer of 1993.

Although the campaign to lift the military ban ultimately failed, and although momentum for gay rights on Capitol Hill was seriously affected by its defeat, 1992 and 1993 were critically important years for the development of a gay civil rights bill. But most of that development took place behind the scenes, in strategy sessions and drafting meetings.

In the summer of 1992, before the gay military ban campaign was even a glimmer in anyone's eye, Patrisha Wright, a lobbyist for the Disability Rights Education and Defense Fund and the lead strategist on the ADA, and Tim McFeeley, then executive director of HRCF, met with Ralph Neas, executive director of LCCR, to discuss the possibility of LCCR supporting a gay civil rights bill. When HRCF and NGLTF had been admitted to LCCR in 1982, the deal had been struck that LCCR would not be asked to take a position on gay rights legislation right away. But ten years had passed, and the gay rights groups had worked side by side with LCCR on a range of other civil rights issues during that time. Wright and McFeeley felt the time was right to raise the question of LCCR support.

Neas was open to raising the question of supporting gay rights legislation with LCCR's twenty-three-member Executive Committee, but wanted time to prepare the groundwork for an affirmative answer to the question. All decisions of the Executive Committee are made by consensus, and so the next several months witnessed a series of careful conversations with key players on the committee. The end result was a classic incrementalist strategy—classic because it so often works so well. At its November 1992 meeting, the Executive Committee voted to add "supporting gay and lesbian antidiscrimination legislation" to its list of new issue priorities, but explicitly noted that the "specific legislative vehicle" for the issue would be "determined later." The Executive Committee also voted to establish a new LCCR steering committee that would be responsible for drafting the proposed "gay and lesbian antidiscrimination legislation."[92]

The Executive Committee vote was brilliant. It allowed LCCR to begin focusing on a gay civil rights bill without committing the organization to any particular piece of legislation. This provided those LCCR members that might have had some concern with endorsing such legislation, such as the U.S. Catholic Conference, the sense that no final vote to endorse legislation had yet been taken. While that day of reckoning would come, there would be time to build bonds and create trust during the drafting period.

The LCCR Executive Committee's vote in the fall of 1992 changed the legal landscape of the gay civil rights bill in one other dramatic way: it ensured, for the first time in the bill's history, that gay rights lawyers and mainstream civil rights lawyers would come together to develop the content of the bill. This partnership would ultimately affect every provision in the bill, but would also ultimately result in the broadest range of support a gay rights bill had ever garnered.

B. Drafting a New Gay Rights Bill

Late one night in December 1992, I received a call from Tim McFeeley. Would I be willing, McFeeley asked, to work as HRCF's consultant in helping to draft a gay civil rights bill with the LCCR steering committee? The committee had met once or twice already, and McFeeley wanted HRCF to have a strong legal presence at those meetings. The committee was meeting again the next day, and McFeeley wanted to know how quickly I could start.

I jumped at the chance to be involved. I had spent three years researching, drafting, and negotiating the Americans with Disabilities Act and had developed the concept of "legislative lawyering" based on that experience. I was more than happy to turn that knowledge now to the development of a gay civil rights bill. But I hated going to meetings that did not have materials available to move a meeting forward productively. I had seen the previous gay civil rights bills and knew from my experience with the ADA that the civil rights community would never accept legislation that amended existing civil rights laws. That approach was simply too dangerous as it exposed existing civil rights laws to unfriendly changes, and it was the reason the ADA had been written as a freestanding piece of legislation.

The previous spring, I had written a broad gay civil rights bill as an exam for my legislation class. I had used the ADA as a template and then inserted a number of mistakes into the legislation as the basis for my exam questions. I pulled up the old exam, fixed the mistakes, and brought copies of a proposed omnibus gay civil rights bill to the LCCR drafting session the next day. Because no one else in the group had yet offered legislative language to begin the discussion, the text from the old exam became the basis for our deliberations.

The proposed bill we were considering covered most of the same areas that had been covered in previous bills: employment, housing, federally funded programs, and public facilities. These areas were identical to those covered in the Civil Rights Acts of 1964 and 1968, but simply described the areas directly instead of through an amendment. In the area of public accommodations, the bill explicitly followed the ADA, rather than the Civil Rights Act of 1964, because the ADA's coverage of private businesses was much broader.

During the early part of 1993, the time and resources demanded by the gay military ban fight made it difficult for the gay rights advocates on the LCCR drafting committee to find time to work on the omnibus civil rights bill. Nevertheless, work on the bill proceeded sporadically, and some of the key issues that would need to be resolved began to surface. Key among these were the type of exemption for religious organizations the bill would include, how the bill would address health benefits for same-sex partners in employment settings, and how the legislation would deal with issues of affirmative action, statistical disparities, and quotas. Other issues that would later come to dominate discussions on the bill were given short shrift. For example, in one early meeting, the decision was made not to include marital status or transgendered status as prohibited grounds for discrimination. While the group felt such discrimination was wrong, the LCCR mandate had been to develop legislation that dealt with "gay and lesbian discrimination" and the group chose to adhere strictly to that mandate.

Work on the omnibus civil rights bill heated up during one month in 1993. A major gay and lesbian march on Washington had been planned for April 1993, and gay rights advocates wanted the bill to be introduced prior to the march. Jeff Blattner and Michael Iskowitz, Senator Kennedy's staff people, began to work closely with the LCCR drafting committee members in March 1993 to try to finalize the bill's substance. But major issues remained in contention. About two weeks before the march, the drafting committee finally concluded it would not be possible to get a bill ready in time. With the pressure of the march lifted, the drafting sessions were again put on a back burner.[93] The gay rights advocates from the committee returned our full focus to the gay military ban fight, where it remained until the fall of 1993 when the final sad vote on codifying the gay military ban was taken.

C. The Birth of the Employment Non-Discrimination Act

By the fall of 1993, prospects for a broad gay civil rights bill did not look good. Indeed, it was unclear what was feasible to achieve at all on the federal legislative front. Washington politics are fickle. If an issue is perceived to "have momentum," more people will support it; conversely, if an issue is perceived to have "lost momentum," people who should support the issue will desert it.

It is fair to say that gay rights was not perceived, in the fall of 1993, as having *any* momentum on Capitol Hill. The loss of the gay military ban had weakened the perceived political power of the gay rights organizations. Given the reality of the political situation, many gay rights advocates (including me and HRCF's newly hired political director, Daniel Zingale) felt the omnibus gay civil rights bill was no longer a viable proposal to present to LCCR and to members of Congress. Rather than gathering any momentum, that bill would likely sink upon introduction.

So the painful decision was made to excise all portions of the omnibus bill other than the employment section. Polls had consistently indicated the highest level of public support for employment nondiscrimination, and presenting a narrowly targeted bill that had the greatest public support would be seen as pragmatic and welcome by our friends on Capitol Hill.[94]

The first six months of 1994 was thus an active period of research, drafting, phone calls, meetings, and negotiations on a range of issues in an employment-only gay rights bill. A broad religious exemption was finally agreed to, although the for-profit, taxable activities of a religious organization remained covered under the bill. The bill explicitly stated that "quotas" and "preferential treatment" based on sexual orientation would not be allowed under the law. The bill also disallowed any "disparate impact" claims. In other words, a claim could not be based on statistical disparities between the number of gay people in a particular workplace and the number of gay people generally. Finally, the bill avoided two potential areas of serious conflict: it chose not to address the issue of benefits for same-sex partners, and it excluded the military from its coverage.

And the bill finally got a name sometime in May 1994. We had been calling the omnibus gay civil rights bill the Civil Rights Act of 1993, based on the Civil Rights Act of 1991 that had been most recently passed by Congress. But we now wanted the title to make clear the more limited scope of the proposed bill. After several attempts, we settled on the Employment Non-Discrimination Act, with the acronym ENDA.[95]

There was still the important issue of LCCR endorsement. While the broad religious exemption was critical to obtaining that endorsement, some LCCR members were still not comfortable with supporting the legislation. Ralph Neas led the way in negotiating with these organizations a statement of LCCR endorsement with which they felt comfortable. Used a few times in LCCR's history, this type of endorsement ultimately made clear that while a majority of LCCR members supported the legislation, the endorsement could not be presumed to reflect the position of every one of the 185 organizational members of LCCR.[96]

The press conference at which ENDA was introduced, in June 1994, was an electrifying moment. For the first time in history, the broad range of the civil rights community stood with gay rights advocates to proclaim their endorsement of a nondiscrimination bill based on sexual orientation. As Coretta Scott King proclaimed eloquently during the press conference:

> I support the Employment Non-Discrimination Act of 1994 because I believe that freedom and justice cannot be parceled out in pieces to suit political convenience. As my husband, Martin Luther King Jr., said, "Injustice anywhere is a threat to justice everywhere." On another occasion he said, "I have worked too long and hard against segregated public accommodations to segregate my moral concern. Justice is indivisible." Like Martin, I don't believe you can stand for freedom for one group of people and deny it to others.[97]

The press conference was notable not only for the range of mainstream civil rights support on display, but for the number of senators and members of the House of Representatives who had signed on to the bill as original cosponsors. The theory that a more limited, targeted piece of legislation, with many significant concessions made early in the process, would garner a broader range of support and momentum had proven true. In June 1994, ENDA was introduced by Senators Edward Kennedy (D-MA) and John Chafee (R-RI) with twenty-eight cosponsoring senators, and by Representatives Gerry Studds (D-MA), Barney Frank (D-MA), and Connie Morella (R-MD) with 107 cosponsors. This was the highest number of cosponsors that had ever been achieved for a gay civil rights bill upon introduction.

One month after the press conference, Senator Kennedy held a hearing on ENDA in the Senate Labor and Human Resources Committee. Because none of the gay rights advocates working on ENDA in 1994 had been present at the hearings in either 1980 or 1982, a sense of historic momentum was in the air. Indeed, it was historic in the sense that this was the first time a hearing had been held on a gay civil rights bill that had a realistic chance of passage.

The hearing was marked by moments of passion, rationality, law, and simple heroism. People had lined the hallways for several hours before the hearing in an effort to ensure a spot in the hearing room. A group of African-American men wearing orange stickers that proclaimed "There is no comparison" had arrived with antigay activist Lou Sheldon. When it became clear the hearing room had already filled up and this group would not be able to enter, one of the Republican staff members led the group into the hearing room through a staff entrance, and the group lined the entire back wall during the hearing.

But supporters of ENDA clearly outnumbered opponents, both in the hearing room and on the witness list. As always occurs in Congress, the majority party controls the substance of the hearing. Because Senator Kennedy was the Chair of the Labor and Human Resources Committee, and the chief sponsor of ENDA, it was no surprise that most of the hearing was dominated by supporters of the legislation. This time, the hearing started out with compelling, personal cases of discrimination. Cheryl Summerville, her voice cracking at times, recounted how she had been fired by Cracker Barrel Old Country Store in Douglasville, Georgia, after the chairman of Cracker Barrel sent a memo directing the firing of all employees "whose sexual preference fails to demonstrate normal heterosexual values." Ernest Dillon recounted how he had been subjected to antigay harassment, and ultimately beaten, by coworkers at his post office job. Dillon explained he had sued under Title VII of the Civil Rights Act, only to be told by the Sixth Circuit Court of Appeals that "these actions, although cruel, are not made illegal by Title VII."[98]

The hearing then moved to a steady drumbeat of support for the legislation by civil rights leaders and business leaders. Justin Dart Jr., the Republican chairman of President George Bush's Committee on Employment of People with Disabilities, testified against "acquiescing in vicious discrimination against American citizens because you disagree with their personal views and activities, activities which in no way infringe on the rights of others." Warren Phillips, the chief executive officer of Dow Jones and Company, and publisher of *The Wall Street Journal* for fifteen years, testified that while many businesses had voluntarily adopted policies of nondiscrimination based on sexual orientation because it made good business sense, the lack of explicit legal protection for gay men and lesbians "leaves a gaping hole in America's commitment to equal opportunity and is an invitation to the perpetuation of prejudice and stereotypes." His views were echoed by Steve Coulter, vice president of Pacific Bell. Finally, Richard Womack, director of civil rights for the AFL-CIO, reaffirmed the unions' support for employment nondiscrimination legislation, noting that "gay and lesbian Americans do not want to be ushered in secretly through the servants' entrance; they want to walk through the front door."[99]

The hearing concluded with a legal panel that included the only opponents to the legislation, Joseph Broadus from George Mason School of Law and Robert Knight from the Family Research Council. I was also on that panel, representing LCCR, and had the job of answering the opponents' objections. Broadus's main claim was that the bill would prohibit employers from firing employees who engaged in bizarre sexual activity (on or off the job) or those who engaged in child molestation.[100] Broadus also claimed the bill would ultimately require employers to adopt quotas based on sexual orientation.

In his written testimony, Broadus used the old marketing statistics to claim that gay people were "an elite" who had no need of special civil rights legislation. During one of the more emotionally charged moments of the hearing, Senator Paul Wellstone (D-MN) challenged Broadus's focus on the economic status of gay people, noting that, as a Jew, he had a real problem with that approach because "that is precisely the kind of argument that was made [about Jewish people] in Germany." Broadus's only response was that Congress had to answer the "basic question of whether . . . engaging in various kinds of sexual acts . . . reflects upon character."[101]

Robert Knight's testimony was more coherent than Broadus's, but was premised on the same moral concerns. As Knight explained, his organization saw ENDA "as less about tolerance than about the federal government forcing acceptance of homosexuality on tens of millions of unwilling Americans." As Knight clearly and correctly explained, "The bill essentially takes away the right of employers to decline to hire or promote someone who openly acknowledges . . . indulging in behavior that the employer or the employer's customers find immoral, unhealthy, and destructive to individuals, families, and societies."[102]

My testimony did not directly engage either opponent on their moral assessments of homosexuality. Rather, my testimony systematically answered all the other objections raised by Broadus and Knight. I explained the methodological flaws in studies used by opponents to claim that gay people are an economic elite; I pointed out that a legislative policy decision to ban discrimination need not depend on a "hierarchy of oppression" (that is, have gay people suffered more than African-Americans), but rather should depend on whether evidence exists that employment discrimination is occurring based on a characteristic that has no relevance to job performance (I had lengthy appendices demonstrating this fact); and finally, I noted that employees could certainly be disciplined for bizarre or disruptive sexual acts under ENDA, as long as both gay and straight employees were similarly disciplined for similar sexual acts.

On the moral question of homosexuality, I never explicitly agreed with Knight that passage of ENDA reflects a governmental policy that "gay is good," and that *because* "gay is good" employers may not use sexual orientation as grounds for employment discrimination. But I also refrained from asserting that passage of ENDA could not possibly be seen as an endorsement of homosexuality, a statement supporters of the gay civil rights bill repeated often in 1980 and 1982. Instead, I stayed with the tried-and-true rhetoric of tolerance and liberalism. Thus, in response to a question from Senator Nancy Kassebaum about whether ENDA was unique and dangerous because it would be the first civil rights law to protect "behavior," I first explained that civil rights law already protected religious behavior. But instead of then pushing the point that religious behavior and gay sexual behavior are *equally morally neutral*, I retreated to endorsing the schizophrenic position consistently manifested in public opinion polls. I explained that "a lot of people in America . . . do not want their sons and daughters to be gay. A lot of them do not like their behaviors. But they think it is wrong for people to be fired from their jobs. And that is really all that we are saying with this piece of legislation."[103]

The 1994 hearing on ENDA felt momentous to gay civil rights advocates. For the first time, we were working hand in hand with the general civil rights community, we had an administration that had conveyed its support for the bill, and we seemed to be in striking distance of a majority of the House and sixty senators (enough to block a filibuster). But everything changed in November 1994. In a surprising election result, the Democratic Party lost control of both the House of Representatives and the Senate. This transfer of power was particularly devastating for ENDA's prospects in the House, where strict procedural rules make it practically impossible for any legislation ever to be considered by the full body without the approval of the leadership of the party in power.

The two years following the Republican congressional takeover in 1994 were hard years for progressive organizations generally. The legislation that made up the Contract with America, including welfare reform, occupied much of Congress's time. Gay and civil rights organizations in Washington again found themselves fighting an array of antigay and anti-AIDS amendments that now found more fertile legislative ground in which to flourish.[104] And on ENDA, a new internal war was being waged. Members of the transgender community were outraged when ENDA was introduced in 1994 without explicitly providing employment protection to individuals whose birth sex did not match their internal feelings of gender identity. Over the previous year, the transgender community had become politicized over this issue and had waged a mini-war against HRCF, protesting through the Internet and through public demonstrations their exclusion from ENDA.

Early in 1995, a summit meeting was held between HRCF and representatives of the transgender community to see if a resolution on the issue could be reached. Although HRCF refused to agree that ENDA would include protection based on gender identity when it was reintroduced, HRCF did agree not to oppose any amendment that added such protection were such an amendment to be offered. HRCF also agreed that I, as their legal consultant, could work with members of the transgender community to help develop such an amendment. Because ENDA needed little legislative-lawyering work by that point, I spent the majority of 1995 meeting with several transgender advocates to develop such an amendment.

With Congress held so tightly in the Republican grasp during this time, it was hard to do any proactive work on ENDA. After much effort, a hearing was convened in June 1996 by Congressman Peter Torkildsen, the Republican chairman of the Subcommittee on Government Programs of the House Small Business Committee. Although the subcommittee could barely claim jurisdiction over ENDA, Torkildsen was the one sympathetic Republican who could be found to hold a hearing. Once again, the hearing was compelling because of individual cases of discrimination recounted by five separate witnesses.[105] It was also memorable because the ranking Democrat on the subcommittee, Congressman Glenn Poshard, was unusually direct in exposing his personal, moral struggle about voting for ENDA. Poshard noted that, as a Christian, he believed that the "homosexual lifestyle is essentially unacceptable," and yet also that he must "do justice." But to Poshard, doing justice by voting for ENDA created a significant moral dilemma: "If we pass a law preventing discrimination against homosexuals in the workplace, does this mean then that we as a society give more legitimacy to the practice of the lifestyle?"

I had recently written an article on sexual orientation, law, and morality and had briefly explored in that piece the manner in which advocates such as myself shrank from answering such questions about ENDA.[106] But, although I testified that day at the House hearing and acknowledged the force of Poshard's question, I did not feel prepared to depart publicly from the "party line" on the bill. Indeed, everyone else who testified that day delivered to Poshard the same message advocates have consistently delivered: passage of ENDA would convey no endorsement of homosexuality, and thus Poshard could continue both to believe homosexuality was morally wrong and to vote for ENDA. To me, however, those answers lacked both resonance and credibility, and I began to question more seriously whether advocates would do better to modify their moral rhetoric regarding ENDA.[107]

An unlikely confluence of events pushed ENDA suddenly to the fore in the summer of 1996. In 1993, the Hawaii Supreme Court had ruled that denying marriage licenses to same-gender couples presented a possible violation of the state's constitutional guarantee of equal protection based on gender. Throughout the spring of 1996, the case was pending in the Hawaii court system, where the state had been forced to present "compelling reasons" to justify its refusal to recognize same-gender marriages. Although final resolution of the case would be years away, congressional Republicans decided the fall of 1996 (conveniently situated just before the November 1996 election) would be an excellent time to put Congress on record as opposing same-sex marriage. Hence, during the summer of 1996, Congress took up the Defense of Marriage Act (DOMA), a bill providing that no state would be required to give effect to a same-sex marriage legally recognized in another state and providing that the term *marriage* or *spouse* in federal law would apply only to a union between a man and a woman.

Among the strategies we considered in the fight against DOMA was to propose a host of unrelated amendments to the bill. Procedurally, it would be next to impossible to offer such amendments in the House of Representatives. But in the Senate, any amendment—no matter how unrelated to the underlying bill—could be offered. Thus, we began to develop a series of amendments, based on pending Democratic legislation on issues ranging from gun control to health care, that we felt could pose embarrassing votes for Senate Republicans. During this process, Daniel Zingale, political strategist for HRC, posed a question to a small group of gay and civil rights advocates: "What about offering ENDA as an amendment to DOMA?"

Zingale's idea was dramatic, and ultimately brilliant. The decision was made that ENDA would be offered as an amendment to DOMA only if vote-counting indicated the amendment could garner affirmative votes in the mid-to-high forties. While we did not need to have ENDA necessarily pass, we did need to know it would make a respectable showing. The strategic, lobbying, and grassroots teams of the LCCR organizations (of which the gay rights organizations were now an integral part) swung into action to begin collecting votes; the legislative-lawyering team began to develop a few modifications to ENDA to respond to concerns that the opposition had raised. By August 1996, we had an ENDA ready that was rapidly gaining support.

The biggest break for the vote on ENDA resulted from the political machinations surrounding DOMA. The Republican leadership wanted to bring DOMA up for a vote, but were not interested in subjecting the bill to potentially embarrassing votes on gun control or health care. Thus, the Republican leadership offered Senator Edward Kennedy, who was leading the fight for ENDA, a simple deal: an up-or-down vote on DOMA, with no extraneous amendments to be offered to DOMA (other than ENDA), in return for an up-or-down vote on ENDA, with no extraneous amendments to be offered to ENDA. Senator Kennedy took the deal, with the agreement of LCCR and the Washington-based gay rights organizations. The opportunity to have a "clean" vote on ENDA, without amendments on teachers or youth or religion or whatever, would be remarkable, and worth giving up the opportunity to offer extraneous amendments on DOMA that might not have made any difference to ultimate passage of the legislation.

Indeed, the debate and vote on ENDA was remarkable. In September 1996, the United States Senate debated ENDA for two days in a serious and comprehensive fashion. For the first time in history, televised proceedings of a full body of the U.S. Congress relayed to the American people discussions related to a *positive* piece of legislation about gay people. The silence of sixteen years ago was gone; the quiet acquiescence to antigay amendments of ten years ago was gone.

But the gut-wrenching aspect of the debate was that a serious, positive discussion of employment discrimination against gay men, lesbians, and bisexuals was sandwiched between a debate and an affirmative vote on DOMA—an explicitly antigay bill. Indeed, if anything demonstrates the limitations of the rhetoric on ENDA, it is the juxtaposition of the debates on DOMA and ENDA. Numerous senators had no problem voting for *both* DOMA and ENDA and proudly proclaiming the consistency of their votes. A vote for DOMA, after all, was seen as an endorsement of the good of heterosexual marriage, and implicitly, as a rejection of the good of gay coupling. Since a vote for ENDA had consistently been described (even by advocates) as *agnostic* on whether gay people and gay coupling were good, a senator could logically vote for both bills. What a far cry from Art Agnos's assessment in 1980 that an antidiscrimination law on employment and housing and a law allowing same-sex marriage are different only in degree, not kind.

The debate on ENDA culminated with a heartbreaking vote of 50–49 against the legislation. Senator David Pryor (D-AR) had indicated he would vote in favor of the bill, but was absent the day of the vote because his son was undergoing surgery. And while Vice President Al Gore was standing ready to cast the tiebreaker if the vote was 50–50, Pryor's absence deprived Gore of that opportunity.[108]

Despite ENDA's failure to pass in the fall of 1996, the close Senate vote gave the bill important political legitimacy. This was no longer a bill that did not have the slightest chance of passage. Rather, it was a bill that simply needed the right opportunity in the Senate and had a realistic hope of passage in the House were the Democrats to again take control. So work on ENDA proceeded slowly and steadily. The bill was reintroduced in the Senate in 1997 with Senator Jim Jeffords, a Republican from Vermont, as the lead sponsor, and in the House with Congressman Christopher Shays, a Republican from Massachusetts, as one of the lead sponsors. Senator Jeffords held a hearing on ENDA in October 1997, which followed the usual pattern of previous hearings.[109] And over the following two years, various provisions of ENDA were tinkered with and changed as new questions arose from potential sponsors or opponents of the legislation. For example, during the first six months of 1999, we worked solely on modifying one provision of ENDA that prohibited affirmative action on the basis of sexual orientation. Although a policy decision about affirmative action had been made six years before, questions about the technical, legal impact of the bill necessitated hours of tinkering and negotiation.

On June 24, 1999, ENDA was reintroduced by Senators Jeffords and Kennedy with thirty-six cosponsors, and by Representatives Shays, Morella, and Frank with 166 cosponsors. By that point, some of the internal fights on ENDA had broken into the open, with NGLTF noting it could not endorse the bill without inclusion of antidiscrimination protection for transgendered people. But the game plan on ENDA remains the same: a slow and steady effort toward collecting votes. And the official line on the bill remains the same: one can vote for ENDA without such a vote indicating anything about one's view about whether gay is good.

So what have we learned in the twenty-five years from Bella to ENDA? Some of our lessons are similar to those learned by other social movements. First, we have learned that change usually occurs only in incremental steps. Indeed, if one tries to achieve change too quickly, one often achieves no change at all. Moreover, positive legislation usually depends on some positive change having already occurred in societal attitudes and beliefs. For gay people, creating that societal change has been inextricably linked with coming out and becoming visible. The presence of gay people living open and honest lives has inevitably affected, in a positive manner, the attitudes of nongay people. And that the gay community has been represented in Washington over a number of years by people who are proudly out and comfortable has made a profound difference in changing the attitudes of other civil rights advocates with whom the gay rights advocates have worked in coalition.

Second, we have learned that change usually occurs most readily when we build coalitions with other groups, and that we must pay our dues with those groups to become full members of the team. Becoming sophisticated members of the team has also meant becoming politically savvy and involved in electoral politics—both through financial contributions and through the mobilization of votes.

But taking incremental legislative steps, forming coalitions with other groups, and using electoral power require patience, pragmatism, and compromise. These are not easy characteristics to adopt when one yearns for a complete victory in the shortest time possible. Moreover, these characteristics are sometimes in tension with frankness. For me, the most difficult tension has been between the rhetoric surrounding ENDA, which consistently proclaims that a vote for ENDA displays no affirmative position that gay sex is a moral good, and my personal belief that being gay is as morally neutral as being heterosexual, and that the love manifested in *both* heterosexual and gay relationships *is* a moral good.

Pragmatism counsels that the rhetoric around ENDA remain the same, since many members of Congress apparently feel comfortable voting for the bill only as long as they are permitted to make the assertion that such a vote carries no moral message about gay sexuality. But the rhetoric supporting ENDA seems somehow behind the times. In so many venues, we are essentially proclaiming that gay love and gay coupling *is* a moral good. Indeed, the more that gay people and gay couples live open and honest lives, the more we are living embodiments of the moral goods of love, caring, pleasure, and commitment.

So perhaps, beyond Capitol Hill, we are beginning to change the world a little. ENDA may well pass based on the old rhetoric, and passage of the law will then help other gay people to continue to change the world by coming out and changing the attitudes of others across the country. But we should hope for an even better outcome. We should hope ENDA itself will be welcomed into a new world where both rhetoric and beliefs have *already* changed, and where the idea plastered on buttons in 1969—Gay Is Good—is not so revolutionary anymore.

CHAPTER 9

Government v. Gays: Two Sad Stories with Two Happy Endings, Civil Service Employment and Security Clearances

Franklin E. Kameny

MANY PEOPLE COMING INTO MATURITY DURING THE past quarter century are unaware that starting during and just after World War II, and with much heightened intensity after about 1950, our federal government implemented policies that banned gay people from civil service employment, and from holding security clearances whether they worked inside or outside the government. Those policies were as rigidly and rigorously administered as the current ban on gays in the military, and as ferociously enforced, and provided an unfortunate example that has been followed by many private employers nationwide to this day.

The two issues, civil service employment and the issuance or retention of security clearances, although often confused and lumped together, were separate and distinct, based upon different rationales, laws, and regulations; they were very differently administered and affected different, although overlapping, populations. However, many gay people were hit by both forms of disqualification, with the government utilizing whichever one seemed most effective under the facts of the particular case. The two issues will be considered separately here.

CIVIL SERVICE EMPLOYMENT

The ban on homosexuals in federal civil service employment began over a century ago. About 1869, even before the creation of the formal civil service, Walt Whitman was fired by the Department of the Interior because, in part, of the gay overtones of his *Leaves of Grass*. In 1881 a disappointed federal office seeker assassinated President James A. Garfield. Two years later, under Garfield's successor, President Chester A. Arthur, Congress created the United States Civil Service Commission (CSC), establishing uniform employment standards and procedures throughout the executive branch, and ending the "spoils system" in which each new president fired all existing employees in order to reward political cronies with federal jobs. Included in these standards, as a basis for disqualification and dismissal, was "immoral conduct," which included homosexuality. For the next two-thirds of a century, insofar as homosexuality was concerned, this standard was utilized sparingly, and in no widespread, crusading fashion.

The question of homosexuality began to attract significant governmental attention during World War II, mostly in connection with the uniformed military. Following the war, the first Kinsey report appeared at the beginning of 1948, with its then-shocking claims that homosexual sexual conduct was far more widespread than was generally believed. In a socially and morally conservative era, well before the onset of the sexual revolution, this was a profoundly disturbing revelation that produced significant backlash. That was reinforced and augmented by psychiatry and, particularly, psychoanalysis, which were in their heyday, with their relentless characterizations of homosexuality (often under the rubric of "sexual perversion") as a profound emotional disorder. It was supposedly accompanied by a variety of other disorders and general instability, rendering those "afflicted" with it mentally, morally, and emotionally unsuitable for employment, and certainly not to be entrusted with government secrets. Finally, the Cold War was rapidly heating up, with its conflation of any kind of nonconformity with disloyalty, as subsumed under what has come to be termed McCarthyism.

In 1950, two Senate committees, chaired by Senators Clyde Hoey and Kenneth S. Wherry, held hearings on the employment of gay people in the federal civil service. Broadly, the Hoey Committee Report dealt with policy on the employment of gays by the federal civil service; the Wherry Committee Report dealt with practical aspects of the implementation of that policy. The Hoey Committee Report (Senate Document 241, December 15, 1950) was entitled "Employment of Homosexuals and Other Sex Perverts in Government." It set out its purpose: "To determine . . . why the employment [of homosexuals] by the Government is undesirable." Not "whether," but "why." The committee had made up its mind in advance. It then stated, "It is the opinion of this subcommittee that those who engage in acts of homosexuality and other perverted sex activities are unsuitable for employment in the Federal Government" and "One homosexual can pollute a Government office."

The Wherry Committee hearings were highlighted by the testimony of Roy E. Blick, then chief of the Morals Division of the D.C. Metropolitan Police Department (MPD), in which he provided what he later admitted was a completely imaginary number of several thousand gays employed in the civil service, shocking that committee. The reports of both committees urged that strong measures be taken to eliminate "sexual perverts" from federal employment. The Wherry Committee Report urged that the MPD set up a squad to ferret out gay federal employees so that their names could be reported to the government so that they could be fired. In compliance with Wherry's directive, the MPD established as part of its Morals Division a "Perversion Squad," which terrorized Washington gays until it was forced into inaction around 1972 and into demise in 1975 by political pressure from the local gay community. Thus commenced a quarter century of intense travail for gay people in the employment of our government, not fully resolved for almost half a century, and with adverse impact far beyond just the federal civil service.

Under D.C. law, solicitation for "lewd or immoral conduct" is a misdemeanor; solicitation for homosexual conduct was then considered such solicitation. Therefore, pursuant to the directives of the Wherry Committee, plainclothes policemen went out to solicit solicitations for which they then made arrests. Once someone was arrested, he was intensively questioned as to identities of other gay people whom he might know. The purpose of the entire operation was to compile lists of gay people to be turned over to the civil service so they could be fired.

Similarly, gay employees, once identified, were also intensively questioned by agency or CSC investigators in order to identify other gay employees, all of whom were then fired. Thus commenced a quarter-century witch-hunt—a reign of terror for gay federal civil service employees—which resulted in the firings of large numbers of competent gay people. Unfortunately, but understandably, in the social climate of the times, not one fought back.

Most extreme in its antigay policies was the State Department, which had been especially traumatized by Senator Joseph McCarthy in the early 1950s. In testimony before Congress in 1965, a representative of the department testified that homosexuality was "an absolute bar" to State Department employment; even a "latent homosexual" or a person merely with "homosexual tendencies" was disqualified, even if he had never acted upon his tendencies; anyone who had had even one homosexual experience past his eighteenth birthday was unemployable by the department.

The effects of these gay-exclusionary employment policies extended far beyond just the federal civil service. They set the tone for employment policies and practices throughout all of American business. After all, if the federal government could exclude gays, and did, then private employers not only could, but should. And they did. The general rule of thumb, almost universally valid, was that if you were known to be gay, you never obtained or retained a job. This left a legacy of antigay employment discrimination throughout America that has persisted long after the federal government was finally brought to heel. While the efforts of gay movement activists have significantly mitigated this pattern, and increasing numbers of larger companies are adopting gay-friendly employment polices, antigay employment discrimination is still extensive.

I became one of the victims of those federal antigay employment policies when, in 1957, as a first-year probationary employee, with a superior performance rating, I was fired from a position as an astronomer with the Army Map Service because of homosexuality. I took that as a declaration of war against me and my fellow gays and became the first person, to my knowledge, to fight back on this issue. This became an eighteen-year war, which I fought victoriously by every possible method: litigation, legislation, negotiation, and demonstration; cunning, conniving, and cajolery; hounding and harassment. The formal victory was followed by yet another quarter century before the matter was brought to a final, happy, definitive closure. The remainder of this section is the story of my war.

Following my dismissal from the Army Map Service in December 1957, I appealed administratively not only through the limited formal channels but beyond them, to the top of the executive branch—the president—and to the top of the legislative branch—the House and Senate Civil Service Committees—all without effect. The national office of the American Civil Liberties Union (ACLU) referred me to an attorney who agreed to take my case to court. After we had lost at the district and appeals court levels, and correctly foreseeing no success at the Supreme Court, the attorney backed out. Guided by a pamphlet that he gave me describing Supreme Court rules for filing petitions for writ of certiorari, and phoning the Court itself whenever I needed further guidance, I wrote my own petition. To my knowledge, this was the first gay rights brief ever filed with the U.S. Supreme Court. It was long (the Justice Department, in reply, complained of its length), but even today, over thirty-seven years later, it still reads well. Writing it forced me to formulate my ideas on gay rights, and to begin to create my rhetoric and "word bites"; I have been well served by it in the ensuing years. It was filed in January 1961; predictably, the Supreme Court denied certiorari in March, thereby ending my personal case. The writing of that petition started a long course of informal, on-the-job training in law, which opened the door to an informal, unofficial, but enormously productive career as a "lawyer without portfolio," leading to my handling of hundreds of cases at the administrative level, as formal counsel, over the next thirty-five years.

In the late 1950s, I had been slightly in touch with the tiny gay movement of the day—a handful of organizations on the East and West Coasts. When I was in intense financial need following my firing from the Map Service, one of them had donated a small sum to help me out. Having now faced the realities of antigay discrimination, and having lost personally, I decided to operate organizationally. So, along with a small group of people, on November 15, 1961, I founded the Mattachine Society of Washington (MSW), and with it, the gay movement locally in Washington, D.C. Because we were in Washington, we made the federal government and its antigay policies one of our prime targets, in the areas of civil service employment, security clearances, and the military.

The battle against the CSC took off immediately. Bruce C. Scott had seen the brief announcement in the *Washington Star,* in late March 1961, of the denial of certiorari in my case. He contacted me in regard to his loss of a job at the Labor Department, on the basis of homosexuality, and became centrally involved in the formation and work of MSW, of which he was an officer for a number of years. Contact with the just-formed Washington affiliate of the ACLU resulted in their support of his case and assignment of an attorney. In 1965, we achieved our first victory in *Scott v. Macy I* (349 F.2d, D.C. Circuit) when the U.S. Court of Appeals reversed Scott's CSC disqualification. The CSC immediately reinstated its action against Scott, leading to another victory, in 1968, in *Scott v. Macy II* (402 F.2d 644). The CSC told us that they were giving up in that case and would not try again. Scott moved back to Chicago, whence he had come, worked for the Illinois Labor Department in a job that led him back into the federal government, and long ago retired.

In 1965, consistent with the rising level of public expressions of dissent nationally, on many issues, MSW commenced a program of picketing at the White House and in other locations. In June 1965, a much publicized demonstration was held in front of CSC headquarters in Washington. Under heavy pressure, CSC officials agreed to a meeting with MSW representatives, and CSC chairman John W. Macy issued a letter responding publicly to demands from MSW for a reversal of CSC exclusionary policy, in which he provided a feeble rationale for that policy. Exclusionary policies and practices remained firmly in place.

MSW had published and widely distributed a leaflet giving advice on how to handle an interview or interrogation by federal investigators. This leaflet was sent out to various parts of the country, was placed on bulletin boards in government buildings, and was distributed at gatherings of gay people, such as at local D.C. gay bars. Its major four-part advice was "Say NOthing; sign NOthing; get counsel; fight back," supplemented by warnings against "diarrhea of the mouth": "Everything you say [to an investigator] should be true, but everything that is true need not be said and often should not be";

and "do not answer questions with a book-length chapter out of your autobiography if a single word—yes, no, or maybe—will do." We were successfully insistent, over strong initial resistance, in establishing the right of employees to be accompanied by counsel at such interviews, thus enabling strong control over the damaging information conveyed, and techniques for exercising such control were gradually developed and evolved continuously over the next three decades. I accompanied many people into such interviews, for both civil service employment and for security clearances, over the next thirty years.

Meanwhile, Clifford L. Norton, a NASA employee, had been arrested in 1963 on a trumped-up solicitation charge and fired. He contacted me at the time of his arrest. We arranged legal counsel, and in 1969 we won a resounding victory in *Norton v. Macy* (417 F.2d 1161, D.C. Circuit) when the same Court of Appeals as in *Scott* said that an agency cannot support a dismissal "merely by turning its head and crying 'shame.' " This decision thus required that the agency demonstrate some rational connection between "the efficiency of the service," the underlying statutory criterion, and the conduct at issue. It set the direction for future law and policy and created a high hurdle for the government.

By this time, Stonewall had occurred, in 1969, the sixties had swept change over America, and profound changes were affecting American attitudes on many matters, including sexual ones generally, and homosexuality specifically. Gay people were becoming increasingly militant and no longer willing to accept adverse governmental actions cringingly and secretively. The number of administrative and judicial challenges to the CSC disqualifications was rising, and while we were by no means always successful, a number of cases were won.

The road to the denouement opened about 1972, when two cases arose almost simultaneously: *Baker and Rau v. Hampton* on the East Coast, and *SIR and Hickerson v. Hampton* (63 F.R.D. 399; N.D. Calif.; aff'd 528 F. 2d 905, Ninth Circuit) on the West Coast. The Society for Individual Rights (SIR) was a San Francisco gay organization that entered the case as a litigant to make it a class action. I had been involved in both cases as counsel and consultant at the administrative level. When the cases went to court, I helped to arrange for formal legal counsel, put the attorneys in touch with each other, and helped orchestrate the two cases jointly through the courts. The result was a victory in both cases, accompanied by an injunction issued about November 1973, and technically still in effect, against the implementation by the CSC of its antigay exclusionary policies. The CSC recognized that this was the effective end of a quarter century of gay exclusion. The general counsel of the CSC phoned me to tell me that it would take eighteen months for them to work things through, and in fact, it did take just about that long. In June 1975, I received another call from the general counsel, informing me that resolution was at hand.

On July 3, 1975, with public fanfare, CSC made its move, in three parts. (1) Its formal suitability regulations were amended by deletion of "immoral conduct" and "infamous conduct" as criteria for exclusion, and a redefinition of "notoriously disgraceful conduct." (2) A lengthy, formal internal policy directive was issued, making clear that homosexuality, including homosexual sexual conduct, was no longer a basis for exclusion from federal civil service employment. (3) A news release was issued, announcing the end of the antigay federal employment policy.

Except for a small number of cases still in the pipeline, that ended the exclusion of gays from federal employment on the basis of suitability, although it still left many vulnerable on grounds of security.

Early in the Carter administration, legislation was introduced to restructure the administration of the federal civil service. The Civil Service Reform Act of 1978 abolished the Civil Service Commission, created the Office of Personnel Management (OPM), separated out certain functions, and made other changes. At that time it was not considered politically practical to address the matter of the employment of gays head-on, although in light of the events of the immediately preceding years, and the climate of opinion at the time, the issue had to be dealt with. Therefore, the new law provided (5 USC 2302 [b] [10]) that, for federal employment, it is a "prohibited personnel practice" to "discriminate for or against any employee or applicant for employment on the basis of conduct which does not adversely affect the performance of the employee or applicant or the performance of others." In 1980, Alan K. Campbell, director of the OPM, stated formally that this directive specifically included homosexual sexual conduct, and homosexuality generally.

While this ended the formal exclusion of gays from federal employment, a deeply and viscerally felt legacy of fear remained, and government gays tended, by and large, to remain very much in the closet for almost exactly another eighteen years. In part, they feared loss of promotions and other advancement, and in part they feared the loss of security clearance, resulting in the loss of jobs requiring such clearance, since the issue of security clearances for gays was slowly being clarified but was not yet at all finally resolved.

Commencing about 1992 or 1993, with high visibility, there suddenly appeared on the scene a group of organizations of openly gay federal employees, characterized by the acronym GLOBE, standing for Gay, Lesbian, Bisexual Employees of the Federal Government. These were formed in a growing number of governmental departments and agencies, along with a global GLOBE that served as a unifying umbrella for the whole structure. With the formation of these groups came a veritable eruption of openly gay federal employees. Department and agency heads were persuaded to hold public ceremonies, often addressed by the agency heads themselves, celebrating diversity in their employment rosters, including gay people. Many agencies instituted sensitivity training programs, directed at offsetting homophobia among employees.

With the arrival of the Clinton administration, two further developments occurred. First, a gradually growing number of publicized high-level openly gay appointments were made, up to the levels of agency directors and assistant secretaries of departments. Second, individual departments and agencies, including OPM itself, were encouraged to issue policy statements disavowing and prohibiting antigay discrimination. This was intentionally done in a somewhat informal, piecemeal fashion because it was perceived that, were such a policy directive issued on a government-wide basis at that time, it might well have been struck down by a homophobic Congress, as had just then happened with respect to lesbian and gay service members.

Illustrating the changes taking place, and particularly gratifying to anyone who had followed these matters, were the almost identical 1992 and 1993 announcements for the State Department Foreign Service Officer Program entrance examination. Both stated, "The Department of State is committed to equal opportunity and fair and equitable treatment for all without regard to" a list of characteristics (race, religion, etc.). The 1992 list did not include sexual orientation. The 1993 list did include sexual orientation. Thus in twenty-eight years, the State Department had been moved from an absolute exclusionary bar not only of gay people but of anyone even suspected of being gay, to equal opportunity and equal treatment of gay people.

The final bridge was crossed on May 28, 1998, during the second Clinton term, when the president issued executive order 13087, which prohibited discrimination in federal employment on the basis of sexual orientation. This was the latest of a series of amendments, over the years, to EO 11478, first issued by President Nixon in 1969, and amended by EO 11560 and in 1978 by EO 12106. The thrust of EO 11478 and its pre-Clinton amendments was to establish as government policy the provision of equal employment opportunity in federal employment, to prohibit discrimination in employment because of race, color, religion, sex, national origin, handicap, or age, and to extend outreach to ensure that members of the groups named perceived that they were welcome and were, in fact, welcome.

EO 13087 added sexual orientation to the previously listed bases upon which discrimination was prohibited and upon which outreach was extended. In so doing, it actually added nothing that had not earlier been provided by the courts, by the Civil Service Commission, by Congress, and by the earlier actions of the Clinton administration. It merely tied up loose ends and ensured uniformity throughout the executive branch and brought the issue to final, formal closure.

Not surprisingly, EO 13087 was attacked by homophobic religious conservatives, who mounted a hysterical series of factually unfounded claims that the executive order would establish affirmative action programs and quotas for the hiring of gays, would apply to contractors, and exceeded the president's authority by going beyond congressional and judicial mandates. An amendment to an appropriations bill was introduced in the House of Representatives to overturn EO 13087. Had this succeeded, the basis would have been created for moving fifty years backward in one fell swoop. The amendment was defeated on August 7, 1998, by a comfortable majority vote of 252 to 176, thereby in effect creating the congressional authority for the pro-gay nondiscrimination policy, even if the Civil Service Reform Act had not done so twenty years earlier. It squelched the religious fanatics and put the policy on a sound, secure legal basis.

Thus, over just short of half a century, we have moved from a viciously and ferociously enforced absolute ban on the employment of gays in the federal civil service as "polluters of government offices" to a policy of affirmative welcome of gays into the federal civil service as valued employees with much to offer. A long, sad, disgraceful story, littered with human tragedies, has had a truly happy ending, with the prospect of a bright future.

SECURITY CLEARANCES

The legitimate existence of governmental secrets has been recognized from the very first days of our nation, even before the Constitution. All presidents have had them, from Washington onward. However, with the vast development of modern technology since World War I, and especially during and since World War II, an orderly means for safeguarding and disseminating those secrets has had to be devised. That means is our security clearance system.

It has generally been considered that, constitutionally, the secrets at issue belong to the executive branch, and that therefore they are the property of the president. Accordingly, the security clearance programs, as they have grown, are largely, although not entirely, a creature of executive orders issued by various presidents, and only minimally a creature of statute. Security programs have grown haphazardly, starting with the Employee Loyalty Program initiated under President Roosevelt in 1939. The current, highly institutionalized program began to take shape during World War II. Especially after the dropping of the first atomic bombs, we began to hear of classifications of secret information such as top secret, secret, confidential, and restricted. Further executive orders have created a hodgepodge of boards and other entities, covering not only government employees, but also employees of firms with federal contracts.

President Eisenhower systematized these programs with what became the definitive order, EO 10450, issued on April 27, 1953. This has shaped and guided our entire security clearance system for the ensuing forty-five years and remains at least nominally in effect in 1998. The scope of the order was large. It provided for investigation of all government employees, even if they had no access to classified information, and established the adjudication standards and criteria for clearances for employees in government and in private industry. The Supreme Court quickly narrowed its application only to employees requiring access to classified information.

The EO 10450 criteria for adjudicating eligibility for a clearance included, among others:

- Any behavior, activity, or association that tended to show that the individual was not reliable or trustworthy.

- Any criminal, infamous, dishonest, or notoriously disgraceful conduct, habitual use of intoxicants to excess, drug addiction, sexual perversion, or financial irresponsibility.

- Any facts that furnished reason to believe that the individual might be subjected to coercion, influence, or pressure that might cause him to act contrary to the best interests of the national security.

The first of these became a general catchall, included ritualistically in all statements of reasons for proposed clearance denials or revocations. The second and third were used specifically to target gays. Thus the stage was set for conversion of our security clearance programs into an open war against gay Americans that went on for some four decades.

EO 10450 suffered from two major defects. First, by delegating its implementation to the heads of agencies and departments, rather than establishing some centralized, government-wide adjudication structure, it created a chaotically fragmented system with almost as many independent security clearance programs as there are government agencies and departments, none of which recognized the clearances that others issued. The battle against its pernicious effects became multifaceted in practice, fought agency by agency and department by department, with the outcome of one case often providing little if any benefit for another.

Second, EO 10450 provided for no due process, leading to some appalling abuses. For example, employees were asked to defend their eligibility for a clearance while being refused information as to the basis for the proposed denial and the alleged facts that they had to defend themselves against; statements of anonymous witnesses were used with no opportunity for cross-examination.

The latter defect was resolved for employees in private industry by the 1959 Supreme Court decision in *Greene v. McElroy* (360 U.S. 474), which indicated that an employee in private industry has a property interest in a job and a career of which he cannot constitutionally be deprived through loss of clearance without due process. This led to the issuance of EO 10865 in 1960, which set up extensive requirements for the processing of industrial security clearance cases. This process was particularly implemented by the Department of Defense, which set up an elaborate system, including the functional equivalents of an indictment and an evidentiary trial before an administrative law judge (usually called a hearing examiner), followed by a written decision (determination), and recourse to an appeal board. The Department of Energy established a different but comparably complex system for review. Since some 90 percent of all security clearances involve the Defense Department, and some 90 percent of those, in turn, are industrial clearances, this meant that the majority of clearance holders then had at least the show of full due process, although as actually administered, this was an empty promise not only for gays, but for others who might be unpopular in various ways.

The adjudication criteria established by EO 10450 quickly converted the security clearance programs into what I termed "social and sexual conformity programs," which, in many instances, became "get the gays" programs (although the word *gay* had not yet come into common parlance, and *perverts* was more often used in this context). In their different ways, all three of the criteria above were utilized for this purpose.

First: The primary rationale for denying clearances to gay people was the universally accepted image of gays as cringing, submissive victims of endless blackmail attempts (i.e., of attempts at "coercion, influence, or pressure"). Accepted as self-evident truth, the hypothesis seemed plausible for the times and was universally accepted, even by gays of that day. It became the formal driving force behind the denial of security clearances to gay people.

Second: With the enormous influence of psychiatry, especially psychoanalysis, at the time, the medical model of homosexuality as an emotional disorder was also universally accepted. From this was derived the judgment that gay people were inherently "unreliable and untrustworthy."

Third: Sodomy (always construed as referring only to homosexual conduct) was not merely criminal, but was a felony in all fifty states and the District of Columbia. A security clearance could not be issued to a habitual criminal because if the clearance holder would violate the criminal laws to suit his convenience, then he might violate the security regulations to suit his convenience as well. The tiny gay movement of the time had had no effect whatever on public attitudes, and between the moralists and theologians, the lawyers and psychiatrists, there was no voice raised to offset or mitigate the relentless onslaught of a uniformly negative assessment of homosexuality as "criminal, infamous, immoral, and notoriously disgraceful conduct." That hostile judgment was nailed down by the unchallenged pejorative characterization of homosexuality as a "sexual perversion."

All three of these rationales had to be successfully challenged before the exclusion of gays from the ranks of security clearance holders could be reversed. Separately, each of these three bases for clearance denial was demolished. It took some three decades, from about 1965 until 1995, to accomplish this, starting with the psychiatrists in 1973, and ending with the blackmail allegation in the early 1990s, but the battle was finally won.

As with the ban on gays in the federal civil service, the effort to reverse the ban on security clearances for gays started with MSW, in August 1962, when it announced this as one of its goals. Meetings were held with top-level Pentagon security clearance officials. The issue was structured into the 1965 MSW picketing demonstrations at the White House and elsewhere. MSW also worked to get the word out as to the best way to handle investigative interviews. Thus began the three-decade-long process of erosion and attrition of a government-wide policy, leading finally to its reversal.

Matters took a more formal turn about 1966, when Barbara Gittings and I were appointed cocounsel for a security clearance holder whose clearance was to be revoked because he was gay. Consistent with regulations issued in pursuit of EO 10865, a formal, evidentiary hearing was scheduled in the Pentagon. At that time, such hearings were closed to the public; only the hearing examiner, counsel for both sides, the clearance holder (technically, the "applicant"), a court reporter, and witnesses while testifying were allowed into the hearing room. In the first trial of a technique that we utilized numerous times thereafter, to address the blackmail allegation head-on we announced a news conference to be held just before the start of the hearing in the Pentagon corridor just outside the hearing room. There the applicant announced that he was gay: now that the media were informed, he was not subject to blackmail because of fear of disclosure. Then, during the hearing itself, the fact of the news conference and the disclosure made there were made part of the formal case record, thereby rendering moot the claim of susceptibility to blackmail. This was the first of a series of such hearings over the next several years, mostly in Defense Department cases, but also at other agencies.

At this hearing, as its expert witness, the department presented the infamous psychoanalyst Dr. Charles Socarides, whom Gittings and I had never before heard of. Openmouthed, dumbfounded, and incredulous, we listened to his appalling characterizations of homosexuality and gay people. We cross-examined him for some three hours, further to elicit views from which he has not departed by so much as a syllable in the three decades since. Some years later, during the American Psychiatric Association (APA) proceedings on removal of homosexuality from its manual of mental and emotional disorders, we circulated a transcript of his testimony opposing gay people as security clearance holders, in order to discredit his claims to be a supporter of gay rights. Following this hearing, the Defense Department dropped Socarides from its roster of expert witnesses on homosexuality.

Despite efforts to mount compelling cases for issuance or retention of Defense Department industrial security clearances, we lost them all. The reason became clear a few years later. In response to our tactic of public announcement of homosexuality at news conferences, a secret policy directive was issued from the top levels of the Pentagon security clearance establishment dictating the outcome of these cases. This was prior to the enactment of the Freedom of Information Act, and the greater governmental openness that ensued from it, so the directive did not come to light until much later. That policy directive stated:

> Homosexuals
> As previously announced, proof of recent homosexual activities establishes conclusively, as a matter of present policy, that the applicant cannot be granted access authorization.
> In some instances, the applicant acknowledges the status, recognizes that it is publicly known, and argues that since he cannot be blackmailed, he presents no security risk. In this case, Department Counsel will have little to do but emphasize the proof that the applicant is a homosexual; the Field Board will act in accordance with established policy as stated in the preceding paragraph.

In short, for noncelibate gay people, the due process required by the Supreme Court and set out in EO 10865 and the regulations derived from it was a travesty and a farce given the predetermined negative outcome—what came to be known as the "per se rule" by which clearances were automatically denied to gay people.

Starting in 1971 and 1972, three Defense Department industrial security clearance cases emerged for which I served as counsel at the administrative level. These were the cases of Benning Wentworth, Richard L. Gayer, and Otto H. Ulrich, in New Jersey, Philadelphia, and Washington, respectively. At least two of these went to hearing, preceded by news conferences. When, consistent with the per se department policy, we lost all three, lawyers were obtained, and the three cases were won in federal district court. A hysterical Defense Department appealed through its official lawyers, the Justice Department. The Court of Appeals joined the three cases together and issued a long, rambling decision (*Gayer, Ulrich, and Wentworth v. Schlesinger*, 490 F.2d 740, 1973), which did not give a clear victory to either side, but resulted in the ultimate acquisition of all three clearances. The court ruled out some of the offensively intrusive questions that had routinely been asked. More importantly, they ruled that administrative determinations in these cases are "to be explained in such manner that a reviewing court may be able to discern whether there is a rational connection between the facts relied upon and the conclusions drawn."

This requirement forced upon the government a level of accountability not previously present and significantly curtailed the impact of the per se rule, although the court denied its existence altogether because the department denied its existence in perjurious testimony.

The watershed case that finally broke the back of the Defense Department's absolute ban on gay people as security clearance holders, and by extension antigay policies throughout the executive branch, was the Tabler case, which originated in 1973.

Otis Francis Tabler was an openly gay man working in an engineering capacity for a small company in the Los Angeles area. When the Defense Department denied him a security clearance because he was gay, he lost his job. The company had no uncleared employment for him. Tabler decided to fight. As his formal counsel, I asked for the optional hearing in the case and then demanded that the hearing be opened up to the public and the media. The department denied our request. With the assistance of the ACLU, we took the department to court. The Justice Department, having more sense than the Defense Department's Industrial Security Review Office, realized that they had a loser on their hands and settled out of court, with an agreement (a) to have an open hearing in the Tabler case, and (b) to revise the department's regulations to permit open hearings in all cases in which the applicant so requested. The stage was set for putting the Defense Department and its homophobic security clearance policies on trial in the media.

The four-day hearing took place in the first week of August 1974, in the Federal Building in downtown Los Angeles. We had publicized it widely, and so each day's session was preceded by a news conference and often followed by Tabler's appearance on radio or television, where we lambasted the department and its homophobia. On one occasion, department counsel chastised me for "crucifying" him in our publicity. With great satisfaction, I thanked him and told him that was exactly what I had intended to do, and what would continue to happen to other publicly named department officials who victimized gay people with their homophobia. To address the various issues raised by the department, we presented a large array of witnesses, including Dr. Evelyn Hooker, a psychologist noted for her research demonstrating that mental health professionals could not reliably distinguish gay from nongay men using standard mental health diagnostic techniques; local gay activists; some of Tabler's coworkers; the investigative agents in the case; and Tabler's mother.

The department had raised three major issues: (1) that Tabler was guilty of criminal conduct because his sexual activity violated the California sodomy law; (2) that his sexual activity, of itself and because it was criminal, rendered him susceptible to blackmail; and (3) that homosexuality was indicative of mental and emotional instability such as to render him unreliable and untrustworthy.

With respect to (1), we showed that the laws applied to both gays and nongays, but were unequally enforced in California and invoked by the department against gays only, that the district attorney for Los Angeles County had publicly pledged, as a matter of formal policy, not to enforce the sodomy laws against anyone at all with respect to private, consensual adult conduct, and that such laws were generally unenforced the country over. Heterosexual witnesses holding security clearances testified under oath to routine and frequent violations of the California sodomy law; we dared the department to revoke their clearances on that account.

With respect to (2), we put into the record the public hearing and Tabler's radio and television appearances, with the argument that these rendered null any rational claim to susceptibility to blackmail because of fear of disclosure.

With respect to (3), we introduced a resolution, initiated and largely written by me and submitted to the American Psychiatric Association (APA) in May 1973. This resolution covered numerous issues, but included language specifically directed to the claims put forward by the government in cases such as this, and was adopted for the APA by their Board of Trustees in December 1973. This resolution read:

> Whereas homosexuality per se implies no impairment in judgment, stability, reliability, or general social or vocational capabilities, therefore, be it resolved that the American Psychiatric Association deplores all public and private discrimination against homosexuals in such areas as employment, housing, public accommodation, and licensing, and declares that no burden of proof of such judgment, capacity, or reliability shall be placed upon homosexuals greater than that imposed on any other persons.

In December 1974, we won a favorable determination in the Tabler case. The department immediately appealed to its own appeal board. While we prepared for the appeal, the California legislature repealed the state's sodomy law in May 1975. In early July came the decision from the Civil Service Commission rescinding its ban on the employment of gays. The Defense Department gave up. Counsel for the department indicated that regulations were being amended, and that the policy of denial of clearances to gay people was reversed. Once again, a small number of cases still in the pipeline were pursued by the department to the bitter end pro forma, but they were all won. Almost a decade later, Tabler obtained a court judgment awarding him back pay for loss of wages ensuing from his original clearance denial.

The outcome of the Tabler case had a ripple effect throughout the government, although unevenly. Over the next few years, it became possible in almost all agencies for gays to obtain clearances. The road to final resolution, however, was not smooth. Much unease remained among those administering security clearance programs at the agency level, ranging from persistent acceptance of the blackmail myth to simple, overt homophobia, so that while clearances were almost always ultimately granted, the process was often excessively long and beset with obstacles not faced by heterosexual applicants. Specifically, (1) at investigative interviews, gays continued to be subject to much more intrusive questioning than nongays, especially about the details of their sexual activities, and how widespread was knowledge of their homosexuality; and (2) the holdout agencies—mostly the intelligence agencies, such as the National Security Agency, the Central Intelligence Agency, and the Federal Bureau of Investigation, for which issues of security clearance eligibility and employment suitability are inseparable—remained intransigent. It took more than a decade and a half to work those through. In addition, two adverse court decisions came down, one specifically gay-related, the other more general, both of which seemed to bode ill in the short run. In the long run, however, they seem to have had little actual effect.

After the Tabler decision, large numbers of gay-related security clearance cases continued to arise. Unlike in earlier years, when the victims often ran away from negative actions and decisions, these tended to be fought. Our techniques for handling the investigative interviews that opened most cases became increasingly refined. Barring additional complicating factors, there were few ultimate denials in gay-related clearance cases. Even that former bastion of entrenched homophobia, the State Department, issued clearances, in some cases to high-level openly gay officials.

However, increasing resentment developed over the extensive, intrusive, often degrading questions administered discriminatorily to gay applicants. A group of gay people employed in high-technology positions in northern California formed an organization called High Tech Gays. Along with several individual, named plaintiffs, they brought suit, commencing about 1983, against the Defense Department, asking that the department be enjoined from conducting special, intrusive investigations of gay applicants solely on the basis that they were gay. The case was initially won at the district court level. As a result, on Octoberr 23, 1987, John F. Donnelly, assistant deputy undersecretary of defense for counterintelligence and security, issued a memo indicating that questions asking about specific positions and other details of sexual encounters are irrelevant and should not be asked.

The Defense Department appealed, winning in 1990. In its decision (*High Tech Gays et. al. v. Defense Industrial Security Clearance Office, et al.*, 895 F2d. 563, 1990), the Ninth Circuit Court of Appeals bought into all of the mythology relating to the susceptibility of gays to blackmail, and also to the persistent myth of the targeting of gays by the KGB and other hostile

204 | Franklin E. Kameny

intelligence services, as justification for permitting the continuation of discriminatorily burdensome processing of gay applicants.

Fortunately, this was offset almost immediately by the January 9, 1991 memo from Michael A. Sterlacci, Defense Department assistant general counsel. At the conclusion of text generally favorable to the issuance of security clearances to gay people, the memo says, "It is prudent to treat homosexuals and heterosexuals the same with respect to the questions put to them about sex. These questions should ascertain the identity of a cohabitant, if any, and the names of other partners when there may be reason to suspect sexual involvement with citizens of foreign nations."

This immediately provided the means for challenging intrusive questions put to gay applicants by ascertaining, through formal objection, that such questions were not routinely put to heterosexuals or asked about heterosexuality. This tactic was extremely useful and was successfully employed in a number of instances.

Over the years, we had always viewed recourse to the courts as the final trump card available to us when the administrative process failed to result in a just outcome. That had served us well in the Gayer cases, and in others. However, in 1988, the U.S. Supreme Court issued a disconcerting decision in *Department of the Navy v. Egan* (108 S.Ct. 818), a nongay case, which said that while clearance applicants were entitled to judicial review of their cases if procedural improprieties or irregularities were alleged, they were not entitled to such review on the substantive merits of their cases. This seemed to open the door to all kinds of arbitrary action, including official denials based upon pure homophobia, with no recourse whatsoever. In fact, I was told by one arrogant security official, "Now we can do anything we want to." While the Egan decision caused profound unease and anxiety, at least in the context of gay-related cases it apparently caused no problems.

Meanwhile, the assault upon the holdout agencies had begun in 1980. The National Security Agency had sought to revoke the security clearance of a gay employee and fire him. As counsel for the employee, I informed this pathologically secretive agency that if they did not decide this matter favorably and quickly, they would be subjected "to a torrent of publicity of my making and not to their liking." As narrated in *The Puzzle Palace* (Bamford, 1982, pp. 81–85), the case was won, accompanied by a barrage of publicity that served to press the issue further, not only at the NSA, but throughout the government. In the ensuing decade, several other gay-related cases arose at NSA, some of which were successfully resolved, some not (although all should have been), but at least this agency showed that it was capable of being worked with, albeit with great difficulty.

Some grudging flexibility on the part of the traditionally recalcitrant FBI began to be manifested in 1988 in the case of a low-level gay employee whom

I represented. In this case, the adverse agency decision was reversed at the Justice Department, the parent agency of the FBI, and the employee retained his clearance and kept his job. Subsequently, an out-of-court settlement was arrived at in the much publicized case of *Frank Buttino v. FBI*, which included stringent requirements for the adoption of nondiscrimination policies both for FBI employment and FBI security clearances. The Justice Department issued a pro-gay employment policy statement, binding on the FBI, and the FBI, under new director Louis Freeh, issued a stronger policy. Around 1995, the FBI appointed an openly gay activist to a high-level position in the agency, and while, at this writing, it is reported that cultural homophobia on the part of its fading old guard remains, problems for gays and the FBI seem to be a thing of the past.

Most intransigent of all was the CIA. Well into the 1980s, under its pathologically homophobic director William Casey (who, according to his published, official biography, was psychologically incapable of even uttering the word *homosexual*), the CIA remained particularly vicious in implementation of its ban on gays. However, even there, the groundwork for mitigation was being laid gradually, going back to 1975. CIA security clearances, as well as those of some other agencies, are called SCI access, where SCI means "secret compartmentalized information," and represents a level of secrecy and clearance above top secret. SCI access is governed by a document called Director, Central Intelligence Directive 1/14, commonly referred to as the DCID (pronounced "dee sid"), first issued about 1975 and revised irregularly thereafter. In general, insofar as gays are concerned, the DCID has been better than those administering it. While harshly and explicitly antigay in its earlier versions, it grew increasingly reasonable and less homophobic in later years, to the point where later revisions no longer even mentioned homosexuality explicitly and could be utilized to support issuance of SCI access to gay applicants.

Once Casey was gone, and without fanfare or publicized action, the CIA quietly became gay-friendly, and open gays, once subjected to intensive polygraph examination as to the details of their homosexuality, received clearances without the subject even being raised, or if raised, not pursued.

The stage was thus set for the denouement, which, again, was multifaceted.

By the 1980s, it had become obvious, as it was not in the 1950s when there was not yet a database, that the attribution to gays of susceptibility to blackmail was truly fictional. There had been numerous espionage cases, and in fact, a compendium of them had been published by a congressional committee. With one or two trivial exceptions, they all involved heterosexuals. The motivations were almost always greed, not sex. To the extent that sex was involved, it was heterosexual.

In point of fact, the only instance of gay-related blackmail in the entire history of Western espionage was that of Colonel Alfred Raedl, in the Austro-Hungarian army in 1912. For over three-quarters of a century, American gays have been denied security clearances solely in consequence of Raedl.

As the 1970s and 1980s progressed, a distinction began to be made between closeted and uncloseted gays. Applicants were questioned as to the extent of knowledge of their homosexuality by those around them—family, business colleagues, etc. In some instances, they were required to inform family members of their homosexuality as a condition for receipt of a clearance. However, as data accumulated, and compendia of the mounting number of espionage cases—all heterosexual—began to be compiled, the point began to be made strongly that, even in the 1950s and into the 1960s, when all gays were in the closet, there had not been one single instance of the submission of a gay person to blackmail for espionage. Our collective record was perfect, which was more than could be said for heterosexuals, and the mythology that gays, particularly closeted gays, were poor security risks because of the omnipresent possibility for submission to blackmail attempts was proven truly fictional.

This had been obvious long before 1990. Why then did the security clearance establishment continue to press the disproven accusation that gays were potential blackmail victims? Perhaps the answer can be found in the observation of the German philosopher and satirist Georg C. Lichtenberg, some two centuries ago: "How do we spend our old age? In defending opinions not because we believe them to be true, but simply because we once said we thought they were true."

It took someone of influence to say that this particular opinion was not true. In July 1991, during a congressional hearing, in response to questions from Representative Barney Frank, Secretary of Defense Richard Cheney termed the characterization of homosexuals as security risks "a bit of an old chestnut." This was widely publicized. It promptly killed the blackmail accusation once and for all and doomed the whole exclusionary policy, although it took another four years for the process to come to complete fruition.

It had long been evident that the security clearance programs, as they had developed in the decades since the issuance of EO 10450, were archaic and badly in need of revision and modernization. The Carter administration attempted it, but was defeated by a security clearance establishment who perceived the changes as threatening to their little empires and fiefdoms. The Reagan administration failed similarly. The Bush administration proposed changes that were so truly totalitarian and with such shameless complete denial of due process that they elicited widespread opposition, even from congressional hearings in 1989 at which I was invited to testify as a recognized authority with wide experience on security clearances generally, and on security clearances for gay people specifically. Those proposals died without enactment.

In 1989, as a result of these efforts and of the continuing need for changes in the security clearance system, the American Bar Association (ABA) established a committee to make recommendations to the White House. While not a lawyer, I was invited to participate and did so actively. The committee, which took a clear pro-gay position with respect to security clearances, met monthly for several years, occasionally with government officials, including high-level White House personnel, so we were heard. Ultimately proposals were adopted, were approved by the ABA, and were forwarded to the White House, where they were influential in framing the action finally taken during the Clinton administration.

All of this led, after about 1990, to a gradual fading of the effort to make homosexuality a factor in the issuance of security clearances. Such new cases as arose were almost all at the investigative level, resulted in issuance of the clearance, and never proceeded further. The stream of new gay-related cases that characterized the 1980s dwindled and, by about 1993, had ceased entirely.

In March 1995, a draft of a new EO on access to classified information was issued. Finally, on August 2, 1995, President Clinton issued EO 12968. Unlike the later EO 13087 (see above), which was exceedingly brief, EO 12968 was long, instituting significant changes in the handling of security clearances. It was far from perfect and was evidently the result of compromises with conflicting interests in the executive branch. Not only did it not repeal EO 10450, but it gave the earlier order a favored status. Nevertheless, it stated, in two provisions (emphasis added): "The United States Government does not discriminate on the basis of race, color, religion, sex, national origin, or *sexual orientation* in granting access to classified information. No inference concerning the standards in this section may be raised solely on the basis of the *sexual orientation* of the employee."

Thus, by a 180-degree about-face, four decades of uncompromising exclusion of gay people from access to the secrets of their government have been transmuted into affirmative protection of that access. And so this second sad story, littered with the unnecessarily blighted careers of many competent people with much to offer our country, has also come to a happy ending.

CHAPTER 10

AMERICAN IMMIGRATION LAW: A CASE STUDY IN THE EFFECTIVE USE OF THE POLITICAL PROCESS

BARNEY FRANK

INTRODUCTION

Case studies are one of the methods by which political scientists draw lessons from and about the workings of American politics. One consequence of our having only recently confronted the problem of homophobia at the national level is that we have few cases to study. This chapter focuses on one of those. Interestingly, it is both the least well known of all the legislative battles that supporters of gay and lesbian rights have fought, and it is also the one that was the most successful. This linkage is not accidental. People—including gays and lesbians—know little about our successful fight to repeal the anti-gay-and-lesbian provision of immigration law in large part because we won: in our time, failure generates a good deal more attention than success. This is a characteristic both of the reportage on American politics in general and on the gay, lesbian, bisexual, and transgendered movement in particular.

The causes and consequences of the pronounced negative bias in the American media—both gay and mainstream—are of serious concern, but they are not relevant here. The predilection of gay, lesbian, and bisexual people to dwell far more on our defeats than our victories, on the other hand, bears directly on the concerns of this volume. This is a case where negativism begets negatives. Our preference for gloom in the telling of our story weakens our chances of success in the fight against homophobia because it undercuts our ability to work through the political process. I am aware of the deep skepticism with which many will greet this assertion, but I believe that the events that led to a substantial diminution of the homophobic elements of American immigration law help make the case for political action as our best weapon against anti-gay-and-lesbian prejudice.

Anyone looking for evidence that the Stonewall resistance in 1969 marked a watershed in the fight for fair treatment for gay, lesbian, and bisexual people has American immigration policy as exhibit A.

From 1963 to 1967, all three branches of the federal government collaborated to tighten the prohibition that existed in American law against homosexuals coming to America, whether as visitors or as potential citizens. And it is noteworthy that this broad-based effort to make sure that American law contained no loopholes through which gay or lesbian foreigners could slip was initiated by two liberal Democratic presidents and was ratified by the predominantly liberal Congress elected in the anti-Goldwater landslide of 1964. To complete the picture, it was the Warren Court—the most liberal Supreme Court in our history—that held in 1967 that these efforts to tighten the anti-gay-and-lesbian provisions were unnecessary, ruling by 6 to 3 that the existing imprecise, insulting statutory language, designed to protect America against the pollution of foreign homosexuality, met all the relevant constitutional standards.

Twenty-five years later, in 1990, I had the enormous satisfaction of sponsoring a successful amendment to American immigration law that repealed the homophobic provisions of that statute in all of its permutations. And one measure of the distance we have traveled in our fight to defeat homophobia is that just as the homophobic provision of the 1965 Immigration Act was so widely supported by a national consensus that no one in Congress even sought in any serious way to delete it, twenty-five years later the anti-gay-and-lesbian bigots recognized that blatant discrimination based on sexual orientation was not sustainable, and they put up only token resistance.

The history of the provisions of American immigration law that made it illegal for gay, lesbian, or bisexual people to come to the United States from abroad has been told elsewhere.[1] Only one part of that history needs to be emphasized here: prior to 1963, Congress had contented itself with language prohibiting the entry of foreigners "with psychopathic personalities" as a sufficient basis for excluding, among others, homosexuals and bisexuals. While I do not know this as a fact, my strong suspicion is that distaste for us early in this century was so strong that even using the word *homosexuality* was considered an intolerable intrusion upon the sensibilities of polite society.

But by the 1960s, with a Supreme Court presided over by Earl Warren, and including as members Hugo Black, William O. Douglas, William Brennan, and Abe Fortas, gay and lesbian people hoped and public officials feared that this linguistic delicacy might become a serious gap in America's antihomosexual bulwark. Those hopes and fears were given strength when a Canadian national who was a legal resident, Richard Boutilier, sued to prevent a deportation order that had been entered against him by the INS based on his having engaged in homosexual activity.

Fortuitously for the antigay majority, President Kennedy was then preparing a major overhaul of American immigration law. Since the earlier part of this century, and especially since the 1920s, that law had been explicitly racist. Admission to the United States from foreign countries was based on ethnic quotas, roughly reflecting the composition of the United States in the 1920s. This favored Northern and Western Europe and discriminated against Eastern and Southern Europe. And even Southern and Eastern Europe fared better than the nonwhite parts of the world.

Ironically, a movement initiated and supported by liberals appalled at this racial and ethnic bias embedded in American law became the vehicle for a tightening of the statutory exclusion of bisexuals, lesbians, and gay men. A bill prepared by the Kennedy administration and ultimately steered into law by the Johnson administration knocked out the old quota system and replaced it with a set of rules for immigration that was free of this ethnic bias and, in every way but one, morally superior to the bigoted statute it replaced. Frightened by the possibility that the Warren Court would agree with Mr. Boutilier that it was unconstitutional to exclude him as "a psychopath" because of consensual sexual activity between himself and other adults, the Kennedy administration proposed, and the Johnson administration endorsed, an amendment to the law that explicitly banned practitioners of "sexual deviation" from legal entry into the United States.

The liberalization of the immigration law that contained this harshening of the homophobic provision passed in 1965, with the ardent support of the most liberal members of Congress and all of the organizations in the United States dedicated to racial justice, civil liberties, and fairness. When I began my efforts to repeal this discriminatory legislation on being elected to Congress in 1980, I researched the history of this law, and specifically the "sexual deviation" provision, to get a sense of what the debate had been at the time. Not entirely to my surprise, I found that there was not only no vote on including this provision, but also that no effort was made by any of the liberals in Congress to delete it from the bill. There was not even any debate on the matter that I could find.

Note that this immigration law was legitimately considered to be a considerable liberalization and was strongly supported by a number of people then in Congress who were within a few short years to become champions of the rights of gay and lesbian people to be free from discrimination. These advocates-in-waiting included Senator Edward Kennedy, and Congressmen Don Edwards and Phil Burton of California. Thirty-four years after that legislative fight, I have been unable to determine whether some of these people realized how homophobic the bill was but decided not to make a fight because they were destined to fail, or whether the prevailing anti-gay-and-lesbian attitude at the time was so strong that this simply did not occur to anyone as an issue. Congressman Phil Burton of San Francisco was, according to Dudley Clendinen and Adam Nagourney in *Out for Good,* beginning to work with the gay and lesbian community in his city on discrimination issues at the time, but the focus of these efforts according to their book was on local practices, not on national concerns. The central point in either case is that at this stage of American history, a significant tightening of federal anti-gay-and-lesbian policy was enacted as a completely noncontroversial step, obviously reflecting a lack of any significant political support for gay and lesbian rights in the country as a whole.

Often in legislative situations where a provision that legislators find obnoxious is being enacted, the better part of valor is simply to ignore it, lest the debate over it add to its prominence and to the visibility of its support, leading potentially to stronger enforcement after enactment.

And there's further proof of the strength of the view that discrimination based on sexual orientation was entirely reasonable, and of the general consensus that homosexuals were bad people with no rights that the federal government had to respect. In 1967 the Warren Court decided Boutilier's case in favor of the government. Since he had brought the case before the addition of the phrase "sexual deviation," the court was deciding whether it was constitutional to exclude us from this country as "psychopaths," and while three justices did object to this, a six-member majority found it wholly unobjectionable. Included in that majority were Earl Warren and Hugo Black.

While the tightened exclusion in the 1965 act does not seem to have been systematically enforced, it was used from time to time to exclude people, particularly those potential visitors or immigrants to the United States who made the mistake of triggering the suspicion of immigration officials that they were other than 100 percent heterosexual. Carrying gay literature in one's luggage, dressing in ways other than those dictated by conventional sex roles, or appearing to be affectionate with someone of the same sex were all bases on which entrants were harassed at best and in some cases prevented from entering at worst.

The first break in this anti-gay-and-lesbian regime came during the

Carter administration, and it was a by-product of one of the early post-Stonewall victories in the fight against antigay bigotry. This victory was the result of the successful campaign waged by gay and lesbian leaders against the psychiatric diagnosis of homosexuality as a mental disorder. This had particular significance for the immigration exclusion: prohibiting gay men and lesbians from entering the United States in any capacity was far from the only seriously stupid part of American immigration law. Beginning around the turn of the century, and culminating in outrageous legislation passed over two Harry Truman vetoes at the height of the McCarthy era, American law contained a large number of exclusions to protect what legislators apparently thought was a fragile citizenry from all manner of dangerous foreign influences. Anarchists, people who believed in polygamy, Communists, people who knew people who were related to Communists, people who thought and said unpleasant things about America—the list of those kept out of America was egregious and in total violation of the spirit of free expression by which we purport to govern ourselves. Indeed, my own attention to this list of wholly unjustified exclusions in immigration law was first drawn not by cases involving homosexuality, but rather by those in which American immigration officials used the law to keep various literary and cultural figures from coming to our country in the 1950s and 1960s, lest they subvert our democracy.

The exclusions were divided into several categories: ideological, economic, moral, and health-related. While the effect of the 1965 amendment was to put us into the morally undesirable category, the original basis for our being excluded was purportedly health based. *Psychopathic* is a term with medical roots, no matter how badly misplaced in this instance. And the statutory and administrative scheme for enforcing the anti-gay-and-lesbian exclusion called for the U.S. Public Health Service to certify potential immigrants as homosexuals as a basis for their exclusion. By the 1970s, public health professionals were increasingly reluctant to engage in this practice, and when Jimmy Carter took office, he appointed a surgeon general who decided that the Public Health Service, over which he presided, would refuse to do so, citing as a justification that the psychiatric profession no longer considered homosexuality an illness. This of course made it entirely inappropriate for the Public Health Service to be the enforcer of the exclusion. (The Public Health Service had shown no such reluctance and was an active participant in drafting the anti-gay-and-lesbian exclusionary language in both the 1950s and 1960s.)

What ensued during the Carter years was the pattern of two steps forward, one step backward we have frequently seen in our effort to do away with homophobic restrictions. The Public Health Service refused to cooperate; the Immigration Service was uncertain how to respond; federal circuit courts issued conflicting rulings on whether exclusions could proceed in the absence of public health certification; and the result was an inconsistent pattern of enforcement, with the prohibition being invoked less often, but nonetheless remaining on the books. Finally, in 1980, high-ranking officials of the Carter Justice Department ruled that the Public Health Service's scruples notwithstanding, the law remained the law and we remained officially prohibited from visiting or immigrating to the United States.

This is the situation I encountered when I came to Congress in 1981. I do not remember exactly when I first became aware that American law flatly banned gay, lesbian, and bisexual foreigners from coming to the United States, and did so in the most inaccurately insulting terms. But I do know that by 1981 I was aware that as a gay American I had joined an institution—the U.S. Congress—that had sixteen years before done everything it could to protect my fellow citizens from foreigners who were like me. And I was determined to do everything that I could to abolish this abomination.

The general climate on gay and lesbian issues in 1981 was not good. Twelve years after Stonewall, while gains had been made at the state and local level in some metropolitan areas and some smaller university communities, the national scene was still bleak. President Carter had made some tentative steps toward dealing with antigay prejudice, but congressional sentiment to the extent that it existed was overwhelmingly hostile. Evidence of this came early for me when the House of Representatives voted by 281 to 119 to overrule a District of Columbia City Council repeal of the city's sodomy law.

This obviously did not bode well for an effort to repeal the homophobic immigration exclusion, so I did not at that point introduce legislation to do so. But another route toward accomplishing that repeal soon became clear. By 1980 widespread dissatisfaction existed with immigration law. Illegal immigration was becoming a problem in the minds of many, as the attractive force of the American economy brought to our shores foreigners in pursuit of economic progress.

In addition to the problem of illegal immigration, some of the ethnic groups that had found their overseas cousins in a less favored position after the 1965 revision were unhappy. Indeed, a prestigious congressionally created national commission had called for a complete revision of immigration law in a widely publicized report in 1980. It occurred to me that just as the antigay exclusions had been first written and then tightened as part of a comprehensive overhaul of immigration law, my best chance to wipe them out was to do it in that same comprehensive context.

I was in a position to do so because I had agreed in 1981 to become a member of the Judiciary Committee, and specifically to serve on the subcommittee that dealt with immigration. As it turned out, my membership on that subcommittee was a critical factor in my being able to lead this fight to a successful conclusion. Had I not been over the next ten years one of those handful of House members intimately involved with immigration reform, I would not have had the leverage to insist that repeal of the antigay exclusion be included as part of the final package. I could of course have argued for that as a member of the House in general, but it is much harder to be the advocate of a potentially controversial piece of legislation from the outside than it is for one who is sitting at the table when the package deal on a complex and controversial bill is put together. I note this because it underlines a point that is too often lost when history is written: accidents not only happen, they are often an indispensable link in the chain of events that cause other, more important things to happen. When I came to Congress, I was committed publicly to serving on the House Banking Committee, which had jurisdiction over urban affairs, having promised to do that during my campaign in a district that included a number of cities. Ordinarily, service on the Banking Committee would have precluded service on the Judiciary Committee, but I was asked by the House leadership to accept a membership on both. This was a time when school prayer, busing, abortion, and other divisive issues were being used by the right wing against Democrats with some success. This put the Democratic leadership in the position of trying to find people who would serve on the Judiciary Committee who felt sufficiently strongly about these issues, and sufficiently secure politically, or some combination of both, to vote against antiabortion and pro-school-prayer legislation in committee to keep it from reaching the floor of the House where more politically vulnerable members would have to vote on it. When I raised the objection at the time to House Speaker Tip O'Neill that I was no more eager than my colleagues to put myself in the line of fire of these various conservative groups, he noted, perfectly reasonably, that the members of those groups generally didn't like me anyway, and so I had little to lose.

Thus, while the overwhelming vote to repeal the District of Columbia's anti-sodomy action was a bad sign for pro-gay-and-lesbian legislation, the consensus that a comprehensive immigration overhaul was necessary, and my service on the subcommittee that would deal with it as a favor to those who were most interested in seeing it happen, meant that I would have a significant role in shaping this package.

I set about to do two things in this regard. First, of course, was to become familiar with the overall issues involved in redrafting immigration law. Second, I began to talk with my colleagues, at first privately and informally, to gauge how much resistance I would encounter in trying to reform the exclusionary provisions in general, and the antigay piece in particular. I was pleasantly surprised by what I found. The national commission itself, chaired by Father Theodore Hesburgh, had indicated its disapproval of the approach to immigration exclusions that the McCarthyite laws of the 1950s embodied, although to avoid entangling their broader immigration objectives in controversy, they had refrained from any specifics. I also found widespread agreement among the mostly liberal Democratic members of the Judiciary Committee that the anti-gay exclusion was unjustifiable, and even among several of the Republicans I found an unwillingness to defend it. Most interesting, even some of those who did defend it did so in a way that revealed that the intellectual and moral underpinnings for the policy were being eroded by the post-Stonewall assault on homophobia in the culture at large. Their argument was that the exclusion was so rarely enforced that it was not a serious obstacle to gay men and lesbians in reality and thus served the useful symbolic function of making clear our national disapproval of homosexual behavior.

One other fact proved indispensable in my ability to take the lead in a successful drive to abolish the antigay exclusion: I was in broad agreement with the approach to immigration that had been recommended by the Hesburgh Commission, and which was supported by both the Reagan administration and the leading congressional advocates of immigration reform. I was thus able to become part of the coalition that was to rewrite immigration law over the next ten years. The notion in the early 1980s was that a single bill would be produced that would seek to retard illegal immigration and would also make some changes in legal immigration. The exclusions were part of the legal-immigration provisions, and as a member of the Democratic majority on the immigration subcommittee, I asked for and was accorded by my colleagues the right to take the lead in rewriting the exclusion provisions.

My intention was to take the legitimate bases for excluding people from this country—namely, that they would in some real way be dangerous to our well-being—and embody them in a new section that would replace the existing obnoxious sections. I would deal with the antigay exclusion simply by leaving it out of the redraft. Thus, no separate vote would be taken on whether to repeal this provision, because its abolition would be accomplished by omission. And since I was part of the majority that would be presenting the new bill, the burden in Congress would thus be shifted to those who sought to preserve this homophobic aspect. That is, since my draft would be part of the committee's proposal, any member or members who wanted to reinsert the ban on gays and lesbians would have to offer their proposal as an amendment.

Because I remained sufficiently in tune with majority sentiment in the immigration subcommittee, and ultimately in Congress as a whole, I could promise to be a strong supporter of the final package, so long as I was satisfied by the redraft of the exclusion provisions, which meant among other things a total repeal of the anti-gay-and-lesbian language. Had I disagreed with the basic outlines of the legislation, my leverage would have been negligible—a threat to withhold your support from a bill you are going to oppose in any case does not buy you much.

Adding significantly to my leverage as a supporter of the overall bill who had a particular set of interests that I wanted included was that the comprehensive package was controversial with or without the exclusion language. The congressional leadership and the Reagan and Bush administrations needed all the help they could get to get the bill passed. Just as I could have expected to win little in bargaining over a bill that I was determined to oppose no matter what, I could not have expected to gain significant attention by threatening to withhold my support from a bill that was certain to pass without me.

The nature of legislative bargaining is a key element here. If all participants feel equally intensely about all parts of the legislation under consideration, bargaining is difficult. In this case I was in an ideal situation because while I was in favor of the overall bill, I cared most of all about the exclusions, and I was prepared to try to defeat the bill if I was not successful in reforming what I considered to be the most outrageous aspect of American immigration law, the antigay, anti-free-speech McCarthyite hangover. On this issue, the main priority of the Democratic and Republican leadership was passing the overall bill. My priority was reform of the exclusionary provisions. In the end they accommodated me on the exclusion issue because I was prepared to be a loyal soldier in their battle for the comprehensive legislation.

But even this would not have sufficed if we had not been making progress in our overall fight against homophobia. Indeed, if the immigration legislation had come to a vote as quickly as had been anticipated, in 1981 or 1982, the antigay exclusion would probably have been retained. The committee leadership would have been supportive, but in an antigay climate, any member in either the House or the Senate might have offered a reinstatement of some or all of the exclusions, specifically including the antigay exclusion. It would have been one thing for me to threaten to withhold my support if the leadership had failed to accommodate me. But if the leadership had tried to be supportive and they and I together had been overruled by a House or Senate vote, my leverage would have been substantially less.

We were helped when the reform of immigration took so much time—partly because the issue proved to be so politically difficult—that the Judiciary Committee decided in 1982 or so to deal with it in two separate bills. Because of the perceived crisis caused by illegal immigration, the illegal-immigration issue was dealt with first in the Simpson-Rodino bill of 1986. Not until 1990 did the question of legal immigration come to a vote on the floor of the House of Representatives, and by that time, opinion both in the country and in Congress had increased significantly—although obviously not nearly enough—against discrimination based on sexual orientation.

The single most important thing I have learned in eighteen years of fighting for gay and lesbian rights in Congress is the interaction of the cultural and political aspects of this fight. This is no chicken-egg conundrum—the cultural element clearly comes first; without changes in attitude, politics is unavailing. But it is also clear to me that as much progress as we make in the culture—as effective as we are as a people in cutting away the intellectual and moral underpinnings of prejudice—we do not automatically profit in law or politics from cultural change. Cultural changes create the opportunity. Intelligent political action is necessary to take advantage of it. In this situation, my being strategically placed in the midst of the coalition pushing for an overhaul of immigration law was an essential element in our getting rid of the antigay exclusion, but nothing I did would have made any difference had it not been for the broad assault on prejudice that millions of gay, lesbian, and bisexual people and our straight allies had been waging in the twenty years between Stonewall and 1990.

The first sign that society's willingness to question homophobia was having an impact on Congress came in 1984 and 1985, in the debate about AIDS. One of the problems we had in lobbying members of Congress to vote against anti-gay-and-lesbian prejudice was their lack of understanding about how serious a problem it was. This is not entirely surprising. For most of American history, we had done a good job of hiding precisely that fact from mainstream America. Closets work all too well. Politicians who did not know that they knew any gay or lesbian people understandably had no real grasp of the pain that homophobia inflicted on these invisible beings. I first learned this in lobbying colleagues for gay rights legislation in the Massachusetts legislature in the 1970s, and I found when working to preserve the D.C. sodomy repeal in 1981 that these attitudes were even more pronounced in Congress. Essentially I was often told, "Look, pal, I don't think it's right to discriminate against those people. [I was myself in the closet until 1987 and my membership in "those people" was not widely known in 1981.] But I don't think this is a real problem and I'm not going to get into political trouble over symbolism." This view, that legislation to protect the rights of gay and lesbian people was much more symbolic than real, prevailed among many politicians who argued that they should not be expected to incur the political damage they thought would result from a pro-gay voting stance in the absence of a real problem.

Then came AIDS. The first votes in which advocates of fairness for gays and lesbians were successful in both the House and the Senate came when gay bashers such as Jesse Helms in the Senate and William Dannemeyer in the House sought to add hate-filled amendments to the earliest AIDS legislation. This presented many of my colleagues with a dilemma. By the mid-eighties sensible politicians understood that AIDS was a serious killer, and they understood that many of these amendments were designed to prevent effective legislation from being adopted to deal with AIDS. In this context, no one could argue that we were fighting over symbolism. Lives were at stake, a point reinforced by the generally courageous position taken by the medical profession, including the American Medical Association, which usually spoke out strongly against these killer amendments. Because most members of Congress are serious people who got into politics because they wanted to do good things, we were able to defeat many of the worst of the amendments that would have hobbled AIDS policy. In fact, I know that many of my colleagues voted against these homophobic assaults expecting that they would pay a price for it at the polls, but believing that they had no moral right to endanger the lives of innocent people just for their political advantage. And this is where the change in public attitudes comes in. To their surprise, members of Congress who had voted against the Helms-Dannemeyer-Burton et al. amendments found that their fears were either greatly exaggerated or just plain wrong. They paid no price at the polls for resisting homophobic efforts to interfere with sound medical treatment. Members of Congress began casting votes on these issues in 1984, and the results of both the 1984 and 1986 congressional elections helped dispel the notion that a pro-gay vote would be significantly politically damaging in all but a handful of highly sophisticated urban districts.

In 1986, I was first able to take advantage of this new confidence that homophobia was politically resistible. The illegal-immigration bill had first been voted on in both chambers in 1984, but the House and the Senate versions were very different and a conference committee was unable to bridge the gap. I was not eager to see the gap closed at that point. First, I was sensitive to the complaints of the Hispanic-American community that imposing sanctions against employers who hired people who are here illegally would foster anti-Hispanic discrimination. To alleviate this problem, I supported amendments that would have greatly strengthened protection against such discrimination and created a new agency to enforce these protections. But the Senate was controlled by Republicans who were deeply skeptical of antidiscrimination efforts and did not wish to increase the government's power in this regard.

I was also concerned about losing my leverage on the issue of exclusions. The Democratic leadership in the House had promised to support my efforts when we proceeded to the part of the legislation dealing with legal immigration, but in the political climate that existed in 1984, especially with regard to homosexuality, that support alone was not a guarantee of success. Had we voted on the antigay exclusion in 1984, while I would have been supported by most Democrats, there might well have been enough Democratic defections along with overwhelming Republican opposition to defeat us. I needed assurances that the House Republicans would support an effort to avoid a floor vote on the issue when the bill came up in the House, and I needed equally that the Republicans would agree to removing the antigay exclusion in the House/Senate conference. In 1984 the Republicans were not ready to give me that commitment, and I was thus extremely reluctant to agree to the reduction in my bargaining strength that would have been occured with passage of the bill dealing with illegal immigration.

During these years—1981 through 1984—I had made clear to the leaders of the immigration-policy coalition my strong feelings on the exclusions. What I found was ambivalence. Few people outside of the hard right were prepared to defend them. The ideological exclusions in particular had been a great embarrassment, and in a number of cases the United States had been made to look foolish because the law had required immigration officials to ban notable literary figures from visiting us. And while the antigay exclusion had not received a great deal of attention in the public debate, partly because those who had been subjected to it were often unwilling to make a public issue of the matter, I raised it with all of those involved. The first reactions I got were of the sort I described above—an acknowledgment that it was unjustified, but a reluctance to take on the political damage that could come from announcing that America was now open to touring homosexuals. But most of all I realized that these were people whose primary goal was to get an immigration overhaul written into law, and their position on the exclusions—including the antigay exclusion—would be influenced by the impact this would have on the overall bill.

All of this strengthened my view that the critical factor in getting rid of the antigay exclusion and rewriting the others would be the willingness of myself and others to make our support of this set of changes a condition of our overall support for the bill. That is, with those most interested in immigration repeal regarding the exclusionary issue as secondary to their overall goal, my job was to make it clear to them that they would be far better off from the standpoint of getting the basic legislation enacted by accommodating my position than by ignoring it. In the early 1980s, I am afraid I would have lost in their calculation. But by the mid-1980s things were changing, as homophobes were increasingly put on the defensive in society at large and as my colleagues learned through the AIDS battle that it was possible to survive casting votes that their opposition would take as support for the "gay agenda."

It thus began to seem possible to me to use my position in the midst of this debate over immigration to remove the antigay exclusion. And a test of that came in 1984. An Englishman legally resident in the United States named Richard Longstaff resisted an effort by the Immigration Service to deport him because of his homosexuality. He was ably represented by lawyers who took advantage of the different approaches that had been followed by different federal circuit courts. But there was no assurance that the legal route would protect him, especially since the U.S. Supreme Court's only ruling on the subject was so negative to us. While he obviously was not being well treated by the U.S. government, there was one fortuitous thing in his relationship to the federal government—he lived in the Texas district of the late Mickey Leland, who was an early and staunch champion of gay and lesbian rights. Congressman Leland, who was tragically killed in a plane crash in Ethiopia on one of his many missions to fight world hunger, approached me to ask for my help in protecting his constituent. I urged him to file a private immigration bill, granting Mr.

Longstaff the right to remain a legal resident, the statutory provisions to the contrary notwithstanding. At no point did we think such a bill could become law, because private bills must pass both chambers with virtual unanimity. A single objection buries a bill, and two objections will kill it. But under the rules of the Immigration Service and the immigration subcommittee, favorable action by that subcommittee on a private bill freezes matters for an indefinite period. That is, I knew that if I could get the immigration subcommittee to pass Mr. Leland's bill, action against Mr. Longstaff would be stopped, giving us time to negotiate, change the underlying statute—which did not require unanimity—or maybe even win a lawsuit.

And so the first test of congressional sentiment, especially among those focused on the immigration bill, came with this private bill. As one does when one is serious about legislation, I spoke privately with my colleagues before introducing the bill to try to prepare the way. At this point we were deeply enmeshed in the negotiations over the passage of the illegal-immigration bill, after the difficulties with the first version had prevented its passage in 1984. Thus, my importance to the ultimate success to the coalition was clearly established. And I was fortunate in having an excellent case with which to test support for repealing the antigay exclusion. Mr. Longstaff was a model citizen who had done nothing wrong, and whose deportation from the country would obviously have been an outrageous injustice. Elected officials are often strongly moved by individual examples of injustice, even when those individual examples represent routine applications of laws that they have supported.

Mr. Leland, who was also well thought of by his colleagues, of course joined me in lobbying strongly for the Longstaff relief bill, and the immigration subcommittee passed it unanimously. The bill then went to full committee, where it also passed, although not before one of the most conservative members of the committee, James Sensenbrenner of Wisconsin, noted that he would not object to this bill's going forward in committee, but that he wanted to serve notice on those who saw this as a way of beginning to repeal the antigay exclusion that he would not support that.

After first seeing his comment was a negative sign, I then realized that it was in fact positive, because it meant that the committee, without dissent other than his, had approved the first legislative step ever taken in contradiction to the antigay exclusion. Mr. Longstaff was ultimately allowed to live in peace. In part because my relationship with immigration officials in both the Reagan and Bush administrations strengthened as we worked together on the legislative package, I was able to help lift all practical restrictions on Mr. Longstaff.

With the initial gauge of sentiment favorable, I was then ready to push for legislative action attacking the entire exclusionary scheme, including the antigay provision. And my opportunity to do so came in 1986 when Congress finally passed the illegal-immigration part of the bill. Several million people who had entered illegally before a certain date, and who had not otherwise committed crimes in the United States, were given legal status by this bill. But the question arose as to the interaction of the legal-amnesty provision with the exclusions. Unless Congress specifically legislated on this subject, those eligible for legalization of their status in general would not qualify if they fell within one of the excludable categories. It was too early to attempt a total rewrite of the exclusions; the exclusion issue was not technically a part of the illegal-immigration bill, which was already controversial. Adding something that could potentially cost votes such as the rewrite of the exclusion legislation thus violated the norm of working together to get the bill passed. But I had a claim for the matter to be dealt with in the illegal bill so that the people being granted amnesty would not be damaged by the exclusions. My argument was that while I was prepared not to press for a total repeal, it would betray my commitment to legislative reform to create a whole new category of people—in the millions—who would then be subject to these unfair exclusions.

By the mid-eighties the partisan divisions over gay and lesbian rights that have become so prominent a part of our fight had appeared. Then as now, the Democratic members of Congress were much better on this subject than our Republican colleagues. In fact, during the 1980s and 1990s, the Democrats have increasingly supported gay and lesbian rights, while the Republicans have sadly stayed the same or even eroded when one does vote analysis. In the mideighties, the gap was not as wide as it is now between the Democratic congressional party largely supporting antidiscrimination measures and a Republican party overwhelmingly backing homophobia, but there was still a difference.

The Democratic leadership in the committee agreed to designate me the lead negotiator on this subject and promised me strong Democratic support for my effort to prevent the full set of exclusions from applying to those getting amnesty. I then negotiated with the Republicans, led by Dan Lungren of California, and Hamilton Fish, since deceased, who was then the senior Republican on the Judiciary Committee. Hamilton Fish was one of what is unfortunately now a rare breed of Republican: a man thoroughly committed to civil rights for all. He used his position as the senior Judiciary Committee Republican to great advantage in that regard. He was also one of those most devoted to getting an immigration bill passed, and he was among my strongest allies in our ultimate success in defeating the antigay exclusion. Dan Lungren, though conservative, and at that time an antigay vote on most issues, was not personally homophobic and was eager to see the overall bill passed.

Congressmen Fish and Lungren agreed that we should try to find a way to prevent the exclusions from interfering with the amnesty provision, even though we were not then ready to repeal them. In consequence, the illegal-immigration bill included a section that explicitly waived many of the exclusions in this amnesty. There were three categories. A few exclusions were continued—those dealing legitimately with public health and safety, which would ultimately be continued in the bill after we rewrote the exclusion section in 1990. A second set were waived automatically, and a third were made waivable by the immigration commissioner. Reflecting the uncertainty of our political strength at the time, the antigay exclusion went into this third category. But it did so only after I had conversations with Alan Nelson, then commissioner of the INS. While he was a Reagan appointee and generally conservative, he and I agreed on some important immigration issues, and he was a reasonable man who saw the inequities and unfairness of many of the exclusion provisions. Indeed, from the early days of our work on immigration, he agreed to moderate enforcement of the antigay exclusion. I use the word *moderate* because as long as it remained on the books, if an immigration officer chose to apply it and could show that he was acting within the statute, no superior could overrule him. High officials may not order law enforcement agents—as Immigration Service people are—simply to disregard laws when those agents find violations, stupid as the laws may be. But Commissioner Nelson did do all he could to minimize the damage the exclusion did, pending our success in repealing it. I was thus assured that if we gave him the discretion to waive the antigay exclusion with regard to those seeking amnesty, he would do so in every case.

Commissioner Nelson proved true to his word. When from time to time cases came to our attention where lower-level immigration agents tried to use the antigay exclusion as a barrier to amnesty, we were always able to get this overruled, since under this law the commissioner had the statutory authority to order such a waiver. And when one of the lawyers concerned with immigration called to my attention that immigration officials were still in some cases using a form that asked people about their homosexuality, I complained quickly to the Commissioner, who just as quickly ordered that these forms be destroyed and never used again.

One example that came to my attention stays with me. A Cuban Marielito who had been expelled by Castro and was covered by the amnesty had been interviewed by an Immigration Service official using one of these "are you now or were you ever a homosexual" forms. The man did not speak English. He was asked by the immigration agent if he had ever had homosexual relations. His answer—as translated—was that he had "fooled around some with guys" but had never had a real relation. A note in the margin of the form indicated that he had then sought to withdraw that answer on advice of counsel, but had not been permitted to do so. The immigration agent promptly decided that he should not get amnesty because of this admission of sexual relations with men. The commissioner, per our agreement, used his waiver authority to overrule this decision and then make clear that this exclusion should not apply.

As a consequence of all this, as the amnesty took effect, it did so with no exclusion of homosexuals. At the same time, the various gay and lesbian organizations and individuals were progressing in our fight against homophobia. Of course we were not then—nor now—anywhere near where we should be in this fight. But we had won an important philosophical and semantic victory, which was to be a decisive factor in our being able ultimately to repeal the exclusion in 1990.

We were at some advantage here because we were dealing with an explicit antigay provision put in by the bigots, rather than an effort by ourselves to enact protective language as with the Employment Non-Discrimination Act, or a hate crimes statute. In logical terms this does not make a great deal of difference. In political terms, it is significant.

Note that this was not the case before Stonewall. In a society in which homophobia is generally accepted, removing an antigay exclusion is no easier than enacting a pro-gay protection. Both are simply rejected on the rationale that homosexuals are bad people doing bad things, and that the law should reflect this attitude. Once we have rendered homophobia generally unacceptable, there similarly will be no difference between enacting a protection and repealing a discrimination. Once society is generally convinced that homophobia is a bad thing and that people should not be disadvantaged because of their sexual orientation, it will make little political difference whether one is trying to undo a disadvantage that is written in law, or protect people against discrimination.

But we are now in what I genuinely believe will be a transitional period, in which homophobia still exists, but in which we have done enough to cut away its support so that the homophobes recognize the need to disguise their position. Thus, in the debates we now have on public policy regarding anti-gay-and-lesbian discrimination, our opponents are rarely as honest as they used to be. When the anti-gay-and-lesbian exclusion in the immigration law was adopted in the 1950s, and even when it was tightened in the 1960s, no one felt the need to engage in any elaborate explanation. Homosexuality was bad; people who indulged in it were, if anything, worse; and while the country could not automatically expel all American homosexuals—although it could make their lives miserable—it could certainly prevent any of those bad people who were not already here from joining us. And in this climate, those members of Congress who by the 1960s obviously knew this was outrageous bigotry simply lacked any intellectual, cultural, or political context in which to make the argument, so they remained silent.

I encountered similar blatant bigotry in the early 1970s when I first introduced gay rights legislation in the Massachusetts House, which I joined after the election of 1972. Antidiscrimination legislation then was not met by pseudosophisticated discussions of special rights. The argument was simple: fags and dykes are undesirables and no one ought to have to associate with them, whether in the workplace or any where else. End of argument.

Today, homophobes are very much on the defensive in our culture. The handful of remaining intellectually honest bigots who announce that they wish to be able to fire people because they do not think gays and lesbians ought to have the same rights as others appear almost quaint. Rarely do we encounter this sort of straightforward acknowledgment of anti-gay-and-lesbian feelings. On issue after issue—antidiscrimination, same-sex marriage, service in the military, protecting young people against harassment in schools—our opponents deny that they are "anti" gay or lesbian and insist instead that they are simply trying to "protect" the rest of society from our aggression. Thus, laws to prevent someone from being fired because he or she is gay or lesbian are illogically denounced as conferring special rights. In fact, to bolster the argument that we are seeking special rights, many of those opposed to antidiscrimination laws claim—in almost every case knowing that they are lying—that the law already protects people against being fired because of their sexual orientation. The Defense of Marriage Act was so titled so that its sponsors could argue not that they were seeking to prevent lesbian or gay couples from formalizing their relationships, but rather that they were protecting heterosexual marriage against the terrible influence that would emanate from same-sex marriages. (Interestingly, at last count, five of the House members who voted to deprive us of the right to marry so as to protect the sanctity of heterosexual marriage have been shown to have engaged in adulterous affairs.) And when we seek to institute programs that protect lesbian and gay teenagers from the torment that is often their lot in high school, we are told not that it is a good thing that these bad young people should be abused, but rather that we seek "to promote" homosexuality. This charge is leveled despite the fact that I have yet to meet anyone, straight or gay, who has any idea about how one would promote homosexuality if that is what one wished to do.

It is frustrating to have our opponents dissemble, but in an ironic way it is also encouraging. That bigots no longer feel comfortable in honestly espousing their bigotry is their implicit recognition that the society is moving away from their position. Their political argument is an example of the truth of La Rochefoucauld's maxim "hypocrisy is the homage that vice pays to virtue." They know that if they were straightforward in explaining why they wished to keep gay men and lesbians at a legal disadvantage in our society, they would lose the support they can otherwise get by claiming that they actually favor legal neutrality and simply seek to prevent us from aggression.

Obviously these are difficult issues for us to grapple with in other contexts, especially with a public that has grown somewhat skeptical of government in general and is thus predisposed to agree with those who impute bad motives to people seeking legislative solutions. But in the case of the immigration exclusion, no such artifice was open to the bigots. The law flatly excluded gay men and lesbians from coming to this country, and we were overwhelmingly on the side of legal neutrality in simply asking that it be repealed. In fact, now that we have succeeded in the repeal, the law is of course still less than neutral. Gay or lesbian people who fall in love with non-Americans are seriously disadvantaged compared to our straight fellow citizens, because they can arrange to have the people they love come join them, as long as they are prepared to get married, no matter what immigration quotas apply. We, unfortunately, have no such right, and one of the least noticed but most vicious provisions of the Defense of Marriage Act says that even if a state allows same-sex marriage, American immigration law will not recognize it. Although an amendment I offered to strike that part of the law did significantly better than we were able to do against the overall bill, it still lost by a three-to-one margin, and it will be up to the courts to free us from this provision when a state does allow same-sex marriage.

The stage was thus set for complete repeal of the anti-gay-and-lesbian exclusion in 1989 and 1990, when Congress finally addressed the legal-immigration question.

And while the stage was set, there was one significant alteration in the role of one of the characters—myself. On June 1, 1987, after some months of dithering, I publicly acknowledged that I was gay. By coming out, I enhanced my ability to press for a complete repeal of the anti-gay-and-lesbian exclusion. Legislating is the most personal of all government business. The importance of the personal factor in relations among government officials increases as the breadth of their discretion increases. Where the authority individual public officials have is tightly circumscribed by law, there is not a great deal of room for personality to have an impact. When you are required by your job to do X or Y, the fact that you do not get along with the people with whom you have to do X or Y has a limited effect. Even where officials at the highest levels have discretion over policy choices, their areas of authority are carefully defined in law, thus limiting the extent to which personal factors influence decisions. And the effect of hierarchy also acts greatly to limit the role of personality in the executive branch. Not only do the secretary of defense and the secretary of state each have a sphere in which his or her legal authority is immune from intrusion by the other, in addition both are subject to orders from the president requiring them to resolve differences. By contrast, legislating puts hundreds of men and women together in a position of formal equality, and in a situation in which, while some may specialize in one or another area, all are legally equal in their responsibility for the whole range of issues. To deal with the potential chaos that this represents, legislators put a great deal of emphasis on good personal relations with each other, even in most cases across party, sectional, and ideological lines. Before I came out, my colleagues respected my insistence on the repeal of the antigay provision as they would respect any colleague's strong feeling on an issue. But once I had acknowledged that I was gay, this moved from being simply an issue with which I was concerned to something that was obviously deeply personal. Automatically this meant that those of my colleagues who wished to preserve good working relationships with me understood how important this matter was to me, and their willingness to accommodate me increased accordingly.

Confirmation that all of the factors that I have described had created a favorable atmosphere for the repeal of the antigay exclusion came in June 1988—coincidentally shortly over one year after the day of my coming out. In preparation for putting together the comprehensive immigration reform bill, the Judiciary Committee leadership decided to present my redraft of the grounds-for-exclusion section in the form of a separate bill for consideration in the committee. We did not have any notion that such a separate bill would become law, nor even that it would pass the House of Representatives. What the committee leadership sought was a test vote on these provisions to see if they would be supported by a majority of the Judiciary Committee, so that they could then be inserted into the overall bill without further controversy.

On June 22, I presented the proposal which removed the egregious bias against people with any mental or emotional illness; dropped most of the ideological exclusions, so that the law would no longer be an offense to the American principle of encouraging free debate; and, most important to me obviously, omitted any reference to homosexuality—i.e., it omitted the antigay exclusion, so that there would be no legal basis whatsoever for barring gay or lesbian immigrants. In the Judiciary Committee meeting, Representative William Dannemeyer, an extreme right-winger and the leading House homophobe during the 1980s, offered an amendment to reinsert the antigay exclusion—using the "psychopath and sexual deviant" label. A roll call vote was taken on his amendment, and we defeated it by a vote of 23 to 10. Two of the factors I have previously mentioned accounted for this significant victory. One was the partisan split that had developed over gay and lesbian issues. Every one of the twenty-one Democrats on the committee voted with me, against the Dannemeyer effort to reinsert an antigay provision. Notably included among these Democratic supporters were members from Virginia, Texas, Kansas, and Oklahoma—not always bastions of social liberalism.

Secondly, the two Republican leaders on the immigration issue who had been working with me so that we could maintain our overall coalition broke with the Republican majority to oppose Dannemeyer's amendment. They were, as noted, the senior Republican on the full committee, Representative Hamilton Fish, and the senior Republican on the immigration subcommittee,

Dan Lungren (who later became attorney general of California and an unsuccessful California gubernatorial candidate in 1998). Interestingly, on a subsequent amendment to make it tougher on "subversives," Congressman Lungren voted with the Republican majority, although this amendment was also defeated, by a 23 to 12 vote. Obviously the cooperation that had developed between me and Congressman Lungren on behalf of the overall bill had an influence on his vote on the homosexual exclusion.

Further confirmation that we were likely to succeed ultimately in repealing the gay exclusion came when the Republican members filed their minority report on the measure.[2] Twelve Republicans signed the report—with Congressmen Fish and Lungren again being the exceptions. But most important for our purposes is that the minority view criticized my proposal because they thought it would weaken our ability to deal with Communists and other national security threats, but did not mention the antigay provision. That is, although the great majority of Republicans felt compelled to vote with Congressman Dannemeyer to reinsert an antigay exclusion when he raised the issue, when it came to listing their reasons for opposing the bill, they acknowledged the lack of political support for the antigay provision by failing to include it.

I should note that I had added leverage when we debated the bill in 1988 because I had come out the year before, and that leverage was not diminished by the unpleasantness in which I was involved in September 1989, when a hustler with whom I had been involved in 1985 and 1986 denounced me, coupling some truths about our sexual relationship with a good number of lies. Over the ensuing year I dealt with this at the House Ethics Committee, and I was ultimately reprimanded for having concealed in a letter the circumstances under which I had met him, and for letting him use my parking-ticket privilege inappropriately, but I was able to refute the most serious of his charges, which were untrue. To my pleasant surprise, the majority of my colleagues appeared to understand my explanation that my stupidity had been one of the consequences of my being in the closet, and in some cases this revelation of the irresponsible way in which I had acted when in the closet helped them understand why I had decided two years earlier voluntarily to acknowledge being gay.

Now that I was out and many of my colleagues were sympathetic rather than censorious, I continued to be the leading advocate of a rewrite of the exclusion laws in general and the antigay exclusion in particular. By this time the Bush administration was in power, but the commitment to a reform of legal immigration was as strong in this administration as it had been in the previous one. And by now both the Democratic and Republican Judiciary Committee leadership on the immigration issue were prepared to support my efforts as long as I remained an active and vigorous proponent of passage of the ultimate legislation.

At this point the Senate became relevant, and it was our good fortune to have an extraordinary bipartisan pair of senators dominating immigration policymaking in that body. The chairman of the subcommittee was Senator Kennedy, who has for years been one of the most effective, committed, and forceful advocates of fairness for gay men and lesbians. And we were equally lucky to have as the senior Republican on this subject Senator Alan Simpson of Wyoming. He was then not only the senior Republican on the immigration subcommittee, but also the deputy leader of the Senate—a post he held until 1995 when he was, sadly, defeated by a right-wing assault that replaced him with Trent Lott. Simpson is a mainstream economic conservative who, unusually among leading Republicans today, maintains an equally strong commitment to individual rights, and while he was not originally a supporter of gay and lesbian rights in the Senate, he is one of those who, as he learned more about the issue, became more strongly supportive. He agreed that the exclusions were foolish and discreditable to America, and he was particularly sympathetic to my concern about the gay exclusion.

As a result of the test vote we won so decisively in 1988, and with the strong support of Senators Simpson and Kennedy, when the overall immigration bill was finally adopted in 1990 and signed into law, we had a mirror image of the situation that had accompanied the tightening of the antigay exclusion in 1965. Just as in that year no formal attempt was made to weaken the antigay exclusion, reflecting the overwhelmingly anti-gay-and-lesbian consensus then ruling in America, so in 1990 no effort was made to reinsert any exclusion. When the House and Senate Conference Committee met in 1990 to put together a final version of the bill for passage in both chambers and subsequent presentation to President Bush, Senator Simpson and I were designated as a subcommittee of the Conference Committee to work out the exclusion issues, and we were quickly able to come to agreement on a proposal that closely resembled what the House Judiciary Committee had approved in 1988. Under House and Senate rules, conference reports are not subject to amendment, and so when the bill was approved by both chambers—not before an initial defeat in the House over an unrelated issue that had to be changed—the repeal of the antigay exclusion became fact.

One threat to this result had presented itself the year before, which we were able to thwart. As I mentioned, the exclusions included obnoxious provisions interfering with the right of Americans to invite to our shores people of a variety of viewpoints to participate in free-ranging debate. The American Civil Liberties Union shared the objections of myself and many others to that provision, and before we were able to bring a comprehensive immigration reform to the floor, the ACLU worked with Senator Daniel Patrick Moynihan, a staunch defender of free speech, to get an amendment adopted, as part of the appropriations process, that substantially reformed the ideological-exclusion part of the immigration law. Laudable as the ACLU's goals were, their proposal would not have repealed the antigay exclusion. My fear was that a partial reform would weaken the coalition of forces I had been able to assemble for a complete improvement in this section. That is, if the First Amendment restrictions were to be permanently repealed, interest in reforming the rest of the exclusion bill would be less than it had been. Senator Moynihan was more sympathetic to this objection than the ACLU was and in consequence agreed to a temporary free-speech fix of only a year, during which time we would be bringing the overall immigration bill to the floor. While the ACLU has subsequently become active in its advocacy of gay and lesbian rights, at this point to my dismay they seemed not at all interested in helping me with the anti-gay-and-lesbian exclusion matter and disagreed with my approach. Fortunately, their legislative allies were more amenable to my insistence on making sure that the antigay provision was not left in place, and that prevailed.

Thus, by 1990, immigration law was formally neutral and all anti-gay-and-lesbian references were excluded.

Things remained this way until 1993, with the advent of the Clinton administration. In 1992, I had written to Attorney General William Barr, in the Bush administration, asking that homosexuality be added to the list of causes for which individuals who suffer persecution overseas can get asylum in the United States. The asylum law allows the Justice Department to allow members of designated "social groups" to qualify for asylum, as long as one can prove persecution based on one's membership in that group. The Bush administration refused to act on my request. President Bush had of course signed the overall immigration bill that omitted the anti-gay-and-lesbian exclusion, but he did so because of his strong support for the overall legislation, not because he supported gay and lesbian rights.

When President Clinton took office with a commitment to take action that would support the right of gay, lesbian, and bisexual people to fair treatment, I renewed the request. For much of 1993 we were of course preoccupied with trying to repeal the ban on gays in the military. When that ended badly for us, I spoke with the president and his aides and urged that precisely because we had been unsuccessful in our effort to repeal the military ban due to congressional opposition, it was essential both politically and as a matter of fairness that the president take whatever actions he could on his authority to protect us against homophobia. Three such actions were on my list, based on my experience with the federal government and its interaction with gay and lesbian people. The first was to build on the efforts that Jimmy Carter had begun to make it clear that discrimination based on sexual orientation was illegitimate in the federal civil service. The president responded by having the director of the Office of Personnel Management, Jim King, send a letter to every federal agency pointing out that it was the Clinton administration's view that existing federal law banned such discrimination, and directing agencies to adopt nondiscrimination policies. We have been following through on this in the intervening years, with a formal presidential executive order embodying this being part of the effort, and by now that policy is fairly well established in the federal government.

Secondly, and importantly, the president issued an executive order in 1994 explicitly revoking the section of the executive order first issued by President Eisenhower that cited homosexuality as a negative factor in the granting of security clearances. Millions of Americans have security clearances, since they are necessary not only for certain kinds of government work, but also for work in the private sector for companies that deal with the Defense Department, the Energy Department, etc. The president's issuance of this executive order was thus important in freeing many gay and lesbian people from a severe form of job harassment and, of course, made an important statement in contradiction to one of the negative stereotypes that have plagued us—namely that we are so prone to blackmail that we cannot be trusted. Of course it should be noted that both before and after the president issued the executive order, there have been no cases of any gay man or lesbian betraying the nation's security because of his or her homosexuality, or anyone's threat to reveal it.

Third, I asked the administration to make gay and lesbian people eligible for asylum if they could show that they were being persecuted for their homosexuality in their home country. It should be noted that this could not have been done until we had repealed the antigay exclusion. So long as American law said that homosexuals could not come to America, our chances of getting a policy adopted that allowed people to come to America because they were being persecuted for their homosexuality would have been oxymoronic.

The Justice Department ultimately complied. At first, they sought to do this by having the Board of Immigration Appeals certify as a binding precedent a previous case in which an immigration judge had allowed a lesbian to get asylum because of egregious persecution. Unfortunately, the board, composed of civil servants, refused. To her credit, Attorney General Reno then used her authority to designate gay and lesbian people as a category eligible for asylum. In the years since then, dozens of people have been freed from antigay persecution by being granted legal residence in this country. And this has also led the State Department to include reports on homophobia in their annual human rights reports. Once again this is a matter that is important both substantively and symbolically. Gay and lesbian victims of persecution receive shelter from it, and the United States officially makes clear that it considers anti-gay-and-lesbian persecution a severe violation of human rights, and one from which we will give people refuge.

Countering this good news, there was bad news on the AIDS front. As part of our effort in 1990, Senator Simpson and I secured the repeal of a provision of law, which had been spearheaded by Jesse Helms in 1987, specifically banning people with AIDS from coming to the United States. We repealed the entire list of diseases, including AIDS, that made people ineligible to visit the United States and replaced it with a provision that gave the secretary of health and human services the discretion to determine which communicable diseases would be grounds for excluding people from entering the country. In January 1991, Louis W. Sullivan, the secretary of health and human services under President Bush, proposed regulations to redraw the exclusion list to include only tuberculosis. However, before those regulations became final, President Bush came under intense right-wing pressure to oppose the repeal of the ban on people with AIDS, and as a result of that, Bush directed Sullivan to place AIDS back on the exclusion list.

The following year, however, during his 1992 presidential campaign, Bill Clinton spoke out against this ban, and he pledged to change it. In 1993, President Clinton's secretary of health and human services, Donna Shalala, began the move to take AIDS off the list of dangerous communicable diseases, but anti-AIDS hysteria was at a high point, and Congress over the objection of myself and others passed an amendment that codified the exclusion of people who were HIV-positive, so the administration no longer had any discretion in the matter. This was a difficult issue to fight because the proposed exlusion had some plausibility in terms of immigration law. The contagious-disease prohibition had originally been adopted at the time of the tuberculosis epidemic and was clearly intended to prevent people from coming to the United States when they were infectious in a way that no one could protect themselves against. This sort of infectiousness was not relevant to the spread of AIDS, except in the minds of those who argued that people could get AIDS from being sneezed upon. But the fear of the epidemic's expansion was widespread. In addition, American law before and after our legislative efforts prohibited people from coming to the United States if they would be totally unable to support themselves and would require taxpayers to support them. Since at the time many people with AIDS would ultimately become "public charges" as the law designated them for a variety of reasons, there were two existing provisions of our law that gave some legitimacy to the exclusion.

We sought to fight that by arguing that it made no sense to exclude people who were HIV-positive on the grounds that they could become public charges if they were able to show that they had the means through health insurance or some other way to deal with their situation. But, as I said, in the political climate of the time we were swept aside and Congress re-enacted the exclusion. The president signed the bill that included this—an appropriations bill—and if he hadn't done so, his efforts to stop it would clearly have been overridden. But the administration has shown some sensitivity on this matter by using to the fullest extent whatever waiver authority it has in this regard.

That means that in the case of tourists, for example, or people coming to attend various conferences on AIDS or on gay and lesbian matters, we have been able to persuade the administration to issue waivers. Nonetheless, this exclusion continues on the books as an unfair example of discrimination, and I hope we will at some point be able to complete our work in this regard by repealing it.

CONCLUSION

In one important sense then, the story of the fight against antigay discrimination in immigration is a microcosm of our fight against homophobia in general. We have made significant gains in diminishing the force of the prejudice based on sexual orientation, but we still have a considerable distance to go before gay, lesbian, bisexual, and transgendered people are treated equally. I think the lessons we can learn from the fight to repeal the antigay exclusion in immigration law are relevant to the broader fight. Indeed, because this was the first sustained effort I was able to make against discrimination based on sexual orientation, the experience I gained in this fight has been an important factor in shaping my own central conclusion: the most important thing for us to do is to engage fully in the political process in exactly the same way that other important interests in our society do. What works for the National Rifle Association, the American Association of Retired Persons, and other segments of our society that feel extremely strongly about a particular issue will work for us as well if we act appropriately.

This is why I am troubled by that predisposition to accentuate the negative that I cited in my introductory comments. Part of the reason for this negativism is an entirely understandable emotional reaction—to victims of a blighting, vicious prejudice, a partial diminution of its effect has less significance than its continuation in other areas. But part of it stems from a misperception of how political movements are best built, and it therefore presents a serious obstacle to effective political organizing.

Many activists believe that it is important when engaged in a political crusade always to stress the downside. They fear that if we who are fighting homophobia ever acknowledge that we have won a victory, we encourage complacency among our followers and diminish the sense of obligation felt by the majority community to deal with our issues. This is essentially an oversimplified—and inaccurate—view of the bargaining process. It is a view that says you should always up the ante, always increase the demands you are making on those in power, so that the ultimate result will come closer to your needs.

There are two fundamental problems with such an approach. First, the people whose participation is necessary to make a movement successful can be discouraged by constantly being told that we have failed. The major defect in the gay, lesbian, bisexual, and transgendered political movement today is our failure to participate in the electoral and legislative processes with the same fervor as our opponents. Constantly denigrating politics and telling people that no good can come of it hardly seems the best way to overcome this gap. It is important to acknowledge our gains at the same time that we make clear the work that remains to be done if we are to motivate people to join us politically.

Second, to the extent that we seek to win over politicians who are not wholly with us on the merits, but who are calculating politically, it is a mistake to follow the advice of those who say that advocates should always appear dissatisfied. Politicians who come to believe that a particular group is determined never to acknowledge any gains have no incentive even to try to satisfy that group's demands. While it is important for a group engaged in political bargaining not to be bought too easily, it is an equally grave danger to give the impression that your support can never be won at all. Supporters of gay and lesbian rights are asking politicians to incur some political cost by endorsing our position on issues. If they do not get credit for being supportive on a particular matter, but are immediately placed into the next difficult controversy without any acknowledgment that they have helped, some will decide that trying to win us over is impossible, and our bargaining power will be diminished.

Worrying about our ability to persuade politicians to vote with us by a judicious mixture of credit when they are right and pressure when they are not is of course a distraction to those who think that the political process is a trap and that we should be relying largely on direct action to win our rights. My first response to this view in light of this case study is to note not only what happened, but also what did not happen. We achieved significant successes in our fight against the homophobic immigration law by working entirely within the political process. There were no demonstrations, rallies, or marches. No angry group of gay or lesbian people sat in the offices of those members of Congress or the executive branch who were opposing us. No immigrants facing deportation because of their sexual orientation chained themselves to anything. Indeed, in this instance, we did not even rely on a major effort to generate phone calls and letters, although if it had become likely that we would face a floor vote in either or both chambers on this issue in 1990, we would have sought to mobilize such an effort. But we would have undertaken that with great trepidation, because the view that eschews electoral politics in favor of some form of street militancy has, unfortunately, had enough impact within our community so that the results of such a letter-writing campaign would almost certainly have been meager, especially in 1990. In fact, three years after that, when the question of abolishing the homophobic policy governing the U.S. military did become a congressional issue to be decided by votes on the floor, we were heavily outlobbied by our opposition, which is the central reason why we lost that fight. We brought a million people to Washington in April of 1993 at the height of the fight against the ban on gay and lesbian military personnel, but there is no evidence that any significant number of them bothered to talk to their members of the House or Senate on this issue. While we were demonstrating publicly and feeling much better emotionally as a result, the right wing was flooding congressional offices with mail and phone calls demanding that they vote against us. The letters and phone calls easily defeated the marches and rallies.

I do not mean to argue here that the actions of gay, lesbian, bisexual, and transgendered people in the broader field of social action are irrelevant. Quite the contrary is the case. We would not have succeeded in repealing the anti-gay-and-lesbian exclusion through the political process in 1990 if it had not been for the extremely effective work done by millions of people in the twenty years since Stonewall in confronting prejudice. No one who pays serious attention to our struggle can be in any doubt that the most important thing we can do is to let those with whom we interact daily know that we are gay, lesbian, bisexual, or transgendered, because the reality of our humanity is the most effective weapon we have against the prejudice that would deny that.

Efforts to combat homophobia culturally, intellectually, and socially are essential if we are to gain further victories. The point is not that the broader fight against homophobic attitudes is irrelevant; it is that it is not self-executing in our political system. Persuading significant numbers of the heterosexual majority that we are being unfairly treated and deserve better from a society that professes to believe in equality is a necessary condition for victory. But it is not sufficient. And the dispute within the gay, lesbian, bisexual, and transgendered community is over what more specific actions are necessary to translate a general diminution of societal prejudice into tangible legal gains.

It is from this perspective that we should be evaluating various forms of direct action. Early in our history, from the Stonewall activity itself and for years afterward, it was essential for gay, lesbian, bisexual, and transgendered people to make their presence known. Hidden minorities have little chance to win their arguments. It was essential that we let the broader community know who we were, and what we suffered. And in this we were unique—no other significant minority in American history had to take the step of simply announcing its presence. The problem is that we have stayed in the demonstrative mode far longer than is sensible.

By now, few Americans are unaware of the significant presence of gay and lesbian people among them. And on the whole, the American public has reacted favorably, realizing in increasing numbers that the homophobia with which many of them grew up is inaccurate and unfair. But that realization does not translate automatically into public policy.

That is especially the case because there continue to be significant numbers of Americans who, for reasons I do not understand and do not want to understand, remain devoted to denying us fair treatment. And they have the advantage of being—at least until now—much better at exercising their political rights than many in the gay, lesbian, bisexual, and transgendered community. In most legislative bodies in the United States today, at both the state and federal levels, a large number of members believe that we should be treated equally, and a smaller number believe that we ought to be stigmatized. In my experience, the decisive votes are with members who do not themselves share homophobic prejudice, but fear that their constituents will take into account their votes on gay and lesbian issues at election time, and that the minority who oppose our cause will be a more potent political force than ourselves and our allies. No marches, demonstrations, sit-ins, or rallies in which we largely speak to each other—often with great eloquence and humor—has any effect on this. And the more activists tell their gay and lesbian brothers and sisters that politics is a snare and a delusion, that trying to influence legislators is a waste of time, and that only direct action will have an impact, the greater the electoral advantage of our foes.

Gay and lesbian people who read in the gay press and hear from gay activists only of our losses and never of the gains we have made are more easily convinced than they should be of the futility of politics. And the preaching of political futility is a self-fulfilling prophecy: the more people believe the political process will do them no good, the less they will participate in that process, and then the process will in fact be less useful to us than it can and should be.

There is a further reason for studying our victories, beyond the political importance of acknowledging them. We can learn from success just as we learn from failure. Successful stratagems and techniques are as important to the legacy of a political movement as are failures. While some qualities to the successful fight we waged against the ban on gay and lesbian immigration to America are unique, other aspects indicate things that will be useful in future battles.

SPECIAL THANKS

In writing this chapter, as in everything I do, I received significant assistance from members of my congressional staff. Daniel McGlinchey was a first-rate editor, Peter Kovar and Robert Raben helped me remember the ten-year history of these events, and Maria Giesta deciphered, translated, collated, and otherwise arranged into an intelligible form what I typed, wrote, and dictated.

CHAPTER 11

GETTING IT STRAIGHT:
A REVIEW OF THE "GAYS IN THE
MILITARY" DEBATE

TIM McFEELEY

PERCEPTION'S CONQUEST OF REALITY IS NOWHERE better illustrated than in the mythology that envelops the phrase *gays in the military.* A complex and dramatic history of the triumph of politics over principle has been packaged into a sound bite that signals misleading messages and disguises the painful experiences that the gay community endured during the heady six months following the 1992 presidential election. For politicians and their advisers, particularly those within, or seeking to be within, the White House, the phrase telegraphs a warning to avoid the minefield of social issues in general and the atomic charge of gay issues in particular. For the gay community, the sound bite and its correlative outcome, Don't Ask, Don't Tell, provoke feelings of betrayal and inconstancy by President Clinton in particular and elicit a dangerous and disabling disdain for the political process in general. Misled by media commentators, who report public policy debates as spectator sports rather than substantive issues, the general public believes that "gays in the military" is the perfect example of a government influenced by special interests and out of touch with the priorities of American voters.

In reality, the brief episode of our recent history, during which the Clinton administration attempted, but failed, to end the exclusion of homosexuals from military service, demonstrates the danger and futility of relying on principles alone without regard to politics in trying to effect change in a democracy. The political loss sustained by Clinton and the gay community was the result of inexperience, bad timing, and a romantic but naive conviction that the ideal of fairness could trump the politics of fear. Rather than the first example of Clinton's inconstancy and surrender to politics, the effort to "lift the ban" was an attempt by Clinton—arguably his last attempt—to hold fast to a principled position. Thereafter, Clinton's initiatives were largely tempered by politics as he pursued the attainable rather than the ideal. Whether the gay community has accepted, or should accept, the same lesson is not clear.

As described by Allan Bérubé,[1] Randy Shilts,[2] and others, the saga of gays and lesbians in the military did not start with Bill Clinton. In September 1975, *Time* magazine ran a comprehensive review of the gay rights movement with Leonard Matlovich, an openly gay air force sergeant, on its cover.[3] Several heroic gay and lesbian service members such as Miriam Ben-Shalom and Perry Watkins came out and challenged the policy of government-sanctioned discrimination in federal court long before most Americans had ever heard of the Arkansas governor. The National Gay and Lesbian Task Force, the Human Rights Campaign Fund, Lambda Legal Defense and Education Fund, and allied organizations that were concerned with gay rights, such as the National Organization for Women, the American Civil Liberties Union, and the National Lawyers Guild, had created the Military Freedom Project to monitor and attempt to prevent egregious "witch-hunts" like the one that occurred at Parris Island during the Reagan-Bush years. Women's advocates were especially attuned to the harassing practice of accusing female service members of homosexuality in order to secure sexual favors. The Persian Gulf War and the resulting goodwill that Americans extended to members of the military created an atmosphere that allowed the Bush administration's secretary of defense, Dick Cheney, to admit before Congress that the argument of excluding homosexuals as security risks was an "old chestnut." President Bush and Cheney deftly handled the attempted outing of Pete Williams, the Pentagon's civilian spokesman, by gay activists in 1991 with a dismissive "So what?"

Encouraged by several polls showing that 65 percent of American voters opposed the exclusionary policy,[4] and armed with a June 1992 General Accounting Office report[5] that the policy was costing taxpayers an estimated $27 million a year, some Democratic leaders in Congress were starting to deal with the issue of discharging homosexuals from the armed forces. In addition, foreign countries, including most NATO allies, began retaining openly gay military personnel with no unfavorable results, and the Pentagon's own Personnel Security Research and Education Center (PERSEREC) report, leaked in late 1989 to Congressman Gerry Studds, stated, "The military cannot indefinitely isolate itself from the changes occurring in the wider society."[6] In late 1991 Barbara Boxer, then a U.S. representative from San Francisco, introduced a House resolution to lift the ban, and Senator Brock Adams (D-WA) introduced the Senate version. These were followed in 1992 with bills (one authored by House Armed Services Committee member Patricia Schroeder [D-CO]) and amendments to defense reauthorization and appropriations bills to the same effect.

In June 1992, NGLTF, the ACLU, and other organizations and activists argued in favor of scheduling a House vote on the Schroeder Amendment to the defense reauthorization bill that would require a change in the Pentagon's exclusionary policy. Others, like myself (I was the executive director of HRCF from July 1989 to January 1995) and Congressmen Barney Frank and Gerry Studds, contended that our side would certainly lose such a vote, and that raising the public profile of the issue without a chance of success, in the face of opposition by House Armed Services Committee chairman Les Aspin and in the midst of a presidential and congressional election campaign, would be unwise. Even if both houses of Congress passed the amendment (an unlikely event), President Bush would have vetoed the resulting bill, capitalizing on a potent election-year issue and putting Bill Clinton, the presumptive Democratic nominee, on the hot seat. Moreover, the gay community was not yet prepared for the immense lobbying effort that would have been required to sustain the amendment. The vote was deferred, but the internal debate was reported in the *Washington Blade* and elsewhere, presaging the strategic disputes that would arise a few months later. Our caution was portrayed at best as a lack of conviction, and at worse as cowardice.

Members of Congress, especially those serving on the relevant defense committees, such as Senator Sam Nunn of Georgia, the Senate Armed Services Committee chairman, and House chairman Aspin, were well aware that the issue was gaining momentum and publicity. General Colin Powell was questioned about the policy early in February 1992 by Congressman Frank during hearings before the House Budget Committee,[7] and on March 4, 1992, Senator Chuck Robb, a moderate Virginia Democrat, whose marine combat experience provided credibility, wrote to his friend, General Powell: "The military . . . should not bar individuals from service based on who they are. . . . Like racial or ethnic origin or gender, sexual preference has no bearing on how great a contribution an individual can make to the United States."[8]

In addition, the Pentagon had made some serious blunders in handling the issue. The public viewed as mean-spirited the attempts by the military to seek tuition restitution from ROTC students, such as Robb Bettiker and Jim Holobaugh, who had come out and left the armed forces training program. When the U.S. navy precipitously and inaccurately blamed an explosion aboard the USS *Iowa* on an alleged love affair between two sailors, one of whom, Clayton Hartwig, died in the incident, even the military's defenders were hard-pressed to support its overreaching zealotry. It became increasingly difficult for the Pentagon and veterans groups to assail the character of exemplary gay and lesbian service members, such as Joe Steffan, who had been dismissed from the Naval Academy at Annapolis just weeks before his graduation in 1987,[9] and Karen Stupski, who was a magna cum laude ROTC graduate from Harvard College and had decided to fight her 1990 discharge from the navy. The evidence was mounting in the public's mind that the ban was unnecessary and unjust, and in the public relations battle, the gay community was truly blessed to have some of the most talented and courageous men and women to stand as proxies for the thousands of gay men and lesbians in the armed forces and to personify the issue. I'll never forget appearing with Lieutenant (j.g.) Tracy Thorne and Bob Dornan, a rabidly antigay California congressman, on NBC's *Today* show. While Dornan and I traded barbs and hyperbolized, Thorne spoke convincingly to the viewers—the "very model of a modern major" hero. Our side had seized and held the moral high ground in the debate.

Gays in the military never became a defining issue in the 1992 campaign for the presidency. At a John F. Kennedy Institute forum at Harvard University, candidate Clinton stated publicly in late 1991 what he had told Barney Frank and other potential gay supporters privately, namely, that he was inclined to lift the ban. Clinton was the most conservative of the Democratic contenders—who included Bob Kerrey, Tom Harkin, Jerry Brown, and Paul Tsongas—and since they had all stated in December 1991, in response to a questionnaire distributed by HRCF, that they favored a change in the antigay policy, Clinton's position did not provoke any challenge or debate during the primaries. In a moving and unprecedented address to the gay and lesbian community in Los Angeles in May 1992, Clinton described a vision of America that included gay and lesbian Americans and in which discrimination, particularly the government's own bias-induced policy of keeping homosexuals from serving their country in uniform, would end.

President Bush did not use Clinton's pro-gay position on the military ban against him in the general election campaign, so the media and the public were not aware of their differences in this regard. Clearly, it was not in Clinton's interest to boldly underscore the difference. For the Democrats it was enough to allow the gay organizations to advise their supporters of Clinton's favorable position and to keep the general public focused on the economic, health-care, and welfare debate. Why the Republicans, who had to be well aware of Clinton's stand on gays in the military, let it go is unclear, but the probable explanation was to distance Bush from the vitriol and extremism of the 1992 GOP National Convention in Houston, particularly Pat Buchanan's fuming and foaming in his August 13, 1992, address. Trying to wound Clinton with gays in the military the way Bush had wounded Dukakis in 1988 with Willie Horton would have caused barrels of editorial ink to flow. The assistance that Buchanan provided in the defeat of George Bush in 1992 cannot be overstated.

In San Francisco on Veterans Day, November 11, 1992, federal judge Terry Hatter issued an order preventing the U.S. navy and the Department of Defense from enforcing the antigay policy against Seaman Keith Meinhold. In Little Rock, President-elect Clinton responded to a reporter's question regarding the *Meinhold* case with a favorable comment in support of Hatter's decision, thus setting up the first major controversy of the transition period and precipitating unfavorable responses from Colin Powell, Sam Nunn, and Republican and right-wing leaders around the country.

During the two-month interval between Judge Hatter's *Meinhold* decision and the inauguration, a euphoric gay community indulged in postelection celebrations, while an angry and fearful right wing mobilized to embarrass the president as soon as he tried to move to change the antigay policy. Progressives often fail to understand the animus that motivates right-wing extremists to sacrifice their money, time, and energy to keep gay and lesbian Americans at the margins of society. Political organizers and fund-raisers do know, however, that fear is a potent motivating force, and conservatives' phobia about sexuality in general and homosexuality in particular has allowed right-wing leaders to use this issue to great advantage. By the time of the inaugural on January 20, 1993, those opposed to change, which included the military leadership and veterans groups, virtually all Republicans, and the radical right, had become so strong, and the gay community and its allies remained so overconfident and weak, that the opposition did not wait, but fired the first shot.

Leaders in the gay community, including myself, assumed that Clinton would act on the military issue within the first hundred days of his term and before the April 25, 1993, gay and lesbian March on Washington. David Mixner, who was a friend of Bill Clinton's and had introduced him to, and promoted his candidacy within, the gay and lesbian community, assured gay leaders, service members, and the community at several gatherings between the election and the inauguration that the president would sign an executive order lifting the ban within the first hundred days. Several inconclusive, but substantial, meetings among transition officials such as John Holum, and gay community leaders, Congressmen Studds and Frank, and the newly designated Pentagon leadership were held in December 1992, concerning exactly how and when the president should keep this campaign promise to the gay community.

However, President Clinton lost control of the timing and manner of introducing the policy change for three reasons. One reason was the astute assessment and cunning skill of Minority Leader Bob Dole, who saw this issue as one with which he could wound the president and start his own 1996 campaign for the White House. Senator Dole, not President Clinton, initially presented the matter to Congress. In the week following the inauguration, Dole proposed an amendment to the totally unrelated Family and Medical Leave Act (under Senate rules amendments need not be germane to the subject of the main bill), designated S. 1 because it was such a top priority for Democrats, in order to force a vote within the first two weeks of the new administration.

The second reason was the inexperience and ineptitude of Clinton's team. The examples, as documented in excellent accounts by Bob Woodward[10] and Elizabeth Drew,[11] were rife. Before the inauguration the public became aware that Zoe Baird, Clinton's nominee for attorney general, had employed illegal immigrants as nannies and had failed to pay social security taxes on their earnings. Despite warnings from Senate Democrats, Clinton decided to press the nomination, until two days after the inauguration, when he conceded defeat and Baird's name was withdrawn. His second choice for attorney general, Judge Kimba Wood, withdrew her name even before she was formally nominated because she too had hired undocumented immigrants (although in Judge Wood's case, no laws had been broken). Two days after being sworn in, President Clinton signed a series of executive orders lifting Reagan-Bush restrictions on abortion counseling, fetal-tissue research, and funding UN population programs that included abortion counseling. In thus fulfilling progressive campaign promises to feminists through the use of executive orders rather than congressional action, Clinton infuriated conservatives and put them on red alert for any further liberal executive orders on hot social issues. And during the weeks leading up to the late-January confrontation with Congress over lifting the gay ban, and even after the controversy erupted, the Clinton staff was not coordinating strategies or sharing information with gay lobbying groups.

The third cause was the overconfidence and insufficient grassroots support in the gay community. Despite the incessant warnings of Barney Frank, Pat Schroeder, and others on Capitol Hill, little constituent pressure had been orchestrated with which to support the president's position. For one thing, people assumed the commander in chief could do whatever he wanted, particularly with Democrats in control of both houses of Congress. In addition, the gay community was starting to divide over priorities for the new administration. After years of wandering in the political wilderness, it was not surprising that gay and lesbian leaders would have many pressing demands. What should we push first and hardest—AIDS prevention and funding, protection from employment discrimination, fighting hate crimes?

We will never know whether, when, and under what circumstances President Clinton would have proposed changing the exclusionary policy. There is

242 | Tim McFeeley

no evidence that Clinton would have taken any action on gays in the military before he had his team in place and before his middle-class priorities concerning the budget deficit, health care, and welfare reform had been initiated. The public impression that Clinton proposed the military policy change before these other issues is wrong, since, in fact, Clinton did absolutely nothing to change the status quo before Senator Dole introduced his amendment to S. 1.

The media created and nurtured the myth that President Clinton cluttered his early agenda with an "insignificant," special-interest issue that was advanced to fulfill a campaign promise. Clinton simply chose not to sidestep the questions about the *Meinhold* decision and refused to qualify or disavow the principled position he had taken at least fourteen months before. In the face of an escalating confrontation fueled by the Republican opposition, Clinton took reasonable steps to consult with Senator Nunn, Majority Leader George Mitchell, and the Joint Chiefs of Staff, but the president had not made any final decisions that we are aware of prior to the preemptory attack of those whose motivation was to use the issue to discredit Clinton as early as possible.

In his autobiography, *My American Journey,* Colin Powell notes that he had initiated a conversation concerning gays in the military with the president in their first meeting after the election, and that Powell had advised the president to pull back from an immediate decision and order the secretary of defense to conduct a six-month study to allay the concerns of the Pentagon and the rank and file. The former chairman of the Joint Chiefs also writes that as the controversy escalated, the issue was the subject of a White House meeting among the president and the branch chiefs on January 25, 1993. At that point, however, the battle over gays in the military was already in serious trouble.

The day before, on January 24, 1993, a mere four days after the inauguration, Secretary Aspin declared defeat and unconditionally surrendered on the issue on the CBS Sunday-morning public affairs broadcast, *Face the Nation,* when he admitted that he had advised the president in a memo, which had somehow been leaked to reporters, that fewer than thirty senators would support lifting the ban and stated, in what General Powell has since described as an "odd performance," "If we can't work it [the gays in the military issue] out, we'll disagree, and the thing won't happen."

No member of Congress missed the implication of this declaration of weakness, and the point was driven home the following day when a carefully orchestrated campaign of letters and telephone calls flooded every office on Capitol Hill. On Monday, January 25, 1993, I received many calls from our friends in Congress, including Barney Frank, Pat Schroeder, Maxine Waters, Jane Harman, and Nancy Pelosi, urging us to put everything we could into producing calls and letters from the pro-gay side. The antigay constituent blitzkrieg, largely unanswered by immediate strong responses from the White House and from those who favored lifting the ban, forced members of Congress to take positions on the issue, often before our side had been able to activate its grassroots supporters. Before the end of January, even those who might have been persuadable had responded to their constituents and their local press inquiries with positions largely opposed to lifting the ban. Successful politicians avoid associations with losing causes, especially those that involve issues like homosexuality.

Who leaked the Aspin memo to the press, thus predictably precipitating these events, and why? And why did Aspin confirm the hopeless assessment on January 24, rather than try to finesse or qualify the memo as premature and incomplete? Secretary Aspin is dead, and we can only speculate on sources and motivations. Les Aspin, the former chairman of the House Armed Services Committee, had been elevated to secretary of defense by President Clinton over Sam Nunn, his counterpart in the Senate. As a member of Congress, Aspin had often tangled with the Pentagon during the Reagan-Bush years. The unenviable task of downsizing defense following the end of the Cold War and the growth of domestic priorities would continue to put the new defense secretary at odds with armed forces professionals, defense contractors, congressmen protective of local military installations, and veterans. Aspin had a lot of difficult assignments on his to-do list, and the emotional issue of gays in the military was not one that Aspin was happy to carry for the president. Eliminating this annoying and disabling issue early in 1993 would have made Secretary Aspin's job a lot easier. Senator Nunn had not only been dropped from consideration as secretary of defense and secretary of state by Clinton (in part, at the strong urging of gay and lesbian leaders, which did not endear us to the Georgian Democrat), but his ultimate objective of being elected president as a moderate, southern Democrat, in the tradition of Lyndon Johnson and Jimmy Carter, was itself foreclosed by Clinton's candidacy. As subsequent events clarified, Nunn was an ardent foe of gays in the military and undoubtedly resented Clinton's failure to defer to him as the chairman of the Senate Armed Services Committee on this, and other, defense issues. Aspin, Nunn, members of their staffs who were privy to the Aspin memo, and perhaps moderate members of the White House staff, who sensed political disaster in the president's pursuit of the gay issue, all had motives to leak the memo to the press and set off the inevitable reaction. Speculation is no substitute for facts, however, and what we do know for sure is that the gay and lesbian community was overwhelmed by the strength of the opposition on this issue.

As soon as Secretary Aspin surrendered, Senator Dole quickly assumed leadership of the opposition and threatened the Family and Medical Leave Act with an amendment that would legislate that no change in the antigay military ban could occur without congressional authorization, thus preempting the executive order as a means to end the policy of discharging homosexuals from the armed forces. The Dole Amendment was a cynical, but not surprising, reaction

244 | Tim McFeeley

to the disarray among the Clinton administration, congressional Democrats, and the gay community on the issue. If the Dole Amendment passed, it would force Clinton to choose between accepting it and breaching his promise to the gay community, or vetoing the Family and Medical Leave Act, thus frustrating the enactment of this overwhelmingly popular measure. The White House and Democratic majority leader George Mitchell enlisted the support of Senator Nunn. Only with Chairman Nunn's support could the Democrats defeat the Dole Amendment, and Sam Nunn insisted that the president agree not to issue an executive order or take any other action to change the antigay policy until July 15, 1993, following a study by the secretary of defense and public hearings by the appropriate congressional committees. The Senate likewise agreed not to legislate on the matter until the so-called moratorium period ended on July 15. The president was able to negotiate an immediate end to the practice of asking the sexual orientation of armed service recruits.

On February 4, 1993, the "preemptive" Dole Amendment was defeated, 62–37, in favor of the Mitchell-Nunn "moratorium" compromise. This early vote put thirty-seven senators on record as firmly opposing any relaxation of the ban, only four senators short of a forty-one-vote block that could, by using the filibuster, prevent Senate action on this matter. The vote also gave Senator Nunn control of this issue. For all intents and purposes the debate was over, and Senator Nunn was empowered to write its epitaph.

Prior to the Nunn Amendment, Clinton could have tried to end the ban by issuing an executive order to that effect, just as he had on the abortion issues. Former president Jimmy Carter, whose first executive order in January 1977 granted amnesty to Vietnam-era draft dodgers, urged this course. Such a course would have been foolish for three reasons. First, it would have created a congressional-executive standoff of the kind seen in late 1995 over the budget, with Congress insisting on a rollback of the executive order and the White House vetoing these efforts, sacrificing all sorts of important legislation in the process. A standoff like that would have soured Clinton's relationship with congressional Democrats as well as Republicans. Second, without broad public support, as expressed by congressional acquiescence, the armed forces would have been in revolt against the commander in chief. Not only would this have seriously hurt Clinton, but it would have put gay and lesbian service members at great risk. Third, a presidential insistence on lifting the ban would have eliminated from consideration all other issues that were important to the gay, lesbian, and AIDS communities, since maintaining the executive order would have depleted all political "chits" available to the gay community with Congress and the White House.

Simultaneously with Les Aspin's unilateral January 24 surrender, the gay community belatedly sprang into action by creating the Campaign for Military Service to coordinate the pro-gay effort. The action did not originate within the activist gay community or its beleaguered leaders in D.C. but, instead, from several prominent gay Democrats, including David Mixner, David Geffen, and Barry Diller, who were closely allied with President Clinton. They were convinced that the problem lay not with the White House or the Democratically controlled Congress, but with HRCF, NGLTF, and the other GLBT and allied organizations. They were sure that a new team and an infusion of money could fix the problem, and they weren't bashful about asserting themselves.

Two meetings were held at the Georgetown home of Bob Schrum and Marylouise Oates in quick succession on January 29 and February 3, 1993. Schrum, a highly skilled speechwriter, campaign professional, and media consultant, and his wife, Marylouise, who was a close associate of David Mixner's, hosted the gatherings as a favor to Bob Burkett, a former Democratic Party official who was then in charge of the David Geffen Foundation in Los Angeles. (Unknown to most of us, but later reported by David Mixner in his book *Stranger Among Friends*,[12] top presidential adviser Paul Begala was monitoring the meeting from Marylouise's kitchen.) The stated purpose of the first meeting was to coordinate the pro-gay efforts. Peri Jude Radecic, the interim executive director of NGLTF, and I, representing HRCF, along with our colleagues from the ACLU, People for the American Way, and other allies reported on our efforts and made an assessment of our immediate needs. Money was one requirement, and $50,000 to fund a grassroots alert was raised at the meeting from Geffen and Diller.

Under Burkett's and Schrum's direction the coordination effort smoothly transformed into an undertaking to organize a supervening, ongoing umbrella group that could bridge institutional rivalries among the organizations, draw on untapped, nongay resources, and act as a lobbying "campaign" to effect the desired result. On Monday, February 1, we coordinated a successful press conference followed by personal lobby visits at the Capitol. Among the speakers supporting the effort to lift the ban were Major General (Ret.) Vance Coleman, an African-American who had served during the days of racial segregation in the army, author Colonel Lucien Trescott, several Vietnam-era veterans, Christian and Jewish army chaplains, and Keith Meinhold, who had sued the navy over the exclusionary policy.

At the second meeting, which was attended by David Mixner and Tom Stoddard, the former executive director of Lambda Legal Defense and Education Fund and a lobbyist for the ACLU, the Campaign for Military Service was organized and Stoddard appointed as its executive director. No one at either meeting believed that the game was over, and in retrospect, we had no realistic notion of how difficult it would be to overcome the political forces arrayed against our side. Not only had we failed to anticipate and combat the opposition to Clinton's initiative to lift the ban, but at that time we didn't recognize that we had already lost the debate. Similarly, the participants at these

Georgetown meetings were disinclined to raise or hash out the obvious turf disputes that would arise as a result of the creation of CMS.

In our defense, we were at once inspired by the justice of our cause and the heroism of the many service members who had publicly come out and challenged the military in the wake of Clinton's pro-*Meinhold* statement, as well as energized by our collective desire to be part of the team that would help the president lift the ban. We quite honestly believed at the time that our political deficits were outweighed by our surplus of principles. As gay organizers we had never before had a president say a kind word about gay and lesbian Americans, and now we had the new president fighting Congress and the military establishment on our behalf. It was almost impossible to believe at that time that we could lose.

From its inception, CMS had an ambiguous structure and mission. Tom Stoddard quickly pulled together his own team of managers, and rather than coordinate the efforts of HRCF, NGLTF, NOW, the ACLU, People for the American Way, and the Military Freedom Project consortium, the CMS team largely replaced them. If in Stoddard's place—encouraged by Mixner, Burkett, Shrum, and others, who felt that HRCF and NGLTF were inadequate for the job—I would have followed the same course, largely because it is easier to achieve loyalty and performance from a newly recruited staff than to acquire these from staff members of wholly separate organizations. The Sheridan Group, a lobbying organization led by Tom Sheridan, who had formerly been associated with the AIDS Action Council, was hired to direct all Capitol Hill lobbying, and HRCF, the principal lobbying agent for the gay and lesbian community, was left to fall in line. Similarly, NGLTF's grassroots contacts and expertise were supplanted by CMS initiatives, such as the nationwide gay and lesbian veterans bus tour. Fund-raising became a sore point, and instead of bridging divisions among the existing groups, CMS became another and, with its Hollywood and White House connections, a more potent, fund-raising rival.

On February 7, the Sunday following the CMS-organizing meeting and three days after the defeat of the Dole Amendment, *The New York Times* published a lengthy report and analysis by Jeffrey Schmalz, in which gay leaders, including Tom Stoddard, were critical of the lack of success and weakness of the national gay organizations, thereby creating a zero baseline from which to build.[13] Although many of their criticisms were valid, their publication demoralized the staff members of HRCF and NGLTF and the many Military Freedom Project volunteers and created tensions and resentment that lasted throughout the brief history of CMS. The legal, lobbying, organizing, fundraising, and public relations activities of CMS were executed extremely well and by highly competent individuals and firms. Unfortunately, they and their counterparts at NGLTF, HRCF, and the other groups, including the energetic and resourceful gay and lesbian veterans groups, were preparing for a battle that, in retrospect, was lost before they had been commissioned.

While the president and the White House staff were consumed with the effort to craft a deficit-reduction and budget plan, they seemed to join the gay community in the collective denial that the gays in the military issue was lost and that a long-term compromise with Senator Nunn had to be worked out before the July 15 deadline. On April 16, 1993, President Clinton met with eight leaders of the gay and lesbian community, including myself, Torie Osborn of NGLTF, William Waybourn of the Gay and Lesbian Victory Fund, the organizers of the March on Washington, and Tom Stoddard of CMS, in the Oval Office. The president continued to reassure us that he believed we could prevail in our efforts to lift the ban, despite the fact that Senator Nunn was using the February-to-July moratorium period and the Armed Services Committee hearings to bolster the opposition, embarrass the president, and strengthen his own hand as the not-so-impartial broker. President Clinton inspired us with his sincere and uncompromising stand in support of permitting gay armed forces personnel to serve their country, using anecdotes of various military members who had whispered in his ear their appreciation for his trying to do the right thing. The president felt good about his personal relationship with General Powell, he said, and was confident that he could bring Powell around on this issue. Clinton encouraged us in our lobbying efforts and praised the courage of those exemplary service members who had come out subsequent to his inauguration and as a result of his promise to lift the ban.

No gay or lesbian leaders had ever before in history met with any president of the United States to discuss issues of importance to the gay community, and here we were being treated like comrades in the fight against the forces of darkness. It was inspiring, heady, romantic, and sad to say, totally unrealistic.

Our collective denial that we were losing was so powerful and pervasive that when Barney Frank proposed exploring a compromise in mid-May, he was criticized by CMS and by gay commentators and activists around the country. Even Gerry Studds, the only other openly gay member of Congress, uncharacteristically distanced himself from Frank by stating that it was not the time to "raise the white flag." In the midst of the struggle we marched on Washington, seven hundred thousand strong, on April 25, 1993. Only a few hundred of the marchers bothered to lobby their members of Congress, and the gathering didn't change one vote in our favor. The media coverage predictably reinforced, with a lot of help from foulmouthed entertainers and bizarrely costumed revelers, the average American's bias against having gays and lesbians anywhere near their sons and daughters.

In addition, there were just too many cooks spoiling the broth—Stoddard,

Osborn, Waybourn, myself, Ralph Neas of the Leadership Conference on Civil Rights, David Crane of People for the American Way, Tom Sheridan and attorney Chai Feldblum as CMS consultants, Schrum, and others—so that strategy sessions became unwieldy and unproductive. Nearly all discussions were leaked to the press, including some sensitive discussions with White House staff. Recriminations followed, and by late May tensions between the community leaders and the White House staff sizzled. The gay community failed the test, as well. More people donned their trendy LIFT-THE-BAN dog tags and danced until dawn than ever lifted a pen to write their congressmen.

There were some memorable triumphs. Media leaders published editorial support. Help came from unexpected sources, former senator, air force brigadier general, and 1964 Republican presidential nominee Barry Goldwater being the most conspicuous. Despite the right-wing hyperbole, positive education did occur, such as the unforgettable exchange between Senator John Kerry and Senator Strom Thurmond, in which the Massachusetts Democrat had to explain to the Republican nonagenarian that heterosexuals could, and did, engage in sodomy, just like homosexuals. Nonetheless, our side failed to discuss, let alone dispel, the public's "shower phobia." By laughing at conservative leaders who raised this issue, we appeared to be laughing at most Americans, who were honestly concerned about their sons' showering with gay men—not a winning strategy in a democracy.

The common view that the president betrayed the gay community during the 1993 debate over gays in the military is oversimplified. The president's errors lay, first, in standing by the community on principle far too long after the issue had been lost, and in so doing, putting gay and lesbian service members at risk and losing the chance to effect, perhaps, a more favorable compromise with Senator Nunn; second, in failing to use any of his considerable reserve of political power to back up his avowed principle of fairness; and third, claiming until the last year of his presidency that the resulting Don't Ask, Don't Tell, Don't Pursue policy is an improvement. The president wants accolades for standing with the gay community on principle, but no criticism of his reluctance to fight for those principles, and no censure for the end result.

On July 2, 1993, as the controversy was drawing to its sad conclusion, I found myself at a small, informal White House dinner as the guest of Ellen Malcolm, the founder and head of Emily's List, a powerful women's political organization, and a member of the HRCF board of directors. There were about seventy-five guests, including several senators and other elected officials, White House staff members, assorted political friends, and the president and first lady. Except for a brief greeting, I wasn't able to talk with President Clinton until the dinner ended and he invited us into the White House theater (familiar to CNN viewers as the venue for daily press briefings) to watch a movie

(*The Firm,* based on a novel by John Grisham). As we left the Blue Room, wait-ers appeared with trays of seltzer water, and I approached the president. I asked him what we should expect as a final outcome, and he indicated that there was no escape from Nunn's Don't Ask policy. I suggested that he could, if he chose, reject Nunn's plan and threaten to veto any legislation that incor-porated the Nunn scheme. President Clinton turned and looked at me as though I had lost my senses. He firmly told me that the plan would be part of the defense reauthorization act and there was no way he could veto such an act of Congress. He made it clear that our conversation was over, turning to his right to talk jovially with Senator Bumpers, who had sauntered toward us. The incongruity of the president's declaration of impotence amidst the symbols of power that surrounded us at the White House was disconcerting and unfor-gettable.

On July 19, 1993, the president, flanked by the Joint Chiefs of Staff, sur-rendered to Nunn's policy, and within the hour of his announcement was pub-licly condemned by gay leaders. My own angry declaration that "we elected a president and got a barometer" was one of the most widely quoted barbs, and the following day, along with several other leaders, I was arrested in a protest demonstration in front of the White House. AIDS activists, many of whom had been arrested with me at 1600 Pennsylvania Avenue on World AIDS Day in 1989, and who were angry that so much attention had been diverted from the AIDS fight to the military issue, encouraged the police to cart us off to jail and chanted, "Lock 'em up and throw the key away."

Two weeks later, CMS folded, and NGLTF, HRCF, and their Military Freedom Project partners worked with our congressional allies to soften the blow. Congress wrote the obnoxious Don't Ask, Don't Tell, Don't Pursue policy into law in October 1993 with White House compliance. The final attempt at lifting the ban failed (with the White House lobbying against us) in the Senate (Barbara Boxer, by then a U.S. senator, proposed the amendment) on October 9, 1993, on a 63–33 vote, and in the House of Representatives (on an amend-ment offered by freshman Marty Meehan of Massachusetts) by a margin of 264–169 on October 28, 1993. The new policy, which in essence makes the lives of gay, lesbian, and bisexual armed forces personnel no better and contin-ues to devalue their contributions to our country, is being tested in federal court. For years the president continued to characterize the policy as a good compromise, instead of admitting that he and the gay community simply lost this fight and that the compromise was forced on us by Senator Nunn, the Re-publicans, and the military led by General Powell. Moreover, the Defense De-partment under three successive secretaries has done a poor job in enforcing the new policy and thereby protecting homosexuals in the armed services from harassment. The community-based, privately funded Servicemembers Legal

Defense Network has uncovered a disturbing pattern of failure by DOD to enforce the prohibitions on asking and pursuing and has shown that the rate of discharge for homosexuality has in fact increased since 1994.

Thirty years after Stonewall we are still faced with the essential contradiction that most Americans simultaneously approve of equality for lesbians and gay men, while continuing to disapprove of homosexuality. Public policy changes have had to contend with this difficult dilemma, and none has been more arduous than the issue of permitting gay men and lesbians to serve openly in the U.S. military. The temporized solution—"yes, but don't let anyone know about it"—is emblematic of how Americans view all aspects of the GLBT movement for equality and acceptance. Ironically, it is also the way most homosexuals live. As more and more gay and lesbian Americans conduct their lives honestly and proudly as healthy and productive members of society, and as a result of that conduct, the time when the government will allow gay and lesbian Americans to serve openly in the armed forces of this country comes closer.

Engaging in the political process to change public policies involves more than idealism and principles. It requires tough, honest appraisals of political strengths and weaknesses and realistic strategies that can favorably shift the balance. It mandates retreat in the face of devastating losses, especially where people's lives are in jeopardy, and aggressive advances when the opposition stumbles. Finally, politics often requires compromise to effect incremental change and prevent permanent marginalization. The 1993 experience in attempting to lift the ban on military service by gay and lesbian Americans provides an example that we ignore at our peril.

CHAPTER 12

BRIDGING RACE, CLASS, AND SEXUALITY FOR SCHOOL REFORM

N'TANYA LEE, DON MURPHY, LISA NORTH, AND JULIET UCELLI

LIKE TWO CARS SPEEDING BLINDLY TOWARD A DANgerous intersection, race and sexuality collided in the 1992 elections, leaving the wreckage of identity politics strewn all over. The proponents of Colorado's Amendment 2 and Oregon's Proposition 9, both antigay initiatives, targeted lesbians and gay men as a weak link in the civil rights coalition. In the Colorado campaign, right-wing organizers piloted an effective populist appeal that pitted "rich gays" seeking "special rights" against "truly disadvantaged" people of color.

This theme struck a chord in many communities of color, especially when tied to a political agenda that focused on working-class and low-income communities' anger toward the sorry condition of their schools and services. In New York City, where whites are the minority and public-school students are 80 percent children of color, the right's antigay campaign addressed the rage that many poor parents feel toward a school system that fails to educate their children and has still not removed much of the basic racism in its teaching methods, materials, and tests. The right blamed then-Chancellor Joseph Fernandez's "liberal social agenda"—which they claimed was manipulated behind the scenes by a gay elite in the school bureaucracy and on the school system's Multicultural Advisory Board—for the school system's failures.

The message hit home. One Caribbean parent stood up at a public meeting and denounced AIDS education efforts, stating bluntly, "Rich, white gay men are taking over. Lesbians and gays are going to move forward with their agenda at the expense of people of color." The right soon found the perfect "wedge" issue in a new curriculum guide proposed for the New York City public schools called Children of the Rainbow (COR). The guide included a short section on nontraditional families, including those headed by gay and lesbian couples.

This time, however, progressives were not caught unrepresented. Led by People About Changing Education (PACE), a multiracial organization of parents and educators involved in school reform, a diverse network of gay and lesbian, education-oriented, and community-of-color-based organizations came together to present an alternative scenario.

The ensuing struggle over the Children of the Rainbow guide is probably the most significant example to date of an organizing campaign that successfully united gay men and lesbians with people of color behind an issue of deep concern to low-income and working-class people—in this case, the quality of public schools. The fundamental divides of race and class were bridged in the heat of battle, but holding together organizations representing diverse constituencies was more difficult once the fight ended. Many of the more middle-class and gay/lesbian-identity-based organizations drifted away once the immediate hazard of the right-wing incursion into the public school system subsided. As the New York City public schools sank even deeper into crisis after 1994, the inner-city-oriented education reformers were left to struggle on their own.

Nonetheless, say the activists involved in the COR campaign, simply bringing all the different communities together for a common purpose was a major achievement, and one that offers rich lessons in how to apply the energy and sense of connection typical of identity politics to the nuts and bolts of issue-based grassroots campaigns.

MULTICULTURALISM IN THE SCHOOLS

Between 1988 and 1990, New York City was rocked by a series of hate crimes involving young people: the murder of Michael Griffith, a young African-American, by whites in Howard Beach; the killing of Yusuf Hawkins by white youths in Bensonhurst, Brooklyn; the rape and beating of a white female jogger in Central Park by black and latino youths; and the antigay murder in Queens of Julio Rivera. These incidents put the city and the school system on notice that racial antagonism was becoming an issue that could not be ignored. Demographic trends in the public schools added to this perception.

By the end of the 1980s, a suffering public school system was serving mostly poor students of color with a disproportionately white teaching staff.[1] Students enrolled in high school in the 1992–93 school year were 9.6 percent Asian, 33.6 percent Latino, 39 percent of African descent, and 17.5 percent white. By 1993, 14 percent of all students were immigrants or the children of immigrants, and over 15 percent were classified as having "limited English" proficiency.[2] Meanwhile, 67 percent of teachers were white, as were 73 percent of guidance counselors.

In this context, the New York City Board of Education under Richard Green, the city's first black chancellor, moved to implement a 1985 resolution mandating multicultural reform. The resolution's goal was to eliminate practices and attitudes that discriminate against students, parents, and school personnel on the basis of "race, color, religion, nationality, gender, age, sexual orientation, or handicaps." Although the inclusion of sexual orientation in this list provoked controversy, the board kept it in and established the Office of Multicultural Education and a community-based Multicultural Advisory Council. After Chancellor Green's untimely death in 1989, staff work continued, although with less top-level support and community outreach, and teachers were assigned to prepare new teachers' guides and materials.

One product of this effort was the COR guide, a 441-page first-grade teacher's guide. The guide consisted predominately of background information for teachers and learning activities for students. Despite some opposition, the Lesbian and Gay Teachers Association of the United Federation of Teachers convinced the Office of Multicultural Education to adhere to the original resolution and include sexual orientation form the earliest grades. Elisse Weindling, a lesbian first-grade teacher, was commissioned to author a six-page section on families, a state-mandated topic for first-grade classes. It explained that families are diverse and can be led by a grandmother, a foster mother, an uncle, two mothers, or two fathers, and informed teachers about antigay bias and violence.

By the time the COR guide was ready for review by local school boards in the spring of 1992, Chancellor Fernandez was already embroiled in a conflict with the Catholic archdiocese (which, by tradition, controls the Brooklyn seat on the Board of Education) and other conservatives around his HIV/AIDS education and condom-availability programs. One of his opponents, Mary Cummins, a close ally of the Catholic hierarchy, raised the battle cry against COR by publicly denouncing the guide. In a letter to parents and school board members across the city, she wrote, "We will not accept two people of the same sex in deviant practices as 'family.'"

Cummins, a white Catholic who chaired the all-white Queens School Board 24 in a district that is 70 percent people of color, found a broad array of allies. They included Latino Pentecostal preachers such as Bronx reverend Ruben Diaz, Catholic churches serving both whites and newly integrated Latinos, Christian right groups such as the Concerned Citizens for Accountability in Education, conservative Muslims, and four of the Board of Education's seven members.

THE RIGHT'S BIG PLAN

In churches and rallies, COR opponents represented the guide as an attempt by Manhattan-based gay and lesbian elites to impose their ideas on working-class parents from the outer boroughs by teaching their first-graders about sex.

Flyers, videos, and funds from the Christian Coalition began circulating in New York, leading to an immediate reaction from the city's well-organized and militant gay and lesbian organizations. In demonstrations at the Central Board and local community school board hearings, mostly white and middle-class gay and lesbian direct-action activists from ACT UP and the Lesbian Avengers pitted themselves against a rainbow of poor, working-class, and middle-class parents, often bused in from Bronx and Queens churches. The confrontations soon got ugly. As a gay white man noted after a particular nasty school board meeting, "Black parents were yelling 'white faggots' at ACT UP members, and ACT UP members were yelling back 'black racists.' It was one of the most depressing things I've ever seen."

At this point, progressive activists from various backgrounds who had not been part of the guide's development began to brainstorm about a new coalition strategy that could bridge some of the divisions of race, class, and sexuality being manipulated by the right. PACE initiated the discussions, bringing in such groups as the Black AIDS Mobilization, the National Congress of Puerto Rican Rights, Gay Men of African Descent, Black Nation/Queer Nation, and others.

PACE members, who have long histories in the black, Puerto Rican, and lesbian/gay liberation movements, as well as in community-control struggles with the public schools, noted with alarm that some anti-COR protestors were parents of color who had been PACE allies on other education campaigns, such as the inclusion of African-American history into school curricula, smaller class sizes, and more equitable funding.

Through a series of meetings, PACE and its allies, including gay family networks such as the Education Coalition for Lesbian and Gay Youth (ECO-LaGY) and the Lesbian/Gay Community Center Kids, Gay Men of African Descent, the Panel of Americans, the Hetrick–Martin Institute for Lesbian and Gay Youth, Advocates for Children, the Lesbian/Gay Teachers Association, and antibias peer educators from high schools, came up with a working document that agreed:

- The fight to include the lives and realities of lesbian and gay people in multiculturalism cannot be separated from the fight for educational quality and equality for all children—by teaching black, Latino, Native American, and Asian-American history, ending gender bias, dismantling a special-education system that labels over 120,000 children and helps few, lowering class sizes, and equalizing resources among schools.

- The struggle against homophobia and right-wing incursion in the schools must be led by people of color, and especially by parents of public-school children.

- To build new alliances, the organizing has to consciously subvert the idea that "gays and lesbians" and "working class/people of color" are mutually exclusive categories, and to support and highlight the voices of lesbian and gay people of color.

- Support for inclusive multiculturalism must be built from the bottom up, through grassroots dialogues with parents and communities, not just through lobbying or working in the bureaucracy.

REACHING OUT TO PARENTS

The Campaign for Inclusive Multicultural Education (CIME), founded on the basis of the above agreement in November 1993, was eventually endorsed by over five hundred individuals and organizations. They included clergy, elected officials, Manhattan Board of Education member Luis Reyes, individual parent activists (most parent organizations were too divided internally to take organizational positions), educators, and community leaders. A People of Color Fight the Right Committee within the larger campaign played a leading role in evaluating and revising the overall strategy. It reached out to working-class Latinos, African-Americans, and Asian-Americans by going door-to-door to explain the hidden white-supremacist, anti-public-school education agenda of the right.

To begin turning the tide, CIME immediately implemented a media strategy. It highlighted people of color and parents who supported COR, and who addressed the education needs of all of New York City's children. CIME was working against print and television media that preferred to show nonparent COR supporters screaming at parents, and the well-funded, right-wing deployment of anti-COR working-class Latino parents. Nonetheless, campaign members were able to appear on over one hundred radio and television shows, explaining why the COR guide benefited all children, and black and Latino children in particular. Members consistently emphasized polls that showed broad support for multicultural education including lesbian and gay realities and the narrow support for the full Christian-right education agenda.

As part of a strategy to blunt the right's incursion into the Latino community, CIME members and Latino leaders such as City Council member Guillermo Linares, Richard Perez of the National Congress for Puerto Rican Rights, Board of Education member Dr. Luis Reyes, and Episcopal priest Father Luis Barrios held a meeting with the Spanish-language newspaper *El Diario*. A sympathetic article and editorial in the newspaper resulted.

NEIGHBORHOOD DIALOGUES

Campaign members designed fact sheets, in Spanish as well as English, for community outreach. The first of these, "Myths and Facts About Children of the Rainbow," was used by dozens of parent activists to answer frequently asked questions and to counter the right's distortions in an accessible way. CIME also provided support to open-minded teachers by sharing lesson plans and teaching strategies, and by pressuring the Board of Education and the United Federation of Teachers to provide professional development and teaching materials.

Grassroots support was developed through dialogues with parents and communities around lesbian and gay inclusion issues. Angelica Rovira, a Puerto Rican lesbian and grandmother, now a school board member, describes how she rang doorbells in housing projects to talk to families about the COR guide.

"I experimented with a lot of approaches. I used to start by asking people if they'd read the Rainbow guide. I don't do that anymore, because it makes people defensive, or they think I'm criticizing their reading ability.

"Now I start by asking, 'What's the biggest problem for your family?' They might say someone needs a job, an apartment, health care—it's a pretty short list. Then I ask, 'Has it ever been a problem for you that a homosexual couple was living in your building?' I don't think I ever had anyone say yes. 'Have you had any horrible experiences with a homosexual—rape, sexual abuse?' Again, mostly noes. 'Can you think about someone in your family who might be homosexual? Are they weird, did they bring shame on you, or hurt you?' Again, most noes.

"Eventually, they ask me, 'Are you pro-Rainbow?' Then I reintroduce myself as the mother of a differently abled—mentally retarded—thirty-four-year-old son who had difficulties in getting a good education. And I tell them I'm a lesbian. I talk about the different needs that different kinds of students and parents have. They see me as this nice Puerto Rican grandmother, just like them, and they're grappling with it. And I keep asking questions, so they'll ask themselves, 'How did I come up with the idea that homosexuals are one of my problems?'

"I don't directly challenge people's beliefs. But I ask them to compare their experiences and feelings to their beliefs and look at the inconsistencies."

CHANCELLOR OUT—ELECTIONS COMING UP

By late fall of 1993, it was clear that the Christian Coalition planned to build on the anti-COR mobilization and run candidates for the May school board elections—possibly in all thirty-two school districts. When right-wing forces succeeded in ousting Chancellor Fernandez in February 1994, liberals and progressives across the city began to fear that the attack on the COR guide was actually going to translate into political power for allies of the Christian right.

At the same time, media exposure of the Christian right's "stealth strategy"—getting people elected to local school boards by hiding their opposition to critical thinking, bilingual programs, multicultural education, and ultimately to public schooling itself—got people angry. An antiright coalition built on that anger, broadening as activists and organizers across the city began making the connection between public schools, inclusive of citizenship, and the future of democracy. Progressives who had little or no previous involvement in public-school politics ran for community school boards or supported candidates. CIME allied with liberal foundations, gay and lesbian Democratic clubs, political action committees such as Empire State Pride Agenda, and politicians such as City Council member Tom Duane, Manhattan Borough President Ruth Messinger, and Assemblywoman Deborah Glick, providing the infrastructure that made formal, partisan work possible when school board races actually began.

Groups such as the National Association for the Advancement of Colored People, Commnity Service Society, and Association of Community Organizers for Reform Now did voter registration and education. Because Fernandez's ouster was seen as a blow to then-Mayor David Dinkins, who is black, black activists from traditional religious or culturally conservative sectors, such as the Reverend Al Sharpton, spoke out against the right, although they avoided criticizing the right's homophobia. PACE helped grassroots groups to new education issues to devleop district-specific education-reform platforms, and CIME members helped form SchoolPAC, the first progressive-education political action committee in the city.

As a result of these efforts, the May elections had the highest voter turnout in twenty-three years and dealt a setback to the right. Right-wing candidates did well in some white and other districts that had votted for conservatives in previous elections. But they didn't take over any additional boards. In black, Latino, and mixed communities where opposition to the COR guide had surfaced, several slates that emphasized diversity and a strong antiright campaign won majorities. Although right-wing candidates managed to unite with a few allies in communities of color, such as Roy Innis of the Congress of Racial Equality, their offensive in black and Latino communities was curbed.

At the same time, the situation became more complex for pro-COR parents of color. In some racially mixed districts in which school boards were dominated by white progressives, fighting the right meant putting off the struggle to elect more people of color. People of color won 50 percent of school board seats (the same as in the 1989 election), although they constitute 80 percent of public school students.

COR'S LEGACY

The COR guide was never fully implemented because of all the controversy and, as with most New York City public school curricular initiatives, because its planning never included funding for materials, dissemination, or teacher workshops. As one PACE teacher said at the beginning of the COR controversy, "They're fighting about a teacher's guide? I've been teaching in this system for twenty years and I've never seen a teacher's guide!"

Still, overall, CIME was quite successful in its most limited goal of stopping the right's incursion into the New York City public school boards, but was notably less successful in its larger goal of building a serious force for educational reform in New York. It's natural for coalitions that come together to respond to a crisis to separate into their constituent parts after the crisis has passed. But in CIME, the middle-class parts of the coalition who were able to manage things to their advantage left the lower-income and working-class parts to fend for themselves.

In New York, as in some other cities, the school administration has approved limited plans to set up independently run schools that remain part of the public school system. Some examples include the Harvey Milk School (for gay and lesbian students), the recently founded ACORN School for Social Justice, and a network of selective schools (mostly visible in the Riverdale section of the city) that essentially function to siphon off the best and the brightest of the public school students and teachers, leaving the rest in worse shape than before. The unintended but nonetheless horribly unfair result is that parents who are motivated, connected, and know the ropes can nearly always get their kids into a decent public school, while the kids of the poor, recently arrived, and otherwise shut-out majority have to make do with overcrowded classrooms, antiquated textbooks (if they have any at all), deteriorated buildings, and burnt-out teachers. Voucher programs that allow parents to apply the cost of a public education against tuition at private schools deepen this inequality and are promoted by the right.

But while middle-class white parents actively oppose school voucher programs that would severely defund public education, in many cases working-class and low-income parents of color are in favor of voucher programs, even those pushed by the right, since nobody else is coming to them with what sounds like a plan to make *their* schools better. At the same time, middle-class parents are generally in favor of plans to decentralize the school system, since they have the resources and organization to set up effective school-based management plans or magnet schools in their neighborhoods.[3]

The feeling among many of the education activists who are involved with the inner-city schools is that middle-class forces will willingly join in a battle to save public education from threats from the right, but they are basically oblivious to the fact that once that threat has been beaten back, the public schools are still in awful shape in most places. "They got theirs, so what do they care?" said one bitter CIME activist.

Other PACE members believe that despite the divides of class, the network could be revitalized and moved in a more positive direction if more resources were available. PACE is an all volunteer operation with a minuscule budget, five hundred members, and a limited capacity for sustained reform campaigns; one self-criticism often heard at PACE meetings is that the group should have paid more attention to building its funding base over the past few years.

GETTING OVER INVISIBILITY

Throughout the antiright COR struggle, many PACE members were aware that the visible lesbian and gays of color are generally middle class. With a few exceptions such as Black AIDS Mobilization, now defunct, and Gay Men of African Descent, they remain primarily involved in identity-affirming, social-network activities. While some black gay fathers, predominantly from middle-class backgrounds, were effective spokespeople in the COR struggle, the voices of the thousands of Latina, black, and Asian-American lesbian mothers were heard all too rarely. For most working-class people with children in public schools, the cost of being a public activist around homophobia is unimaginably high. Another aspect of this silence is that there are no organizations of lesbian and gay educators of color or parents of color. In addition, lesbians and gay men are talked about as if it's only sexuality that defines them. On the other hand, when people of color who are lesbian or gay—Langston Hughes, Audre Lorde, James Baldwin—are described as contributors to their communities and culture, their sexual orientation is usually not mentioned at all.

To counter this reality, PACE members decided to produce educational approaches and materials covering the realities and contributions of lesbian and gay people of color, and to help create spaces and dialogues in communities of color that welcome gay and lesbian participation.

In the spring of 1994, PACE cosponsored a public meeting with over fifty parent activists, school board members, teachers, young people, and education advocates about lesbian/gay issues in public school multiculturalism. The efforts emerging from that meeting included an issue of the PACE newspaper *School Voices* devoted to lesbian and gay youth writings and two important community initiatives: parent-led outreach and support groups for relatives of lesbian, gay, and bisexual youth of color, and community-based spaces for lesbian and gay youth, where youth of color can socialize, and get support services, free of harassment and violence, in their own neighborhoods.

Two key elements of an antihomophobia agenda tied to people's real needs in public schools are AIDS education and antiviolence organizing. PACE and other teachers' groups have been actively involved in conducting workshops and seminars on antigay violence and prejudice in the public schools based on material collected by the PACE Lesbian and Gay Curricular Project. For example, in 1994 schoolteacher and PACE member Bert Hunter conducted several staff development workshops using a resource kit called Stonewall 25 (named after the twenty-fifth anniversary of the Stonewall riots in Greenwich Village, which are credited with launching the gay rights movement). He used the workshop to link specific, school-related incidents of antigay violence and harassment with general dialogue on gay and lesbian issues and concerns.

These kinds of people-of-color-led initiatives are a vital part of an overall reform program around curriculum issues in New York City public schools. Curriculum, however, is only part of the struggle. A true dialogue on what it would take to provide every New York City public school student a decent education has yet to emerge. Some organized communities have clearly figured out how to make public education work for them, and these middle-class constituencies can be counted on to defend public education from those who want to destroy it. Will these same forces rally behind a struggle to make New York City public schools work for all children? The experience of the COR struggle suggests that a "united front" around education issues is possible in New York City and elsewhere, but that a strong organization of parents and teachers based in communities of color has to play a leading role.

THE EMERGENCE OF A GAY AND LESBIAN ANTIVIOLENCE MOVEMENT

DAVID M. WERTHEIMER

INTRODUCTION: WHAT IS BIAS-RELATED VIOLENCE?

I still own the dictionary that was the standard reference volume in my home when I was a child. Our family loved the English language, and dinner-table debates often sent one or another of us flying to the bookshelf to look up the precise meaning of a new or unusual word that had been introduced into the discussion. And so, it was not out of place for me to come home and grab the family Webster's one day after several classmates had hurled the word *faggot* in my direction in the school yard.

> **faggot:** 1. a bundle of sticks, twigs, or branches, especially for use as fuel.
> 2. in metallurgy, a bundle or heap of iron or steel pieces to be worked into bars by hammering or rolling at welding temperature.[1]

I now know that thousands, perhaps millions of gay people have shared the identical experience of running to the dictionary as they struggled to understand the taunting playground language of childhood that is the staging area for the patterns of oppression that preoccupy so much of the adult world.

Although I knew the word had not been directed to me in a friendly fashion, I was puzzled why someone would call me a bundle of twigs. I knew it was bad, that it meant *I* was bad, but it would be almost two decades before I learned that I had been taunted with a word steeped in Western civilization's long-term hate affair with sexual minorities. (It would take years before I learned that faggots, during the Middle Ages, were the bundles of sticks used to light fires to burn witches and that men who were identified as sodomites were often rolled up, alive, inside these bundles of twigs as part of the fuel.) And so, my first public identification as a gay person was with a word that is itself rooted in violence of the most extreme nature against sexual minorities.

Bias-related violence may be defined as acts "directed against persons or groups because of their real or perceived race, ethnicity, national origin, religion, sex, age, disability, or sexual orientation."[2] These acts of hatred have particular potency because they do not target solely the individuals who may be the victim of a given crime. Rather, they are intended to target the entire group of which the victim is perceived to be a member. They are attempts to isolate, violate, and depersonalize an entire community such that each member of the group is robbed not only of his/her personal safety but of the larger sense of security required to live, work, play, and pray in any sustained or substantive manner.[3] Until only recently, hate crimes have been classified by the police and prosecutorial authorities as nothing more than attacks on persons or property.[4] And yet, a swastika spray-painted on the side of a Jewish home does not only victimize the owner of the house, who must be reminded of the Holocaust as s/he paints over the familiar Nazi symbol. That swastika is intended to remind every Jew who sees it that someone hates them enough to send them to the gas chambers. The cross burned on the lawn of an African-American family who dares to buy property in a white neighborhood targets not only that brave family, but warns any black person who would contemplate living in that neighborhood that s/he will never be safe or secure.

It is no different for gay, lesbian, bisexual, and transgendered individuals. Although the lesbians who are attacked on the street for walking hand in hand are (hopefully) identified by the police as the survivors of a bias-related assault, the victims of this attack are legion, for the assault is designed to warn all sexual-minority persons that hatred of them is real. That they should remain invisible. That someone wishes they were dead.

As my own early etymology lesson taught me, hate crimes are nothing new. Organized hate groups in the United States have a long and unfortunate history. In 1865, immediately after the end of the Civil War, the Ku Klux Klan (KKK) formed for the specific purpose of attacking and intimidating African-Americans.[5] In response to hostile sentiments and violence against American

Jews, the Anti-Defamation League (ADL) was founded in 1913 to fight anti-Semitism through programs and services that counteract hatred, prejudice, and bigotry. That the KKK has been so successful and continues to survive to this day, that the ADL continues to be so badly needed as waves of anti-Semitism continue to wash across our communities, are indications of the power and impact of bias-related violence. It is, unfortunately, a form of control and intimidation that *works*. Its power is remarkably effective. For example, why are there so few places in the cities and towns of this nation where a same-sex couple feels able to walk down the street holding hands? Is it because they don't want people to know that they love another person? Is it because these individuals are embarrassed about being gay or lesbian? No. The invisibility of sexual minorities on the main streets of America persists because they fear violent assaults against them. In short, getting the living daylights beaten out of you is a predictable consequence of visibility.

Gay, lesbian, bisexual, and transgendered individuals were so completely intimidated by the collective impact of the fear and hatred that defines heterosexism that they suffered for centuries the violence perpetrated against them with virtually no organized response. Whether they experienced the disorganized assaults of marauding bands of teenagers who for some reason felt threatened by sexual minorities or the highly organized agendas of hostility perpetrated by law enforcement officials through bar raids and sanctioned acts of gay bashing, the sexual-minority community accepted these blows to their collective chin in frightened silence. Antigay and antilesbian violence were quietly accepted as the price tag for even marginal visibility in the earliest gay ghettos. Bashings and bar raids were considered the inevitable response to they sexual-minority community's most modest attempts at self-expression. The Stonewall riots during the summer of 1969, largely recognized as the seminal event of the contemporary gay rights movement, were themselves a response to the continuing police harassment of gay establishments in New York City's Greenwich Village.

DOCUMENTING THE EXTENT OF ANTIGAY VIOLENCE

In October of 1998, Americans watched in horror as the mainstream media brought the story of Matthew Shepard into virtually every home in the nation. The country seemed shocked that a fragile, twenty-one-year-old University of Wyoming student, targeted because he was gay, would be brutally beaten and left to die tied to a fence post in below-freezing temperatures. Four months later, America watched with renewed horror as the savagely victimized body of Billy Jack Gaither was found in the woods forty miles south of Birmingham, Alabama. Gaither, once again, was targeted by his assailants because of his sexual orientation. These two incidents began to raise the visibility of violence against sexual minorities in a way that no previous incidents had ever been able to accomplish.

Most disturbing, perhaps, is that although these two homicides helped the mainstream media and the American public to "discover" the issue of bias crimes against sexual minorities, these incidents in and of themselves did not in any way represent something new or different. The full extent of anti-gay, -lesbian, -bisexual, and -transgendered violence has, until only recently, gone unrecognized and undocumented. Historically, official reports of hate crimes targeting sexual minorities are virtually nonexistent. Not only have the police and media largely ignored them, but gay, lesbian, bisexual, and transgendered people themselves have been reluctant to come forward subsequent to victimization. Recent research has confirmed what many have suspected for many years—that almost three-quarters of the individuals victimized by antigay and antilesbian violence rarely report the assaults against them to the police.[6] There are many reasons for this underreporting. In addition to facing the shame and pain of the primary victimization suffered at the hands of the initial assailant, sexual-minority crime victims also face multiple layers of "secondary" victimization. This revictimization can include negative responses from family, friends, and traditional social-service agencies. More devastating still, in most parts of the country, where the civil rights of lesbians, gay men, bisexuals, and transgendered individuals are not protected by law, disclosure of an anti-gay/lesbian assault can lead to the loss of employment, eviction from housing, denial of access to public accommodations, and loss of child custody, all of which can be entirely *legal*.[7] These risks in and of themselves provide an enormous disincentive to the reporting of hate crimes to the authorities. And as the police are willing to tell any crime victim, a crime that isn't reported is a crime that never occurred.

Several studies in the late 1970s began to pull back the veil of invisibility from the problem of violence against sexual minorities and reveal the true nature and extent of this problem. A national survey of 5,400 lesbians and gay men in 1977 included questions about violence. The report determined that 77 percent of the males and 71 percent of the females surveyed had experienced anti-gay/lesbian verbal abuse and that 27 percent of the men and 14 percent of the women had been physically assaulted because they were perceived to be gay.[8] In 1978, Bell and Weinberg published the results of a San Francisco Bay Area study of 977 lesbians and gay men. Thirty-five percent of the men surveyed reported they had been either robbed or assaulted.[9]

These early studies helped to stimulate the first national, organized response to antigay and antilesbian violence. In 1982, the (then) National Gay

Task Force launched a "violence project." The goal of this project was to help both the gay/lesbian and the nongay communities define antigay violence, determine the nature of its scope, and promote local responses to the problem, both among sexual-minority-community activists and local law enforcement authorities. Under the energizing leadership of Kevin Berrill, the NGTF Violence Project quickly evolved into a highly visible catalyst for change at both the local and national levels. Berrill traveled widely throughout the country, educating diverse communities on violence issues and assisting local organizers to mobilize community-based responses to violent attacks against lesbians and gay men.

In 1984, Berrill and the NGTF Violence Project undertook groundbreaking research that began to document the full extent of hate crimes targeting sexual-minority communities around the nation. The results of sampling 1,420 gay men and 654 lesbians in eight American cities (Boston, New York, Atlanta, St. Louis, Denver, Dallas, Los Angeles, and Seattle) were stunning. Ninety-four percent had been victimized by some form of violence from verbal abuse to physical assault. Nineteen percent of the total sample indicated they had been punched, hit, kicked, or beaten at least once in their lives because they were gay or lesbian. Forty-four percent had been threatened with violence, and 84 percent knew other gay or lesbian people who had experienced anti-gay/lesbian victimization. In the years that followed, numerous additional studies confirmed what Berrill's groundbreaking work had determined: violence against lesbians and gay men in the United States was at epidemic proportions. The table below summarizes the findings of six anti-gay/lesbian violence surveys conducted between 1984 and 1987.

TABLE I. SUMMARY OF ANTIGAY
VIOLENCE/VICTIMIZATION SURVEYS: 1984–87[10]

Type of Victimization	Vermont 1987[11]	Alaska 1986[12]	Philadelphia 1985[13]	Wisconsin 1985[14]	Maine 1985[15]	NGLTF 1984[16]
Verbal abuse	81%	58%	80%	83%	84%	86%
Threats of violence	36	24	31	47	45	44
Property vandalized	19	12	10	20	20	19
Targets of objects	21	—	22	21	26	27
Followed or chased	32	14	25	37	38	35
Punched, hit, or kicked	16	11	10	23	16	19
Weapon assault	5	—	4	10	9	9
Victimized by police	8	8	20	24	14	20

Victimization of sexual-minority youth has proven even more difficult to document and measure. The stereotypes of lesbians and gay men as child molesters who keep their communities alive by recruiting unsuspecting children and adolescents into the fold through seduction and abuse are familiar to most of us. These perceptions have had a highly negative impact on organized efforts within the gay community to provide support and guidance to lesbian and gay youth; the emergence and growth of organizations serving lesbian, gay, bisexual, and transgendered youth have come relatively late in the evolution of sexual-minority social-service agencies. Data related to the victimization of sexual-minority youth has been equally scarce. It wasn't until 1987 that the New York State Governor's Task Force on Bias-Related Violence conducted a survey of 2,823 eighth, tenth, and twelfth grade students in New York State high schools and discovered that 31 percent had witnessed acts directed against students or teachers suspected of being gay or lesbian.[17]

In a 1988 study of 500 youths conducted by New York City's Hetrick-Martin Institute, 201 youths (40 percent) reported that they had experienced violent physical attacks. The average age of these victims was 17.1 years. Forty-six percent reported that the attack was antigay or antilesbian in nature, with 61 percent of the assaults occurring *in the family*. Not surprisingly, suicidal thoughts and behaviors were reported by 44 percent of those who had experienced violent assaults, with 41 percent of the females and 34 percent of the males actually attempting suicide.[18]

THE GROWTH AND DEVELOPMENT OF THE GAY AND LESBIAN ANTIVIOLENCE MOVEMENT

Even as an identifiable crime-victims movement emerged in the United States, it failed to address the nature and extent of hate crimes based on sexual orientation. Grassroots organizing efforts during the late 1960s and 1970s, mostly within women's organizations concerned about violence against women (without specifically identifying the needs of lesbians), gave rise to community-based programs offering a modest range of services to heterosexual, female survivors of domestic violence and sexual assault.[19] Several state governments also initiated the earliest crime-victim compensation programs during this time, and after 1975, municipalities around the country began to fund programs providing crisis-intervention services to a variety of crime victims.[20] Labeled "comprehensive," these programs were often affiliated with municipal or county agencies such as local police departments and district attorneys. The federal government added its own voice to the growing expression of concern for the welfare of crime victims when the Justice Department established its Office for Victims of Crime in 1981. The Presidential Task Force on Victims of Crime studied the problem nationally, issuing its final report in 1982.

And yet, despite these advances during the 1970s and 1980s, many crime-victim populations remained significantly unacknowledged and underserved throughout the United States. More often than not, crime victims are members of groups that have historically been among the most vulnerable in our society—women, persons of color, children, the elderly, persons with disabilities—populations whose disenfranchisement has resulted in, among other things, a minimizing of the concerns and needs that have traditionally been addressed through social service agencies. Lesbians and gay men are among these vulnerable and disenfranchised subsets of the general population. Although the data that emerged during the 1980s presented a powerful statistical argument, existing crime-victim service networks largely failed to acknowledge or address the existence and needs of lesbian and gay victims of violent crimes. As a consequence of this and other manifestations of systemic heterosexism, lesbians and gay men continued to suffer the often devastating consequences of victimization in isolation and silence. This systemic failure only compounded the initial physical and psychological injuries that follow any bias-related assault.

Although today more than twenty-five gay, lesbian, bisexual, and transgender-specific antiviolence organizations throughout the United States are organized into the National Coalition of Anti-Violence Programs,[21] the first local antiviolence efforts for sexual minorities in the United States were not organized until almost a decade after the Stonewall riots. The origins of Community United Against Violence (CUAV) in San Francisco, the nation's first successful community organization responding to anti-gay/lesbian hate crimes, may be traced back to the late 1970s when neighborhood "butterfly brigades" were organized, equipping lesbians and gay men with whistles to alert others on the street to bias-related attacks in progress. These concerned citizens responding to local incidents of antigay violence became the foundation of the more organized efforts that followed the massive protests after the assassinations of Mayor George Moscone and openly gay Supervisor Harvey Milk in 1978.[22] By 1979, CUAV had begun to emerge as a structured organization. CUAV was followed in 1980 on the East Coast by the Chelsea Anti-Crime Task Force, later to become the New York City Gay and Lesbian Anti-Violence Project (AVP).[23]

The emergence of the New York City Gay and Lesbian Anti-Violence Project, which in 1998 is the largest program of its type in the nation, is illustrative of how local sexual-minority communities began to identify and respond to the nature of the problem of bias-related violence. Between 1980 and 1990, AVP evolved from a grassroots, neighborhood-specific community network into an agency that is a formally acknowledged member of the larger social-service and crime-victim-service-provider communities.

In the early spring of 1980, lesbian and gay residents of the Chelsea neighborhood of Manhattan's West Side began hearing rumors of a significant increase in antigay attacks. It appeared that men walking in the evening, either alone or in pairs, were being attacked and beaten with alarming frequency by wandering groups of young males who moved through the neighborhood either on foot or in cars. Many area residents had the impression that these young men had come to the neighborhood with the specific intention of harassing and assaulting gay men. As was typical at this time, these bias-related assaults against lesbians and gay men were almost never reported to law enforcement authorities. Because virtually none of these attacks were being reported to the Chelsea police precinct, there had been no official documentation of the problem, and accordingly no official response. News of the assaults traveled by word of mouth, leaving community residents feeling highly intimidated, confused, and uncertain about exactly what was happening. Members of the Chelsea Gay Association, a local lesbian and gay community organization, began to address the problem by sponsoring a number of well-attended town meetings. Numerous assault victims came forward publicly for the first time to report what had happened to them. As a result of these meetings, two members of the Chelsea Gay Association placed a special telephone hot line in their home to take reports from individuals who had been gay-bashed. Volunteers from the group were recruited and trained to respond to messages left on an answering machine, to document incidents of violence, and to provide basic crisis-intervention services to callers. The group decided to provide volunteers who could accompany crime victims who wished to make police reports to the local precinct, and to monitor the progress of any cases that resulted in arrests and entered into the criminal court system. Palm cards with the new hot line number were distributed throughout the community. As word spread, calls came into the hot line from all over the city. The project organizers quickly realized that antigay and antilesbian violence was not limited to any one neighborhood, but was present throughout the city. Nevertheless, the organization remained a special-interest program of the Chelsea Gay Association for the next three years.

In 1983, the Anti-Violence Project incorporated and, through the assistance of a local elected official, received its first grant from the New York State Crime Victims Board. At first, the state refused to issue a check to an organization that had the words *gay* and *lesbian* in its corporate title. The group had incorporated as the New York City Gay and Lesbian Anti-Violence Project; a separate corporation called the Chelsea Anti-Crime Task Force had to be created to first receive these public moneys. This grant enabled the agency to open an office and hire its first paid staff. The organization's newly elected board of directors decided that the agency's mandate would be to provide crime victim services throughout the New York City area. Hot line and volunteer peer-counseling services continued. The organization also began to provide short-term crisis-intervention counseling, continued police advocacy, and court monitoring. The presence of a paid staff also enabled the organization to begin interacting more professionally with other crime-victim service providers as well as with the police and the offices of the various district attorneys. In 1985, when I became the Anti-Violence Project's executive director, AVP hired its first professional mental-health staff. The caseload of the organization grew steadily each year.[24] Between 1984 and 1987, the number of clients served by the Anti-Violence Project grew from 186 to 517, an increase of almost 180 percent.[25] Although much of this can be attributed to the growing strength of the Anti-Violence Project and the growing visibility of the bias-crime issue within the sexual-minority community, the atmosphere faced by gay people in New York was also changing dramatically. Statistics collected suggested that the increasing visibility of the AIDS epidemic, associated at that time largely with the gay male community, was stimulating increasing levels of antigay sentiment and backlash. In 1985, 25 percent of the antigay attacks documented in New York City by the AVP were identified as AIDS-related. Either before or during an assault, epithets hurled at victims would include such statements as "You faggots give us AIDS" or "Here come the AIDS carriers, let's get them!"[26]

Despite the statistical evidence provided by researchers in numerous American cities and the data generated by programs like the New York City Gay and Lesbian Anti-Violence Project and Community United Against Violence, the official response to antigay and antilesbian violence remained minimal. Although several larger police jurisdictions began in the early 1980s to classify and respond to bias crimes based on race, religion, or ethnicity, in New York City the police department's Bias Investigations Unit did not add sexual orientation to its bias categories until July of 1986.[27] Even then, in 1986 the Bias Unit only classified eleven reports as antigay and antilesbian, despite more than 450 cases documented by the AVP.[28]

Even as the gulf remained enormous between community-based organizations documenting the problem of anti-gay/lesbian violence and the timid response of local law enforcement authorities, the momentum behind the gay and lesbian antiviolence movement began to build at the national level. Emerging local community education efforts and victim-service programs joined forces with the NGLTF's Anti-Violence Project to create a national antiviolence presence and agenda. Horrifying personal accounts of bashings publicized in the emerging gay media, combined with local data from fledgling antiviolence organizations, were used by our community's national organizations to force the issue of antigay and antilesbian violence into more mainstream forums. Largely as a result of lobbying done by the American Psychological Association and the NGLTF, Representative John Conyers (D-MI), a member of the House Judiciary Committee, agreed in 1986 to sponsor hearings on antigay and antilesbian violence by the Judiciary Committee's Criminal Justice Subcommittee, which he chaired.

October 9, 1986, was a remarkable day in Congress. The hearing participants included Dr. Gregory Herek from the American Psychological Association, Kevin Berrill from the NGLTF, Joyce Hunter from the Institute for the Protection of Lesbian and Gay Youth (later to become the Hetrick-Martin Institute), Diana Christensen from CUAV, Jacqueline Schafer from the New York County District Attorney's Office, anti-gay/lesbian assault survivors Ed Hassell, Robert Gravel, and Kathleen Sarris, and myself. Members of Congress sat in stunned silence as Washington resident and assault survivor Ed Hassell, sitting in front of the most powerful legislators in the land, offered the following testimony:

> [My assailants] . . . forced me at knifepoint to strip. They beat me. One of them stood on my wrists, leaning over my face, holding the knifepoint at my throat so that any way I moved, it would dislodge him and then he would fall into me, forcing the knife through my throat—while the other one systematically beat me in the groin, the side. They made me address them as "sir." They threatened to castrate me; they threatened to emasculate me. They called me "queer," "faggot." One of them urinated on me. They kept me this way for an hour. There's an old Southern expression called playing possum. I kept trying [to feign unconsciousness] but they were hurting me so badly I couldn't help but to cry out in pain.[29]

Indianapolis lesbian activist Kathleen Sarris offered a similarly chilling account of what happened to her one night as she was leaving and locking up her office. Feeling a gun at the back of her head, she was forced back into the office. Sarris testified:

> For the next three and a half hours, I was beaten, I was assaulted sexually, and I was raped. Throughout the incident, the man kept saying over and over again that the reason he was doing it was to put an end to what was happening [gay rights efforts] in Indiana, and that somebody had to stop the gays and lesbians, and that he, in essence, was going to either kill me or I would walk out of there heterosexual.[30]

NGLTF's Kevin Berrill charged during his testimony that the federal government in general, and the Justice Department in particular, had acknowledged that antigay violence was a major problem but had resisted any efforts to address the issue. Representative Conyers agreed: "Local law enforcement responses to antigay violence have been terrible. Some areas are trying to do a better job than others. Most areas, however, appear to treat the issue as insignificant or somebody else's problem."[31] Berrill presented a set of recommendations on how government could improve its response to antigay and antilesbian violence. These recommendations included:

- Repeal of sodomy laws.

- Passage of local, state, and federal legislation to prohibit gay-related discrimination.

- Passage of legislation to combat antigay violence.

- Establishment of research, education, and programs to monitor antigay violence.

Representative Barney Frank (D-MA), who attended the hearings, called the hearings "an important step forward," adding that "you all deserve better from the system, but your willingness to come forward may help us minimize the number of other people who are victimized."[32]

The national exposure for the issue of bias-related violence against sexual minorities that was generated by these congressional hearings was remarkable. Until this time the mainstream media had not significantly covered this issue, which now began to move into the national spotlight. Shortly after the Conyers hearings, a young New York Times reporter named William Greer called the New York City Gay and Lesbian Anti-Violence Project and inquired "whether or not there is a story in violence against homosexuals." On November 23, 1986, still during the era in which The New York Times identified lesbians and gay men only as "homosexuals," the Times ran the first, major mainstream-media article to address the full scope and extent of antigay and antilesbian violence.[33] The story, buried on page 36, almost didn't make it into print at all. Despite the overwhelming evidence provided to the Times reporter by researchers and service providers around the nation, the Times news editor insisted that the story was not legitimate without corroboration of this data from local and national law enforcement authorities. Yet without official mechanisms for the collection and analysis of hate crimes data involving lesbians and gay men at the local, state, and national levels, such corroboration was impossible. The statistics and case studies cited by representatives of the gay community were considered, by the editor, to represent the subjective political agenda of community activists rather than hard news. Only after heated conversations between the reporter and the editor did the Times relent and run the article,[34] but not without a headline that undercut the force of the story itself: "Violence Against Homosexuals Rising," said the first line of the three-column article, with a second headline stating, "Groups Seeking Wider Protection Say."[35]

With The New York Times providing the groundwork of an "establishing story" on the topic of anti-gay/lesbian violence, mainstream media coverage of the topic began to increase rapidly. Newspapers throughout the nation began to report on the issue, and the topic became briefly popular on daytime television talk shows such as *Donahue, Oprah,* and *Sally Jessy Raphael.* This visibility not only stimulated a larger public dialogue on antigay violence, but also had a substantial impact on the lesbian and gay communities, particularly in areas outside of New York and San Francisco. Antiviolence organizations that followed the examples of New York and San Francisco began to emerge in other cities, including Philadelphia, Boston, Chicago, Los Angeles, and Hartford. These organizations generally followed one of three models:

- **Freestanding antiviolence projects:** Where sufficient interest and energy were present, several communities organized freestanding social-service organizations addressing the needs of crime victims and the issues of bias-related violence (e.g., New York, Hartford).

- **Programs sponsored by local law enforcement:** Prosecutorial authorities in some jurisdictions provided funding, staff, and office space for lesbian and gay crime-victim/witness-assistance services (e.g., San Francisco, New York County district attorney).

- **Programs within larger lesbian and gay community programs:** Many existing lesbian and gay community centers and social service programs began to organize specialized services for lesbian and gay crime victims (e.g., Boston, Chicago, Los Angeles, Philadelphia).

Representative Conyers kept his commitment to sustain momentum at the federal level. Following one of the recommendations made during his landmark congressional hearing, Conyers in 1988 introduced the Hate Crimes Statistics Act, which would require the Department of Justice to collect and publish annual statistics on crimes that manifest prejudice based on race, religion, sexual orientation, and ethnic origin. This bill was finally passed in both houses during the 101st Congress and was signed into law by President George Bush on April 23, 1990, as Public Law 101-275.[36]

BUILDING BRIDGES: BIAS-RELATED VIOLENCE AND THE LARGER COMMUNITY

Documentation of the extent of anti-gay/lesbian hate crimes, the organized community's response to antigay and antilesbian violence in the United States, and the acknowledgment of this issue by Congress have provided extraordinary opportunities. Chief among these was the ability to begin constructing bridges to and alliances among the sexual-minority community and a broad range of other constituencies. The issue of bias-related violence is a remarkable lens through which to view the shared experience of oppression in the United States. As Audre Lorde, noted African-American and lesbian poet and essayist, wrote in her noted essay "There Is No Hierarchy of Oppression":

> I have learned that oppression and the intolerance of difference come in all shapes and sizes and colors and sexualities; and that among those of us who share the goals of liberation and a workable future for our children, there can be no hierarchies of oppression. I have learned that sexism (a belief in the inherent superiority of one sex over all others and thereby its right to dominance) and heterosexism (a belief in the inherent superiority of one pattern of loving over all others and thereby its right to dominance) both arise from the same source as racism—a belief in the inherent superiority of one race over all others and thereby its right to dominance. . . . Within the lesbian community I am Black, and within the Black community I am a lesbian. Any attack against Black people is a lesbian and gay issue, because I and thousands of other Black women are part of the lesbian community. Any attack against lesbians and gays is a Black issue, because thousands of lesbians and gay men are Black. There is no hierarchy of oppression.[37]

The power of this argument helped the lesbian and gay antiviolence movement transcend many of the traditional barriers that had prevented the consideration of sexual-minority concerns in mainstream venues. From progressive religious organizations that condemned violent attacks of any type against innocent citizens to "law and order" Republicans who supported strengthening of local police powers to investigate crimes and incarcerate perpetrators, the issue of decreasing violence against lesbians and gay men was able to gather a powerful set of allies in places where lesbians and gay men had previously found only limited support. As local antiviolence organizations and national groups such as the NGLTF and the American Psychological Association began to disseminate the data and horrifying accounts of bias-related violence that targeted sexual minorities, it became increasingly difficult to exclude anti-gay/lesbian violence from any larger discussions of hate crimes and organized hate groups.

In the wake of the 1986 racially motivated slaying of a young African-American man in the Howard Beach neighborhood of Queens in New York City, Governor Mario Cuomo convened the New York State Governor's Task Force on Bias-Related Violence in 1987. This task force was charged with studying the problem of bias-related violence in New York State through research, analysis, and public hearings and with making recommendations on a broad range of strategies to reduce the incidence of hate crimes throughout the state. As executive director of the New York City Gay and Lesbian Anti-Violence Project, I was one of fifteen members named to the task force by the governor. In its 315-page report, issued in March 1988, the task force issued dozens of recommendations on legislation, education, law enforcement, social services, housing, and the media.[38] After careful deliberation, the task force decided against including specific chapters in its report on bias-related violence against different communities. Rather, hate crimes were considered a class of crimes that have the potential to victimize any person who is or is perceived to be a member of any oppressed community. Sexual-minority concerns were not separated and ghettoized into a separate chapter that any reader could choose to skip over; instead, the issue of antigay and antilesbian violence was sewn into the fabric of each chapter of the report. No one could come away from reading the report without realizing that, when the State of New York referred to bias-related violence, lesbians and gay men were part of the issue. In echoing the wisdom of Audre Lorde, the task force report stated:

> The secrecy, isolation, and fear of discovery plaguing some gay and lesbian victims have an analogue in the experiences of other victims of bias crimes. The horror of reliving the Holocaust strikes the victim of anti-Semitism. The deep historical roots of slavery and oppression and racists' rejection of full citizen status aggravate the pain for Black victims. Hispanic and Asian victims struggle with language barriers, scapegoating that degrades the meaning of success, and a threatened sense of belonging. There are many other pains, some shared by all bias crime victims, others primarily affecting one victim group. There is no hierarchy of pain and suffering. All who suffer deserve full recognition and the best care available.[39]

When, in February of 1990, the U.S. Congress considered the legislation that was to become the Hate Crime Statistics Act, the list of organizations and groups that articulated their support for the inclusion of sexual orientation in this bill was impressive. More than ninety national organizations endorsed the legislation, including the American-Arab Anti-Discrimination Committee, the American Baptist Church, the American Jewish Congress, the NAACP, the AFL-CIO, the National Council of La Raza, the National Urban League, and many others.[40] In the face of such support, even the lengthy rantings of Jesse Helms (R-NC) went virtually unnoticed when he called the bill "the flagship of the homosexual, lesbian legislative agenda."[41] When this legislation was passed and signed by President George Bush, it became the first law in the nation to specifically identify the needs and rights of lesbians and gay men in any positive fashion.

STATUS REPORT: THE PRESENT DAY

Since 1990, incidents of violence against lesbian, gay, bisexual, transgendered, and HIV-positive persons have shown no signs of abating. Documenting the nature and extent of the problem of bias-related violence targeting sexual minorities has been greatly facilitated during the 1990s by the emergence of the National Coalition of Anti-Violence Projects (NCAVP). The model gay and lesbian antiviolence programs developed by larger gay communities in cities such as San Francisco and New York laid the groundwork for replication of these efforts in cities throughout the country. During the late 1980s, organizations documenting incidents of anti-gay, -lesbian, -bisexual, and -transgender violence emerged in such cities as Chicago, Boston, Philadelphia, and Los Angeles. By the late 1990s, organizations documenting incidents of antigay violence and in many cases providing services to survivors of these attacks had emerged in some two dozen cities throughout the nation. Utilizing a uniform data-reporting instrument, the national coalition today provides a vital infrastructure within the sexual-minority community that documents and reports annually on changes in patterns and trends of anti-gay, -lesbian, -bisexual, and -transgender violence.

In 1997, the National Coalition of Anti-Violence Programs documented a total of 2,445 anti-gay, -lesbian, -bisexual, -transgender, and HIV-related incidents in fourteen different jurisdictions throughout the country. Even as the Department of Justice reported that violent crime rates fell dramatically across the country during 1997, reported bias crimes against sexual minorities continued to climb.[42] Perhaps this is not surprising. The more visible our community becomes, the more those who fear or hate us will use violence to render us invisible. Additionally, the increasing visibility of the gay, lesbian, bisexual, and transgender antiviolence movement has stimulated increased community awareness of violence and may be resulting in more reporting of the incidents that do occur. According to the NCAVP, the number of attacks against lesbians and gay men peaks each year in June. June, when most GLBT pride events are held throughout the nation, is the community's month of greatest visibility— and the greatest threat to those who seek to keep sexual minorities powerless in the closet.[43] Nor are the attacks against individuals becoming any less violent. In 1997, 274 incidents nationally involved an assault with a weapon. Seventy of these incidents involved bats, clubs, or blunt objects. Eighty-eight of these incidents involved firearms or knives. Minor injuries were sustained by

505 individuals; 243 individuals reported serious injuries. There were eighteen homicides.

Recent data related to sexual-minority youth may be less dramatic but are equally alarming. In the "1995 Teen Health Risk Survey" of more than seven thousand students conducted by the Seattle, Washington, public school district, 34 percent of 360 students who self-identified as gay, lesbian, and bisexual reported that they had been the target of offensive comments or attacks based on their perceived sexual orientation either at school or on the way to and from school. This compares to a rate of only 6 percent for similar harassment or assault for heterosexual students.[44] The intolerance and lack of acceptance communicated by these hostile acts also appears to have caused suicidal thoughts and behaviors among sexual minority students. A disturbing 36 percent of gay, lesbian, or bisexual students had seriously considered suicide (as compared to 17 percent of the heterosexual students), and 21 percent had actually made a suicide attempt (as compared to 7 percent of the heterosexual students).[45]

Fortunately, the increased visibility of the issue of bias-related violence targeting sexual minorities has led to growth among those organizations providing crime-victim services, criminal-justice-system advocacy, and community education. The New York City Gay and Lesbian Anti-Violence Project, for example, has grown from a struggling organization of one and a half staff in 1985 to a vibrant social service agency with more than a dozen staff members. Direct services are funded through a variety of public and private grants and a strong community donor base. Many private foundations, such as the Joyce Mertz-Gilmore Foundation and the Open Society Institute, made their first gay-funding grants to lesbian and gay antiviolence organizations precisely because these groups are less controversial. These and other foundations have sustained and expanded their support of the sexual minority antiviolence movement.

The increasing levels of support have enabled lesbian and gay victim-assistance organizations to expand the scope of their activities outside the arena of bias-related violence. For example, in 1986, New York's AVP was awarded the first grant from a state public health department to develop services for lesbian and gay survivors of domestic violence.[46] In 1987, AVP received funds to develop services for male survivors of sexual assault. In 1990, AVP became the first program in the nation to receive funding to develop an HIV-related violence program. Resources for the innovative services offered by this program were provided by the New York State Health Department, the New York City AIDS Fund, and the New York Community Trust.[47] In addition to these specialized grants, antiviolence organizations around the nation have also secured resources to strengthen organizational infrastructures. For example, standardized data systems are now able to record and monitor incidents of bias-related violence throughout the nation.

As the inclusiveness of the sexual-minority community has expanded, so has the work of our antiviolence programs. Since 1995, the National Coalition of Anti-Violence Programs has been the first and only national group to collect and report data on violence against transgender persons. In 1997, 102 (3.5%) of the victims reporting to the NCAVP self-identified as transgendered persons.[48] The antiviolence movement has also continued to build stronger bridges to the law enforcement community. Sexual-minority community relationships with the police have expanded from the fragile police/gay community rap sessions held by the AVP and the CUAV in the early 1980s. For example, during 1997, the National Coalition of Anti-Violence Programs worked closely with the Federal Bureau of Investigation and played a leading role in the effort to warn gay communities throughout the nation about the activities of spree killer Andrew Cunanan.[49] Many municipal police departments now actively recruit new officers from the sexual-minority community.

Finally, despite an increasingly conservative atmosphere in local and national legislative bodies, community activism and the broad base of support for antiviolence efforts have kept various legislative initiatives on bias-related violence alive and well. In June of 1998, Senator Edward Kennedy (D-MA) introduced the Hate Crimes Prevention Act of 1998. Under the terms of this bill, it would be a federal crime to harm or attempt to harm someone on the basis of race, color, religion, national origin, gender, sexual orientation, or disability. Offenders could face up to ten years in prison, or life imprisonment if the crime involves kidnapping, aggravated sexual abuse, or murder.[50]

These bills continue to face extensive and powerful opposition. Subsequent to the 1998 murder of Matthew Shepard in Wyoming, several bills were introduced into the Wyoming State legislature to create enhanced penalties for hate crimes committed against individuals because of their race, religion, disability, sexual orientation, national origin, or ancestry. Due to strong opposition to including sexual orientation in this statute, the bill failed to pass a Senate committee. Even a watered-down version of this bill enhancing penalties for bias-motivated crimes committed because of an individual's "membership in a group" failed to win enough votes to pass.[51] In Texas, a statewide hate crimes statute was scuttled in early 1999 so that Republican Texas governor and presidential contender George W. Bush would not have to sign or veto a bill that might be interpreted as being friendly to the gay, lesbian, bisexual, and transgender community. Even after witnessing the bloodied bodies of Matthew Shepard and Billy Jack Gaither, America still resists efforts to call this most extreme form of bigotry by its true name.

Although the struggle is clearly far from over, during the past fifteen years hate crimes targeting lesbian, gay, bisexual, transgendered, and HIV-infected persons have moved from being considered the predictable and accepted consequences of a deviant lifestyle to a legitimate minority-community issue that engenders the outrage of many individuals and organizations throughout the United States. Rather than suffering in invisibility and silence, victims of bias-related attacks are increasingly able to access the services and supports that promote recovery. By working to care for their own wounded while building bridges to other constituencies that understand the nature and impact of crimes motivated by hatred, the lesbian, gay, bisexual, and transgendered communities have further insured their presence at the table of those who seek to guarantee our basic rights to life, liberty, and the pursuit of happiness.

PART IV

FAMILY VALUES

CHAPTER 14

Couples: Marriage, Civil Union, and Domestic Partnership

David L. Chambers

I N THIS COUNTRY, DURING THE LAST DECADES OF THE twentieth century, thousands of lesbians married other women and thousands of gay men married other men. Many of these couples recited traditional vows in churches and synagogues. Others have pledged to each other in their own backyards in words that they wrote themselves. But not one of these thousands of solemn occasions was recognized as creating a legally valid marriage. In the United States, each state has its own statute defining who can marry, and as far as the states were concerned, these couples were playing dress up. One state has now made an abrupt change. Just before this book went to press, Vermont's legislature, prodded by a decision of the state Supreme Court, enacted a statute that permits same-sex couples to enter into "civil unions" and obtain all the legal benefits and burdens of marriage except the name. It is, however, too soon to know whether or when other states will create similar forms of unions or whether Vermont will eventually take the final step and call civil unions "marriage."

Thus, two quite different social histories might be written about this same period. One is of the growth in the numbers of same-sex weddings and commitment ceremonies performed in the United States, as well as the in-

crease in the social acceptance for such unions by gay people, by their constructed and their biological families and by the media. That encouraging story
will not be told here. The story here is the history of the intermittent and
much less successful efforts to secure *legal* recognition of same-sex marriage
in the United States. This is a story in progress, one that may well have a happy
ending. It has some heroes—some courageous couples who have put themselves on the line, some talented advocates who always believe that victory is
near, and the justices of two state supreme courts who went out on a limb.
Overall, however, it is a story of repeated judicial and political defeats and of
tension among gay activists and between national and local groups.

A second and closely related story is also one in progress. It is the more
gratifying story of the movement to secure legal recognition of lesbian and gay-
male couple relationships in ways other than marriage, the history of efforts to
obtain "domestic partnership." In Hawaii today, legal same-sex marriage has
been rejected, but the legislature now permits same-sex couples to register
their relationship and secure many of the benefits that married couples enjoy.
Hundreds of corporations, municipalities, and universities now provide health
and other benefits to the same-sex partners of their employees. Whatever the
final outcome of the story of the efforts to obtain legal recognition of same-sex
marriage, it will inevitably be intertwined with the story of domestic partnership. Indeed, Vermont created civil union as the legal equivalent of marriage,
but civil union can, of course, be seen as the ultimate form of domestic partnership.

THE MOVEMENT FOR LEGAL RECOGNITION OF SAME-SEX MARRIAGE

The 1970s

The first efforts to secure state recognition of gay relationships in the
United States occurred in the early 1970s. The nascent national gay organizations of the time played no role whatever. To some involved in the early
national movement, marriage was just one more tool of the capitalist establishment, a corrupt institution through which men sustained dominance over
women and property. To the extent that gay activists addressed issues of public
policy in the first few years after Stonewall, they focused largely on reducing
harassment of gay people by the police. They hoped that harassment might be
reduced if the police and mainstream society could be led to view gay persons
as simply harmless and pitiable, rather than as immoral and mentally unstable.
By contrast, opening up the institution of civil marriage would have required a
much more radically restructured view of gay people—a view of us as morally

worthy and of our loving relationships as comparable in merit to the most hallowed of relationships in heterosexual society. At the time, few gay people and almost no heterosexual people held such a view.

Still, Stonewall had occurred, and in the largest gay enclaves, more and more lesbians and gay men were living their lives in the open. Some gay couples were holding weddings. Ministers of the Metropolitan Community Church, organized in 1968, had begun performing weddings for their members.[1] The August 1970 issue of *The Advocate* proclaimed that America was experiencing a "gay marriage boom."[2] It was thus inevitable that, despite general public hostility to gay people, some lesbian and gay male couples would be bold and determined enough to present themselves at a city clerk's office demanding a marriage license. And some did. Indeed, during the early 1970s, across the country, close to a dozen couples did—and three couples followed the state's refusal to issue a license by filing a lawsuit. The stories of these three couples are instructive about the state of gay political efforts at the time.

The first case was brought in Minnesota. Jack Baker was a law student at the University of Minnesota. Michael McConnell was a librarian. They had begun dating in 1967. By 1970, they were both involved in gay political activity. At Minnesota, Jack was a member of a gay student group called FREE (Fight Repression of Erotic Expression). Imbued with the spirit of the civil rights era, Jack believed in "equal rights, in all areas of society. . . . We've got to integrate the gay community into the heterosexual community at large."[3] He was also familiar with the activist tactics of the antiwar protesters. Thus, through FREE, Baker tried in various ways "to provoke a heterosexual backlash by rhetorical and psychological confrontation," because backlash, he believed, could lead to educational opportunities.[4] He found, however, that sending demands to state legislators, organizing gay dances on campus, and dancing with his partner at the law school's Barristers' Ball produced little reaction. Openly gay on campus, Jack ran for student association president, and won; Walter Cronkite reported the event as a curiosity on his nightly newscast.

In the spring of 1970, Jack and Michael devised a new tactic. They decided to marry and invited the press to come with them when they applied for a marriage license. With this move, they evoked the reaction they had been hoping for. On May 18, they held a press conference and marched to the city clerk's office with a crowd of reporters. The clerk refused to issue a license without consulting with the county attorney. The event attracted television and newspaper attention across the country. Jack and Michael were, so far as I can find, the first same-sex couple in American history to seek a marriage license openly. Shortly afterward, McConnell reflected that getting married by the state would have been "a political act with political implications. I sincerely believe that my love for Jack is as valid and deep as any heterosexual love, and I think it should be recognized—I demand that it be recognized!—by the state and society."[5] Just as his war-protesting classmates believed they could bring down the military establishment, Baker believed that "within five years we can turn the whole institution of marriage upside down."[6]

The story reached gay audiences through *The Advocate*, then in its fourth year as "the newspaper of America's homophile community." Baker and McConnell were the headline story for the mid-June 1970 issue[7] and probably planted the idea of legal marriage in many gay persons' minds for the first time. The couple reached a vastly wider audience in early 1971, when they were featured in a three-page spread in *Look* magazine, a widely read photo magazine of general circulation, as part of an issue devoted to the American family. Jack and Michael were "The Homosexual Couple," sandwiched between articles on two other growing and culturally unsettling groups—"The Young Unmarrieds" and "The Executive Mother." In a series of attractive pictures, Jack and Michael are lathered up and shaving, snuggling on a couch while a straight friend plays a guitar, chatting with their priest after a mass at the campus Catholic chapel, and presenting themselves at the counter in the city clerk's office applying for the license. For its era, the article is breathtakingly positive. Except for a few lapses when trying to distinguish the two from other gay men ("Neither is a limp-wristed sissy"), the text and photo captions have the same sort of isn't-this-sweet, patronizing tone that we expect today in a story about a gay couple in *People* or *Newsweek*.

When Baker and McConnell's request for a license was eventually refused, they turned to the courts, aided by a local attorney who was unaffiliated with any gay or civil rights organization. The Minnesota trial court, like later courts in other states, rejected both a statutory claim that the state marriage statute permitted same-sex marriage and a constitutional claim that the U.S. Constitution compelled its recognition. The couple appealed to the Minnesota Supreme Court, this time with the help of the Minnesota Civil Liberties Union. The court upheld the trial court's decision in a brief opinion, dismissing arguments under the due process and equal protection clauses.[8] The court justified its decision on the ground that marriage uniquely involves procreation and the rearing of children. It also explicitly rejected analogies between barriers to same-sex marriage and barriers to interracial marriage, which had by then been held unconstitutional by the U.S. Supreme Court. Baker's lawyer had argued that prohibitions on women marrying women when men can marry women were constitutionally indistinguishable from miscegenation statutes that permit blacks to marry blacks but not to marry whites. Miscegenation statutes involve race discrimination, said the court. Sex discrimination is different.

In September 1971, while the *Baker* case was still pending before the Minnesota Supreme Court, Paul Barwick and John Singer applied for a marriage license in Seattle, Washington. Like Baker and McConnell, Barwick and Singer were deeply involved in gay political activities in their local communities.[9] In other ways they were quite different. Jack Baker was in many ways the prototype of the earnest student activist of his day. Barwick and Singer, in the language of the time, were hippies. They lived in a commune with a half dozen others involved in running a new gay community center. They were active in antiwar efforts. Like Baker and McConnell, they recall having been frustrated by the meager news coverage for gay issues in their area.

Their decision to seek a marriage license followed a speech at the gay community center by a local state representative. The legislator boasted that he had recently succeeded in securing legislative language that changed the marriage statute into sex-neutral terms. He implicitly challenged the group to test the reach of the statute. Others at the center were enthusiastic, and Barwick and Singer volunteered because they thought they were in the least vulnerable positions in their jobs. Barwick was working as director of the gay center. Singer worked for the federal Equal Employment Opportunities Commission. Quite unlike Baker and McConnell, who regarded themselves in a marriage-like relationship, Barwick and Singer were simply good friends and housemates who had had sex with each other from time to time. "We were not an item," recalls Singer today. They liked the idea of seeking a marriage license because they anticipated that it would generate public discussion about gay people and gay relationships.

Like Baker and McConnell, they invited the press, presented themselves at a clerk's office, and were rejected. Only then did they face squarely the question whether to file a lawsuit. Some within the local gay community strongly supported the idea of marriage, but feared going to court because they regarded it as seeking too much, too soon. Some feminist and lesbian friends were hostile to seeking marriage rights at all, but were assuaged by Singer's explanation that one of his goals was to challenge mainstream definitions of marriage and the family. Barwick and Singer assumed from the outset that the courts would reject their claims. Indeed, Barwick says he would have been stunned if they had decided otherwise. If the state had permitted them to marry, Barwick reflects, he and John would have been both America's first officially married gay couple and America's first officially divorced gay couple.

They did decide to file a case and approached the local chapter of the ACLU. The chapter considered their request, but, as Singer recalls, thrashed the matter out in many committees with endless "rigmarole" and eventually decided that litigation would be hopeless. A lawyer from the National Lawyers Guild agreed to help them and filed suit on their behalf. In court, he made essentially the same arguments that had by then been rejected by the Minnesota Supreme Court, and in the end the trial court and Washington Court of Appeals rejected their claims.[10] Unlike Minnesota's, Washington's constitution contained a provision that guaranteed equality of rights based on sex, but the court again rejected the analogy to the U.S. Supreme Court decision invalidating miscegenation statutes. No sex discrimination was involved, declared the court, because marriage is inherently the union of one man and one woman. In their view, it was as preposterous for a man to argue that he had a right to marry a man as it would be for a man to argue that he had a right to get pregnant.

Despite the loss in the courts, Singer and Barwick regarded their efforts as entirely successful. They generated just the publicity they hoped for. Like Baker and McConnell, they induced an entourage of reporters to accompany them to the clerk's office for a marriage license. Their request for a license was reported across the country on TV and carried on the AP and the UPI. Barwick remembers that little news articles appeared as "fillers" across the country. Like Baker and McConnell, they recalled being asked which one was the wife and were pleased to be able to say that they were simply two men who were a couple. Singer, who later changed his name to Faygele Ben Miriam, looked back with particular pleasure at their success in reaching closeted gay people, who had few positive images of gay men or gay relationships available to them. He recalled receiving grateful letters from gay men in small cities across the country. He and Barwick also spoke to gay and straight audiences all over the state of Washington and distributed hundreds of copies of their lawyers' brief.

The Minnesota and Washington couples nonetheless paid a heavy price for putting themselves so squarely in the public eye. One member of each couple lost his job. Singer lost his position at the EEOC. He had been hired by the regional office in part because he was gay, but was fired because the U.S. Civil Service Commission still had rules prohibiting federal employment for homosexuals. McConnell lost a promised job as a librarian at the University of Minnesota. Both sued to get their jobs back and both lost.[11] In each case, a federal court of appeals relied on their having "flaunted" their homosexuality publicly in a manner that an employer need not tolerate. In rejecting McConnell's claim that his seeking a marriage license was constitutionally protected behavior, the appellate court scoffed, "This is not a case involving mere homosexual propensities on the part of a prospective employee. . . . It is, instead, a case in which . . . the prospective employee demands . . . the right to pursue an activist role in implementing his unconventional ideas concerning the societal status to be accorded homosexuals and, thereby, to foist tacit approval of this societally repugnant concept upon his employer."

Looking back after a quarter century, the two couples share a similar pride in their efforts and a similar resentment toward others who should have been their allies.[12] Singer and Barwick remained bitter that the ACLU refused to help them in the marriage case. Baker remained bitter that the "so-called gay leaders" in Minnesota at the time of the case were hiding deeply in their closets. Few spoke up on his and Michael's behalf when they were denied a license. Few spoke up for Michael when he was denied his promised job as a librarian at the university.[13] Today, Jack and Michael have totally withdrawn from political activism. They guard their privacy as assiduously as they once promoted their outness.

The one other couple from this period to appeal the denial of a marriage license was very different. The couples in Minnesota and Washington had sought a marriage license to gain public attention for gay issues in general. The third couple, Tracy Knight and Margery Jones, were uninvolved in gay politics and were persuaded to file for marriage in 1970 by a lawyer who wanted public attention for himself. Knight and Jones lived in Louisville. I cannot locate them today, but their attorney, Stuart Lyon, remains a general practitioner in Louisville. According to Lyon, Knight and Jones had consulted him about a legal problem unrelated to their status as a couple.[14] According to Lyon, the two women were "Damon Runyan–type characters" who ran a "flogging operation" for straight masochists. So far as he knew, they had never been involved in gay rights issues.

Lyon, looking back with some embarrassment, says that he was on an "ego trip" at the time. He is not gay and had never previously worked on any issue regarding sexual orientation. He was simply an ambitious young lawyer wanting to bring a high-profile case. He knew that the Kentucky marriage statute directed that licenses be issued to "two adults," not just to "one man and one woman," and he had heard about the Baker case pending in Minnesota. So, as he describes it, he talked the two women into applying for a license and, when the license was rejected, persuaded them to let him take the matter to court. The trial and appellate court smirked at his claims. The appellate court, in a brief opinion, held that despite the sex-neutral terms of the Kentucky act, marriage had always been considered the union of a man and a woman and that was that.[15] In three abrupt sentences, it dismissed a hundred pages of constitutional arguments that Lyon advanced in his brief.

As Lyon recalls, the case received some but not much coverage in the local and national news. No civil liberties or gay rights organization came to his aid. After the loss in the court of appeals, he thought about taking the case to the state supreme court, but by that time, the two women had broken up. Lyon had also realized by then that an appeal would be futile.

A few others in the same era sought to marry. In Wisconsin, a lesbian couple applied for a license, but did not turn to the courts when the license was denied. A friendly city clerk in Boulder, Colorado, issued marriage licenses to at least six same-sex couples, stopping only when ordered by the state attorney general. All the couples lost in later efforts to have their marriages recognized.[16] Thus, by the mid-1970s, several same-sex couples had tried to force a state to recognize them as married but none had succeeded. The law everywhere was just what it had been before. Worse, legal precedents had been set that are still cited a quarter century later. The only positive consequences of the early efforts were the news accounts depicting gay people in a positive manner and informing many heterosexual and gay people for the first time that some gay people were demanding that their relationships be recognized.

The 1980s

Between the mid-1970s and 1987, no further gay male or lesbian couples in the United States appear to have requested a marriage license or filed a case demanding a right to one. The first gay legal organizations organized in the 1970s, and none placed gay marriage on their initial agendas. As William Eskridge has commented, the more "radical" activists within the gay communities continued to reject marriage, and many others gave same-sex marriage a low priority because other political issues seemed more pressing and because none of the litigation from the 1970s had produced even minimally promising results.[17] The early 1980s also marked the beginning of what many came to regard as an alternative strategy for the recognition of gay couples and nontraditional family relationships—the move toward domestic partnership, a movement that is discussed at greater length at the end of this chapter.

In 1986, when Nan Hunter started the ACLU's Lesbian and Gay Rights Project, no marriage cases of any sort were pending or proposed, and nothing existed resembling a "marriage strategy."[18] Indeed, *Bowers v. Hardwick* had just been decided, and its dismissive tone convinced many that little possibility existed for obtaining federal constitutional protection for gay people in any aspect of their sexual or loving relationships.[19] By the end of the decade, however, same-sex marriage had reappeared as a lively political issue among gay people. Lesbians and gay men were celebrating ceremonies of commitment in large numbers. The Metropolitan Community Church had grown throughout the 1970s and 1980s, and its ministers conducted hundreds of marriages every year. In 1987, at the second March on Washington, over one thousand lesbian and gay male couples joined in marriage at the National Cathedral with an accompanying rally at which some speakers demanded legal recognition for gay unions. Large numbers of gay people, unaware of the earlier cases or undeterred by them, were becoming insistent about state recognition of their relationships. The push for recognition was intensified by the tragic case of Sharon Kowalski, who had suffered brain damage in an automobile accident and whose biological family successfully blocked for many years the efforts of her lover, Karen Thompson, to become her caretaker. Had they been married, Thompson would have been recognized as the appropriate guardian as a matter of course.

Thus, by the late 1980s, for the first time, the issue of legal marriage asserted itself in the discussions of gay rights lawyers. The Legal Roundtable, a group of gay rights litigators, first convened by Lambda Legal Defense and Education Fund in the mid-1980s to plan strategy for challenges to sodomy laws, evolved by the end of the 1980s into a general forum for discussing litigation strategy on all gay issues. These discussions came to include debates on same-sex marriage. By all accounts, no other issue produced discussions that were as heated or acrimonious. Evan Wolfson of Lambda, who joined the organization's staff in 1989 and has devoted much of his professional career to the gay marriage issue, argued for filing gay marriage cases now in states most likely to be sympathetic. To a lesser degree, Tom Stoddard, director of Lambda, agreed with Wolfson. They both believed that the issue meant more to more gay people than almost any other. On the other side, Paula Ettelbrick, then the legal director at Lambda, believed that, although gay people should be as entitled to marry as heterosexuals, marriage was a demeaning institution for both groups and should be accorded a low priority. Views similar to Ettelbrick's were held by Nancy Polikoff and many other lesbian feminists.[20]

In 1989, Stoddard and Ettelbrick published a celebrated pair of articles in the magazine *Out/Look*.[21] Ettelbrick argued that marriage undercuts much of what lesbians and feminists have been fighting for ("I do not want to be known as 'Mrs. Attached-to-Somebody-Else'") and that seeking marriage requires arguing that gay relationships are just like straight relationships, when they are not. Stoddard, though acknowledging the stultifying inadequacies of "traditional" marriage, argued that lesbian and gay male couples need marriage's legal protections and that gay relationships will be regarded as less valuable than heterosexual relationships until lesbian and gay male couples secure the right to marry.

Taking a middle ground in the Roundtable deliberations were Nan Hunter and Matt Coles of the ACLU and some others. They disagreed with Ettelbrick's view of marriage as an irretrievably sexist institution, but agreed with her conclusion that seeking marriage should be accorded a low priority. On pragmatic grounds, they believed that, especially after *Bowers,* marriage cases were certain to lose and would simply lead to a longer string of ruinous precedents. As recently as 1988, for example, a state judge in Indiana had indicated his views of the frivolousness of the issue when denying two gay prison inmates a license to marry. He fined them $2,800 and declared that their "claims about Indiana law and constitutional rights are wacky and sanctionably so."[22] Ettelbrick, Coles, Hunter, and others also believed that pursuing domestic partnership advanced important goals for all gay people and was more promising as a strategy for securing benefits for same-sex couples.

The 1990s

By the early 1990s, the Roundtable forums, whatever their staff members' individual views, had coalesced around a position that they themselves would not bring cases seeking marriage rights and that they would actively seek to discourage others from filing such cases. The middle view that such cases were doomed to fail had carried the day. When an attorney in Hawaii hoping to file a marriage case requested support from the National ACLU Lesbian and Gay Rights Project and from Lambda, both groups declined. Over the next few years, the same groups also declined to represent gay male couples who wished to marry in New York, the District of Columbia, and Alaska.

But the couples in Hawaii, New York, the District of Columbia, and Alaska applied for marriage licenses anyway and, when licenses were refused, found other attorneys willing to represent them in court. Years later, the couples in New York, the District of Columbia, and Alaska, remained extremely resentful that the national groups declined to help them. So did some of those in Hawaii who first encouraged a suit. The Hawaii case, filed in 1990 and known initially as *Baehr v. Levin,* led to a decision by the Hawaii Supreme Court that, though preliminary in its holding, reshaped the gay marriage debate in the United States. It made heterosexual people aware of the issue for the first time. It kindled hope and unrealistic expectations in thousands of gay couples. It produced political responses in almost every state of the country. And it forced the Roundtable, caught by surprise, to develop an entirely new set of strategies. A few years later, in the last weeks of the century, the Vermont Supreme Court issued a decision that reached even further. The rest of the marriage section of this chapter deals with the Hawaii and Vermont cases and the reactions to them.

The Baehr of *Baehr v. Levin* is Ninia Baehr.[23] When in her early thirties, Ninia fell in love with Genora Dancel, Genora asked Ninia to marry her. Ninia agreed. They were then taken aback when their life insurance companies refused to permit them to name each other as beneficiaries. They consulted with Bill Woods, a lawyer and gay organizer in Hawaii. Woods had long advocated litigation to secure same-sex marriage in the state. He gave them advice about the insurance and asked them if they would like to challenge the Hawaii marriage law. Although they were not activists at that point, they nonetheless said yes. Eventually two other couples joined with them. Woods claims credit today as the "Creator of the Hawaii Gay Marriage Lawsuit."[24] It was he who was rebuffed by the ACLU and Lambda when he initially sought their assistance.

Baehr and Dancel and the two other couples, Tammy Rodrigues and Antoinette Pregil, and Pat Lagon and Joseph Melilio, applied for licenses at the Hawaii Department of Health in December 1990. Woods had invited the media, who appeared in substantial numbers. The staff of the Department of

Health said that they would have to consult with the attorney general. Woods then invited the press to follow him and the three couples from the Department of Health to the ACLU-Hawaii office. Woods, still furious at the national ACLU's refusal to represent the couples, staged there a public and embarrassing request for the ACLU to represent the six license seekers. At a later point, the ACLU-Hawaii again said no. Dan Foley, a heterosexual private practitioner who had been the previous director of the ACLU-Hawaii, agreed to represent the six license seekers. He has been their principal attorney ever since. In April 1991, when the state formally denied the couples' request, Foley promptly filed a suit on their behalf in court.

The early stages of the litigation resembled the cases previously filed in other states. The trial court dismissed each of the constitutional claims, and the plaintiffs appealed to the state Supreme Court. In his brief, Foley stressed the right to marry and discrimination based on sexual orientation and barely mentioned a claim based on discrimination on the basis of sex. At this point, most lawyers who knew anything about the case believed that, as in all the earlier cases, the state's appellate court would affirm. But, to almost everyone's amazement, the court did not.

In May 1993, the Supreme Court reversed the trial court. Justice Stephen Levinson, writing for a plurality of two judges, began inauspiciously by rejecting the plaintiff's claim that gay people have a constitutionally protected interest in marrying someone of their sex, but then went on to hold that the Hawaii statute presumptively denied the plaintiffs the equal protection of the laws under the Hawaii constitution because it discriminates on the basis of sex.[25] The Hawaii constitution includes a specific provision prohibiting discrimination based on sex, and to the surprise of many, Justice Levinson accepted the reasoning based on the anti-miscegenation cases that had been rejected in the same-sex marriage cases from the seventies: he held that since the Hawaii statute permitted men to marry women but prohibited women from marrying women, the statute constituted unconstitutional discrimination based on sex, unless the state could demonstrate a compelling reason for limiting marriage to persons of the opposite sex. The court remanded the case to the trial court for a hearing at which the state would be permitted to demonstrate a compelling interest. Gay groups in Hawaii and on the mainland were ecstatic about the case's holding. For the first time in American history, a court had suggested that same-sex couples were as entitled to marry as everyone else.

Within Hawaii, the political reverberations from the decision began immediately. Just as gay organizations were much more organized by the 1990s than they had been when the first marriage cases were brought in the 1970s, so too, of course, conservative political and legal organizations were much more organized than they had been twenty years before. These conservative groups had discovered that speaking out against gay rights issues was an effective organizing tool. Between 1993 and 1997, every session of the Hawaii legislature produced new responses to the prospect of gay marriage. Hawaii newspapers ran hundreds of articles. For years, Honolulu's largest paper printed articles or letters almost every week. Television news covered every aspect of the story.

The Hawaii legislature reacted quickly after the Supreme Court decision. Within months, the legislature passed a statute that restated with clarity that marriage was the union of one man and one woman. An accompanying report castigated the justices for usurping the legislature's prerogative to determine important matters of family policy. In the same statute, the legislature established the Commission on Sexual Orientation and the Law to make recommendations regarding the rights and benefits that same-sex couples should have. The statute directed that the commission, when appointed, include, among others, members representing the Mormon and the Roman Catholic Churches. The next year, after the provision regarding church representation was held unconstitutional by the state courts, the legislature created another, smaller commission with much the same mission. The commission issued a report in December 1995 that, contrary to the expectations of the legislature, recommended, by a split vote, that the legislature legalize same-sex marriage or, in the alternative, adopt a domestic partnership law that accords same-sex couples most of the rights of married couples.

Not until the fall of 1996, more than three years after the Hawaii Supreme Court's decision, did the trial court hold the hearing on remand in *Baehr* at which the state was given the opportunity to demonstrate a compelling interest in limiting marriage to opposite-sex couples. The delay of three years before the trial court rehearing flowed largely from requests for extensions of time from the state's attorney general, who was hoping for a political resolution of the controversy. At the hearing, the state made many arguments for limiting marriage to persons of the opposite sex but seriously advanced only one of them: that if gay people were permitted to marry, it would lead to their greater participation in child rearing, and the state has strong reasons for preferring that children be raised by couples composed of one adult of each sex. Each side put on several expert witnesses, but even the witnesses of the state acknowledged that most gay men and lesbians raising children performed in a fully satisfactory manner.

In December 1996, the trial judge, Judge Chang, ruled that the state had failed to demonstrate the necessity of limiting marriage to opposite-sex couples in order to assure that children were satisfactorily nurtured.[26] The decision paints an overwhelmingly positive, albeit traditional, picture of lesbians and gay men as parents and as partners. Judge Chang found that "children of gay and lesbian parents and same-sex couples tend to adjust and develop in a normal fashion" and that "in Hawaii, and elsewhere, same sex couples can, and do, have successful, loving, and committed relationships." Opponents of gay marriage on the right criticized the state for failing to rely, except in passing, on other arguments the right considered stronger, such as that permitting gay marriage would contribute to the destabilization of traditional heterosexual marriage and the collapse of traditional families.

Responding in 1997 to the trial court's decision on remand, the legislature approved a constitutional amendment to be submitted to the voters at the elections in November 1998 that would give the legislature the power to limit marriage to persons of the opposite sex. In the same session, it also enacted a law called the Reciprocal Beneficiaries Act. This act provides to partners in same-sex couples who register several of the rights of married couples, such as intestate succession for a surviving partner, joint tenancy, and some employer-provided health benefits.[27] The act was the first law adopted by a state legislature permitting same-sex couples to register and obtain benefits accorded to married couples.

The waves caused by the Hawaii decision soon traveled from the islands to the mainland. By late 1993, marriage had replaced the military ban as the gay political issue most in the national news. Among national groups, Lambda played the central role. Almost immediately after the Hawaii Supreme Court decision, Lambda changed course and agreed to provide its fullest support to the plaintiffs in the remaining stages of the *Baehr* litigation. Evan Wolfson of the Lambda staff, who had provided informal advice to the plaintiffs' lawyer, Dan Foley, up to this point, joined Foley as cocounsel and worked with him at every later stage. In addition, Wolfson and Lambda took the lead in forming the National Freedom to Marry Coalition, which included virtually all national gay organizations and still meets regularly to discuss strategy.

A first impact of *Baehr* on the rest of the country was to inspire couples in other states to consider bringing litigation in their own courts. At first, the Roundtable and the Coalition tried to discourage such cases, urging that couples wait for a final resolution in Hawaii before deciding whether to litigate. Matthew Coles of the ACLU and Evan Wolfson each recall persuading local groups to postpone filing cases. One group, for example, was from North Carolina, where no hope existed whatever for a positive judicial decision. The Roundtable lawyers were, however, unable to discourage couples in Alaska and New York. The couples there found lawyers who were willing to bring cases without the blessing or participation of national organizations. After this new pair of cases had been filed, the Roundtable group concluded that it should shift its stand and take a proactive role in encouraging and working with local lawyers to bring a case or two in states that might conceivably have receptive courts. Out of these consultations came the Vermont litigation discussed below.

These few efforts at positive litigation to capitalize on *Baehr* have been dwarfed by the efforts required to respond to the legislative attacks on *Baehr* in almost every state. Both the Marriage Coalition and the far right realized that if *Baehr* was affirmed in the second appeal, an issue that would immediately arise would be the recognition by other states of a same-sex marriage conducted in Hawaii. Lambda conscripted lawyers in almost every state to research whether a same-sex marriage conducted in Hawaii would be recognized as valid in their state. It wanted to be ready to defend couples married in Hawaii who returned to (or moved to) other states. It also wanted to be ready to take the initiative to bring cases in states where the courts were especially likely to be supportive.

Right-wing groups, on the other hand, devised strategies that could be implemented before a final judicial resolution of *Baehr*. They provided conservative legislators in every state with draft legislation that would direct their state's courts and other agencies to refuse to recognize a marriage between two persons of the same sex conducted in another state. Promoting this legislation proved to be an extremely successful move by conservative groups, for the legislation not only served as a rallying point for conservatives, but also divided liberal legislators from their gay constituents. Many Democratic state legislators across the country either themselves believed that marriage should be limited to one man and one woman, or at least believed that they could not vote against the far right's bill because of the views of most of their heterosexual constituents. So, just as the far right had hoped, many otherwise liberal legislators voted for the bills and infuriated gay and lesbian voters. Gay groups, local and national, were forced to devote huge amounts of effort in nearly every state to persuade legislators to reject the bills. In some states, they succeeded in keeping bills bottled up in committee, but by late-1999, thirty states had adopted nonrecognition legislation that may be impossible to overturn in the courts and difficult to repeal in the legislatures, and bills or referenda were pending in eight others, including California and New York.[28]

Conservative members of Congress introduced comparable federal legislation with much the same effect. The Defense of Marriage Act (DOMA) was proposed by Republicans and adopted by Congress in the summer of 1996, in the midst of congressional and presidential campaigning.[29] Since, under our Constitution, it is the states, not the federal government, that define who is eligible to marry, Congress did not try to impose a uniform national law limiting marriage to those of opposite sexes. But, in its only two substantive sections, DOMA seeks to limit the effects of any state's judicial decision or legislation that defines marriage in any other way. The first section asserts Congress's authority to enforce the Full Faith and Credit Clause of the Constitution and declares that states need not recognize the marriage of two people of the same sex even if validly contracted in another state. Many legal scholars believe that this section is unconstitutional.[30] The second section, one that may well prove more harmful in the long term, provides that all federal legislation and regulations that mention married persons or spouses shall be read as applying only to persons in opposite-sex marriages. Again, usually liberal-voting legislators supported the bill and angered their gay constituents. President Clinton announced early in the deliberations that he himself believed that marriage should be limited to opposite-sex unions and that he would sign the bill, making it that much easier for Democratic members of Congress to support the bill and further alienating himself from gay supporters.

In ugly hearings leading up to the enactment, members of Congress and witnesses forecast that if men could marry men, they would soon be permitted to marry children and other animals. Several witnesses and senators feared the collapse of Western civilization. Senator Jesse Helms believed that the same-sex marriage movement threatened "the moral and spiritual survival of this nation."[31] Representative Steve Largent warned that "the crosshairs of the homosexual agenda" were aimed at the institution of marriage.[32] National gay political organizations resisted, but not very much. They regarded themselves in a bind. The Human Rights Campaign, for example, spoke out against the bill and devoted some staff support to defeating it, but refused to work against the re-election of the president or of those members of Congress who, though voting for DOMA, supported other legislation HRC wanted (notably ENDA, the employment non-discrimination bill). In the end, DOMA passed by wide margins in each chamber. The president signed the bill but sought to soothe his gay and liberal supporters by omitting the usual Rose Garden signing ceremony. A few weeks later, in one of the televised presidential campaign debates, Clinton's opponent, Robert Dole, tried to demonstrate that he was even more opposed to gay marriage than Clinton by ridiculing Clinton for signing the bill so secretively.[33]

Our nation is a federal republic. Usually states recognize without quibble the laws of other states. In all of American history there have been few occasions when states (or the Congress) have reacted with as much hostility to the decisions or laws of another state as occurred in response to *Baehr*. In the years before the Civil War, somewhat similar hostility was directed at the decisions of judges in New England who refused to return fugitive slaves to their Southern owners. And in the middle of this century, many states sought ways to refuse to recognize divorces granted under Nevada's lax laws. That same-sex marriage has stirred so much resistance demonstrates how widespread within America is the attachment to a narrow vision of marriage and how widespread is the reluctance to accept gay people within the social mainstream. The scale of the expressed resistance is also a testament to the religious right's political acumen.

In November 1998, Hawaii's voters by a 70–30 landslide vote overwhelmingly adopted the constitutional amendment proposed by the legislature. The amendment permits the legislature to fix the definition of marriage as limited to opposite-sex couples. A year later, the Hawaii Supreme Court dismissed the *Baehr* case on the ground that the existing legislation limited marriage to one man and one woman.

THE VERMONT CASE: *BAKER V. STATE*

When the *Baehr* odyssey came to an end in Hawaii, all but one of the marriage cases that had been pending in other states had been resolved unhappily. The District of Columbia plaintiffs, whom William Eskridge served as lead counsel, lost in both the trial and appellate courts, though they did secure a gratifying dissent in the court of appeals. The New York case was dismissed. The Alaska case produced a fine victory in the trial court, with a holding that the statute limiting marriage to one person of each sex violates gay persons' fundamental right to marry, but Alaska's legislature responded by proposing a constitutional amendment to limit marriage to one man and one woman and Alaska's voters adopted the amendment in 1998 by about the same margin as the voters in Hawaii. Only in Vermont did litigation lead to at least a partial victory. The Vermont case, *Baker v. State,* is nonetheless a landmark decision, the first by a state appellate court squarely holding a marriage statute unconstitutional.[34]

In the Vermont litigation, unlike the marriage litigation in other states, national legal organizations and local attorneys collaborated from the outset. Susan Murray and Beth Robinson, law partners in a firm in Middlebury, Vermont, worked with Mary Bonauto of Gay and Lesbian Advocates and Defenders in Boston. They found three Vermont couples, Peter Harrigan and Stan Baker, Holly Puterbaugh and Lois Farnham, and Stacy Jolles and Nina Beck, who were eager to marry. In 1996, the three couples applied for a marriage license in the usual manner, and when it was denied in the usual way, Bonauto, Murray, and Robinson filed a lawsuit on their behalf.

The plaintiffs claimed that the Vermont marriage statute violated the Vermont state constitution and, to prevent eventual review by the United States Supreme Court, made no allegations under the U.S. Constitution. They relied on a two-hundred-year-old Vermont provision that declares that "government is, or ought to be, instituted for the common benefit, protection and security of the people, nation, or community, and not for the particular emolument of any single man, family or set of persons who are a part only of the community." This clause was originally intended to prohibit the giving of privileges to a landed aristocracy, but had been interpreted by the Vermont Supreme Court as a general protection against unjust discriminations of all sorts in much the same manner that the U.S. Supreme Court has interpreted the Equal Protection clause.

The state of Vermont found itself in an awkward position in defending the marriage statute. The Attorney General, a liberal, was unwilling to argue that same-sex couples should be excluded from marriage simply because Vermonters considered their relationships immoral, but had difficulty coming up with other plausible explanations for the law. The state came up with seven possible justifications. In its ruling in December 1997, the trial court rejected six of them, but held that the statute was justified on the ground that sanctioning same-sex marriage would diminish the perception of the link between marriage and procreation and thus reduce men's and women's sense of responsibility for childrearing.

The plaintiffs appealed to the Vermont Supreme Court. In November 1998, Beth Robinson argued the case for the plaintiffs to a sympathetic court. She began by drawing an analogy to a case from the 1950s in which the California Supreme Court became the first appellate court to strike down a statutory ban on interracial marriage. She said that, in the California case, the state had made the same sorts of unfounded claims about harms to children and families that Vermont was making here, and she bravely acknowledged that a positive decision by the Vermont justices would require much the same courage that had been shown by the California justices a half century before, at a time when interracial marriage was regarded by the public even more hostilely than same-sex marriage is regarded today. The justices seemed to hear her message. When counsel for the state began her presentation by claiming that the California case was quite different (because some states had never prohibited interracial marriages while all states prohibit marriage between persons of the same sex), one of the justices interrupted her and asked rhetorically, as to same-sex marriage, "Some state court has to go first, doesn't it?" And, as the state's lawyer groped for a response, another justice asked her whether the uniformity among the states regarding same-sex marriage might not simply demonstrate the depth of the hostile feelings toward gay people in our country. It was not a good day for the state's attorney.

Thirteen months later, in December 1999, the Vermont Supreme Court issued its decision, unanimously holding unconstitutional the state's exclusion of same-sex couples from marriage. The majority opinion, written by Chief Justice Jeffrey Amestoy, rejected all the justifications offered by the state. It found no empirical support or logical plausibility for the claim that only by limiting marriage to one man and one woman could the state sustain in the public mind the link between procreation and parental responsibility. It supported its conclusions for equal treatment by pointing out that the state legislature itself had recently prohibited employment discrimination on the basis of sexual orientation and had permitted adoption by same-sex couples. In a stirring conclusion, the court declared that "The extension of the Common Benefits Clause to acknowledge plaintiffs as Vermonters who seek nothing more, nothing less, than legal protection and security for their avowed commitment to an intimate and lasting human relationship is simply, when all is said and done, a recognition of our common humanity."

Despite this embracing statement, the court did not then enter an order directing the state to issue marriage licenses to same-sex couples. Instead, in a most unusual disposition, the court held that the state must extend all the legal benefits and responsibilities of married persons to same-sex couples, but that it could do so either by permitting gay people to "marry" or by creating a parallel institution known as domestic partnership or something else. It remitted the case to the legislature, telling the plaintiffs that if the legislature did not provide full benefits within "a reasonable period of time," the court would order specific relief. One justice, Denise Johnson, dissented as to the remedy, asserting that the Court should have provided the relief that the plaintiffs had demanded.

The Vermont legislature reconvened in early January 2000 and immediately began considering how to respond. The House and Senate Judiciary Committees held joint public hearings in the House chamber attended by thousands of people. More than two hundred Vermont citizens, chosen by lot, spoke for and against marriage for two minutes each. Gay people told stories of their own lives. The children of gay couples spoke. So did many others who simply prized Vermonters' tolerance of diversity. Conservatives also testified in large numbers, quoting Leviticus, railing against "Adam and Steve," forecasting the collapse of the American family, and threatening revenge in November.

To the legislators' chagrin, almost no one had anything kind to say about domestic partnership. One side sought marriage; the other urged the legislature to ignore the court and to begin the process of amending the state constitution. Conservative legislators strongly resisted creating an expansive form of domestic partnership, saying it would really be marriage in thin disguise. "If it looks like a duck and walks like a duck and quacks like a duck, it is a duck and we should reject it," fumed one Republican legislator from northern Vermont. Of course, the gay organizations would have been glad to call the duck a duck, but came to understand that their supporters in the legislature simply couldn't put together enough votes to do so.

In the end, after receiving signals from gay organizations that they would prefer marriage by another name to nothing at all, the House committee created an entity called "civil unions" available solely to same-sex couples and poured into it every benefit and responsibility attaching to marriage. As with the marriage statute, the civil union bill required not only that the couple register with the state but also that they enter into the relationship in the presence of a minister or a justice of the peace. The bill carried each chamber by a narrow margin and was signed into law by Governor Howard Dean on Thursday,

April 27, 2000. The law went into effect on July 1, 2000, and along with many other couples across the state, Lois Farnham and Holly Puterbaugh, joined together that day in a civil union.

THE DOMESTIC PARTNERSHIP MOVEMENT

As early as the 1970s, some gay people began searching for mechanisms other than marriage to secure legal recognition of their relationships. Some gay men, for example, went to court and adopted their partners, since adoption seemed to be the only available mechanism other than marriage by which one person could form a legally recognized familial relationship with another person to whom he is not biologically related. Even though such adoptions have often been approved by family courts over the years (perhaps because they have been uncontested),[35] few gay men and even fewer lesbians have adopted their partners. The symbolism is unappealing to most people—parent and child, not a relationship of partners. In addition, the adoption of one adult by another, even if it is recognized as valid by the state and federal government, secures for the couple only some of the legal benefits that marriage offers.

Much more appealing have been various forms of recognizing the couple relationship through devices commonly referred to as domestic partnership. Broadly speaking, domestic partnership efforts take either or both of two forms. The first form involves a public registration system for same-sex and sometimes unmarried opposite-sex couples. At its purest, the registration carries no benefits. Instead, it simply provides public recognition of the worthiness of the same-sex or unmarried-couple relationships. In 1982, in the first attempt at such a scheme, the Board of Supervisors of San Francisco voted to permit unmarried couples to register if they affirmed that they were each other's "principal domestic partner" and that they shared "the common necessities of life." The mayor of San Francisco at the time, Dianne Feinstein, vetoed the bill, expressing fears about the impact of domestic partnership on the institution of marriage, but the bill nonetheless provided a model for ordinances that San Francisco itself and many other American cities have since adopted. West Hollywood, California, was the first, in 1983.

The second form of domestic partner recognition focuses on a particular benefit available to married persons or couples and seeks to secure the same benefits for same-sex couples. In 1982, the *Village Voice* in New York City became the first employer to provide health and other benefits to the unmarried partners of its employees on the same terms that they provided them to spouses. In 1985, the cities of Berkeley and West Hollywood became the first public employers to offer such partner benefits.

Piecemeal efforts to secure legal benefits for domestic partners have also taken other forms. In a celebrated case, the New York Court of Appeals held that a regulation that permitted members of a tenant's "family" to remain in a rent-controlled apartment after the death of the tenant should be interpreted to include a tenant's long-term same-sex partner.[36] Similarly, in several states, lesbians have been permitted to become the legal coparent of their partner's biological child, despite statutory language that seems to limit such adoptions to persons legally married to the biological parent.[37] From one view, Vermont's civil union bill is simply an example of domestic partnership legislation that has been fully loaded with all the consequences of marriage.

The varied efforts for recognizing domestic partnership do not reflect a unified ideology. Linking all the efforts is the common goal of securing recognition of the legitimacy and social worthiness of gay relationships. But some proponents have seen the effort to obtain domestic partner benefits or registration as simply a first step toward obtaining legal marriage. For them, marriage remains the one great prize, with domestic partnership viewed as the best that is attainable at the moment. For others, however, domestic partnership has been an end in itself, an effort to secure recognition of an alternative form of union for both opposite- and same-sex couples, or more broadly, one part of an effort to secure the recognition of a wide variety of nontraditional family forms. Tom Coleman of Los Angeles has probably been the most outspoken single advocate in this latter movement. Coleman has also been a supporter of gay marriage, so long as it is combined with the recognition of other relationships. Still others, such as Nancy Polikoff, favor domestic partnership and a broad recognition of other nontraditional family relationships as alternatives to marriage and disagree with Coleman. They distrust marriage and favor significantly reducing the special status attached to marriage in our society. Instead, they wish the state to recognize the relationships that citizens view as significant to themselves, relationships that might include more than two intimately involved persons and relationships that have no sexual component.

Because of the different goals and the different attitudes toward marriage, the relationships among those working on domestic partnership issues have often been uneasy and distrustful. Most would be pleased if states recognized both marriage and domestic partnership. Those, such as Evan Wolfson, who place a high premium on attaining the right to legal marriage fear that governments will eventually accept domestic partnership and stop there, abandoning gay people forever to a second-class form of citizenship. Those, such as Paula Ettelbrick and Nancy Polikoff, who distrust marriage and seek the recognition of other forms of relationships fear that the marriage movement will succeed and that, if it does, legislators and courts will refuse to continue to expand alternative ways of recognizing familial relationships. Each side finds dangers in the other's priorities.

Thus, even within single campaigns the two groups can end up in tension. For example, a common issue in employers' decisions about offering partner benefits is whether to limit the benefits to employees with a same-sex partner or to extend the benefit as well to unmarried employees with an opposite-sex partner. For the employer, the issue is often solely one of costs, but proponents are sometimes divided by ideology. Those whose primary allegiance is to securing marriage for same-sex couples are willing to have domestic partnership benefits limited to same-sex couples, content with the reasoning that only gay people deserve the benefits because only they are unable to marry. Those seeking a wider definition of family want benefits for both unmarried same-sex and unmarried opposite-sex couples (and for other nonmarital family bonds) as a way of affirming an alternative to marriage and advancing an expanded view of family.

Whatever the tensions among the goals of the advocates, the spread of domestic partner registration and benefits has produced immediate and tangible benefits for tens of thousands of gay men and lesbians over the past decade. In the late 1980s and 1990s, at least one municipality or county in over half the states adopted some form of domestic partner registration, and some provided benefits to their employees' partners. Registration and benefits for public employees have been adopted in academic communities such as Ithaca, Cambridge, and Ann Arbor, and large cities including New York, Chicago, Los Angeles, and Seattle. Benefits have also been provided by large counties such as Alameda County, California, and Wayne County, Michigan. San Francisco, which initially rejected registration, adopted both registration and partner benefits in the early 1990s and has now gone further than any other city by requiring that employers who contract with the city also provide partner benefits to their employees.[38]

As we've seen above, Hawaii, in 1997, became the first *state* to adopt partner registration, calling the couple not *domestic partners* but the even more bloodless name *reciprocal beneficiaries* and permitting persons in a wide range of relationships to register. Hawaii's extension of some of the benefits of marriage to same-sex couples is a more significant step than it might at first appear, since most legal benefits and responsibilities of marriage are fixed by state law, not by city or county ordinances. As of mid-1999, four states provide some form of partner benefits.[39]

California's legislature adopted somewhat similar legislation in 1996, but it was vetoed by the governor, Pete Wilson. The efforts for the California legislation offered an opportunity for gay people to work together with others with analogous goals. The California legislation was the result of joint efforts by gay groups and groups representing senior citizens. The seniors groups were interested in protecting older people with a close tie to someone to whom they were not married. By contrast, in the efforts for same-sex marriage, no other groups excluded today from legally marrying offer a potential ally for gay people. No lobby exists for adolescents who want to marry, for siblings who want to marry, or for polygamists.

The actions of cities and counties in providing benefits to employees spread to public and private universities and private businesses in the mid-1990s. The universities that adopted partner benefits included many of the elite private universities and colleges in the country, as well as large public institutions such as the Universities of California, Washington, Iowa, Minnesota, Michigan, and New Mexico. The movement among large commercial employers has been equally swift and extensive. A 1997 survey reported that about a quarter of American companies with over five thousand employees offer partner benefits.[40] Among corporations and to a lesser extent among universities, the decisions of administrators to provide benefits seem largely to have been driven by traditional market forces—by the desire to attract and hold on to the most able employees and, to a lesser extent, to appear progressive to their customers. Thus, partner benefits are particularly widespread in the media, entertainment, technology, and computers industries where large numbers of out gay employees work within a relatively liberal political environment. Partner benefits have, however, also been adopted by several of the largest oil companies in the United States, showing the power of market forces in an industry not noted for its progressive views.

Some companies that have provided benefits have had to respond to market forces of a different sort. In 1996, the Southern Baptist Convention urged its 16 million members to boycott the theme parks, movies, and television productions of the Walt Disney Corporation. The Convention had threatened a boycott previously, but voted to implement one only after Disney adopted benefits for same-sex partners.[41] The boycott seems to have had little impact on Disney's revenues, and boycotts of other companies become less and less plausible as partner benefits become common in mainstream corporations.

The success of efforts to obtain domestic partner benefits is, nonetheless, a little less grand than it appears. As an initial matter, federal tax laws require unmarried employees to report as taxable income the value of health coverage provided to their partners but permit married employees to exclude it. Secondly, even at corporations that have adopted benefits, most report that few employees register. The reason appears to be in part that even when working for progressive companies, many gay employees are still afraid to be known as gay.

HISTORY LESSONS

What can be learned from the movement to secure legal recognition of gay relationships?

In some ways, everything turns on the ultimate outcome. If other states follow Vermont's lead and if, over time, Vermont and some other states permit marriage itself, many will look back and think that all the losing cases and DOMA and the repellent state legislation were worth enduring. They will indeed regard them as skirmishes that had to be lost in building support for a campaign that would inevitably be won. On the other hand, if Vermont stands alone, or worse, if Vermont eventually adopts a regressive constitutional amendment repealing the civil union legislation, those who have cautioned against filing litigation will seem vindicated.

Still, whatever the outcome, a few lessons can be drawn now.

First, the marriage movement has also revealed just how difficult it is to maintain a national strategy on an issue of local policy. Over and over again, a couple somewhere has decided to seek a marriage license and turned to a national gay or civil liberties organization for representation. The national organization, on reasonable grounds, has advised against filing and declined to help. The couple goes ahead—and even though they lose the case just as the national group warned, they and their local allies grumble for years afterward about the arrogant national group that refused to help. It is hard to know what advice to draw from this experience for future marriage cases. After all, on some occasions, local couples or groups have *accepted* the advice not to file, thereby almost certainly avoiding a harmful appellate decision. The national groups could try a middle course—beseeching couples in inauspicious states not to file but telling them from the outset that if they reject the advice and do seek a license, the national group will represent them. The paradoxical effect of this course would probably be that some couples who would have decided not to file if the national group had declined to help will choose to file because the help is (reluctantly) promised. The short of it is that—much as with a parent whose child decides to marry someone whom the parent strongly dislikes—any course the national group takes is likely to feel unsatisfactory.

Second, the marriage efforts, like the efforts to end the military ban, have revealed just how vigorously conservative Americans will resist the efforts of gay people to join the institutions that they hold most dear. We have stepped on the sacred turf of the American right—at home and at war. By the same token, the persistent efforts of gay men and lesbians to enter these essentially conservative institutions demonstrate the depth of our yearning for social acceptance. The marriage efforts are especially touching in this respect. Tens of thousands of gay people have joined together in ceremonies of their own devising, but most still crave to marry with the blessing of the state—less, it seems, for the legal benefits that might flow from it than for the symbolism of formal equality. The tenacity of the conservatives' resistance is the measure of our need.

The final lesson is about the power of the word. For some years, Governor Howard Dean of Vermont has been giving talks to public schools around his state urging tolerance and acceptance of gay people. Yet, on the day after the Vermont Supreme Court's decision, he stated publicly that "like anyone else," he was troubled by the idea of "gay marriage." He would support domestic partnership (and he did, with vigor) but not marriage. His statement was not unusual but is more than a little odd. Why is it that some persons who are completely comfortable with extending to gay couples all the legal rights and benefits of marriage are "troubled" about calling it marriage? All of the substance but not the ultimate affirmation. The starting point for an answer is to recognize that "marriage" is an enchanted term that each society reserves for its most highly valued sexual relationship. All the *legal* rights and benefits of marriage, taken together, are, in honesty, a fairly pallid package. What counts most is the name. Still, even if we recognize that that is so, why is it that some liberals and many moderates who accept our entitlement to legal equality remain reluctant to share with us the magical title? In what way do they find gay people's relationships, though tolerable, not fully equal to their own? I myself suspect that it has something to do with the ways that we gay folks have sex or with the challenge we pose to traditional gender roles, but who knows? In any event, the last hurdle toward full recognition will fall only when many more straight people push beyond toleration, beyond acceptance. They will have to come to see us as themselves. I'm not sure that we should want such an embrace, but that is what it will take.

CHAPTER 15

RAISING CHILDREN: LESBIAN AND GAY PARENTS FACE THE PUBLIC AND THE COURTS

NANCY D. POLIKOFF

IN 1972 I MET AN OPENLY LESBIAN MOTHER FOR THE first time. She was in the feminist consciousness-raising group that evolved out of a women-in-literature course I took in my senior year of college. Like most women in her situation, she was embroiled in a battle with her former husband over the custody of her children, a battle she subsequently lost. Thus began my now almost thirty-year interest in the legal problems facing gay and lesbian parents. Over these years, some of the issues have remained remarkably constant; women and men who entered marriages when they thought—or hoped—they were heterosexual still find their custody and visitation rights challenged when they come out. Other issues have emerged from the phenomenon of planned lesbian and gay families, issues I could scarcely have imagined in the early seventies, such as access to reproduction through assisted conception, joint adoption of children by gay and lesbian couples, and protecting a nonbiological lesbian mother's relationship with her child after her relationship with the child's biological mother ends.

Lesbians and gay men asserting their fitness to bear, adopt, and raise children have engendered myriad responses from the public, policy makers, and the courts. Their responses are often linked to their reactions to all contact between lesbians or gay men and children. Thus the fate of lesbian and gay parenting is connected to the fate of lesbian and gay teachers, Scout leaders, and school board members among others.

The development of policy and law affecting the lives of gay and lesbian parents has been shaped by the distinct place of family law within the U.S. federal system. Embedded in the Constitution is the principle that some aspects of life are governed by state law, determined in each state and not subject to federal uniformity. Family law is one such area. Although Congress passes much legislation that affects families, it cannot determine the standards that courts apply to family disputes, including those involving child custody and visitation. Thus, campaigns to recognize the ability of lesbians and gay men to provide happy and healthy homes for children have been fought primarily on the state level, one state at a time. Determinations are made by state legislatures or, more commonly in the custody and visitation arena, by state appeals courts. With the smallest of exceptions, child custody decisions from a state's highest court cannot be appealed to the U.S. Supreme Court, making each state's highest court the final word for parents and prospective parents in that state.

Given the tenor of the Congress and the makeup of the Supreme Court over the last quarter century, this state control has almost certainly been for the best. At no point in the history of the gay and lesbian rights movement would it have been possible to get a positive vote on gay and lesbian parenting from a majority of the U.S. Congress. That we have been spared the possibility of a negative vote has made it possible to develop good law in some states, thereby increasing the visibility and acceptance of lesbian and gay parents.

The most dramatic consequence of this aspect of the struggle on behalf of gay and lesbian parents is the lack of uniformity among states. Crossing the border from Virginia to the District of Columbia, or from Missouri to Illinois, for example, can mean the difference between losing and retaining custody or being able to adopt as a gay or lesbian couple.[1] Dramatic affirmations of lesbian and gay parenting are irrelevant beyond the borders of the state where they are pronounced; conversely, vitriolic rejection of lesbian and gay child-rearing in one state has no bearing in any other state.

One other fact about lesbian and gay parenting makes any review of the last thirty years imperfect: the stories and rulings in cases reported in law books or even in popular media tell just a small piece of the picture of the lives of lesbian and gay parents. No one can produce an accurate number of gay men and lesbians who are parents, or who are parents who have been involved in legal disputes. Advocates and scholars have been estimating the number of gay and lesbian parents for twenty-five years, but no methodology exists to lend credence to these estimates, and they vary by more than 10 million.

Court dockets are not accurate sources of data. Adoption records are sealed. Divorce disputes are not cataloged according to whether custody or visitation was disputed. Reviewing court files for data is a laborious process that often reveals few facts underlying the parties' disagreements. In the absence of an appeal, no transcript of a court hearing is produced. Furthermore, only a tiny percentage of custody and visitation disputes are actually tried; the overwhelming majority are settled by the parents and their lawyers without a court hearing. Many lesbians have never faced custody problems because their former husbands did not want to raise their children and no other family member challenged them. Others have had supportive former spouses who saw no conflict between homosexuality and good parenting. In anecdotal reports, some lesbian mothers have kept custody by forgoing all child support, and some have obtained generous and unrestricted visitation rather than fight for custody and risk less time and more constraints on their contacts with their children. Many lesbians and gay men have given up almost everything without going to court because they had neither the money nor the stomach to fight. All these decisions to settle have taken place in the shadow of the formal and informal laws of the particular state—the formal laws being statutes and cases reported in official legal publications, and the informal laws being the knowledge of the predilections of specific judges.

As much as decisions vary from state to state, they also vary from county to county and from judge to judge. Family court judges have enormous discretion to make custody and visitation determinations, and they are usually affirmed on appeal. There is no way to know the number of custody and visitation disputes that have been resolved by trial judges both in favor of and against gay and lesbian parents and have never been appealed. In states where the case law is generally good for gay and lesbian parents, a judge opposed to gay and lesbian parenting often has plenty of room to decide against the gay and lesbian parent. Likewise, in states where case law is bad for gay and lesbian parents, a sympathetic judge can often mitigate the effects of what looks like negative precedent. Thus the life of an individual gay or lesbian parent is determined primarily by factors that defy overarching generalizations, including such elements as the lawyer he or she retains or the judge assigned to the case.

THE BEGINNINGS

Lesbian and gay parenting did not appear on the original agenda of either women's or gay liberation. At the end of the 1960s and the beginning of the 1970s, as both movements spawned public-policy and law-reform strategies, the women's movement concentrated on equality in the workplace and under the Constitution, and the gay movement concentrated on the issues that primarily touched the lives of its gay male leaders—decriminalization of sodomy, security clearances for government workers, and civil rights protections. When lesbians pushed for inclusion in both movements, however, they enunciated as their most important issue the ability of lesbian mothers to retain custody of their children upon divorce. Phyllis Lyon and Del Martin's groundbreaking 1972 book, *Lesbian/Woman*, contained a chapter on lesbian mothers.[2] The next year, the two women authored an article on lesbian mothers in the year-old feminist publication *Ms.*[3] Articles in 1973 in *The New York Times* and *Newsweek* discussed lesbian mothers, although these were isolated instances of media coverage.[4]

The Lesbian Mothers National Defense Fund (LMNDF), the first grassroots organization to address exclusively the legal issues facing lesbian mothers, was formed in Seattle in 1974 as an outgrowth of a high-profile custody dispute involving a local lesbian couple. The all-volunteer group became a national clearinghouse for legal decisions and legal and psychological articles; it published a newsletter, maintained a referral service, and raised money that it used to help lesbian mothers with legal bills. That year, the lesbian mother I had met in 1972, Rosalie Davies, formed Custody Action for Lesbian Mothers, in Philadelphia, after she lost custody of her children. Child custody became the first lesbian issue addressed at the National Conference on Women and the Law, in 1974, and later it became the first primarily lesbian issue addressed by the nascent gay legal and policy organizations. Lambda Legal Defense and Education Fund, for example, the first national gay and lesbian legal organization and currently the largest, was founded in 1973 and filed its first friend-of-the-court brief in a lesbian-mother custody case in 1977. The American Civil Liberties Union (ACLU) published a layperson's guide, *The Rights of Gay People,* in 1975, which included a handful of pages for lesbian and gay parents.[5] In 1978, the National Lawyers Guild, a progressive legal organization with roots in the labor and civil rights movements, published a legal guide for lesbian and gay parents; it sold two thousand copies in a year and a half. Because no women's, gay, or progressive legal organization had ever made lesbian custody a priority, the Lesbian Rights Project was founded in 1977 in San Francisco. Although the project addressed a range of issues affecting lesbians, such as employment, immigration, and the military, its major focus was always parenting issues. Pushed by lesbian activists, nondiscrimination in custody determinations became a plank of the Plan of Action adopted at the federally sponsored 1977 National Women's Conference in Houston and one of three principal demands of the first national gay rights march, held in Washington, D.C., in 1979. At that march, the first national gay fathers' group, Gay Fathers Coalition, was formed, primarily as a support network and a convener of annual conferences, rather than as a legal advocacy and defense fund as was LMNDF.

Challenges to the ability of lesbians and gay men to raise children took place initially in domestic relations courtrooms. Although a parent's homosexuality was explicitly acknowledged in a handful of reported cases going back to 1952,[6] cases began appearing more frequently in the early and mid-1970s, as the women's liberation movement and changing attitudes toward divorce made it easier for all women to leave marriages and as the gay liberation movement enabled untold numbers of gay men and lesbians to embrace an identity they had been taught to despise.

As a network of lesbian lawyers and activists began advocating on behalf of lesbian and gay parents, unreported court opinions were passed around the country and written about in law review articles and community publications.[7] Most of the cases took place upon divorce, or sometimes years later, as a child's heterosexual parent would seek to obtain custody from the child's gay or lesbian parent or to dramatically restrict that parent's visitation rights. Because, at the time, mothers usually retained custody of children and fathers usually obtained visitation rights, lesbian mothers generally fought custody battles, while gay fathers generally fought for unrestricted visitation rights. Some of the custody disputes involving lesbian mothers, however, confronted the same issues fathers faced in their visitation cases; a court might be willing to grant custody to a lesbian mother, but only if she refrained from living with a partner. Less frequently, custody disputes took place between a lesbian mother and another relative, such as the father's mother or her own mother or sister, with the relative attempting to obtain custody because of the mother's lesbianism. In a small number of cases a mother's lesbianism was a factor in an action seeking to place a child in the custody of the state.

In cases between parents, judges were required to apply a "best interests of the child" standard, with enormous discretion to view a parent's lesbianism or homosexuality in a negative light. This standard also governed cases in which the issue was whether a gay parent could have unrestricted visitation. In custody cases brought by another relative, the parent was supposed to have the edge, and sometimes a finding of parental unfitness was required before the nonparent could be awarded custody. When the state sought to remove a child from the family, some showing of abuse or neglect was normally required.

Within the boundaries of these standards, there were both failures and successes. In 1972, a lesbian couple in Seattle was permitted to keep custody of six children between them. Although they were ordered not to live together, they set up apartments across the hall from one another, went back and forth between the two apartments, and embarked upon a public campaign to undo the restriction placed on them. They interested a doctor at the University of Washington in their family, and he helped the university get a grant to make a movie, *Sandy and Madeleine's Family*, which included Margaret Mead articulating a supportive position. Local lesbians rallied in support of Sandy and

Madeleine, and their organizing spawned the Lesbian Mothers National Defense Fund. In 1974, their ex-husbands hauled the women back into court, but the judge allowed the couple to keep their children and lifted all restrictions on their custody. When the Washington Supreme Court affirmed the trial judge's order in 1978, the family became the subject of a *People* magazine photo spread. Their movie was entered as evidence in some later custody cases.

States with other successful cases in the mid-1970s included California, Maine, Ohio, Oregon, and South Carolina. In the first victory, and still one of the few, for transsexual parents, in 1973 a Colorado appeals court told a trial court it was wrong to remove custody of four children from a mother simply because she had undergone a sex-change operation and become a man.[8]

Cases in which lesbian mothers lost custody of their children were more numerous and sometimes produced dramatic consequences. For example, Marilyn Koop, an Oregon mother, had three children, ages fifteen, twelve, and ten, all of whom wanted to live with her and her partner rather than with their father. The judge permitted the eldest to live where she wished, but ordered the younger two into the custody of their father. When the children ran away from their father and later told the judge they would not live with him, the judge ordered them placed in a juvenile detention center. They were subsequently placed with their married half sister. The judge called the mother's living arrangement "abnormal" and said it would be "highly detrimental to the girls." In an Ohio case in which the children's father had once tried to commit suicide in front of the children, a judge found the father unfit but awarded custody of the children to their paternal grandmother, who had not testified in the case nor expressed a willingness to raise the children, rather than place them with their lesbian mother, who "boldly and brazenly" set up a home with her partner. In a 1974 New Jersey case, a heterosexual mother requested that her former husband, Bruce Voeller, who was executive director of the newly formed National Gay Task Force, be denied any overnight visitation with his three children. After detailing the exposure of the children to the father's partner, to other gay men, and to gay rights demonstrations, the judge said, "We are dealing in the present case with a most sensitive issue which holds the possibility of inflicting severe mental anguish and detriment on three innocent children." Although the judge discussed extensively that the father had a constitutional right to participate in raising his children, he nonetheless permitted only limited daytime visits that could not be at the home the father shared with his partner. The judge also ruled that the father could not take the children to places where there were other gay men or gay-related activities, and that his lover could not be present when he saw his children.[9]

To win a case, the parent usually had to avoid media coverage, political demonstrations, or other publicity. Lawyers for lesbian mothers asked judges to focus on the best interests of the children, not on the mother's sexual orientation. They sought to prove the many ways in which the children would be better off with their mother, and then to show that nothing about their mother's lesbianism should negate such a ruling. Homosexuality would loom much larger if a parent was public and politically active, as in Bruce Voeller's case. If the trial was publicized, sexual orientation would become the focus of the trial—exactly what lawyers wanted to avoid.

Although this strategy probably resulted in winning cases that would otherwise have been lost, it came with a cost. A judge could be educated about lesbian and gay parenting in an individual case, but no widespread educational campaign could take place if each case occurred in a vacuum. Gay and lesbian parents were also denied the opportunity to learn about others like themselves who faced possible court battles. Still, no parent could be expected to become a poster child for custody rights if it would make it more likely that she would lose her children. Even a parent who was successful could not publicize her victory in the hope of educating others; custody decisions are never final, and the willingness to be public could itself result in a reopened court case in which the mother would lose. Sandy and Madeleine, who kept their children even though they went public, were the exception, not the rule.

The rule was almost certainly exemplified by Minnie Bruce Pratt, whose volume of poems about the loss of her children garnered the Lamont Prize from the Academy of American Poets in 1989.[10] Minnie Bruce came out in Fayetteville, North Carolina, in 1975. When she spoke with lawyers about obtaining custody of her two young sons, one read her the North Carolina sodomy statute; another told her that the world was not ready for someone like her. She did not know any other lesbian mother; she did not know that there had ever been successful lesbian-mother custody cases; she faced the prospect that her own mother would testify against her in court. Instead of fighting, she relinquished custody and obtained restricted visitation.

One mother who lost custody and then went public was Mary Jo Risher. Texas is the only state in the country in which a jury, rather than a judge, can decide child custody matters, and in 1975 a Texas jury gave custody of Risher's nine-year-old son to her former husband. Risher sought national publicity, resulting in, among other things, the first *Time* magazine article on lesbian and gay parents.[11] Her story became a book and then a made-for-TV movie, *A Question of Love*, starring Jane Alexander and Gena Rowlands, which aired in 1978 and which portrayed Risher in a sympathetic light. *A Question of Love* spawned additional media interest in the topic.

Several developments in the early 1970s assisted legal advocates for lesbian and gay parents. In 1970, responding to changing attitudes toward divorce, lawyers and legal scholars wrote a model law, the Uniform Marriage and Divorce Act, that formed the basis for revision of many state laws. Responding to changing sexual mores and undermining the decades-old rule that an adulterous parent was unfit to be a child's custodian, the act provided that "the court shall not consider conduct of a proposed custodian that does not affect his relationship to the child."[12] Additionally, in 1973, the American Psychiatric Association removed homosexuality from its list of mental illnesses in its *Diagnostic and Statistical Manual*. These two changes formed the backbone of the legal strategy for custody and visitation rights for gay and lesbian parents, as advocates asked courts to disregard a parent's sexual orientation unless it was shown to have an adverse impact on the child.

At the same time, mental health professionals sympathetic to lesbian and gay parents began conducting research on gay and lesbian parents and their children. Although a few studies comparing the overall mental health of lesbians and heterosexual women had been published, the first research on lesbian mothers was published in 1973.[13] The first study on children raised by gay, lesbian, or transsexual parents would not appear until 1978,[14] but in 1976 the American Psychological Association passed a resolution opposing use of sexual orientation as a primary component in custody, adoption, or foster-parenting determinations. Effective use of mental health experts to combat myths about lesbians and gay men, and to offer opinions that children would not be psychologically harmed by living with a gay or lesbian parent, became a cornerstone of the trial strategy for representing gay and lesbian parents.

During the mid-1970s, on the legislative front, the burgeoning gay rights movement was seeking civil rights ordinances in many cities. Meanwhile, divorce and custody laws were being reformed, often along the lines proposed in the Uniform Marriage and Divorce Act. Advocates in the District of Columbia, after obtaining inclusion of sexual orientation in a broad antidiscrimination law passed in 1974, succeeding in adding sexual orientation to the list of factors prohibited from determining custody and visitation when the family law code was revised in 1976. That law remains the only statutory protection for gay and lesbian custody in the country, as the backlash against the early successes of gay rights advocacy began in earnest in 1977.

Although custody and visitation were the principal parenting issues gay men and lesbians faced in the 1970s, issues of adoption and foster parenting first surfaced then. Shortly after its founding in 1973, the National Gay Task Force, in conjunction with New York City child welfare agencies, developed a network of gay foster homes for homeless gay teenagers who were not functioning well in city group homes. A *New York Times* article about the program appeared in 1974 and included both praise and skepticism from a variety of child welfare professionals.[15] Although the extent of such programs is not well documented, New York's was not the only one. In 1974, a Washington State judge approved the placement of a gay teenager with gay foster parents. A year later, however, another Washington State judge denied such a placement, sid-ing with the child's father, who opposed it. In spite of favorable testimony from social workers, juvenile parole officers, a psychiatrist, and a psychologist, the judge reasoned that "substituting two male homosexuals for parents does violence not only to the literal definition of who are parents but offends the traditional concept of what a family is."[16] As a new practicing attorney in Montgomery County, Maryland, in 1976, my first contested gay family case was similar to the one in Washington State. The county had placed a gay teenager whose parents had kicked him out of their home with a single gay man as a foster parent. Although the parents still did not want the child at home, they asked the judge to remove him from the foster home and place him with a heterosexual family. Both the county social worker and an independent psychiatrist opposed the child's removal, and the judge denied the parents' request.

There is no record of an adoption by an openly gay or lesbian parent during this period. It is likely, however, that gay men and lesbians who were not open were able to adopt. Every state permits single adults to adopt, and state adoption agencies would happily have approved a single parent, especially for a hard-to-place child or for a child related to the adopting parent, such as a niece or nephew, whose parents died or were otherwise unable to raise the child.

1977: THE BACKLASH BEGINS

"Save Our Children" was the battle cry of Anita Bryant, singer and spokesperson for Florida orange juice, who spearheaded the drive to repeal a Dade County, Florida, gay rights ordinance. Within five weeks, with inflammatory rhetoric about molestation and recruitment by lesbians and gay men, to whom she referred as "human garbage," she had collected the sixty-five thousand signatures necessary for a referendum. On June 7, 1977, the referendum was held and the ordinance repealed. The next day, Florida's governor signed into law a ban on adoption by lesbians and gay men, the first such statewide ban.

The next year, another attack on gay and lesbian civil rights also capitalized directly on fears about children. Just after the Florida bill was signed into law, California state senator John Briggs announced his initiative, which appeared on the November 1978 ballot and would have banned both openly gay teachers and all teachers who spoke positively about homosexuality. The breadth of the proposal drew opposition from civil libertarians and most mainstream politicians, including Ronald Reagan, and the initiative was defeated. But the rhetoric of the campaign filled the air with vicious attacks: "Homosexuals want your children. . . . If they don't recruit children or very young people, they'd all die away. They have no means of replenishing." More quietly, the Oklahoma legislature that year passed a virtually identical bill.

The backlash against gay and lesbian rights meshed with two related backlash movements that had begun in 1973: one against abortion that developed after the Supreme Court's *Roe v. Wade* decision and the other to prevent ratification of the Equal Rights Amendment. Opponents of gay rights correctly calculated that the Achilles' heel of a movement for gay civil rights would be anxiety about children, both fear of sexual molestation and fear that gay men and lesbians would "recruit" children to homosexuality.

While these concerns had surfaced in the child custody, visitation, and foster-parenting cases of the early and mid 1970s, those cases had garnered little public attention. In individual cases, advocates could sometimes dispel the fears of judges with sympathetic expert witnesses.[17] Vocal, public antigay campaigns, however, presented new challenges for advocates for lesbian and gay parents. Victory for lesbian and gay parenting in the legislative arena became impossible; attempts to duplicate the District of Columbia law would have met powerful organized resistance anywhere. Although it is more than twenty years later, and the resources devoted to advocacy on behalf of gay and lesbian rights have increased dramatically, no group has ever proactively attempted to gain explicit antidiscrimination protection for gay and lesbian parenting in state legislatures. Rather, throughout the eighties and nineties, as the structure of lesbian and gay families evolved and presented new legal and policy challenges, the focus has remained in the courts, where cases might be won both at trial and on appeal state by state; on educating gay and lesbian parents and their lawyers about strategies that might be successful for individual parents; and, when necessary, on defeating legislative proposals that would circumscribe the ability of lesbians and gay men to raise children.

By the end of the 1970s, controversy surrounding lesbian and gay families surfaced on a national level. President Jimmy Carter's 1976 campaign promise to convene a White House Conference on the Family evolved through many disagreements between liberals and conservatives, including a name-change battle won by the liberals, into the White House Conference on Families, held in three cities in 1980. The conference structure included a National Advisory Committee, delegates from each state, and a national task force that was to take reports from the conferences, in Baltimore, Minneapolis, and Los Angeles, and make recommendations to the president and Congress. While lesbian and gay parenting was not explicitly part of the agenda, acceptance of lesbians and gay men as forming families was. Conservatives sought to define the family as "persons related by blood, marriage, or adoption," a definition that passed in Minneapolis but failed in Baltimore, where conservatives walked out rather than lend credibility to a conference they considered "pro-ERA, pro-abortion, pro–sexual preference, pro–a guaranteed annual income, and pro–national health insurance." Gay rights supporters in Baltimore, however, failed to win approval of a definition of *family* that would have explicitly included gay men and lesbians. Conference debates received national media attention.[18]

In spite of the backlash, custody and visitation cases toward the end of the 1970s continued to produce victories as well as defeats. In what remains one of the most eloquent expressions of the positive aspects of having a lesbian mother, a New Jersey appellate court reversed a trial court order removing the children from their lesbian mother, reasoning in part that children could benefit from being raised by a gay or lesbian parent. The judge stated:

> [These children may] emerge better equipped to search out their own standards of right and wrong, better able to perceive that the majority is not always correct in its moral judgments, and better able to understand the importance of conforming their beliefs to the requirements of reason and tested knowledge, not the constraints of currently popular sentiment or prejudice.[19]

During the late seventies, the first mental health research on the well-being of children raised by lesbian mothers was published, and strategies for persuading judges through the use of expert witnesses were refined. Advocates were able to identify recurring myths in court decisions against lesbian mothers—that lesbians were mentally ill or emotionally unstable; that a lesbian mother would sexually molest her child or demonstrate sexual behavior in front of her child; that children raised by lesbian mothers would become gay or lesbian, would be confused about their gender identity, or would be socially stigmatized—and to use expert witnesses to rebut these myths. Also during this time, more mainstream legal publications acknowledged lesbian mothers; *Family Advocate,* a publication of the American Bar Association that goes to all members of its Family Law Section, published its first article on representing a lesbian mother in 1979, and in both 1978 and 1979, articles on gay child custody cases appeared in a journal aimed exclusively at judges.

By the late 1970s numerous factors coincided to launch a new form of lesbian and gay parenthood not tied to heterosexual marriage. The gay rights movement enabled many young adults to embrace, rather than reject, their sexual orientation. Men and women who, in an earlier period, would have married out of convention, fear, or denial no longer did so. While it may initially have appeared that parenthood would never be an option for such men and women, other cultural and medical phenomena soon resulted in a new frame of mind. Specifically, births of out-of-wedlock children no longer carried the stigma they had in earlier decades, and medical technology opened the possibilities for conception without sexual intercourse. At some point in the late

1970s, therefore, open lesbians in significant numbers began contemplating planned motherhood, primarily using alternative insemination as the means of conception.

Although there are accounts of decisions by lesbian couples to raise children together as far back as 1965,[20] this form of planned motherhood probably first took hold in the San Francisco area about 1978. Word spread through pamphlets describing alternative insemination. Women who could not find doctors or sperm banks that would service lesbians, or any unmarried woman, learned how to do the procedure themselves with semen obtained from a willing donor. A 1979 *Newsweek* article described this phenomenon,[21] as did a 1980 article in the *New York Times Magazine,* which estimated that 150 lesbians had become pregnant through this method.[22] The legal issues this method of family formation raised, including access to sperm banks and the parental relationships that would or would not be recognized, became the subject of law review articles beginning in 1980.

Lesbians considering motherhood chose adoption as well as alternative insemination. Although many private adoption agencies would work only with married couples, others were open to single parents. Public agencies, often entrusted with finding homes for hard-to-place children, almost always accepted applications from single men and women. Lawyers advised adoption applicants not to lie but also said that it was not necessary to volunteer information that was not asked. Many social workers, privately supportive of gay adoption but concerned about unsympathetic judges, asked no questions that would require revealing sexual orientation so that they could write reports that portrayed a lesbian or gay applicant simply as a single parent. Although states had not followed Florida's lead in banning all gay adoption, few prospective adoptive parents wanted to risk rejection by judges empowered to grant or deny adoptions. Most, therefore, described themselves without reference to their sexual orientation.

THE "GAYBY" BOOM AND THE RISE OF THE RELIGIOUS RIGHT

Shortly after Ronald Reagan was elected president in 1980, the first national campaign in which the Christian right was a significant force, two conservative senators, Paul Laxalt of Nevada and Roger Jepsen of Iowa, introduced into Congress the Family Protection Act, the right wing's blueprint for a conservative family agenda. Among other things, it would have required withdrawal of federal funds from any entity involved in "advocating, promoting, or suggesting homosexuality, male or female, as a lifestyle," and it would have forbidden the use of Legal Services Corporation funds for any litigation involving "homosexual rights." In his speech before the Senate as he introduced the bill, Senator Jepsen warned that the move to a broader definition of family, which his legislation sought to combat, would lead to the ability of "homosexuals and lesbian couples to adopt children."[23]

In the early eighties, even as the influence of the Christian right grew, the openness and pride of lesbian and gay families also grew. By the mid-1980s, increased media attention widened the exposure of planned lesbian and gay parenting, creating possibilities for lesbians and gay men around the country. In 1982, the Oakland, California, Feminist Women's Health Center opened a sperm bank that provided frozen semen and shipped it anywhere in the country, without discriminating on the basis of sexual orientation. Two videos were produced, *Choosing Children*, in 1984, and *Alternative Conceptions*, in 1985; *Choosing Children* was reviewed in *The New York Times*. Also in 1985, the first book devoted to helping lesbians decide whether and how to become parents was published.[24] Gay newspapers reported numerous regional conferences on choosing children. The National Lesbian Health Care study, conducted in 1985, showed that about one-third of the lesbians studied wanted to become mothers through adoption or alternative insemination. Legal issues for planned lesbian and gay families gained popular attention during this time, as *The New York Times* reported a judge's approval of an adoption by an openly gay man in 1982 and a visitation dispute in 1984 between two women who had raised a child conceived through alternative insemination.[25] By 1985, several legal conferences had addressed the issues caused by this new family form.

Meanwhile, the number of reported cases of custody and visitation disputes between a heterosexual parent and a gay or lesbian parent grew; about twenty states had reported decisions in the first half of the 1980s. New forms of lesbian and gay families confronted the courts for the first time, but the traditional disputes, precipitated when lesbians and gay men came out after they had married and had children, still constituted the greatest number of legal challenges to lesbian and gay parenting. Decisions during this period were no more favorable than those of the 1970s. Some courts eschewed discrimination, such as those in Massachusetts, Alaska, and New York. In 1980, the Massachusetts Supreme Court permitted a lesbian mother to regain custody from a guardian who had cared for her children while the mother was suffering from mental and physical illness. Reversing the trial court decision that would have kept the children with the guardian, the court said that the mother could not lose her children because her household failed to meet "ideals approved by the community" or because she had a lifestyle "at odds with the average."[26] The Alaska Supreme Court ruled in 1985 that a mother's lesbian relationship should be considered only if it negatively affected the child and that it was "impermissible to rely on any real or imagined social stigma attaching to [the] mother's status as a lesbian."[27] A 1984 New York appeals court decision also articulated the requirement of an "adverse effect" before a parent's sexual orientation could be a basis for denying custody, and an appellate case the next year lifted a trial court order prohibiting the presence of the father's partner or any other gay person during visitation.[28]

Most courts, however, ruled against gay parents. Cases from appellate courts in Indiana, North Dakota, South Dakota, and Virginia overturned trial court judges who had awarded custody to lesbian, gay, or bisexual parents. In 1985, the Virginia Supreme Court held that a gay parent living with a partner was always an unfit parent.[29] In Tennessee and Oklahoma, appellate courts affirmed transfers of custody from lesbian mothers to heterosexual fathers. An Ohio trial judge who granted a gay father visitation rights with the restriction that "unrelated" males could not be present during visitation was reversed by an appeals court that found that the judge had not imposed enough restrictions on the gay father. The appeals court, in its 1985 decision, said the state had a "substantial interest in viewing homosexuality as an arrant sexual behavior which threatens the social fabric, and in endeavoring to protect minors from being influenced by those who advocate homosexual lifestyles."[30]

In the early 1980s, Missouri appellate courts issued three opinions against lesbian and gay parents. These would be joined by an additional six in the second half of the 1980s, making Missouri the single worst jurisdiction in the country in which to litigate on behalf of a gay or lesbian parent. A 1980 decision changing custody to a heterosexual father because a lesbian mother permitted her partner to be around her children compared the presence of the mother's partner to the presence of "a habitual criminal, or a child abuser, or a sexual pervert, or a known drug pusher."[31] A 1982 decision affirmed severely limited visitation rights for a gay father, disregarding two expert witnesses who testified, among other things, that there was no reason to fear that the children would be sexually molested by the father or his friends. In spite of the evidence, the court reasoned that "every trial judge, or for that matter every appellate judge, knows that the molestation of minor boys by adult males is not as uncommon as the psychological experts' testimony indicated."[32] Another 1982 decision upheld restrictions on a lesbian mother's visitation, referring to her home as an "unwholesome environment."[33]

As the number of cases grew, it became increasingly important to reach parents and child custody litigators around the country, to arm them with positive precedent from other jurisdictions, and to suggest strategies that held the most likely chance of success. The National Lawyers Guild reprinted its Lesbian and Gay Parent's Legal Guide to Child Custody in 1980 and again in 1985. In 1980, the Lesbian Rights Project published its first annotated bibliography of legal and psychological materials on lesbian mothers and their children. In 1982, the Lesbian Rights Project published the first edition of its

Lesbian Mother Litigation Manual. A year later, it published the second edition of its annotated bibliography. In 1985, in conjunction with the National Lawyers Guild, a publisher of legal books for practitioners produced the volume *Sexual Orientation and the Law* with sections on representing gay and lesbian parents. These materials made it possible to transmit more effectively a decade of accumulated experience and wisdom about the legal climate for lesbian and gay parents.

Sustained national attention to the suitability of lesbians and gay men raising children emerged in 1985 in the context of foster parenting. Many states, chronically short of foster homes, licensed lesbian and gay foster parents in the decade from 1975 to 1985, a practice supported by both the American Psychological Association and the National Association of Social Workers. But in May 1985, neighbors of a gay couple in Boston who served as foster parents went to the *Boston Globe* to express their disapproval. The ensuing publicity, in print media and on television, sparked widespread debate about gay men and lesbians raising children. The Massachusetts Department of Social Services removed the children from the home, and the Massachusetts state house voted to prohibit children's placement in lesbian and gay homes, explicitly defining homosexuality as a threat to children's well-being. Although that bill did not become law, Massachusetts changed its policy, issuing regulations that made it almost impossible for lesbians and gay men to become foster parents.[34]

In the wake of that controversy, in 1986 the New Hampshire legislature enacted a law prohibiting adoption, foster parenting, or ownership of a child care facility by lesbians or gay men. Although the child-care-facility provision was struck down as unconstitutional, the bans on adoption and foster parenting were upheld. The state Supreme Court was unwilling to credit the undisputed studies that growing up in a gay or lesbian home would not make a child become gay. Rather, it reasoned that a gay role model might affect a child's sexual orientation, and that this consideration could properly inspire the legislature to prohibit gay and lesbian adoption and foster parenting.[35] New Hampshire became the second state with an adoption ban and the first with a legislatively mandated ban on gay foster parenting. In 1987, President Reagan's Interagency Task Force on Adoption issued its report, which contained a recommendation that "homosexual adoption should not be supported."[36]

As in the past, advocates for gay and lesbian parents continued to represent individual gay and lesbian parents in custody and visitation disputes, hoping to improve the law state by state through appellate court decisions. But during this time they also developed new legal approaches to protect gay and lesbian families in which, from birth, a child had two parents of the same gender. The number of such families continued to grow in the 1980s, and lawyers developed theories using existing adoption statutes in attempts to ensure that both partners would be legally considered the parents of their child.

Lawyers coined the term *second-parent adoption* to describe the equivalent of a stepparent adoption, in which a biological parent's partner adopts her child. The term *joint adoption* was used to designate adoption of a child by both members of a couple, a practice unheard of earlier unless the couple was legally married. The first second-parent adoption was granted in Alaska in 1985, and within months there were others in Oregon, Washington, and California. All these were granted by trial court judges without written opinions, making them of limited precedential value. The adoption decrees were circulated among a small group of legal advocates, who used them to help develop the law in an increasing number of jurisdictions. Although law review articles first discussed these cases in 1986, there was no reported opinion granting a second-parent adoption until 1991.

The mid-1980s also saw the first disputes between separating lesbian mothers who had raised a child together and between a lesbian mother and a semen donor, often a gay man, when disagreements arose about the donor's relationship with the child. These cases would become more prominent in the late 1980s and into the 1990s.

The U.S. Supreme Court's 1986 decision in *Bowers v. Hardwick* upheld the constitutionality of a Georgia statute prohibiting sodomy between two consenting adults of the same gender. The decision thus left standing criminal sodomy laws in twenty-four states and the District of Columbia. In some states, these statutes had been used explicitly to justify denials of or restrictions on custody or visitation. A positive decision in *Bowers* would have given advocates in those states a powerful weapon for asserting the rights of gay and lesbian parents. Instead, the Court's decision gave tacit approval to reasoning such as that applied by an Arizona appeals court just a few months after the *Bowers* decision. The court affirmed a trial court's unwillingness to certify a bisexual man as an appropriate adoptive parent, reasoning that Arizona had a criminal sodomy statute, that such a statute was constitutional under *Bowers*, and that "it would be anomalous for the state on the one hand to declare homosexual conduct unlawful and on the other create a parent after that proscribed model, in effect approving that standard, inimical to the natural family, as head of a state-created family."[37] The New Hampshire Supreme Court also cited *Bowers* in upholding the state's legislative ban on gay adoption and foster parenting.

Although *Bowers* gave ammunition to courts inclined to disapprove of lesbian and gay parenting, those courts did not need *Bowers* to rule against a gay or lesbian parent; they had been doing so for more than a decade. Conversely, *Bowers* did not require a court to deny the ability of lesbians and gay men to be good parents. The year after *Bowers* a trial judge in South Carolina, a state with a criminal sodomy statute, awarded custody of a child to her lesbian mother, and the appeals court affirmed because it found, among other things, no evidence that the child's welfare was being adversely affected.[38]

Thus, although a victory in *Bowers* might have facilitated a step forward for lesbian and gay parents, the defeat preserved the state-by-state status quo.

In the decade or so between the beginning of organized advocacy on behalf of gay and lesbian parents and the decision in *Bowers,* lesbians changed their outlook on sodomy law reform. In the early 1970s, many lesbians resented and considered irrelevant the early gay rights legal movement's emphasis on eradicating criminal sodomy statutes. By the time of *Bowers,* however, the two issues—the right to parent and the right to sexual privacy—did not seem quite so distinct. Sodomy statutes were sometimes cited in custody and visitation cases. Even if the parent in the case was a gay father, the reasoning of the case denying custody or restricting visitation would apply with equal force to a lesbian mother in a subsequent case. Sodomy law reform thus became connected to advocacy on behalf of lesbian and gay parenting.

Since the second half of the 1980s, advocates for lesbian and gay parents have divided their resources between the issues facing parents with children from prior heterosexual relationships and the issues facing planned lesbian and gay families. Because the former issues had been around for more than a decade, by the late 1980s they were well defined; there was both an extensive body of literature analyzing court decisions and a growing number of studies comparing the mental health of children raised by divorced heterosexual mothers to children raised by divorced lesbian mothers. In 1988, the District of Columbia held the first judicial education program in the nation, mandatory for all trial and appellate court judges, designed to overcome myths and bias about lesbian and gay parents.

These developments did not mean that, nationwide, there were more successes. Appellate court decisions from the late 1980s continued to add up both for and against lesbian and gay parents. In 1986, the Nevada Supreme Court terminated a father's parental rights solely because he underwent a sex change operation.[39] In 1987, the Arkansas Supreme Court awarded sole custody to a heterosexual father, reasoning that it was proper to presume the children would be harmed living with their lesbian mother in an "immoral" environment.[40] Missouri continued its rampage of decisions against lesbian and gay parents, adding six between 1987 and 1989 to the three from earlier in the decade.

Meanwhile, there continued to be some successes. In 1988, a New Mexico appeals court overturned a trial judge's refusal to place a neglected child in the custody of his adult brother who was gay. The court reasoned that a proposed custodian's sexual orientation was not enough to conclude that the person would be unable to provide a child with a proper environment.[41] During this period, decisions in California and Washington overturned restrictions on a gay or lesbian parent's visitation rights. A 1987 Ohio court rejected a heterosexual mother's request that her former husband be denied all overnight visitation. The mother specifically urged, and the court specifically rejected, the following arguments: that overnight visitation would trigger "homosexual tendencies" in the children, that they might contract AIDS, that they would suffer social stigma, and that no proof of adverse impact should be required. While the reasoning of the court was extremely positive, the overnight visitation order prohibited the presence of nonrelated males, which the father did not appeal and the court, therefore, did not address.[42] The case was thus a limited victory.

The issues facing couples in planned lesbian and gay families during this time were too new for there to be published resources, such as manuals or law review articles, or even much reported law. Like lesbian-mother custody disputes in the 1970s, the development of legal theories took place among a small group of advocates who disseminated their work. An enormous change since the 1970s, however, made this work of dissemination much easier than it had been a decade earlier. The small, informal networks of the mid-1970s, formed by those who met at Women and the Law or National Lawyers Guild conferences or through word of mouth, and the handful of lawyers associated with fledgling gay legal groups, were enhanced by an extensive and coordinated network encompassing local practicing attorneys, increasing numbers of advocates working for national organizations, and openly gay students and faculty at law schools. The ACLU added a Lesbian and Gay Rights Project in 1986. The National Lesbian and Gay Law Association (NLGLA) was formed at a meeting held in conjunction with the 1987 March on Washington. It linked both an increasing number of local gay bar associations and individual attorneys who represented lesbian and gay clients. In 1988, NLGLA held its first Lavender Law conference, which included panels addressing both traditional custody and visitation disputes and the issues facing planned gay and lesbian families— access to alternative insemination, surrogacy, and adoption; second-parent adoptions; termination of a coparenting relationship through death or dissolution. It took Lambda Legal Defense and Education Fund ten years, from 1973 to 1983, to hire its first full-time attorney, but by 1989 it had four. By the end of the 1980s, a monthly publication of legal developments affecting lesbians and gay men, entitled *Lesbian/Gay Law Notes* and compiled by New York Law School professor Arthur Leonard, had a national circulation of more than a thousand attorneys and legal groups.

Thus, more attorneys had the resources to assist planned lesbian and gay families. Dozens of second-parent adoptions were granted in Alaska, Oregon, Washington, and California, including one granted in Washington in 1989 over the objection of a guardian ad litem appointed to represent the child; the judge found "overwhelming" evidence that the adoption was in the child's best interests.[43] In a 1989 case, a trial court judge in Broward County, Florida, awarded custody of ten-year-old Kristen Pearlman to Janine Ratcliffe, her nonbiological mother. Janine and her former partner Joanie had decided to raise a child together, and Joanie had conceived through anonymous donor insemination. They raised Kristen together until she was six, when Joanie died and a court awarded custody to Joanie's parents. Janine instituted further custody proceedings four years later, after Kristen's emotional health had deteriorated and the grandparents had terminated all contact between Kristen and Janine. In chambers, the child pleaded with the judge to permit her to live with Janine. The judge found that Kristen continued to view Janine as her primary parent figure, that it would be detrimental to Kristen to continue her separation from Janine, and that there was no evidence Janine's sexual orientation would have any detrimental effect on Kristen.[44]

In 1989, the media discovered planned gay and lesbian families. Articles appeared in *The New York Times, The Wall Street Journal, The Boston Globe,* the *San Francisco Examiner, The Washington Post,* and *Newsday.* The *Donahue* show and 20/20 (in a show entitled, "I Have Two Moms") featured lesbian couples raising children. In that year, the first children's book appeared whose central character was a child born of anonymous-donor insemination to a lesbian couple, and its initial printing of four thousand copies sold out before publication. In 1990, at the annual conference of Gay and Lesbian Parents Coalition International (GLPCI), a group of children of lesbian and gay parents held their own series of meetings out of which emerged a national organization called Children of Lesbians and Gays Everywhere (COLAGE). The first generation of children raised by lesbian mothers and gay fathers who came out in the early and mid 1970s had reached adulthood.

Inexorably, the formation of lesbian and gay families with children resulted in the subsequent dissolution of some of those families. Beginning in the late 1980s and continuing throughout the 1990s, these dissolutions have presented courts with two options—recognize planned lesbian and gay families and modify family law principles to protect the interests of parents and children in such families, or maintain a rigid definition of parenthood grounded in a biologically based, heterosexual norm and thereby obliterate the reality of children's lives with their lesbian and gay parents. Courts have usually chosen the latter option. In most states that have faced the issue, courts have refused to look beyond biology or the legal status conferred by formal adoption.

Disputes about parenthood have arisen primarily in two contexts. The first is a claim by a nonbiological parent to continue a relationship with a child when she and the child's biological parent separate. The second is a claim by a biological father, usually a semen donor, who demands legal parental status in disregard of an agreement with the lesbian couple that he would not assert formal parental rights based on biology.

These cases initially posed a dilemma for gay and lesbian legal organizations. The National Center for Lesbian Rights, for example, had a policy of not representing one lesbian against another. Yet it became apparent early on that in lesbian breakups the parent with the legal status was using doctrine designed to protect parents from outsiders, such as relatives or temporary childcare providers, for the purpose of excluding from the child's life a former partner who had functioned as the child's parent. Even if the legally unrecognized mother stayed home with the child, or if the child called both women "Mommy," or had the last name of the legally unrecognized mother, or asked to live with, or at least visit, the person s/he clearly considered another parent, courts rejected such claims through a narrow definition of parenthood tied to a heterosexual paradigm of family. Thus NCLR reexamined its policy and determined, as did the other legal organizations, that it would advocate upholding the family deliberately formed by the couple and their children and oppose a legal parent's attempts to write the legally unrecognized parent out of the child's life.

This advocacy has been largely unsuccessful. Appellate courts in California and New York, the states with the largest number of planned lesbian and gay families, have both closed the door on all claims by nonbiological mothers and recognized the claims of semen donors. Claims on behalf of nonbiological mothers have also been rebuffed in Ohio, Texas, and Florida. The measure of the vulnerability of legally unrecognized parents is the celebration engendered by a 1995 Wisconsin Supreme Court decision permitting such parents to request visitation rights, even though the decision also foreclosed any request for custody, even if the nonbiological parent was the child's primary caretaker. In Vermont, the first state whose Supreme Court approved second-parent adoptions, the Supreme Court has also ruled that in the absence of such an adoption, no factual scenario, no matter how compelling, would require a legally recognized parent to continue contact between her child and the child's legally unrecognized parent.

Advocacy for the integrity of planned lesbian and gay families has posed a dilemma for advocates for lesbian and gay parents. Doctrine that makes it difficult for nonparents to obtain custody has historically protected lesbian mothers from claims by their own relatives or relatives of a child's father. A lesbian mother whose former husband does not challenge her for custody is protected from claims by other relatives by doctrine that makes it difficult for a nonparent to challenge the custody rights of a parent. It is precisely this legal doctrine, however, that courts apply to rebuff the claims of a lesbian who has functioned in every way as a child's coparent but who lacks legal status. The distinction between a coparent and, for example, a grandparent could be made in carefully written legislation, but because lesbian and gay advocates cannot use the political process on behalf of lesbian and gay families without incurring political backlash, this avenue had been largely foreclosed. Advocates are left asking courts to walk a fine line between opening the door in true coparenting situations while not opening it so far that more lesbian and gay parents are vulnerable to claims by antigay relatives. Almost all courts have declined this invitation in the absence of legislative guidance, leaving lesbian and gay coparents in the category of all other nonparents and therefore without legal recourse.

The most extreme example of a biological mother's attempt to write a nonbiological mother out of her child's life occurred in North Carolina in 1997. In 1993, in Washington, Shifra Erez gave birth to a child and consented to the child's second-parent adoption by her partner, Aviva Starr. The adoption was granted under Washington law. The couple and their child moved to North Carolina in 1995 and separated in 1996. Erez left their daughter with Starr, who filed a petition for custody. Erez responded by asking the court to find that Starr's adoption of the child was contrary to the public policy of North Carolina and should therefore not be recognized by a North Carolina court. She argued that North Carolina courts would not have granted the second-parent adoption and that North Carolina did not recognize same-sex marriages. Although the North Carolina judge upheld the Washington adoption, the biological mother has appealed that ruling, and the case illustrates the lengths some individual gay men or lesbians are willing to go to use legal arguments, even blatantly homophobic ones, to negate an already vulnerable planned gay or lesbian family.[45]

In almost every state the rigid definition of parenthood that excludes a legally unrecognized lesbian mother includes not only the biological mother but also the biological father. Lesbians who use anonymous semen donors through their doctors or through sperm banks are protected from paternal claims, but those who have chosen known donors, who are often gay men, are vulnerable to a paternity claim by the donor that could lead to court-ordered visitation rights or even a transfer of custody. When the intent of the parties at the time of conception has been clear, the lesbian and gay legal organizations have argued that the parties' agreement should be carried out, but they have again been thwarted by the dominant heterosexual paradigm. The rights and responsibilities of parenthood cannot be contracted away, and therefore courts will refuse to enforce agreements, even if written, that the semen donor will not claim legal parental status. This doctrine stems partly from the laudable goal of ensuring that heterosexual fathers will be unable to walk away from their obligation to financially support their children. But the doctrine reflects a larger theme in the contemporary contest over "family values." At a time when policy makers can blame all social ills on single mothers and the lack of fathers in the lives of children, the courts are unlikely to affirm the ability of a lesbian couple, or indeed any unmarried woman, to raise a child alone if there is a man clamoring for the right to parent. Thus courts have almost uniformly embraced semen donors' claims to the rights of fatherhood. This ideological conflict, between recognition of the inherent worth of a variety of family structures and dogmatic adherence to the supremacy of a child-rearing model with one mother and one father, forms the core of the policy disputes over lesbian and gay parenting into the 1990s.

THE 1990S

The 1990s have been filled with incongruity for lesbian and gay parents. The number of planned lesbian and gay families has skyrocketed, bringing unprecedented visibility in the media, in schools, in churches and synagogues, and in the courts. In November 1996, Grammy Award–winning singer Melissa Etheridge appeared on the cover of *Newsweek* with her pregnant partner, Julie Cypher. Dozens of articles appear in daily papers each year, in such places as Dayton, Ohio, Sarasota, Florida, and Greensboro, North Carolina, as well as all major cities, describing local lesbian and gay families and their children. News coverage this decade has included the relatively recent phenomenon of gay fathers raising biologically related children born to a surrogate mother, a practice that captured the attention of the major national media with the opening in 1996 of a Los Angeles–based agency devoted exclusively to matching prospective gay fathers with surrogate mothers.

With this visibility has come an increased number of heterosexual allies, people in positions of power able to influence mainstream organizations, as well as ordinary people whose children become friends with children of gay and lesbian parents, thereby learning about gay and lesbian families in ways that break down myths, stereotypes, and fear. In 1995, the American Psychological Association issued *Lesbian and Gay Parenting: A Resource for Psychologists,* a review of forty-three empirical studies and numerous other articles that concluded that "not a single study has found children of gay and lesbian parents to be disadvantaged in any significant respect relative to children of heterosexual parents."[46] In some parts of the country, joint and second-parent adoptions for lesbian and gay couples have become routine, and lesbians and gay men have been welcomed as adoptive and foster parents for the growing number of children needing good homes.

With increased visibility has come increased political volatility. Legislatures have had more opportunities to debate lesbian and gay parenting. Related issues concerning children and homosexuality, such as the content of school curricula, the sexual orientation of school board members, and whether gay men can serve as Boy Scout leaders, have increasingly seeped into social discourse. Courts considering the fate of lesbian and gay parents have issued rulings in the context of these public debates.

Disputes between gay and lesbian parents and their heterosexual former spouses or other family members have continued unabated, and while supportive opinions have emerged in some states, the decisions in other states contain antigay rhetoric more vicious and vitriolic than anything written in the early 1970s. In many parts of the country it is no more possible for a lesbian mother to retain custody of her children now than it was twenty-five years ago. Several states whose child welfare agencies have approved lesbians and gay men as adoptive and foster parents, and in which judges have granted lesbian and gay adoptions on a case-by-case basis, are now considering outright bans on adoption and foster parenting by lesbians and gay men.

The legal and policy disputes about lesbian and gay child-rearing are taking place amidst a larger conversation about the role of family structure in society. The religion-based right-wing backlash of the late 1970s and 1980s was joined by, and in part has given way to, a right-wing movement claiming to be based in social science. This movement decries not only lesbian and gay families but no-fault divorce, single-parent families, out-of-wedlock birth, and, indeed, anything not based in a heterosexual marital unit. Its rhetoric blames all social ills, including poverty and violence, on the existence of alternatives to the heterosexual marital unit for rearing children.[47]

These positions are represented by such groups as Focus on the Family, based in Colorado Springs, and the Family Research Council, based in Washington, D.C., voices of the radical right. The crude claims of the 1970s that gay men and lesbians sexually molest and "recruit" children, and the religious objections of the 1980s that trumpeted the Bible, have not disappeared, but in the mainstream media and academic press have been replaced by claims that the healthy development of children demands support only for heterosexual marital units. In 1992, when Vice President Dan Quayle criticized the television character Murphy Brown for giving birth without shame out of wedlock, he was generally perceived as morally anachronistic. Later that year, Arkansas governor Bill Clinton accepted his party's nomination for president in a speech that extolled an America that included "every family. Every traditional family and every extended family. Every two-parent family, every single-parent family, every foster family." Just one year later, however, the media was trumpeting that "Dan Quayle was right" for recognizing that children need fathers both for their own development and as the solution to society's social and economic problems.[48]

Public awareness of lesbian and gay parenting increased as a by-product of the impassioned debate over lesbian and gay marriage that captured public attention after the Hawaii Supreme Court in the 1993, in *Baehr v. Lewin*, issued a ruling making lesbian and gay marriage a real possibility in that state. The ruling stated that a same-sex marriage ban could stand only if the state of Hawaii could prove that it was necessary to achieve some compelling state interest, a difficult legal standard to meet.[49] Congress responded by passing the Defense of Marriage Act (DOMA) in 1996, giving states the authority to disregard marriages between same-sex couples even if those marriages were legal in another state, and limiting marriage for purposes of federal law to unions between a man and a woman. In state legislatures around the country, lawmakers debated whether they would recognize same-sex marriages from Hawaii or any other state legalizing same-sex marriage; as of 1998, about thirty states had passed laws prohibiting recognition.[50]

To advocates on behalf of lesbian and gay parents, marriage raised issues distinct from those related to bearing and rearing children. With planned gay and lesbian families well into their second decade and with twenty years of developing often-successful legal strategies to support custody and visitation rights for gay and lesbian parents, advocates wished to keep right-wing attacks on gay and lesbian marriage from spilling over into the parenting arena. This proved impossible. Some opponents of lesbian and gay marriage, at both the federal and state levels, explicitly articulated as their basis children's "need" to be raised in heterosexual homes. A poll published in *Newsweek* in 1996 found support for adoption by lesbians and gay men at 48 percent, well under the 84 percent that support nondiscrimination in employment. Furthermore, the state of Hawaii sought in the trial that followed the state Supreme Court's opinion to justify the same-sex marriage ban on the theory that heterosexual marriage was the preferred unit for child-rearing. This turned the trial into a contest about lesbian and gay child-rearing. After hearing witnesses from both sides, the trial judge rejected the state's claim, finding that lesbians and gay men make good parents and that banning same-sex marriage would not further the state's interest in providing for the welfare of children. Although Hawaii's progress toward same-sex marriage was halted by a public referendum, the trial court's decision remains as a validation of the ability of lesbians and gay men to raise healthy children.

In addition to DOMA, congressional attention to lesbian and gay parenting arose from the particular status of the District of Columbia, which falls largely under congressional control.[51] Although the District has a local legislative body and a local court system, Congress retains the power to control its budget, write local legislation, and veto legislation the elected city council passes. In 1995, the District of Columbia appeals court ruled in a case involving a gay couple that joint and second-parent adoptions were permissible under the D.C. adoption statute.[52] Shortly thereafter, as part of the District's budget process on Capitol Hill, House Republicans attempted to pass a provision prohibiting joint adoptions by any unmarried couple. Although the provision was consistently defeated in committee that year and in each subsequent year, in 1998 Representative Steve Largent of Oklahoma introduced it as an amendment to the District's budget on the floor of the House. Speaking in favor of the restriction, Largent invoked the passage of DOMA.[53] Although several members of Congress cited the American Psychological Association's support of lesbian and gay parenting, and although the Child Welfare League of America opposed the restriction because it would "unnecessarily limit the pool of families available for [children],"[54] the restriction passed, 227–192. It was saved from enactment in the House-Senate conference only because President Clinton, after lobbying by gay and lesbian organizations, included it on the short list of items he would not support, thereby persuading the conference committee to drop it from the final legislation. The next year, 1999, the same language, again introduced by Representative Largent, was defeated on the House floor by a vote of 215 to 213, with 36 Republicans voting against it.[55]

The greatest legal accomplishment for lesbian and gay parents in this decade has been the availability in some parts of the country of joint and second-parent adoption. After many unreported trial court decisions in the last half of the 1980s, the first second-parent adoption by a lesbian couple to be reported in a legal publication occurred in 1991 in the District of Columbia. Other reported decisions came shortly thereafter, and in early 1992 the first New York decision granting a second-parent adoption to a lesbian couple was reported in *The New York Times* and applauded on its editorial page. Appeals courts in New York, New Jersey, Vermont, Massachusetts, Illinois, and the District of Columbia have approved such adoptions and instructed trial judges to grant them under the same best-interests-of-the-child standard used in all adoptions. Although appellate courts in Wisconsin, Colorado, Connecticut, and Ohio have rejected such adoptions, in decisions narrowly construing their adoption statutes, trial courts in more than a dozen other states have granted such adoptions, and in some counties, such as those in the San Francisco Bay Area, there have probably been thousands over the last fifteen years.

The success of second-parent adoptions is largely attributable to the context in which they arise and the limited role of the judge in any individual case. A petition to make a nonbiological mother a legal parent to the child does not ask a judge to express any opinion about lesbian and gay parenting generally; it simply asks the judge whether the child will be better off with one parent or with two. No heterosexual parent is vying for the child, who will be raised in a lesbian home regardless of the parents' legal status. In that context, the decision is usually easy for a judge. Also, the judges who hear adoption petitions are often the same judges who, in other cases, hear allegations of abuse and neglect and see children whose lives have been destroyed by myriad factors. The judge who granted the first second-parent adoption in New York put it this way:

> Today a child who receives proper nutrition, adequate schooling, and supportive sustaining shelter is among the fortunate, whatever the source. A child who also receives the love and nurture of even a single parent can be counted among the blessed. Here this court finds a child who has all of the above benefits and two adults dedicated to his welfare,

secure in their loving partnership, and determined to raise him to the very best of their considerable abilities. There is no reason in law, logic, or social philosophy to obstruct such a favorable situation.[56]

When a couple seeks to adopt a child together, they usually want a joint adoption, in which they will both be the child's legal parents. Most agencies that permit individual lesbians and gay men to adopt do not permit such joint adoptions, reasoning that marriage is a prerequisite for joint adoption and that therefore no unmarried couple may jointly adopt. Couples are unlikely to challenge such a policy for fear that no child will be placed with them, and thus most children adopted into lesbian and gay families have, in the eyes of the law, only one parent.[57] If the state permits second-parent adoption, the couple can achieve legal status for both parents through a two-step process, first an adoption by one of them and later a second-parent adoption.

Michael Galluccio and Jon Holden faced such a prospect when the New Jersey state agency that had placed with them a drug-addicted, lung-damaged, HIV-positive three-month-old foster child, Adam, told them two years later that it would approve only one of them as an adoptive parent. Michael and Jon knew that New Jersey approved second-parent adoptions, and the agency told them they could go through that procedure, but they did not want the extra expense or the gap during which Adam would have only one legal father. In a class-action suit filed by the ACLU, Michael and Jon challenged the state's regulations. The judge granted Michael and Jon their joint adoption. The state agency had nothing but praise for the care the couple had provided the child, and the judge found that the adoption was both legally permissible and in the child's best interests. Two months later, the state and the ACLU reached a settlement in which the state agreed to evaluate gay and lesbian, as well as unmarried heterosexual, couples by the same criteria used to evaluate married couples. Although the settlement was widely reported, incorrectly, as making New Jersey the first state to permit joint adoption by gay couples, the case did make New Jersey the first state with a written policy from its child welfare agency requiring equal treatment for gay and heterosexual prospective adoptive parents.

Michael Galluccio and Jon Holden could pursue their case with the confidence that, whatever the outcome, New Jersey would not remove Adam from their home. The state agency knew they were gay when Adam was placed with them, and that fact had not kept them from being licensed as foster parents. Throughout the 1990s, lesbians and gay men became increasingly visible as foster parents for the growing number of abused, neglected, and abandoned children in state social-service systems. In settlement of a lawsuit, Massachusetts in 1990 abandoned its regulations that made placement of a child with gay or lesbian foster parents almost impossible. A 1994 Florida court decision

struck down that state's unwritten policy against licensing gay and lesbian foster parents. In 1996, an Iowa gay male couple were named foster parents of the
year by the state's Foster and Adopted Parents Association. They were nominated by their seventeen-year-old foster son, and over the preceding seven
years they had fostered thirteen children, one of whom they had adopted.[58]
What began in the 1970s as advocacy for licensing of gay foster parents to meet
the needs of gay teenagers unwanted by their parents and ill served by other
placements such as group homes had been broadened by the nineties—and by
the boom in planned gay and lesbian families—to include the desires and abilities of lesbians and gay men to help meet the desperate need for placements
for children in state care.

For the most part, lesbians and gay men became licensed as foster parents
by state agencies, without publicity or fanfare, in keeping with the longstanding
position of the National Association of Social Workers, which condemns discrimination based upon sexual orientation. In a few instances, however, the existence of gay and lesbian foster parents has garnered national media attention. In
1997, a Texas child-welfare supervisor, Rebecca Bledsoe, ordered the emergency
removal of an infant from his foster home upon discovering that the licensed foster parent was a lesbian, in spite of the report by the child's caseworker that he
was thriving under the care of the foster parent and her partner. The agency defended its practice of licensing lesbian and gay foster parents, overruled Bledsoe,
and demoted her from supervisor to caseworker. The incident received nationwide publicity, with antigay organizations coming to the defense of Bledsoe, who
subsequently challenged her demotion in court, albeit unsuccessfully.

From the mid-nineties on, the marriage debate (including the success of
antigay forces in state legislatures) and the increasing, high-profile coverage of
lesbian and gay families (including the New Jersey adoption settlement and
the Texas foster-parent incident) provoked an escalation of attacks on the ability of lesbians and gay men to adopt children and serve as foster parents. Legislation proposing statewide bans on adoption and/or foster parenting were
introduced between 1995 and 1997 in Oklahoma, Missouri, South Carolina,
Tennessee, and Washington. None passed. In 1998 and 1999, however, on the
heels of the nationwide publicity accorded the settlement of the New Jersey
litigation which required equal treatment of gay adoption applicants, prohibitions were proposed in Arizona, Arkansas, California, Indiana, Georgia, Missouri, Idaho, Oklahoma, Texas, and Utah. Restrictions passed in Utah and
Arkansas in 1999, and court challenges have been filed in both states.

Although the increased visibility of lesbian and gay families has engendered primarily hostile responses from state legislatures, a handful of positive
developments reflect the distinctly local character of disputes over contact between lesbians and gay men and children. For example, in 1994, the Montgomery County, Maryland, council voted to delete the portion of its 1984

antidiscrimination law that permitted employers to refuse to hire anyone who would work with children of the same sex and who advocated homosexuality and bisexuality. Most significantly, however, in 1998, a New Hampshire state legislator introduced a bill to repeal the state's ban on lesbian and gay adoption and foster parenting. With a Democratic governor and a legislature that in 1997 had enacted a statewide ban on discrimination based on sexual orientation in employment, housing, and public accommodations, New Hampshire looked like a different place from the one in which the 1986 ban could be enacted with one legislator arguing that lesbians and gay men wanted to "raise their own meat" to sexually molest. The repeal bill passed in 1999. Upon signing the bill into law, Governor Jeanne Shaheen commented that foster and adoptive families would now be selected based on fitness, "without making prejudicial assumptions."

Although child-rearing by openly gay men and women has become increasingly common, and although young gay men and lesbians have an increasing number of positive images and role models that allow them to affirm their sexual orientation, large numbers of adults still do not come out as gay or lesbian until after they have married and had children within heterosexual marriages. Their life stories look strikingly like those of their counterparts in the 1970s, and as in earlier decades, their fate will be determined more than anything else by the state in which they live and the judge who hears their case.

Measured by media coverage alone, the most important dispute about lesbian and gay parenting in the 1990s was the custody battle between Sharon Bottoms and her mother, Kay Bottoms, who challenged Sharon's right to continue raising her two-year-old son, Tyler. Sharon was divorced from Tyler's father when Tyler was one and received custody by consent. Even after he learned of Sharon's lesbianism, Tyler's father, who had little to do with the boy, believed that Sharon should continue to raise him. Sharon had relied on her mother for assistance in raising Tyler, but told her mother she was concerned about the time he spent in her mother's home because her mother's longtime live-in boyfriend had sexually molested Sharon as a child and as a teenager. Upon hearing that Sharon planned to curtail Tyler's visits to her home, Kay Bottoms filed for custody, accusing Sharon of unfitness because she was living with her partner, April Wade.

For longtime advocates on behalf of lesbian and gay parents, there was nothing unusual about Sharon's case; disputes over custody between lesbian mothers and their own mothers had been litigated and reported since the early 1970s. After losing custody at an initial hearing, and with no funds to hire a private attorney, Sharon received assistance from the ACLU in Virginia and was willing to discuss her case publicly. Perhaps because of the increased visibility of lesbians and gay men raising children, and because a dispute between a lesbian mother and her own mother appeared dramatic and extraordinary, media across the country covered the case. The 1993 *Time* magazine cover story "Gay Parents: Under Fire and on the Rise" used the Bottoms case as a jumping-off point to discuss the nationwide status of gay and lesbian parenting.

Sharon lost at trial, but won in the Virginia Court of Appeals, in a decision that credited the years of research on the well-being of children living with lesbian mothers.[59] The victory was short-lived, however, as the Virginia Supreme Court in 1995 reinstated the trial court's ruling, which included a prohibition on Sharon's visitation with Tyler in the presence of April.[60] In the opinion of advocates for gay and lesbian parenting, this loss was tempered only slightly by the editorials in major newspapers around the country that supported Sharon's right to raise her son.

The continuing danger to lesbian and gay parents in some parts of the country was reinforced by a series of state supreme court decisions in 1998 and 1999 from Indiana, Missouri, North Carolina, Alabama, and Mississippi. Each affirmed either a change in custody or a severe restriction on visitation rights based upon the parent's homosexuality.

In one of the Alabama cases, custody was transferred from a mother who had raised her daughter with her partner for six years to a father who had remarried, in spite of the opinion of the child's therapist recommending that custody remain with the mother. The court explicitly condemned the mother for establishing "a two-parent home environment where their homosexual relationship is openly practiced and presented to the child as the social and moral equivalent of a heterosexual marriage." The court cited the state's criminal sodomy statute, its DOMA, and a statute requiring that sex education in schools emphasize that "homosexuality is not a lifestyle acceptable to the general public and that homosexual conduct is a criminal offense under the laws of the state." Then the court concluded that the mother was exposing her daughter "to a lifestyle that is neither legal in this state, nor moral in the eyes of most of its citizens." Although an expert testified concerning the many studies supporting the positive mental health of children raised by lesbian mothers, the court adopted the position that "the degree of harm to children from the homosexual conduct of a parent is uncertain . . . and the range of potential harm is enormous."[61]

To be sure, there have been positive court decisions during the 1990s. A 1998 opinion from the highest appeals court in Maryland overturned a trial judge's order that a gay father's partner be prohibited from being present during the father's visitation with his children, citing similar decisions from California, Illinois, Oregon, Pennsylvania, and Washington.[62] Nonetheless, evaluation of disputes between gay and straight parents in the nineties demonstrates that neither the increased visibility of lesbian and gay families, nor the mental health research on the well-being of children raised by lesbian and gay parents, nor the successes in the areas of adoption and foster parenting have decreased the risks to a lesbian mother or gay father battling a heterosexual former spouse over custody or visitation. It is as true in the nineties as it was in the seventies that the results of such a dispute depend largely on where the case goes to court.

CONCLUSION

For a moment in the mid-1970s, it looked as though the struggle for lesbian and gay rights, including the right to raise children, might evolve organically from the civil rights gains, the reemergence of feminism, and the sexual revolution of the previous ten years. The backlash that began in 1977, however, irrevocably altered that course. The story of the last thirty years is the story of advances followed by repercussions. The present assault on lesbian and gay parenting, exemplified by an increasing number of states considering bans on adoption or foster parenting, is taking place as unprecedented numbers of gay men and lesbians are choosing to raise children. Child-rearing by lesbians and gay men has drawn opposition from the religious right and from secular groups espousing "family values" ideology that glorifies heterosexual marriage and blames all social ills on marital dissolution (or nonformation) and the absence of fathers in the lives of children. On the other hand, such child-rearing has garnered the support of the principal mainstream organizations committed to positive outcomes for children—the American Psychological Association, the National Association of Social Workers, and the Child Welfare League of America.

The state-by-state nature of family law has always produced a checkered legal and political climate for lesbian and gay parents. This remains as true today as it was in the 1970s. Then, as now, states in the South are more likely than other states to severely limit the parental rights of lesbians and gay men. Regional generalizations, however, should not be overstated. For example, a recent proposal to ban lesbian and gay foster parenting and adoption in South Carolina failed, and that state has appellate case law going back to 1987 prohibiting courts from presuming harm to a child from living in the custody of a lesbian mother. Indeed, there are fifty-one separate legislative battlefields, each requiring its own strategy, and hundreds of appellate judges and thousands of trial judges, all of whom must be educated. While ground is being and will be lost in some states, lesbians and gay men are raising children in increasing numbers, even in states without friendly legal climates, and there is no evidence that this trend is letting up. To the Alabama mother who lost custody of her daughter last year, it is no consolation that lesbian moms in California or Massachusetts do not face such judicial hostility. But gay and lesbian couples in Vermont or New Jersey or the District of Columbia who take for granted not only their custody rights but their ability to jointly adopt children should not be complacent. The struggle for recognition, acceptance, and appreciation of all forms of families, including those in which lesbians and gay men raise children, is far from over.

CHAPTER 16

FAMILY VALUES: FROM THE WHITE HOUSE CONFERENCE ON FAMILIES TO THE FAMILY PROTECTION ACT

THOMAS J. BURROWS

THE YEARS 1977–80 MARKED A CRITICAL POINT, IDE-ologically and chronologically, in the tensions between lesbian/gay civil rights activists and the New Right. Following the conservative Republican administrations of the Nixon/Ford years, the presidency of Jimmy Carter brought renewed national attention to family and other social-policy concerns. Carter included promises in his 1976 presidential campaign to investigate and implement policies to help the American family. The White House Conference on Families organized by his administration served as a focal point for the gay and lesbian community's growing concern about families as well as the New Right's efforts to impose conservative "pro-family" values on the nation. These efforts included the introduction of the Family Protection Act (FPA). The National Gay Task Force and other gay rights organizations began to work in coalition with other social justice movements, and family and youth issues became a significant part of the national lesbian and gay community's agenda during this period. The demands of the National March on Washington for Lesbian and Gay Rights, held on October 14, 1979, included an end to discrimination in lesbian and gay child custody and protection of gay and lesbian youth. In a direct counterpoint, the Moral Majority–sponsored march on Washington during the weekend of April 28–30, 1980, focused on lifestyle and family issues and was called the Washington for Jesus march.

FAMILIES, GAYS, AND THE CARTER PRESIDENCY

The presidential campaign of Jimmy Carter involved active and visible participation of lesbians and gay men. In the early days of the Carter administration, the Dade County, Florida, commissioners brought increased national attention to the gay and lesbian civil rights movement by passing a sexual orientation nondiscrimination ordinance in January 1977. This ordinance became a major rallying point for the antigay and New Right forces and was loudly attacked by Anita Bryant, the spokesperson for the Florida orange growers. Bryant formed the Save Our Children organization and traveled the United States attacking gay people and calling for the public to vote against rights for gay men and lesbians. Rallies across the country on both sides of the issue focused on the Dade County ordinance and thrust the issue of gay rights into the national debate. The antidiscrimination ordinance was repealed as a result of a public referendum in June 1977.

During this period of heightened national awareness of the issue of gay rights, members of President Carter's staff met with representatives of gay and lesbian organizations. Fourteen gay leaders met with Carter administration aides at the White House on March 26, 1977, to educate the Carter administration about the concerns of the lesbian and gay community and to lobby for an end to discrimination against homosexuals. This was the first time that gay and lesbian leaders had a meeting at the White House. Participants at this meeting included Presidential Assistant for Public Liaison Midge Costanza and the coexecutive directors of NGTF, Bruce Voeller and Jean O'Leary. The group also included Charlotte Spitzer, of Parents of Gays of LA, who shared with the president's aides the hardships experienced by parents and their gay children as a result of discrimination and the needs of families with gay children. O'Leary stated that the group was "highly optimistic that the meeting would soon lead to complete fulfillment of President Carter's pledge to end all forms of federal discrimination on the basis of sexual orientation."[1]

The New York Times in its reporting of the meeting reminded its readers that Carter had earlier expressed concern for preserving the traditional values of the American family and had urged federal workers living out of wedlock with a member of the opposite sex to get married. The White House meeting was loudly denounced by Anita Bryant. She stated, "Behind the high-sounding appeal against discrimination in jobs and housing—which is not a problem to the closet homosexual—they are really asking to be blessed in their abnormal lifestyle by the Office of the President of the United States." And, she added, "What gays really want is a right to propose to our children that there is an acceptable alternate way of life."[2] This was a rallying cry of Bryant's Save Our Children organization.

During President Carter's Father's Day interview in 1977, he was asked how he regarded homosexuality in relation to the family. "I don't see homosexuality as a threat to the family," he said. "What has caused the highly publicized confrontations on homosexuality is the desire of homosexuals for the rest of society to approve and to add its acceptance of homosexuality as a normal sexual relationship. I don't feel that it's a normal interrelationship. But at the same time, I don't feel that society, through its laws, ought to abuse or harass the homosexual." When asked if he thought homosexuals should be able to adopt children or teach school, the president replied: "That's something I'd rather not answer. I don't see the need to change the laws to permit homosexuals to marry. I know that there are homosexuals who teach and the children don't suffer. But this is a subject I don't particularly want to involve myself in. I've got enough problems without taking on another."[3] However, Carter would see this subject continue to be a problem for his administration and to be a particular concern in the White House Conference on Families.

Marilyn Haft, Carter's associate director of the White House Office of Public Liaison and one of the participants at the spring 1977 meeting with gay leaders at the White House, clarified Carter's views at a joint meeting of Washington, D.C.'s Gertrude Stein Democratic Club and the Capitol Hill Chapter of NOW. Haft stated that President Carter separated his personal beliefs about whether gay people were "normal or not" from his support for gay civil rights.[4]

During this period a growing number of New Right organizations were organized while others expanded their reach, and the leaders of these organizations created a network that became known as the Pro-Family Coalition. Among the main targets of the New Right were gay men and lesbians. In one of his fund-raising mailings, Jerry Falwell, the founder of the Moral Majority, asked contributors to join him in declaring "war on homosexuality." He continued: "Hundreds of thousands of men and women in America today flagrantly boast their sin and march in public view. We Americans are indeed sick if we allow this sin against God to be 'normalized' and go uncontrolled. Homosexuality is unnatural and is Satan's diabolical attack on the family and God's order in Creation. And the children of America will be the targets."[5] Some of the other members of the New Right network were Christian Voice; the March for Jesus; the Praise the Lord Club (PTL), headed by Jim Bakker; Phyllis Schlafly's Eagle Forum; Jerry Falwell's Religious Roundtable; and the Library Court, organized by Connaught "Connie" Marshner.

During this same period, NGTF leadership was in transition. Jean

O'Leary resigned as the coexecutive director in December 1978, and Bruce Voeller resigned in January 1979. Charles Brydon was chosen as one of the new codirectors in March 1979, and Lucia Valeska was chosen in June 1979. In the midst of the growing New Right hostility to gay men and lesbians and congressional legislation such as the FPA, which included specific provisions regarding gay men and lesbians, NGTF had two new directors with significantly different political philosophies. Valeska's experience working with the feminist and pro-choice communities expanded and strengthened NGTF's coalition efforts, not only in support of gay and lesbian issues but also feminist and pro-choice concerns. These efforts were countered by the position held by Brydon and many longtime members that NGTF should limit its focus to the fight for gay rights and not involve itself in other social justice and feminist issues.

Amidst the background of controversy over Carter's position on gay and lesbian civil rights were his difficulties in fulfilling his campaign promises of helping the American family and convening a White House conference on families. In a speech made in August 1976, during his campaign for president, Jimmy Carter promised that he would restore respect for the family system, which he said had been degraded and weakened in the United States. He announced that Joseph Califano would serve as a "special adviser" on how federal programs could aid and support the American family.[6] "We're going to reverse the trend . . . that has destroyed the American family. . . . I believe we can restore human values, respect for one another, intimacy, love, respect for the law, patriotism, good education, strong churches, a good relationship among our people and our government." In October 1976, in another campaign speech, Carter told the National Conference of Catholic Charities of his plans to convene a White House conference on the family. He stated, "A White House conference can be a first step in focusing federal policies that help families, not hinder them, and can also begin a long-overdue dialogue between government and private agencies that work with families."[7]

Califano, who was Carter's special assistant for family issues, was named Carter's Secretary of Health, Education, and Welfare (HEW). HEW was given the responsibility for organizing and conducting the conference on families and had originally scheduled it for December 1979. In June 1978, the conference was postponed from the original date until 1981. The early planning of the conference was delayed because of personnel fights based in part on the appointment of conference chairmen who did not appear to meet the concerns of some participating groups, particularly Catholics. There was particular objection to the appointment of Patsy Fleming as the executive secretary. Fleming was black and a divorced mother of three teenage sons. Some suggested that having a divorced person as the head of the families conference would be detrimental to the purposes of the conference.

Disputes over the purposes of the conference and the difficult substantive issues had to be addressed. Controversial issues included abortion and the desire of homosexual groups to participate in all facets of the conference.[8] President Carter had originally defined *family* as the traditional nuclear family. However, early in the conference planning the definition was broadened to include "diverse family forms." This included not only nuclear families but extended families, single-parent families, community families, ethnic families, and lesbian and gay families.[9] The original name, the White Conference on the Family, was changed in early 1979 to the White House Conference on Families (WHCF).

COALITION FOR THE WHITE HOUSE CONFERENCE ON FAMILIES

To represent and support the network of moderate and liberal organizations involved in the planning and activities of the conference, the Coalition for the White House Conference on Families was organized. The Coalition, representing nearly fifty diverse moderate and liberal organizations from the American Red Cross to Catholic Charities, voted early on to include NGTF in its membership. NGTF's commitment to and active involvement in the Coalition resulted in scores of organizations getting a better understanding of gay and lesbian families as well as developing a cooperative working relationship with NGTF. The Coalition membership included American Home Economics Association, Zero Population Growth, Planned Parenthood, National Association of Social Workers, National Education Association, National Organization of Women, Urban League, National Military Wives Association, American Red Cross, Future Homemakers of America, and the National Council of State Committees for Children and Youth. The official name of the Coalition for the White House Conference on Families was changed to the Coalition for Families in January 1981.

NGTF coexecutive director Lucia Valeska and I, as her special assistant, participated in virtually every planning and organizing meeting of the Coalition. We served on various committees and did a great deal of behind-the-scenes work at the three regional conferences. Together with other gay and lesbian members of the Coalition, we debated, studied, wrote proposals, circulated petitions, drew up minority reports, and devised amendments to resolutions. In the formal workshops at the regional conferences many of the chairpersons had worked with the Coalition and with NGTF and were familiar enough with particular individuals to know when they were present in a room and, consequently, when to call the vote on particular resolutions. Coalition volunteers, including NGTF representatives, had observer status at the conference and could enter the workshops and were able to let the chairpersons know when all Coalition members were present to vote.

NGTF had attempted to become an official member of the forty-member National Advisory Committee to the WHCF. When the Carter administration was seeking recommendations for appointments to the National Advisory Committee, the Coalition for Families proposed NGTF and lobbied for its inclusion. The administration declined to admit NGTF to the official body. The Advisory Committee for the White House Conference on Families was organized in July 1979. Jim Guy Tucker of Arkansas became chairman; John Carr, former coordinator of urban issues for the United States Catholic Conference, became executive director.[10] Deputy chairmen included Lieutenant Governor Mario Cuomo of New York, Detroit city councilwoman Maryann Mahaffey, social work professor Guadalupe Gibson, Coretta Scott King, and JCPenney chair Donald Seibert. The forty-member National Advisory Committee included former House member Patsy Mink, NOW president Eleanor Smeal, and Jesse Jackson.[11] Carr was a devout Catholic and the National Advisory Committee also included a Catholic bishop, a Catholic Charities director, Lutheran pastor Richard John Neuhaus, a high-ranking Mormon official, a representative of the Church of the Brethren, and the head of the Christian Life Commission of the Southern Baptist Convention.[12]

The Coalition for Families passed a resolution asking the National Advisory Committee to spell out for state conference organizers the groups that should be included under "diverse family forms" and to include gay families. NGTF also proposed that a statement be included in the instructions sent to each state conference specifically barring discrimination based on sexual orientation in delegate selection. The Coalition met before the first meeting of the National Advisory Committee, and NGTF urged the Coalition to vote on a recommendation that gays specifically be included as a "diverse" family form and be listed in outreach programs. This was passed by the Coalition and was the only official recommendation made to the Advisory Committee. The Advisory Committee chair, Jim Guy Tucker, forestalled the motion by announcing a "nondiscrimination" clause in delegate selection. The conference rules would not mention gay or any other "diverse" family unit but stated that state conferences could not discriminate against potential delegates on the basis of sexual orientation.[13]

In preparation for the national conference, NGTF had urged local and state gay and lesbian activists and their supporters to become involved in state and local conferences to introduce gay-supportive resolutions and to elect gay and lesbian delegates. NGTF staff and board members helped coordinate gay and lesbian participation and built coalitions with feminist and pro-choice groups to elect not only gay and lesbian delegates but also feminist and pro-choice delegates who supported NGTF positions. At one point, Lucia

Valeska was invited to participate in a planning meeting for the WHCF state coordinators. She was scheduled to present a workshop on new lifestyles in an effort to bring the concerns of gay families across to the state coordinators. At the last minute this workshop was canceled because of "scheduling conflicts."[14]

REGIONAL HEARINGS

The National Advisory Committee held seven regional hearings throughout the country in 1979 to identify the issues and problems to be addressed at the WHCF. The issues addressed at these hearings ranged across a whole field of potential pressures on the family, including abortion, drug abuse, domestic violence, gay rights, poverty, and the family life of the elderly.[15] At the regional hearings held in Washington, D.C., on November 30 and December 1, 1979, gay advocates urged a broadening of the definition of "the family" to include stable long-term gay relationships. Six gay rights defenders out of four hundred people testified at the hearings. Speakers included Melvin Boozer of the Gay Activists Alliance; Clint Hockenberry of the Gay Law Students Association; Frank Kameny and Carolyn Handy for the National Gay Task Force; Billy Jones of the National Coalition of Black Gays; and Mayo Lee representing the National Committee for Sexual Civil Liberties. Clint Hockenberry testified regarding gay marriage and argued that the "the right of homosexuals to marry is dictated" by the Fourteenth Amendment to the U.S. Constitution. Hockenberry and others argued that "gay people were being legally excluded from the legal and economic benefits of marriage." Other speakers did not directly argue for gay marriage but did urge that benefits afforded married couples be extended to committed same-sex couples. The NGTF statement presented by Carolyn Handy attacked the inability or unwillingness of many state government agencies to help conventional families cope with gay and lesbian youth.[16]

NGTF and local activist participation in the regional hearings increased gay visibility and consciousness of gay and lesbian family issues. As a result of the efforts of NGTF, the diverse groups involved with the conference were made aware of gay families, increasing the likelihood that their concerns would be included in any further discussions. One NGTF member commented, "If Middle America can get it through their heads that homosexuals can form families, then we have accomplished a great deal by participating in the conference."[17]

Many activists involved in the hearings and the delegate selection stages of the conference were frustrated by the apathy of the gay community. Mel Boozer was quoted as saying, "I don't think people appreciate how polarized the family issue has become. The 'family' is to the eighties what 'law and order' was to the Nixon era." Clint Hockenberry remarked, "Gay people by and large don't look at each other as families." Tax laws, legal rulings, credit and employment policies, housing, child custody, health care, insurance, and mental health rules are all affected by how society defines "family," and all are used to discriminate against gays.[18]

STATE CONFERENCES

The state conferences became battlegrounds, with professional counselors, teachers, and social workers on one side and antiabortion, antifeminist conservatives on the other. At the Virginia conference, the Pro-Family Coalition elected twenty-two of the twenty-four representatives.[19] District of Columbia mayor Marion Barry appointed to the D.C. planning committee gay leaders, including Mel Boozer, Clint Hockenberry, Gene Baker, and Billy Jones. Unfortunately, the apathy of the gay community and the New Right's declaration that delegate selection to the WHCF was a priority resulted in an antigay, antifeminist, and antiabortion slate of delegates for the District. Barry later did appoint Mel Boozer and gay rights supporter Ngina Lythcott as D.C. delegates to the Baltimore Regional Conference. In Oklahoma, the Pro-Family Coalition captured all eight elected delegates. In South Dakota, the moderates prevailed, getting three out of four elected delegates. New York State held five regional conferences with feminists and ethnic minorities winning a preponderance of the twenty-four delegates selected to represent New York City. They included Mary Bighorse, American Indian; Goldie Chu, Chinese-American; Noreen Connell, former president of NYC NOW; Rhonda Copelon, the attorney who won the federal district court case that struck down the congressional amendment prohibiting medicaid financing for abortion; Marcella Maxwell, chair of the NYC Commission on Women; and Josephine Williams, of the Sisterhood of Black Single Mothers.[20] Ilene Margolin, who was the executive director of the New York State Council on Children and Families, coordinated New York's role in the WHCF. Margolin later proved effective in the regional conferences as a chair of various issue workshops.

On the opposing side, the National Pro-Family Coalition on the White House Conference on the Family opposed ratification of the proposed equal rights amendment, legalized abortions, feminism in all forms, and access for teenagers to contraception or sex education in the schools. This coalition consisted of 150 organizations including the Moral Majority, the National Christian Action Coalition, Family America, FLAG (Family, Life, America, God), and Phyllis Schlafly's Eagle Forum. The basic dispute between the "pro-family" movement and the government was whether *family* should be defined.[21] Other pro-family issues at the WHCF ranged from the content of school textbooks and classroom prayer to feminism, homosexuality, "permissiveness," and big government.[22] All of these issues were addressed in major provisions of the Family Protection Act.

The WHCF fight stemmed, in part, from the supposed feminist domination of the 1977 National Women's Conference and their foes' counter-rally under pro-family colors. As part of the International Women's Year, a National Women's Conference was held in Houston in November 1977. As with the WHCF, delegates were elected in state conferences and appointed by a national committee. Bella Abzug was the chairperson of the conference and featured participants included feminists Betty Friedan and Eleanor Smeal.

At the convention, feminists and pro-family women squared off over the ERA, abortion rights, and gay and lesbian rights. Final recommendations included a resolution calling for an end to any sort of discrimination against lesbians, including judicial prejudice in child-custody disputes. As a result, the New Right directly linked the feminist agenda with lesbian and gay rights. Beverly LaHaye, head of Concerned Woman for America, observed, "The lesbians flooded into that conference and attached themselves to the feminist movement, and never again were the feminists able to shake the lesbians from their agenda."[23]

Following the Women's Conference, NGTF coexecutive director Jean O'Leary was appointed by President Carter to the National Advisory Committee on Women. Her involvement with the Women's Conference and the Advisory Committee led to a strong friendship with Eleanor Smeal. This friendship proved helpful when Smeal strongly advocated for NGTF involvement in the WHCF and the Coalition for Families.

The pro-family coalition was kept informed of the activities related to the WHCF by the *Family Protection Report* newsletter edited by Connaught "Connie" Marshner. This newsletter monitored the impact of government policies on family life and helped members of the pro-family network stay in touch with each other. Marshner used the newsletter to alert members to the WHCF delegate process and to urge pro-family forces to get as many elected delegates as possible. This included churches busing in large delegations to state conferences to elect pro-family delegates. The delegate selection process was established early in the planning of the conference. There were 2,000 delegates with 1,669 chosen from fifty states and seven territories by population. Thirty percent of the delegates were to be elected and 30 percent appointed by the governor. The state steering committees were to determine how the next 35 percent were to be chosen. The remaining 5 percent were at-large delegates appointed by the National Advisory Committee. Approximately 250 of the 1,500 delegates who attended the three regional conferences were from conservative Christian backgrounds. Connie Marshner herself was appointed an at-large delegate.

The conservative participants at the state conferences followed a prepared "script" provided by the Pro-Family Coalition. The conservative forces sought to limit the definition of *family* to people related by blood, adoption, or marriage, and to establish the basic unit of husband, wife, and children as the norm to be adhered to when possible. The main concern of the New Right was to make sure that unmarried partners, unwed mothers and their offspring, and most importantly homosexual relationships were not recognized as legitimate.[24]

At their state conferences, thirteen states made recommendations on how *family* should be defined. West Virginia proposed, "A family consists of a person or group of persons who are related by blood, marriage, adoption, or legal custody." Arkansas, Oklahoma, Washington, and Iowa recommended, "Government should not redefine the legal term of *family* to include homosexual marriage." California, the District of Columbia, and Maryland proposed legal recognition of nontraditional family forms.[25]

NATIONAL CONFERENCES

Baltimore, June 5–8, 1980

The Coalition for the White House Conference on Families, made up of moderate to liberal organizations, including the National Gay Task Force, had expected a tough fight in Baltimore. The approximately seven hundred delegates at Baltimore had been selected at nineteen state conferences. The elected delegates were balanced by appointed representatives. The close proximity of the conference site to Washington, D.C., made it possible for many staff and volunteers of national organizations, both liberal and conservative, to attend as observers and to assist delegates in preparing for the issue sessions and the votes. As I was quoted to have said at the time, "We were prepared for the worst."[26]

The majority of the delegates and public opinion at the time felt that the most pressing family problem was the economy. However, leading up to the regional conference, bitter disputes arose at state conferences between conservative forces who favored defining *family* as persons related by blood, marriage, or adoption and who opposed abortion and the proposed federal Equal Rights Amendment, and the more loosely affiliated and ideologically mixed groups considered to be liberal. The Pro-Family Coalition claimed 20 percent of the delegates. A memorandum was prepared and provided to these delegates with instructions on how to tie the pro-family goals into any recommendation raised in any workshop. As in the state conferences, members of the Pro-Family Coalition followed the script they were provided to assure that the New Right agenda was included in every workshop and every recommendation. One of their top priorities was to get the conference to adopt a definition of *family* covering only the traditional nuclear family of husband, wife, and children.[27] The Pro-Family Coalition agenda also urged passage of the antigay Family Protection Act.

The Coalition for the White House Conference on Families, on the other hand, urged its members to avoid single-issue debates and to find areas of consensus.[28] To prevent the pro-family forces from dominating the conference and to prevent damaging recommendations, most importantly a narrow definition of *family,* from being passed, Coalition for Families member organizations worked closely with delegates to assure that they were briefed on the issues and made aware of the tactics of the Pro-Family Coalition. Organizational observers and volunteers also made sure that delegates were always present at workshops when votes were taken. While the delegates slept, the representatives of the member groups discussed workshop recommendations, scoped out the opposition, and prepared issue papers. These groups also attended the numerous press conferences of the Pro-Family Coalition to ensure balanced reporting.

One of the strategies of the Pro-Family Coalition was to first try to win as many delegate seats as possible and then vote in their agenda at the regional conferences. When this strategy failed, they then denounced the conference as rigged and walked out, claiming the results were illegitimate. On the second day of the Baltimore conference Connaught Marshner, at-large delegate and organizer of the Library Court, called for a walkout of the pro-family delegates. In explaining her reasoning, Marshner was quoted as saying, "Our delegates told us that in some of the workshops ideas like freedom of sexual preference were approved." She added, "This is equivalent to an endorsement of homosexuality. We wanted to be fair but only the point of view of the conference staff could be heard."[29] However, this strategy of denouncing the process and then walking out of the conference backfired on the Pro-Family Coalition.

At the start of the conference, of the 671 delegates in attendance in Baltimore, seven were openly gay and came from New Hampshire, Connecticut, Massachusetts, New York, Pennsylvania, and Washington, D.C. Activist Eric Rofes was an openly gay delegate from Massachusetts. Billy Jones, a D.C. gay activist and delegate, reported that about thirty other delegates had "come out of the closet" to him during the conference.[30] David Cunningham was one of those who did come out at the conference. David, the executive director of the Connecticut Collaboration for Children's Justice, was quoted: "For me the White House Conference was my Stonewall. . . . I wasn't at Stonewall in 1969, and I hadn't gotten involved in gay political organizations. I was just living a pretty comfortable life in Connecticut, very accepted by my family and friends. But, just like the people at Stonewall, something about the attacks at the White House Conference on Families had me say to myself, 'I am not going to put up with this!'"[31]

The presence of professional representatives from NGTF and its active and open participation in the Coalition for Families created an opportunity for closeted gay and lesbian delegates to be members of a supportive coalition without being forced to come out. While many delegates did come out of the closet during the conference, many others could not because of their jobs, their relationship to other delegates, and their positions in their hometowns. Yet they were able to communicate confidentially with NGTF staff and board members through their participation in the Coalition. Gay delegates and their supporters drafted gay-supportive statements in their workshops. These included proposals such as one drafted in the Family and Major Institutions work group that stated "community institutions . . . have a responsibility to make available a choice of public and community services which take into account individual preferences and differences in family makeup and community pluralism."

The strongest pro-gay proposal was one in which five "legal and human rights" were listed. This included support for the ERA, the right to choose abortion, and the "elimination of discrimination and encouragement of respect for differences based on sex, race, ethnic origin, creed, socioeconomic status, age, disability, diversity of family type and size, sexual preference, or biological ties."[32] However, the joining of the ERA, abortion, and gay rights in one proposal was a bone of contention for at least one of the delegates who had been appointed, in part, because of her support of gay rights. In a speech on the final morning of the conference, Ngina Lythcott, appointed by Mayor Barry of D.C. with the support of the gay and lesbian community, spoke out against passage of the resolution saying that she could not "allow the hookup of the ERA and abortion." She later did vote in support of the resolution.

Susan Bruce, a delegate from New Hampshire, spoke to the conference of her experience as an illegitimate child and a lesbian. Delegates such as David Cunningham spoke effectively to the other delegates and the media about gay and lesbian issues from their personal experience, particularly the concerns of gay and lesbian youth. Gay men and lesbians who were the heads of other major child-care agencies were further able to educate conference delegates about the issues and concerns of gay and lesbian youth and their families. One of our greatest supporters and hardest workers was Lisa Desposito of Planned Parenthood NYC, whose cousin was gay. Positive resolutions for gay and lesbian families were passed and the controversy around the Pro-Family Coalition walkout inspired other gay and lesbian delegates to come out. Some supportive proposals were defeated, but language was introduced in workshop sessions that would be repeated later. One delegate had proposed a definition of *family* as "two or more persons who share resources, responsibility for decisions, values and goals, and have commitment to one another over time."[33]

Some of the language for proposed resolutions was worked out in nightly meetings of Coalition members. It is important to note that within the Coalition for Families there was extensive discussion of the choice of the term *sexual orientation* or *sexual preference*. Feminists, including Betty Friedan, argued that the Coalition should use the term *sexual preference* in its proposals. At the time the feminist community was debating women identified women "choosing" to have sexual relations with women, and therefore the decision to use *sexual preference* was made. This language was also used at the National Women's Conference.

Fifty-seven recommendations were finally approved at the Baltimore conference including the "liberal" proposal concerning abortion, gay rights, and the proposed Equal Rights Amendment.[34] The recommendation that included nondiscrimination against gays was passed by a vote of 292 to 291. Without the long and active involvement of NGTF in the Coalition for Families, the education and coordination of delegates, and the personal relationships delegates made with gay men and lesbians, this vote would not have happened.

Economic concerns, including national health insurance and the elimination of the "marriage penalty" in the income tax, were the top issues at the Baltimore conference. However, on the front pages of national newspapers such as the *Los Angeles Times* and *The Washington Post*, "nondiscrimination against homosexuals" was in the lead paragraph of articles reporting on the White House Conference on Families.[35]

Minneapolis, June 19–21, 1980

Six hundred delegates from thirteen Middle Western and Southern states attended the Midwestern Conference on Families held in Minneapolis. The Pro-Family Coalition was much stronger at this regional conference. Half of the Minnesota delegation was antiabortion. Twenty of the twenty-six elected delegates from Illinois were in the Pro-Family Coalition. The Pro-Family Coalition had also caught on to a strategy of the Baltimore conference and claimed that work-group chairpersons were ruling their proposals out of order. Chairpersons responded that according to the rules only those subjects directly dealing with the specific topic in a workshop could be discussed.[36]

In Minneapolis, as they did in Baltimore, Pro-Family Coalition delegates again walked out to protest their claim that the conference was stacked against them. Conference delegates did defeat a proposal that called for an amendment to the Constitution, the Human Life Amendment, that would have outlawed abortion. The Minneapolis conference endorsed the ERA, but also approved a definition of families that specifically excluded homosexual relationships and denounced "secular humanism" in public institutions.[37] Two recommendations to define *family* as "two or more persons related by blood, heterosexual marriage, adoption, or extended families" were narrowly approved. But also passed was a recommendation to prohibit housing discrimination against all members of minority groups, single people, and people unrelated by blood, marriage, legal ties, or adoption.[38] Having anticipated that the Midwest conference would lean more to the right than Baltimore, the members of the Coalition for Families had been more willing to moderate their views.

The Coalition for Families included in its membership two groups who had first proposed the idea of a family conference to Jimmy Carter when he was a presidential candidate. These were the United States Catholic Conference and the National Conference of Catholic Charities. Both of these groups withdrew from the Coalition following the Minnesota conference, claiming that the Coalition had instructed delegates to oppose a number of church-supported recommendations. Coalition members and delegates always caucused on the night before the final session. At the Minneapolis conference some Coalition delegates had asked for a written guide for voting at the plenary session. Observers and delegates of some of the member organizations of the Coalition, including NGTF, Planned Parenthood, and NOW, stayed up late into the night writing up and printing a guide. This guide was distributed to Coalition delegates but was not endorsed by the Coalition. The confusion regarding the origin of this guide resulted in the two Catholic groups quitting the Coalition for Families.[39]

Minority reports were also included with the final recommendations of the entire conference and required at least fifty delegate signatures. Bill Kelley, a gay delegate from Illinois and former NGTF board member, submitted a minority report signed by fifty-six delegates. He prepared, circulated, and spoke in favor of this report, which advocated an end to sexual orientation discrimination in a comprehensive range of areas and the conferral of family benefits on any two or more persons functioning and defining themselves as a family. Kelley was pleasantly surprised at how easy it was to collect the necessary signatures, including one from a woman from Paragould, Arkansas, a rural town only a few miles from his Missouri birthplace. Kelley was also a member of Illinois State Planning Committee for his state's follow-up to the WHCF.[40]

Los Angeles, July 10–12, 1980

The Western White House Conference on Families was composed of 615 delegates from nineteen Western states and four Pacific territories. Again I represented NGTF at the conference, with the assistance of my domestic partner,

Randy Gardull. NGTF assisted in the operation of the Coalition suite and helped coordinate the efforts of not only the gay and lesbian delegates but all Coalition member organization delegates. Volunteers and staff of the Los Angeles Gay and Lesbian Community Services Center provided invaluable assistance to NGTF and the Coalition. Members of the Los Angeles community also provided housing and transportation for the NGTF representatives. Planned Parenthood Federation vice president Jane Trichter and her assistant Amy Goldstein were active supporters of NGTF positions in the Coalition for Families at all three regional conferences. Gay and lesbian representation at the Western Conference was larger than at Baltimore or Minneapolis, and there was excellent cooperation of delegates from NOW and other feminist organizations. The Coalition worked to defeat proposals that called for a prohibition against gay teachers and the "removal" of any presentations of homosexuality in the media. A proposal calling for the end of discrimination in housing based upon sexual preference was approved. And in aging-related recommendations, language pointed out the need for an awareness of the sexual differences among the aged.

Delegates at the Western regional conference included lesbian activist Roberta Bennett, who, with the support of the White House, was appointed by the National Advisory Committee, and Adele Starr, president of Parents of Gays of Los Angeles. Los Angeles mayor Tom Bradley appointed Starr as a delegate to the conference after receiving numerous endorsements for her from the gay community. She clearly remembers how eye-opening an experience it was and how she was attacked by many of the Pro-Family Coalition delegates. She noted that she was "very naive" about the conference and observed that many of the participants were experienced in these processes. In her work groups, the right-wing delegates and other special interests block-voted to assure that their particular issues would be passed. She also was disappointed that many of the supportive delegates at the conference didn't always vote. She made a three-minute speech to the delegates regarding the needs of families with gay and lesbian children.[41]

At this regional conference, there continued to be a tug-of-war between the traditional and liberal views of what constituted a family. Coalition for Families members had agreed to avoid red-flag words for the right wing and attempted to include gay and lesbian issues in ways that could not be voted down. As a result, references to the needs of "nontraditional" family forms and "extended" families were used in drafting workshop recommendations.[42] Flashpoint issues continued to be abortion, ERA, homosexuality, and family values.[43]

In another attention-getting ploy, twenty-one Pro-Family Coalition delegates from Kansas challenged the seating of that state's official delegation because they said the selection process was "undemocratic."[44] This group was called the "rump" delegation and was notable for the large sunflowers that they wore throughout the conference. Pro-Family Coalition delegates did not walk out of the Western Conference, but during the final vote session, fifty-one did walk up to the front of the conference room and tear up their ballots in protest.

The top recommendations of the Western regional conference were focused on education, housing, awareness of the disabled, media responsibility, and taxes. However, the *Los Angeles Times* reported, "The White House Conference on Families endorsed the Equal Rights Amendment, the right to government-funded abortions, and nondiscrimination against homosexuals in housing."[45]

Following the regional conference in Los Angeles, conservative and New Right groups held an alternative conference in Long Beach called America's Pro-Family Conference. Tim LaHaye, of Californians for Biblical Morality, stated, "The White House Conference on Families does not represent the more traditionalist viewpoint of the family, but instead favors the feminist and pro-homosexual viewpoints espoused by the liberal establishment."[46] LaHaye continued, "Jimmy Carter has falsely used his born-again image to hoodwink people into thinking that he is one of us." Most of the Pro-Family Conference leaders supported the Republican presidential nominee-apparent at the time, Ronald Reagan. At this same time, the Republican Platform Committee, under heavy pressure from Reagan supporters, adopted planks that opposed abortion and overturned Republican support for the ERA.[47]

THE FINAL REPORT

As discussed above, NGTF, with the backing of the Coalition for Families, had attempted to gain membership on the National Advisory Committee and the National Task Force, which was to gather the recommendations from the three regional conferences and prepare a final report to the White House. One hundred delegates were chosen to write the final report. Final recommendations included more flexible work schedules and revision of the marriage tax. The White House conference leadership tried to stress throughout the two-day National Task Force meeting that the recommendations of the three regional conferences focused on "mainstream family issues" and not on the more controversial ones.[48] A call for employment policies more responsive to working parents received the strongest support of the three regional conferences. There was strong support for the elimination of the "marriage penalty" in the tax code and for nondiscrimination for all minorities in employment and housing.

The final report was issued on October 22, 1980. The top five recommendations were family-oriented employment policies, efforts to control alcohol and drug abuse, tax code changes including elimination of the "marriage tax," tax policies to encourage home care, and assistance to families with disabled family members. The subjects that generated the most controversy and media coverage—the ERA, abortion, and sex education—received secondary priority. President Carter stated, "We are already working to implement the recommendations."[49] However, the chair of the conference conceded that the future of Federal self-evaluation was "subject to the results of the election." Carter had also proposed future White House conferences on children and on the aging. Shortly thereafter, Reagan, with the support of the Pro-Family Coalition, won the election for president.

The 250-page final report, *Listening to America's Families, Action for the 80's,* only lightly touched upon gay rights, abortion, and the ERA. Billy Jones, delegate from the District of Columbia, in his assessment of the report stated, "What was important to me is that the recommendations that came out of the WHCF didn't exclude us."[50] The Baltimore conference had barely passed a resolution calling for the end of antigay discrimination. Minority reports supporting gay and lesbian nondiscrimination did receive more than fifty signatures at both the Minneapolis and Los Angeles conferences and were included in the final report. The importance of the conference for gays was not in the resolutions passed but in the contacts with people and organizations that had never dealt with openly gay and lesbian people before.

THE FAMILY PROTECTION ACT

Even before the regional conferences had convened, conservatives were looking for other ways to move their agenda forward. In December 1979, the Family Protection Act (FPA) was introduced in the U.S. Senate by Senator Paul Laxalt (R-NV). Senator Laxalt served as the national campaign chairman for Ronald Reagan in both 1976 and 1980. Cosponsors of the act were Senator Jake Garn (R-UT); Senator Thad Cochran (R-MS), and Senator Jesse Helms (R-NC). At the same time, the FPA was introduced in the House of Representatives by Representative Steven Syms (R-ID).

The Family Protection Act was a major project of the conservative movement. Connie Marshner, chair of the Library Court and director of the Family Policy Division of the Free Congress Foundation, worked closely with Senator Laxalt in drafting the bill. The FPA of 1979, according to Stephen Endean, then executive director of Gay Rights National Lobby, was "officially the brainchild of the Moral Majority. However, the Free Congress Foundation, particularly Connie Marshner, may have done the real work of putting it together."[51] Richard Viguerie in his book *The New Right: We're Ready to Lead* stated, "The act will be a benchmark for years to come for the kind of sensible actions the federal government should be taking to preserve traditional family values in

America. It reasserts the rights of parents in rearing and educating their children. It seeks to protect the rights of private schools. It gives the parents a greater role in textbook review. It denies government favoritism for homosexuality."[52] Paul Weyrich, a leading pro-family conservative activist, included the experience of the White House Conference on Families as one of the reasons why the Family Protection Act was needed. Weyrich quoted New Right leader Joann Gasper in charging that the White House Conference on Families was an event organized "to drum up support for more federal spending, more federal regulations, and more political power for 'alternative lifestyle' groups like homosexuals and women's libbers."[53]

This comprehensive bill was seen as a "Christmas tree for the New Right." The original FPA of 1979 had included three provisions specifically directed against the rights of gay people. The first provision would have barred the Legal Services Corporation from granting money to "provide legal assistance to any proceeding or litigation which seeks to adjudicate the issue of gay rights." This proposal had been contained in prior House bills sponsored by Larry McDonald (D-GA). A second provision incorporated another McDonald proposal and would have amended the Civil Rights Act of 1964 so that the term "unlawful employment practice" could not be applied "with respect to an individual who is a homosexual or proclaims homosexual tendencies." This section would further have forbidden any "agency, bureau, commission, or other instrumentality of the Government of the United States . . . to enforce nondiscrimination with respect to individuals who are homosexuals or who proclaim homosexual tendencies." This provision's proposed restrictions on the Legal Services Corporation also included the other two red-flag issues of the New Right. The FPA would have prohibited the provision of legal services to the poor in matters involving the ERA and abortion.

In a supporting memorandum supplied by the sponsors of the act, the reasons listed for this provision included: "the right of normal citizens to be able to choose their associates does exist," "the public has a distaste for self-proclaimed homosexuals," "parents are desirous of protecting their children from association with known homosexuals," and "individuals filling sensitive positions in government need to be screened very carefully on any number of qualifications and characteristics. Homosexuality is a weakness—like alcoholism—which might interfere with an individual's ability to do the job effectively."

The third antigay section was new to the Congress. Section 507 of the FPA would have required that "no Federal funds may be made available under any provision of Federal law to any public or private individual, group, foundation, commission, corporation, association, or other entity which presents homosexuality, male or female, as an acceptable alternative lifestyle or suggests that it can be an acceptable lifestyle." This section was a direct response to the provision of federal CETA funds to organizations such as the Los Angeles Gay Community Services Center.

In the memorandum in support of the FPA, proponents cited a number of factors showing the need for a provision denying federal funds to homosexual organizations. This included: "Homosexuality is a crime in many states. Since at least 1974 the federal government has been allowing funds to aid the underprivileged to be used to support numerous 'gay community centers.' It is impossible for such a 'gay community center' to avoid proselytizing. The question of the legitimacy of homosexuality is one that the people of our nation must deal with. Allowing federal funds—the taxes of hardworking citizens—to be used to give legitimacy to what was traditionally considered a perversion is offensive to many Christian and Jewish citizens. Continuation of such practice by the Federal government is an unjust and immoral use of public money and abuse of public trust."

Other sections of the FPA attacked public education. This included a provision that declared that "no funds authorized under any applicable program or any provision of Federal law shall be made to any State or local educational agency which does not provide for parental review of textbooks prior to their use in public classrooms." Another provision barred the use of federal funds for "any program which produces or promotes courses of instruction or curriculum seeking to inculcate values or modes of behavior which contradicts the demonstrated beliefs and values of the community." A third provision of the FPA would have barred federal funds for "purchase or preparation of any educational materials . . . if such materials would tend to denigrate, diminish, or deny the role difference between the sexes as it has been historically understood in the United States."[54] These issues had also formed the outline for the efforts of the Pro-Family Coalition at the White House Conference on Families. The first version of the FPA died at the end of the Ninty-sixth Congress.

Ronald Reagan, with the strong support of the New Right organizations, was elected President in 1980. Homosexuality was not the only target of the New Right. Reagan's secretary of health and human services (HHS) not only opposed abortion, which the Human Life Statute would have made a capital crime, but sex education as well. The Human Life Statute, introduced in 1981, sought to declare the fertilized egg equal to a person under the Fourteenth Amendment. The 1980 Congress also considered legislation to require capital punishment for adultery. The New Right–sponsored Family Protection Act (FPA) not only contained the family and social policy agenda of the New Right but also contained most of the tax and budget policies proposed by Reagan's budget director, David Stockman.

A revised Family Protection Act was introduced into the Ninety-seventh Congress in June 1981. The Senate bill was sponsored by Roger Jepsen (R-IA), and a companion bill was introduced in the House of Representatives by Albert Lee Smith (R-AL). The revised act did not include the statement that discrimination against declared homosexuals would never be considered an "unlawful employment practice." The sponsor of the bill, Senator Jepsen, said that this provision was removed because it was "an example of government intrusions and it's not our intent to keep people out of any kind of employment." He went on to point out that the supporters of the revised FPA "in no way condone" homosexuality and believed that "problems with homosexuality" were addressed in two other provisions. Senator Laxalt, who had introduced the first version of the FPA in 1979, did not reintroduce the bill. An article in *Ms.* magazine reported that "Capitol insiders say that the FPA is too much for even Reagan to stomach and that Laxalt, after his heady days as Reagan's campaign manager, does not want to propose major legislation that lacks the President's full support."[55]

Of the two antigay provisions that remained, one stated that "no entity receiving funds" from the Legal Services Corporation "shall . . . provide legal assistance with respect to any proceeding or litigation which seeks to adjudicate the issue of homosexual rights." The second provision stated that "no federal funds may be made available under any provision of federal law to any public or private individual, group, foundation, commission, corporation, association, or other entity for the purpose of advocating, promoting, or suggesting homosexuality, male or female, as a life style."

Neither the original nor the revised Family Protection Act was ever passed by Congress. However, in both the Ninety-sixth and Ninety-seventh Congresses, as well as at the White House Conference on Families, it served as the outline of demands and pressure points for New Right leaders and their organizations to build their membership and create public awareness of their conservative vision for America.

ANTI-NEW RIGHT COALITIONS

Leaders of the National Gay Task Force and the Gay Rights National Lobby called the Family Protection Act both repressive and unconstitutional.[56] The National Gay Task Force and Gay Rights National Lobby joined and worked together with coalition groups including Interchange, the Coalition for Families, and People for the American Way to oppose this and other New Right–sponsored legislation. NGTF leadership was active in the initial formation and the continued activities of these and other coalition groups that were formed during the WHCF and in response to the growing New Right.

Interchange was established in 1978 to challenge and inform on the growing strength of the New Right. Its purpose was "to know, to understand, to reverse the momentum of the New Right." Interchange functioned as a clearinghouse and referral service on the New Right. Interchange published the *Interchange Report,* with articles reporting on the Family Protection Act, the White House Conference on Families, and the activities of the Coalition for Families. Interchange membership included representatives from education, labor, human services, church, women's, consumer, and civil liberties groups. Its over 150 organizations included Metropolitan Community Church, Gay Rights National Lobby, National Education Association, National Women's Political Caucus, National Organization for Women, National Association of Social Workers, United States Students Association, and National Abortion Rights Action League.

People for the American Way was established in 1980 to celebrate and protect Americans' First Amendment rights and individual freedoms. The most well known of its founders was Norman Lear, but many of the organizations and individuals active in the Coalition for Families contributed to the development of People for the American Way. Its initial concerns, at the time of the growing New Right influence in American politics, were the freedom of belief and the separation of church and state. One of the provisions of the Family Protection Act would have denied federal education money to states that prohibited prayer in public buildings. The FPA would also have required parental review of school textbooks. People for the American Way continues to educate and organize around First Amendment issues.

NGTF was involved in other coalition activities focused on political issues of the time. Partially because of its location in New York City, NGTF was invited to participate in seminars conducted by the Institute for the Humanities at New York University. During the late seventies and early eighties the Institute conducted at least two seminars that addressed issues of concern to NGTF and of gay and lesbian families. One was the Institute's "Homosexuality" seminar. Lucia Valeska, the coexecutive director of NGTF, and Charlotte Bunch of the NGTF board, were members of this seminar. Another of the Institute's seminars, "The New Right: Scenarios and Responses," was attended regularly by, at first, Lucia Valeska, and then by me. This seminar was cochaired by Barbara Ehrenreich and Alan Wolfe. The participants included leading journalists from the mass media as well as specialized publications and academics from various disciplines such as Frances Fox Piven, Allen Hunter, Frank Donner, Frances Fitzgerald, and Ellen Willis. The seminar focused on what might earlier have been thought to be "nonpolitical" issues: the family, sexuality, and religion. The inclusion and active participation of NGTF representatives informed the other participants at every session of the linkages between the struggle for lesbian and gay rights and the struggle for all progressive issues. This knowledge was included in articles, books, and other writings of the participants of these seminars.

CONCLUSION

The active and open participation of gay men and lesbians in Jimmy Carter's presidential campaign in 1976 led to unprecedented access to the White House and presidential staff. The involvement of gay men and lesbians throughout the country in all stages of Carter's White House Conference on Families assured that gay men and lesbians were included in all aspects of this conference. NGTF, through its newsletter *It's Time* and appearances by staff and board members, urged gay men and lesbians across the country to testify and be elected as delegates at the state and national conferences. NGTF participated in national coalition efforts to see that a broad variety of families were included in the discussions about American families and that gay men and lesbians were active participants in all aspects of the conference. The contacts and connections made with the Carter White House and, to some extent, the office of New York lieutenant governor Mario Cuomo, provided powerful behind-the-scene connections to assure that our voices were heard. As a result, NGTF was able to get the White House Conference on Families to listen to the needs and aspirations of gay and lesbian families at conferences held across the country and to include these concerns in the final report to the president.

The coalitions and connections that NGTF made at the White House Conference on Families were strengthened and extended after the conference through continued cooperation with various national groups fighting the New Right. These connections proved to be important in preventing the passage of the New Right agenda as outlined in the Family Protection Act. These connections were also needed to preserve whatever gains had been made during the Carter years as the nation began a long period of Republican administrations and conservative Congresses.

PART V

THE POLITICS OF HEALTH

CHAPTER 17

ADVOCATING FOR LESBIAN
HEALTH IN THE CLINTON YEARS

MARJ PLUMB

LESBIAN HEALTH ORGANIZING IN THE 1990S WAS, IN many ways, not unlike previous decades of lesbian activism; much of the organizing was infused with the feminist principles of self-help and peer education, collectivism and collaboration, and the overarching pursuit of parity. But it also reflected new strategies developed mostly by gay and bisexual men in the HIV movement. It's also true that some of the same feminist principles were evident in the work of gay and bisexual men in responding to HIV. The activist group AIDS Coalition to Unleash Power (ACT UP) looked eerily similar to the feminist Women Take Back the Night, and Shanti Project and Project Open Hand operated on similar principles as the Black Women's Health Project or any number of feminist women's health projects. All of these organizations had at their core behavior-marginalized communities doing for themselves what mainstream society wouldn't. And given the stigmatization of those affected by the HIV epidemic (gay and bisexual men, IV drug users, etc.) a kind of "homegrown" health industry was probably the only effective way to reach and care for individuals with HIV.

But exploring what impact feminism had on the HIV/AIDS movement wouldn't explain all its successes nor its tremendous impact on the lesbian health movement. While the homophobia evident in the early stages of the HIV epidemic is clearly documented, white gay men infected with the disease had, often prior to their diagnosis as closeted gay men, access to levels of power unprecedented among marginalized health-care movements. It was not uncommon in the early days of the epidemic, for instance, for directors of research institutes, senior staff at federal health agencies, and scientists at pharmaceutical companies to be on a first-name basis with gay and bisexual male leaders in the HIV/AIDS movement. These relationships were not the panacea anyone had hoped for (homophobia still ruled the epidemic), but they obviously had tremendous impact as evidenced in such changes as the Food and Drug Administration's (FDA) speeding up their drug-approval policies and federal funding for the epidemic that has outstripped any other disease to date. While these successes cannot be claimed totally by those who had access to the halls of power (activism was certainly a force to be reckoned with), those successes would not have occurred without the internal power brokers. The simple fact is, up until the 1990s, no marginalized community—not even the predominately white feminist women's health movement—could claim as much access.

It wasn't until the late 1980s, when female legislators in Congress called for a General Accounting Office audit of research funded by the National Institutes of Health (NIH), that the astounding lack of gender parity in research was first revealed. The disparity was never more strikingly clear than in the federally funded research project on heart disease (the single greatest killer of women) that included fifty-five thousand men and not one single woman. Soon after the GAO report was published, in what could be considered the beginning of the second wave of the women's health movement, women gained access to the health-care bureaucracy. In the early 1990s Congress passed the Women's Health Equity Act, which, in effect, funded Offices of Women's Health (OWH) throughout agencies of the federal health department.

The convergence of these two movements, the AIDS movement and the second women's health movement, created the birth (or perhaps the void) for the lesbian health movement of the 1990s. By the end of the 1980s, after the first wave of AIDS relief hit (the discovery of the drug AZT and the belief that it would slow the devastation of the disease), many lesbian and bisexual women began taking stock of their activism and found that women's health issues had been vastly ignored by the co-gender lesbian and gay movement (and certainly within the HIV movement) and that while gay men had achieved access to power, it had not been shared with lesbians. Similarly, lesbians realized that the OWHs, built on the idea that gender parity in health care and health research is an important concept, had no such awareness of the importance of parity for lesbian and bisexual women's health. The very beginnings of the lesbian health movement, reflected in the struggles within and among the lesbians-and-breast-cancer movement and the lesbian HIV movement, were forged with conflicts about race and class, and definitional disagreements about lesbianism and inclusion. The access that was gained, however, led to remarkable advances, including a report by the esteemed Institute of Medicine (IOM) on the importance and need for research on lesbian health.

Lesbian health can be defined as the way in which specific health issues such as cancer, HIV, or alcohol use impact differently on women who identify as lesbian than on women who identify as heterosexual. Because *lesbian* is a social-political term that has many different meanings to many people, in its broadest sense it can include lesbians, bisexual women, and all women who have sex with women (WSW), whether they identify or not. While there are no known biological differences between women of different sexual identities or behaviors, health advocates and providers believe that current research and clinical experience suggests that lesbians and bisexual women may have some significant differences in rates of disease, access to health care, and disease outcomes as compared to heterosexual women.[1]

Research suggests that populations of lesbians and bisexual women have higher rates of cigarette, alcohol, and other drug use than heterosexual women.[2] Some clinicians and researchers have posited that lesbians and bisexual women might also have higher rates of diseases associated with those behaviors, such as lung cancer, breast cancer, heart disease. Lack of access to sensitive care, lack of insurance, and lack of routine usage of traditional women's family-planning services can all be significant barriers for this population to overcome to receive care.[3] Barriers to care for other populations of women (e.g., ethnic minorities, poor women, etc.) can delay women from seeking care, even when symptomatic, until a disease is often at such a late stage that treatment is more costly and less successful. This might be true for lesbians and bisexual women as well.

The contention that there are disparities in health care and health status between lesbian/bisexual women and heterosexual women is actually not all that new; what's new is the movement to organize specifically on lesbian health issues and to take available evidence of disparity to federal health authorities.

THE LESBIAN HEALTH MOVEMENT: FROM SELF-HELP TO ADVOCACY

Lesbian health activism began in the early 1970s as a part of the women's self-help movement. Lesbians working in women's health clinics developed programs to address the specific health needs of lesbians, which were frequently overlooked in mainstream health care.[4] During this decade, women's health clinics, often at the urging and organizing of the lesbian staff in the clinic, would hold "lesbian health nights," which were clinic times that were preserved and promoted as lesbian-only space. Advertised in local feminist and lesbian newspapers, these evenings provided the only place a lesbian could be assured she would receive nonjudgmental, nonhomophobic gynecological care.

During the 1970s there were clinics for gay men (such as Fenway in Boston and Howard Brown in Chicago), but they were primarily sexually transmitted disease (STD) clinics that had somewhat of a "revolving door" ethic. As with women's health clinics, health education was obviously within the framework of the services provided, but STD treatment, which was quick and efficient, didn't really require a tremendous peer support or education. In 1978 gay men and lesbians had an opportunity to begin seeing whether these two health movements could come together when the newly formed National Lesbian and Gay Health Association (NLGHA) held the first annual National Lesbian and Gay Health Conference. The conference was intended as a place for gay and lesbian health organizers, educators, and health-care providers from throughout the country to come together to share information and health-education strategies. The lesbian health and gay male health movements had grown independently throughout the seventies, so the advent of a joint conference was viewed as, perhaps, a place where co-gender organizing could take place.

But the coexistence was short-lived: the path of each movement was abruptly altered in the early 1980s by the AIDS epidemic. It was obvious early on that the epidemic's toll would be especially great on the gay and bisexual male communities. Many in the lesbian community joined in the fight against HIV/AIDS as volunteers, activists, donors, and caregivers. This was important to the success in the early stages of fighting the epidemic as the very self-help philosophies of the women's and lesbian health movements—health education, prevention, and even medical care—were so quickly utilized in this new health crisis. And with good reason. Certainly the public health establishment was not prepared to talk about anal sex, an early suspected mode of transmission, or homosexuality in general, and was therefore slow to respond to the epidemic. But before long gay and bisexual men, acting out of an assumption of privilege and access as men (especially the white men), confronted the public health establishment and mainstream medicine to force them to deal with the growing HIV epidemic. To all the ways the women's health movement focused on individual change through self-help and peer-service provision—and those strategies provided the bedrock for the initial response to the HIV epidemic—the HIV/AIDS movement added a key strategy for health-care organizing: if the health-care institution won't help, change it!

After a decade of work in the HIV movement, the lesbian community began reviving its own health movement, increasingly as a community aware of its own vulnerability to HIV, and most visibly in response to a very female disease—breast cancer. The movement's reemergence was really a natural growth of experiences from previous movements. It combined the self-help aspects of the women's health movement in the seventies and the "fight the establishment" strategy of the HIV movement in the eighties to create a lesbian health movement of the nineties ready to continue encouraging and supporting grass-roots health organizing while at the same time, for really the first time, demanding a piece of the public health pie.

The first reason for a "call to arms" for lesbian and bisexual women was that gay men in the HIV/AIDS movement were sexist. Some believed the time and energy lesbians devoted to HIV/AIDS activism would never be returned by gay and bisexual men, was a waste of a decade, and was responsible for derailing the lesbian health movement. Others believed that as lesbian and bisexual women HIV activists began working more closely with lesbian health activists, their experience would instill the lesbian health movement with the appreciation of class and race politics that had been missing in much of the 1970s lesbian health movement. The lesbian and bisexual women who were infected with the HIV virus were, for the most part, of color and/or poor. They were women not traditionally found in gay and lesbian community centers, let alone lesbian cancer projects. One thing was clear, however, as the 1990s approached: the knowledge, skills, and access that lesbian health activists learned in the HIV/AIDS movement would play a pivotal role in advancing the lesbian health movement.

LESBIANS AND HIV:
IS THIS REALLY A LESBIAN HEALTH ISSUE?

Given that most people thought women with HIV had been infected by a male partner or through IV drug use, it literally never crossed their minds that these women could identify as lesbian. Yet throughout the 1980s, it was obvious to lesbian and bisexual women working in the HIV movement that something was amiss: there seemed to be a disproportionate number of lesbians among the women with HIV. Those who tried to make this point visible, however, were often considered hostile to the HIV movement, traitors to gay men, or were scoffed at with disbelief. One man even remarked that lesbians had "virus envy." The few reporters who covered lesbians and HIV, and lesbian HIV activism, tended to reveal a hint of ridicule as well. One of the problems with getting the issue of lesbians and HIV taken seriously was the ongoing polarity of dismissing or overemphasizing female-to-female sexual transmission.

Women who have sex with other women, whether they call themselves lesbian or bisexual or nothing at all, have been infected with the HIV virus since the beginning of the epidemic. This is incontrovertible. These infections have occurred mostly through sharing needles and having unprotected sex with men. But due to the lack of understanding among public health epidemiologists about lesbianism (i.e., that some lesbians have sex with men and that some lesbians shoot drugs), they dismissed lesbian HIV issues because of the dual beliefs that (1) female-to-female transmission was the only lesbian HIV issue and (2) was irrelevant, as it was, at best, infrequent. This complete dismissal often created an overemphasis on barrier-based safer sex for lesbians (i.e., dental dams) by many lesbian health advocates, which, in effect, further marginalized the issue of lesbians and HIV.

Most published research focused on female-to-female transmission and suggested that it was "possible" yet "unlikely" that a woman could sexually transmit the virus to another woman. Even though in the mid-to-late eighties four letters were published in peer-reviewed journals that documented four separate cases of female-to-female transmission—so health educators knew that transmission could indeed happen—the research continued to emphasize how unlikely it was rather than exploring why it happens when it does happen—far more important information for HIV prevention. One of the most misinterpreted pieces of research was published in 1990 by Dr. Susan Chu, a researcher at the Centers for Disease Control (CDC), who had reviewed CDC-reported AIDS cases and found that all infections of WSW were probably due to either sex with men or sharing needles. Other researchers found flaws in Dr. Chu's analysis, especially because of the large percentage of missing data in the CDC database on sexuality, yet the research was still considered the most conclusive evidence that female-to-female transmission doesn't happen, or at least not often. In an amazing turn of events, however, this research fueled the lesbian HIV movement for well over a decade. In the report, Dr. Chu stated that only a woman who had had sex with another woman since 1978 would be classified as lesbian. This definition, referred to by the lesbian and bisexual women's communities as the "CDC's definition of *lesbian*," was actually just a research definition and was only used this one time by Dr. Chu, yet it ignited outrage (and often hysterical laughter) throughout the country.

In the early nineties, mostly at the urging of lesbian members of the activist group ACT UP, a few AIDS agencies added activities geared toward lesbians (safer-sex brochures, flyers, and events). At Gay Men's Health Crisis in New York City, the oldest and largest not-for-profit AIDS organization in the country, the Lesbian AIDS Project (LAP) was founded in 1991. Through the directorship of activist and author Amber Hollibaugh, LAP grew to provide services for women most often marginalized by the lesbian community and all but invisible to the gay male community: lesbians of color, poor lesbians, institutionalized lesbians, and lesbian drug users. The materials developed by LAP and other lesbian HIV projects began to take a broader view of the epidemic and include prevention messages to lesbians about sex with men and how to clean needles rather than just safer-sex messages for female-to-female sexual activity. The integration of LAP into GMHC's services was always problematic, however, as GMHC claimed they wanted to serve lesbians but were concerned about the project's inclusion of drug-using and incarcerated women.

In April 1993 the lesbians and bisexual women of ACT UP took the issue of lesbians and HIV to Washington, D.C., during that year's march on Washington for gay, lesbian, and bisexual equal rights. The Women's National Network of ACT UP organized a demonstration at the Department of Health and Human Services (DHHS) and a meeting with Secretary Shalala to draw attention to HIV-infected WSW. The purpose of the meeting was largely to address a primary ACT UP concern, that "the voices of lesbians with AIDS/HIV are rarely heard." Videotape from the meeting with the secretary shows a roomful of lesbians with HIV telling the stories of their lives, including living with HIV, in poignant and stark detail. The secretary, visibly moved, expressed her desire to do something about their concerns.

Yet, it wasn't until April 1995—two years later—after a nationwide letter-writing campaign by AIDS and gay and lesbian organizations, that the CDC finally held a meeting to address HIV-related issues for lesbians. The meeting was organized to bring together experts in epidemiology, behavioral science, lesbian health issues, lesbian substance-abuse issues, and women's health. In contrast to the meeting with the secretary, only one lesbian with HIV was represented at the meeting, although activist organizers of the meeting called for greater representation. The meeting culminated with a list of recommendations, including changing surveillance methods to better capture possible female-to-female exposure to HIV, a written report to be published through official CDC channels about the variety of ways that lesbians are infected with HIV, funding for research to investigate the behaviors and sexual practices of HIV-infected WSW, and research to investigate how lesbianism is a cofactor in risks associated with sex with men and sharing needles.

Two studies have finally been funded. One study, funded by the National Institutes of Drug Abuse, is a three-year ethnographic study of WSW IV-drug users (IDU) in New York City and Seattle. This study will examine the high rates of HIV infection among WSW IDUs. The CDC has also recently funded a retrospective female-to-female transmission study that will be carried out in San Francisco, New York City, Baltimore, and Washington, D.C. Through the use of more advanced laboratory tests, the researchers will test women who think they transmitted the virus sexually and compare their viral strain with the women they think they infected. And while there have been no changes in the primary surveillance practices of the CDC with regards to female-to-female transmission, the No Identified Risk units of the Surveillance Branch are routinely trained to investigate their cases with an eye toward this risk factor.

Significant concern remains, however, about the CDC's official silence on this issue. Even though staff at the CDC have continued to publish research and papers on lesbians and HIV (the most recent an excellent overview by Megan Kennedy et al.[5]), there has still been no official report from the CDC about lesbians and HIV. Without a report, distributed through official channels to state and local health departments, community prevention-planning groups, and researchers, regarding what is already known about lesbian HIV risks, especially lesbian IDU needle-sharing risk, this population will continue to be neglected in prevention and treatment initiatives.

The CDC's continued silence could probably be challenged more effectively if a serious and steady advocacy effort were once again waged. But the lesbian HIV movement lacks organizational stability. Lesbian HIV projects have always existed, if at all, within larger HIV programs or agencies. With recent well-publicized declines in funding for AIDS services, marginal issues such as lesbians and HIV receive fewer and fewer resources, certainly none to spare to continue fighting the CDC. Additionally, the fact that most women with HIV are women of color and poor, and traditionally not taken seriously in policy arenas, makes a sustained fight for recognition tremendously difficult.

LESBIANS AND BREAST CANCER: THE *OTHER* EPIDEMIC?

AIDS in the United States was often characterized by women as a male disease, therefore creating a need for help on a women's disease. Women's cancer issues received a boost in 1990 when women legislators pushed Congress to enact the Breast and Cervical Cancer Mortality Prevention Act (Public Law 101-354). This legislation authorized the CDC, through a program called the National Breast and Cervical Cancer Early Detection Program (NBCCEDP), to provide state health agencies with funds to increase breast and cervical cancer screening among women. Underserved women were the target population, particularly women who were elderly, had low incomes, were underinsured or uninsured, or were members of racial/ethnic minority groups. Lesbians were not at that time identified as a target population.

While this legislation was being enacted, lesbian cancer projects had begun springing up throughout the country. The catalyst for the development of many of these projects was the diagnosis or death of a local lesbian, famous or not, to breast cancer, and the ensuing organizing drive by widowed lovers and friends. For some, it just felt important to begin working on behalf of lesbians again. The issue of breast cancer ended up being a perfect organizing tool for lesbians—it truly was for women only. And after a decade of working with gay men in the AIDS movement, many lesbians were looking for a movement that didn't require negotiating through all the sexism.

In contrast to the lesbian HIV movement, success would be fast and relatively easy. At the 1992 NLGHF Conference in Los Angeles, Dr. Susan Haynes of the National Cancer Institute (NCI) presented research on lesbians and cancer, and the lesbian cancer movement exploded. Having been encouraged by lesbian cancer activists, Dr. Haynes reviewed past research on lesbians and compared the data to the NCI suspected risks for breast cancer. Her presentation included the hypothesis that, given data on lesbian nulliparity (never having children), high alcohol use, and obesity, she could conclude that lesbians might have a two to three times greater risk of breast cancer. Because of Dr. Haynes's position with the NCI, her use of actual data (even if the research is not considered representative of all lesbians), and the dearth of information about lesbian health in general, the gay and straight media reporting on her presentation fell all over themselves to report that, like gay men, lesbians had a health epidemic too—breast cancer.

In fact, one mainstream reporter conjectured that Dr. Haynes's presentation could mean that lesbians had a one in three chance of developing breast cancer. *The Advocate* (a national gay and lesbian magazine) actually called breast cancer "The Other Epidemic." Even after Dr. Haynes's presentation was understood more broadly by lesbian health advocates as being preliminary and the reporter's one-in-three estimate as misleading, *The Advocate* continued to report on lesbians and breast cancer as an epidemic in 1998 with a cover story that announced how many lesbians could be expected to get breast cancer that year. Most of the women in the lesbian health movement knew this to be media hyperbole at its best. It was probably accepted as fact, however, by thousands of lesbians throughout the country, thus sending another wave of panic through a community that had been through it once before.

This presentation contributed to an ever-growing rift between the lesbian HIV movement and the lesbian cancer movement along color and class lines. Dr. Haynes's presentation used several pieces of research on lesbians, all of which was mostly on white, middle-class, middle-age lesbians.

Behind the scenes, lesbian cancer advocates took advantage of the increasing attention to lesbian cancer issues while trying not to be irresponsible and compound the misinformation about the issue. The increased attention did open doors as representatives from national gay and lesbian advocacy groups, health clinics that provided services to lesbians, and lesbian cancer projects met with program staff from the NBCCEDP in January 1994 to discuss ways they could include lesbians as a target population. Specific recommendations were made during this meeting, including selecting a lesbian health speaker to present at their national conferences, identifying a lesbian resource person in every state program, and sharing educational materials that address the unique health needs of lesbians with the state projects. After a tremendous amount of work by supporters inside the CDC and advocates such as the executive director of the Mautner Project for Lesbians with Cancer, Susan Hester, by March 1995 the CDC published a paper that provided background on the development of lesbians as a target population for the NBCCEDP and discussed strategies for reaching this population.[6]

The CDC also announced the availability of special project funds for four state health departments to work with four local city-based YWCAs to develop model strategies for outreach to lesbians. This three-year project was the first time the federal health department had a specific funded initiative on a lesbian health issue. The YWCAs were chosen to house these projects because of their integral role in the NBCCEDP programs and their long-standing history of pro-lesbian consciousness. It is expected that research from the four projects will be used in other states to initiate lesbian outreach projects.

The culmination of ongoing advocacy efforts by staff at the Mautner Project (most notably Susan Hester and Bev Baker, the second executive director of Mautner) was the selection by the CDC in September 1997 of the Mautner Project as one of ten nationwide partners. Of these ten organizations in this grant cycle, the Mautner Project is the only lesbian organization. Other grantees include the National Education Association, Baylor College of Medicine, the National Asian Women's Health Organization, and the National Caucus and Center on Black Aged, Inc.

As an example of what federal funding means, the first year's grant of $235,000 doubled the Mautner Project's budget. "Removing the Barriers" is the Mautner Project's CDC-funded program, which is designed to increase the ability of health care providers to adequately serve lesbians and to reduce the heterosexism of health care institutions. The project will include the development of a provider training curriculum that focuses on lesbians and the specific barriers lesbians face with regard to access to clinical breast exams, Pap tests, and mammograms. The curriculum will be pilot-tested for two years at a variety of sites around the country.

The significance of this grant to the Mautner Project and to the entire lesbian health movement can not be overstated. No one really knows if lesbians are more likely to get breast cancer than heterosexuals. What we do know is that lesbians deserve sensitive, nonjudgmental health care services, and because of federal funding, gotten through intensive and directed advocacy, projects such as Removing the Barriers will make them more likely to get it.

DEPARTMENT OF HEALTH AND HUMAN SERVICES: LET THE SUN SHINE IN

While lesbian HIV activism, and the emerging lesbian cancer movement, were independently winding their way through lesbian communities and into the halls of power, the modern lesbian health advocacy movement officially arrived in Washington, D.C., shortly after the 1992 election of President Clinton. After twelve years of Republican administrations, optimism from gay and lesbian health activists could be felt throughout the country as all signs pointed to increased support for gay and lesbian health issues (including HIV/AIDS) within the federal health establishment. The optimism wasn't completely naive. Even before the president began appointing new administrators in the various agencies, there was evidence of greater interest in working on gay and lesbian health issues.

In January 1993, as executive director of the Lyon-Martin Women's Health Services, I and San Francisco Board of Supervisors member Barbara Kaufman met with acting DHHS secretary Dr. Audrey Manley to discuss women's health issues (including lesbian health). Dr. Manley and others present in the meeting had all been high-ranking health department officials in the Bush administration, which was not known for its open-door policies toward gay issues. Yet the meeting was filled with support and confidence in the department's ability to begin working on gay and lesbian health issues. As one attendee stated, "the blinds had been raised" with the election of a Democratic president. When Clinton appointed Donna Shalala as the head of DHHS, advocates began feeling even more hopeful.

Organizing on lesbian health issues had begun immediately after the elections. The National Gay and Lesbian Task Force (NGLTF) had been asked by Susan Hester of the Mautner Project for Lesbians with Cancer and Amelie Zurn of Lesbian Services at Whitman-Walker Clinic to help organize a national meeting of lesbian health activists during the gay and lesbian march on Washington that was to be held in April 1993. The purpose of the meeting would be to begin formulating a national lesbian health policy agenda that could be presented to DHHS. NGLTF arranged for a series of conference calls with individuals from around the country, and using the Public Health Service Women's Health Report as a guide (which I had received during my meeting with Dr. Manley), approximately twenty lesbian health activists formulated a lesbian health agenda. When the secretary's appointment was announced, the Human Rights Campaign (HRC) quickly set up a meeting between her and members of the gay and lesbian health leadership for April 23, 1993. Because of the organizing that had been going on for months, the lesbian health agenda was already developed and ready for the meeting.

The meeting with Shalala included presentations on people of color, youth, substance abuse and mental health, aging, sexually transmitted diseases, lesbian and gay health clinics, health care reform, antigay violence, HIV/AIDS, and lesbian health. Susan Hester, Kate O'Hanlan of the Gay and Lesbian Medical Association (GLMA), Joyce Hunter of NLGHF, and I presented the "1993 Lesbian Health Agenda" to the secretary. The document detailed health issues for lesbians and recommendations for the inclusion of lesbians in DHHS-funded services and research. It was laid out in an agency-by-agency format so that implementation of the recommendations could easily be accomplished. In handing the report to the secretary, I stated, "We've done everything but assign staff!"

The secretary was incredibly responsive to the entire meeting, appointing Patsy Fleming, then special assistant to the secretary, the gay and lesbian liaison to the department. This was a first for DHHS and the lesbian/gay community; it provided an unprecedented level of access outside of the HIV movement.

Immediately following this meeting, lesbian health advocates began planning for their next advocacy activity: the first Lesbian Health Roundtable, which was held February 27–March 1, 1994, at George Washington University in Washington, D.C. The event was sponsored by NGLTF, the National Center for Lesbian Rights (NCLR), HRC, and NLGHF. An organizing committee of eight individuals represented national organizations, community-based agencies, and public health departments. Over seventy women were invited from across the country to participate. The purpose of the roundtable was to broaden the participation of lesbian health activists in the further development of the lesbian health policy agenda. It was also an opportunity to expand the skills of lesbian health activists, and to move the agenda, by setting up meetings with high-ranking officials at several of the agencies within DHHS and individual members of Congress.

On the first day of the roundtable it was obvious that lesbian health organizing would look different from organizing within mainstream health. This day began with presentations and discussions about how class and race differences impact not just the development and delivery of health programs, education, outreach, and research, but health advocacy organizing itself. I began the meeting by reading a statement from the organizing committee that addressed some of the conflicts that had occurred in organizing the event. The statement began: "Often, conflicts that are inherent to the organizing of a meeting like this remain hidden and then explode. Instead, the organizing committee would like to make some of our conflicts and shortcomings visible. This is a new agreement about organizing—that we don't get so panicked by guilt or ignorance that we try to ignore where we messed up or stop organizing altogether."

While 50 percent of the organizing committee were women of color and over 50 percent of the participants in the meeting were women of color (a re-markable feat for a lesbian health event), Asian/Pacific Islander (API) and Native American women were notably absent. Efforts had been made at the last minute and API women did attend the roundtable, but the lack of inclusiveness from the beginning of the organizing needed to be addressed so that trust could be reestablished for the remainder of the work.

The second issue raised by the organizing committee was its decision not to specifically include bisexual women's health issues. While several bisexual women were invited to the roundtable, and bisexual women's health issues were included in the agenda, the event itself was billed as a "lesbian health roundtable." The organizing committee acknowledged that this was a conflict for them. Some members of the organizing committee felt that it would be appropriate to change the title to be more inclusive, yet others felt that it would be tokenistic and not truly inclusive if the committee wasn't truly prepared to fully include bisexual women's health issues in all the work at the roundtable. The view to exclude bisexuality from the title of the roundtable was supported by many of the lesbians from inside the health bureaucracy. Their fear was that lesbian issues wouldn't really be addressed by the administration and that "confusing" the issue would only make it worse. In the end, it had been decided to exclude the word *bisexual* in the title but to make sure that bisexual women were invited to and visible at the roundtable.

After the statement was read, activists Carmen Vazquez and Amber Hollibaugh presented an overview about race, class, and sexuality to further frame the issues that have often divided lesbian health organizing. The agenda for the meeting was then put on hold as the participants spent the next few hours discussing the implications of the two areas of conflict on the organizing of the meeting and the movement. And, as always, opinion was divided about whether this time was well spent. Some individuals (mostly white) felt that the time spent listening to the pain that was caused by the lack of inclusive organizing was not a productive use of the meeting and sat impatiently through it. Others (some white women, as well as significant leadership from African-American women, who were well represented) felt that it was the right thing to do—individuals and communities had been hurt, they deserved time to share their grievances. The value to the roundtable of having the discussion up front and with honest dialogue was evident throughout the rest of the roundtable as women then got down to the business at hand.

Day two of the roundtable was spent discussing and identifying lesbian health issues, developing recommendations on policy directions for DHHS, and discussing and identifying legislation that would improve the quality and availability of health services for lesbians. Using the policy agenda previously developed, participants added new recommendations and expanded many of the original ones. One of the most strained presentations was that of Nan

Hunter, who was at that time working at DHHS on health care reform. Many women at the roundtable felt distrustful of the administration for not including sexual orientation in the nondiscrimination language in the bill, for not including same-gender relationships in the definition of *family*, and for not including Indian Health Services and the prison health system within the plan. Here was a high-ranking official of the DHHS, an out lesbian, at a historic lesbian health event, but in some ways at odds with many of those present.

On the third day, roundtable participants were dispatched to an array of prearranged meetings. Patsy Fleming had assisted in setting up the meetings with DHHS and in making sure that senior staff at the various agencies were available to meet with the roundtable participants. DHHS oversees 250 programs, ranging from AIDS research, cancer treatment, and alcohol and drug abuse prevention to immunizations, Medicare, Medicaid, and Social Security. To infiltrate such a large bureaucracy effectively, meetings were targeted to agencies that funded programs that could have an immediate impact on lesbian health: NIH, the Health Resources and Services Administration (HRSA), Substance Abuse and Mental Health Services Administration (SAMHSA), Agency for Health Care Policy and Research (AHCPR), the Office of Women's Health (OWH) at DHHS, the Office of Personnel Administration, and the National AIDS Policy Office (AIDS czar). Almost all of the meetings were attended by the highest-ranking personnel at those agencies including, often, the director of the agency, as well as the director of women's health within the agency, and many other key staff.

Dr. Harold Varmus, director of the NIH, and Dr. Vivian Pinn, director of the NIH Office of Research on Women's Health (ORWH), met with roundtable participants and immediately began implementing several of the recommendations that had been made. Dr. Pinn delayed issuing ORWH's supplemental proposal, which had already been printed, until she had a chance to ask the advisory committee to add lesbians to the list of target populations. This proposal was aimed at currently funded researchers to give them more money so that they could include target underresearched communities (women of color, poor women). Dr. Pinn's efforts to include lesbians in that was significant as it meant that currently funded NIH researchers could receive additional grant monies for adding lesbians to their projects. She also offered to have Dr. Kate O'Hanlan, who had been a speaker at the workshop "Recruitment and Retention of Women in Clinical Research," write up her talk so that Dr. Pinn could ensure its inclusion in the report from the workshop.

Also arranged for that day were over forty meetings with key congressional representatives and/or their staff. This was, in effect, the first lesbian health lobby day in history! Of utmost concern to the roundtable participants was the Clinton health reform plan. Participants asked members of Congress to ensure that sexual orientation was included in the nondiscrimination clause, that confidentiality protections be strengthened, and that the incarcerated and undocumented be included in coverage.

One of the most important discoveries for the lesbian health advocacy movement during the roundtable was recognizing the importance and openness of the various Offices of Women's Health. Because these offices had only recently been established, they were not staffed by career bureaucrats. The staff were fresh and already taking on gender inequity. Once we made the case for a lesbian health agenda, they began to take on some of the work.

Immediately after the lesbian health roundtable the D.C.-based lesbian health advocates (then formally known as the Lesbian Health Advocacy Network or LHAN) requested to meet with the DHHS Coordinating Committee on Women's Health (CCWH). This coordinating committee included the women's health coordinators from the major health agencies: the Centers for Disease Control and Prevention (CDC), FDA, NIH, SAMHSA, AHCPR, and HRSA. The CCWH also included women's health staff from other parts of the DHHS, including the assistant secretary of health's office, Dr. Phil Lee, and the Office of AIDS Policy.

The committee had not met, due to internal staffing problems, for over a year. The LHAN asked for and received permission to have the first meeting of the CCWH, scheduled for January 25, 1995, focus on lesbian health issues. The nervousness of the office that coordinates this meeting was obvious; although there was an out lesbian in that office at the time of the meeting, the official agenda did not include the word *lesbian* but was titled "Agency Briefings and Discussion on Health Issues Affecting Special Populations." Whether this was due to the suspected homophobia of the office's director or was, as stated, necessary to shield the meeting from intrusive congressional eyes and oversight, we don't really know, but the meeting did help to continue to keep the lesbian health agenda on the front burner of the DHHS agencies.

Dr. Kate O'Hanlan of the Stanford University Medical Center opened the meeting with an overview of the status of lesbian health research, identifying lesbians as an underserved population of women. She pointed to the absence of research data that includes information about lesbian identity and behavior and stressed the importance of including same-gender sexual behavior in analyses of women's health research. She also presented a compilation of research that identifies homophobia as a serious health hazard for lesbians. As a LHAN participant and director of the NYC Office of Lesbian and Gay Health Concerns, I recapped the history of DHHS efforts on lesbian health to date and encouraged those present to avail themselves of the expertise available among lesbian researchers, doctors, nurses, and community activists, who could assist their agencies in addressing lesbian health issues.

Members of the LHAN further challenged DHHS to review and monitor its activities with regard to lesbian health, and to identify lesbians as a target population for research, prevention, education, and treatment services. Three agencies (CDC, SAMHSA, and NIH) that had already begun including lesbian health issues in their work were asked to present case studies.

This was an important meeting, demonstrating both access and advocacy muscle on the part of lesbian health activists. The *Washington Blade* attempted to report on the meeting after it occurred, but DHHS staff instructed LHAN members not to overemphasize the importance of the meeting for fear of right-wing reprisals. The LHAN issued the following statement to the press: "The meeting was productive and informative. We look forward to continuing the dialogue with DHHS staff and other representatives of our government to further their understandings of lesbian health issues." In reality, the participants all went back to their respective agencies boasting of the boldness of this young movement to secure the very first meeting of this coordinating committee for the topic of lesbian health.

In 1995 gay men and lesbians were once again on different sides of the same issue; the president appointed Shalala's special assistant Patsy Fleming to the AIDS-czar position. While seen as a positive move by many AIDS activists, the loss of someone in the secretary's office who had operated as a liaison to the lesbian health movement was a serious blow. Throughout the first two years of advocacy with DHHS, the lesbian health movement had relied heavily on Fleming's access to the secretary, her willingness to use the secretary's name to open doors at the various DHHS agencies, and her availability in educating lesbian health advocates as to the inner workings of the department. The advocates waited for a year for Shalala to appoint another liaison until they finally asked Elizabeth Birch, executive director of the HRC, to use her personal access to the secretary as a "chit" to request a meeting to discuss the secretary's plan for filling the vacancy Fleming left.

The meeting between the LHAN and the secretary was held on September 17, 1996. The primary objective of the meeting was to encourage the secretary to appoint another special assistant who could serve as a lesbian/gay liaison. The meeting did not begin well, however, when Shalala explained that she was reluctant to appoint a liaison as she felt that integration, not segregation, was the way to go. Undaunted by her opening statement, the LHAN members explained one by one how the successes over the past three years could not have come about without Fleming and her position. The LHAN agreed that integration was an important goal but stressed that, until lesbian health professionals, advocates, and activists had full knowledge of and access to all levels of the federal health bureaucracy, and until lesbian health issues could be openly discussed without fear of congressional opposition, a liaison was not only important but essential.

The meeting was relaxed and somewhat spirited in a way that took us all by surprise. The secretary asked questions and showed her awareness of this issue by commenting on work she knew the department was already doing. Presentations by LHAN members, in particular Rea Carey of the National Youth Advocacy Coalition on lesbian youth, Sabrina Sojourner of the Black Gay and Lesbian Leadership Forum on lesbians of color, Beverly Baker of the Mautner Project for Lesbians with Cancer, Amber Hollibaugh of the Lesbian AIDS Project, and Beverly Saunders Biddle of the National Lesbian and Gay Health Association on provider education, engaged the secretary and reinforced through many examples how Fleming's position helped to achieve various levels of access to DHHS on these issues.

The meeting included a surreal moment when the secretary's assistant came into the room to inform her that Senator Helms was on the phone needing to speak about an urgent matter. Shalala went to her office to take the call and everyone nervously laughed—not wanting to believe that he had somehow learned of this meeting and was calling to interrupt it. It was a good lesson that the paranoia we sometimes criticized the administration for having was, grudgingly, understandable. As it was, the senator was calling because of mosquito problems in his home state.

Mosquito problems apparently under control, in January 1997 the secretary announced the appointment of Dr. Marsha Martin, an African-American lesbian from New York City, as her special assistant who would, among other tasks, assist lesbian health advocates in continuing their educational work within the department. The September meeting with Shalala was historic—the first meeting solely on lesbian health with a DHHS secretary. How even more amazing that this historic meeting would result in the reinstatement of the liaison position.

LESBIAN HEALTH RESEARCH:
WE DON'T KNOW WHAT WE DON'T KNOW

Given the lack of research on lesbian health issues, it is really quite remarkable that lesbian health advocates have been so successful in convincing federal health bureaucrats of the health risks and inequities that lesbians face. After all, it wasn't until 1984, when NLGHA supported the work of two lesbian health researchers, Caitlin Ryan and Judith Bradford, that the first national lesbian health survey was conducted.

Four major challenges have historically confronted researchers who have attempted to study lesbian health: their institutions do not see lesbians as an important community to research so they could not get professional support to do research; racism within the lesbian community and within the health care community has limited the ability of researchers to include lesbians of color in research samples; researchers lack funds; and few publications are willing to publish lesbian health research once it's completed.[7]

Dr. Vickie Mayes and colleagues found that it wasn't until 1991 that studies on lesbian health began to appear regularly in medical journals (more than half of the 371 articles that discussed lesbian health research found on a Medline search between 1969 and 1995 were not published until after 1991).[8] Several prominent changes appear to have brought about such a significant increase in publishing on lesbian health issues. In particular, the HIV epidemic helped to "normalize" a research field with a large homosexual component. The congressional investigations into the serious disparities between women's and men's health research opened the door more widely to population-based health advocacy. And the greater social acceptance of lesbians and gay men since the late eighties and early nineties meant that lesbian medical providers and health researchers could be more comfortable coming out, which many did, by beginning to focus on lesbian-themed research topics. But even these studies, published and accessible via Medline, did not provide the research weight that many thought was needed to prove that lesbian health was a serious and important field of study and medical scholarship.

In 1994, Dr. Kate O'Hanlan (then president of GLMA) and Paula Ettelbrick (then public-policy director of the NCLR) led a national letter-writing campaign to convince the principal investigators of two large NIH-funded women's health studies, the Women's Health Initiative and the Harvard Nurses' Health Study, to include sexual orientation or sexual behavior questions in their surveys. A year later these advocacy efforts proved successful, and the investigators of the Women's Health Initiative, a longitudinal study of 163,000 women, agreed to include questions about sexual behavior in their study and to assist each of the forty study sites to actively recruit lesbian and bisexual participants. That same year, the investigators heading the Harvard Nurses' Health Study, the longest ongoing study of women's health in the United States, agreed to ask study participants (127,000 female nurses) about their sexual orientation. The presence of academic physicians and researchers, including out lesbians, who believed in and provided scientific—rather than activist—arguments for the inclusion of these questions proved crucial in persuading investigators to ask about sexual practice and identity.

The principal investigators of these studies were originally concerned that adding questions about sexual behavior or identity to their studies would distress heterosexual participants perhaps to the point of their not being involved in the study. Additionally, the researchers questioned the importance of using these large research projects to study this negligible population. Their reluctance has turned into acceptance, however, as researchers have reported no attrition in either study that can be attributed to the inclusion of the sexual orientation/behavior questions. The lack of attrition in either study after the inclusion of lesbian subjects and/or questions should provide ample evidence to researchers who have similar concerns. Additionally, preliminary data analysis of the Harvard Nurses' Health Study suggests significant differences in some areas between the lesbian/bisexual women and heterosexual women studied, thus proving the value of research on this population.[9]

Throughout the 1990s the field of lesbian health has been aided by the creation of projects within the lesbian community specifically designed to promote lesbian health research. Dr. Kate O'Hanlan and other lesbian leaders associated with the GLMA started the Lesbian Health Fund in 1992 to fund lesbian and bisexual women's health research. Through the work of lesbian health researcher Liza Rankow, NCLR published a Lesbian Health Bibliography in 1994 and an update in 1996 so that those interested in lesbian health research would know what was available. Caitlin Ryan and Judy Bradford started an international Lesbian Research Network in 1996, which is designed to assist and support lesbian researchers by providing access to information, mentoring, and technical assistance. And in March 1997 the *Journal of the Gay and Lesbian Medical Association* began publishing as the world's first peer-reviewed multidisciplinary journal dedicated to lesbian and gay health issues. This journal provides lesbian health researchers with a viable publishing opportunity for work that may still not be accepted by other journals.

These changes notwithstanding, the field of lesbian health will not gain respect nor have any real impact on medical training and the provision of health services without more and better research. And the ongoing problem with getting better research is the age-old problem with methodology: the gold standard methodology in mainstream research is the random or probability sample (a sample that resembles the population it was drawn from). But random samples of oppressed, stigmatized, invisible, and marginalized communities are almost impossible to achieve. No one, at this point, can draw a sample of lesbians and claim it represents every one in the United States who identifies as or acts like a lesbian. Is there any kind of research we could do then that would be considered good research?

To get this question answered, lesbian health advocates pressured Dr. Pinn to hold a methodology conference on lesbian health research. She decided, however, that to ensure that any report on lesbian health research methodology was given the most serious attention of researchers throughout the world, and not considered some political offering by the Clinton administration, that she would contract with the prestigious and independent Institute of Medicine (IOM) to develop a report.

Even after this contract was signed between the NIH (with additional support from the CDC) and the IOM, advocacy on the project did not end. This was the first time the IOM had ever included lesbian health in any report it had ever worked on. The staff, while interested and clearly competent, simply did not have access into the often closeted world of lesbian researchers and lesbian health. One of the first activities of the IOM was to select the nine-person committee who would be responsible for writing the report. Yet, the experts in lesbian health were largely unknown to the IOM. In a matter of weeks, the loose-knit lesbian health advocacy network had generated hundreds of résumés of interested lesbian and lesbian health researchers. As a result of receiving such a significant pool of interested and important individuals, and to enhance the work of the committee, the IOM started a "public liaison group" for the development of the report—a first for the IOM.

The selection of the committee, however, was not without conflict in the lesbian community. The IOM was prepared to select several individuals with expertise in lesbian health research but made it clear that they were not going to select only lesbian health researchers. Several individuals on the committee had no known relationship to lesbian health issues at all: Dr. Ann Burgess, professor, University of Pennsylvania School of Nursing; Dr. Larry Norton, chief, Breast Cancer Medicine, Memorial Sloan-Kettering Cancer Center; and Dr. Bruce McEwen, Rockefeller University. Many in the lesbian health movement were angry at what they considered a slap in the face to lesbian health researchers, yet others felt that the report's credibility in the mainstream health research field would only be guaranteed with notable and "unbiased" health researchers on the committee. That out of a committee of nine only four were lesbian health researchers meant the jockying for those four spots was intense.

Others in the lesbian health movement were furious that only researchers were allowed on the committee. The movement had been built on peer-advocacy models of care, and grassroots models of research, and it seemed significant that the community's voice would not be heard inside the committee discussions. Other professionals, lesbian health providers in particular, felt that they had carried the issue of lesbian health into the fields of medicine, often at great detriment to their own careers, and that their voice should be at the table as well.

But of most harm to the final report, and a great frustration to many in the lesbian health movement, was that only two nonwhite individuals were on the committee. If lesbian health research is scarce, to say the least, research on lesbians of color is as close to nonexistent as you could come. With the notable exception of a few researchers who have focused on lesbians of color, almost all of lesbian health research is on white women. Without equitable racial balance on the committee the issues of lesbians of color had significant disadvantages to being a part of the report. This was of such great concern that many highly placed lesbians of color, including in DHHS, threatened to attempt to stop the IOM report altogether. That the problems identified are certainly endemic to every other report of the IOM was of no consolation.

The committee met for the first time in 1997 to begin discussions and to develop their work plan. I was honored to be the sole representative from the lesbian community to be invited to present at that first meeting. It was important to me, therefore, to be sure that the members of that committee understood both the historical significance of what they were doing as well as the potential pitfalls. My greatest fear after advocating with the NIH, and then working with the IOM, to have an authoritative voice speak on lesbian health was that they would make the same mistake Dr. Chu had made at the CDC years earlier—a definition of *lesbian* that didn't fit the reality of our lives.

In 1999 the IOM finally published its report on lesbian health.[10] It included an intriguing reanalysis of the sexual behaviors study that had been published in 1994 to much fanfare.[11] This study had created tremendous harm during the first term of the Clinton administration because, for lesbians, it reported that less than 1 percent of women surveyed could be considered lesbian (women who had all of the three identified variables of same-gender sexual orientation—same gender desire, behavior, and identity). In an interesting turn of events, the IOM committee reanalyzed the data and used all the different combinations of those variables (women with one, two, or three of the variables) to identify almost 9 percent of the women surveyed as having some same-sex orientation. It's interesting to note that most of the lesbian health advocacy in this decade occurred while some believed that lesbians were only 1 percent of the female population!

The IOM report also called for more research funding to address lesbian health issues, better methodology to improve the quality of research on sexual orientation, more inclusive research, and finally, for all researchers to "routinely include questions about sexual orientation in data collection."

And now, a movement originally begun by grassroots lesbians in towns and cities across America, building health care services and providing health education for lesbians in their own communities, returns after this brief foray into the federal health bureaucracy. Armed with the IOM report, lesbians throughout the country are confronting their local health establishments (from public health departments to local medical schools) and are demanding to be a part of the research agenda.

CHAPTER 18

CONTESTED MEMBERSHIP: BLACK GAY IDENTITIES AND THE POLITICS OF AIDS

CATHY J. COHEN

ONLY FAIRLY RECENTLY HAVE SCHOLARS IN THE social sciences begun to recognize that the concept of group identity in its essentialist core is in crisis. Influenced by postmodern and deconstructive discourse, historical analyses focusing on marginal groups, and a new emphasis on identity in social movement theories, researchers are beginning to understand that the idea of group identity that many of us now employ is markedly different from the conception of a stable, static, and homogenous group previously assumed in the social sciences.[1] Just as most scholars have finally become accustomed to including in their analyses simple conceptions of identity coded in binary form (e.g., white/black; man/woman), we now face the realization that identities of difference (race, class, gender, sexuality) are themselves fragmented, contested, and of course, socially constructed.

Social constructionist theory provides the framework and the intellectual incentive to identify and examine those social, political, and economic processes that lead to the promotion of certain conceptualizations of group membership and group meaning at particular historical moments.[2] Social constructionist models can also be used to analyze internal debates over membership within marginal communities.[3] Using this approach, constructionist frameworks help us recognize and understand indigenous definitions of group membership and group meaning encapsulated under the rubric of group identity.

While previously, most of the work on the social construction of group identity came from scholars in the humanities, researchers in the social sciences, especially those of us interested in the topics of race, gender, class, and sexuality, must find ways to incorporate such insight into our analyses. Moreover, we are being challenged by a rapidly expanding understanding of group identity not only to recognize and examine the socially constructed character of group identity, but also to investigate the stratification found in groups and the implications of such fragmentation on attempts at group mobilization and political action.[4] Thus, beyond examining the ways in which dominant groups and institutions change or alter their imposed definitions of marginal groups within different historical contexts, we must also understand how marginal group members define and redefine themselves, setting their own standards for "full group membership."[5]

This article takes up the topic of indigenous constructions of group membership and its impact on the political attitudes and mobilization of marginal group members. In particular, I am interested in how the concept of "blackness," as it is defined and refined within black communities, is used to demarcate the boundaries of group membership. As a second point of examination, I want to know how these indigenous definitions of blackness influence, shape, and lend legitimation to the political attitudes and behavior of community leaders and members.

Indigenous definitions of blackness, while of course building on dominant ideas or definitions of who *is* black, employ a more expansive, but at the same time often less inclusive, understanding of black group identity. They center not merely on easily identifiable biologically rooted characteristics, but also use moralistic and character evaluations to appraise membership. Individuals employ a "calculus" of indigenous membership that can include an assessment of personal or moral worth, such as an individual's contribution to the community, adherence to community norms and values, or faithfulness to perceived, rewritten, or in some cases newly created African traditions. Thus, indigenously constructed definitions of black group identity seek to redefine and empower blackness to the outside world by policing the boundaries of what can be represented to the dominant public as "true blackness." And it is through *public policing*, where the judgments, evaluations, and condemnations of recognized leaders and institutions of black communities are communicated to their constituencies, that the full membership of certain segments of black communities are contested and challenged.

Let me be clear that examples of the indigenous construction of blackness and contests over such definitions abound in our everyday interactions.

Whether it be the challenge to the authenticity of those black students who choose not to sit at "the black table" in the cafeteria or the looks of contempt or concern encountered by black group members seen walking with their white mates, informal or "hidden transcripts" of blackness guide interactions in black communities, as they undoubtedly do in all communities.[6] However, in most cases full-scale contestation is not the norm in black communities. Instead, those whose position in the community is challenged exist silenced and regulated for years. Only when the subgroup experiencing ostracization or *secondary marginalization* has alternative means for securing resources, such as an external network of support, will the full battle over inclusion be fought.[7] Thus, in most cases those individuals deemed to be on the outside of "acceptable blackness"—either because of their addiction, their sexual relationships, their gender, their financial status, their relationship with/or dependency on the state, etc.—are left with two choices: either find ways to conform to "community standards" or be left on the margins where individual families and friends are expected to take care of their needs.

Again, my concern here is not that these group members will be rejected by dominant groups as not being part of the black community. Most marginal group members know that racism in the dominant society functions with essentialist principles in its assessment of black people. Thus, men and women who meet basic dominant ideas of what black people look like and "act" like rarely have their "blackness" evaluated, except to have it negated as a reward for assimilation into dominant white society (e.g., Michael Jackson, Clarence Thomas, and formerly O. J. Simpson). Instead, my concern is with the process employed by other marginal group members to evaluate someone's blackness. Will certain group members be rejected by other marginal group members because of their inability to meet indigenous standards of blackness? Are there processes through which the full "rights" or empowerment of group members becomes negated or severely limited *within* black communities because of a stigmatized black identity?[8]

As stated earlier, the objective of this analysis is not only to understand the processes through which indigenous constructions of group membership come about, but also to explore how these definitions impact on the behavior, in particular the political behavior, of marginal group members. To this end, I have chosen to center this analysis on the black community's response to the AIDS epidemic. Specifically, I will explore how indigenous contests over black gay male identity have framed and influenced black communities' conception of and response to AIDS.[9]

Throughout this article I use examples and quotes from community leaders in black churches, electoral politics, activist organizations, and the academy to examine the relationship between indigenous definitions of blackness, a public black gay identity, and the political response to AIDS in black communities. Has the emergence of a public, empowered black gay identity, perceived and defined by many community leaders, activists, and members, as standing outside the bounds of generally recognized standards of blackness been used by these leaders to justify their lack of an aggressive response to this disease? Do community leaders interpret a public black gay identity as a direct threat to the acceptability or "cultural capital" gained by some in black communities, in particular by the black middle class? In the minds of indigenous leaders and activists, does embracing or owning AIDS as a disease significantly impacting on members of black communities also mean owning or finally acknowledging that sexual contact and intimate relationships between men are something found in, and inherently a part of, black communities?[10]

My central claim is that contestation over identity, in this case indigenous racial identity, has tangible effects, influencing the distribution of resources, services, access, and legitimacy within communities. In the case of AIDS, without the support of established leaders and organizations in black communities, underfunded community-based education programs encounter limited success, facilitating the continued infection and death of black men, women, and children. Further, in the absence of political pressure from leaders, organizations, activists, and mobilized members of the black community, the federal government is allowed to continue its shameful dealings, neglecting to provide the full resources needed to effectively fight this disease in black communities. Thus, those failing to meet indigenous standards of blackness find their life chances threatened not only by dominant institutions or groups, but also by their lack of access to indigenous resources and support. Therefore, scholars who profess to be concerned with the conditions of marginal group members face the monumental challenge of recognizing and examining indigenous group definition without reifying the group as an essentialist and exclusionary category.

Furthermore, the importance of disputes over community membership and the importance of groups should not be understood only at an abstract, theoretical level where discussions of identity, authenticity, and essentialism are often held. This examination of the intersection of AIDS, black gay identity, and indigenous constructions of "blackness" provides us with an empirical example of the importance of group membership and group resources for marginal group members, as well as the dangers of identity politics. In this case we must be concerned with politics that only recognize and respond to the needs of those segments of black communities judged by our leaders to meet indigenous standards of group membership. This issue is of critical importance because it represents what I believe to be one of the more pressing political challenges currently facing marginal communities in the twenty-first century, namely how to maintain and rebuild a principled and politically effective group unity. How do marginal communities, still struggling for access and power from dominant institutions and groups, maintain some pseudo-unified political base in the face of increasing demands to recognize and incorporate the needs and issues of members who were previously silenced and made invisible in structuring the politics of the community? How do marginal communities make central those who are the most vulnerable, and often the most stigmatized, members of the community, when many of the previous gains of marginal group members have been made through a strategy of minimizing the public appearance of difference between the values, behavior, and attitudes of marginal and dominant group members? How do we build a truly radical, liberating politics that does not re-create hierarchies, norms, and standards of acceptability rooted in dominant systems of power? These are the questions that frame this analysis.

DECONSTRUCTION AND THE CRISIS OF ESSENTIALISM

Before proceeding, I want to take up what I consider an important criticism of group analysis. For some scholars, attention to the construction of identity, instead of the deconstruction of such bounded categories, seems misplaced. These researchers call for the deconstruction of both dominant and indigenous categories that are viewed as excluding certain marginal group members and reinforcing hierarchies of power. Thus, activists and academics adhering to a deconstructionist framework embrace a more fluid and transgressive understanding of identity.[11] In the case of black Americans, these scholars argue that the variation found in definitions of who qualifies as black and what that is to mean, as well as the variation in the actual life chances and lived experience of those identified through history as black, demands that we abandon the use of race as a category of analysis. Barbara Jeanne Fields, who I doubt would label herself a deconstructionist, writes at the end of her essay "Slavery, Race and Ideology in the United States of America":

> Those who create and re-create race today are not just the mob that killed a young Afro-American man on the street in Brooklyn or the people who joined the Klan and the White Order. They are also those academic writers whose invocation of self-propelling "attitudes" and tragic flaws assigns Africans and their descendants to a special category, placing them in a world exclusively theirs and outside history—a form of intellectual apartheid no less ugly or oppressive, despite its righteous (not to say self-righteous) trappings, than that practiced by the bio- and theo-racists; and for which the victims like slaves of old are expected to be grateful.[12]

In contrast to Fields, I argue that calls for the deconstruction of categories and groups ignore not only the reality of groups in structuring the distribution of resources and the general life chances of those in society, but also ignore the importance of group membership in promoting the survival and progress of marginal group members. If one exists, as many of us do, without the privilege and the resources to transgress socially erected boundaries or categories, then we learn at an early age to rely on, and contribute to, the collective material resources/power/status of other group members who share our subject position. Thus, to argue that race or blackness is not "real" in some genetic or biological form (which I do) is not to believe that race or blackness, in particular as an ideological construct of grouping and separation, has not massively structured the lives of those designated black as well as the rest of American society. Omi and Winant in their book *Racial Formation in the United States* write, "The attempt to banish the concept [of race] as an archaism is at best counterintuitive. . . . A more effective starting point is the recognition that despite its uncertainties and contradictions, the concept of race continues to play a fundamental role in structuring and representing the social world."[13]

Nonetheless I share some of Fields's concerns about the re-creation and legitimization of categories used primarily to exploit and oppress. Many within black communities, whether they be cultural nationalists, religious leaders, politicians, or the average person trying to make it day to day, adhere to some form of a less stigmatized notion of group essentialism. Scholars ranging from Molefi Kete Asante to Patricia Hill Collins to those of us who use statistical analyses to examine the condition and progress of black people invoke some nonbiologically based definitions of "*the* black experience."[14] Undoubtedly, much of our focus on a unified black community reflects that, compared to white communities, black people do in fact exhibit a significant political cohesiveness. Clearly, this observed homogeneity of black political attitudes, for instance, is forced in part by the survey questions that researchers ask, and more forcefully by the shared history of oppression that has framed our worldviews. However, we have reached a time when the issues faced by black communities demand that we look below the unified surface so often referenced by social scientists. Issues that currently frame the political agenda of black communities are often rooted in those points of social cleavage—class, gender, sexuality, language, country of origin—that problematize, at the very least, any conception of a unified, essential core of blackness as well as any assumption of shared lived experience.

Thus, it seems that this examination and others like it must be understood as an attempt to walk the thin line between two important constraints. First is a recognition that essentialist theories of the black community have at best limited relevance to understanding the structure and condition of black communities. Second, we must also understand that strict adherence to deconstructive approaches, which call for the complete negation of groups as a unit of analysis, risks ignoring the importance of indigenous group structure to the living conditions of marginal groups.

EMERGENCE OF A VISIBLE BLACK GAY IDENTITY

The perceived existence of a unifying group identity cannot be overstated when trying to explain the structured politics of black communities. Systems of oppression from slavery to redemption, to legal and informal Jim Crow segregation, and other more recent forms of segregation and deprivation have dictated that most African-Americans share a history and current existence framed by oppression and marginalization. However, even as a unifier, blackness, or what qualifies as indigenously constructed blackness, has always been mediated or contested by other identities that group members hold. And at no time did both the primacy and the fragility of a unified group identity become more evident than in the liberation politics and social movements of the late 1960s and early 1970s. Whether it be civil rights institutions, black liberation organizations, or even the electoral campaigns of black candidates, one primary identity—"blackness"—was understood to be the underlying factor joining all these struggles. Each organization espoused in its own way a commitment to the liberation of black people, and anything thought to detract from this goal was dismissed and in some cases denounced. However, the uniformity during this period of such a political worldview can also be challenged.

During the 1960s and 1970s the black community experienced increasing stratification. Whether that stratification was based in the deindustrialization experienced in urban centers or the politicized nature of the times, which helped to promote consciousness of members' multiple identities, a segregated and seemingly unified black community had to deal openly with fragmentation. All across the country we witnessed the beginning of extreme bifurcation in black communities, with an expanding middle class and an expanding segment of poor black people. However, beyond economic segmentation, other identities or social locations became visible in defining the lived experience of black people. In black communities, as well as in the political groups of the time, individuals increasingly began to recognize and acknowledge the multiplicity of identities upon which their oppression was based. Unfortunately, it was the inability of many of the race-based organizations to recognize and act on perceived tears in "unity" that led in part to the dismantling of many of these organizations.[15] However, it was also in this changing environment that the visibility of lesbian and gay people, including black lesbian and gay people, began to take shape in the community.

It is important to recognize that black gay men and lesbians have always existed and worked in black communities, but these individuals had largely been made invisible, silent contributors to the black community.[16] When faced with the devastation of racism, the cost of silence and invisibility seemed a willing payment from lesbian and gay community members for the support, caring, and protection of members of the black community and, more importantly, the support and acceptance of immediate family members. In her book *Talking Back,* bell hooks discusses the dilemma that many black lesbians and gay men confronted:

> The gay people we knew did not live in separate subcultures, not in the small, segregated black community where work was difficult to find, where many of us were poor. Poverty was important; it created a social context in which structures of dependence were important for everyday survival. Sheer economic necessity and fierce white racism, as well as the joy of being there with the black folks known and loved, compelled many gay blacks to live close to home and family. That meant however that gay people created a way to live out sexual preferences within the boundaries of circumstances that were rarely ideal no matter how affirming.[17]

Thus, if one was willing not to "flaunt" one's sexual orientation in front of family members and neighbors (although many would secretly suspect that you were "that way"), the primarily verbal abuse—like taunts of "faggot" and "bull dyke"—was generally kept to a minimum. Again, I do not want to minimize the importance of even such conditional support on the part of family, friends, and community. The prospect of facing continuous residential, occupational, and social exclusion as a manifestation of widespread racism, even in primarily white lesbian and gay communities, underscores the importance of some feelings of safety and familiarity. These were the feelings of support bought by our silence.

However, the willingness and ability of black lesbians and gay men to remain quiet and invisible has radically changed. These changes have resulted in part from many of the factors that have spurred new identities as well as politicized identities of old. One major factor has been the proliferation of liberation and social movements demanding access and control for groups long pushed out of dominant society. Cornel West speaks of this situation when he argues, "During the late fifties, sixties, and early seventies in the USA, these decolonized sensibilities fanned and fueled the Civil Rights and Black Power movements, as well as the student antiwar, feminist, gray, brown, gay, and lesbian movements. In this period we witnessed the shattering of male WASP cultural homogeneity and the collapse of the short-lived liberal consensus."[18]

Closely connected to involvement and association with organized social movements was the more formal establishment of an institutionalized, socially connected, and in many cases monetarily secure gay community in many of the nation's urban centers. These "ghettos" provided a space in which ideas of rights and political strategies of empowerment could be generated and discussed. These enclaves, as well as other dominant institutions such as universities, were integral in creating space for the exploration of independence away from local communities and families.[19]

In conjunction with the continued development of gay enclaves was the emergence of an outspoken and brave black lesbian and gay leadership who openly claimed and wrote about their sexuality (Audre Lorde, Cheryl Clarke, Barbara Smith, Pat Parker, Joseph Beam, Essex Hemphill . . .). These individuals were intent on creating new cultural voices. When they were denied the right to speak openly through traditional avenues in black communities, these cultural leaders found and created new avenues to affirm their presence and connection to black communities. Books such as *This Bridge Called My Back, Home Girls, Brother to Brother, In the Life,* and more recently videos such as *Tongues Untied* all sought to detail from various perspectives the struggle to consistently mesh one's black and gay identities.[20] All of these factors helped create an environment in which the silence that had structured the lives of many black lesbian and gay men seemed unacceptable.

The conditions listed above, however, did not lead to a massive coming out in black communities. In fact, the level of silence among black lesbian and gay men is still an immediate and pressing concern for those organizing in the community today. However, the environment that developed through the sixties and seventies created a situation in which some black women and men choose to identify publicly as black *and* gay. The choice, or in many cases the perceived need, to embrace publicly a black gay male or black lesbian identity undoubtedly escalated with the emergence of AIDS, an issue that demands either recognition and empowerment or death. Thus, after spending years affirming themselves, building consciousness, and contributing to black communities that had too often refused to embrace their particular needs, gay brothers and lesbian sisters faced an issue, AIDS, that threatened to kill black gays and lesbians as well as generally wreak havoc throughout black communities if we did not speak out and demand recognition.

It would be this political, social, and economic environment that would heighten the contestation over an open black gay male identity. This social context, where black gay men in particular were experiencing the destruction of AIDS, produced many of the early pioneers who saw it as their responsibility to provide the first level of response to AIDS in the black community. Ernest

Quimby and Samuel Friedman, in their article "Dynamics of Black Mobilization against AIDS in New York City," document much of the early organized activity around AIDS in people-of-color communities.[21] The authors note, "In the
epidemic's early days, media reports that AIDS was a disease of white gay men
reduced the attention blacks paid to it. . . . By 1985, however, some leaders of
the minority gay and lesbian community began to challenge this denial and
helped set up some of the first minority-focused AIDS events.[22]

Two of the earliest national conferences on AIDS in people-of-color communities were organized by lesbians and gay men of color. The Third World
Advisory Task Force, a primarily gay group out of San Francisco, organized a
Western regional conference in the early part of 1986.[23] The National Coalition of Black Lesbian and Gays, a progressive national membership organization structured around local chapters, organized the National Conference on
AIDS in the Black Community, in Washington, D.C., in 1986. This conference, which was cosponsored by the National Minority AIDS Council and the
National Conference of Black Mayors, was funded in part from a grant from
the U.S. Public Health Service.[24] Further, black gay men across the country,
from Washington, D.C., to New York to Oakland to San Francisco to Los Angeles, were instrumental in establishing some of the first AIDS service organizations explicitly identifying minority communities as their target population.
Additionally, black gay organizations such as Gay Men of African Descent
(GMAD) of New York City have been and continue to be essential in educational efforts seeking to reach large numbers of black men.[25]

A number of factors were helpful in laying the groundwork for the response from black gay men and lesbians. The information this group received
from white gay activists was extremely helpful. The realization that some black
gay men and lesbians also possessed limited access and economic privilege was
useful in developing contacts and pooling resources. Further, the personal experiences of loss that brought together and raised the awareness of black lesbians and gay men were undoubtedly instrumental in motivating some
response. Finally, "out" black gays and lesbians were less vulnerable to the
moral judgments of traditional institutions in the black community. Because of
their public identity as black lesbians or gay men, these individuals stood ready
to challenge the marginalizing ideology associated with AIDS. Thus, as they attempted to speak to the entire black community about the dangers of this
growing epidemic, the silence and invisibility that had once been a part of the
survival contract of black lesbians and gay men could no longer exist if lives
were to be saved.

AIDS AND POLICING BLACK SEXUALITY

In spite of the activities initiated by black lesbian and gay men in response to AIDS, it has devastated black communities, which is clearly represented in the numbers. In New York City, as in other major metropolitan areas, AIDS is now the number one killer of black men ages 25–44 and women ages 18–44. Nationally, over one hundred thousand (114,868) black Americans have been diagnosed with AIDS, accounting for 32 percent of all AIDS cases, nearly three times our 12 percent representation in the general population. Black women comprise 54 percent of all women with AIDS nationally, with black children constituting 55 percent of all children with AIDS, and black men accounting for 28 percent of men with AIDS. If these numbers were not sobering enough, the trend of increasing representation of those with AIDS from people-of-color communities suggests that these numbers will only continue to increase.[26]

Thus, in the face of such substantial and increasing devastation being visited upon the black community by AIDS, one might expect members or at least leaders of black communities to mobilize community support for more resources, attention, and action in response. However, the evidence suggests that the response from black community leaders and activists has been much less public, confrontational, collective, and consistent than the statistics might dictate. Further, any cursory comparative examination of the political response emanating from predominately white lesbian and gay activists to this disease suggests that black organizations and institutions have been less active. Over the years, members of gay and lesbian communities have found old and new ways to make officials, institutions, and at times the general public answer some of their demands.[27] Gay activists have developed sophisticated political tactics to respond to the indifference and hostility that the government and other institutions display toward people with AIDS. Rallies, sit-ins, lobbying, private meetings, civil disobedience, "phone zaps"—few things seem too far out-of-bounds to make people listen and respond.

And while the gay community has mounted a coordinated effort of traditional politics and public collective action to the AIDS epidemic, the response in the black community has been much less pervasive, public, and effective. Again, through the work of primarily black gay activists, important conferences and forums have been sponsored to educate members of black communities on the dangers of AIDS. Organizations such as the Minority Task Force on AIDS and the Black Leadership Commission on AIDS have been established to provide services and develop educational programs for members of black communities. National leaders have even on occasion made mention of AIDS in their speeches to black constituents. However, generally there has been no substantial and sustained mobilization around this crisis in African-American communities. There have been few, if any, rallies, sit-ins, or petitions in black communities to bring attention to the devastation created by AIDS. There has been no sustained lobbying effort by national black organizations such as the NAACP or the Urban League. Instead, many in the black community continue to see AIDS as a horrible disease, believing that we should extend sympathy and compassion to its "victims," but claim no ownership as a community. AIDS is generally not understood as an internal political crisis that necessitates the mobilization of black communities. Even when AIDS is seen as a conspiracy against black communities, by the government or some other entity, no mobilization accompanies such suspicion. [28] For most in black communities, AIDS is still a disease of individuals, usually "irresponsible, immoral, and deviant" individuals, some of whom happen to be black.

Quite often, when trying to explain the response to AIDS in black communities, authors retreat to the familiar and substantively important list of barriers preventing a more active response from community leaders and organizations. Regularly topping this list is the claim that because black communities have fewer resources than most other groups, they cannot be expected to respond to AIDS in a manner similar to "privileged" lesbians and gay men. And while there is truth to the claim that most black people operate with limited access to resources, this explanation is based on a narrow conception of resources and a limited understanding of the history of the black community. Most of the cities hardest hit by this disease (New York, Los Angeles, Washington, D.C., Detroit, Chicago, Atlanta) have been or are currently headed by black mayors. Thus, while black individuals suffer from limited resources, black elected officials control, or at least have significant input into, decisions about how resources will be allocated in their cities. Further, while individuals in the black community still suffer from marginalization and oppression, organizations such as the NAACP, the SCLC, and the Urban League have been able to gain access to national agencies and policy debates. Thus the claim that black people have fewer resources than other groups, while accurate at the individual level, does not appropriately account for the institutional resources controlled or accessed by black elected officials and traditional organizations.

A second explanation that is sometimes offered focuses on the numerous crises plaguing black communities. Proponents of this view argue that members of the black community suffer from so many ailments and structural difficulties, such as sickle-cell anemia, high blood pressure, diabetes, homelessness, persistent poverty, drugs, crime, discrimination . . . that no one should expect community leaders to turn over their political agenda to the issue of AIDS. Again, this position has merit, for we know that black communities do suffer disproportionately from most social, medical, economic, and political ills. It is, however, specifically because of the inordinate amount of suffering found in black communities that we might expect more attention to this disease. Because AIDS touches on, or is related to, so many other issues facing, in particular, poor black communities—health care, poverty, drug use, homelessness—we might reasonably expect black leaders to "use" the devastation of this disease to develop and reinforce an understanding of the enormity of the crisis facing black communities. Rarely does an issue so readily embody the life-and-death choices facing a community and rarely is an issue so neglected by the leadership of that community.

Another explanation suggested is that the dominant media sources as well as many community papers portray AIDS as a disease of white gay men, which thus does not threaten and need not interest the majority of black people. Further, when coverage around AIDS and black communities is provided, it often continues the historical practice of associating black people/Africa with disease (e.g., discussion of the origin of AIDS in Africa) and helps reinforce a look-the-other-way attitude by indigenous leaders and organizations.[29] Again while both of these factors clearly play a part in understanding the community's response, I contend they still leave vacant a central component in this puzzle over black communities' lack of mobilization around AIDS.

Recently, scholars who study AIDS and black communities have begun to point to homophobia in the black community as the missing piece in our puzzle.[30] Their concern is not just with homophobia among individuals, but more importantly with the homophobia rooted in indigenous institutions such as the black church, fraternal and social organizations, as well as some national political organizations. Different variants of this argument suggest that the black community's homophobia significantly structures its response, or lack thereof, to AIDS.[31]

While homophobia in the black community is something we must pay attention to, I do not believe that the concept or explanation of homophobia adequately captures the complexity of sexuality, in particular lesbian and gay sexuality, in black communities. This is not to say that homophobia, which we all endure in socialization, is not a part of black communities. However, homophobia as the fear or even hatred of gay and lesbian people does not represent the intricate role that sexuality has played in defining blackness throughout the years. Sexuality, or what has been defined by the dominant society as the abnormal sexuality of both black men and women—with men being oversexed and in search of white women while black women were and are represented as promiscuous baby producers when they are not the direct and indirect property of white men—has been used historically and currently in this country to support and justify the marginal and exploited position of black people.

Scholars such as Takaki, Steinberg, Davis, Lewis, and Omi and Winant have all attempted, through various approaches, to detail the ways in which dominant groups, often with state sanctioning, have defined and redefined racial classification for their benefit and profit.[32] Whether it be the one-drop rule, one's maternal racial lineage, simplistic evaluations of skin color, or some other combination of biological, cultural, or behavioral attributes, ideas of who is to be classified as black have had a long and varied history in this country. However, beyond the mere designation of who belongs in a particular group, dominant groups have also defined racial-group meaning. Those characteristics or stereotypes propagated as representing the "essence" of black people have been constructed by particular historical needs. Ideas about the laziness, inferiority, and in particular the sexual or abnormal sexual activity of black people have been advanced to justify any number of economic, political, and social arrangements.

This systematic degradation, stereotyping, and stigmatization of black Americans has all but dictated that attempts at incorporation, integration, and assimilation on the part of black people generally include some degree of proving ourselves to be "just as nice as those white folks." Thus, leaders, organizations, and institutions have consistently attempted to redefine and indigenously construct a new public image or understanding of what blackness would mean. This reconstruction or (im)provement of blackness relies not only on the self-regulation of individual black people, but also includes significant "indigenous policing" of black people. In the writings of black academics we consistently hear reference to the role of the black middle class as examples and regulators of appropriate behavior for the black masses. Drake and Cayton, in their 1945 classic, *Black Metropolis,* discuss the attitude of the black upper class toward the behavior of black lower classes:

> The attitude of the upper class toward the lower is ambivalent. As people whose standards of behavior approximate those of the white middle class, the members of Bronzeville's upper class resent the tendency of outsiders to "judge us all by what ignorant Negroes do." They emphasize their *differentness*. . . . The whole orientation of the Negro upper class thus becomes one of trying to speed up the process by which the lower class can be transformed from a poverty-stricken group, isolated from the general stream of American life, into a counterpart of middle-class America. [Emphasis in original.][33]

Regulation of the black masses was often pursued not only by individuals, but also by an extensive network of community groups and organizations. James R. Grossman details how the Urban League in conjunction with black and white institutions worked to help black migrants "adjust" to urban standards of behavior:

The Urban League and the *Defender*, assisted by the YMCA, the larger churches, and a corps of volunteers, fashioned a variety of initiatives designed to help—and pressure—the newcomers to adjust not only to industrial work, but to urban life, northern racial patterns, and behavior that would enhance the reputation of blacks in the larger (white) community. . . . The Urban League, through such activities as "Stranger Meetings," leafleting, and door-to-door visits, advised newcomers on their duties as citizens: cleanliness, sobriety, thrift, efficiency, and respectable, restrained behavior in public places. . . . Under the tutelage of the respectable citizens of black Chicago, migrants were to become urbanized, northernized, and indistinguishable from others of their race. At the very least, they would learn to be as inconspicuous as possible.[34]

It is important to remember that a substantial amount of indigenous policing focused on what would be represented publicly as the sexual behavior of black people. Community leaders and organizations, fighting for equal rights, equal access, and full recognition as citizens, struggled to "clean up" the image of sexuality in black communities. Cornel West in *Race Matters* discusses the unwillingness of most black institutions to engage in open discussions of sexuality in black communities.

But these grand yet flawed black institutions refused to engage one fundamental issue: *black sexuality*. . . .

Why was this so? Primarily because these black institutions put a premium on black survival in America. And black survival required accommodation with and acceptance from white America. Accommodation avoids any sustained association with the subversive and transgressive—be it communisms or miscegenation. . . . And acceptance meant that only "good" negroes would thrive—especially those who left black sexuality at the door when they "entered" and "arrived." In short, struggling black institutions made a Faustian pact with white America: avoid any substantive engagement with black sexuality and your survival on the margins of American society is, at least, possible.[35]

Thus, individuals who were thought to fulfill stereotypes of black sexuality as something deviant or other often had their morality questioned by leading institutions in black communities. For instance, sexuality thought to stand outside the Christian mores as set down by the black church was interpreted as an indication of the moral character of that individual and his or her family as well as an embarrassment to the collective consciousness and cultural capital of the black community. Hazel Carby discusses the moral panic and threat to the collective respectability of black communities attributed to uncontrolled migrating black women in her article "Policing the Black Woman's Body":

> The need to police and discipline the behavior of black women in cities, however, was not only a premise of white agencies and institutions but also a perception of black institutions and organizations, and the black middle class. The moral panic about the urban presence of apparently uncontrolled black women was symptomatic of and referenced aspects of the more general crises of social displacement and dislocation that were caused by migration. White and black intellectuals used and elaborated this discourse so that when they referred to the association between black women and vice, or immoral behavior, their references carried connotations of other crises of the black urban environment. Thus the migrating black woman could be variously situated as a threat to the progress of the race; as a threat to the establishment of a respectable urban black middle class; as a threat to congenial black and white middle-class relations; and as a threat to the formation of black masculinity in an urban environment.[36]

While these examples may seem dated, we need only look around today to see the great efforts many black leaders and academics engage in to distance themselves from those perceived to participate in "inappropriate immoral sexual behavior." Examples of such distancing efforts are evident not only in the absence of any sustained writing on black lesbians and gay men by black authors and academics, but is also found in the counterexperience of unending writing and policy attacks on the "inappropriate" and "carefree" sexuality of those labeled the "underclass" and more generally black women on welfare.[37]

I want to be clear that contests or opposition to the public representation of black gay male sexuality in particular and nonnormative sexuality in general is significantly motivated by a genuine threat to the cultural capital acquired by some in black communities, where cultural capital symbolizes the acceptance, access, and privilege of primarily black middle- and upper-class people.[38] Thus, for many black leaders and activists, visible/public black homosexuality is understood to threaten that "cultural capital" acquired by both assimilation and protest. The policing or regulation of black gay and lesbian behavior/visibility is seen as the responsibility not only of dominant institutions, but also of leaders of indigenous institutions, who can claim that they are protecting the image and progress of "the race/community." Through the fulfillment of these communal duties, internal ideas and definitions of blackness, thought to help with the task of regulation, emerge. These definitions set the rules that to be a "good" or "true" black person you must adhere to some religious standards of appropriate sexual behavior. To be a true black man is antithetical to being gay, for part of your duty as a black man is to produce "little black warriors in the interest of the black nation." The rules suggest that to be gay is to be a pawn of a white genocidal plot, intent on destroying the black community. To be gay is to want to be white anyway, since we all know that there is no tradition of homosexuality in our African history. Thus, to be gay is to stand outside the norms, values, and practices of the community, putting your "true" blackness into question.

In his article "Some Thoughts on the Challenges Facing Black Gay Intellectuals," Ron Simmons details just some of the arguments made by national (and nationalist) black leaders such as Nathan Hare, Jawanza Kunjufu, Molefi Asante, Haki Madhubuti, Amiri Baraka, and Yosuf Ben-Jochannan that seek to undermine claims of an empowered, fully recognized black gay identity.[39] Specifically, Simmons outlines what he considers the four major reasons provided by these scholars for the development of homosexuality in the black community:

> In reviewing African-American literature, one finds that black homophobic and heterosexist scholars believe homosexuality in the African-American community is the result of (1) the emasculation of black men by white oppression (e.g., Staples, Madhubuti, Asante, Farrakhan, and Baraka); (2) the breakdown of the family structure and the loss of male role models (e.g., Kunjufu, Madhubuti, Farrakhan, and Hare); (3) a sinister plot perpetuated by diabolical racists who want to destroy the black race (e.g., Hare); and (4) immorality as defined in biblical scriptures, Koranic suras, or Egyptian "Books of the Dead" (e.g., Farrakhan and Ben-Jochannan).[40]

It is important to recognize that while these authors all see homosexuality as something devised and infiltrated from outside the black community, none or few are advocating directly that black gay men and women be fully rejected and excluded from the community. And that is not the claim I seek to make with regards to the contested nature of black gay identities. Instead, many of the scholars in Simmons's analysis argue that homosexuality must be understood as a threat to the survival of the black community. Thus, they ask that black lesbians and gay men suppress their sexuality, keep quiet, remain undemanding, and make their needs subservient to the "collective" needs of the community. Simmons cites Molefi Asante as directly promoting such a subservient position in his book *Afrocentricity*:

> Afrocentric relationships are based upon . . . what is best for the collective imperative of the people. . . . All brothers who are homosexuals should know that they too can become committed to the collective will. It means the submergence of their own wills into the collective will of our people.[41]

Simmons identifies similar ideas of inclusion without empowerment for black gay men and lesbians in Nathan and Julia Hare's book *The Endangered Black Family*:

> On the other hand—and this is crucial—we will refuse to embark on one more tangent of displaced contempt and misdirected scorn for the homosexualized [*sic*] black brothers or sisters and drive them over to the camp of white liberal-radical-moderate-establishment coalition. What we must do is offer the homosexual brother or sister a proper compassion and acceptance *without advocacy.* . . . Some of them may yet be saved. And yet, we must declare open warfare upon the sources of [their] confusion. [Emphasis added.][42]

Again, the proscription these authors offer is not the complete rejection of black lesbian and gay men. Instead, they suggest a quiet acceptance "without advocacy." It is within this analysis that we again see the conflictual nature of black gay identity as it has been repeatedly defined in the black community. It is an identity that allows inclusion, but only under certain restrictions— denying any attempt at the empowerment of this segment of the black community. For these leaders, homophobia or the hatred of black gays and lesbians does not fully explain their position of silent inclusion. Thus, the "sin" that black lesbians and gay men commit is not just rooted in the inherent wrongness of their sexual behavior, but instead or just as importantly in their perceived weakness and cost to black communities.

We can now understand why homophobia, as a simple makeshift explanation to represent the complexity of sexuality in black communities, is inadequate. Instead, to analyze black communities' response to AIDS we must address a whole set of issues, including dominant representations of black sexuality, how these ideas/stereotypes have been used against black communities, and the perceived need to regulate black sexuality through indigenous definitions of blackness. From this starting point we may be better able to understand, although never accept, the range of opposition black gay men encounter as stemming not only from people's repudiation of the idea of sex between men, but also from the use of sexuality by dominant groups to stigmatize and marginalize further a community already under siege.

Again, it is important to note that what is at stake here is the question of membership, full empowered membership in black communities. Thus, visibility, access to indigenous resources, participation and acknowledgment in the structuring of black political agendas—all are put into question when one's blackness is contested. Undoubtedly, many factors contribute to the black community's response to AIDS, including a real deficiency in community resources as well as a real mistrust of government-sponsored information on health care and disease in black communities.[43] However, I believe that a significant part of the explanation for the lack of forceful action around AIDS is directly tied to ideas and definitions of "black identity" put forth by indigenous leaders, institutions, and organizations. These definitions of blackness stand in direct contrast to the images and ideas associated with those living with AIDS or HIV in black communities. In particular, these indigenous constructions of blackness define behavior linked to the transmission of HIV as immoral and an embarrassment, threatening to the status and survival of community members.

Having laid out this argument concerning the contestation of black gay identity and its impact on political responses to AIDS in black communities, it is important to provide, even briefly, a concrete example of the way an indigenous institution such as the black church defines and responds to the needs of black gay men in the era of AIDS. I will also try to highlight a few of the ways black gay men have responded to the secondary marginalization they have experienced through black churches. Again, I use the church merely as an illustration of the marginalization and identity contestation in which numerous indigenous institutions engage.

THE BLACK CHURCH

Activists and scholars have often focused on the activity of the black church to understand and explain the political behavior of members of the black community, since traditionally the church has been perceived as the glue and motor of the community. If any activity was to touch every segment of the community, it was believed that such efforts had to be based in the black church. The work of Aldon Morris linking the black church to the civil rights movement is a classic example of the role the black church is thought to play in struggles for liberation and rights.[44] However, even prior to the civil rights movement the black church was used to build movements of freedom. The black church acted as meeting space, school, health care facility, and distributor of food from slavery to Reconstruction, through the years of Northern migration and the decades of Jim Crow segregation. In her article on the new social role of black churches, Hollie I. West comments, "African-American churches have traditionally served as a refuge from a hostile white world, beehives of both social and political activity."[45]

However, with the advent of AIDS, drug epidemics, and the increasing poverty and stratification of black communities, some organizers and activists are beginning to question the central authority given to the church. West suggests in her article that AIDS is a problem that pulls the church in two directions: "Some clergymen privately acknowledge the dilemma. They recognize the need to confront AIDS and drugs, but conservative factions in their congregations discourage involvement."[46] A conservative ideology, based on strict norms of "moral" behavior, has often framed the church's response to many of the controversial social issues facing black communities. Gail Walker briefly delineates the contradictory nature of the black church: "The dual—and contradictory—legacy of the African-American church is that it has been among the most important instruments of African-American liberation and at the same time one of the most conservative institutions in the African-American community."[47]

While the position of the black church on homosexuality has seemed fairly straightforward, it has both public and private dimensions. Holding with the teaching of most organized religions, members of black churches assert that homosexual behavior is immoral and in direct contrast to the word of God. Black ministers have consistently spoken out and preached against the immorality and threat posed to the community by gays and lesbians. Recently, black ministers from numerous denominations in Cleveland, Ohio, organized in opposition to federal legislation to include gay men and lesbians under the protection of the 1964 Civil Rights Bill. These ministers, representing themselves as "true leaders" of the black church, wrote in the local black newspaper, the *Call and Post*:

> We as members and representatives of African American protestant congregations reaffirm our identity as THE BLACK CHURCH. . . .
> We view HOMOSEXUALITY (including bisexual, as well as gay or lesbian sexual activity) as a lifestyle that is contrary to the teaching of the Bible. Such sexual activity and involvement is contrary to the pattern established during creation. Homosexual behavior in the Bible is forbidden and described as unnatural and perverted. . . .
> Our attitude toward any individuals that are involved in/with a HOMOSEXUAL LIFESTYLE is expressed through tolerance and compassion. The church's mission is to bring about RESTORATION. . . . [48]

However, at the same time that condemnation of gay and lesbian sexual behavior is a staple of the black church, it is also well-known that black gay men, in particular, can be found in prominent positions throughout the church. Thus, black gay men in black churches can be quietly accepted as they sing in the church choir, teach Sunday school, and in some cases even preach from the pulpit, or they can be expelled for participating in blasphemous behavior. Nowhere does the idea of inclusion as fully recognized and empowered members exist. Thus, according to religious doctrine, black lesbian and gay members of the community are to be embraced and taken care of in a time of need. However, their gay identity places them outside the indigenously constructed boundaries of both Christian and black identification as recognized by the church.

Nowhere recently has this principle of silent acceptance and care at the expense of a public denunciation of homosexuality been more evident than in struggles around the church's response to AIDS in black communities. The contradictory nature of church actions and rhetoric continues to frustrate many AIDS activists, who looked to the church initially for a swift, compassionate, and empowering response. Activists and those providing services claim that the church did little to nothing early in response to the epidemic. Further, when members of the church elite finally did mobilize, it was with negative judgments and pity.

Dr. Marjorie Hill, former director of New York City's Office of Lesbian and Gay Concerns under Mayor David Dinkins, explains that the church's history of activism is muted with regards to AIDS because of its insistence on denying public recognition of lesbian and gay community members: "Historically, activism in the black community has come from the church. However, the reluctance of the church to respond to AIDS means they are not following the mission of Christ. . . . The church has not dealt with the issue of homosexuality. Many have gays who sing in the choir and play the organ and that is fine until they need the church's help and recognition. . . . Denial only works for so long; the reality of gay men and women will eventually have to be dealt with."[49]

Others argue that the church is making progress. Church members point to the numerous AIDS ministries that have been established to deal with AIDS in black communities. They highlight what seem like revolutionary strides in the ability of black ministers to even mention AIDS from the pulpit. And while black lesbian and gay leaders commend those attempting to identify comfortable ways for black ministers and congregations to deal with the devastation of AIDS in their communities, they still contend there's no full recognition of the rights and lives of those infected with this disease. The saying "love the sinner, hate the sin" is paramount in understanding the limited response of black clergy. Gay men are to be loved and taken care of when they are sick, but their loving relationships are not to be recognized nor respected. Most individuals affected by this disease can tell at least one story of going to a funeral of a gay man and never having his being gay recognized as well as never hearing the word AIDS mentioned. Family members and ministers are all too willing to grieve the loss of a son or church member, without ever acknowledging the totality of that son. Lost to AIDS is not only the son loved so dearly, but the totality of his life, which included lovers and gay friends who also grieve for that loss.

The fundamental obstacle to the church's wholehearted response to AIDS is its adherence to a strict middle-class Christian code that holds behavior that transmits the virus is immoral, sinful, and just as importantly for the argument presented here, costly to the community's status. Until church leaders are ready to discuss issues of sexuality, drug use, and homosexuality in an inclusive discourse, their ability to serve the entire community as well as confront, instead of replicate, dominant ideologies will be severely inhibited. The Reverend James Forbes of Riverside Church in New York City has been one of the few black clergy who has openly called on the church to open up its dialogue concerning AIDS. In a keynote address at the 1991 Harlem Week of Prayer, he declared that until the black church deals with fundamental issues such as sexuality in an inclusive and accepting manner, it will never be able to deal adequately with the AIDS epidemic in the black community.

While ministers like the Reverend Mr. Forbes preach the need for the church to reevaluate its stance on fundamental judgments of human sexuality, others believe that we may have seen the church move about as far as it's going to go. Except for those exceptional congregations committed to a liberation theology, the provision of services for those with AIDS may be the extent of the church's response, because for many clergy there is no way to reconcile behavior that can lead to the transmission of the virus to the doctrine of the Christian church. The Reverend Calvin Butts of Abyssinian Baptist Church in Harlem explains:

> The response of the church is getting better. At one time the church didn't respond, and when the church did respond, it was negative. Ministers thought that a negative response was in keeping with the thinking that AIDS was transmitted by homosexual transmission, drugs, you know. But as more thoughtful clergy became involved, issues of compassion entered the discussion and we used Jesus' refuge in the house of lepers as an example. People became more sympathetic when people close to the church were affected. Also the work of BLCA [Black Leadership Commission on AIDS] brought clergy together to work on our response. Unfortunately, there are still quite a few who see it as God's retribution.[50]

However, in an environment where their identity is contested and their full rights and connection with black communities is negated, many black lesbian and gay leaders are actively developing ways to ignore the dictates and challenge the power of the church, especially as it affects AIDS organizing. One such strategy has focused on how black gay and lesbian leaders as well as AIDS activists can do effective work in the community without the help of the church. Some suggest that it does not matter whether the church responds because the church no longer touches those parts of the community most at risk for this disease. Colin Robinson, former staff member at Gay Men's Health Crisis and currently executive director of Gay Men of African Descent, explains, "The church is still hooked on sin, but compromised by sin. They will take care of you when you get sick, but they won't talk about it, and that is no way to provide effective education."[51] George Bellinger Jr., a member of GMAD and former education director of the Minority Task Force on AIDS in New York, suggests, "We put too much status in the church. They aren't connected to the affected populations, and they bring with them all kinds of middle-class values."[52]

Others in the community have gone beyond developing AIDS education strategies to focus directly on challenging the teaching of the church about homosexuality, especially as black gay identities are offered as a contrast to the indigenous constructed image of "good black Christian folk." These individuals seek out leaders inside the community, such as the Reverend James Forbes, who have publicly challenged the representations of more conservative clergy. These activists seek a leadership that will embrace an empowered black lesbian and gay community. In the absence of these individuals, black gay activists have begun building their own religious institutions, in such cities as New York, San Francisco, and Los Angeles, to put forth a different interpretation of the Bible.

All of these oppositional strategies contest the stigma of a black gay identity as constructed by the black church. Black gay activists understand that to engage the black community on AIDS as well as lesbian and gay rights they must contest and challenge the church's labeling of gay and lesbian lifestyles as immoral. Further, black lesbian and gay activists must redefine themselves as integral, connected, and contributing members of the community, so as to access the community support we most desperately need.

CONCLUSION: A FEW LAST COMMENTS

The goal of this paper was to explore, in some concrete fashion, the contested nature of identity within marginal communities. For far too long we have let assumptions of a stable, homogeneous group direct our attention to a framework of analysis that focuses on struggles between dominant and marginal groups. Left largely unexplored by social scientists are the internal struggles within marginal communities threatening to severely change the basis and direction of group politics. Throughout this paper I have attempted to explore how identities are constructed and contested, and how in this case such disputes influenced the politics of AIDS in black communities. Central to this entire discussion has been the idea that group identity, or at least the way many of us conceptualize it, has changed over the years. We can no longer work from an essentialist position, in which all marginal people, in particular all black people, are assumed to have the same standing within their communities. Instead, we must pay attention to the battles for full inclusion waged within these communities, because these battles provide important signals to the future political direction of the community. In the case of AIDS, the vulnerable status and contested identities of those most often associated with this disease in the black community, IV-drug users and gay men, severely impacts the community's response to the epidemic. And while indigenous institutions and leaders have increasingly demonstrated a willingness to fight political battles over AIDS funding and discrimination, these same leaders have made few attempts to redefine the community's battle against AIDS as a political fight for the empowerment of the most marginal sectors of the community.

However, the battle around AIDS and who has full access to the resources and consciousness of the community does not stand alone. Similar battles are being waged around other issues, such as the "underclass." Those on the outside, those designated "less than, secondary, bad or culturally deviant," are developing new ways to politically challenge a cohesive group unity that rejects their claims at representation and in many cases ignores their needs. These individuals, like the black gay men discussed in this paper, can no longer afford to support a leadership that is content to have them seen, in some cases blamed, but not heard.

Thus, if there is one larger implication of this work that needs further investigation, it is how marginal groups facing increasing stratification and multiple social identities will adjust to build a somewhat unified identity for the pursuit of political struggles. The importance of groups in our political system cannot be denied. In a pluralistic political system access is usually based on the grouping of individuals with some shared interest, with these individuals pooling resources and influence to impact policy. Collective mobilization becomes especially important for marginal groups with a history of being denied access to dominant political structures. These marginal groups often find themselves excluded and defined out of the political process. Thus, African-Americans grouped together by the socially constructed category of race have found their political access restricted. Only through coming together to redefine their marginal identity into a new identity that both unified and empowered the multiple segments of the community could any political battles be won.

In black communities the presence of increasing stratification and heterogeneity, as is evident in the community's mixed response to AIDS, raises the question of the utility of race as a basis upon which to build political movements. Some scholars suggest that race is of dwindling importance in understanding the life choices and conditions of most black people and instead argue that class as it interacts with urban (inner-city) residency should be regarded as the defining explanation of the "black experience" in the contemporary United States. While I do not subscribe to the school that race is unimportant, I do believe that African-Americans face a crisis in identity. Other social identities, such as gender, class, sexual orientation, and geographic location, are taking on greater significance in determining the experiences of group members. Without some increased recognition of the broadening of identities through which people exist in and understand the world, black leaders, scholars, and activists may end up so out of touch with the experiences of most people that they fill no real function in the community and thus are left to talk to themselves.

Thus, as social scientists we must proceed with our study of groups and group identity in new and innovative ways. First and foremost, we must again see the group as a unit of analysis with special attention paid to the internal structure of marginal groups. Second, we must pay attention to and recognize new or newly acknowledged identities. Where once we struggled to include gender, race, and class into our multivariate regressions as well as our class-room discussions, we now have the opportunity to explore group identities, such as lesbian and gay identities, that were once thought to be outside the realm of importance to "real" political scientists.[53] And finally, as we focus on the group and include more groups in the picture, we must accept that ideas of essentialist, stable identities in which homogenous groups act as one in calculating risk and determining strategy must be dismissed or revised. Gone are the biological and essentialist conceptions of group formation. They have been replaced with an emphasis on social construction and contextual meaning.

Overall, I believe that we must develop a new approach to understanding identity and its role in structuring politics and political behavior. This new approach assumes that identities are not only constructed, they are also challenged and contested. As reluctant as we political scientists often are to incorporate change into our understandings of politics, this new approach to understanding and studying group identity both promises and threatens to reconstruct our social science playing fields. There are new players to identify, there are old groups to redefine, and there are new actions that should be interpreted as political. Undoubtedly, our old favorites of race, class, and gender will remain, but the internal restructuring of those identities may change as common agendas and assumed "unity" are challenged. In the end what all of this may mean is that those of us interested in the group as a unit of analysis, those of us interested in the developing agenda of marginal groups as they struggle for inclusion and/or equality, even those interested primarily in the individual, assessing the role of group identity through dummy variables representing race, class, and gender in multivariate equations, may have to look a bit closer at what is really happening in these communities and groups. Who is being counted? Who is shaping the political agenda? How are stratification and contests over identity impacting on the internal unity needed to address a dominant system? And finally, how will this affect the politics of these groups as well as the larger society in the twenty-first century?[54]

CHAPTER 19

THE RYAN WHITE CARE ACT: AN IMPRESSIVE, DUBIOUS ACCOMPLISHMENT

JOHN-MANUEL ANDRIOTE

IN THE EARLY YEARS OF THE AIDS EPIDEMIC, VOLUN-teers in communities throughout the country offered practical assistance and emotional support to their friends and neighbors with AIDS because "someone has to do it." They channeled their concern and energy into small AIDS service organizations whose shoestring budgets were cobbled together from fund-raising events such as walkathons, auctions, and drag shows. Money from the federal government was scarce, and even private philanthropies—despite their greater ability to respond quickly and flexibly as needs arise in their communities—didn't start contributing significant amounts of money for AIDS services until the end of the eighties.

With the 1990 passage of the federal Ryan White CARE (Comprehensive AIDS Resources Emergency) Act, hundreds of millions of public dollars were suddenly made available for AIDS services. Existing AIDS service organizations expanded, employing more staff, offering more services. New organizations sprang up, and tottering social service agencies were buttressed by CARE Act funds. These funds provided a lot of jobs and became the largest single budget item at the Health Resources and Services Administration, the federal agency that disseminates CARE Act funding and oversees CARE Act–funded programs in the nation's cities and states.

Among the services paid for by CARE Act funding are primary medical care, substance-abuse treatment, food and nutrition services, housing services, and medications. Like the models upon which it was based, the CARE Act mandates that states and communities receiving AIDS-services funding must pull together "planning councils" to assess local needs and determine how the funding should be apportioned among service providers. The CARE Act consists of four major sections or "titles": title I covers grants to urban areas reporting 2,000 or more cumulative AIDS cases since the beginning of the epidemic, or a cumulative rate of 250 cases per 100,000 population; title II provides funding to each state, the District of Columbia, Puerto Rico, and eligible territories, as well as to Special Projects of National Significance, a program intended to advance knowledge and skills by supporting innovative models of care delivery; title III(b) provides grants supporting outpatient early-intervention HIV services; and title IV offers support to children, youth, women, and families with HIV.[1]

The CARE Act grew out of service models created largely by gay people operating AIDS service organizations, and out of lobbying efforts aimed at institutionalizing the variety of coordinated, community-based AIDS services put together by gay people in San Francisco in the earliest years of the epidemic. The vast amount of money made available through the CARE Act was a great reward for the efforts of gay-activists-cum-AIDS-lobbyists who had learned to "do politics" in Washington because of the AIDS crisis. In playing the game of Washington politics, though, these advocates were forced to operate within a system that doesn't value the lives of gay people because it doesn't treat gay people as equally protected by the Constitution.

After Rock Hudson's July 25, 1985, announcement that he had AIDS, *Life* magazine announced on its cover, "Now No One Is Safe." Those words encapsulated the political strategy adopted by AIDS lobbyists in Washington in the late 1980s, who then "de-gayed" AIDS in their pitches to lawmakers—emphasizing the (relatively few) women and children with AIDS in this country, downplaying the hundreds of thousands of gay men with the disease. If they could successfully (despite the epidemiology) convince politicians that heterosexuals were equally at risk for AIDS, the lobbyists believed (correctly, it turned out) the politicians would pay attention. Indeed, attention was given to the so-called innocent victims—particularly the children born to HIV-infected women—and diverted from gay men so as not to alienate the "moral" folk in Congress who simply didn't care to know that gay men have sex.

The CARE Act has had many positive benefits—most obviously that it pays for social services and treatments that sustain the lives of people with HIV/AIDS. But the CARE Act has been a mixed blessing. It spawned a seemingly permanent AIDS industry under the federal government's only disease-specific program. Rather than working to integrate HIV/AIDS services into the framework of "mainstream" health-care and social-service programs—the original goal of AIDS advocates—the AIDS industry now lobbies hard to continue the carve-out that pays for salaries as well as services. As a result, the CARE Act is increasingly criticized as an example of "exceptionalism," a program that supports only a specific segment of the population even as others without such a program must fend for themselves or, if they're lucky, rely on federal poverty programs such as Medicaid, Medicare, and Social Security. These issues have become thornier as HIV/AIDS affects increasing numbers of poor people, and not merely the white middle-class people by and for whom CARE Act programs were designed.

From a gay civil rights perspective, the efforts of activists to pass—and now perpetuate—the CARE Act go to the heart of what "gay liberation" has stood for, raising anew some of the movement's most fundamental questions: Are we fighting for our rights alone, or for the freedom and dignity of *all* Americans? Do we take ours and run, or do we stick to it, form strategic alliances with others who support our interests and whom we support, and push for systemic change that will improve the quality of life for everyone?

The Ryan White CARE Act is a big program, but it nevertheless represents only a fraction of the money the federal government spends on AIDS services. In 1998, CARE Act funding totaled $1.15 billion, or 18.6 percent of the $6.18 billion the federal government spent altogether for HIV/AIDS-related care and assistance (including cash assistance, health care, and housing). In contrast, $4.9 billion—nearly four-fifths of all federal AIDS services funding—was provided through combined state and federal Medicaid funds and Medicare.[2] Clearly, many more people are served by federal "poverty" programs than by the CARE Act.

Why, then, has the CARE Act been the single-minded focus of AIDS advocates in Washington? To find an answer, let's look at where the CARE Act came from, how funds are allocated, the services they pay for, why advocates are so invested in the act's continuation, and finally, why it's unlikely the CARE Act will continue indefinitely and what might replace it.

In 1982, well before anyone knew what was causing the mysterious and fatal outbreak of immune-deficiency disease among formerly healthy gay men, Pat Norman, the first director of the office of lesbian and gay health concerns in San Francisco's public health department, pulled together a group of five people in San Francisco to lay out a plan for providing a range of services for those afflicted by AIDS. Called simply the San Francisco Plan, it united health and social service organizations throughout the city to offer a range of services. If someone was worried about possibly having AIDS—of course in 1982, no sexually active gay man could be sure he didn't have it—he was sent to the Mission Health Center in the Castro District. The Shanti Project offered emotional support and housing. The newly formed Kaposi's Sarcoma Foundation (now the San Francisco AIDS Foundation) provided supportive social services. KS patients would be sent to the new KS Clinic at the University of California–San Francisco. Those with *Pneumocystis carinii* pneumonia would be sent to San Francisco General Hospital.

The central coordinating committee, together with the community organizations in San Francisco providing AIDS services in those early years, were central components of what became known as the San Francisco model of AIDS care. Also called a continuum of care, the various services offered throughout the community were intended to keep someone with AIDS out of the hospital, living at home, and functioning as well and long as possible. These services included case management, information hot lines, resource materials, workshops, attendant care, "buddy" programs to assist with practical needs, meal services, ambulette services to get to medical appointments, nursing, hospice care, support groups and peer counseling, recreation or activity programs, legal and financial services, and group or scattered-site housing.[3]

In November 1985, the Princeton, New Jersey–based Robert Wood Johnson Foundation (RWJ), the nation's largest philanthropy devoted to health care issues, launched a $17.1 million AIDS Health Services program to stimulate the development of community-based AIDS services throughout the country. The foundation's board invited Dr. Philip R. Lee, then director of the Institute for Health Policy Studies at the University of California–San Francisco (later the assistant secretary for health in the first Clinton administration), to meet with them in Princeton to discuss the San Francisco model of AIDS care. RWJ vice president for programs Paul Jellinek recalled in an interview, "We saw that we could play an important role by helping others to learn about what had been done in San Francisco, and testing the viability of the San Francisco model in other communities that were beginning to see increased AIDS cases."[4]

In November 1986, RWJ made awards to nine projects serving eleven communities with the country's highest AIDS caseloads—Atlanta, Dallas, Fort Lauderdale, Jersey City, Miami, Nassau County (N.Y.), Newark (N.J.), New Orleans, New York City, Seattle, and West Palm Beach.[5] AID Atlanta was the only gay-community-based AIDS organization to be selected as an RWJ program's coordinating agency; in most other cities, the public health department administered the program. To help replicate the San Francisco model of coordinated AIDS services, the foundation hired some of the architects of the San Francisco model. Dr. Mervyn Silverman, who was director of San Francisco's public health department, came on board to direct the AIDS Health Services program. A bridge-builder since his days in the Peace Corps, Silverman was ideally suited to RWJ's efforts to build cooperation among various health-care and social-service providers in its participating cities. Silverman brought with him Cliff Morrison, the former director of nursing at San Francisco General Hospital, who had set up the hospital's famous AIDS ward in July 1983.

Morrison's job was to visit the participating cities to help coordinate their AIDS services. He soon recognized that RWJ's goal of replicating the San Francisco model was limited by social, political, and financial differences. Morrison recalled, "People would say, 'You can do those things in San Francisco that we can't do here.' "[6] Perhaps the biggest difference was that no other city had a gay community as visible, politically influential, and full of willing volunteers as San Francisco's. Recognizing the limited extent to which the San Francisco model could be replicated elsewhere, RWJ revised its goal to simply build on a community's existing service structures and networks.

In 1989, the Health Resources and Services Administration (HRSA) funded four demonstration projects—in Los Angeles, Miami, New York, and San Francisco—modeled directly after RWJ's AIDS Health Services program. By providing public funding, HRSA hoped to stimulate existing nonprofit community-based organizations to develop a comprehensive out-of-hospital service-delivery system for people with AIDS. Joseph O'Neill, a gay physician long involved in caring for AIDS patients and now the director of HRSA's AIDS Bureau—which administers Ryan White CARE Act funding and programs—describes the HRSA demonstration projects as a "primordial" version of the CARE Act.[7]

Before the AIDS epidemic, gay people had little experience lobbying as a bloc in Washington on their own behalf and no experience whatsoever with federal budgets, appropriations, or the Department of Health and Human Services (HHS). The only gay political presence in the nation's capital was Steve Endean's Gay Rights National Lobby (formed in 1978) and the National Gay Task Force (the word *lesbian* was added later), which pushed the federal gay and lesbian civil rights bill, first introduced by the late Representative Bella Abzug in 1975, and worked with federal agencies during the Carter presidency to implement policy changes. Not only did gay people have to learn about Washington politics, but they had to make a major shift in their thinking about the role of the federal government in their lives. Jeff Levi, who became NGTF's Washington director in 1983 and later its executive director, said, "The traditional gay and lesbian agenda is 'Stay out of our lives.' "[8] When AIDS appeared, gay leaders suddenly realized how essential the federal government's involvement—particularly its money—would be to deal with a crisis of such magnitude. Ginny Apuzzo, director of the Task Force at the time, told me, "Getting people to change their perspective was like trying to turn a ship around."[9]

Besides sharpening their skills in lobbying Congress, gay politicos in Washington cultivated relationships with people inside the executive branches, particularly HHS. Apuzzo recalls that when she first met Ed Brandt, the assistant secretary for health in the first Reagan administration, "He looked at me like I'd lost my mind." But Apuzzo wouldn't leave the conservative Republican doctor alone. "I kept working on him," she said, "giving him data, giving him facts." Brandt eventually came to support Apuzzo's efforts, though he had to do so furtively to avoid being caught by other Republicans. Apuzzo recalled that after Brandt sent what was supposed to be a confidential memo to HHS secretary Margaret Heckler, in 1984, asking for $55 million more than the administration's $51 million request for AIDS, "It ended up in our mailbox in a plain brown envelope." Shortly afterward, Brandt announced his resignation from HHS. Before he left, though, he spent his last day with Apuzzo—and later sent her a handwritten letter saying he wished he'd spent more time with her.

Gay rights advocates in Washington took on AIDS issues because so many gay men were affected and the often appalling treatment they received illuminated the very issues the advocates were calling attention to. Meanwhile, the new AIDS service organizations springing up around the country realized they would need representation of their own. To provide a means of networking with one another, thirty-eight community-based AIDS organizations formed the Federation of AIDS-Related Organizations (FARO) at the June 1983 "Second National AIDS Forum," held in conjunction with the annual national lesbian and gay health conference, in Denver. The group also wanted a presence in Washington and in August 1983 hired a health lobbyist to singly staff their "lobby project," which they called the FARO AIDS Action Council.

Former diplomat Gary MacDonald was hired as the first executive director of what today is known simply as AIDS Action Council. Besides lobbying Congress and the administration to increase funding for AIDS research and education, MacDonald spent a great deal of time educating people in the government about homosexuals. He told me, "There was enormous ignorance in the early days: 'Who are these people? How many of you are there? Where do you live?' I'd get calls from people at CDC asking, 'What percentage of the population is gay male?' "

Two years after the formation of AIDS Action Council, the group's board in late 1985 decided to form a second national organization devoted to sharing information among and providing technical assistance to the hundreds of AIDS service organizations already in existence. Launched with a minuscule budget of $5,000 from the nation's largest AIDS organizations, the National AIDS Network (NAN), based in Washington, was dedicated to teaching local groups how to manage the *business* of providing AIDS services.

In October 1987, NAN cosponsored a meeting of 150 representatives from government and private-sector organizations to map out a plan for addressing "AIDS into the Nineties," as the meeting and the report produced from it were called. NAN brought together representatives of the American Medical Association, the federal Centers for Disease Control, gay rights groups, the insurance industry, public health organizations, minority organizations, Burroughs Wellcome, and many others in this first-ever major collaboration among the various "players" involved in the nation's response to AIDS. The interorganizational collaboration, as well as the technical assistance NAN provided to community groups, would provide the federal government with another model for coordinated AIDS services under the Ryan White CARE Act. The group concluded that community-based AIDS service organizations would remain the backbone of the nation's response. They noted, however, that those organizations needed to look to "a broader future when the AIDS response is concentrated within traditional mainstream institutions."[10]

Despite the perception by everyone in Washington that AIDS Action Council was a gay organization representing gay-run AIDS organizations, Mac-Donald said, "The council had deliberately decided not to position itself as a gay organization. That was a board decision, which I supported."[11] While AIDS Action represented organizations that grew out of the gay community, the council didn't see itself as a gay organization—a distinction beyond the ken of many Americans who, to this day, see AIDS as a "gay disease." When Jean McGuire, then identifying herself privately as bisexual and with two children, was hired in early 1988 to be AIDS Action's executive director, the council's board members were overjoyed to have a woman perceived as being heterosexual simply because she had children (today she lives with a female partner). Fortunately, McGuire was a savvy, experienced Washington lobbyist who knew about the power of coalition politics and would position AIDS Action at the center of the AIDS lobby.

The pieces were in place, the models available, for the federal government finally to do something to address the nation's need for AIDS services in a way that would be commensurate with its resources. To urge it along, AIDS Action Council in the late eighties spearheaded a political coalition that was effective and powerful and would accomplish important feats in Washington that would have far-ranging benefits for people with AIDS. Unfortunately, the strategy of "de-gaying" or "mainstreaming" AIDS used to win support and funding for AIDS—and ultimately the CARE Act—would wind up alienating many gay people who were already tired of feeling scolded, slighted, and generally viewed as second-class Americans.

AIDS Action's Jean McGuire and her right-hand man at the council, Tom Sheridan, were instrumental in organizing a coalition of national trade and professional organizations in Washington that in some way had a vested interest in AIDS, either because of the nature of their business (medical groups, for example) or the clients they represented (such as disability organizations). Called National Organizations Responding to AIDS (NORA), the coalition included the national gay rights groups. But for the first time since the beginning of the epidemic, those groups weren't the principal spokespeople on AIDS. Like AIDS Action itself, NORA depended on a strategy of "mainstreaming" or "de-gaying" AIDS to get the attention and support of members of Congress.

McGuire, Sheridan (who was in the closet at the time), and lesbian lawyer/ activist Chai Feldblum (who, like McGuire, was then identifying herself as bi-sexual) steered NORA in its efforts to de-gay AIDS by emphasizing—despite the epidemiology of AIDS in this country at the time and, largely, still today— that "everyone is at risk" for AIDS and "it's not only a 'gay disease.'"

From his vantage point in the House of Representatives, Tim Westmore-land worked with the AIDS advocates to ensure the passage of the Ryan White CARE Act. As chief counsel to the Subcommittee on Health and the Environ-ment—the body that oversees the nation's medical research institutions and health care systems—Westmoreland told me the advocates were helpful in three major ways in making the case for what became the CARE Act: they demonstrated to representatives that AIDS was a problem in their districts; strategized on appropriate language that would defang hostile amendments in-troduced by conservative members (in the Senate, for example, Jesse Helms wanted mandatory HIV-antibody testing in prisons, for health care workers, and mandatory notification of sexual partners); and provided legislators with "snapshots" of how CARE Act funding would be used in effective programs.

After what Westmoreland said were "dozens of meetings on the San Francisco model," political wrangling inside Congress, and lobbying pressure from AIDS advocates, Congress was ready to act. Title I, geared to hard-hit cities, appealed to members of the House—not surprising since the dense pop-ulations of urban areas mean they have the overwhelming number of votes in the House. Title II appealed to senators—only two to each state—because it wasn't tied to urban areas but considered states as a whole. Title III would pro-vide funding to clinics and community-based health centers already serving poor people and people with sexually transmitted diseases. And title IV would provide health care for pregnant women and children.

The naming of the bill was a sticking point. Senator Dan Coates of Indi-ana was a conservative Republican linchpin who would bring other conserv-atives on board to support the legislation. To do so, however, Coates insisted the bill be named after Indiana teenager Ryan White, who had died from AIDS only months before the bill was finally passed in August 1990. Westmoreland recalled that Representative Henry Waxman, chair of the House subcommit-tee, was angry about naming the bill after Ryan White. "He went on record to make clear his reluctance to sign a bill named for an 'innocent victim,'" said Westmoreland.[12] White had contracted HIV from the blood products he took to treat his hemophilia. Despite the far greater attention his diagnosis and death brought to AIDS, it was politically inconceivable that there would be a "Rock Hudson CARE Act."

The CARE Act changed the landscape of AIDS services and service providers. Organizations that had struggled to make ends meet were suddenly flooded with money. HRSA, the federal agency overseeing the CARE Act, became as it were the headquarters for the AIDS industry, with CARE Act funding and programs accounting for its largest single budget item. In fiscal 1991, the first year CARE Act funds were available, the nation's hardest-hit state, New York, received nearly $63 million. California, the second-hardest-hit state, received $44.7 million under all the titles and programs for which the state was eligible. By fiscal 1994, California had nearly tripled its CARE Act funding to just under $123 million. By the end of the CARE Act's first five-year funding cycle, California and New York together had received more than half a billion title I dollars alone.[13]

Besides bolstering the existing AIDS service organizations, the availability of so much money under the CARE Act on a competitive basis brought many people and agencies into the AIDS industry that had never been involved in—or even interested in—providing AIDS services. By the mid-nineties, an estimated eighteen thousand organizations throughout the country were providing some kind of AIDS-related services—two hundred of them in San Francisco alone. How and why did all these organizations appear? The how had to do with the availability of vast amounts of money from the CARE Act. As for the why, there was a widespread belief in the AIDS service community—largely unchallenged by left-leaning AIDS activists—that individuals should have "culturally competent" care, ideally from service providers who "looked like" themselves. This gave rise to territoriality and the assertion that only organizations based in a client's racial, ethnic, or socioeconomic community could provide what were deemed appropriate services. Often new organizations arose from the ashes of anger and accusations that a particular AIDS service agency wasn't meeting a particular population's specific needs (at least the needs as they were defined by AIDS activists and those employed by AIDS service organizations). Paul Kawata, former director of the National AIDS Network and, since 1989, director of the National Minority AIDS Council, told me, "There was so much rage and anger, and it felt like there was a lot of dollars. So if you weren't going to meet my needs, I'll go off and start my own organization."[14]

Anger and large amounts of CARE Act funding fueled a lot of activists and a lot of AIDS organizations. I asked HRSA AIDS Bureau director O'Neill whether the country can sustain the multitude of AIDS service providers now drawing down CARE Act funding. "You can't," he said, "at least not on the public dole." As an example, he referred to the extraordinary number of agencies providing AIDS services in San Francisco. "We can't pay two hundred executive directors out of Ryan White money," he said. To continue getting Congress's support of the CARE Act, O'Neill foresaw a coming time of "painful discussions" and consolidation. "I'm not referring to the care and maintenance of organizations," he said. "I'm referring to the care and maintenance of sick individuals."[15]

The sometimes competing interests of AIDS service organizations and the clients they serve have given rise to the question that was asked at the time the CARE Act was being considered in Congress: Is the best approach to funding AIDS services a disease-specific program like the CARE Act? Or would it be more effective to reform public entitlement programs—Medicaid in particular—in a way that benefits people with AIDS as well as those with other life-threatening illnesses? This would go far toward changing the increasing public perception that AIDS is being treated as an "exception," a special-interest carve-out of the federal budget for a politically astute group.

When the CARE Act came up for reauthorization, in 1995, AIDS advocates in Washington spoke out about the "special populations" who need the AIDS services provided by their organizations. Strangely, gay men were no longer considered a special population—as if they didn't still account for the greatest number of AIDS cases in this country, had prevented all new HIV infections, and had received all the services they might need. Even more strangely, gay men and gay-run organizations were regularly referred to as "mainstream" by AIDS advocates. Before the CARE Act, gay lobbyists in Washington encouraged politicians to feel good about doing something for women and children, downplaying the vast numbers of gay men afflicted by AIDS to win support and funding. Now AIDS service providers themselves championed people with AIDS who were poor, female, ideally prepubescent ("innocent victims," they were called)—and definitely not white or gay. The strategy of "de-gaying" AIDS had succeeded in winning the CARE Act, but it resulted in the needs of gay men (of all races) being shunted aside as others stepped forward and demanded "their" share of funding—as disproportionate as it may have been given the distribution of AIDS and HIV cases according to CDC-defined risk categories.

Besides their internecine squabbling over which "special populations" deserved more than others, the advocates were also fighting amongst themselves over whether to push Congress for a new funding formula to determine how CARE Act funds would be allocated. AIDS Action Council supported a new appropriation process being considered in the Senate that would have jointly funded AIDS services in cities and states, rather than separately as had been done in the CARE Act's first five years. Advocates representing organizations based in hard-hit cities wanted to leave the formula alone, arguing that taking money from the cities where most people with AIDS live would give a disproportionate amount of money to rural areas and smaller towns. San Francisco AIDS Foundation director Pat Christen resigned from AIDS Action's board after eight years because she believed this new funding formula would harm her organization.

To advocates representing organizations in rural areas and smaller towns, the new formula would reflect the changing demographics of the epidemic and loosen the grip that cities such as San Francisco had on CARE Act funding because of their big caseloads and big, influential AIDS organizations. In an egregious conflict of interest, the chair of AIDS Action's policy committee, Doug Nelson, who was director of the AIDS Resource Center of Wisconsin, pushed the council to lobby for the new formula. Nelson also was the head of the Campaign for Fairness, a group whose goal was to increase federal funding for AIDS organizations in rural areas that felt "ripped off" because they were receiving less under the CARE Act than the cities that had tens of thousands of AIDS cases. The new formula would be of great benefit to Nelson's own organization—even if it threatened to split the national AIDS lobby down the middle.

Former AIDS Action staff were hired to represent the competing interests in the battle for reauthorization of the CARE Act. Former director Dan Bross, then employed by a lobbying firm run by two former congressmen, both Republicans, pushed for the funding-formula changes on Capitol Hill. On the other side, Tom Sheridan's new lobbying firm, the Sheridan Group, lobbied for reauthorization of the CARE Act with no changes to the way funding was allocated.

When the CARE Act was finally reauthorized, in May 1996, through fiscal year 2000, it seemed the best that could be said for the AIDS advocates who lobbied for it was that they had united to resist the cuts in funding that were rumored to be in the works by hostile Republicans. The rifts among them were revealed for what they truly were: competing organizational interests, frequently masked in rhetoric about the "needs of people with AIDS." In actual fact, they spoke on their own behalf, which sometimes included the interests of people with AIDS, but at other times seemed to have much more to do with their board members' personal priorities and the expectations of their now-large staffs to be paid regularly.

Certainly no one could deny that services for people with AIDS are vitally important. But one had to question why the AIDS lobbyists focused exclusively and tenaciously—ripping one another to shreds, if necessary—on CARE Act funding. They had never managed to find the same passion for mounting a major push to get the federal government finally to pay for HIV prevention campaigns that were relevant to people's real lives. Could it have had something to do with the fact that funding cuts would mean they'd have to find ways to collaborate so that one or a few organizations could serve multiple populations—rather than there being a different AIDS service organization for every possible variation on the theme of personal identity? More to the point, would it have meant their own organizations, paychecks, and perks would have to be scaled back?

Ralph Payne, formerly Senator Dianne Feinstein's (D-CA) staff person for gay and AIDS issues, told me in late 1995 that although he had probably attended a hundred meetings about the CARE Act, advocates didn't seem interested in, for example, AIDS research. While advocates were "blackening the sky with planes" to fly into Washington "to argue about minutiae and funding formulas in the Ryan White CARE Act," Payne said, they weren't interested in other federal entitlement programs that support people with AIDS, such as welfare and Medicaid. He noted, "There's as much money flowing into California Medicaid dollars as in all Ryan White dollars. Medicaid is by far the biggest AIDS program in the country."[16]

In fact, 40 percent of people with AIDS end up on Medicaid as their sole means of support, according to Tim Westmoreland, who in the fall of 1999 was appointed director of the national Medicaid program. "Ryan White is a drop in the bucket compared to Medicaid," he said.[17] Why, then, have advocates been overwhelmingly focused on the CARE Act? After all, they claim that the "needs of people with AIDS" are their first priority. Could it have to do with the fact that Medicaid provides health care for individuals—and doesn't provide operating revenue for AIDS service organizations?

Or is it because AIDS lobbyists have focused on winning as much as they could for AIDS alone, with little regard for people with other diseases or whose financial precariousness has left them as dependent upon the government as so many people with AIDS? Discussing the "exceptionalism" underlying the CARE Act, Jean McGuire said she was upset by the way AIDS activists had so single-mindedly—and myopically—pushed for their piece of the pie without regard to other Americans in as much need for medical and social services as people with HIV/AIDS. McGuire, who had long worked on Medicaid issues in her pre–AIDS Action Council career, felt it was wrong to carve out exceptions for people because they happened to have the "right" disease. "What did it mean," she asked, "to say this particular disease elevates the status of your poverty above someone else's poverty?" McGuire said AIDS advocates resisted framing the struggle for protection against discrimination and destitution in a broader "poverty discourse"—what it means to be both sick and poor in the wealthiest nation in history—because they viewed the broader systemic reforms that are so clearly needed in the nation's health and social welfare programs as beyond either the scope of their concern for AIDS or their ability to effect change.

Yet, as McGuire pointed out, one can't really talk about AIDS without talking about issues of poverty, disenfranchisement, and the cracks in the nation's social welfare infrastructure that can swallow someone who is sick and poor.[18] Thoughtful leaders in the gay civil rights movement have said similar things about how the struggle for equal rights for gay men and lesbians is ultimately about the struggle for the dignity and freedom of all people.

Before AIDS forced young, white, middle-class gay men to confront both mortality and the inequities of America's health care and social welfare systems, they didn't think much about programs like Medicaid or welfare. But they were outraged and appalled when they saw professionally successful, sometimes affluent, gay men lose their jobs, their homes, and be forced to spend themselves into poverty to be eligible for federal assistance to pay for exorbitantly priced AIDS treatments and to get from gay community organizations the supportive, nonjudgmental services they couldn't receive from mainstream health and social service providers. AIDS advocates successfully persuaded the federal government to fund special programs for people with AIDS under the CARE Act. But as the epidemic continued to spread among nongay, nonwhite, non-middle-class people, their arguments began to seem shortsighted, even selfish. What they wound up with is a parallel system of services created especially for AIDS—even as people who are poor and sick with the "wrong" disease (that is, not AIDS) continue to struggle with inadequate health care and social welfare programs.

At the time the CARE Act was being debated in Congress, Tim Westmoreland said there were questions among AIDS advocates as to whether they ought to pursue an expansion of the Medicaid program or to push for the special AIDS program. We know the answer they settled on. But there is some regret among those who pushed the CARE Act through Congress, among people whose political vision of a just society looks beyond AIDS alone. Westmoreland calls the CARE Act a "safety net for the Middle class." He points out that whereas Medicaid in some places will pay only $15 for a doctor's visit, the CARE Act will pay $50 for massage. "Something is wrong here!" he said. Westmoreland noted that the CARE Act reflects the middle-class values of the AIDS advocates who pushed for its passage. Looking back to the late eighties when the CARE Act was being considered in Congress, Westmoreland said, "Who becomes an AIDS advocate in America? Not poor people. [It was] people who could take time and money to lobby in Washington. It was a class issue." But with AIDS now affecting more poor people, said Westmoreland, "expanding Medicaid could have helped more people with AIDS." He added, "We're at a crossroads to choose between Medicaid versus Ryan White."[19]

One might reasonably expect that an important lesson from the gay community's experience with AIDS would be a recognition that everyone who is in need is equally deserving of assistance and support. Pushing for a broader reform of federal entitlement programs that will benefit *everyone* with AIDS (as well as those with other health needs) would seem a logical extension of the gay movement's traditional philosophy. But AIDS advocacy has gone well beyond the gay community that initiated it. AIDS service organizations now comprise an industry whose lobbyists in Washington work to make sure their employers get all they can. They play up or play down whichever "special population" suits their needs of the moment. If they are speaking to members of Congress, women and children are still a sure bet to win support. If they speak to a group of gay people—who are still good for generous donations—they might actually acknowledge that gay men (of all races) continue to bear the overwhelming brunt of the epidemic in this country. As with the seasoned lobbyists in the halcyon days of the NORA coalition, whatever it takes to win is what they do.

They operate within a system that rewards those with political and financial resources—even as those who lack them are forced to languish without a CARE Act to meet their particular needs. The AIDS advocates talk a good line about race and poverty and all the isms and phobias that, for them, neatly explain the AIDS epidemic and the nation's response to it. But they don't ask the most obvious questions: Why should AIDS services now get more than $1 billion a year under the nation's only disease-specific funding measure? Is it because of the disease's infectiousness? Or because of the young age and productive years lost of its victims? Those are certainly compelling reasons to make AIDS a top priority. One final question, though, is avoided because of the discomfiting implications of its answer: Is AIDS an "exception" because of the political and financial resources of the AIDS industry—and because the CARE Act is now the largest budget item at the Health Resources and Services Administration, the biggest funder of the AIDS industry and every bit as invested as the advocates in the continuation of the CARE Act? Are so many now invested in the CARE Act's continuation that working for genuine health care reform, rather than merely perpetuating the "exceptions" made for AIDS, is more than they care to do?

Perhaps such questions will be sorted out and answered in time. For now, AIDS advocates likely will continue fighting to keep their own piece of pie, arguing that AIDS is exceptional and the CARE Act is the most effective way to fund services despite the figures for such programs as Medicaid that I cited earlier in this chapter. The status quo, even after it was shaken up and altered by AIDS activists in the late eighties, is usually so static because it feels so familiar and safe. But isn't it time to take the vision of equality that gay people brought to AIDS and expand it to ensure that anyone in need of health and medical services is able to access an equitable delivery system? "We may still be too scared to ask those questions," said Jean McGuire. "They are ultimately about giving up privilege."[20]

PART VI

BUILDING MOVEMENT

CHAPTER 20

LESBIANS TRAVEL THE ROADS
OF FEMINISM GLOBALLY

CHARLOTTE BUNCH AND
CLAUDIA HINOJOSA

W HEN WE MET IN 1980 IN COPENHAGEN, DENMARK, at the Non-Governmental (NGO) Forum held parallel to the Mid-Decade United Nations World Conference on Women, there was a spark of recognition between us that we shared a common vision and drive to connect our feminism with our lesbianism. Both of us had come eager to see feminism develop globally and determined that lesbianism be discussed there. We also knew that this issue can be used to divide women, especially along North-South lines, and wanted to challenge the stereotype that lesbians are all white, middle class, and Western. Our lesbian feminism had developed within the women's movements in our respective countries—the USA and Mexico—and we saw its growth linked to the emergence of feminism around the world. In Copenhagen we not only found that we shared common views but also connected with lesbians from other countries with whom we have worked ever since.

This article tells the story of lesbians within the context of the UN World Conferences on Women. Lesbians organized at all these events from the International Women's Year (IWY) World Conference in Mexico City in 1975, where a UN Decade for Women was launched, through the end-of-the-decade events in Nairobi, Kenya, in 1985 and the Fourth World Conference on Women in Beijing ten years later. We alternate voices telling the story as each of us saw it. We use the framework of the UN World Conferences because this is an experience we share, and it is a common reference point for women in diverse countries. Further, the events (especially the nongovernmental ones) surrounding these conferences became gathering places that reflected the growth in women's activities around the world during those years.

The United Nations certainly did not create either feminism or lesbian activism globally, and its officials have often been hostile to both. Nevertheless, it has provided a focus on women worldwide and expanded the public space in which feminist groups could work, as well as sponsored events where women developed international contacts and political savvy. Similarly, women's movements in almost every region have been fearful of lesbianism, yet feminism has provided both the ideological and organizational context for lesbians to become more visible and to challenge homophobia. Thus, both the UN World Conferences and the growth of women's movements around the globe have, often in spite of themselves, assisted in the development of lesbian feminism globally.

Clearly, lesbian activism internationally does not occur only in relation to women's movements and the UN World Conferences. Much of it is cultural, and some relates to gay organizations or is autonomous. While we make references to other types of lesbian organizing, it is beyond the scope of this article to cover the incredible richness and diversity of lesbian political life internationally. Rather, we focus on lesbianism in relation to feminist movements as reflected in a particular context since we know that best and see it as playing a crucial role in advancing lesbian status globally.

UNEXPECTED TURBULENCE

Mexico City, June–July, 1975: "We can only regret the way in which some feministoid groups have turned the Tribune [the nongovernmental event that ran parallel to the official UN conference] into a cheap cabaret or an indecent carnival. In the name of Women's Liberation, these groups came to exhibit their cynicism and shamelessness. . . . What are the lesbians doing here? What can they ask for? Do they want now to inscribe their pathologic irregularity in the Charter of Human Rights? Are they claiming the pathetic 'right' to boast about their sexual aberration? This unawareness of their illness just proves how severe these clinical cases are. . . . They have discredited this Conference and distorted the true purposes of women's emancipation." So read the report of Pedro Gringoire in *Excelsior* (7/1/75), Mexico's largest-circulation newspaper at the time.

Having lived all my life in Mexico City, I observed the International

Women's Year (IWY) Conference, with all its "outrageous incidents," from the dark corners of the closet. I had fully acknowledged my lesbian feelings, "confessed" them to myself, to my partner, and to a couple of friends. But that was all I could afford then, as an urban middle-class music student who had managed to achieve a precarious economic independence. I was definitely not prepared to participate in what came to be the first public discussion in Mexico on lesbianism.

While I have no firsthand impressions of it, I have learned about that event from an article by Frances Doughty in the first edition of *Our Right to Love* ("Lesbians and International Women's Year: A Report on Three Conferences"), material provided by Judith Friedlander and by the Lesbian Herstory Archives in New York, and through an interview with Nancy Cardenas, a prominent Mexican theater director who had not planned to attend the conference but went to the lesbian workshop at the urging of a friend.

Nancy reported, "I was suddenly surrounded by forty, sixty, or probably one hundred journalists. They all asked very direct questions, one after the other. I couldn't even answer them: 'Are you one of them?' 'Where are the others?' 'How did you decide to come here?' 'What does this mean?' "

This "meant," among other things, that Nancy was the only familiar face for the troops of Mexican journalists who had clustered outside the room where the first lesbian workshop was about to take place. Her presence there as a well-known public figure in Mexico provided not only the possibility of titillating news but also a confrontation to the way the press had been handling the lesbian issue during the conference. They had approached it as an imported extravagance, completely alien to Mexican women and to the legitimate interests of Third World women.

The emergence of lesbianism at the Tribune took everyone by surprise. It was not easy to predict that this gathering would become the frame for the first fruitful exchange between Mexican lesbians and organized lesbians from several countries. Consider the setting: the Mexican government appointed as president of the official conference Mr. Pedro Ojeda Paullada, the attorney general, and the Tribune's meeting was opened by the president's wife, Maria Ester Zuno de Echeverria, who proclaimed that "man and woman cannot be conceived separately. . . . The participation of women as citizens is a task that cannot accept deviations."

Through a Latin American feminist living in the United States, contact had been established between the lesbian visitors and the lesbian underground community in Mexico. After a few days of research, this feminist had obtained Nancy Cardenas's phone number and invited her to the lesbian workshop at the Tribune. Nancy had been working for almost four years with a gay and lesbian group that was discussing Mexican law, reading and writing about principles of sexual liberation and consciousness-raising, and undertaking "cultural guerrilla" actions: informing journalists and intellectuals about homosexuality and opening private debates with influential psychologists and psychiatrists.

In coverage of the IWY Conference, the word *lesbian* was printed for the first time in a "respectable" mainstream Mexican newspaper. The front page of *Excelsior* read: GIRLS FROM THE US DEFEND HOMOSEXUALISM. The L-word, with all its reverberating effects, also appeared in an inside article featuring Laurie Bebbington, national women's officer of the Australian Student Union, who "bravely stepped up on the platform to defend lesbianism and to demand that society not keep women with this tendency 'invisible and forbidden.' "

Another major Mexican newspaper, *Novedades,* under the headline ARMÓ LA GORDA (hell broke loose), reported that Frances Doughty, from the U.S. National Gay Task Force Women's Caucus, demanded that the Tribune's program include the issue of lesbianism. The article also included long excerpts of Bebbington's speech on sex-role stereotyping and the family: "In this room there are single women, there are childless women, and there are women who choose to love other women. Acceptance of a compulsory marriage and motherhood for all women not only denies us the possibility of choice. It downgrades and insults the lifestyles of many of our sisters present here. . . . I am proud to say that I am a lesbian: that I have chosen to love other women." The wave of applause that preceded that statement, as well as the verbal abuse that followed, were also reported, e.g.: "Throw her out!" "Go see a doctor!"

The International Lesbian Caucus, formed by women from several countries at the beginning of the Tribune, had challenged the exclusion of lesbianism from the agenda in an article published by *Xilonen,* the Tribune's daily newspaper: "Everywhere it is assumed that we do not exist or that we are a very small group of deviants. . . . All women are assumed to be heterosexual. . . . Sex-role stereotyping is the principal way that [these] oppressive relationships are maintained. This conference has reinforced this stereotyping by choosing to ignore lesbians in the planned schedule. The real issues of this conference have been raised by the participants themselves through free time at the microphone and through workshops."

After several interventions by lesbians in the large plenary sessions, lesbian workshops were scheduled and organizers were overwhelmed at the positive response as people poured out of the small workshop rooms. Not only was it the first time that lesbianism had been openly discussed in Mexico, but the workshops provided the only space at the Tribune for discussion by women of their own sexuality. The panelists addressed different aspects of lesbian feminism, including the experience of two lesbian mothers. A group of Mexican lesbian feminists wrote a statement that they asked the panelists to read, speaking about their struggle against self-loathing. In addition, private meetings were held where lesbians celebrated what had happened, talked more intimately about their lives, and discussed further the possibilities of organizing a movement.

While the Tribune and the government conference did not talk further about lesbianism or take any actions to support the issue, which most still viewed as outrageous, the L-word had been introduced into the UN Women's Year and the UN Decade for Women to follow. Nancy Cardenas recalled being nearly "pulled out of the closet" by circumstances "which simply surpassed me." So it was for many lesbians at the time of the Mexico conference. The moment to transform our individual self-rediscoveries into a collective enterprise and a public presence in the Mexican political scenario, as well as in the international lesbian feminist movement, would come some years later.

During the years that followed the Mexico City conference, I discovered feminism as a new understanding of politics. It began reshaping my life, validating my sexual experiences, empowering my social imagination, and articulating my political desires. This is how I was able to participate in the coming out of the Mexican lesbian and gay movement in 1978. The movement also emerged that year in other Latin American countries, such as Brazil, Colombia, and Costa Rica.

Besides the growth of the feminist movement, other conditions favored the appearance of the lesbian and gay movement in Mexico during the late seventies: the opening of "democratic spaces" through political reform, a brief period of temporary economic affluence, and an atmosphere of rising social expectations. The years 1978, 1979, and 1980 were full of intense activity for the movement. We introduced the discussion of heterosexism and the importance of the lesbian issue to feminist groups, we participated in coalitions such as the National Front for Women's Liberation and the National Front against Repression, and we challenged the agenda of the university trade unions and the new sexological institutions. The first gay and lesbian pride march was organized in 1979 in Mexico City. At an international level, I made connections with the Spanish movement in 1977, when I participated in the first gay and lesbian demonstration of the post-Franco era in Barcelona. In 1979, I experienced meaningful exchanges as part of a small Mexican contingent at the U.S. Third World Gay and Lesbian Conference, followed by the first national march on Washington, D.C. So, in a rather euphoric spirit, I arrived in Copenhagen in 1980 for the Mid-Decade Conference on Women, mobilized more by the promise of getting in touch with feminists from all over than by the UN's call for "equality, development, and peace," the official conference themes.

—C.H.

LESBIANS NETWORK INTERNATIONALLY

One hot Tokyo night in July of 1971, I slipped away from the meetings that had taken me there to go to a lesbian bar with a straight U.S. feminist and her gay male friend who knew the place. I had become a lesbian six months earlier within the women's movement in Washington, D.C. I was part of The Furies, a lesbian collective eager to find lesbians everywhere with whom we could build "a new world." As I struggled through my gay male interpreter to explain our political ideas to a bar hostess dressed in a finely tailored pin-striped suit, she kept asking if there really were women in my country who "loved only women." Her eagerness to know there were lesbians elsewhere was so great that she could not get past that question, forcing me to see the isolation that so many lesbians experience in the world.

During the 1970s, I worked in the lesbian/gay and women's movements in the United States, but I yearned for a broader perspective and wanted to know more about lesbian reality elsewhere. In preparation for the 1975 International Women's Year Conference in Mexico City, Frances Doughty and I cowrote an article on how North American feminists and lesbians might approach that event and make our issues visible without dominating it as *gringas*. We suggested that groups choose people to represent them rather than flooding the conference with USAmericans, so I found myself staying here doing support work while Frances went to be our lesbian presence. I followed the reports from Mexico, feeling proud that the word *lesbian* had made it onto the floor and feeling sad that it was dismissed by many as outrageous and Western.

Following the Mexico City Conference, the U.S. Congress authorized a National Women's Conference to be held in Houston, Texas, in 1977 as part of International Women's Year and the UN Decade for Women. After intense lobbying of the Carter administration by lesbian and gay leaders, Jean O'Leary of the National Gay Task Force (NGTF) staff was selected to be one of forty-seven members of the National Commission for the event. As a member of the Board of Directors of NGTF and one of the leaders of its women's caucus, I saw this as an opportunity to advance lesbian rights in the United States. I worked closely with Jean and with lesbian, gay, and feminist groups around the country to ensure that lesbians were delegates and that our issues were included in the Houston Plan of Action.

Throughout 1977, conferences open to all women voters were held in every state. Many women got involved, and feminist coalitions formed in response to growing pressures from right-wing women's organizations, who also sought to control the agenda. Lesbians all over the country participated in their state conferences—proposing resolutions, getting elected as delegates, and building coalitions with other feminists. A significant number of out lesbians were elected as delegates, and the national lesbian caucus we organized out of

NGTF played a key role as part of the Feminist Pro-Plan Coalition in keeping "Sexual Preference" one of the twenty-six planks approved in the National Plan of Action. It was one of the most unifying moments in the U.S. women's movement and a highpoint for lesbians, marking both a maturity in our organizing and mainstream feminist acceptance of our presence and power. However, it also foreshadowed the intensity of the backlash against feminism and lesbian/gay rights that has dominated much of U.S. and international women's politics ever since.

By the time of the Copenhagen conference in 1980, I had begun to work more internationally and sought to find a path for lesbian visibility within the UN Decade similar to what we had achieved in Houston. I worked with two international women's organizations, the International Women's Tribune Centre and ISIS, to set up an explicitly feminist international networking section at the NGO Forum, where controversial issues such as lesbianism and abortion could safely be discussed. In addition, the Forum organizing committee had accepted five or six proposals for lesbian workshops in the regular schedule of events. These were well attended, primarily by lesbians from industrialized countries but with some Third World participants. In addition, women who did not identify as lesbians asked for other sessions to discuss the issue since they felt intimidated or hesitant to attend lesbian workshops. Several small groups met near the end of the Forum with women from a wide range of countries, including more from the Third World, for lively dialogues where women seeking to end their ignorance asked basic questions about how lesbians live, have children, and age.

Thus, lesbians moved from outrageous scandal in Mexico to low-key networking in Copenhagen. The 1980 sessions were productive, but they were perhaps too quiet. Although the press sought to inflame antilesbian sentiment at the end with a photo of women at the Forum sunning shirtless, many who attended the conference never knew the subject had been discussed. It did not become a controversy and did not garner much media attention. With some ten thousand participants and over two thousand separate workshops and no room that held more than six hundred, the decentralized structure of the Forum contributed to this invisibility. The major controversies that grabbed headlines and divided women were over the Middle East and Zionism specifically, and the definition of feminism and women's issues generally. These divisions were serious, and Western domination of the conference precluded their resolution. Still, important pockets of constructive exchange between women of the North and the South occurred that the press ignored, but that led to global networks and projects during the 1980s and 1990s. Some of those exchanges laid the groundwork for various global lesbian activities as well.

Several European lesbians present at Copenhagen were from groups affiliated with the International Gay Association (IGA), founded in England by gay men in 1978. IGA, a gay civil rights organization based in the Netherlands, was holding a conference every year. During the early 1980s, a number of lesbians working with IGA challenged its sexism and in 1981 formed a separate organization, ILIS—International Lesbian Information Secretariat (later changed to Service). From 1980 to 1985, IGA and ILIS both held conferences every year, which, while mostly European, did include a growing number of North and South Americans, and a few participants from elsewhere. The IGA and ILIS conferences were the only ongoing international gay events in this period, although increasingly, lesbians also met across national lines at other events such as women's studies conferences. In 1986 the IGA changed its name to ILGA (International Lesbian and Gay Association), and its programs have come to reflect a larger concern with lesbians, although women are still a minority in its affairs.

The ILIS conferences in the eighties were lively arenas with raging debates over whether to work with men or straight women, the role of culture and politics in the movement, etc. Unfortunately, ILIS had organizational and financial difficulties and was dependent on the viability of its home offices, which have rotated over the years. Perhaps its greatest success in terms of global lesbianism was the last conference held in 1986 in Geneva, which had a significant number of Third World participants due to the work of the Geneva organizers. ILIS represented lesbian desires for global visibility and played an important role both in Nairobi and through the 1986 Geneva conference.

Between the Copenhagen (1980) and Nairobi (1985) conferences, lesbian consciousness and organizing in the Third World expanded. At the first Latin American and Caribbean Feminist Encuentro (Conference), held in Bogotá, Colombia, in 1981, lesbianism was discussed in a small session as part of the workshop on sexuality and health. During the second Encuentro held in Lima, Peru, in 1983, the subject was not on the agenda so lesbians called for a mini-workshop. The session began in a bar after dinner but drew so much interest that it reconvened in the plenary hall, where over half of the six hundred participants present spent a moving evening in what was perhaps the largest ever coming-out event in the region. Following that opening at the Encuentro, a number of lesbian feminist groups formed throughout Latin America from Chile and Peru to Brazil, Mexico, and the Dominican Republic. Visible parts of the women's movement in the region, they have continued to demand that lesbian oppression and homophobia be understood as issues for the whole movement and not just questions of a sexual minority.

Prior to the Nairobi conference in 1985, Asian lesbians also began to speak out, often first as communities in the West and then in their native countries. For example, Asian Lesbians of the East Coast (of the USA) brought forth a slide show on the history of lesbians in the region. A short-lived but vibrant South Asian newsletter, *Anamika,* published out of New York, reflected the spirit of making lesbianism everywhere visible. Its inaugural issue, published in May 1985, in time for the Nairobi conference, declared: "We aim to provide information by and about Indian, Pakistani, Bangladeshi, Afghani, Sri Lankan, Bhutanese, Nepalese, and Burmese lesbians. . . . Lesbianism has been a part of our histories for thousands of years. We refuse to continue to be invalidated as a 'Western phenomenon.' "

The 1980s saw increased lesbian visibility in the world but also of growing complexity within the movement. The AIDS crisis reshaped the gay movement, raising difficult issues for lesbians about our role in responding to it. The growth of lesbian consciousness and organizing in many Third World countries was paralleled in the United States by a greater visibility of lesbians of color. As the movement became more diverse, the breadth of issues it addressed and people it reached widened, but these changes added to the complexity of determining what is a lesbian agenda. Further, the conservative climate in the West symbolized by Thatcher and Reagan required that lesbians spend more time defending ourselves, often at the expense of moving forward in new areas. In much of the Third World, the worsening economic situation heightened difficulties for lesbians, who as women often lacked the economic independence necessary to live openly as lesbians. All of these developments set the stage for the 1985 Nairobi World Conference on Women, which began with rumors that out lesbians might be prevented from going but became an exciting arena for lesbian discussion globally.

—C.B.

GLOBAL LESBIANISM COMES OUT

In July 1985, more than fourteen thousand women gathered in Nairobi, Kenya, for the Non-Governmental Forum held parallel to the UN End of the Decade World Conference. One of the most appealing aspects of this unprecedented event was the diversification of the lesbian presence, related to the emergence of feminism in many Third World countries. In contrast to the low-key networking that took place in Copenhagen, lesbianism was an issue in Nairobi that hardly escaped anyone's attention. On the first day of the conference, the Forum '85 newspaper confirmed "reports appearing in two Kenyan daily papers of the presence of lesbians at the NGO Forum. At least two hundred of them have already arrived in spite of the reports that their presence has offended other Forum participants."

There were initially some edgy responses from the organizers due to rumors and fear of the Kenyan government's interference with and objection to lesbian activity. This uneasiness led to some misunderstandings that the press exploited. But the Forum Organizing Committee scheduled and respected official workshops on lesbians and employment, health, racism, education, and international lesbian networking.

As in Mexico in 1975, this was the first public discussion of lesbianism in Kenya. There was so much interest that informal sessions on the lawn at the University of Nairobi's Great Court were organized daily. This "lesbian spot" remained crowded throughout the conference, mostly by Kenyan women (and some men), who asked *all* sorts of questions, answered by lesbians from different countries. Though sometimes exhausting, this was one of the activities I enjoyed most because of the informal, direct, and often playful exchange. There were also daily meetings of lesbians at five o'clock, which provided the best space to talk among ourselves and also served as a place to check out problems and rumors.

For many of us, the highlight of Nairobi was the Lesbian Press Conference, where women from all over the world spoke about their situation in front of the press. One of my most striking memories of that contagiously encouraging session was when a powerful Peruvian leader of the urban popular movement stood up to state publicly for the first time that she enormously enjoyed being a lesbian. Another outcome of the press conference was the Third World lesbians' statement: "It has often been assumed that lesbianism is a product of decadent capitalist societies. We refute this argument and make our existence as Third World lesbians and lesbians of color everywhere known. . . . If it seems that lesbianism is confined to white Western women, it is often because Third World lesbians and lesbians of color come up against more obstacles to our visibility. . . . But this silence has to be seen as one more aspect of women's sexual repression and not as a conclusion that lesbianism doesn't concern us. . . . The struggle for lesbian rights is indispensable to any struggle for basic human rights. It's part of the struggle of all women for control over our own lives."

Being in Nairobi provided the opportunity to learn about different ways lesbians live and keep inventing daily forms of resistance or struggle within diverse cultural, economic, and political realities. One inspiring experience was witnessing the success of the Dutch lesbians' strategy to get their official delegation to speak out on behalf of lesbian women. The Dutch delegate's speech included a call for defending lesbian rights and was the first historic mention of lesbianism at a United Nations conference. It also produced concrete results when the Dutch government followed up its policy statements made in Nairobi by providing travel funds for about twenty women from around the world to attend the ILIS lesbian international conference held in Geneva in March 1986.

In Geneva, approximately eight hundred lesbians attended the ILIS conference from no less than thirty countries, making it the most diverse lesbian conference to date. This eighth ILIS conference was hosted by the group

Vanille-Fraise and housed at the University of Geneva. The organizers spent more than a year contacting lesbians from around the world, drawing substantial participation by lesbians of color from the West, a number of lesbians from Asia and Latin America, and one woman from Kenya.

There were twenty scheduled workshops, plus several spontaneous events and caucuses, along with films, slide shows, and dramatic presentations during that intense weekend. New contacts, friendships, and exchanges gave shape to the Asian Lesbian Network and the Latin American Lesbian Network. The resulting enthusiasm led us, the Latin American Network, to propose on the spot the First Latin American and Caribbean Lesbian Encuentro to take place in Mexico, in 1987.

The Encuentro, an event that couldn't even have been imagined some years before, was held in Cuernavaca, Mexico. The first such conference in the region, it drew around 250 lesbians from Mexico, South and Central America, the Spanish- and English-speaking Caribbean, as well as Chicanas, Latinas, and non-Latinas from the United States, Europe, and Canada. Rebecca Sevilla, from Peru, wrote in the 1988 ILIS newsletter: "Lesbian mothers, lesbian feminists, lesbian Marxist-Leninists, lesbians working in gay movements or trade unions, individual lesbians without a group. . . . were meeting each other, sharing experiences, fighting, making love . . . and helping with the practical organization of the conference. The setting up of a Latin American lesbian network was a very important, but slow and difficult process."

The Lesbian Latin American Network set a number of long-term goals. These included breaking down isolation through the publication of a newsletter and directory, supporting international actions against the oppression of lesbians, strengthening our public presence through increasing participation in the feminist movement and other progressive movements, and organizing periodic lesbian *encuentros* in the region.

The second lesbian *encuentro* was to take place in Peru in 1989, but due to the difficult economic and political situation there, it was held in Costa Rica in 1990. During the 1990s, three more lesbian feminist regional meetings were held: Puerto Rico in 1993; Argentina in 1995; and Brazil in 1999. These *encuentros* required considerable efforts from the organizing committees, who struggled with scarce resources and often hostile and repressive local environments. In the midst of such adverse conditions, the *encuentros* became the space for meaningful and sometimes polarized debates, as the movement grew, diversified, and faced new challenges, such as the severe impact of structural-adjustment policies and increasing violence in the region. Some of the critical questions raised at the *encuentros* included the meaning of political autonomy and the need to make alliances with other social movements, dealing with ideological diversity within the movement, problems of organizational structure, leadership, and representation, and the role of lesbian visibility within the women's movement. These continue to be challenges to lesbian organizing in Latin America as well as in other parts of the world.

—C.H.

AFTER THE DECADE—A CENTURY

The UN Decade conferences proved useful to lesbian networking globally, but they were also sober reminders of how far we still have to go to get respect for the human rights of lesbians and gay men. While the issue was raised at all the NGO parallel events, no overall consideration of it took place that was endorsed or recorded by the conferences as a whole. Too often the L-word was still unspeakable—avoided or referred to only euphemistically in many women's groups, and lesbian issues were often marginalized as special interests rather than incorporated as part of the whole picture.

Yet, if we measure progress by how far we have come away from the isolation of lesbians prior to the UN Decade, there has been significant change. In the years between the Nairobi (1985) and Beijing (1995) World Conferences, lesbians became more visible in many ways, often utilizing the space opened by feminism. Lesbian groups emerged in industrialized countries in North America, Europe, Australia, and New Zealand alongside women's movements during the 1970s and similarly in Latin America in the 1980s. As Eastern Europe became more open, lesbian groups in Poland and East Germany surfaced quickly, as did the Yugoslav organization, which had hoped to sponsor an ILIS conference in 1990. With the end of the Cold War, the 1990s have seen the growth of lesbian and gay groups in Eastern Europe, but the erosion of women's economic independence in the region has made it hard for many women to survive as open lesbians.

Asian lesbian networking, which was encouraged at the ILIS conference in Geneva, has continued to expand, and several regional conferences for Asian lesbians have been held in the nineties in different countries from Thailand to Japan. Lesbians in this region face societies where they are labeled Western in spite of cultural roots that can be traced back as far as 500 B.C. when Buddhist nuns wrote lesbian love poetry. In India, two working-class lesbian policewomen in Bhopal, India, who married in 1988, were discharged from their jobs amid an uproar that forced more open discussion of the issue in the women's movement as well as among the general public. Some lesbians in the region report that this union, registered as *a maitrikarar* ("marriage of friendship"), inspired other lesbian unions in a country where young women facing forced marriages sometimes commit suicide together or run away. In the 1990s, a number of Indian lesbian and gay groups have formed, and the first anthology of lesbian writing from India was published in 1999.

Another important development can be seen in the global women's networks that have given recognition to the importance of lesbian issues. Soon after Nairobi, an open letter from the Third World caucus of the Fifth International Women and Health Conference in Costa Rica in 1987 included the statement: "We reject a definition of sexuality as synonymous with heterosexuality. We demand that lesbianism be recognized as a political issue, and that sexuality be considered as socially determined." Similar positions have been taken at all the International Women and Health Conferences since, which incorporate lesbian issues as a matter of course.

In the early 1990s, women's networks began organizing to bring feminist perspectives into all types of UN activities that were not woman-specific, including UN world conferences. I have been active in one of these efforts—the Global Campaign for Women's Human Rights—which developed around the concept that "women's rights are human rights" and first sought to put women onto the agenda of the UN World Conference on Human Rights in Vienna in 1993. While the NGO activities of this campaign have included lesbian rights as women's/human rights, we did not succeed in raising this issue at the governmental level in Vienna. A year later, an effort by the international women's health movement to gain respect for "sexual rights" on the Programme of Action from the International Conference on Population and Development in Cairo failed as such but did generate considerable attention and advanced the document's commitment to women's rights and empowerment.

All of these developments set the stage for the first open governmental debate about lesbianism at a UN World Conference, which took place at the Fourth World Conference on Women in Beijing in September of 1995. Rumors about lesbians abounded in China, where the general public had been told to expect bare-breasted lesbian demonstrations, and the police were rumored to be equipped with blankets to toss over any such offenders. While this preparation proved unnecessary, lesbians were highly visible in the NGO Forum held outside Beijing as well as well prepared for the debates in the official government meeting.

Activists for lesbian rights coming from every continent and a variety of organizations operated within a global women's movement that had developed considerable experience at UN conferences. Lesbians were present in the regional and international preparatory events for the Beijing conference to argue for inclusion of references to sexual orientation, and a network was formed in preparation for Beijing that was facilitated by the International Gay and Lesbian Human Rights Commission. Many lesbian activists of an earlier generation such as me were now deeply involved in the larger agenda of women's rights and counted on collaboration with a newer generation whose energies were more directly focused on lesbian rights.

One of the new generation of activists was Ara Wilson, who wrote about the lesbian caucus in Beijing: "At the preparatory meetings, activists for sexual rights (guided by friends in high places) had been rapidly learning and improvising tactics to ensure that violations of women's basic rights based on sexuality were addressed by this official forum. The drafts for the official document held five paragraphs with the terms *sexual orientation, sexual rights,* or *sexual autonomy* marked for debate by brackets. In Beijing, in a bordello-like room above a disco, the lesbian caucus met daily to plan lobbying to include these phrases. Inspired by the direct-action method of politics, lesbians staged a peaceful protest within the UN meeting itself, displaying a banner and placards." The lesbian caucus was also allotted an NGO slot to speak in the plenary. Palesa Beverley Ditsie, a young lesbian from South Africa, used it well to remind the assembly, "No woman can determine the direction of her own life without the ability to determine her sexuality."

While the space for debate over the inclusion of the term *sexual orientation* in the intergovernmental conference was a victorious first, this discussion was put off until the early hours of the morning on the last night, and it was often venomous. None of the references survived, but there was support from some thirty countries, including an extremely moving statement by a South African delegate that they had just emerged from a struggle against discrimination and would never sanction it against another group. Such support was critical given the effort by some to label this a white, Western issue—an accusation that often turned ugly as when an older African leader attacked Ditsie after her speech, saying she must have some "white blood" as there are no real African lesbians. The virulence of the homophobia of some opponents and the way that they used it to try to oppose women's rights more generally educated some delegates about the importance of the issue.

The supporters of sexual rights did win some battles, such as paragraph 96 in the health section of the Platform for Action, which reads: "The human rights of women include their right to have control over and decide freely and responsibly on matters related to their sexuality, including sexual and reproductive health, free of coercion, discrimination, and violence." Further, several governments entered interpretive statements noting that they considered references to the prohibition of discrimination on the basis of "other status" where it appears in the Platform to include sexual orientation. These victories and the coalitions built among lesbians and other women in preparation for and during the Beijing conference provide a strong place from which to build in the future.

I cannot leave the discussion of Beijing without saying a word about the lively "lesbian tent" that was one of seven "diversity tents" in the permanent meeting area of the NGO Forum. While regrettably I did not have much time to spend there, Ara Wilson offers a vivid description of the vital role it played in advancing lesbian visibility and understanding throughout the ten days of the Forum: "The tent served as the place to meet, to hold workshops, to provide information, and to prepare lobbying strategies. . . . But the existence of this tent was especially critical to the many women who must remain quiet, or 'closeted,' about this part of their lives. . . . [It] hosted a continuous flow of visitors, including fascinated onlookers and reporters eager to file a sensationalist story. Anjana, the Thai organizer, prepared a 'lesbianism for the curious' meeting where attendees were able to ask questions about this thing called lesbianism. African lesbians and bisexuals met for the first time. For the most part, the neighboring tents, passersby, and the larger NGO community received the lesbian presence with warmth and welcome. These exchanges at the lesbian tent or the 'curious' workshops were important ways to demonstrate that lesbians come from all regions, classes, and ages; to show that they can be happy, well adjusted, and have children; and to convey that the problems we face come from society or the state, not from our sexuality itself." Beijing was a long way from Mexico, Copenhagen, and Nairobi, and yet it was a familiar story of lesbians coming together and talking with others along the pathways of global feminism.

Lesbians are of course everywhere, and the impetus for making our realities and views known keeps growing around the world. Clearly, that so much has happened in just over two decades indicates how much can be done when lesbians find spaces to come together and to come out. The context for this work, however, is often discouraging, as violence and hostility still greet efforts to establish our human rights. Nevertheless, the means of resistance and survival among our sisters throughout the world are remarkable. While lesbian activity does not take the same form everywhere, we can learn from the great diversity of ways that we continue to assert our rights and visions. We must look beneath the surface of descriptions of our reality and particularly the denials of our existence to see the strength of what lesbians are doing. Thus we will come to know, as the Japanese bar lesbian discovered, that, yes, women who love women are in all parts of the world, and we are changing the face of that world as well.

—C.B.

RECOMMENDED READING

A list of recommended reading appears in the Notes, pages 516–17.

CHAPTER 21

Three Marches,
Many Lessons

Nadine Smith

E VER SINCE DR. MARTIN LUTHER KING'S VOICE
echoed across the Reflecting Pool and through the living rooms of
America in 1963, social justice movements have come to view massive gatherings in our nation's capital as rites of passage. Immortalized by King's "I Have a
Dream" speech, the March on Washington for Jobs and Freedom in August
1963 became a watershed moment in American history. The stark moral con-
trasts were inescapable: peaceful freedom marchers armed with love, courage,
and commitment vs. the glowering, hate-filled segregationists armed with fire-
hoses and tear-gas bombs and flanked by attack dogs. With that march, mass
media finally provided the civil rights movement sufficient coverage to shame
a nation. The country heard in it a clarion call to its better nature, as well as a
formal declaration of moral authority by those who had been victims but maintained the grace to, in King's words, "inject a glorious new dimension of love
into the veins of society."

Even among those who know little else about the civil rights movement,
images of that grand moment in Washington, D.C., are familiar and powerful.
A desire to replicate or at least match the power of that march has fueled a
steady parade of similar events in the nation's capital over the past three

decades. Vietnam War opponents, women's liberationists, economic-justice activists, African-American men, animal rights groups, nuclear disarmament proponents—all have used gatherings in Washington as a sort of holy grail for the disenfranchised and a national spotlight for a long and varied list of issues, movements, and causes.

But what is the net effect of these massive gatherings? Do they result in political change, cultural definition, spiritual healing? All, part, or none of the above?

The backbone of the modern queer movement was formed by individuals who cut their activist teeth in the 1960s and 1970s marching for a variety of progressive causes. No longer content to put energy into causes that welcomed them only as long as they parked their queer identities at the door, they felt an increasing need to connect and be visible. Mass national actions offered them not only a platform for queer political organizing, but an irreplaceable opportunity to break through isolation, to rejuvenate, and to heal the psychic damage of discrimination and alienation. Many have described participation in national marches as a turning point that launched them out of the closet and headlong into activism.

Gay and lesbian activists (bisexual and transgender activists had not yet emerged on the scene as organized and recognized political forces) were buoyed by the political climate, emboldened by queer cultural and political advancements, and moved by the impact of the 1963 march. They began to look for ways to increase the visibility of issues specific to sexual orientation. In 1965, roughly a dozen gay and lesbian pioneers donned suits and dresses and held up picket signs in front of the White House and the Pentagon, calling for an end to the government prohibition on hiring homosexuals. This small event paid homage in tone and demeanor to the 1963 march. The strict code of dress and conduct was designed to present a nonthreatening image to a country whose only concept of gays was as warped, depraved, and sinister people to be reviled or pitied.

But this clean-cut, carefully orchestrated, and courageous picket line is not the moment we recount when we commemorate the beginning of the modern gay movement. Instead, we usually look to the rowdy, cross-dressing, gender-bending, multiracial howl of pain and defiance that erupted at the Stonewall Inn in 1969. Perhaps our embrace of the Stonewall riot as the beginning of the modern queer liberation movement is at the foundation of the conflicts that often erupt over what our national marches are supposed to accomplish and signify today.

Unlike race, sexual orientation carries with it the double-edged sword of the closet. While it can protect most of us from the daily confrontations with discrimination, it also blunts our ability to define starkly the oppression we face. Even the most "out" generally keep the closet door unlocked for emergencies.

As a consequence, visibility—breaking through the assumption of heterosexuality—has often been viewed as our ultimate political act.

But as political and cultural gains lead sexual minorities out of the closet, increasing numbers lack the knowledge of, or the allegiance to, the liberationist roots of the movement. There is conflict between those who believe the movement is about visibility as a political act that challenges compulsory heterosexuality and those who tend more toward assimilation and believe equality will come from asserting we are more like heterosexuals than we are different. Left vs. right, progressive vs. conservative, liberationist vs. assimilationist—however the conflict is defined, it gets played out most dramatically during the national dialogues provoked by march organizing. Much of the current dissension over the value and purpose of national marches comes down to a battle over how we define ourselves and to whom our marches are supposed to speak. Who is the audience? Those of us gathered on the Mall? The isolated teen in the heartland watching the event on television who now knows she's not alone? Straight America? Politicians? Depending on how one answers this question, the three national marches have been remarkable successes, disappointing failures, or something of both.

Those who evoke the 1963 march and wonder aloud "Where is our movement's Martin Luther King?" tend to argue that our marches must present a nonthreatening image that causes Middle America to acknowledge our commonalities and consequently support our equality. Implicit in this message is a desire to present a carefully crafted image in which nonmainstream images of the lesbian, gay, bi, and trans community are invisible or at least minimized. But in times of crisis it is easier to table those differences to focus attention on the most imminent danger.

THE FIRST NATIONAL MARCH: 1979

While critical strides and activism occurred long before the Stonewall rebellion in 1969, the years immediately preceding and following the riots were filled with a rapid succession of cultural and political advances for the lesbian, gay, bisexual, and transgender (LGBT) communities. There were groundbreaking literary works. The first openly gay person appeared on national television. The Gay Liberation Front, the Metropolitan Community Church, the National Gay Task Force, and Lambda Legal Defense Fund were among the national organizations that formed. The first openly gay person was elected to office. Lesbians successfully challenged homophobia in NOW. The American Psychiatric Association stopped labeling homosexuality a disease. And Florida saw the passage of one of the nation's first local bans on antigay discrimination in the Dade County Human Rights Ordinance.

Beauty-queen-turned-orange-juice-spokesmodel Anita Bryant used the Dade County law to launch her Save Our Children campaign in 1977. A self-described born-again Christian, Bryant was the darling of the far right wing, whose religious fundamentalists vilified homosexuals and tried to rescind the advances of the previous decade. The effort succeeded in repealing the Dade County ordinance, and within two years, Florida's became the first state legislature to specifically ban adoptions by gays and lesbians. (Today, Florida is the only state that continues such a ban.) Bryant's efforts emboldened right-wing homophobes around the country and issued a challenge to the queer community to stand up to the backlash. Coupled with the antigay Briggs initiative in California, the Bryant campaign fueled activists' discussions of a national gathering in Washington, D.C.

While the prospect of marching had been raised in a variety of places, Harvey Milk is generally acknowledged as the first to call for the national march during his 1978 Pride Week speech in front of San Francisco's City Hall. Two months later, an ad hoc committee gathered in Minneapolis to begin organizing, but internal struggles caused the group to disband. Then, in November 1978, Harvey Milk was assassinated. The need to react in a unified way caused activists in San Francisco, Philadelphia, and New York to rekindle the organizing efforts. By March, a steering committee, coordinating committee, and several working committees had been formed.

The national office was opened by the spring of 1979 and regional offices were soon established. Area conferences were organized to select delegates to a national steering committee to be held in July at the University of Houston. The 1979 March Program book described the meeting and process: "There, 128 delegates, 48 percent women and 28 percent Third-World persons, plus observers and press, discussed questions concerning lesbian visibility and the inclusion of Third-World people in all leadership and policy positions within March planning. That conference was cochaired by six persons on a rotating basis to allow the broadest facilitation of the meeting. Since March organizing was being done by many transpersons (transsexuals, transvestites, transgenderists, drag queens, and female impersonators) along with all the other various organizers in the country, there was considerable discussion about a policy of nondiscrimination towards them. Out of those discussions came the inclusion of transpersons within all March literature, and on advisory boards to the structure of the organization of the March." Permits for the march and rally were secured in late July, and a national information center was established by the Houston conference. As a result of the Houston conference, the National Gay Task Force, Gay Rights National Lobby, the National Organization for Women, Metropolitan Community Church, the National Lawyers Guild, and the Mobilization for Survival decided to endorse the march on Washington. The involvement of these significant organizations within the march planning placed the movement in a new relationship to the struggle for civil liberties in the United States.

The march was now on sure footing to make broad advances in the fight for gay rights. The organizing of the march on Washington gave a diverse community a new wave of energy and coalition building and established a structural guideline for how other groups should work. A minimum of 50 percent women and 20 percent Third World people were to be included in all planning and leadership of the march. There would also be advisory groups of other underrepresented groups from the community: youth, older persons, physically challenged people, and transpersons. This inclusion allowed for more representative decision making and maximized the flow of information throughout the community. For national organizing, the country was broken down into seven regions to insure urban as well as rural input. Thus, when the marchers finally strode down Pennsylvania Avenue before the White House, they had done much to assure that our entire community, with all its diversity and humanity, was showcased.

In that spirit, the 1979 march on Washington became the first national mass action for queer liberation. If Stonewall marked the beginning of the modern gay movement, the first national queer march in 1979 was its coming-out party. The impact was profound for those who traveled from Greenwich Village, the Castro, and other queer enclaves along the coasts. We Are Everywhere was no longer just a slogan. It was a very visible, dramatically proven fact. "After Stonewall, the 1979 march took us to a new level. It put us on the map as a large and serious movement," says Leslie Cagan, an organizer who has attended all three marches and was a key organizer for the 1987 event. "Even for those who lived in the urban centers, this was a new experience. We were just finding out that we really were everywhere."

While marches today are measured by attendance and media coverage, a more accurate accounting can be made in the aftermath of an event. The remnants of the organizing structure are usually transformed into local, state, and national groups. Even though the community's information infrastructure— newspapers, community centers, the Internet—for the most part did not yet exist, the 1979 march still drew approximately one hundred thousand participants, largely from well-known queer enclaves where some measure of community, anonymity, and safety existed. Thus, the event was not just about presenting our face to society but, perhaps even more importantly, to each other. The sheer number of those who gathered fearlessly in the heart of government power was, in itself, a life-changing experience for most.

THE SECOND NATIONAL MARCH: 1987

Just as 1979 was spurred by the Anita Bryant crusade and Harvey Milk's assassination, the 1987 march was unmistakably a response to the AIDS epidemic. The Reagan/Bush administration had refused to acknowledge the plague, let alone marshal resources to end it. The horror of it galvanized the community across many lines of division and moved many who considered themselves apolitical to action. This would not only be a march but an act of civil disobedience with mass arrests to confront the government's willingness to stand idly by while AIDS decimated the gay community.

The 1987 march on Washington built on the grassroots organizing structure of its predecessor. A committee organized a national meeting to which representatives of all sexual minority organizations—local, state, and regional as well as national—were welcomed. Organizational representatives voted, but otherwise, all in attendance were invited to participate in these open meetings. The meetings established the need, set a date, and began the process for identifying the issues the march would include in its platform. Local committees formed to get the word out, and national and state organizers marshaled resources to bring people to the capital. Roughly six hundred thousand gathered from across the country to march, rally, and view the AIDS Quilt for the first time. Over six hundred people were arrested in a demonstration in front of the Supreme Court building to protest the high court's 1986 ruling in the *Hardwick* case. That decision had upheld sodomy laws that outlaw private sexual relations between consenting same-sex adults. Plans for the 1987 march were already under way when that infamous Supreme Court decision was handed down, but it no doubt bolstered attendance and intensified the rage.

For those who traveled from the smaller towns, the march was a life-affirming revelation. Every conceivable segment of the community was there among the hundreds of thousands gathered. It was an antidote to the isolation so acutely felt by those who lived far, both physically and emotionally, from the large urban centers to which queers escaped. And, in the aftermath of the 1987 march, grassroots organizations proliferated around the country, spreading far beyond major urban areas.

THE THIRD NATIONAL MARCH: 1993

The circumstances that had fueled organizing for the 1987 march remained five years later, and once again, talk of a national march began. The change from a Reagan presidency to a Bush White House had prompted virtually no change in AIDS policy, and Senator Jesse Helms's amendments were as ubiquitous as they were homophobic. Increasingly, the far right was taking its antigay crusades to state legislatures—Oregon, Colorado, Florida, Maine, Arizona, Michigan, Ohio, Idaho, Washington, and Montana. In Colorado, voters passed by ballot measure an amendment that repealed any existing anti-discrimination protections that covered gays in that state and prohibited any future ones, thus triggering a national boycott of the state.

As with previous marches, the decision on whether and when to march was hotly debated. Some thought such an event would detract from the 25th Anniversary of the Stonewall Riots, scheduled for New York in 1994. Others looked at the shift toward state-based attacks and questioned the effectiveness of another national march. The issues pro and con were aired out during three open national meetings in 1991. By May, the consensus was clearly in favor of a D.C. march in April 1993, and the structure of the march on Washington was adopted. By the January 1992 meeting, the full national steering committee (NSC) was established with thirty national-organization seats, fifteen constituency seats, four seats for each of seventeen geographical regions, a thirteen-member executive committee, and a hired national organizer. The gender parity and minimum 50 percent people-of-color requirement applied to the entire 127-member NSC. Regions chose their own representatives and raised funds to send their representatives to the NSC meetings.

The platform of the 1993 march differed little from that of the 1987 march. (The end of apartheid was the only platform item that had been achieved.) But the right-wing shift in the country was mirrored in the gay community as well, and the platform became a target of strong criticism. Conservative gays described it as a utopian left-wing laundry list sure to become fodder for far-right homophobes. A gay rights focus, they argued, ought to be the narrow plank on which we all organized. Others countered that it was the height of classism, racism, and sexism to decide that only those issues of concern to gay white men make up the agenda on which the entire community should organize. No one argued that AIDS was a health issue, not a "gay issue." Why then should poverty, racism, sexism—equally life-and-death issues to sexual minorities—be considered outside the scope of the "gay movement"?

This time, the ideological rift that had been subsumed by the AIDS crisis was on the front burner. Was the movement part of a progressive social-justice coalition, or a single-issue identity movement aimed at reforming antigay laws? The support for a broader vision was ultimately reflected in the preamble to the 1993 platform: "The Lesbian, Gay, Bisexual, and Transgender movement recognizes that our quest for social justice fundamentally links us to the struggles against racism and sexism, class bias, economic injustice, and religious intolerance. We must realize if one of us is oppressed we all are oppressed. The diversity of our movement requires and compels us to stand in opposition to all forms of oppression that diminish the quality of life for all people. We will be vigilant in our determination to rid our movement and our society of all forms of oppression and exploitation, so that all of us can develop to our full human potential without regard to race, religion, sexual orientation, identification, identity, gender and gender expression, ability, age or class."

The march's demands reflected the philosophy of the preamble. They stated: "(1) We demand passage of a Lesbian, Gay, Bisexual, and Transgender civil rights bill and an end to discrimination by state and federal governments including the military; repeal of all sodomy laws and other laws that criminalize private sexual expression between consenting adults; (2) we demand massive increase in funding for AIDS education, research, and patient care; universal access to health care including alternative therapies; and an end to sexism in medical research and health care; (3) we demand legislation to prevent discrimination against Lesbians, Gays, Bisexuals, and Transgendered people in the areas of family diversity, custody, adoption, and foster care and that the definition of family includes the full diversity of all family structures; (4) we demand full and equal inclusion of Lesbians, Gays, Bisexuals, and Transgendered people in the educational system, and inclusion of Lesbian, Gay, Bisexual, and Transgender studies in multicultural curricula; (5) we demand the right to reproductive freedom and choice, to control our own bodies, and an end to sexist discrimination; (6) we demand an end to racial and ethnic discrimination in all forms; (7) we demand an end to discrimination and violent oppression based on actual or perceived sexual orientation, race, religion, identity, sex and gender expression, disability, age, class, AIDS/HIV infection."

As organizing for the 1993 march proceeded, something unexpected began to occur that changed the face of the event. George Bush was riding high in the polls, buoyed by the conflict with Saddam Hussein, and was expected to claim another four years in office. But an Arkansas governor whose campaign had several times seemed on the verge of scandal-driven collapse was suddenly emerging as a significant challenger. Dubbed the Comeback Kid, Clinton was not only immune to attack, but controversy seemed only to make his candidacy stronger. When he publicly reached out to the LGBT community, he sparked a cautious optimism. When he casually announced he would as president lift the ban on gays in the military and spoke of a vision for the future that included gay people, the response from the community was overwhelming and unprecedented. By the time Clinton entered the White House, the mood of dread that had inspired the organizing of the 1993 march was replaced with hope, optimism, and expectation. While some on both the left and right of the gay community seemed skeptical of Clinton's promise and immune to his charisma, the overwhelming majority were enamored. The tone of the march was shifting from one of protest to one of celebration and hope.

The day of the march, a record-breaking 1 million LGBT and allied marchers converged in the capital. While the media had failed to give appropriate coverage to previous marches, they turned out in droves in 1993. C-SPAN covered the event live, while national and international press made the event a front-page story. Even national newsmagazines, notorious for ignoring past marches, provided advance coverage and postevent wrap-ups. Despite the embrace of Clinton, significant fault lines were visible by the time the march arrived. Clinton refused to speak at the march, and angry AIDS activists were continuing to draw attention to his Arkansas AIDS policies. The lifting of the antigay military ban was devolving into an ill-conceived Don't Ask, Don't Tell compromise. While it was a significant part of the march platform, the military issue disproportionately overshadowed all other concerns. Accustomed to being marginalized outsiders, leaders seemed not to know how to respond when they found the door ajar. Activists appeared either too enamored of the new level of access or far too disdainful of it.

Under the slogan, A Simple Matter of Justice, the 1993 march had continued and expanded the grassroots structure of its predecessor but was not infused with the same sense of crisis. Consequently the fissures in the community were perhaps more visible than ever before. And something else had shifted, as well. The movement had largely been defined by activists in urban gay enclaves and D.C.-based national organizations that often owed their origin and funding largely to those same communities. But marches and the activism they had spurred had drawn hundreds of thousands out of the closet and into action. Rather than flee to metropolitan areas, activists had increasingly begun to organize in their hometowns by introducing human rights ordinances, challenging school board policies, and running for elective office. The failure of televangelist Pat Robertson's 1992 presidential bid had caused the far right also to turn to local and state initiatives. Consequently, state and local activists claimed a larger role in shaping the movement's direction and a louder voice in the use of the community's resources. Marriage, an issue few thought could be broached, became a galvanizing issue—not because national groups placed it in on the agenda, but because local organizers took the matter to a Hawaiian court.

While tension caused by this shift has been viewed as a debate about the relative value of national vs. state organizing, it was more accurately a reflection of a maturing movement. Some argued that national organizing was the only way to avoid creating a crazy patchwork, rights à la carte, with employment protections in one county, domestic partnership in another. The reality was that national organizing without strong state and local work was a paper tiger constantly on the verge of having its bluff called. Those working for equality and justice at the national level need grassroots mechanisms to mobilize voters, impact elections, lobby their legislators. By the same token, local and state organizations need to know that national organizations will be responsive and respectful of grassroots experience and expertise. As the movement matures, the challenges of organizing in a racially, ethnically, politically, economically, culturally, and spiritually diverse community can no longer be dodged.

The three national marches have illustrated that the events are less important than the sum of the organizing parts. Democracy is messy and challenging and fractious, but in national organizing we have been able to have the difficult conversations. In 1993, for instance, the debate on transgender inclusion was painful and necessary. There existed no other real forum for such intense and sustained discussion.

In 1991 Billy Hileman, one of the national cochairs for the 1993 march, wrote a short statement in response to the growing clamor from vocal white men who argued that the organizational structure should be streamlined and efficient without any meaningful action to promote diversity. "Diversity and empowerment were more important than efficiency," Hileman wrote. "Without a commitment to diversity from the beginning, marginalized people will be positioned once again to fight for their place at the table. The organizational structure cannot allow the final process to commence while anyone is still on the outside. The success of the 1993 march—how many thousands show up in D.C. in April—hinges directly on our commitment to diversity and empowerment, as well as efficiency. The March will be bigger, better, and a far more lasting achievement for our community if it builds on the foundation of all of these principles."

CONCLUSION

Three marches since 1979, and what do we have to show for them? Not much, or a great deal, depending on whom you ask. If history judges these mass gatherings in the nation's capital by the number of demands that have been achieved, the statistics are fairly grim. Only the end to apartheid can be struck from the list. Not only has Congress failed to respond to the marches by passing a comprehensive civil rights bill or employment protection, it has added the Defense of Marriage Act to lawbooks and codified the military exclusion policy. On the other hand, three marches on Washington have also brought hundreds of thousands of women and men out of the closet, sparked the formation of hundreds of organizations to fight for equality at every level of government and society, and spawned countless activists across the country.

But these changes may also mean that marches on Washington no longer serve the same purpose of empowering personally and challenging politically through visibility. Politicians who once ran from addressing gay issues now actively campaign on our issues. The LGBT community has unprecedented visibility and has, to the joy of some and dismay of others, become a highly sought-after niche market. These developments have heightened the divide in our communities between haves and have-nots, between those who believe that homophobia is just an aberration in a basically decent and equitable system and those who believe it is the inevitable result of a system founded on inequity and corrupt at its core.

In the past, such division meant heated organizational meetings between volunteers with opposing viewpoints. Today, the debate is increasingly shaped by paid staff with sizable budgets and by a moderate-to-conservative board of directors with little accountability outside their own organizations. Such structure allows the organizations that shape the perceived agenda to ignore or overshadow the voices of dissent in the community. The infusion of a corporate mentality is not coincidental. National groups turn increasingly to the corporate world rather than the activist community to scout for their next leaders, raising questions about who shapes the agenda and how it is shaped.

Just as the community has begun soul-searching about the meaning and function of annual pride events each June, many have begun to question whether another national march is what is needed now. When a private producer wanted to launch a fourth march on Washington for 2000, the idea was not embraced by grassroots activists, who were instead eager to build strong local and statewide organizations through a coordinated national day of action in the state capitals. Others supported the concept of a march but considered the timing poor, since it would conflict with local community election-year efforts. So the idea was marketed instead to the wealthiest national groups—the Human Rights Campaign and the Metropolitan Community Church, the leaders of which jumped enthusiastically at the idea of building membership, increasing funding, and seizing the opportunity to shape the message of such an event outside the grassroots democratic model used by previous marches. For those who viewed the prior marches as a left-wing exercise driven by a mind-numbing consensus process, this was viewed as great progress. It was seen as an opportunity to bring corporate structure and efficiency to a way of organizing they saw as obsolete. To others it was seen as the hijacking of a democratic movement, a dramatic and dangerous shift to the right, an abandonment of the civil rights and progressive coalitions that had been forged over decades, and an attempt to manage which voices and which images of the queer community were considered worthy and acceptable.

Washington marches, which historically had been events launched to draw the community together, have now become one of the most divisive issues in our community. A number of national organizations first provided, but then withdrew, endorsements for the 2000 march. Corporations lined up behind the proposed Millennium March and Rally, providing financing in exchange for marketing opportunities. At the same time, a growing group of longtime movement leaders began to raise questions about the proposed march and prompted increased debate. Organizers point to polls that show support for a march, while opponents claim the polling speaks more about past marches than about the proposed event in 2000. Dissenters point out, and rightly so, that it is possible to support national marches and oppose this specific event as it is conceived and executed.

Is this where three national marches have led us? Will the next national march be produced by a national corporation just as eager to tap the "lucrative gay market," similarly lacking accountability, with a media machine and deep enough pockets to outlast the criticisms of a loose-knit network of grassroots activists? In 1835, Tocqueville wrote an essay titled *Democracy in America*. In it he warned of the dangers of abandoning democratic values in the smaller details of life. It is a warning that resonates in the queer organizing community, as so much of the agenda, strategy, and message of the movement is now controlled by a smaller group of people operating in a closed, unaccountable system. "It must not be forgotten that it is especially dangerous to enslave men in the minor details of life," Tocqueville wrote. "For my own part, I should be inclined to think freedom less necessary in great things than in little ones, if it were possible to be secure of one without possessing the other. Subjection in minor affairs breaks out every day and is felt by the whole community indiscriminately. It does not drive men to resistance, but crosses them at every turn till they are led to surrender the exercise of their will. Thus their spirit is gradually broken and their character enervated."

While this may serve as rebuttal to those who dismiss opponents of the proposed march in 2000 as petty and process obsessed, it points to a much larger challenge to the movement as a whole. Much of the oppression the LGBT community faces comes not in spectacular showdowns with bigots but in small skirmishes that are often easily ducked. Holding hands on the street, a picture of a partner/lover/spouse on one's desk, going to a gay bar or event are fraught for most of queer America with an unarticulated sense of danger. A majority of us circumscribe our lives to avoid oppression to such a degree that we overwhelmingly do the bigot's job. We are indeed crossed at every turn in so many little ways that the spirit to challenge the bigger injustices ebbs and wanes. The issues of marriage and the military hold so much power primarily because the source of the oppression is crystal clear. Consequently, the demands to access these two institutions have become the battlefields that most closely evoke the spirit of past civil rights struggles.

But we do not fill the clerks' offices with demands for wedding licenses only to be carted off to jail. We do not crowd the recruiter's offices daily announcing we are homosexuals who demand to serve. The closet has prevented us from exposing discrimination in all its forms. While it may protect us from the daily humiliation and targeting, it also has the effect of "crossing us in countless minor ways" that alone do not seem to add up to a powerful confrontation with evil. It is important to remember that the 1963 march, whose memory is so often invoked, was the culmination of local battles, not a replacement for them. That march was not called because it was safer to go to D.C. than Main Street, but to draw attention to the brutality and daily humiliation of segregated hometowns.

Many people lament what they see as rampant apathy in the LGBT community and wonder what horrible event will have to occur to get people to mobilize. I don't believe people are apathetic. I believe most people don't see the connection between the work they are asked to do and improving their everyday lives. I think the challenge of organizing is connecting the work to people's real lives and helping them to see how circumscribed all of our lives are by the ever present homophobia. We, as a community, have to understand that it is not just the heinous acts of violence or the outrageous incidents of discrimination that demand our action. It is the constant and relentless subjection in "minor affairs."

To the degree we fail to build the local and state infrastructures in which people can do the work, we have squandered the momentum, inspiration, and motivation built by national marches. To the extent we fail to empower through democratic organizing, we short-circuit our communities' power. But, to the extent we succeed in linking actions to improving daily life, people dedicate themselves to ending discrimination with a boundless passion. When activism is viewed as the province of a small cadre of expert or political wonks, the community is disempowered and disinterested.

Facing Discrimination, Organizing for Freedom: The Transgender Community

Phyllis Randolph Frye, Esq.

INTRODUCTION

I was the second son of three children. I became an Eagle Boy Scout, my high school's ROTC commander, a multischolarship university student, a career military officer, a licensed civil engineer, a husband, and a father. I am now in my fifties and have lived as a woman for almost one-half of my life.

Afraid of becoming the woman whom I had felt was inside me since I was approximately age six, and afraid of being labeled a queer in the 1950s and 1960s, I struggled throughout my youth to suppress my really inner self. I also feared that my family would reject me. To avoid detection, I took on the attitudes that I had been taught were acceptable for a straight, white, Protestant, American man: a Catholic-Jew-queer baiter with overt chauvinism, racism, and sexism and the superior attitude of someone with that privileged social status.

By the early 1970s, I allowed the woman who was inside me to openly express herself part-time. This resulted in my being divorced by my first spouse, discharged by the U.S. army, and blackballed by engineering employers. When my she came out full-time in the mid-1970s, all of the fears of my youth came true. Society did label me a queer and did mistreat me as a queer. My family did ostracize me so completely that my father took his disgust with him to his grave in 1998. I was transformed into a person without any civil rights and certainly without any privileged social status.

Transgendered individuals will suffer vast amounts of short-term discomfort and cultural punishments to attain the long-term comfort of a close fit between their inner sense of gender identity and gendered behavior that society has deemed inappropriate for them. Cultural punishments as a child can be the mild clues of not allowing play with the culturally defined wrong-gendered toys. Cultural punishments as an adolescent can be severe teasing, ostracism, and violence.

Cultural punishments as an adult are called discrimination and can take many forms and can last for ten to twenty years or longer. The forms of discrimination include unemployment or underemployment or less pay for the same work. Also included are loss of child custody or visitation, loss of housing, loss of community services that are gender-based, such as medical clinics for the poor or homeless shelters, and mistreatment by or lack of protection by the police. Ostracism and threats of violence from parents or siblings are frequent. Vandalism from previously nice neighbors is also common. And there is a continuing search for a safe place to go to the bathroom when away from home or when seeking to retain employment.

The bathroom situation is not a jest. It, and the use of a shower stall at work or at the gym, recur as the largest hurdles that most anti-transgender-rights people place before us. As you will read later herein, it is the reason that transgenders—as recently as the June 24, 1999, reintroduction of a federal job nondiscrimination bill—remain purposefully excluded from proposed protective legislation.

In 1997, at the Tenth Annual Creating Change Conference in San Diego sponsored by the National Gay and Lesbian Task Force (NGLTF), Jamison Green, Shannon Minter, and I held a workshop to ask the question "Is sexual orientation a subset of gender identity?"[1] In a nutshell, the question turns on its head the common misperception that transgenders are kind of a hang-on or add-on group to the lesbian, gay, and bisexual civil rights movement and but for society lumping us all together as queer, there would be nothing in common. Instead of that, this question supposes that lesbians, gays, and bisexuals are actually the subsets and members of the larger gender identity community.

I had so titled the workshop to generate controversy because there are still a lot of queer people who did not consider transgenders to belong to the lesbian, gay, and bisexual civil rights movement. I wanted to make them think, and I wanted to spotlight their misperception. I expected a small group and a lot of negative debate. In actuality, the large room filled to overflowing. Every gender-variant lesbian, gay male, and bisexual who was not overwhelmingly drawn to another workshop was there at our workshop. And more came after they completed their other workshop. They entered the room agreeing with the workshop title and seeking the community of others who felt the same way. The silent majority had come to speak out.

Speaker after speaker from the audience confirmed that the discrimination they felt as a lesbian, gay man, or bisexual was not because of who they had sexual intimacy with, but was instead because of the gender expectation that society imposed. The culture did not see them actually having sex, but the culture did see and reacted angrily at two women holding hands, at two men dancing, and at any people who stretched the range of allowable gender expression.

Today, most activists in the transgender community and many activists in the lesbian, gay male, and bisexual community agree that people who hate, despise, feel ashamed of, preach from the pulpits against, or otherwise act in a disparaging manner toward transgenders, lesbians, gay men, and bisexuals simply do not distinguish among the categories of queers. In the struggle to stay employed, maintain family relationships, stay out of jail, stay with children or adopt children, and not be verbally abused by people who wield some form of holy writ, all transgenders, lesbians, gay men, and bisexuals are labeled *queer*.

FACING DISCRIMINATION

The transgendered face discrimination from straight people in the form of violence and hate crimes. Several deaths illustrate the point. Brandon Teena was a young FTM (female to male) who was murdered in Nebraska several years ago. Prior to his death, he had sought police protection and had been refused. Tyra Hunter was a MTF (male to female) who was in an automobile accident in Washington, D.C. As she was bleeding to death, paramedics on the scene stopped treatment when they discovered that her genitalia did not match their expectation. In both cases huge public outcries finally got the authorities to act. Brandon's murderer was convicted, and the city that hired Hunter's paramedics was found liable. In most cases the murderer is not found. In many cases the families do not want the body or they bury the body dressed as the former incorrect self.

The transgendered face discrimination from straight people in the form of employment discrimination. In the introduction, I referred to the military and engineering careers that I lost. The engineering firing was typical in that it was over which rest room I would use at the office. I still appeared as a man to my employers, but I had told them about who I was and that a transition was in my future. They would not let me use the men's or the women's rest room, so I was fired.

As a lawyer and as a transgender rights activist, I receive lots of letters, calls, and E-mail from people who are about to lose their jobs because the employer cannot solve the rest room problem. I advise them to ask for the use of just one rest room that is close to where they work and give notice that they will either lock the door or put up a Post-it note when they enter. What usually happens in a company that is willing to try to keep the transitioning employee is that friction is generated by just a few folks who make a lot of noise. After the transition, if time is given for this matter to settle down, and if the company insures that employees know the company wants to keep the transgendered employee, it becomes a nonissue. Unfortunately most companies will not invest that time, and the transgender is fired. Diana Cicotello has written some pamphlets to help employers through this transition.[2]

Finding work for the recently transitioned or just-fired transgender is difficult. Most employers simply do not want to take the initial risk of having a problem while they are trying to incorporate a new employee into the workplace. As a result, most transgenders apply and interview by hiding as much of their past as possible. At that point identification documents become crucial. Because of immigration law, most companies ask for identification at the time of application. If a judge only changed George's name to Susan and refused to change the M to an F, then the judge gave her an incomplete change of name, and she will probably not get the job. Or if a judge only changed Janette's name to Ralph and refused to change the F to an M, then the judge gave him an incomplete change of name, and he will probably not get the job.

Fortunately, I am beginning to see evidence of change. Even though more transgenders lose their jobs than keep their jobs, and even though more transgenders have difficulty getting new jobs, I am noticing a shift. The numbers of successfully employed transgenders who are using their full skill packages and not having to accept less pay for the same work is increasing. Although they are still in a minority, what I see in my office or in my mail or on the Internet suggests that their numbers are increasing.

In the family law area, many transgenders are forced into divorce. That cannot be helped if one spouse wants a divorce, but sometimes the divorce is from the misperception that the couple has to divorce. This misperception used to be promulgated widely within the medical profession. Doctors would tell married transgenders that they would not begin the alterations because that would make an illegal, same-sex marriage. Over the years, as a lawyer, I have fought this misperception vigorously. Once a person with male genitalia is legally married to a female-genitaled person, they will remain legally married regardless of whether one has genitalia-altering surgery and it then becomes a de facto same-sex marriage. The state cannot force a divorce. The first time that I promoted this idea publically, outside of the Transgender Law Conferences,[3] was in my platform speech at the 1993 march on Washington. Since that time Mary Coombs has expanded upon it in her 1998 law review article.[4]

But many were forced to divorce and many others simply were divorced. In those cases, the fear of exposure often left the transgendered spouse fair game in the divorce settlement. Often children were involved, and the courts would only allow supervised visitation. This aspect of transgender discrimination is getting a little better, but it is still not that good. I get lots of letters and calls and E-mail from people who are being forced into lopsided property settlements and out of partial custody or visitation of their children. It remains another uphill climb.

Straight parents, siblings, and children are often unsure about how to respond to their transgendered family member. If they come around to acceptance at all, it is usually long after the transgender has struggled by herself or himself through transition. Recently the Parents, Familys and Friends of Lesbians and Gays became transgender inclusive. The PFLAG Transgender Special Outreach Network also published a helpful pamphlet.[5] Evelyn Lindenmuth and Mary Boenke are both straight parents of transgendered children, and they have written helpful books that I recommend.[6, 7] Even so, initially accepting parents, siblings, and children of the transgendered remain the exception.

Discrimination is rampant in homeless shelters, and therefore homeless transgendered often have nowhere to go but the streets. Homeless shelters will not take them except if they go to a matching-genitalia facility. Imagine the harassment, beatings, and rape that would go on in those situations.

The unemployed homeless or the underemployed transgenders get little help from public medical clinics. They are often ridiculed by staff in the waiting rooms and do not come back. I know of FTMs who could not afford male hormones after being fired and began menses again several months later. They could not get help because they were laughed at or refused. An MTF with prostrate problems is out of luck at a public medical facility.

Transgenders are often harassed or arrested by police. This usually occurs on trumped-up charges of hitchhiking or using the wrong public rest room. Imagine being an MTF on female hormones for several years, but being unable to get a good job because some judge will not give you a complete change of name. The judge gave you identification of a Susan with an *M* or of William with an *F*. Therefore, if you did want genital surgery, you could not afford it. Imagine being arrested and spending the night in the side of the jail that matches your genitalia. Prisons are doubly hard on transgenders. Prisons usually refuse to allow transgenders to continue on their hormones. The rationale is to conserve taxpayer money or some such inappropriate reason. The Transgender Law Conference did a prison study and published standards for prison care for transgenders.[8] So far, no prison authority has expressed interest.

I am always amazed at how straight people can carve out exceptions to allow them to do whatever they wish. The following tongue-in-cheek exception brings a perspective to gender cross-dressing. Most folks who don country-and-western garb do not own cows, horses, farms, or ranches. And yet some people cross-dress in this country-and-western manner part-time, while others do it full-time. When folks are asked why they cross-dress in country and western, a common response is, "I like the way it makes me feel." Often there are sexual undertones to the expressions. People vent feelings of virility, coquetry, or flirtatiousness when so dressed. Men frequently wear cowboys boots with their Manhattan business suits—a great way for a man to be socially permitted to wear a high heel. There are country-and-western clothing stores, catalogs, bars, dancing, music, and literature—all readily utilized by people who do not own cows, horses, farms, or ranches. And yet these social cross-dressers do not fear loss of jobs, friends, and families. They do not fear religious persecution whether they wear country and western some of the time or all of the time. I call them the trans*west*ites.

Discrimination from the lesbian and gay community comes in many ways. For instance, some lesbian and gay political leaders want the homosexual transgenders to host events to raise funds for lesbian and gay political needs.[9] And yet, frequently, those same political leaders distance themselves from us or shun us when the media turns the cameras on us at queer pride community events.

Frequently we are left out of proposed local, state, or national antidiscriminatory legislation that is sponsored by lesbian and gay political leaders. During the late 1980s and most of the 1990s legislation was almost always in the form of protection on the basis of sexual orientation only. The most important exception was in Minnesota.[10] Sexual orientation, unless specifically defined, does not protect gender identification.

Interestingly, and this has been difficult for some lesbian and gay leaders to understand, sexual orientation protection without an accompanying gender-identification protection leaves all gender-variant lesbians and gender-variant gay men unprotected for their gender variance, which can then be used as a legal cover for discrimination against them. With time and with the actions discussed in subsequent sections of this chapter, more lesbian and gay leaders are understanding this gap.

I have never noted or been aware of any discrimination from bisexuals. Many years ago leaders of the bisexual community and the transgender community met to discuss that both of our communities were marginalized by the lesbian and gay community. Bisexuals get mentioned more often than do transgenders, but they still feel left out. Therefore we made a mutual pledge that we would support each other. The transgenders would always speak out for the rights of transgenders and bisexuals, and the bisexuals would always speak out for the rights of the bisexuals and the transgenders.

ORGANIZING FOR FREEDOM

Some Background—Prior to the Fall of 1993

Most transgenders have remained hidden in their races and cultures throughout much of recorded history. Those who have come out and been recognized have had to do so in brazen ways to be acknowledged as transgendered. Usually they have come out in a piecemeal fashion, and most often they have been confused with or mistaken for just another homosexual, even if they were heterosexuals. As a result, a great deal of transgender history has been lost or has become intermingled into the backdrop of what is called gay history. Either way, the bigotry against transgenders by most Western cultures has been intense, but it usually has been called homosexual discrimination. It has not been recognized as discrimination against transgenders.

The modern queer rights movement began in 1969 with the riots in New York City at the Stonewall Inn, a queer bar. It has often been incorrectly called a gay bar, but the initial police abuse during that riot was directed at the bar's heterosexual transsexual patrons and homosexuals with extreme expressions of gender variance. So, from the very beginning, and ever since, in the history of the gay rights movement transgenders have been present. And yet, even though a large contingent of people who threw the first stones at Stonewall were transgender, the transgender community soon began to be segregated from the modern queer rights movement.

In the heterosexual transgender community, the most noted and earliest education activist was Virginia Prince (formerly Charles Prince) of California. After many years of cross-dressing, he combined his small organization, Feminine Personality Expression (FPE), with Carol Beecroft's larger Ma'mselle Society to form the Society for the Second Self (SSS or Tri-Ess) in the 1970s. Tri-Ess is known as a group for the heterosexual cross-dresser and his wife.[11] Charles Prince then decided to live the rest of his life as Virginia, but without genital surgery. Thus Virginia Prince came into the world and the term *transgenderist*—as a distinction from the transvestite and the transsexual—was coined by her in the 1970s to describe her decision.

Virginia Prince's early educational work was so fundamental that she is considered the godmother of the heterosexual transgender community. The International Foundation for Gender Education (IFGE), created by Merrissa Sherrill Lynn in 1987, named its highest award for lifetime achievement after

Virginia Prince, who was also its first recipient.[12] Today at eighty-six, Ms. Prince is still active in shaping the community.

Others in the heterosexual transgender community also formed groups and began to hold social events, some local and some regional. Many of the first groups were formed in the 1970s and 1980s with names such as Be All You Can Be, the Texas T-Party, California Dreaming, or Southern Comfort. Also there were national organizations called the Renaissance Transgender Association (RTA)[13] and the American Educational Gender Information Service (AEGIS),[14] led by JoAnn Roberts and Dallas Denny, respectively. Tri-Ess was renewed largely through the efforts of Jane Ellen and Mary Frances Fairfax. Most of the local, regional, and national heterosexual transgender newsletters and magazines were concerned with fashion or how to keep your family or where to get hormones or surgery. There were also some early attempts made to bridge the gaps between the heterosexual transgender community and the gay, lesbian, and bisexual community.

There were spots of local transgender legal and political activism during the 1970s and 1980s, but little was of a national sweep. In the 1970s, some brave and valiant transgenders lost federal court cases. Most of this history was compiled in 1995 by JoAnna McNamara.[15] McNamara reported that in *Holloway*[16] (1977), *Sommers*[17] (1982), and *Ulane*[18] (1984) three federal appellate courts ruled that the Title VII prohibition against sex discrimination did not apply to transgenders. The courts held, in effect, that discrimination against post-surgical transsexuals was not discrimination based on sex, which would be prohibited by Title VII. They held that this was change-of-sex discrimination upon which Title VII was silent.

Defeats were balanced by successes. During that time, the California Department of Motor Vehicles was persuaded to change its regulations so that names and gender identities of preoperative transsexuals could be changed if they were undergoing their real-life tests. The lobbyist was a veteran of the U.S. navy, now a MTF nun in the order of the Sisters of Saint Elizabeth. Sister Mary was acting as the chair of the Transsexual Rights Committee of the Southern California Chapter of the ACLU. She also tirelessly lobbied the California state legislature to allow the amendment of birth certificates to reflect new gender identities after genital surgery. In addition, she published an early work on transgender law in 1990.[19]

Other legal work was done by men and women who were lawyers in gender transition in the 1970s and 1980s and fought in their states for similar legal rights. But there was still not a national focus on transgender legal and political rights.

Local work centered around municipalities with antimasquerade laws that made cross-dressing illegal. These ordinances were used by police to make life miserable for any transgenders thought to be in the homosexual community. Vagrancy ordinances were used to harass poor people, and people of color. In a similar manner, police used these ordinances to hassle queers. Any gay man who remained cross-dressed after a performance was subject to arrest, and this frequently occurred. The same attitude greeted lesbians wearing fly-front (rather than side- or back-zippered) pants. Heterosexual cross-dressers visiting gay bars were often arrested. Even full-time preoperative transsexuals with name changes, on hormones, and carrying letters from their physicians were often arrested. After much trial and appellate court work, and lobbying of city councils and state legislatures, most, but not all, of those ordinances have been repealed.[20]

Most queer civil rights political activity by transgenders was done by homosexual transgenders and by those heterosexual transgenders who had by now consciously decided that they would not be concerned with the queer stigma. This recognition that transgenderism already carried a queer taint has steadily increased. Some were simply tired of the oppression and ready to make a stand. They assumed that fighting for gay rights in the sixties, gay and lesbian rights in the seventies, and gay and lesbian and bisexual rights in the eighties was also a fight for transgender rights. All of their contributions, therefore, to all of the gains made by the gay, lesbian, and bisexual movement remain invisible, but inextricably intertwined.

As the 1980s drew to a close, the attitudes of many transgenders began to change and they started to assert and acknowledge their contributions as transgendered men and women. They realized that they had been segregated and determined that they would no longer tolerate such treatment. The shift came about in dozens of local situations. The common scenario involved overt discrimination by police or an employer against an out and open full-time transgendered person. The transpersons experiencing discrimination were often already active in local queer political caucuses, and they mistakenly assumed that their colleagues would join in the fight for their civil rights when they were wronged. Sometimes that was the case, but often enough, in many places around the country, the response was that it was not a gay problem.

And on the national level, the invisibility of transgenders to the gay and lesbian communities grew more obvious. Perhaps the biggest examples have come from the queer marches on Washington. The planning meeting for the first march on Washington was held in the summer of 1979. There was a protracted floor fight over whether transgenders would even be mentioned in the event brochure. In the 1987 march, transgenders were again left out. By the 1990s many transgender leaders—mostly heterosexual at this time and mostly MTF—recognized that the queer freedom train was leaving the station without them, and it was time to become vocal. They saw numerous organizations, local, state, and national, that used "lesbian and gay" in their names, but typically omitted any reference to bisexuals or transgenders.

The first national act of defiance by transgenders, I would argue, was the protest of Susan Stryker, Anne Osborn, and others at the 1993 March on Washington for Lesbian, Gay and Bi Rights. Transgenders had once again been left out of the name of the event, but we were visible in the event's written "Purpose and Goals." Big deal, who in the media wrote about that? Stryker, Osborn, and their friends were planning to lie down in front of the march and be arrested to protest the transgender omission in the name of the event.

I wish now that they had done it, but I was one of many who helped talk them out of it. I should have joined them then, and as you will read, I was moved to do so one year later. I believe that such an act then would probably have moved the transgender reintegration movement ahead by several years. And that is a worthwhile point to discuss. Transgenders were seeking to be reintegrated into the queer rights movement. We were not fighting for our initial, first-time inclusion in the queer rights movement.

Transgenders have never fought to be included. Instead, after Stonewall, and as the help of transgenders became necessary for fund-raising even as we remained a politically embarrassing subgroup, the segregation began. It reached full-blown proportions in the late 1980s, and we have been seeking ever since our rightful place in a greater, reintegrated lesbian, gay, bisexual, and transgender (LGBT) queer community. A thousand times I have wished that I had not been a party to convincing Stryker and Osborn to call off that protest, but I did.

In summary, the status of national transgender legal and political activity in the fall of 1993 was as follows. The homosexual transgenders still thought of themselves as homosexual first and foremost, and they put up with the verbal slaps from their political leaders and kept raising money. Most of the heterosexual transgenders tended to their local or regional gatherings, but the leadership was beginning to push for a merge with the homosexual and bisexual communities. Most national heterosexual transgender organizations dealt with everything except legal strategy and political action. Most transsexuals went from one closet to another. And most FTMs were still holding back and presenting either as androgynous straights or as butch lesbians. But the shift was building.

Our Time Has Come—Beginning in the Fall of 1993

In 1993, there were activist people like Stryker and Osborn all around the country needing a national focus. The Congress of Transgender Organizations (CTO) had been formed in the late 1980s. Unfortunately it did not meet often, and it did not fill the national legal and political vacuum.

The International Conference on Transgender Law and Employment Policy (ICTLEP) was formed in 1991 because all of the national homosexual law groups had omitted the transgender community. By 1993, ICTLEP had held two annual conferences designed to bring transgender leaders together to focus on strategies, and to train them for progressive legal change.

Also, JoAnn Roberts and Sharon Stuart had each independently drafted and published different versions of an International Bill of Gender Rights. Later, with the blessing of both, and the continuation of the work by Stuart under ICTLEP's flag, the bill evolved to read, in part, as follows:

> 1. The Right to Define Gender Identity—All human beings carry within themselves an ever-unfolding idea of who they are and what they are capable of achieving. The individual's sense of self is not determined by chromosomal sex, genitalia, assigned birth sex, or initial gender role. Thus, the individual's identity and capabilities cannot be circumscribed by what society deems to be masculine or feminine behavior. It is fundamental that individuals have the right to define, and to redefine as their lives unfold, their own gender identities, without regard to chromosomal sex, genitalia, assigned birth sex, or initial gender role.[21]

The document goes on to demand the following:
   —the right to free expression of gender identity
   —the right to secure and retain employment and to receive just compensation
   —the right of access to gendered spaces and participation in gendered activity
   —the right to control and change one's own body
   —the right to competent medical and professional care
   —the right to freedom from psychiatric diagnosis or treatment
   —the right to sexual expression
   —the right to form committed, loving relationships and enter into marital contracts
   —the right to conceive, bear, or adopt children; the right to nurture and have custody of children and to exercise parental capacity.

By the fall of 1993 the FTM community was beginning to organize nationally and under the guidance of Lou Sullivan formed FTM International.[22] In the fall of 1993, bitterly recalling that *transgender* had been left out of the 1993 march name, transgender activists began planning for June 1994—the celebration of the twenty-fifth anniversary of the Stonewall riots, and the Gay Games. Both were scheduled to occur in New York City at the same time that year. Both events were going to exclude transgenders in some fashion. Jessica Xavier, Denise Norris, Riki Wilchins, Sharon Stuart, myself, and others did a huge amount of work.

Sharon Stuart and I took a page from the Stryker book. We threatened to lie down and obstruct the Stonewall march and be arrested. Upon our arrival the day before, our attorney advised us that although our goals were not fully met, the point had been made forcefully over the preceding six months, and that we should declare a victory and march. Wilchins, who lived in New York City, told us later that the point had been made so well that the Stonewall march organizers were going to assign a team to encircle Stuart and me when we lay on the street so that the marchers could go around us. The organizers recognized our protest but did not want us to suffer being arrested.

A month later in July 1994, after the third ICTLEP conference had been held, Karen Kerin and I went to Washington, D.C., to attempt to speak before the Senate hearings on the Employment Non-Discrimination Act (ENDA). Transgenders had been omitted from the ENDA language, and Kerin and I felt that if we showed up, we could address the problem. Even with the help of Senator Jim Jeffords, we could only watch as ENDA was discussed. Transgenders had been omitted, and much of the anti-ENDA attacks were centered around cross-dressing at work. Kerin and I met with people who told us about a coalition of human rights organizations for ENDA that was being led by the Human Rights Campaign (HRC), and that a year earlier the decision had been made by the HRC-led coalition to omit transgenders. Kerin's close ties to Senator Jeffords, the ranking Republican on the committee considering ENDA, allowed us to work for a transgender-inclusive ENDA that would be ready for introduction in the 1995 congressional session.

In October 1994, ICTLEP was invited to present transgender legal workshops at the Lavender Law Conference sponsored by the National Lesbian and Gay Law Association (NLGLA) at their meeting in Portland, Oregon. Between sessions, Melinda Whiteway, JoAnn McNamara, Sharon Stuart, and I met with a small group of gay political law leaders. Prominent among them was Professor Chai Feldblum of the Georgetown Law School, who had drafted ENDA as a contractor for the HRC. We confronted the group with the news that we were aware of the HRC-led meetings of the previous year when it was decided to omit transgenders from ENDA. Feldblum acknowledged this and stated that it was felt at the HRC-led meeting that transgender inclusion would cost thirty votes. From this revelation, transgender leaders began to criticize HRC in thirty pieces of silver/votes traitor arguments.

During that time, a political action group called the Transsexual Menace was conducting other protest demonstrations against transgender discrimination in New York City. Transgender Menace, along with Martine Rothblatt, also began to protest the American Psychiatric Association (APA) for continuing to include "gender dysphoria" as a diagnosis for transgenders in its official list of disorders, the *Diagnostic and Statistical Manual (DSM)*.[23] Anne Osborn and others were arrested at another such protest. The APA has not changed its damaging diagnosis. Many transgender activists feel that it should be an anatomical or endocrinological diagnosis rather than a damaging mental diagnosis.

Through 1994, the Internet was still a fledgling tool of communication. Until 1995, the cheapest and fastest way to get out the word to other community leaders was by fax. The fax machines were hot during those times. Not until the summer of 1995 did the groundwork laid by such people as Gwen Smith at America Online, and others, come to fruition. She and people using other servers fought for the right to have transgender keywords and chat rooms. Through the Internet, closeted transgenders began to discover how many others like themselves were out there, and they began to come out. The Internet gave a jump start to the FTM community, and it has rapidly been catching up in numbers and organization. Very notable is the rapid growth of The American Boyz, an organization of female-to-male transgenders.[24]

In January 1995, the NLGLA became the first national organization to unanimously pass a board resolution calling for transgender inclusion in ENDA. Shortly after that the National Gay, Lesbian, and Bisexual Veterans Association (NGLBVA) amended its bylaws at the request of Tere Fredrickson to include transgender.

From October 1994 to March 1995, Sharon Stuart attempted to create an organization that she called the Transgender Education and Advocacy Coalition (TEAC). Her aim was to get us all moving together and pick up the momentum that ICTLEP had generated. In March of 1995, a meeting was called in Washington, D.C., for folks who might want to move TEAC along. The meeting was also called because Riki Wilchins wanted to organize a transgender march on Washington. Karen Kerin attended, as did Riki Wilchins, Jessica Xavier, Sharon Stuart, Jane Fee, and myself. Jane Fee had recently been instrumental in persuading Minnesota politicians to become the first to enact statewide antidiscrimination legislation that was transgender inclusive.[25] TEAC never came into being, and neither did the transgender march on Washington. Instead, Karen Kerin from Vermont, Riki Wilchins from New York, Jane Fee from Minnesota, myself from Texas, and two others preferring anonymity went to the congressional offices of our four states over two days and lobbied. That was the first organized transgender lobbying event in our nation's capital.

During the spring of 1995, the faxes continued between leaders as we slowly began to convert to the Internet. Most of us agreed that the national leaders would meet at the fourth ICTLEP conference, and all but three national transgender leaders actually came to the conference. We already had a transgender-inclusive ENDA ready for Jeffords to introduce. It was a particularly propitious time, because Jeffords was now the chair of his Senate committee due to the Republican sweep of the Senate in the previous national election. Wilchins had been so turned on by our lobbying successes in March that she and Kerin and I agreed to tri-chair the organization of a second and vastly larger transgender lobbying event in October. We were all feeling pretty proud of ourselves. We were all pretty sure that this would slide through without much resistance.

Our bubble burst on Thursday, June 15, 1995, in Houston, Texas. That evening, all but three transgender national leaders assembled at the fourth ICTLEP conference. We were shocked to learn that the HRC had pushed their non-transgender-inclusive version of ENDA through for introduction in Congress. I believe that was the defining and galvanizing moment for the national political and legal movement of the transgender community. Feelings of betrayal and anger were palpable. From that moment to the end of the year was a blur of hectic activity. The Internet came to life. Many of our personal businesses suffered radically during those months. New people from towns and states across the nation came on-line and asked to be a part of the movement. HRC became the whipping post, and we whipped hard. By September, HRC asked for a meeting. They paid for the hotel rooms and airfares. The following transgender leaders went to HRC offices for a daylong meeting: Kitt Kling, Gary Bowen, Sarah DePalma, Sharon Stuart, Karen Kerin, Jessica Xavier, Riki Wilchins, Tere Fredrickson, and myself. It was a long and anger-filled meeting. HRC agreed to have Jessica Xavier and Sharon Stuart work with Chai Feldblum on drafting a transgender-inclusive ENDA.

The second lobbying event was in October. It was the largest and the best up to that point. Over one hundred transgenders, MTF, FTM, people of color, and spouses and children from thirty-five states came for the two-day event. We trained them on Sunday evening, assigned them to teams, and gave them score sheets and handout materials. Wilchins had organized a press conference for Monday, and Kerin, through Jeffords's office, insured that the Capitol Hill police would leave us alone. We lobbied over 95 percent of the House and Senate offices and had no negative incidents. In November, at the annual Creating Change Conference of the National Gay and Lesbian Task Force, I received an award. The presenter, NGLTF staff director Tracey Conaty, stated that "1995 was the year that the transgender community had stood the lesbian and gay community on its ear." Even though I was the recipient, the honor went to all of us who had worked at a fever pitch for the previous six months.

In 1996, the homosexual portion of the transgender community was beginning to catch on that they were not going to be protected by ENDA the way it was written. Later, at the 1998 Lavender Law Conference, Chai Feldblum addressed the Plenary Civil Rights Roundtable. She confirmed that gender-variant lesbians, gays, and bisexuals would not be covered by ENDA. More lesbian, gay, and bisexual leaders across the nation also began to pick up on this huge omission. They began to urge transgender inclusion in ENDA. And more heterosexual transgenders began to recognize their need to merge politically into the LGBT movement.

In the fall of 1996 came the trade-off vote in the U.S. Senate. Some senators traded their votes on the anti-same-sex marriage act called the Defense of Marriage Act (DOMA) for a vote on ENDA. DOMA prevented federal recognition of same-sex marriages. In the trade-off, ENDA got forty-nine votes. ICTLEP had been arguing since 1993 that legal same-sex marriages already existed. As the leader of ICTLEP, I also worked to convince the homosexual leaders to use the transgender same-sex marriages as an equal-protection argument in court cases. I suggested that during news programs and talk shows homosexual leaders should use the legality of transgender same-sex marriage to combat the opposition, which frequently argued that same-sex marriage could not work. To date, most homosexual leaders continue to ignore this resourceful argument.

Although a lot of transgender political activity had been ongoing, there was still no umbrella organization of transgender groups that would provide political clout. In late 1996, JoAnn Roberts sought to form a group called Gender PAC (GPAC). Unfortunately there was distrust amongst some of the major leaders, and the new executive director did not take direction from the provisional board. As a result, Roberts dropped the idea. Even so, Riki Wilchins and Dana Priesing continue to use GPAC as their banner as they do their work in the D.C. area.

In November of 1996, the next large transgender community meeting with HRC took place. There was a dramatic attempt to insure that the transgender delegates truly represented the geographic, racial, and sexual diversity of the transgendered. Eleven people from the Atlantic to the Pacific attended, including people of color, MTFs and FTMs, cross-dressers, and postsurgical transsexuals. They were Allison Lange, Phyllis Dickason, Yosenio Lewis, Gary Bowen, Jon Banks, Stephanie Young, Jamison Green, Janice Galeckas, Shannon Minter, Melissa Dixon, and myself. The thrust of the meeting was to reposition old stances. HRC was not going to put us into ENDA. We, on the other hand, were going to settle for nothing less. The upshot of the meeting was that this group decided to meet with other groups in the D.C. area, including the NGLTF.[26] As a result of that display of diversity, the NGLTF and other national LG groups (not HRC) began to amend their mission statements and bylaws to include transgenders and bisexuals if they had not already done so.

In February 1997, I organized a third gathering of transgenders to come to Washington, D.C. Twenty people came, and in two days we met with the offices of the forty-six senators remaining out of the forty-nine who had voted for ENDA in the fall of 1996. Time and time again we were told that if Senator Ted Kennedy and Representative Barney Frank put transgenders into the next

ENDA bill, they would still support it. Time and time again we were also told that if Kennedy and Frank left us out, they would still support it. It was up to Kennedy and Frank.

Some of us met with Kennedy's staff. And we met with Barney Frank. No movement. We went to the commissioners of the Equal Opportunity Employment Commission (EEOC). Jo Anne McNamara argued that with rule-making power, the EEOC could find that Title VII protected transgenders and essentially override the *Ulane* trio. The commissioners understood, but declined, noting that the Republican Congress would retaliate by reducing appropriations for the EEOC in the next budget. In the fall of 1998 the Department of Justice (DoJ) announced that it would begin to do pretty much what we had asked EEOC to do. In May 1997, GPAC had the fourth gathering of transgenders in D.C. to lobby primarily about hate crimes and ENDA. Later the new ENDA was introduced, omitting transgenders once more.

Even though the 1998 DoJ decision could make the ENDA struggle moot as to the issue of transgender inclusion, most transgender leaders are painfully aware that a DoJ case could easily meet the same ultimate fate as the *Ulane* trio if it went to the Supreme Court. Therefore, we still believe that having transgender placed into a Title VII law like ENDA is needed. Also, we choose to remain in the fight alongside our gender-variant lesbian, gay, and bisexual sisters and brothers who are not protected by the current ENDA language.

In 1997, ICTLEP held its sixth and last conference. Much of what it had formed to do was happening. In addition, the NLGLA was beginning to embrace many of ICTLEP's goals. Lavender Law Conferences became increasingly transgender inclusive in the workshop subjects and in panelists. By 1999, transgenders and bisexuals were in the mission statement, bylaws, and literature. Over a quarter of NLGLA's directors were transgender lawyers, and one of its current cochairs, Melinda Whiteway, is a transgender director of ICTLEP. NLGLA's affiliation with the American Bar Association has opened the door, and NLGLA now presents GLBT workshops at the ABA conventions and midyear conferences.[27] ICTLEP is still a corporate entity, but in 1999 it went into stasis until it is needed again. In 1997 the National Organization of Women (NOW) adopted in convention a strong resolution of support for transgenders. In 1999, the NOW Lesbian Conference was strongly transgender inclusive.

In 1997, the Roundtable of Executive Directors for National Gay, Lesbian, Bisexual and Transgender Organizations, concerned with national public policy, began. Before the first meeting, I lobbied hard for more than three transgender representatives. At that first meeting ICTLEP, It's Time America (ITA—a grassroots transgender political organization founded at the third ICTLEP conference)[28], FTM International, GPAC, The American Boyz, and Transgender Officers Protect and Serve (TOPS—for transgender police, fire, and military officers)[29] were represented. The executive director of the Intersex Society of North America was also present.[30]

In 1997, Maggie Heineman, Mary Boenke, Jessica Xavier, Nancy Sharp, Sharon Stuart, and others began to work with the Parents, Family and Friends of Lesbians and Gays (PFLAG), which was also bisexual inclusive in its by-laws. In 1998, PFLAG became transgender inclusive.[31] In late 1998, PFLAG became active in the movement to persuade Senator Kennedy and Representative Frank to include transgender in ENDA for 1999.

The momentum continues. There are a host of transgender activists. Some are working quietly and behind the scenes, and others are working boldly and openly in their towns and states to effect change and transgender protections or inclusion in GLBT legislation.

While HRC continues to resist transgender inclusion in ENDA and in its own mission statement and bylaws, it is now working to have transgenders covered in federal hate crimes legislation. It has also published a transgender employment guide authored by Dana Priesing.

Trying to stop transgender political activity at this point will be like trying to stop the ocean's tide. Even in Texas, complete with its stereotype of independence and the Old West, the State Bar allowed the creation of a Section on Sexual Orientation and Gender Identification Legal Issues.[32] This was the first LGBT state bar section to have transgender in the name. In January of 1999, fifty-plus Texas transgenders lobbied their Austin statehouse on a number of bills and were included in the proposed Texas ENDA. As Texas transgenders loudly proclaim, if we can do this in Texas, you can do it where you live. In addition, newer law journal articles are appearing, such as those by Elvia Arriola[33] and Mary Coombs,[34] that are being written by people who actually know the transgender community.

In 1999 the fight for ENDA inclusion remains and is refocused. Interestingly, the resistance has been focused on Barney Frank and rest-room policy. When President Clinton took office, gays in the military became an issue. Barney Frank took a lot of heat on this issue concerning rest rooms and showers. It seems that men who gawk at women do not like the idea that they may be gawked at themselves. And for such noncompelling reasons, gays are being run out of the military. Now, in 1999, the main resistance to transgender inclusion in ENDA is that Barney Frank does not want to revisit the rest room and shower issue again.

Rest rooms and showers are an interesting issue for Americans. When I grew up in the South, I noticed that businesses made accommodations for bigotry and spent the money to build three rest rooms—(white) men, (white) women, and colored (men and women). Concerns for privacy did not require gender segregation when the goal was racial segregation. Now with the Americans with Disabilities Act (ADA) there is often a handicapped rest room—

unisex with a lock. So why are transgenders continuing to face legal job discrimination by being omitted from ENDA simply because businesspeople cannot provide a lock on a door or maintain rest room stall door locks? What is the cost of a lock compared to the cost of unemployment benefits?

On Friday, June 25, 1999, ENDA was introduced to the new Congress. Transgenders and other gender-variant lesbians, gays, and bisexuals were again omitted. On June 28, 1999, five years passed since I began the ENDA fight. Let right be done.

ACKNOWLEDGMENTS

I wish to thank Kim Stuart, JoAnn Roberts, and Jamison Green for their editing assistance.

CHAPTER 23

ORGANIZATIONAL TALES: INTERPRETING THE NGLTF STORY

JOHN D'EMILIO

THE HISTORY OF THE NATIONAL GAY AND LESBIAN Task Force is important.[1] As many of the chapters in this volume make clear, no account of the changes in the laws and public policies that shape gay and lesbian life in the United States would be complete without attention to the Task Force. It played a critical role in the campaign to eliminate the sickness classification of homosexuality. It worked to lift the prohibition on federal civil service employment for gays and lesbians. It strove in the 1970s to make the Democratic Party responsive to the gay community. It took the lead in the 1980s in national organizing against homophobic violence. The Task Force shaped the first serious efforts in Washington to address the AIDS epidemic. It was a founding member of the Military Freedom Project, which prepared the ground for the gays-in-the-military debate of 1993. It has worked with the administrations of presidents from Carter to Clinton. Some of the most effective and dynamic leaders of the gay and lesbian movement have made NGLTF their organizational home.

At the same time, the identity of the Task Force is elusive. Most lesbians and gay men are, admittedly, unaware of what any of their national organizations do. But, among the minority who do pay attention to such things, some groups are more readily described than others. Lambda Legal Defense and Education Fund, for instance, is easily perceived as an ACLU of the gay movement. It fights through the courts to win equality and justice on issues involving sexual orientation. The Human Rights Campaign is a national gay PAC. It endorses candidates, works on congressional campaigns, and lobbies in Washington, D.C. Parents, Family and Friends of Lesbians and Gays (PFLAG) provides support for straight family members, educates them, and mobilizes them as a force for change. But what exactly is a "task force"? What does it do and what does it stand for? What niche has it filled in the evolving gay movement? How has it gone about its work? In what ways has it succeeded, and in what ways has it not?

Like the Task Force itself, the answers to these questions are both important and elusive. They are important because they can help elucidate one of the critical mechanisms through which change has occurred over the last generation. And they are elusive because little serious sustained examination of gay and lesbian organizations has occurred.

For social movements that sustain themselves for any length of time, organizations are key to survival and effectiveness. An individual might lay claim to being a feminist or a gay liberationist by virtue of her beliefs, or how she conducts her life each day, or having marched on Washington. But what keeps a social movement chugging along are its organizations. They are the mediating institutions between the big cause and the individual. Through organizations, an amorphous entity called a movement is able to frame missions, define goals, develop strategies, implement campaigns, achieve objectives, and, above all, mobilize lots of individuals to act. Organizations help set the direction of social movements. And while individuals can and do shape an organization, organizations also set up constraints within which individuals work. Understanding organizations, then, is an essential element in any assessment of how a movement succeeds in creating change.[2]

All of these issues—creating change, the dynamics of social movements, the role of organizations—are compelling to me. I study and teach about social movements. I have written extensively about the history of the gay and lesbian movement. I have been both the scholarly observer and the impassioned participant. I am especially drawn to understanding the role of the National Gay and Lesbian Task Force because, for the last dozen or so years, NGLTF has been a primary place in which I have expressed my activist impulses.

My own history has intersected with the history of the Task Force at a number of points. In 1973, as a newly minted gay activist in New York City, I remember the founding of what was then called the National Gay Task Force. At the time, I saw it as one more sad indicator that the radicalism and militancy that had drawn me to gay liberation was dying. In 1976, when the Democratic Party held its national convention in New York, I was one of many thousands demonstrating noisily outside the convention. NGTF was inside the convention hall, working with a party that I saw as bankrupt and compromised. In the early 1980s, I found myself taking a second look at the Task Force after Ginny Apuzzo, an activist whom I knew and respected, became executive director. I did my first work for NGTF in 1983 when Apuzzo commissioned a report from me detailing the history and impact of federal antigay policies.

My involvement with the Task Force escalated dramatically toward the end of the 1980s. In 1987 I helped Sue Hyde, the director of NGLTF's Privacy Project, plan a "town meeting" on sex and politics to coincide with the national march on Washington. The event drew an overflow crowd of many hundreds. Moderating it, I found myself marveling that a seemingly mainstream organization devoted to legislation and lobbying would take on the issue of sex. In 1988, I joined the board of the organization, served as cochair for two years, and stayed for five years. They were five intense years in the life of the gay movement in the United States. I left the board in the fall of 1993, but returned to the organization in 1995 for a two-year stint as a staff member, charged with launching a policy institute or think tank. Today, I continue to work with the organization on discrete projects, such as its national policy roundtable. I think it safe to say that, through my participation in NGLTF, I have learned more about social movements and their organizations than any amount of study alone could have provided.

This essay is motivated, at least in part, by an effort to make sense of my experience with the Task Force, particularly during the decade between 1988 and 1997 when it drew from me as much commitment as did my academic career. NGLTF won me over because it seemed to be doing what social movement organizations rarely attempt. It was combining outsider and insider stances into an elegantly choreographed—and compellingly innovative—strategy for change. Not content with the constraints that the unwritten rules of inside-the-beltway politics imposed, and unwilling to accept the marginality that often came with grassroots protest, NGLTF tried to play with both. It lobbied and it agitated. It negotiated and it mobilized. It supported breaking the law and changing the law. It tinkered with the system to effect small immediate changes, and it expressed a commitment to a more expansive vision of social justice.

Maintaining this stance was, and is, no easy matter. Many board and staff members, whether from temperament or political philosophy, inclined toward one direction or the other. But the years from the late 1980s into the early 1990s seemed especially conducive to this balancing effort. Through ACT UP and other local groups, there was a resurgence of direct action militancy, while in Washington, in some state capitals, and in many cities, the legislative process was newly hospitable to queer lobbying. These years, roughly extending from the 1987 march on Washington to the 1992 national elections, witnessed

shifts as profound as those that came in the aftermath of the Stonewall uprising. And NGLTF's influence could be detected everywhere.

For a brief season, the election of Clinton seemed to multiply the opportunities for change. I say this not because of Clinton himself, since little in his
previous career suggested any strong commitment to a progressive political
agenda. Rather, Democratic control of both the White House and Congress
ought to have shifted the political calculus just enough to make the victories of
the previous few years pale in comparison to what might lie ahead.

It didn't happen. Some of the other chapters in this book help explain
why. But from inside the Task Force, the "gay moment" of 1992–93 was a disaster. Instead of seizing the moment, NGLTF almost imploded. Over the next
three years it shrunk precipitously in size, influence, and effectiveness. Why?

At the time, caught within the drama of the internal debates, I interpreted
the near collapse of the Task Force as the result of poor political choices. The
emotional intensity of Washington—and movement—politics in the face of the
gays-in-the-military debate, the seductive accessibility of the new president, and
the magnitude of the 1993 national march seemed to destabilize the precariously
crafted balance of insider-outsider strategies. In the effort not to become, as the
Human Rights Campaign appeared to be, a tool of an unreliable Democratic
Party, NGLTF moved far in the other direction. It saw itself only as oppositional,
and it seemed to regard marginality and outsider status as valuable. In other
words, I interpreted the travails of NGLTF through the very lens with which we
participants framed, and debated, the story.

Now, a number of years and many hours of reflection later, I have come
to see these events differently. They need, I believe, to be placed in the context
of the organization's whole history. And they need to be understood not in the
terms that participants used to debate political choices, but through the unarticulated fundament that lies at the core of NGLTF's organizational culture.

Though often a passionate advocate in many of the debates that shaped
the organization's direction over a number of years, in the rest of this essay I
will try to look at those debates, and the larger history of the organization, with
some measure of detachment. I will provide an overview of the organization's
history, detailing the key issues, people, and events. I will then suggest—and
discard—a number of common ways of interpreting a social movement organization's history. I will pick up the concept of organizational culture, suggest
how one might define this in relation to NGLTF, and detail the ways I think
this can help us understand the history of the Task Force. Finally, I will suggest some lessons. Because I care so much about the organization, decoding
the history of NGLTF is important to me. But I also think it is vital to raising
the organization's effectiveness—and the efficacy of other organizations as
well.

AN OVERVIEW

The National Gay Task Force was founded in New York City in October 1973.[3] In the four years that had elapsed since the Stonewall uprising in Greenwich Village, militant gay and lesbian organizations had proliferated across the country, their numbers approaching a thousand. The gay liberation movement of those years, full of bravado and daring, was given to the dramatic gesture. Its hit-and-run tactics, its in-your-face rhetoric, succeeded in capturing media attention. The movement also won for itself an expanding body of recruits, especially among younger lesbians and gay men affected by the radical cultural politics associated with the sixties. But its style and methods were not particularly suited to the long, sustained march through institutions that the battle against homophobia, heterosexism, and gay oppression also required.

The key founders of the Task Force—Bruce Voeller, Nath Rockhill, Ron Gold, and Howard Brown among them—were New York City activists. Voeller, Rockhill, and Gold were all closely associated with the Gay Activists Alliance, one of the premier post-Stonewall organizations. They had grown tired of GAA's chaotic style of operation in which every proposal could be debated endlessly and mass membership meetings seemed to stand in the way of the coordinated pursuit of long-term goals. Brown was a former health commissioner for the city of New York, a professionally successful gay man who had just come out on the front page of *The New York Times*.[4] He was looking for a vehicle to express his political commitments.

Voeller and the others saw the organization they were launching as a new departure.[5] Until the founding of the Task Force, volunteer energy had sustained the gay liberation movement, and almost all of its work had been local. The Task Force was conceived as a national organization, designed to work on issues beyond the reach of local groups, with a paid staff who would provide a measure of continuity and professionalism to the work of gay advocacy.

The Task Force came into being at a promising time for national gay advocacy efforts. Everything in America was up for grabs. An unpopular war was ending. The racial status quo had been shaken. Feminists were bringing a new brand of sexual and gender politics into everyday life. The conservative Nixon administration was unraveling in the wake of the Senate Watergate hearings. Everywhere, it seemed, traditional sources of power and privilege faced challenges. Could a national civil rights organization of lesbians and gay men capitalize on the moment and win concessions from a range of American institutions?

The early years of the Task Force fueled the optimistic sense that anything was possible. Despite its small size (a handful of staff members with an annual budget of a couple of hundred thousand dollars in its first years), it was able to nudge change forward in several critical areas. In December 1973, two months

474 | John D'Emilio

after NGTF was formed, the national board of the American Psychiatric Association voted to remove homosexuality from its list of mental disorders. When dissident psychiatrists insisted on an association-wide referendum, the Task Force worked with allies in the profession to win support for the change and defeat the referendum. Supporting the efforts of Frank Kameny, one of its board members, it pushed successfully to have the federal Civil Service Commission reverse, in 1975, the ban on the employment of lesbians and gay men in federal jobs. Other achievements included successful lobbying within the American Bar Association to put the organization on record in favor of sodomy law repeal (1974) and eliciting from the National Council of Churches a resolution condemning antigay discrimination (1975).

As the above examples suggest, NGTF cast its net widely. It saw change as coming not only through government, but through a range of institutions in American life. In 1975 Ginny Vida, its media director, coordinated one of the first national protests against the media, in response to a homophobic episode of *Marcus Welby, M.D.*, a popular television series of that era. The Task Force won a reversal of an Internal Revenue Service policy that denied tax-exempt status to organizations that argued that homosexuality was acceptable. It conducted the first national survey of major corporations to determine their hiring practices, then began to advocate for explicit nondiscrimination policies. It worked with Bella Abzug and, later, with Ed Koch, members of the House of Representatives from New York City, to introduce a comprehensive gay rights bill into Congress.

Jean O'Leary, a founder of Lesbian Feminist Liberation in New York City, joined the staff in 1975 and became coexecutive director the following year.[6] O'Leary brought a strong interest in party politics and in feminism to the organization. Focusing on the Democratic Party, which in these years seemed to offer the most likely opportunity for dialogue, she initiated a convention project in 1976. NGTF surveyed the party's candidates for the presidential nomination, organized constituent meetings in a number of districts, and maintained a communications center at the convention. Although the platform made no mention of gay and lesbian issues, O'Leary and the Task Force gathered signatures from six hundred delegates in support of gay rights and sodomy law repeal.

O'Leary also worked closely with other female staff and board members (gender parity existed on the board almost from the beginning) to agitate within the women's movement for lesbian visibility and support for lesbian rights. Focusing attention on President Carter's International Women's Year activities, O'Leary managed to get herself appointed as the only openly lesbian delegate on the president's IWY commission. O'Leary and other Task Force women coordinated the passage of sexual preference resolutions at thirty state conferences and, at the national conference in Houston in 1977, won over-whelming support for lesbian rights. The Houston conference was a milestone in the effort to make equality for lesbians a key feature of mainstream feminist advocacy.

The late seventies saw both new opportunities and dramatic challenges. O'Leary's work within the Democratic Party had cracked open a door to the Carter administration. The Task Force was able to engineer a series of meet-ings with officials in executive agencies, initiating a dialogue about issues rang-ing from access to gay publications for inmates of federal prisons to the implementation of immigration and naturalization policy. At the same time, the gay movement encountered new resistance to its advocacy efforts in the form of an emerging New Right that deployed a rhetoric of family and morality to challenge both feminism and gay liberation. The first major battle came in 1977 in Dade County, Florida, where Anita Bryant, a popular singer, was spokeswoman for a campaign to repeal a gay rights ordinance. While the cam-paign brought sustained media attention to gay rights for the first time, it also was the opening battle in a continuing struggle that has stretched now for more than two decades. Voeller traveled to Florida frequently to help local activists craft a winning strategy. But in Dade County, as well as in Wichita, St. Paul, and Eugene, Oregon, in the following year, gay activists proved unable to pre-vent repeal of antidiscrimination ordinances.

Just when the shifting political winds began to constrict the opportunities for gay activists, NGTF experienced a turnover in leadership. Both Voeller and O'Leary, who had worked effectively together, left in 1979. As replacements, the board of directors chose Charles Brydon, a businessman who had built an organi-zation of gay professionals in Seattle, and Lucia Valeska, a grassroots activist from New Mexico with long experience in the women's movement.[7] Very different from one another in temperament and political perspective, the two were a poor pair for jointly running an organization. Yet, the Task Force especially needed forceful leadership for the new decade. Reagan was about to enter the White House, and Republicans were winning control of the Senate for the first time in a generation. Powered by a newly mobilized fundamentalist constituency, the Re-publican Party was coming to dominate politics just as AIDS emerged in the lives of gay and bisexual men.

The few achievements of the Task Force during these years rested on de-cisions made earlier. In October 1979, the Task Force cosponsored the first na-tional conference of Third World gays and lesbians, which in turn helped spur autonomous organizing in the 1980s within people-of-color communities. NGTF worked with other organizations to sustain a strong presence at the 1980 Democratic National Convention, which saw the incorporation of some gay issues into the party's platform. The Fund for Human Dignity, a nonprofit educational arm of NGTF, became fully operational. Mel Boozer was hired as a lobbyist, giving the New York–based organization a Washington presence for the first time.

But Brydon and Valeska were poorly suited to the new era. The differences between them meant that internal conflicts—between men and women, between proponents of more cautious approaches to change and more assertive ones—consumed much of the organization's energies. Instead of focusing attention outward, on the increasingly well-organized opponents of the gay movement, the Task Force often found itself engaged in internecine quarrels with other gay organizations. Brydon and Valeska each committed a series of very public gaffes, which lowered the credibility of NGTF. By the early 1980s, the budget of the organization was shrinking, unable to keep pace with inflation. Important areas of work, such as media advocacy, were dropped because of financial constraints. Brydon quit as codirector in 1981. The following year, Valeska was fired by the board of directors after a disastrous performance in Dallas at the first national forum on AIDS.

With the Task Force in disarray and close to collapse, the board hired Virginia Apuzzo to restore NGTF's credibility. Apuzzo possessed a number of strengths. She held the respect of both lesbians and gay men. She was a dynamic speaker who could rouse an audience to action. She combined a commitment to using conventional modes of politics with a visionary rhetoric of radical social change.

Apuzzo also displayed an uncanny knack for identifying cutting-edge issues. For instance, as gay men and lesbians became more visible in the 1970s, homophobic violence against them seemed to escalate. Police were often unsympathetic, blaming the victim rather than the perpetrator, and gays and lesbians were often reluctant to report crimes. In cities like New York and San Francisco, local antiviolence groups formed to address the issue. Apuzzo took a small volunteer-staffed initiative at NGTF and supported its development into a major national organizing effort. Under the direction of Kevin Berrill, the Anti-Violence Project provided technical assistance to local groups, coordinated the first national surveys of homophobic violence, and worked to put the issue on the radar screen of the Justice Department and other law enforcement organizations. Years of patient coalition-building eventually led to the inclusion of sexual orientation in federal legislation, the Hate Crimes Statistics Act of 1990. For many years, the Task Force's antiviolence project stood as a model of the partnership that could develop between local and national advocacy efforts.[8]

Above all, Apuzzo focused the energy of NGTF on the AIDS crisis. When she took the job at the Task Force, AIDS was not yet a major story in the mainstream media or the gay press. The nationally reported caseload was still below a thousand, and beyond a few big cities, the epidemic had hardly registered in the consciousness of the community. But Apuzzo sensed that a crisis of massive proportions was in the making, and its solution was beyond the capacity of local groups, such as the Gay Men's Health Crisis in New York City, to solve. AIDS required resources that only the federal government was large enough to provide.

Apuzzo hired Jeff Levi, an activist in Washington, D.C., as a lobbyist to focus on AIDS. Together with Levi, a small number of other activists, and some friendly congressional staff, she began to craft a response by building key relationships within the federal government, mobilizing gay community organizations, and reaching out to likely coalition partners. At an early congressional hearing in Washington in 1983, Apuzzo wore a flaming red dress to dramatize her anger as she blasted the neglect and apathy of the Reagan administration. She found the money to help launch, with the support of other gay organizations, AIDS Action, which became the key lobbying organization in Washington. AIDS Action in turn, with Levi playing a critical role, formed the NORA coalition (National Organizations Responding to AIDS), which brought together a wide range of organizations whose work was affected by the AIDS epidemic. While the rewards of this work were great, the price was also high. It almost bankrupted NGTF, weakening the organization's infrastructure.

After Apuzzo left the Task Force in 1985, the job of organizational rebuilding fell to Levi. The board approved the move of the organization's offices to Washington, in response to the increasing emphasis on work at the federal level. It also changed the name, to the National Gay and Lesbian Task Force, to make clear the commitment to gender parity and lesbian issues. Meanwhile, mounting frustration over AIDS, and anger over the *Hardwick* decision of 1986, in which the Supreme Court sustained the constitutionality of Georgia's sodomy statute, was enlarging the pool of gay men and lesbians willing to support the work of an organization like NGLTF.

Through the rest of the 1980s, Levi slowly added staff, augmenting the scope of the organization's work. Urvashi Vaid was hired as communications director and used the position for an assertive brand of media advocacy. After *Hardwick,* Sue Hyde came on as director of a newly created Privacy Project, designed to work state by state for sodomy law repeal. Levi brought in Peri Jude Radecic, a lobbyist with the National Organization for Women, to handle the expanding volume of legislative and executive-branch work in Washington. Ivy Young became the director of a new Families Project, providing resources for activists seeking to win domestic partnership benefits and to expand their right to parent. And Kevin Berrill continued his work on hate-motivated violence.

By the end of the 1980s, the Task Force occupied a unique niche in the gay and lesbian movement. It played an important role in Washington, D.C., where, along with the Human Rights Campaign Fund, it maintained a presence on Capitol Hill and worked with a broad range of federal agencies. But through its organizing projects, it increasingly saw its role as mobilizing the grass roots to make change. Radecic, for instance, not only lobbied members of Congress. She issued "report cards" grading them based on their votes on gay and AIDS issues, then circulated the reports to local constituents as a way of holding legislators accountable. As organizations like ACT UP adopted direct action tactics as part of the practice of politics, the Task Force lobbied on the inside and supported militancy on the outside.

When Urvashi Vaid succeeded Levi as executive director in 1989, she pushed the Task Force more strongly in the direction of movement-building.[9] The growing power of the religious-based New Right and the attacks on the gay community from politicians like Jesse Helms, William Dannemeyer, and Robert Dornan made it clear that a Washington-based politics alone would not succeed. Under Vaid, the Task Force devoted itself to strengthening the local infrastructure of the gay and lesbian movement. Creating Change, its annual conference, became the major site each year in which activists learned skills, shared strategies, and concocted joint organizing campaigns. Project directors at NGLTF spent much time on the road, working to strengthen local organizations and build statewide coalitions. At the same time, Vaid's tenure (1989–92) coincided with important legislative victories. Among them were the Hate Crimes Statistics Act, the Americans with Disabilities Act, the Ryan White CARE Act, and important changes in immigration law.

Between the summers of 1992 and 1993 came "the gay moment" in American national politics. Bill Clinton, the Democratic candidate, embraced the gay community as no other presidential nominee had done before. By contrast, the Republican National Convention in Houston witnessed an orgy of fiercely homophobic rhetoric and references to "culture wars." Early in 1993 the military exclusion policy became the subject of national debate. As hundreds of thousands marched in Washington for gay, lesbian, and bisexual rights, and as Clinton invited gay leaders to the White House, Congress was relentlessly moving toward support for the continued ban on gay, lesbian, and bisexual service members. For the gay community, the year was marked by a dizzying oscillation between exhilarating optimism and terrifying vulnerability. Many organizations, local and national, expanded dramatically during this period, as more gays and lesbians than ever before were politically mobilized. Despite the defeat over the military issue, organizations by and large emerged from this period larger, stronger, and better positioned to shape policy and public discourse.

But not the Task Force. The years 1993 to 1997 were difficult for the organization. Leadership was unstable at a time of tremendous opportunity. Vaid's successor as executive director, Torie Osborn, stayed for only six months. The next two executive directors, Peri Jude Radecic and Melinda Paras, also had relatively brief tenures. They presided over a staff that was rent by internal debates over the direction the organization should take in this new era of national attention. Should the organization emphasize national work or focus on grassroots mobilization and movement-building? Should the Task Force work closely with the Clinton administration or position itself as a progressive opposition? Should it continue its issue-oriented projects or devote its resources to fighting and exposing an increasingly powerful religious right? Should its focus remain on gay issues, or should it work in coalition on a range of issues to build a strong progressive movement?

The effects were debilitating. Appearing directionless and ineffective to many on the outside, the Task Force shrank precipitously. The opportunities for growth that the events of 1992–93 brought proved temporary for NGLTF, even as other movement organizations became permanently larger. Between 1994 and 1996, its budget shrank by almost 50 percent, and its staff was cut in half. Organizing projects that had been very successful—such as the Anti-Violence and Campus Projects—were terminated. The Task Force lost its leadership of issues that had long been associated with the organization. Its lobbying presence in Washington, formerly visible and effective, faded away. It played no role of consequence in the negotiations over reauthorization of the Ryan White CARE Act, the debates over the Defense of Marriage Act, or the lobbying for ENDA, the Employment Non-Discrimination Act.

Even during this period of crisis, some important initiatives were taken. Under Melinda Paras, the board approved the creation of a policy institute, a combined think tank and research arm. Its mission was to produce fresh perspectives on critical issues, create academic-activist partnerships, and encourage innovative strategies for change. NGLTF also made the building of effective statewide federations a priority, as state legislatures in the 1990s became key arenas for the making of policy on gay, lesbian, bisexual, and increasingly, transgender issues.

Under the leadership of Kerry Lobel, who became executive director at the end of 1996, the organization slowly began to grow again. Finances improved, and new staff were hired. Urvashi Vaid returned to the organization, this time as director of the policy institute. She initiated a national policy roundtable that brings together the leaders of more than three dozen key organizations, and a religious roundtable that is welding activists in communities of faith into a more effective force for change. State organizing has continued, and in 1999 NGLTF led the planning for Equality Begins at Home, the first-ever coordinated set of lobbying events, public rallies, and conferences in state capitals around the country. Whether this work is a prelude to a new era of effective advocacy for NGLTF, or whether its historical era as a leading national organization has passed, remains to be seen.

INTERPRETING THE TASK FORCE STORY

Much more could be written, of course. But even this brief overview suggests a few things. NGLTF has been involved in some of the key issues facing the gay and lesbian community since the mid–1970s. At particular moments, and on certain issues, it has played a key role in focusing attention, mobilizing support, and provoking policy change. But it also has a checkered organizational history. In some periods the Task Force was anything but effective, dropping the ball, becoming mired in internal squabbles, relinquishing its leadership role to other organizations. What accounts for this oscillation between peaks and troughs of organizational effectiveness?

One way of intepreting the history of NGLTF is by looking at leadership eras. Under Voeller and O'Leary, the Task Force accumulated a credible record as a national voice for gay and lesbian advocacy efforts. It compiled some important achievements and broke new ground. Under Brydon and Valeska it stumbled badly and accomplished little. Under the successive regimes of Apuzzo, Levi, and Vaid, it gathered a great deal of momentum, thrusting itself into important policy debates. It led nationally and worked closely with grassroots activists to craft a variety of strategies for change. Under Osborn, Radecic, and Paras, NGLTF almost imploded and became increasingly marginal even as gay issues were agitating the body politic as never before. Most recently, under Lobel, the Task Force has been rebuilding, recouping lost ground. and carving out a new niche for itself.

Another way of approaching the Task Force story is through the prism of politics, the series of conflicting perspectives variously thought of as left or right, liberationist or assimilationist, grassroots militancy or professional lobbying, multi-issue coalition-building or single-issue identity politics. NGTF was founded specifically to free itself from the excessive democracy of local gay activist organizing, addressing national issues as a professionalized advocacy group. Lesbians brought more feminist styles of politics to the organization, and for a while in the 1970s, it blended a national lobbying perspective with efforts to mobilize local activists. Under Brydon and Valeska, these two perspectives clashed rather than cooperated. By the mid–1980s, a conscious effort was being made to keep both insider and outsider approaches to change in balance, so that both were in the Task Force tool kit of advocacy methods. Thus, NGLTF was willing to negotiate with the Food and Drug Administration over its approach to testing and approving AIDS drugs, at the same time that it was actively supporting militant ACT UP demonstrations against the agency. It helped train local activists and build local organizations even as it worked for change inside the beltway. In the 1990s, faced with the rise of an extremist right wing, the disarray of Democratic Party liberals, and the perception of betrayal by the Clinton administration that the military debate engendered, the tensions involved in this balance exploded. NGLTF emphasized grassroots organizing rather than lobbying Congress or the executive branch. It self-consciously defined itself as "the queer voice of the progressive movement and the progressive voice of the queer movement," while it floundered over how to translate this perspective into an effective program and organizational mission. Today it seems to have emerged from this turmoil. It has reconstituted itself as an organization committed to progressive coalition-building, even as much of its day-to-day work focuses on issues of concern to gays, lesbians, bisexuals, and the transgendered.

Yet a third way of understanding the history of NGLTF is to place Task Force activities within the shifting social and political world of the last generation. How attentive has it been to the changing needs of the gay and lesbian community? Has it picked issues that mattered to its constituents? Has it read the political climate well enough to know where it could negotiate change and which victories were achievable? How has it responded to the falling fortunes of the Democratic Party and American liberalism in the 1980s and 1990s, and the simultaneous rise to political power of the Republican Party and a new American conservatism? Exploring questions such as these combine issues of leadership and political perspective with historical context to allow us to chart the varied fortunes of NGLTF.

Each one of these angles is useful. That the quality of leadership matters for an organization seems self-evident. The head of an organization sets a tone, shapes the environment in which staff works, and provides the public with a face, personality, and character. Other key staff can build—or destroy—credibility with the people whom they are trying to mobilize and the figures they are trying to influence by the skill and style they bring to their work. There is no single formula or profile for good leadership, but without effective leadership no organization will thrive and achieve significant goals. Leadership may not be the only thing that matters, but it is essential to an organization's welfare.

Similarly, the politics of an advocacy organization will shape its focus and position it in the world of public policy. A self-definition as liberal or conservative, reform-oriented or radical, influences goals, tactics, the choice of coalition partners, and the target of one's activities. An organization's political orientation also will affect its relation to the kind of conflicts that an identity-based constituency confronts, such as the tension between a liberationist vision and assimilationist aspirations.

Finally, any incisive analysis of a movement organization will be attuned to the shifting historical context. The most compelling issues of one decade can fade away in the next, even if one's objectives have not been achieved. Successes open up new horizons. Generational shifts require rethinking one's goals as younger cohorts come of age with new expectations of how they would like the world to be. Meanwhile, a new balance of forces in national politics, or changes in the cultural fabric, or shifts in economic or social life, will often require a rethinking of strategy, tactics, and goals. Without the ability to grasp the significance of these trends, the most successful organization of one era will be dust in the next.

Let me propose, however, that even combining all three of these perspectives will leave the Task Force story indecipherable. For something else has been at play in the workings of NGLTF that has, as much as anything, shaped the contours of its history and molded its identity. The Task Force has a *culture* that drives it.

To describe this culture in a nutshell: NGLTF exists to fill a void. Its purpose from its inception has been to do what needs to be done, but what no one else is doing. This sense of purpose propels it forward, creating a sense of daring, innovation, and living on the edge. It also generates an atmosphere of missionary zeal and of sacrifice: the organization is there to serve selflessly the community's needs. Its periods of greatest achievement have come during those times when the void it chose to fill coincided with work that most needed doing and when the organization has been able to achieve consensus internally about what to do. But the imperative to innovate, to be on the edge, also has its drawbacks. It can lead to crisis and disarray as an organization tries to reinvent itself for the changing times. It prevents an organization from developing expertise and longevity in an area, as the work of one era comes to feel old and stale while the new beckons. And it keeps the identity of the Task Force elusive precisely because its work keeps shifting. An organization always in search of the new, or always rushing to fill a void, will experience recurring difficulties. Supporters will peel away as the organization no longer speaks to them, and new supporters will always have to be found. Rather than build steadily, it will periodically have to start over again.

The need to fill a void animated the organization from its inception. No organization had national work as its mission when NGTF was founded in 1973. The absence of competitors and the sense of breaking new ground created an élan, a sense of excitement and achievement over virtually every initiative. But, in time, the thrill evaporated as the slow, plodding work of extracting policy change from the federal bureaucracy moved to the foreground. The Task Force found itself paralyzed. Should it continue or abandon the work it had started in Washington? Or should it rush to fill a new void that had appeared—helping local organizations counteract a rising right-wing assault on gay rights legislation? Unable to stick with the old or embrace the new, the organization floundered.

The solution came when the need to craft AIDS policy—a new, bigger, more menacing void—emerged in the 1980s. No movement organization was seizing the initiative in Washington, where the federal government, for better or worse, held the future of the epidemic in its hands. Apuzzo's decision to embrace the issue, to rush to fill the gap, made a historic difference in the evolution of AIDS policy over the next several years. It also saved NGTF, restoring its sense of missionary fervor, creating an environment of desperate activity commensurate with the danger of AIDS.

By the late 1980s the Task Force had succeeded so well that it was no longer working alone. In Washington, AIDS Action Council and the NORA coalition were advocating for AIDS, while in communities throughout the country ACT UP chapters were engaging in direct action protest, drawing major media attention to the issue. AIDS activism was still a life-and-death issue, but the field was now crowded. No longer did it satisfy the need to be on the frontier, or to lean over the edge of the precipice, staring into the unknown and uncharted.

Instead, AIDS had spawned something new. As the 1987 march on Washington revealed, a whole new generation of gays and lesbians had come out of the closet and were prepared to make of their identity a political statement. But the infrastructure to sustain local activism was still weak in much of the country. Toward the end of the decade NGLTF began reorienting itself away from AIDS work and toward nurturing grassroots activism. Partly it did this through its annual Creating Change conference, which not only taught skills but built desperately needed networks among activists. Partly it did this through emphasizing issue-oriented organizing projects. These projects—antiviolence, sodomy law repeal, families, and campus—provided local organizations with resources and technical assistance so that the generalized desire to do something could be more effectively translated into concrete action to change policy and institutions. NGLTF staff spent a lot of time on the road. Going to the "heartland" and aiding the building of a strong movement fed the need to be doing what no other national organization was doing in the way that, earlier, going to Washington had nourished the same impulse.

The powerful combination of AIDS, a proliferating grassroots movement, and a politically aggressive radical right together created the "gay moment" of 1992–93. Gay and lesbian issues received unprecedented national attention, posing both great dangers and great opportunities. The moment required leadership of the most flexible sort. It required imaginative strategizing. And it required skilled and determined mobilization. With a history of working in Washington, and with its ties to local activists around the country, NGLTF might have shaped a creative response that maximized the opportunities while containing the dangers. Instead, it found itself imploding.

This was the period of my own heaviest involvement with NGLTF. As I described at the start of this essay, what had won me over to the Task Force in the late 1980s was the profile of the organization at that time. Insider and outsider perspectives were elegantly balanced within it. NGLTF seemed committed to doing what rarely happens within one movement organization. It was holding on to a full range of strategic and tactical options. It believed in working through the legislative process and with government bureaucrats to make change. It believed in the need to build a vibrant democratic social movement in which local people were empowered. It was willing to endorse direct action as a legitimate form of political activity. Now, in 1993, we seemed to be confronted with the rare political moment when such a broad conception of how to make change was most needed.

It surprised, puzzled, and disappointed me when the Task Force essentially abandoned its work of the previous decade. As a participant in these years, I saw the conflicts and debates that were erupting in NGLTF in political terms. They seemed to be variations of familiar political divisions that had often recurred in social movements. Should an organization work closely with those in power (in this case, the Clinton administration) to shape policy, or should it remain an independent voice? Can "the system" be trusted to reform itself, and can meaningful change be achieved through insider lobbying and negotiation with those in power? Or, must those with grievances always battle from the outside, building a power base that rests upon substantial grassroots mobilization? Were Democratic Party liberals able to deliver the goods, or did a new progressive politics need to emerge, sufficiently robust to arouse Americans and to counteract an increasingly powerful extreme right wing?

These political issues had an internal analogue as the staff fought among itself about the nature of the organization's work culture. Was Torie Osborn, the new executive director, trying to create a hierarchical professionalized organization? Was she too attached to inside-the-beltway conceptions of social change? Would big donors and high-priced fund-raising events come to shape the organization's outlook?

To me, it seemed that the issues being debated, overtly and covertly, were creating a sense of mutually exclusive alternatives rather than building on what I saw as NGLTF's strength, namely its ability to reconcile and synthesize approaches that often seem incompatible. It made no sense to me that one should have to choose between working with the national government and mobilizing the grass roots. This choice seemed especially destructive of the Task Force's progressive political goals since, if the organization abandoned Washington-based work, more conservative organizations such as the Human Rights Campaign Fund were bound to dominate the scene and shape the agenda. Yet the organization seemed impervious to such arguments. Instead, over the next two years, NGLTF jettisoned significant policy work at the national level, allowing responsibility for it to devolve upon other organizations. It also permitted its issue-oriented projects, which had given the Task Force its working connection with local activists, to atrophy and die. In its place, NGLTF devoted itself to "fighting the right." Its purpose became to expose the danger that the extreme right wing posed to democratic values and visions of social justice and to mobilizing the grass roots to respond.

At the time, I thought that the wrong political perspective triumphed, that a poor strategic path had been chosen. Retrospectively, the debates seem less about the overt content and much more about something never clearly articulated. For the outcome revealed that, once again, the Task Force was shaping its program not in relation to a long-range vision of change, nor in terms of immediately realizable goals that might build the organization, but to fill a void. This time the void was combat against a more powerful, aggressive, and threatening right wing. Fighting the right not only was work that no other important queer organization was taking on. It also fed the need to be on the edge, to be brave warriors, to exhibit the passion and fervor of missionaries. It certainly was more appealing than the humdrum tasks of moving the Washington bureaucracy during a friendly Democratic administration, or of patiently following a few issues all the way to success.

"Fight the right" proved a disaster as a program. For one, the Task Force was far too small an organization to have any noticeable impact on what the right did. It also made the organization's program thoroughly reactive, completely dependent on what one's political opponents did rather than on what queer communities wanted or needed. It offered few tangible achievements that the organization could claim for itself or deliver to its constituency. It made many of the organization's partners angry as commitments to preexisting work, such as the antiviolence project or the campus project, were dropped. Finally, it created within the organization a sense of embattlement, of being besieged by enemies, of daily being on the verge of Armageddon.

Since these years in the mid–1990s, the Task Force has attempted to reinvent itself once more. Today, its program and direction include several elements. It is putting resources into a policy institute, conceived as a combination research arm and think tank that produces high-quality innovative analysis of issues and fosters new strategic thinking. It is working to develop a strong infrastructure of state-level gay, lesbian, bisexual, and transgender organizations to facilitate legislative and policy change in state capitals across the country. It is committed to coalition-building and multi-issue organizing, believing that justice is indivisible and that a queer policy agenda will move forward to the degree that the gay movement is aligned with a broad array of social movements. And it has become a voice for inclusion, arguing that agendas must be developed that embrace the perspectives of bisexuals and the transgendered.

As at various other points in its history, NGLTF today has a program that can make a credible claim to representing a strategic perspective on how best to achieve significant change in the long run. Successes in each of the above areas would have a major impact on law, public policy, and the political climate.

But, this program could just as easily be the latest in a long series that have all, I believe, been ultimately shaped by the unacknowledged culture of the organization: its need to fill a void, to do what no one else is seriously doing, to see itself as taking risks and living on the edge.

CONCLUSION

There is nothing wrong with an organization having as its central driving impulse the desire to fill a void. At different points in its history, NGLTF has been able to translate this impulse into effective work and impressive achievements. This has been most true in the earliest years of the organization, when it pioneered advocacy at the national level, and in its middle period, when it crafted a political response to AIDS and encouraged the revival of effective local activism.

But such an impulse, and the culture that surrounds it, is problematic when it goes unacknowledged. It is hard on the people who work there, since the flip side of being pioneers who struggle on the edge is high, almost constant, stress. It is hard on an organization's survival, too, since the expertise that brings accomplishment, name recognition, and fund-raising capability is regularly discarded as one moves on to new challenges and new issues that appeal to a different constituency. Thus, it is not surprising that NGLTF has experienced recurring budgetary constraints, more so than many other national organizations. Finally, the compelling urge to rush toward where the void is has serious effects on the movement to which NGLTF is devoted. It has meant that the Task Force has periodically abandoned the constituents it has nurtured, ironically creating voids of its own as it leaves one arena of advocacy work to pursue something newer and edgier.

In doing so, the Task Force unwittingly betrays the leadership role that it has, with justification, often claimed for itself. Periodically, its track record of success has brought it to a point where it could decisively affect the direction of the movement as a whole. Instead of embracing a higher level of influence and power, which have accrued to it because of its effective work, it has backed away. In an era when the mainstream of the gay movement seems to be accommodating to the conservative spirit of the times, steady, reliable leadership from a progressive organization is more critical than ever. Wouldn't that be a void worth filling?

1. MIRROR IMAGES: LESBIAN/GAY CIVIL RIGHTS IN THE CARTER AND REAGAN ADMINISTRATIONS

1. Photocopy of letter, Robert Strauss to C. F. Brydon and Lucia Valeska, 3/3/80, in file "Gays [CF, O/A 728]," box 211, Eizenstat papers, Domestic Policy Staff (cited hereafter as DPS), Jimmy Carter Library (cited hereafter as JCL).

2. Press release, 10/14/76, announcing O'Leary's and other appointments, in file "Gay Rights: Jimmy Carter's views on," box 4, Office of Public Liaison papers (cited hereafter as OPL), JCL. As the name suggests, this file contains extensive information about Carter's position, mostly from the 1976 campaign. On the 51.3% committee, see Emily Walker Cook, "Women White House Advisors in the Carter Administration: Presidential Stalwarts or Feminist Advocates?" (Ph.D. diss., Vanderbilt University, May 1995), 38n11.

3. Press release, n.d., "California Gay People for Carter-Mondale," in file "Gay Rights: Jimmy Carter's views on," box 4, OPL, JCL. On Perry and the Universal Fellowship of Metropolitan Community Churches (commonly known as MCC), founded in 1968, see very brief mentions in Barry D. Adam, *The Rise of a Gay and Lesbian Movement* (Boston: Twayne, 1987), 136; and D'Emilio, *Sexual Politics, Sexual Communities* (Chicago: University of Chicago Press, 1983), 227. On Martin and Lyon founding the DOB, see D'Emilio, 101–5; for their own account, see "Lesbians United," chapter 8 in Del Martin and Phyllis Lyon, *Lesbian/Woman* (1972; Twentieth Anniversary Edition, Volcano, Calif.: Volcano Press, 1991), 217–55.

4. Letters, Robert S. Havely, campaign coordinator for national issues and policy, to Jean O'Leary, co–executive director, NGTF, 10/4/76; Julie Michel, New York issues coordinator, to Allen Roskoff, 5/24/76; both in file "Gay Rights: Jimmy Carter's views on," box 4, OPL, JCL.

5. Message from O'Leary and Voeller to Carter, 8/18/76, file "[Gay Rights: Correspondence] 5/76–7/78 [O/A 5771]," box 4, OPL, JCL.

6. Letters, 6/28/77, Haft to R. Adam DeBaugh, resigning from Gay Rights National Lobby; 2/14/77, Haft to organizers of Women & Law Conference; both in file "FG 6-1-1/Haft," White House Central File (cited hereafter as WHCF), JCL.

7. File "[Gay Rights & Vice Mayor Costanza of Rochester, N.Y.] 1/76–8/76 [O/A 5771]," and material in file "[Gay Rights: Memos, Correspondence, Clippings] 5/76–8/78 [O/A 5771]," both in box 4, OPL, JCL.

8. Letter, 2/1/77, O'Leary and Voeller to Costanza referring to "your deep humanity at the Platform Committee and the Democratic National Convention"; and memo from Costanza, no date or recipient specified, describing her activities on Platform Committee; both in file "[Gay Rights: Correspondence] 5/76–7/78 [O/A 5771]," box 4, OPL, JCL.

9. Cook, "Women White House Advisors," 41–50. Quotation comes from transcript of Jody Powell's appearance on television show *Face the Nation*, 3/27/77, in file "[Gays, Jimmy Carter on] 3/76–3/77 [O/A 4499]," box 22, OPL, JCL.

10. See memos exchanged between Costanza, and Voeller and O'Leary, both dated

2/8/77, in file "[National Gay Task Force Correspondence] 9/76–2/78 [O/A 4499]," box 27, OPL, JCL.

11. All of the files in box 28, OPL, JCL, contain briefing booklets on these issues that NGTF representatives left after their meeting at the White House. See also memo, 2/8/77, Voeller and O'Leary to Costanza. See also memo, 3/25/77, Haft to Costanza, describing likely issues for meeting; and memo, 4/8/77, Costanza to the president, reporting on meeting, both in file "[Gay Civil Rights], 10/76–2/78 [O/A 4609]," box 22, OPL, JCL; handwritten notes by Bob Malson, aide for Civil Rights on Domestic Policy Staff, copy sent to Haft on 4/4/77, in file "[Haft, Marilyn G.] 1/77–4/77 [O/A 4499]," box 23 OPL, JCL.

12. Transcript, file "[Gays, Jimmy Carter on] 3/76–3/77 [O/A 4499]," in box 22, OPL, JCL.

13. See draft, file "[Homosexuality—Gay Rights & Public Health] 8/76–1/78 [O/A 5772]," box 5, OPL, JCL.

14. Copy of poll and results, 4/77, in file "[Gay Rights: Correspondence] 5/76–7/78 [O/A 5771]," box 4, OPL, JCL.

15. File "Mail [Count Sheets]—Midge Costanza, 11/77–1/78," box 27, OPL; letters from Koch, 3/21/77; Holtzman, 4/4/77; and Burton, 3/11/77, to president, all in file "3/1/77 to 4/30/77," box HU-5, WHCF/Subject File (hereafter, SF), JCL.

16. See various memos, beginning with Haft to Costanza, 4/11/77, describing general outline for future NGTF meetings with agencies, meeting with Justice already scheduled, 4/28/77; memo, 4/28/77, reminding Costanza of meeting with Justice, notifying of meeting with Civil Rights Commission, 5/15–16/77, all in file "[Gay Rights: Memos, Correspondence, Clippings] 5/76–8/78 [O/A 5771]," box 4, OPL, JCL.

17. Voeller and O'Leary describe the IRS requirements in their memo, 2/8/77, to "the White House" detailing their proposed agenda for the initial meeting. File "[National Gay Task Force Correspondence] 9/76–2/78 [O/A 4499]," box 27, OPL, JCL. Haft told Costanza that "counsel," not clear whose, told her that the White House could not intervene in IRS policy decisions, memo, 3/25/77, in file, "[Gay] Civil Rights 10/76-2/78 [O/A 4609]," box 22, OPL, JCL. William Kelley, who attended the 3/26/77 meeting to present the issue of discrimination in the granting of tax-exempt status, reports that Carter aides may have worried about any appearance of political meddling with the IRS because it would evoke comparisons to the Nixon administration. Kelley, personal correspondence with author, 6/24/98. For the announcement of the policy change, see the *Cumulative Bulletin*, 1978-2: 172–73.

18. Memo, 4/11/77, Haft to Costanza, "[Gay Rights: Memos, Correspondence, Clippings] 5/76–8/78 [O/A 5771]," box 4, OPL, JCL.

19. On Justice and Civil Rights Commission, see note 17. On the Public Health Service, see memo, 9/14/77, Haft to Costanza, in file "[Gay] Civil Rights 10/76–2/78 [O/A 4609]," box 22; on FCC, see letter, 2/24/78, Ginny Vida, NGTF media director, to Belle O'Brien, consumer affairs officer, FCC, in file "[Gay Rights—Federal Communications Commission, 2/78 [O/A 4499]," box 22; on INS, see memo, 8/8/77, Haft to Costanza, reporting on meeting, 7/18/77, in file "[Gay Rights: Memos, Correspondence, Clippings] 5/76–8/78 [O/A 5771]," box 4; all OPL, JCL.

20. Memo, Haft to Costanza, 10/7/77, file "[Gay] Civil Rights 10/76–2/78 [O/A 4609]," box 22, OPL; see also file "10/1/77 to 12/31/77," box HU-5, WHCF/SF; both JCL.

21. Memo, Malson to Eizenstat, 4/19/80, in file "Gays [CF, O/A 728]," box 211, Eizenstat papers, DPS, JCL.

22. Memo, Wald to Keuch, 3/10/78, in file "National Gay Task Force: Prisons [Carl-

son Case] 3/78 [O/A 4499] [3]," box 28, OPL, JCL. This file, and its two counterparts, contain extensive information, including some of the pleadings from the lawsuits, as well as further correspondence among participants in the meeting.

23. Memo, Haft to Doug Huron, 6/6/77, file "5/1/77 to 6/30/77," box HU-5, WHCF, JCL.

24. File "[National Gay Task Force: Military] 3/77 [O/A 4496]," box 28, OPL, JCL.

25. Mike Hippler, *Matlovich: The Good Soldier* (Boston: Alyson Publications, 1989).

26. For an overview of these changes, see National Defense Research Institute, *Sexual Orientation and U.S. Military Personnel Policy: Options and Assessment* (Santa Monica: Rand, 1993), 3–9.

27. "Homosexuals [File 1]" and "Homosexuals [File 2]" in Federal Records, Records of the Cuban-Haitian Task Force, box 22, Record Group 220, JCL.

28. On the initial meeting, see memo, Haft to Costanza, 6/31/77, in file "1/20/77–1/20/81," box FG-114, WHCF/SF, and Bob Malson's notes, 7/12/77, in file "Gay Views," box 8, Malson files, CR/DPS, JCL. I have told the story of activists' efforts to change INS policy in more detail in "Lesbian/Gay Rights and Immigration Policy: Lobbying to End the Medical Model," *Journal of Policy History*, 7, no. 2 (1995): 208–25. Frank describes his role in the 1990 legislation in chapter 10.

29. "NGTF Action Report," 12/76, in file "National Gay Task Force Flyers and Publications, 12/76–3/77 [O/A 4499]," box 27; "Fourteen Gays Attend White House Meeting," *It's Time*, NGTF newsletter, 3/7, April-May 1977, file "National Gay Task Force 4/77–5/77 [O/A 4461]," box 91; both OPL, JCL.

30. For example, letter, Harvey Milk to president, 6/28/78, enclosing copy of Milk's speech from San Francisco Gay Pride Day, in file "[Gay Rights—Harvey Milk Speech & Letter] 6/78–7/78 [O/A 5771], box 4, OPL; letter, Del Martin, chairperson, Commission on the Status of Women, City and County of San Francisco, 7/13/77, to president, in file "9/1/77 to 9/30/77," box HU-5, WHCF; letter, Joanie Parks Hughes, secretary of Westfield, N.J., chapter, National Organization for Women, to president, 7/31/77, in file "7/1/77 to 9/30/77," box HU-7, WHCF/SF; telegram, Donald Russell Frost to president, 6/12/78, and letter from Rhode Island Gay Political Caucus to president, 2/14/78, both in file "1/1/78 to 6/30/78," box HU-8, WHCF/SF; all, JCL.

31. Ad appears in *Time*, 1/9/78; copy included with material from Rhode Island Gay Political Caucus, ibid. On Bryant and fight over Dade County ordinance, see extensive clippings, including story by Bill Peterson, "Gay Rights Law Loses 2–1 in Miami," *Washington Post*, 6/8/77, in file "Gay Views," box 8, Malson files, CR/DPS, JCL.

32. Milk's speech from San Francisco Gay Pride Day, in file "[Gay Rights—Harvey Milk Speech & Letter] 6/78–7/78 [O/A 5771], box 4, OPL, JCL. On Briggs initiative, see extensive information in file "7/1/78–12/31/78," box HU-8, WHCF/SF, JCL.

33. William Claiborne, "For Carter, a Folksy Foray to Major Fund-Raiser," *Washington Post*, 6/24/77, A8; David S. Broder, "Mondale in California: Hecklers, Smog, Space Travel," *Washington Post*, 6/19/77, A2.

34. Jean O'Leary, conversation with author, May 13, 1999. For NGTF's own accounts of the initial meeting, see "Fourteen Gays Attend White House Meeting," *It's Time*, NGTF newsletter, 3/7, April-May 1977, in file "National Gay Task Force 4/77–5/77 [O/A 4461]," box 91, OPL, JCL.

35. On this issue, see Cook, "Women White House Advisors," 58–76.

36. For example, see memos, Wales to file and to Mike Chanin and Tom Beard, both 1/8/79, describing meeting, which Weddington arranged, with Bob Kuntz, gay activist in Miami, in file "1/20/77 to 1/20/81," box HU-5, WHCF/SF, JCL.

37. See memo, Anne Wexler and Stu Eizenstat to the president, 12/19/79, getting his

approval for draft response to NGTF questionnaire, in file "Gay Rights," box 58, Sarah Weddington files, JCL. See also draft responses to letter in file "Gay Views," box 8, Malson papers, DPS/CR, JCL.

38. Memo, Malson to Eizenstat, 4/19/80, in file "Gays [CF, O/A 728]," box 211, Eizenstat papers, DPS, JCL.

39. Discussion of this issue began with memo, Seymour Wishman to Costanza, n.d., in file, "[Gay] Civil Rights 10/76–2/78 [O/A 4609]," box 22, OPL, JCL.

40. Memo, Rick Hutcheson to Costanza and Eizenstat, 2/27/78, returning their memo to the president on subject of "Civil Service Reform Legislation and Gay Rights," with various comments attached—Pettigrew's is last page. In file "2/27/78 [2]," Office of the Staff Secretary, Handwriting File, JCL.

41. See esp. Erwin C. Hargrove, *Jimmy Carter as President: Leadership and the Politics of the Public Good* (Baton Rouge: Louisiana State University Press, 1988).

42. Letter to Haft from Dr. J. Rogers Conrad, vice president for political affairs, Gay People of Columbia, Md., 6/22/77; and from Thomas J. Herndon, 6/23/77, both complimenting Haft while chiding the president, in file "[Homosexuality—Gay Rights and Public Health] 8/76–1/78 [O/A 5772]," box 5, OPL, JCL.

43. Haft to Pettigrew, 11/28/77, in file "[Gay Rights: Jimmy Carter's views on] 10/76 [O/A 5772]," box 4, OPL, JCL.

44. William Raspberry, "Anita and Gays Should Cool It," *Washington Post*, 6/17/77.

45. See Harvey Milk speech, in file "[Gay Rights—Harvey Milk Speech & Letter] 6/78–7/78 [O/A 5771]; message, Voeller and O'Leary to Carter, 8/18/76, in file "[Gay Rights: Correspondence] 5/76–7/78 [O/A 5771]," both in box 4, OPL, JCL.

46. Jimmy Carter, "It's Fundamentally Christian to Reject Politics of Hate," *Los Angeles Times*, 2/23/96, B9.

47. On IWY, see memo, Jane Simpson to Hugh Carter, 6/17/77, file "Mail [Count Sheets]—Midge Costanza, 11/77–1/78," box 27, OPL, JCL; on Bryant and the ERA in Florida, see photocopy of *Miami News* story, 3/17/77, "Fears Gay Marriages Would Be Legalized"; and press release from Transperience Center, both in file "[Gay Rights: Memos, Correspondence, Clippings] 5/76–8/78 [O/A 5771]," box 4, OPL, JCL.

48. "Opening Space," *The Advocate*, 2/7/80. Photocopy of article, and copy of Reagan's official statement condemning Briggs initiative, appear in file "Homosexuals/Gay Rights," Douglas Bandow files, box 6, Ronald Reagan Presidential Library (cited hereafter as RRL).

49. Eric Marcus, *Making History: The Struggle for Gay and Lesbian Equal Rights, 1945–1990, an Oral History* (New York: Harper Collins, 1992), 312.

50. Letter, 7/17/80, Timothy Drake and Charles Thompson to Governor Reagan; Gay Vote 1980: The National Convention Project, "The 1980 Republican Platform: Implications for the Civil Rights of Gay Americans," undated, both in file "Homosexuals/Gay Rights," Douglas Bandow files, Box 6, RRL. The absence of any attached correspondence from the campaign back to the Convention Project suggests that the campaign did not bother to respond.

51. Michelangelo Signorile, *Queer in America: Sex, the Media, and the Closets of Power* (New York: Random House, 1993).

52. Taylor Branch, "Closets of Power," *Harper's*, October 1982, 34–50, 47.

53. Randy Shilts, *And the Band Played On: Politics, People, and the AIDS Epidemic* (New York: St. Martin's Press, 1987), 407, 473.

54. Letter, 9/14/81, Bill Green to Elizabeth Dole, with handwritten note attached, and letter, 10/7/81, Lozano to Green, all in file "National Gay Task Force," White House Office of Records Management (WHORM), Alpha File, RRL.

55. See Rhonda Brown, "The Family Protection Act: Blueprint for a Moral America," *The Nation*, 5/23/81, 630.

56. Family Protection Act, Section 507, as quoted in Rosalind Pollack Petchesky, "Antiabortion, Antifeminism, and the Rise of the New Right," *Feminist Studies* 7 (1981), 206–246, 225.

57. Lee Edelman, "Capitol Offenses: Sodomy in the Seat of American Government," in *Homographesis: Essays in Gay Literary and Cultural Theory* (New York: Routledge, 1994), 129–137.

58. See letter, meeting notes, and memos in file "AIDS OA U288," Faith Whittlesey files, RRL.

59. For American Legislative Exchange Council, see "Gay Rights," box 12399, Jane Carpenter files; for Exodus International, see HU010—Human Rights (Equality), WHORM, Subject File; for Cameron's claims about gay men, see "Homosexuals (3)," box 9088, Morton Blackwell files; all RRL. On Cameron's expulsion from the APA, see "The Man Behind the Myths: A Report on the Chief Anti-Gay Researcher of the Religious Right," Log Cabin Republicans briefing paper by Mark E. Pietrzyk, 1/26/94, copy in author's possession.

60. Randy Shilts, *And the Band Played On: People, Politics, and the AIDS Epidemic* (1987; reprint, New York: Penguin Books, 1988).

61. Ibid., 273, 292–93, 298, 345–46, 354, 363–64, 370–71, 455, 463, 471–72, 521, 536, 554–55, 572, 574.

62. Letter, Howard Phillips to Margaret Heckler, 8/22/83, in file "Gay Rights," box 11286, Faith Whittlesey papers, RRL. On conservative activists' dislike for Heckler, see Shilts, *And the Band Played On*, 526.

63. Shilts, *And the Band Played On*, 349.

64. Memo, 3/31/87, Ralph C. Bledsoe to Edwin Meese, file "Health Policy Working Group: AIDS #2, [2 of 6]," OA 16629, Robert Sweet files, RRL. As a member of the Domestic Policy Council's Health Policy Working Group, Sweet kept voluminous files detailing the administration's work on AIDS, largely confirming Shilts's portrayal of individuals intent on subordinating public health expertise to the political demands of their ideological positions.

65. John D'Emilio, interview with Jeff Levi and Tim Westmoreland, 2/2/99. Transcript by Wayne van der Meide in my possession, esp. p. 13.

66. Minutes of Domestic and Economic Policy Council meeting, 12/19/85, in file "Working Group on Health Policy, AIDS [5 of 13]," OA 16630, Robert Sweet files, RRL. For legislative message, see "Message to Congress on America's Agenda for the Future," *Public Papers of the Presidents of the United States: Ronald Reagan*, 1986, 2 vols. (Washington, D.C.: United States Government Printing Office), 1:155.

67. Memo, 2/11/87, from Edwin Meese to the Domestic Policy Council, in file "Health Policy Working Group: AIDS #2 [3 of 6]," OA 16629, Robert Sweet files, RRL

68. U.S. Department of Education, "Preventing the Spread of AIDS Through Routine and Voluntary Testing," attached to memo, 2/16/88, Gary Bauer to members of the Health Policy Working Group, in file "Health Policy Working Group: AIDS #2 [1 of 6]," OA 16629, Robert Sweet files, RRL.

69. Ibid., 2.

70. "Surgeon General's Report on Acquired Immune Deficiency Syndrome" (Washington, D.C.: United States Public Health Service, n.d. [1986]), 31, 33.

71. William J. Bennett, "We Need Routine Testing for AIDS," *Wall Street Journal*, May 26, 1987.

72. Memo, 3/30/87, from the Working Group on Health Policy to the Domestic Policy

Council, in file "Health Policy Working Group: AIDS #2 [3 of 6]," OA 16629, Robert Sweet files, RRL.

73. Assistant Secretary for Health, "Improving AIDS Policy Oversight," 3/20/87, attachment to memo, ibid.

74. See Burton Kaufman, *The Presidency of James Earl Carter, Jr.* (Lawrence: University Press of Kansas, 1993), 29, 110–13.

75. Costanza described herself as the defender of traditional Democratic New Deal and civil rights constituencies to me during an interview on 6/6/97. For the circumstances of her resignation from Carter's staff, see Cook, "Women White House Advisors."

76. Patrick Buchanan, "Nature's Retribution," *Washington Times,* May 27, 1983.

77. Preliminary Report of the Presidential Commission on the Human Immunodeficiency Virus Epidemic, Admiral James D. Watkins (retired), chairman, 12/2/87: 10–11. There is a copy, along with Watkins's letter of transmission to the president, also dated 12/2/87, in file "Working Group on Health Policy: AIDS, 8 of 13," OA 16630, Robert Sweet files, RRL.

2. BEATING AROUND BUSH: GAY RIGHTS AND AMERICA'S 41ST PRESIDENT

1. Michael Nelson, *Congressional Quarterly's Guide to the Presidency,* 2nd ed. vol. 2 (Washington, D.C.: Congressional Quarterly, Inc., 1996), 1527–29.

2. Alessandra Stanley, "AIDS Becomes a Political Issue," *Time,* 3/23/87, 24.

3. From the Republican Party platform, "The Restoration of Competence and the Revival of Hope," excerpted in Michael L. Closen et al., *AIDS: Cases and Materials* (Houston: John Marshall Publishing Company, 1989), 219.

4. Ibid., 221.

5. Larry David Smith, "The Party Platforms as Institutional Discourse: The Democrats and Republicans of 1988," *Presidential Studies Quarterly* 22 (1992): 536.

6. Ibid., 536-537.

7. Closen, *AIDS: Cases and Materials,* 223.

8. Robert W. Stewart, "Dannemeyer Suggests White House Policy Encourages Homosexuality," *Los Angeles Times,* 7/1/89, I28.

9. Ibid.

10. Randy Shilts, "Advisory Commission Is Complete: Bush Names Patient to AIDS Panel," *San Francisco Chronicle,* 7/21/89, A9.

11. June E. Osborn, "AIDS and Public Policy," *AIDS* 3, suppl. 1 (1989): S297.

12. Henry Miller, "Anti-Medicine Man: Commissioner David A. Kessler; Politics, Favoritism and the Food and Drug Administration," *National Review,* 10/9/95, 48.

13. Victoria A. Brownworth, "Does George Bush Have a Clue About AIDS?" *The Advocate,* 9/8/92, 40.

14. Ibid., 42.

15. For an analysis of AIDS activism, see M. Kent Jennings and Ellen Ann Andersen, "Support for Confrontational Tactics among AIDS Activists: A Study of Intra-Movement Divisions," *American Journal of Political Science,* 40 (May 1996): 311.

16. For example, see William McGurn, "Mr. Bush's Cautious Embrace?" *National Review,* 5/28/90, 22; Denise Hamilton, "President Jokes Through Caltech Protests," *Los Angeles Times,* 6/15/91, A14; Jeffrey Schmalz, "Gay Rights and AIDS Emerging as Divisive Issues in Campaign," *New York Times,* 8/20/92, A1; *The Advocate,* 9/22/92, 18.

17. McGurn, "Mr. Bush's Cautious Embrace?" 24.

18. Ibid.

19. *Bragdon v. Abbott,* USSC no. 97–156.

20. David Tuller, "Gays Note Successes in Congress," *San Francisco Chronicle,* 12/24/90, A8.

21. 115 S.Ct. 2338 (1995).

22. 116 S.Ct. 1620 (1996); striking down Colorado's Amendment 2, which prohibited statutes and ordinances intended to protect gays and lesbians from discrimination.

23. For a discussion of this history, see Allan Bérubé, *Coming Out Under Fire: The History of Gay Men and Women in World War Two* (New York: The Free Press, 1990).

24. Randy Shilts, "Military May Defer Discharge of Gays: Pentagon has 'Operational Needs' in Gulf," *San Francisco Chronicle,* 1/11/91, A19.

25. Randy Shilts, "In Wake of War, Military Again Targets Gays," *San Francisco Chronicle,* 8/5/91, A1.

26. David Tuller, "Ex-Student Fights ROTC's Gay Policy: Battle Over Demand to Repay Scholarship," *San Francisco Chronicle,* 10/11/90, A23.

27. Jim Doyle, "Fired Agent Files First Lawsuit Accusing FBI of Anti-Gay Policy," *San Francisco Chronicle,* 10/3/90, A18.

28. *New York Times,* 3/23/94, A17.

29. Eve Kosofsky Sedgwick, "How to Bring Your Kids Up Gay: The War on Effeminate Boys," in *Tendencies* (Durham: Duke University Press, 1993), 144.

30. Ibid.

31. Robert A. Bernstein, "Family Values and Gay Rights," *New York Times,* 6/26/90, A23.

32. *New York Times,* 8/12/92, A1.

33. Chris Bull, "Why Bush Hates You: The Religious Right's Stranglehold on the Presidency and the GOP," *The Advocate,* 10/20/92, 40.

34. Ibid.

35. Richard W. Waterman, "Storm Clouds on the Political Horizon: George Bush at the Dawn of the 1992 Presidential Election," *Presidential Studies Quarterly* 26, no. 2 (Spring 1996), 337.

36. Schmalz, "Gay Rights and AIDS," A1.

37. Ibid., A21.

38. *The Advocate,* 9/22/92, 18.

39. Schmalz, "Gay Rights and AIDS," A21.

40. Ibid.

41. Paul Cellupica, "The Political Dawn Arrives for Gays," *New York Times,* 11/7/92, I21.

42. Schmalz, "Gay Rights and AIDS," A21.

43. Torie Osborn and David M. Smith, "At Last, the Mainstream Agenda Opens to Gay and Lesbian Issues," *Los Angeles Times,* 6/3/92, B7.

44. Waterman, "Storm Clouds," 341.

45. Ibid., 347.

46. Dean C. Hammer, "The Oakeshottian President: George Bush and the Politics of the Present," *Presidential Studies Quarterly* 25, no. 2 (Spring 1995): 301.

3. A "Friend" in the White House? Reflections on the Clinton Presidency.

1. Chris Bull and John Gallagher, *Perfect Enemies: The Religious Right, the Gay Movement, and the Politics of the 1990's* (New York: Crown, 1996), 77–78.

2. Charles Kaiser, *The Gay Metropolis: 1940–1996* (New York: Houghton Mifflin, 1997), 330.

3. Ibid., 330–331.

4. Ibid., 333–334.

5. See Craig A. Rimmerman, *Presidency by Plebiscite: The Reagan-Bush Era in Institutional Perspective* (Boulder: Westview Press, 1993), 17.

6. David Rayside, *On the Fringe: Gays and Lesbians in the Political Process* (Ithaca: Cornell University Press, 1998), 221.

7. Craig A. Rimmerman, "Introduction," in Craig A. Rimmerman, ed., *Gay Rights, Military Wrongs: Political Perspectives on Lesbians and Gays in the Military* (New York: Garland Publishing Co., 1996), xix.

8. See Craig A. Rimmerman, "Promise Unfulfilled: Clinton's Failure to Overturn the Military Ban on Lesbians and Gays," in Rimmerman, *Gay Rights, Military Wrongs*, 112.

9. Concrete examples of such policies are Clinton's commitment to welfare reform via workfare, support for the death penalty, and a willingness to question the overall effectiveness of the 1960s Great Society programs.

10. The Campaign for Military Service was organized by lesbian and gay leaders in early 1993 to lobby the president in an effort to force him to keep his promise.

11. Kaiser, *Gay Metropolis*, 334.

12. Rimmerman, *Gay Rights, Military Wrongs*, 119.

13. Ibid., 120–21.

14. C. Dixon Osburn and Michelle Benecke, "Conduct Unbecoming Continues: The First Year Under 'Don't Ask, Don't Tell, Don't Pursue,'" ibid., chapter 9. For a good overview of the implementation of the current military policy, see Francine D'Amico, "Sexuality and Military Service," in Craig A. Rimmerman, Kenneth Wald, and Clyde Wilcox, eds., *The Politics of Gay Rights* (Chicago: University of Chicago Press, 2000), chapter 10.

15. Clyde Wilcox and Robin M. Wolpert, "President Clinton, Public Opinion, and Gays in the Military," in Rimmerman, *Gay Rights, Military Wrongs*, 129.

16. Kaiser, *Gay Metropolis*, 331.

17. Lou Chibbaro Jr., "The Clinton Quandry," *Washington Blade*, 11/1/96, 21.

18. Ibid., 24.

19. Sheryl Gay Stolberg, "Clinton Decides Not to Finance Needle Program," *New York Times*, 4/21/98, A1.

20. Personal interview with author, 3/4/97.

21. Mark Strasser, *Legally Wed: Same-Sex Marriage and the Constitution* (Ithaca: Cornell University Press, 1997), 127.

22. For a good overview of the president's decision to sign DOMA, see Todd S. Purdum, "Gay Rights Groups Attack Clinton on Midnight Signing," *New York Times*, 9/22/96, A16.

23. Chibbaro, "Clinton Quandry," 24.

24. John Gallagher, "Speak Now," *The Advocate*, 6/11/96, 21.

25. For a good overview of the background of Clinton's decision, see Lisa Keen and Lou Chibbaro Jr., "White House in Raging Debate Over Support in Colorado Case," *Washington Blade*, 6/2/95, 1, 30, 31.

26. Chibbaro, "Clinton Quandry," 24.

27. Lou Chibbaro Jr., "Clinton: Being Gay is 'Not a Security Risk,'" *Washington Blade*, 8/4/95, 1.

28. Peter Freiberg, "President's Order Protects Workers," *Washington Blade* 6/5/98, 1.

29. Ibid., 29.

30. Chibbaro, "Clinton Quandry," 21.

31. See Lou Chibbaro Jr., "White House Chides Lott for Statements," *Washington Blade*, 6/19/98, 1, 14, for a discussion of the White House's response.

32. For articles examining the Scott appointment, see Betsy Billard, "Shooting Straight," *The Advocate*, 7/25/95, 26–28; and J. Jennings Moss, "Picking Up the Pieces," *The Advocate*, 10/31/95, 25–27.

33. For an overview of the Socarides appointment, see Lou Chibbaro Jr., "White House Gay Liaison Named," *Washington Blade*, 6/21/96, 1.

34. Peter Baker, "Echoing Truman on Race, Clinton Calls for Gay Rights," *International Herald Tribune*, 11/10/97, 2.

35. John D'Emilio, "Cycles of Change, Questions of Strategy: The Gay and Lesbian Movement After Fifty Years," in Rimmerman, Wald, and Wilcox, *Politics of Gay Rights*.

36. Personal interview with author, 2/4/98.

37. See Rimmerman, in Rimmerman, Wald, and Wilcox, *Politics of Gay Rights*.

4. From *Bowers v. Hardwick* to *Romer v. Evans*: Lesbian and Gay Rights in the U.S. Supreme Court

Case References

Baker v. Wade, 553 F. Supp. 1121 (N.D. Tex. 1982), reversed, 769 F.2d 289 (5th Cir. 1985), cert. denied, 478 U.S. 1022 (1986) (Texas sodomy law case contemporary with *Bowers v. Hardwick*).

Bowers v. Hardwick, 478 U.S. 186 (1986) (Georgia sodomy law decision).

Buchanan v. Batchelor, 308 F. Supp. 729 (N.D. Tex. 1970), vacated and remanded, 401 U.S. 989 (1971) (early Texas sodomy law decision).

Campbell v. Sundquist, 926 S.W.2d 250 (Tenn. Ct. App. 1996) (post-*Hardwick* Tennessee sodomy case).

City of Dallas v. England, 846 S.W.2d 957 (Tex. App. 1993) (post-*Hardwick* Texas sodomy case).

Commonwealth v. Wasson, 842 S.W.2d 487 (Ky. 1992) (post-*Hardwick* Kentucky sodomy case).

Doe v. Commonwealth's Attorney for City of Richmond, 403 F. Supp. 1199 (E.D. Va. 1975), affirmed, 425 U.S. 901 (1976) (early Virginia sodomy law decision).

Egan v. Canada, 2 S.C.R. 513 (1995) (holding that sexual orientation is an "analogous ground" to the enumerated grounds of forbidden discrimination in the Canadian Charter of Rights).

Eisenstadt v. Baird, 405 U.S. 438 (1972) (contraception/privacy case).

Equality Foundation of Greater Cincinnati v. City of Cincinnati, 838 F. Supp. 1235 (S.D. Ohio 1993); perm. inj. granted, 860 F. Supp. 417 (S.D. Ohio 1994); rev'd, 54 F.3d 261 (6th Cir. 1995); vacated and remanded, 116 S.Ct 2519 (1996); 128 F.3d 289 (6th Cir. 1997); 1998 U.S. App. Lexis 1765 (6th Cir. Feb. 5, 1998); cert. denied, 119 S.Ct. 365 (1998) (upholding constitutionality of Cincinnati charter amendment similar to Colorado Amendment 2).

Griswold v. Connecticut, 381 U.S. 479 (1965) (contraception/privacy case).

Gryczan v. State, 942 P.2d 112 (Mont. 1997) (post-*Hardwick* Montana sodomy case).

Hurley v. Irish-American Gay, Lesbian and Bisexual Group of Boston, 515 U.S. 557 (1995) (Boston St. Patrick's Day parade case).

Manual Enterprises, Inc. v. Day, 370 U.S. 478 (1962) (gay publications should not automatically be excluded from the U.S. mail on grounds of obscenity).

Nabozny v. Podlesny, 92 F.3d 446 (7th Cir. 1996) (upholding equal-protection claim of gay high school student).

One, Inc. v. Olesen, 355 U.S. 371 (1958), summarily reversing 241 F.2d 772 (9th Cir. 1957) (rejecting contention that gay publications are automatically obscene).

Padula v. Webster, 822 F.2d 97 (D.C. Cir. 1987) (denial of equal-protection claim by government-employment applicant).

People v. Onofre, 51 N.Y.2d 476, 415 N.E.2d 936 (1980), cert. denied, 451 U.S. 987 (1981) (pre-*Hardwick* New York sodomy case).

Plessy v. Ferguson, 163 U.S. 537, 559 (1896) (famous dissent from "separate but equal" ruling).

Powell v. State, 510 S.E.2d 18 (Ga. 1998) (sodomy law violates state constitutional right of privacy).

Roe v. Wade, 410 U.S. 113 (1973) (abortion/privacy case).

Romer v. Evans, 517 U.S. 620 (1996) (Colorado Amendment 2 violates Equal Protection clause).

Rose v. Locke, 423 U.S. 48 (1975) (early Tennessee sodomy law decision).

Stanley v. Georgia, 394 U.S. 557 (1969) (privacy of the home case).

State v. Morales, 869 S.W.2d 941 (Tex. 1994), 826 S.W.2d 201 (Tex. App., 1992) (post-*Hardwick* Texas sodomy case).

State v. Smith, 729 So.2d 648 (La. App. 1999) (Louisiana sodomy law violates right of privacy under state constitution).

Thornburgh v. American College of Obstetricians and Gynecologists, 476 U.S. 747 (1986) (pre-*Hardwick* abortion decision).

U.S. Department of Agriculture v. Moreno, 413 U.S. 528 (1973) (Congress may not disqualify "hippie communes" from entitlement for food stamps).

Wainwright v. Stone, 414 U.S. 21 (1973) (early Florida sodomy law decision).

Weigand v. Houghton, 1999 Westlaw 47748, 1999 Miss. Lexis 69 (Miss. Supr. Ct. 1999) (family-law decision relying on sodomy law to deny joint child custody to gay father).

Williams v. Glendening, No. 98036031 (Md., Baltimore City Cir. Ct. Oct. 15, 1998) (sodomy law does not apply to private, consensual adult sex; case settled by government agreement to desist from enforcing sodomy law against consenting adults).

7. A WHEEL WITHIN A WHEEL: SEXUAL ORIENTATION AND THE FEDERAL WORKFORCE

1. http://www.opm.gov/er/orientation.htm.

2. http://www.pub.whitehouse.gov/uri-res/I2R?urn:pdi://oma.eop.gov.us/1998/6/1/8. text.2, for the order; and for the president's statement on the order: http://www.pub. whitehouse.gov/uri-res/I2R?urn:pdi://oma.eop.gov.us/1998/5/29/16.text.1.

3. And it is a work very rich. Space and format did not allow for a history of the programmatic elements of Federal and the agency GLOBEs, which include IRS GLOBE's tax workshops for HIV-positive people and PWAs, the Smithsonian History of the Month case exhibit for Stonewall 25, responses to religious right attacks, and so much more. That will have to be another publication.

4. First the homophile movement, now the lesbian, gay, bisexual, transgender rights movement.

5. See Greg Lewis, "Lifting the Ban on Gays in the Civil Service: Federal Policy Toward Gay and Lesbian Employees, Since the Cold War," *Public Administration Review* 57 (1997): 387–95, for a detailed analysis of the policy and the movement toward its reform.

6. See John D'Emilio, *Sexual Politics, Sexual Communities* (University of Chicago Press, 1983), for an excellent analysis of this period.

7. Similar arguments are used to justify exclusion of gays from the military. For the

Civil Service, the concern was public trust in the government; in the military, it is the impact on unit cohesion. It is interesting to note that as this argument has been shown faulty, the conservatives have been moving toward a justification of exclusion of gays and lesbians from the military using an in loco parentis argument—parents who do not want their children living with open homosexuals should have their wishes considered. Hopefully, this will backfire since parental concerns about military conditions have never been grounds to change policy.

8. As June has been chosen as pride month to commemorate the June 27–30, 1969, Stonewall riots, October 11 has been designated National Coming Out Day to commemorate the October 11, 1987, March on Washington for Lesbian and Gay Rights.

9. After just a little debate, the group voted not to call itself Smithsonian Institution Queers.

10. The O in GLOBE does *not* stand for *or*. The August 1992 meeting where the name was adopted included a multihour debate on that point.

11. The sordid history of the U.S. government and its persecution of lesbians and gays through the security-clearance process is dealt with in chapter 9 of this book.

12. Craig Howell is one of the unsung heroes of the lesbian and gay movement. He has been an activist in Washington, D.C., now for decades, playing major roles in the formation of GLOBAL, the Department of Labor GLOBE chapter, and having leadership roles in the Gay and Lesbian Activists' Alliance and the Gertrude Stein Democratic Club. He has taken up the mantle from Frank Kameny and leads the charge whenever a discriminatory act or amendment is proposed within the District.

13. In 1993, a senior official in a federal Civil Rights office recalled to me a 1981 meeting at the Old Executive Office Building where they were told to "put the memo in the back of the file cabinet."

14. Note that this was signed by an appointee of President Bush!

15. In November 1993, the Gay and Lesbian Victory Fund had a reception at the National Press Club introducing twenty-two open lesbians and gay men, including the two who had to get Senate confirmation, Roberta Achtenberg and Bruce Lehman. Over the course of the administration, there have been over a hundred openly lesbian and gay appointees.

16. As this is being written, in summer 1999, there is a controversy raging in the queer community around Congressman Frank and ENDA, the Employment Non-Discrimination Act. The act does not mention transgender issues and is seen as not protecting transgender people. The National Gay and Lesbian Task Force has come out against the legislation for this reason, while Frank is a major proponent to move the agenda forward even if everything is not perfect. Frank is a politician, and politics is the art of the possible.

17. The loss of Gerry Studds in Congress certainly adds to the importance of Frank's office. Kolbe's office is beginning to do some of the lifting, and with Congresswoman Baldwin coming into Congress this year, the potential for more burden-sharing among the offices increases. But seniority counts, and Frank will be the lead for some years to come.

18. The country and the community lost immeasurably when Secretary Brown's airplane crashed in 1996. His leadership and simple appreciation of the power of diversity and equality were stirring and effective.

19. We look at five categories from which antigay behavior might arise: *ignorance* or lack of knowledge of the issues; *heterosexism* or the assumption of the normality of heterosexism and therefore the unimportance of making a workplace welcome to homosexuals; *homophobia* or the fear of queers, usually based on misinformation, myth, and peer pressure; *homo-hatred* or the visceral dislike of gays, potentially brought on by repressed feelings or jealousy; and *conscientious objection* founded in real ethical considerations. We have found

that people of conscience do follow the adage of hating the sin but loving the sinner and can work well with lesbians and gays in the workplace without hostile interactions.

20. And our own continually evolving understanding of the issues and the ways to make a more equal union.

21. One of the first questions we are asked when we do training for these offices is, "What should we call you?" This is a legitimate concern and underscores the potential for failure. *Queer,* when used by queers, is affirming and a repatriation of the term (though often not liked by a sizable percentage of the community). *Gay* is seen by some as exclusionary, as is *lesbian and gay. LGBT* is awkward and opens up debate on transgender issues. If *we* cannot agree and ease the situation, it is hard to expect others to be welcoming.

22. Members of the Board of Directors of Federal GLOBE jokingly call this the 32 million points of light, since some of them felt that anything more than one page was too daunting for senior executives and that it needed to be shortened.

23. Mancur Olsen, *The Logic of Collective Action: Public Goods and the Theory of Groups* (Cambridge, Mass.: Harvard University Press, 1965).

24. The 1998 Voter News Service exit poll, conducted for ABC, CBS, NBC, CNN, Fox, and the Associated Press, found that 4 percent of the voters asked self-identified.

8. THE FEDERAL GAY RIGHTS BILL: FROM BELLA TO ENDA

1. 120 *Congressional Record.* H14647 (daily ed., 5/14/74). Two months later, in July 1974, the gay newspaper in Washington, D.C., ran a brief story about Abzug's introduction of the bill: "Federal Gay Rights: Bella's New Bill," *Gay Blade,* 7/74, 2. The *Gay Blade* went through several name changes: from the *Gay Blade* to the *Blade* and then to its current name, the *Washington Blade.* All names refer to the same newspaper.

2. 140 *Congressional Record.* E1311-02 (daily ed., 6/23/94); 140 *Congressional Record.* S7561-02, *S7581 (daily ed., 6/23/94).

3. A Lexis search at the time this chapter was researched found 185 news stories on ENDA (8/9/99; search request "Employment Nondiscrimination Act").

4. 142 *Congressional Record.* S10129-02 (daily ed., 9/10/96).

5. "My Fellow Americans . . . State of Our Union Is Strong," *Washington Post,* 2/20/99, A12.

6. Molly McGarry and Fred Wasserman, *Becoming Visible: An Illustrated History of Lesbian and Gay Life in Twentieth-Century America* (New York: Penguin Studio, 1998), 156 (hereinafter *Becoming Visible*).

7. Ibid., 157.

8. Ibid., 163; Dudley Clendinen and Adam Nagourney, *Out for Good: The Struggle to Build a Gay Rights Movement in America* (New York: Simon & Schuster: 1999), 31–32 (hereinafter *Out for Good*). Jonathan Katz, *Gay American History: Lesbians and Gay Men in the U.S.A.* (New York: Avon Books, 1976), 426–27.

9. *Becoming Visible,* 167–68; *Out for Good,* 71–76.

10. *Becoming Visible,* 200; *Out for Good,* 188–95.

11. John D'Emilio, "After Stonewall," in D'Emilio, *Making Trouble: Essays on Gay History, Politics, and the University* (New York: Routledge, 1992), 247.

12. 42 U.S.C. §2000a (public accommodations), §2000b (state facilities), §2000c (public schools), §2000d (programs receiving federal financial assistance), and §2000e (employment).

13. 42 U.S.C. §2000c (public education) and §2000e (employment).

14. H.R. 14752, 93rd Cong., §11 (1974); 120 *Congressional Record.* H14647 (5/4/74).

15. 121 *Congressional Record.* H188 (1/15/75).

16. *Out for Good*, 256–60.

17. 123 *Congressional Record*. H6832 (3/9/77).

18. "Gay Civil Rights Bill Gathers Momentum," *Blade*, 4/77, 8. In the early years of the *Blade*, stories often reflected cheerleading for the gay rights movement, rather than simple journalistic observing, reporting, and investigating. This approach changed significantly under the leadership of Lisa Keen, who brought journalistic rigor to the paper.

19. "Bias Against Homosexuals Is Outlawed in Miami," *New York Times*, 1/19/77, 14; *Out for Good*, 231.

20. Grace Lichtenstein, "Poll Finds Public Split on Legalizing Homosexual Acts," *New York Times*, 7/19/77, 17. For consistency of poll results, see "American Values: 1998 National Survey of Americans on Values," *Washington Post*/Kaiser Family Foundation/Harvard Survey Project. See Kaiser Family Foundation (visited 6/22/99) at http://www.kff.org:80/kff/library.html?document_key=2146&data_type_key=433.

21. Lichtenstein, "Poll Finds Public Split," 17.

22. William Safire, "Now Ease Up, Anita," *New York Times*, 6/9/77, 21.

23. This type of statistical disparity had been used with significant frequency in race-discrimination challenges through the 1970s, with the argument that such disparity was either evidence of an intentional pattern of discrimination or evidence of a disparate impact from a seemingly neutral rule or practice. See, e.g., *Williams v. Tallahassee Motors, Inc.*, 607 F.2d 689 (5th Cir. 1979); *Griggs v. Duke Power Co.*, 401 U.S. 424, 91 S.Ct. 899 (1971).

24. H.R. 7775, 95th Cong. §12 (1977). On July 13, 1977, Koch introduced two new bills, H.R. 8268 with fifteen cosponsors and H.R. 8269 with nineteen cosponsors, with the new section added to both bills. 123 *Congressional Record*. H22734 (7/13/77).

25. 123 *Congressional Record*. H18855 (6/14/77).

26. Ibid.

27. Ibid. (quoting Prime Minister Pierre Trudeau of Canada).

28. 123 *Congressional Record*. 20919 (6/27/77).

29. Ibid.

30. "Gay Leaders Plan Strategy with Civil Rights Groups," *Washington Post*, 7/12/77, A9.

31. Sidney Brinkley, "The 'Art' of Building Civil Rights Coalitions," *Washington Blade*, 4/23/93, 23.

32. "National Gay Lobby Regroups," *Blade*, October 1978, 7; *Out for Good*, 397.

33. "National Gay Lobby Regroups," *Blade*, October 1978, 7.

34. E-mail from Bruce Wolpe to the author, May 1999.

35. "Republican Co-Sponsors Sought," *Blade*, 11/8/79, A4.

36. Don Leavitt, "GRNL: Digging In for the Long Haul," *Washington Blade*, 5/1/80, 6 (describing development of a nationwide computer listing of gay rights supporters).

37. Lou Chibbaro Jr., "'Mover and Shaker' Steve Endean," *Washington Blade*, 5/1/92, 23.

38. Leavitt, "GRNL," 6.

39. Ibid.

40. Steve Martz, "First Hearings on Gay Rights Bill Slated," *Washington Blade*, 9/25/80, A5.

41. *Civil Rights Amendments Act of 1979: Hearings on H.R. 2074 Before the Subcommittee on Employment Opportunities of the Committee on Education and Labor*, 96th Cong., 1980, 8 (hereinafter *1980 Hearings*) (statement of Art Agnos, assemblyman and Democratic Caucus secretary, California Assembly).

42. Ibid., 9, 10.

43. Ibid., 16.

44. Ibid., 17, 18 (statement of Congressman Ted Weiss).

45. Ibid., 17 (statement of James M. Stephens, minority associate labor counsel).

46. Ibid., 17, 18 (statement of Art Agnos).

47. M. V. Lee Badgett, *Income Inflation: The Myth of Affluence Among Gay, Lesbian, and Bisexual Americans* (National Gay and Lesbian Task Force Policy Institute, 1998); Yankelovich Monitor, "Gay/Lesbian Report, Demographic Profile, June 9, 1994" (finding that gay men had a lower personal income and lower household income than heterosexual men in certain categories).

48. The organist sued, but the court ruled in favor of the church based on its constitutional right to the free exercise of religion. *Walker v. First Orthodox Presbyterian Church of S.F.*, 1980 WL 4657 (Cal. Super. 1989).

49. *1980 Hearings*, 32–35 (statement of Rev. Charles A. McIlhenny, pastor, First Orthodox Presbyterian Church, San Francisco).

50. Ibid., 40, 42.

51. Ibid., 74 (statement of Gwen Craig, vice president, Harvey Milk Gay Democratic Club).

52. Don Michaels, "Falwell Distorts Rights Bill Objectives," *Washington Blade*, 10/24/80, A4. Falwell also asserted the bill would "require employers to hire a particular quota" of gay people. The *Blade* story pointed out that both the House and Senate bills included a provision that precluded the use of quotas.

53. Steve Martz, "House Gets New Rights Bill, Support Lags," *Washington Blade*, 2/6/81, A3.

54. *Civil Rights Amendments Act of 1981: Hearings on H.R. 1454 Before the Subcommittee on Employment Opportunities of the Committee on Education and Labor*, 97th Cong., 1982, 8 (hereinafter *1982 Hearings*) (statement of Jean O'Leary, director, National Gay Rights Associates).

55. Ibid., 8.

56. Ibid.

57. Ibid., 18 (statement of Congresswoman Millicent Fenwick).

58. Ibid., 22–23 (Tsongas); 27 (Wells-Schooley); xx (Weinberg); 36 (Post); 58–60 (Christensen).

59. Ibid., 40–41 (Marshner).

60. Lichtenstein, "Poll Finds Public Split," 17. See also "Gay Rights Support Has Grown Since 1982—Gallup Poll Finds," *San Francisco Chronicle*, 10/25/89, A21.

61. *1982 Hearings*, 51.

62. Larry Bush, "Events Have Taken a Nasty Turn and They May Become Nastier," *Washington Blade*, 8/6/82, 5.

63. "GRNL Seeking to Join Civil Rights Group," *Washington Blade*, 5/28/82, 13.

64. Sidney Brinkley, "The 'Art' of Building Civil Rights Coalitions," *Washington Blade*, 4/23/93, 23.

65. "News You May Have Missed," *Washington Blade*, 8/20/82, 9; Lou Chibbaro Jr. et al., "PAC Scores Well in First Outing," *Washington Blade*, 11/5/82, 1; Larry Bush, "Tuesday's Election the Most Significant One Yet for Gays," *Washington Blade*, 11/5/82, 1.

66. Lou Chibbaro Jr., "Senate Rights Bills Introduced," *Washington Blade*, 2/4/83, 1; "Additional Sponsors Sign House, Senate Bills," *Washington Blade*, 4/15/83, 4; 129 *Congressional Record*. H156 (1/6/83)(H.R. 427); 129 *Congressional Record*. H8961 (4/19/83) (H.R. 2624); 129 *Congressional Record*. S1659 (2/4/83).

67. Lou Chibbaro Jr., "'Mover and Shaker' Steve Endean," *Washington Blade*, 5/1/92, 23; Lou Chibbaro Jr., "Endean to Give Up HRCF Post; Will Retain Two Others," *Washington Blade*, 3/11/83, 1. Vic Basile was hired as HRCF's executive director in May 1983.

Steve Martz, "GAA's Basile to Head Reorganized Campaign Fund," *Washington Blade*, 5/20/83, 1.

68. John-Manuel Andriote, *Victory Deferred: How AIDS Changed Gay Life in America* (Chicago: The University of Chicago Press, 1999), 220–21 (hereinafter *Victory Deferred*).

69. Chibbaro, "'Mover and Shaker' Steve Endean," 23.

70. History might also fault Bush as an active participant in the political drama surrounding Endean and gay politics. *Out for Good*, 489–93.

71. Larry Bush, "U.S. Mayors: Increase Research Funds for 'Cause and Cure,'" *Advocate*, 7/21/83, 71.

72. Ibid.; Larry Bush, "Dallying with Dollars: Reagan's Threatened Veto Holds Up $12 Million for AIDS," *Advocate*, 8/4/83, 14.

73. Lisa M. Keen, "Goodstein Asks for Endean's Ouster," *Washington Blade*, 6/3/83, 1.

74. Steve Martz, "GRNL's Endean Set to Resign," *Washington Blade*, 10/21/83, 1.

75. Dave Walker, "Endean Resignation Accepted; GRNL Faces Financial Woes; Possible Merger," *Washington Blade*, 10/21/83, 1; Lou Chibbaro Jr., "Endean 'Laid Off' As GRNL Woes Continue," *Washington Blade*, 1/20/84, 1.

76. Lisa M. Keen, "Hollings Joins Senate Gay Rights Bill," *Washington Blade*, 10/7/83, 7; Lou Chibbaro Jr., "Mondale Will Back Federal Gay Bill," *Washington Blade*, 2/17/84, 1; Dave Walter, "Hart Signs On as Co-Sponsor to Federal Gay Rights Bill," *Washington Blade*, 5/4/84, 1.

77. AIDS Action Council was established in 1983 and was essentially the trade association of AIDS service providers from around the country. See *Victory Deferred*, 224.

78. 133 *Congressional Record*. 27771 (10/14/87).

79. "Legislative lawyering" refers to the art of combining a sophisticated knowledge of legal text with a well-honed sense of politics to create legal and policy solutions for difficult legislative situations. See Federal Legislation Clinic (visited 4/27/99) at http://www.law.georgetown.edu/clinics/flc/leg_lawyering.html.

80. 44 *Congressional Quarterly Almanac* 710 (1988).

81. *School Board of Nassau County v. Arline*, 481 U.S. 1024 (1987).

82. 133 *Congressional Record*. 5027 (3/6/87).

83. *Grove City College v. Bell*, 465 U.S. 555 (1984).

84. S. Rep. No. 100-64 (1987), 27–28, 31.

85. 134 *Congressional Record*. 1988, 383–84.

86. The NORA coalition was first established by Jeff Levi from NGLTF. In 1987, the coalition was reinvigorated and expanded by Jean Maguire and Tom Sheridan at AIDS Action Council. At that point, I was a legislative attorney with the AIDS Project of the American Civil Liberties Union (ACLU), based in the ACLU's national Washington office. I was active in the NORA coalition and drafted most of the legislative materials used by the coalition.

87. H.R. Rep. No. 100-711 at 28 (1988); 134 *Congressional Record*, 1988, 16496–504.

88. 136 *Congressional Record*, 1990, 10911.

89. 136 *Congressional Record*, 1990, 17033, 17058.

90. As Eric Rosenthal from HRCF noted at one point in 1989, "The antigay tactics of Helms and others in the 100th Congress diverted the lobbyists' attention [from the gay civil rights bill]." Lisa M. Keen, "Gays Gearing Up for Battles on Capitol Hill," *Washington Blade*, 2/17/89, 1, 9.

91. See Federal Legislation Clinic (visited 4/27/99) at http://www.law.georgetown.edu/clinics/flc/five_circles.html.

92. Memorandum from Benjamin L. Hooks and Ralph G. Neas to LCCR presidents and representatives, *LCCR Priorities,* 12/10/92.

93. Activity did continue on the drafting of the gay civil rights bill through the summer of 1993, primarily through the hard work of Bobbie Bernstein, who was working for me as a research assistant through HRCF. Bobbie's research on disparate impact laid the groundwork for the final resolution of that issue in 1994.

94. Ironically, there was such little knowledge of the past history of gay rights bills among those of us working on the bill that we did not realize we were repeating a pragmatic decision that had been made many years before with regard to the Senate gay rights bill.

95. Actually, the acronym was first END, but we realized such an acronym could be perceived as ominous and foreboding (which is certainly how the religious right viewed the bill). Unfortunately, we realized this after HRCF had already made several hundred buttons that proclaimed: "Support END/Employment Non-Discrimination Act."

96. LCCR's statement of endorsement included the following sentence: "A number of organizations in the Leadership Conference have not taken a position at this time and do not join in this statement." Statement of Ralph G. Neas, executive director of the Leadership Conference on Civil Rights, on behalf of the Employment Non-Discrimination Act, June 23, 1994.

97. Remarks of Coretta Scott King, press conference on the introduction of the Employment Non-Discrimination Act of 1994, Washington, D.C., June 23, 1994, reprinted in *Hearing on S. 2238 Before the Committee on Labor and Human Resources,* U.S. Senate, 7/29/94, S. Hrng 103-703, 62 (hereinafter *1994 Hearings*).

98. Ibid., 4–7 (Summerville); 8–11 (Dillon).

99. Ibid., 13–16 (Dart); 18–20 (Phillips); 20–22 (Coulter); 22–24 (Womack).

100. Broadus made his claim partly based on the fact that *sexual orientation* was defined in the bill to mean "lesbian, gay, bisexual, or heterosexual orientation, real or perceived, as manifested by identity, *acts*, statements, or associations" (emphasis added). Although these acts referred simply to sexual acts between persons of the same gender, Broadus used the definition to misrepresent the protections afforded by the bill. In later bills, therefore, the definition was changed to read "homosexuality, bisexuality, or heterosexuality, whether such orientation is real or perceived."

101. *1994 Hearings,* 28–33 (Broadus).

102. Ibid., 34–38 (Knight).

103. Ibid., 38–45 (Feldblum).

104. I continued to work for HRCF during this time as a legislative lawyer, as a consultant. My work now included not only activity on ENDA, but also helping to fight anti-gay amendments. In July 1998, I did not renew my consultancy agreement with HRC (the name of the organization changed in 1996) and instead began doing legislative-lawyering work for the National Gay and Lesbian Task Force, beginning in January 1999.

105. *Hearings on H.R. 1863, the Employment Non-Discrimination Act, before the Subcommittee on Government Programs of the Committee on Small Business,* U.S. House of Representatives, 7/17/96, No. 104-87, 25–40.

106. "Sexual Orientation, Morality and the Law: Devlin Revisited," *University of Pittsburgh Law Review* 327 (1996): 57.

107. I described this hearing and explored alternative modes of answering Poshard in "The Moral Rhetoric of Legislation," *New York University Law Review* 992 (1997): 72.

108. Carolyn Lochhead, "Senate OKs Gay Marriage Restrictions; Job Discrimination Bill Fails by One Vote," *San Francisco Chronicle,* 9/11/96, A1.

109. *Hearings on S. 869, Employment Non-Discrimination Act of 1997, Before the Committee on Labor and Human Resources,* U.S. Senate, 10/23/97, S. Hrg. 105-279.

10. American Immigration Law: A Case Study in the Effective Use of the Political Process

1. See for example William Turner, "Lesbian/Gay Rights and Immigrant Policy," *Journal of Policy History* 2 (1995).

2. House of Representatives, Committee on the Judicary, Report 100-882, 8/12/88.

11. Getting It Straight: A Review of the "Gays in the Military" Debate

1. Allan Bérubé, *Coming Out Under Fire: A History of Gay Men and Women in World War Two* (New York: The Free Press, 1990).

2. Randy Shilts, *Conduct Unbecoming: Lesbians and Gays in the U.S. Military* (New York: St. Martin's Press, 1993).

3. "Gays on the March," *Time*, 9/8/75, 32–43.

4. Human Rights Campaign Fund poll, conducted by Penn & Schoen, 1992.

5. General Accounting Office, *Defense Force Management: DOD's Policy on Homosexuality*, 6/12/92.

6. Personnel Security Research and Education Center, "Non-Conforming Sexual Orientation and Military Suitability," 1989.

7. Hearings of the House Budget Committee, U.S. Congress, 2/5/92.

8. Letter from Senator Charles Robb to General Colin Powell, 3/4/92.

9. See Joseph Steffan, *Honor Bound: A Gay American Fights for the Right to Serve His Country* (New York: Villard Books, 1992).

10. Bob Woodward, *The Agenda: Inside the Clinton White House* (New York: Simon & Schuster, 1994).

11. Elizabeth Drew, *On the Edge: The Clinton Presidency* (New York: Simon & Schuster, 1994).

12. David Mixner, *Stranger Among Friends* (New York: Bantam Books, 1996), 288.

13. Jeffrey Schmalz, "Gay Groups Regrouping for War on Military Ban," *New York Times*, 2/7/93, 26.

12. Bridging Race, Class, and Sexuality for School Reform

1. Of a total enrollment of 995,000 students, 590,000 were eligible for the free lunch program and 421,000 came from families collecting public assistance. Figures on the New York public schools from the Population Studies Unit of the Department of Education.

2. Four out of the top six countries of origin for immigrant students are countries with predominantly black populations: the Dominican Republic, Jamaica, Guyana, and Haiti.

3. See Jonathan Kozol's book *Savage Inequalities* for a harrowing trip through the worst of the public schools, including some New York City schools, and a description of how "magnet schools" can actually work to worsen conditions for the majority of students.

13. The Emergence of a Gay and Lesbian Antiviolence Movement

1. *Webster's New World Dictionary of the American Language*, 1962.

2. New York State Governor's Task Force on Bias-Related Violence, *Final Report*, March 1988, 1.

3. Ibid.

4. New York State Governor's Task Force, *Final Report*, "Bias Violence Legislation", 217ff.

5. Herek and Berrill, eds., *Hate Crimes: Confronting Violence Against Lesbians and Gay Men* (Newbury Park: Sage Publications, 1992), xiii.

6. Gary Comstock, "Victims of Anti-Gay/Anti-Lesbian Violence," *Journal of Interpersonal Violence* (1989) 4: 101–6.

7. Herek and Berrill, *Hate Crimes*, 289–305.

8. K. Jay and A. Young, *The Gay Report* (New York: Summit Press, 1977).

9. A.P. Bell, and M.S. Weinberg, *Homosexualities: A Study of Diversity Among Men and Women* (New York: Simon & Schuster, 1978).

10. Herek and Berrill, *Hate Crimes*.

11. Survey of 58 men and 75 women by Vermonters for Lesbian and Gay Rights, 1987.

12. Survey of 323 men and 411 women in Alaska by Identity, Inc., 1986.

13. Survey of 87 men and 80 women by Aurand, Adessa & Bush, 1985.

14. Survey of 213 men and 75 women by Wisconsin Governor's Council on Lesbian and Gay Issues, 1985.

15. Survey of 176 men and 147 women in Maine by Steinman & Aurand, 1985.

16. Survey of 1,420 men and 654 women by NGLTF, 1984.

17. New York State Governor's Task Force, *Final Report*, 77.

18. Joyce Hunter, "Violence Against Lesbian and Gay Male Youth," in Herek and Berrill, *Hate Crimes*, 78–79.

19. Boston Women's Health Collective, *The New Our Bodies, Ourselves* (New York: Simon and Schuster, 1984).

20. J. Stark and H. W. Goldstein, *The Rights of Crime Victims* (New York: Bantam, 1985).

21. National Coalition of Anti-Violence Programs, "Anti–Lesbian, Gay, Bisexual and Transgendered Violence in 1997," March 1998.

22. Gregory Herek, "The Community Response to Violence in San Francisco," in Herek and Berrill, *Hate Crimes*, 241.

23. David Wertheimer, "Treatment and Service Interventions for Lesbian and Gay Male Crime Victims," *Journal of Interpersonal Violence*, September 1990, 386.

24. Ibid., 386–87.

25. *New York Post* editorial, 5/6/88, 20.

26. Carl Siciliano, "An Epidemic of Violence Against Homosexuals," *The Catholic Worker*, May 1987, 3.

27. William Greer, "Violence Against Homosexuals Rising, Groups Seeking Wider Protection Say," *New York Times*, 11/23/86, 36.

28. Ibid.

29. Ed Hassell, quoted by Dave Walter, "Gays Testify on Homophobic Violence," *The Advocate*, 11/11/86, 13.

30. Kathleen Sarris, quoted, Ibid.

31. Ibid.

32. Ibid.

33. Greer, "Violence Against Homosexuals Rising," 36.

34. David Wertheimer, as recalled from telephone conversations with William Greer, November 1986.

35. Conversations between David Wertheimer and *New York Times* staff, November 1986.

36. John Conyers, "Foreword," in Herek and Berrill, *Hate Crimes*, xiii–xv.

37. Audre Lorde, "There Is No Hierarchy of Oppression," *Interracial Books for Children Bulletin* 14, nos. 3, 4.

38. New York State Governor's Task Force, *Final Report*.

39. Ibid., 8.

40. *Congressional Record,* Senate, 2/8/90, S1067–68.

41. Ibid. S1076.

42. National Coalition of Anti-Violence Programs, "Anti–Lesbian, Gay, Bisexual and Transgendered Violence in 1997," March 1998, 3.

43. Ibid., 12.

44. Seattle Public Schools, "1995 Teen Health Risk Survey," April 1996, III–14.

45. Ibid., V-8.

46. Peter Freiberg, "New York State Grants $40,000 to Gay Anti-Violence Group," *The Advocate,* 10/14/86, 14.

47. New York City Gay and Lesbian Anti-Violence Project, "HIV-Related Violence," March 1992.

48. National Coalition of Anti-Violence Programs, "Anti–Lesbian, Gay, Bisexual and Transgendered Violence in 1997," 17.

49. Ibid., 1.

50. Joseph Altman, "Lawmakers' Plan Toughens Federal Law on Hate Crimes," *The Seattle Times,* 6/17/88, A11.

51. National Gay and Lesbian Task Force, "Wyoming Legislature Kills Hate Crimes Bills" (press release), 2/3/99.

14. Couples: Marriage, Civil Union, and Domestic Partnership

1. Kay Tobin and Randy Wicker, *The Gay Crusaders* (New York: Arno Press, 1975), 13–27.

2. Suzanne Sherman, "Lesbian and Gay Marriage," *The Advocate,* August 1970, 7.

3. Tobin and Wicker, 141–42. The story of Baker and McConnell told here is drawn from Tobin and Wicker's account and from a phone interview of Baker conducted by the author in January 1999. For another recent book reporting on the marriage of Baker and McConnell and their other gay political activities at the time, see Dudley Clendinen and Adam Nagourney, *Out for Good: The Struggle to Build a Gay Rights Movement in America* (New York: Simon and Schuster, 1999), 70–71, 226–38.

4. Tobin and Wicker, 141.

5. Ibid., 144.

6. Ibid.

7. *The Advocate,* June 10–23, 1970, 1.

8. *Baker v. Nelson,* 191 N.W.2d 185 (Minn. 1971).

9. The author interviewed Singer by telephone, 7/23/98, and Barwick by telephone, 7/24/98. All the personal information in the text comes from these interviews. Singer, who had changed his name to Faygele ben Miriam, died in June 2000.

10. *Singer v. Hara,* 522 P.2d 1187 (Wash. Ct. App. 1974).

11. *Singer v. U.S. Civil Service Commission,* 520 F.2d 247 (9th Cir. 1976) (at the request of the U.S. government, the Supreme Court vacated the circuit court decision when new civil service regulations were adopted at the beginning of the Carter administration); *McConnell v. Anderson,* 451 F.2d 193 (8th Cir. 1971), cert. denied, 405 U.S. 1046 (1972).

12. See note 9 for interviews with Singer and Barwick. The author interviewed Jack Baker by telephone, 1/24/99.

13. Interview. See note 11. Some gay activists in Minnesota probably remain bitter

toward Baker, for he was not a dependable ally. In the spring of 1973, Baker testified against a legislative bill to bar discrimination against "homosexuals" because he considered the word *homosexual* insulting. Other gay activists were stunned. See Clendinen and Nagourney, *Out for Good,* 229.

14. The author interviewed Lyon by telephone, 8/17/98.

15. *Jones v. Hallahan,* 501 S.W.2d 588 (Ky. Ct. App. 1973).

16. William N. Eskridge Jr., *The Case for Same-Sex Marriage: From Sexual Liberty to Civilized Commitment* (New York: Free Press, 1996), 55–56.

17. Ibid., 57.

18. The author interviewed Hunter by telephone, 7/16/98. Writing in 1989, Tom Stoddard, then executive director of Lambda, wrote, "As far as I can tell, no gay organization of any size, local or national, has declared the right to marriage as one of its goals." Stoddard, "Why Gay People Should Seek the Right to Marry," *Out/Look,* fall 1989, 9.

19. 478 U.S. 186 (1986).

20. See, e.g., Nancy Polikoff, "We Will Get What We Ask For: Why Legalizing Gay and Lesbian Marriage Will Not 'Dismantle the Structure of Gender in Every Marriage,'" *Va. L. Rev.* 1535 (1993):79; Ruthann Robson, *Lesbian (Out)Law: Survival Under the Rule of Law* (Ithaca, N.Y.: Firebrand Books, 1992), 124–27; Kath Weston, *Families We Choose: Lesbians, Gays, Kinship* (New York: Columbia University Press, 1991), 209–10.

21. Stoddard, "Why Gay People Should," and Ettelbrick, "Since When Is Marriage a Path to Liberation," *Out/Look,* fall 1989, 9.

22. See William Rubenstein, ed., *Lesbians, Gay Men and the Law* (New York: Free Press, 1993), 418 (note 3).

23. A fuller account of the lives of Baehr and Dancel and how they came to be involved in a lawsuit is provided in Eskridge, *Case for Same-Sex Marriage,* 1–5.

24. Woods's Web site; see, e.g., marriage-digest@abacus.oxy.edu, 9/30/96.

25. *Baehr v. Levin,* 852 P.2d 44 (1993).

26. *Baehr v. Miike,* 1996 *Westlaw* 694235 (Haw. Cir. Ct. 1996).

27. After the bill was enacted, the state attorney general ruled that private employers could not be required to provide health benefits. A federal district court upheld the attorney general's decision.

28. See "Legislative Reactions to Suits for Same-Sex Marriage," www.buddybuddy.com.

29. Defense of Marriage Act, Pub. L. no. 104-199, 110 Stat. 2419 (1996) (codified as 28 U.S.C. section 1738C and 1 U.S.C. section 7).

30. See, e.g., Barbara Cox, "Same-Sex Marriage and Choice of Law: If We Marry in Hawaii, Are We Still Married When We Return Home," *Wis. L. Rev.* 1033 (1994).

31. See 142 *Cong. Rec.* S10,068 (daily ed., 9/9/96).

32. *Defense of Marriage Act: Hearing on S. 1740 Before the Senate Committee on the Judiciary,* 1996 *Westlaw* 387295 (7/11/96). (Representative Largent, the bill's sponsor, spoke at the Senate hearings in support of the bill.)

33. Presidential debate, San Diego, 10/16/96. ("As far as special rights, I'm opposed to same-sex marriages—which the president signed well after midnight one morning in the dark of night. He opposed it.")

34. 744 A.2d 864 (Vt. 1999).

35. For an example of an appellate decision refusing to permit a man to adopt his partner, see *In re the Adoption of Robert Paul P.,* 471 N.E.2d 424 (N.Y. 1984).

36. *Braschi v. Stahl Assocs. Co.,* 543 N.E.2d 49 (N.Y. 1989).

37. See chapter 15 by Nancy Polikoff in this volume.

38. See Nancy Knauer, "Domestic Partnership and Same-Sex Relationships: A Marketplace Innovation and a Less than Perfect Institutional Choice," *Temple Political & Civil Rights Law Review* 7 (1998):337, 341.

39. Hawaii, New York, Oregon, and Vermont. See Lambda Legal Defense and Education Fund Web site, www.lambdalegal.org.

40. Knauer, "Domestic Partnership and Same-Sex Relationships," 339.

41. See "Baptists Vote to Boycott Disney over Gay Benefits," *Wall Street Journal*, 6/13/96, A23.

15. RAISING CHILDREN: LESBIAN AND GAY PARENTS FACE THE PUBLIC AND THE COURTS

1. This is not to suggest that a lesbian or gay parent can simply drive across state lines and be successful. All states have residency requirements before their courts can hear custody or adoption cases. For example, under the Uniform Child Custody Jurisdiction Act (UCCJA), which has been enacted in some form in every state, a custody proceeding should usually be brought in the "home state" of the child, which is the state where the child has lived for the six months preceding the litigation. Upon moving with the child to a new state, the former residence of the child remains the child's "home state" for six months, and litigation concerning the child would usually take place there. Furthermore, once a state issues a custody decision, that state is probably the only state that can ever decide custody matters concerning the child, unless the child and both of the parents move out of the state.

2. Del Martin and Phyllis Lyon, *Lesbian/Woman* (Glide, 1972).

3. Del Martin and Phyllis Lyon, "Lesbian Mothers," *Ms.* 2, no. 4 (October 1973): 78.

4. Judy Klemesrud, "Lesbians Who Try to be Good Mothers," *New York Times*, 1/31/73, 46L; "The Lesbian as Mother," *Newsweek*, 9/24/73, 75–76.

5. E. Carrington Boggan, Marilyn G. Haft, Charles Lister, John P. Rupp, and Thomas Stoddard, *The Rights of Gay People* (New York: Bantam Books, 1975), 94–103.

6. *Commonwealth v. Bradley*, 91 A.2d 379 (Pa. Super. Ct. 1952).

7. See, e.g., R. A. Basile, "Lesbian Mothers I," *Women's Rts. L. Rep.* 8 (1974): 3; Nan D. Hunter and Nancy D. Polikoff, "Custody Rights of Lesbian Mothers: Legal Theory and Litigation Strategy," *Buffalo L. Rev.* 25, (1976): 691.

8. *Christian v. Randall*, 516 P.2d 132 (Colo. Ct. App. 1973).

9. These cases are discussed in Hunter and Polikoff, "Custody Rights of Lesbian Mothers," 696–97, n. 7, 698–700, 704.

10. Minnie Bruce Pratt, *Crimes Against Nature* (Ithaca, N.Y.: Firebrand Books, 1990).

11. "Briefs," *Time*, 1/12/76, 54.

12. Uniform Marriage and Divorce Act, *Uniform Laws Annotated*, vol. 9.

13. Bernice Goodman, "The Lesbian Mother," *American Journal of Orthopsychiatry*, 43 (1973): 283–84.

14. Richard Green, "Sexual Identity of 37 Children Raised by Homosexual or Transsexual Parents," *American Journal of Psychiatry* 135 (1978): 692–697.

15. Lucinda Franks, "Homosexuals as Foster Parents: Is New Program an Advance or Peril?" *New York Times*, 5/7/74, 47.

16. These cases are discussed in Rhonda R. Rivera, "Our Straight-Laced Judges: The Legal Position of Homosexual Persons in the United States," *Hastings L. J.* 30 (1979): 798, 907–8.

17. In individual cases judges also had to determine the best interests of the child

within the complex context of that child's life. A judge might say, as several did, that an award of custody to a lesbian mother did not represent a gay rights victory but rather a simple judgment that the mother would provide a better home for that child than would the father. The use of this reasoning by trial judges in specific cases is discussed ibid., 899–900.

18. E.g., Spencer Rich, "Strife, Touchy Issues Sank Conference on Families," *Washington Post*, 6/24/78, A3; Lynn Langway, "Family Politics," *Newsweek*, 1/28/80, 78.

19. *M.P. v. S.P.*, 169 N.J. Super. 425, 438, 404 A.2d 1256, 1263 (App. Div. 1979).

20. The earliest examples of lesbian couples choosing to raise a child together almost certainly involve conception by one member of the couple through sexual intercourse with a man for the express purpose of becoming pregnant. A 1973 *New York Times* article about lesbian mothers describes a couple raising an eight-year-old daughter conceived deliberately with the help of a mutual male friend (Klemesrud, "Lesbians Who Try to Be Good Mothers," 46). A 1977 custody dispute between a child's nonbiological mother and the biological mother's sister after the biological mother died concerned a child born in 1970 after the biological mother had sexual intercourse with a student she met on vacation. The lesbian couple had contacted an adoption agency in 1968 about adopting a child; when that was unsuccessful, they used casual sexual intercourse. "In re Hatzopolous," *Fam. L. Rep.* 4 (12/6/77): 2075.

21. Diane H. Shah, Linda Walters, and Tony Clifton, "Lesbian Mothers," *Newsweek*, 2/12/79, 61.

22. Anne Taylor Fleming, "New Frontiers in Conception," *New York Times Magazine*, 7/12/80, 14.

23. 127 *Congressional Record*, S12697 (daily ed., 6/17/81) (statement of Senator Jepsen).

24. C. Pies, *Considering Parenthood* (San Francisco: Spinsters/Aunt Lute, 1985).

25. "Homosexual Adopting a Son," *New York Times*, 12/27/82, D10; "Lesbians' Custody Fight on Coast Raises Novel Issues in Family Law," *New York Times*, 9/9/84, 44.

26. *Bezio v. Patenaude*, 410 N.E.2d 1207 (Mass. 1980).

27. *S.N.E. v. R.L.B.*, 699 P.2d 875 (Alaska 1985).

28. *Guinan v. Guinan*, 477 N.Y.S.2d 830 (1984); *Gottlieb v. Gottlieb*, 488 N.Y.S.2d 180 (1985).

29. *Roe v. Roe*, 324 S.E.2d 691 (Va. 1985).

30. *Roberts v. Roberts*, 489 N.E.2d 1067 (Ohio Ct. App. 1985).

31. *N.K.M. v. L.E.M.*, 60 S.W.2d 179 (Mo. Ct. App. 1980).

32. *J.L.P.(H) v. D.L.P.*, 643 S.W.2d 865 (Mo. Ct. App. 1982).

33. *L. v. D.*, 630 S.W.2d 240 (Mo. Ct. App. 1982).

34. For extensive discussion of the people involved in the Massachusetts foster-care controversy, see Laura Benkov, *Reinventing the Family* (New York: Crown, 1994), 86–98; and Neil Miller, *In Search of Gay America* (New York: Harper & Row, 1989) 121–30.

35. *In re Opinion of the Justices*, 530 A.2d 21 (N.H. 1987).

36. Judith Havemann, "Task Force Opposes Adoption by Homosexuals," *Washington Post*, 12/10/87, A20.

37. *Matter of Appeal in Pima County, Juvenile Action B-10489*, 727 P.2d 830 (Ariz. Ct. App. 1986).

38. *Stroman v. Williams*, 353 S.E.2d 704 (S.C. Ct. App. 1987).

39. *Daly v. Daly*, 715 P.2d 56 (Nev. 1986).

40. *Thigpen v. Carpenter*, 730 S.W.2d 510 (Ark. Ct. App. 1987).

41. *In re Jacinta M.*, 764 P.2d 1327 (N.M. Ct. App. 1988).

42. *Conkel v. Conkel*, 509 N.E.2d 983 (Ohio Ct. App. 1987).

43. *In re E.B.G.*, discussed in Nancy Polikoff, "This Child Does Have Two Mothers: Redefining Parenthood to Meet the Needs of Children in Lesbian-Mother and Other Nontraditional Families," *Geo. L. J.* 78 (1990): 459.

44. "In re Pearlman," *Fam. L. Rep.* 15 (1989): 1355 (Fla. Cir. Ct. 1989).

45. *Starr v. Erez*, no. 97 CVD 624 (N.C. Durham Co. Dist. Ct., 8/29/97).

46. American Psychological Association, *Lesbian and Gay Parenting: A Resource for Psychologists* (Washington, D.C.: 1995), 8.

47. The best analysis of the evolution of the right-wing so-called family values movement is in Judith Stacey, *In the Name of Family* (Boston: Beacon Press, 1996).

48. The phrase was coined in a cover story by Barbara Dafoe Whitehead in the April 1993 *Atlantic* magazine.

49. *Baehr v. Lewin*, 852 P.2d 44 (Haw. 1993).

50. National Gay and Lesbian Task Force Policy Institute, *1998 Capital Gains and Losses: A State by State Review of Gay, Lesbian, Bisexual, Transgender and HIV/AIDS-Related Legislation in 1998* (1999), 5.

51. On the Senate side, hostility to lesbian and gay parenting killed one of President Clinton's federal court nominees. In 1994, upon the recommendation of Senator Barbara Boxer, Clinton nominated Judith McConnell, the presiding judge of the San Diego County Superior Court, as a federal district court judge. In 1987, while a juvenile court judge, McConnell had awarded guardianship of a sixteen-year-old boy, Brian Batey, to the life partner of the boy's biological father after the father died. The father had raised Brian with his partner since Brian had been four years old, and Brian wanted to stay with the partner rather than live with his mother, who opposed the guardianship petition. The partner was represented by the local ACLU chapter, and the judge's decision was reported in the press. Upon learning of McConnell's decision, Senate Republicans stated that they would be unwilling to confirm her. When it became clear that the Clinton administration would not fight for her confirmation, McConnell withdrew her nomination.

52. *In re M.M.D.*, 662 A.2d 837 (D.C. 1995).

53. 144 *Congressional Record*, H7382 (daily ed. 8/6/98) (statement of Representative Largent).

54. Ibid., H7384–85.

55. Eric Lipton, "House Rejects D.C. Marijuana, Needle Efforts," *Washington Post*, 7/30/99, B-1.

56. *In re Adoption of Evan*, 583 N.Y.S.2d 997, 1002 (N.Y. Sup. Ct. 1992).

57. Obviously, when a lesbian or gay prospective adoptive parent is not out to everyone in the adoption process, that person goes through the process as an ostensibly single adult. Although adoption applicants are advised not to lie, many social workers do not ask directly about sexual orientation. If the applicant's partner has a separate bedroom, the social worker may write up the partner as a roommate, regardless of his or her suspicions about the true nature of the relationship. Also, social workers and private agencies that know the applicant is gay may intentionally omit that information from the home study to facilitate adoptions from other states, or even other countries, where a lesbian or gay man would not be accepted as an adoptive parent. For these reasons, it is impossible to know how many gay men and lesbians have adopted children; the vast majority of them are simply counted as single adoptive parents in any statistical compilations.

58. Holli Hartman, "Gay Couple Top Foster Parents," *Des Moines Register*, 6/1/96, 1.

59. *Bottoms v. Bottoms*, 444 S.E.2d 276 (Va. Ct. App. 1994).

60. *Bottoms v. Bottoms*, 457 S.E.2d 102 (Va. 1995).

61. *J.B.F. v. J.M.F.*, 730 So. 2d 1190 (Ala. 1998).

62. *Boswell v. Boswell* 721 A.26 662 (Md. 1998).

16. Family Values: From the White House Conference on Families to the Family Protection Act

1. *New York Times*, 3/27/77, 13.
2. *Washington Blade*, 4/77, 1.
3. *New York Times*, 6/19/77, 16.
4. *Washington Blade*, 7/19/77, 1.
5. *Washington Blade*, 11/21/80, A1.
6. *New York Times*, 8/4/76, 12.
7. *U.S. News & World Report*, 5/5/80, 88.
8. *New York Times*, 6/19/78, 1.
9. *Washington Blade*, 11/8/79, A1.
10. *New York Times*, 7/21/79, 20.
11. *Washington Post*, 8/21/79, A3.
12. William Martin, *With God on Our Side* (New York: Broadway Books, 1996), 180.
13. *Washington Blade*, 9/13/79, 3.
14. *Washington Blade*, 11/8/79, 1.
15. *Washington Post*, 12/1/79, B1.
16. *Washington Blade*, 12/6/79, A7.
17. *Washington Blade*, 11/8/79, 1.
18. *Washington Blade*, 2/21/80, A4.
19. *Washington Post*, 11/15/79, C1.
20. *New York Times*, 1/28/80, D10.
21. *New York Times*, 1/7/80, D8.
22. *Washington Post*, 1/18/80, A2.
23. Martin, *With God on Our Side*, 164.
24. Ibid., 178.
25. *Listening to America's Families: Action for the 80's, the Report of the White House Conference on Families*, 1980.
26. *Washington Blade*, 6/12/80, 1.
27. Ibid.
28. *New York Times*, 6/6/80, B4.
29. *New York Times*, 6/7/80, 46.
30. *Washington Blade*, 6/12/80, A1.
31. Martin, *With God on Our Side*, 185.
32. Ibid.
33. *Time*, 6/16/80, 31.
34. *New York Times*, 6/8/80, 24.
35. *Los Angeles Times*, 6/8/80, 1; *Washington Post*, 6/8/80, 1.
36. *New York Times*, 6/20/80, 18.
37. *New York Times*, 6/22/80, 24.
38. *New York Times*, 6/23/80, II8.
39. *New York Times*, 6/27/80, 20.
40. Personal communication from Bill Kelley, 8/3/98.
41. Personal communication from Adele Starr, 9/26/98.
42. *It's Time*, 9/80, 2.
43. *Los Angeles Times*, 7/11/80, I3.
44. *New York Times*, 7/11/80, A14.
45. *Los Angeles Times*, 7/13/80, I3.

46. Ibid.

47. Ibid.

48. *Washington Post,* 8/21/80, A33.

49. *New York Times,* 10/13/80, III1.

50. *Washington Blade,* 11/7/80, A3.

51. *Gay Community News,* 4/4/81, 3.

52. Richard Viguerie, *The New Right: We're Ready to Lead* (Falls Church, Va.: The Viguerie Company, 1980), 200.

53. Ibid., 205.

54. *Washington Blade,* 12/20/79, A1.

55. *Gay Community News,* 4/4/81, 3.

56. *Washington Blade,* 6/26/81, A5.

17. Advocating for Lesbian Health in the Clinton Years

1. See R. Denenberg, "Report on Lesbian Health," *WHI* 5, no. 2 (summer 1995); E. J. Rankow, "Lesbian Health Issues for the Primary Care Provider," *Journal of Family Practice* 40, no. 5 (May 1995); J. C. Whiate and W. Levinson, "Lesbian Health Care: What a Primary Care Physician Needs to Know," *Western Journal of Medicine* 162, no. 5 (May 1995): 463–66; Council on Scientific Affairs, American Medical Association, "Health Care Needs of Gay Men and Lesbians in the United States," *JAMA* 275, no. 17 (May 1, 1996): 1354–59.

2. M. Plumb, E. Rankow, R. Young, "Drug Use and Increased Risk of HIV Among Lesbians, Bisexual Women, and Women Who Have Sex with Women," in *Proceedings of the Conference on Drug Addiction Research and Women's Health* (Rockville, Md,: National Institutes of Drug Abuse, 1998).

3. P. E. Stevens, "Protective Strategies of Lesbian Clients in Health Care Environments," *Research in Nursing and Health* 17, no. 3 (June 1994): 217–29; and P. E. Stevens, "Marginalized Women's Access to Health Care: A Feminist Narrative Analysis," *Advances in Nursing Science* 16, no. 2 (December 1993): 39–56.

4. R. Denenberg, "A History of the Lesbian Health Movement," in *The Lesbian Health Book: Caring for Ourselves* (Seattle, Wash.: Seal Press, 1997), 3–22.

5. M. Kennedy, M. Scarlett, A. Duerr, and S. Chu, "Assessing HIV Risk Among Women Who Have Sex With Women: Scientific and Communication Issues," *Journal of the American Medical Women's Association,* May/August 1995, 103–7.

6. D. Knutson, "Framework for Outreach Strategies to Reach Lesbians" (available from the CDC, 4770 Buford Highway NE, Mailstop K-57, Atlanta, GA 30341).

7. J. White, "Challenges and Opportunities in Clinical Research on Lesbian Health" (paper presented at the Institute of Medicine Workshop on Lesbian Health Research, Washington, D.C., October 6, 1997).

8. V. Mayes, S. Cochran, C. Pies, S. Chu, and A. Ehrhardt, "The Risk of HIV Infection for Lesbians and Other Women Who Have Sex with Women: Implications for HIV Research, Prevention, Policy, and Services," *Women's Health: Research on Gender, Behavior, and Policy* 2, nos. 1 & 2 (Mahweh, N.J.: Lawrence Erlbaum Associates, 1996), 119–39.

9. P. Case, "Disclosure of Sexual Orientation in the Nurses' Health Study II," and Deborah Bowen, "Cancer and Lesbians" (papers presented at the Institute of Medicine Workshop on Lesbian Health Research, Washington, D.C., October 6–7, 1997).

10. Institute of Medicine, *Lesbian Health: Current Assessment and Directions for the Future,* Andrea Solarz, ed. (Washington, D.C.: National Academy Press, 1999).

11. E. O. Laumann, J. H. Gagnon, R. T. Michael, S. Michaels, *The Social Organization of Sexuality: Sexual Practices in the United States* (Chicago: University of Chicago Press, 1994).

18. Contested Membership: Black Gay Identities and the Politics of AIDS

1. For discussions of postmodern and deconstructive approaches see for example Sylvia Walby, "Post-Post-Modernism? Theorizing Social Complexity," *Destabilizing Theory: Contemporary Feminist Debates*, M. Barrett and A. Phillips, eds. (Stanford, Calif.: Stanford University Press, 1992), 31–52; Jane Flax, "Postmodernism and Gender Relations in Feminist Theory," *Feminism/Postmodernism*, L. J. Nicholson, ed. (New York: Routledge, 1990), 39–62; and Steve Seidman, "Identity and Politics in a 'Postmodern' Gay Culture: Some Historical and Conceptual Notes," *Fear of a Queer Planet: Queer Politics and Social Theory*, M. Warner, ed. (Minneapolis: University of Minnesota Press, 1993), 105–42.

2. First, it is important that we remember that social constructionist theories come in different forms and different degrees. For such a discussion see Carole S. Vance, "Social Construction Theory: Problems in the History of Sexuality," *Homosexuality, Which Homosexuality?* (London: GMP Publishers, 1999), 13–33.

Second, it is also important to recognize that social constructionist theory is still relatively new to many fields within the social sciences. So in the field of American political science, where quantitative analysis dominates as the methodology of choice, rivaled by formal theory, social constructionist approaches to the study of groups has at best tangentially made any appearance.

Finally, for examples of variants of social constructionist approaches to the field of race and black studies, see among others Stuart Hall, "Race, Articulation and Societies Structured in Dominance," *Sociological Theories: Race and Colonialism* (Paris: UNESCO, 1980), 305–45; Paul Gilroy, *Small Acts: Thoughts on the Politics of Black Cultures* (London: Serpent's Tail, 1993); and Evelyn Brooks Higginbotham, "African-American Women's History and the Metalanguage of Race," *Signs* 17, no. 2 (winter 1992): 251–74.

3. By marginal communities I mean those groups with an ascribed and certainly constructed identity that has historically and institutionally served as the basis for the exclusion, deprivation, and a distinction of "other."

4. See for example Iris Marian Young, "The Ideal of Community and the Politics of Difference," in *Feminism/Postmodernism*, L. Nicholson, ed. (New York: Routledge, 1990), 300–323; Shane Phelan, "(Be)Coming Out: Lesbian Identity and Politics," *Signs* 19 no. 30 (spring 1994): 765–90; Kimberle Crenshaw, "Demarginalizing the Intersection of Race and Sex: A Black Feminist Critique of Antidiscrimination Doctrine, Feminist Theory and Antiracist Politics," *University of Chicago Legal Forum* (1989): 139–67; Lisa Lowe, "Heterogeneity, Hybridity, Multiplicity: Marking Asian American Differences," *Diaspora* 1, no. 1 (spring 1991): 24–44.

5. See for example Maria Lugones, "Purity, Impurity, and Separation," *Signs: Journal of Women in Culture and Society* 19, no. 2 (1994): 458–79; and E. Frances White, "Africa on my Mind: Gender Counter Discourse and African-American Nationalism," *Journal of Women's History* 2, no. 1 (spring 1990): 73–97.

6. James C. Scott, *Domination and the Arts of Resistance: The Hidden Transcript* (New Haven: Yale University Press, 1990).

7. For a full discussion of secondary marginalization see Cathy J. Cohen, "Power, Resistance and the Construction of Crisis: Marginalized Communities Respond to AIDS" (unpublished manuscript, 1993), 72–75.

8. See Henry Louis Gates Jr., "Two Nations . . . Both Black," *Forbes* 150 (9/14/92), 132–35, for a subtle example of the *indigenous* evaluation and separation of members of the community into categories of "good" and "bad" or "industrious" and "culturally deficient" black people.

9. While several different segments of the black community have been associated with AIDS, I focus this inquiry on the struggle around black gay male identity because it seems most illustrative of the ways in which contests over indigenously defined identities can impact on the politics of marginal communities.

10. I should be clear that any number of organizations or leaders have constructed ways to "deal" with AIDS without directly confronting or embracing those stigmatized segments of black communities associated with this disease. Thus, you are much more likely to find "leaders" talking about the innocent children and women who are the victims of this disease in black communities than the gay men and intravenous drug users who suffer disproportionately in our communities.

11. Judith Butler, *Gender Trouble* (New York: Routledge, 1990); Warner, *Fear of a Queer Planet*; Teresa de Lauretis, "Queer Theory: Lesbian and Gay Sexualities," *Differences* 3 (1991).

12. Barbara Jeanne Fields, "Slavery, Race and Ideology in the United States of America," *New Left Review* 181 (May/June 1990): 115–16.

13. Michael Omi and Howard Winant, *Racial Formation in the United States: From the 1960s to the 1990s,* (2nd ed.) (New York: Routledge, 1994), 55.

14. See for example Molefi Kete Asante, *Afrocentricity* (Trenton, N.J.: African World Press, 1988); Patricia Hill Collins, *Black Feminist Thought: Knowledge, Consciousness, and the Politics of Empowerment* (New York: Harper Collins Academic, 1990).

15. See for example Cheryl Clarke, "The Failure to Transform: Homophobia in the Black Community," *Home Girls: A Black Feminist Anthology,* B. Smith, ed. (New York: Kitchen Table: Women of Color Press), 197–208.

I would caution the reader, however, not to discount the role that state-sponsored repression also played in leading to the destruction of many of these groups. It is now well-documented that the FBI through the counterintelligence program (COINTELPRO) helped destroy many liberation groups, such as the Black Panther Party.

16. See Eric Garber, "A Spectacle in Color: The Lesbian and Gay Subculture of Jazz Age Harlem," in *Hidden from History: Reclaiming the Gay and Lesbian Past,* M. Duberman, M. Vicinus, and G. Chauncey Jr., eds. (New York: Meridian Books, 1990), 318–31; Jonathan Ned Katz, *Gay American History: Lesbians and Gay Men in the U.S.A.* (New York: Meridian Books, 1992).

17. bell hooks, *Talking Back: Thinking Feminist, Thinking Black* (Boston: South End Press, 1989), 120–21.

18. Cornel West, "The New Cultural Politics of Difference," in *Out There: Marginalization and Contemporary Cultures,* R. Ferguson, M. Gever, T. T. Minh-ha, and C. West, eds. (Cambridge: MIT Press, 1990), 25.

19. John D'Emilio, *Sexual Politics, Sexual Communities: The Making of a Homosexual Minority in the United States, 1940–1970* (Chicago: University of Chicago Press, 1983).

20. Cherrie Moraga and Gloria Anzaldua, eds., *This Bridge Called My Back: Writings by Radical Women of Color* (Latham, New York: Kitchen Table: Women of Color Press, 1981); Smith, *Home Girls*; Essex Hemphill, ed., *Brother to Brother: New Writings by Black Gay Men* (Boston: Alyson Publications, 1991); Joseph Beam, ed., *In the Life: A Black Gay Anthology* (Boston: Alyson Publications, 1986).

21. Ernest Quimby and Samuel R. Friedman, *Social Problems* 36, no. 4 (October 1989).

22. Ibid., 405.

23. Ibid. This conference was organized "with the assistance of the city health department and the University of California."

24. Guy Weston, "AIDS in the Black Community," *Black/Out* 1, no. 2 (fall 1986): 13–15.

25. There are conflicting views on the effectiveness of GMAD during the AIDS crisis. Some argue that in a crisis of this proportion GMAD should be a leader in this fight, holding programs whenever possible. Other GMAD members suggest, however, that there are more dimensions to the lives of black gay men than just the threat of AIDS. Thus it is the responsibility of GMAD to provide a supportive environment in which black gay men can dialogue and work on the opportunities and obstacles that structure their lives.

While this debate will probably not be settled anytime soon, I still believe, every time I see seventy-five black gay men at one of their meetings, that this is an example of the success of struggle. An example that needs work and adjustment, but a success all the same.

26. U.S. Department of Health and Human Services, Public Health Service, Centers for Disease Control and Prevention, "HIV/AIDS Surveillance Report" 5, no. 4 (year-end ed., 1993).

27. Undoubtedly, the organization most recognized as contributing to the organization of people in lesbian and gay communities is ACT UP (AIDS Coalition to Unleash Power). See for example Josh Gamson, "Silence, Death, and the Invisible Enemy: AIDS Activism and Social Movement `Newness,'" *Social Problems* 36, no. 4 (October 1989), 351–67.

28. Responses to a question from the 1993–94 National Black Politics Study on the origin of AIDS found that nearly one-quarter (22 percent) of African-American respondents agreed that "AIDS is a disease that is a result of an antiblack conspiracy."

29. Renee Sabatier, *Blaming Others: Prejudice, Race and Worldwide AIDS* (Washington: The Panos Institute, 1988); Cindy Patton, *Inventing AIDS* (New York: Routledge, 1990).

30. Harlon L. Dalton, "AIDS in Blackface," *The AIDS Reader: Social, Political and Ethical Issues,* N. F. McKenzie, ed. (New York: Meridan, 1991), 122–43; Evelynn Hammonds, "Race, Sex, AIDS: The Construction of 'Other,'" *Radical America* 20, no. 6 (1987): 328–40; Phillip Brian Harper, "Eloquence and Epitaph: Black Nationalism and the Homophobic Impulse in Responses to the Death of Max Robinson," in *The Lesbian and Gay Studies Reader,* H. Abelove, M. A. Barable, and D. M. Halperin, eds. (New York: Routledge, 1993), 159–75.

31. Now, before engaging in any discussion of homophobia in the black community, these authors, as I myself do, make their obligatory claim that while we can talk about homophobia in the black community, this is not done to suggest that the black community is "more" homophobic than any other community, in particular white "communities." In fact, there is a reasonable argument that marginal groups, either because of an understanding of the outsider position or a lack of power to enforce their prejudices, have been more inclusive and accepting of lesbian and gay members *relative to* other groups rooted in dominant society.

32. See Ronald Takaki, *Strangers From a Different Shore: A History of Asian Americans* (New York: Penguin, 1990); Stephen Steinberg, *The Ethnic Myth: Race, Ethnicity, and Class in America* (Boston: Beacon Press, 1989); F. James Davis, *Who Is Black? One Nation's Definition* (University Park, Pa.: Pennsylvania State University Press, 1991); Earl Lewis, "Race, the State, and Social Construction: The Multiple Meanings of Race in the Twentieth Century" (unpublished manuscript 1994); Omi and Winant, *Racial Formation.*

33. St. Clair Drake and Horace R. Cayton, *Black Metropolis: A Study of Negro Life in a Northern City* (Chicago: University of Chicago Press, 1993), 563.

34. James R. Grossman, *Land of Hope: Chicago, Black Southerners, and the Great Migration* (Chicago: University of Chicago Press, 1989), 145–46.

35. Cornel West, *Race Matters* (Boston: Beacon Press, 1993), 86.

36. Hazel V. Carby, "Policing the Black Woman's Body," *Critical Inquiry* 18 (summer, 1992): 741.

37. For such a critique see Adolph L. Reed Jr., "The 'Underclass' as Myth and Symbol: The Poverty of Discourse about Poverty," *Radical America* (summer 1991). For an example of such distancing see Gates, "Two Nations."

38. Pierre Bourdieu, "The Forms of Capital," in *Handbook of Theory and Research for the Sociology of Education,* J. G. Richardson, ed. (New York: Greenwood Press, 1986), 241–58.

39. Ron Simmons, "Some Thoughts on the Challenge Facing Black Gay Intellectuals," in *Brother to Brother,* Hemphill.

40. Ibid., 212.

41. Molefi Kete Asante, *Afrocentricity: The Theory of Social Change* (Buffalo: Amulefi, 1980), 65. As cited in Simmons, "Some Thoughts," 213.

42. Nathan Hare and Julia Hare, *The Endangered Black Family: Coping with the Unisexualization and Coming Extinction of the Black Race* (San Francisco: Black Think Tank, 1984), 65. As cited in Simmons, "Some Thoughts," 214.

43. We need only remember the Tuskegee Syphilis Experiment to understand where such mistrust is rooted. See James H. Jones, *Bad Blood: The Tuskegee Syphilis Experiment—a Tragedy of Race and Medicine* (New York: Free Press, 1981); David McBride, *From TB to AIDS: Epidemics Among Urban Blacks Since 1900* (Albany: State University of New York Press, 1991); Hammonds, "Race, Sex, AIDS," 28–36.

44. Aldon D. Morris, *The Origins of the Civil Rights Movement: Black Communities Organizing for Change* (New York: Free Press, 1984).

45. Hollie I. West, "Down from the Clouds: Black Churches Battle Earthly Problems," *Emerge,* 5/90, 51.

46. West, 1990, p. 51.

47. Gail Walker, "'Oh Freedom': Liberation and the African-American Church," *Guardian,* 2/26/92, 10.

48. Rev. C. Jay Matthews, "The Black Church Position Statement on Homosexuality," *Call and Post,* 6/10/93, 5c.

49. Interview with Dr. Marjorie Hill.

50. Interview with the Reverend Calvin Butts.

51. Interview with Colin Robinson.

52. Interview with George Bellinger Jr.

53. This formal recognition of groups, in particular marginal groups, has led to the inclusion of race, gender, and class into traditional studies of politics. Unfortunately, in many cases those scholars who studied these topics long before they were fashionable, in particular women and people of color, have not found their way into traditional routes of power within political science organizations and departments.

54. The author would like to thank Franny Nudelman, Joshua Gamson, Debra Minkoff, Gordon Lafer, Vicky Hattam, Ian Shapiro, Rogers Smith, Alex Wendt, and members of the Yale University Ethics, Politics and Economics Summer Reading Group for their helpful comments. All shortcomings are the full responsibility of the author.

19. The Ryan White CARE Act: An Impressive, Dubious Achievement

1. Health Resources and Services Administration, *HIV/AIDS Programs and Accomplishments: FY91–FY95 State Profiles* (Washington, D.C.: U.S. Government Printing Office, 1995).

2. Henry J. Kaiser Family Foundation, *Federal HIV/AIDS Spending: A Budget Chartbook* (May 1998).

3. Lewis Katoff, "Community-Based Services for People with AIDS," *Primary Care* 19 (March 1992): 231–43.

4. Paul Jellinek, telephone interview with author, 2/10/95.

5. Ruby P. Hearn, "An Overview of AIDS Programs Receiving Support from the Robert Wood Johnson Foundation," in *Proceedings: AIDS Prevention and Services Workshop, February 15–16, 1990,* Vivian E. Fransen, ed. (Princeton, N.J.: Robert Wood Johnson Foundation, 1991).

6. Cliff Morrison, telephone interview with author, 8/15/95.

7. Joseph O'Neill, opening remarks to the Special Projects of National Significance "Objective Review Panels" review of grant proposals, at the Radisson-Barcelo Hotel, Washington, D.C., 6/26/96.

8. Jeffrey Levi, interview with author, Washington, D.C., 2/24/95.

9. Virginia Apuzzo, telephone interview with author, 8/8/95.

10. Michael E. Carbine, Peter Lee, *AIDS into the 90s: Strategies for an Integrated Response to the AIDS Epidemic* (Washington, D.C.: National AIDS Network, 1988).

11. Gary MacDonald, interview with author, Washington, D.C., 2/7/95.

12. Timothy M. Westmoreland, interview with author, Washington, D.C., 9/9/98.

13. Health Resources and Services Administration, *HIV/AIDS Programs and Accomplishments.*

14. Paul Akio Kawata, interview with author, Washington, D.C., 3/24/95.

15. Joseph O'Neill, M.D., interview with author, Washington, D.C., 8/29/95.

16. Ralph Payne, interview with author, Washington, D.C., 9/24/95.

17. From Tim Westmoreland's remarks at a February 14, 1995, breakfast "roundtable" at the offices of the National Gay and Lesbian Task Force, Washington, D.C.

18. Jean McGuire, interview with author, Cambridge, Massachusetts, 7/25/95.

19. Westmoreland interview.

20. McGuire interview.

Chapter 20: Lesbians Travel the Roads of Feminism Globally

Recommended Reading

Dorf, Julie, and Gloria Careaga Perez. "Discrimination and the Tolerance of Difference: International Lesbian Human Rights," *Women's Rights–Human Rights: International Feminist Perspectives,* Julie Peters and Andrea Wolper, eds. New York: Routledge, 1995.

Rosenbloom, Rachel, ed. *Unspoken Rules: Sexual Orientation and Women's Human Rights.* USA: International Gay and Lesbian Human Rights Commission, 1995.

Sukthankar, Ashwaini, ed. *Facing the Mirror: Lesbian Writing from India.* New Delhi: Penguin Books India, 1999.

Tambiah, Yasmin. "Sexuality and Human Rights," in *From Basic Needs to Basic Rights: Women's Claim to Human Rights,* Margaret A. Schuler, ed. Washington, D.C.: The Institute for Women, Law and Development, 1995.

Wilson, Ara. "Lesbian Visibility and Sexual Rights at Beijing." *Signs: Journal of Women in Culture and Society* (University of Chicago Press) 22, no. 1 (autumn 1996).

22. FACING DISCRIMINATION, ORGANIZING FOR FREEDOM: THE TRANS-GENDER COMMUNITY

1. This session was tape-recorded by HMR Duplications, 18 Gregory Place, Oakland, CA 94619, tel. 510-482-8732. From the NGLTF, 10th Annual Creating Change Conference #231, session: "Sexual Orientation Subset of Gender."

2. Diana Cicotello "Why Is S/HE Doing This to Us?: An Employer's Handbook" and "What is S/HE Doing?: An Informational Booklet for Co-Workers." Both are reprinted with permission in International Conferences on Transgender Law and Employment Policy, *Proceedings I and II*. Cicotello may be contacted at E-mail dainna@aol.com.

3. The Transgender Law Conference is the International Conference on Transgender Law and Employment Policy, Inc., or ICTLEP, at P.O. Box 1010, Cooperstown, NY 13226. Executive Director Sharon Stuart, E-mail ictlephdq@aol.com. Although now in stasis, for a review of much of ICTLEP's work and for a free downloading of an index to its five volumes of *Proceedings*, go to www.abmall.com/ictlep.

4. Mary Coombs, "Transgenderism and Sexual Orientation: More Than a Marriage of Convenience," *National Journal of Sexual Orientation Law*, 3, no. 1 (1998), found at http://sunsite.unc.edu/gaylaw/issue5/coombs.html.

5. Transgender Special Outreach Network of Parents, Family and Friends of Lesbians and Gays (PFLAG), "Our Trans Children." PFLAG may be contacted at E-mail communications@pflag.org.

6. Evelyn Just, *Mom, I Need to Be a Girl* (ISBN: 0-9663272-09) (Imperial Beach, Calif.: Walter Trook Publishing, 1998). Evelyn Just may be contacted at E-mail justevelyn@earthlink.net.

7. Mary Boenke, ed., *Trans Forming Families: Real Stories About Transgendered Loved Ones* (ISBN: 0-9663272-1-7), (Imperial Beach, Calif.: Walter Trook Publishing, 1998). Boenke may be contacted at E-mail MaryBoenke@aol.com.

8. The report on prison conditions for transgenders is in ICTLEP, *Proceedings II*. The "Policy for the Imprisoned Transgendered" states:

1. Segregation in the interest of an inmate's safety and dignity shall not deprive any inmate from the rights, privileges, and facilities afforded to other general population inmates.
2. Access to counseling shall be allowed all transgendered inmates and shall include peer support group participation by those from inside the institution and those from the outside where possible. Counseling professionals should be qualified with respect to the current in gender science.
3. Transgendered inmates shall be allowed to initiate or to continue hormone therapy, electrolysis, and other transgender treatment modalities as prescribed by the involved professionals.
4. The transgendered inmate shall have access to clothing, personal items, and cosmetics that are appropriate to the gender presentation of that inmate and appropriate within the institutional setting.
5. Special care shall be taken not to make a spectacle of transgendered inmates to the amusement of others, or to deny or to deprive transgendered inmates of their dignity.
6. A process shall be established to afford a hearing of grievances to the above policy items and appropriate resolution shall be made.

9. The Imperial Court system is the best known of these groups. Originating in San Francisco in 1965, it was intended mainly for "camp" fun. From that beginning came the camp titles and coronation. The Court system raises and contributes tens of thousands of dollars each year to local community services. The International Imperial Court and links to its individual service organizations is at www.impcourt.org.

10. Minnesota Statutes 1992, section 363.01, was amended to add subdivision 45 to read as follows: "'Sexual orientation' means having or being perceived as having an emotional, physical, or sexual attachment to another person without regard to the sex of that person or having or being perceived as having an orientation for such an attachment, or having or being perceived as having a self-image or identity not traditionally associated with one's biological maleness or femaleness. 'Sexual orientation' does not include a physical or sexual attachment to children by an adult."

11. Tri-Ess is the Society for the Second Self, 8880 Bellaire B2 #104, Houston, TX 77036, E-mail jeftris@aol.com.

12. International Foundation for Gender Education, P.O. Box 540229, Waltham, MA 02454-0229, tel. 781-899-2212. Web address www.ifge.org.

13. Renaissance Transgender Association, Inc., 987 Old Eagle School Road #719, Wayne, PA 19087. Web address www.ren.org.

14. AEGIS, P.O. Box 33724, Decatur, GA 30033-0724. Web address www.gender.org/aegis.

15. JoAnna McNamara, "Employment Discrimination and the Transsexual," appendix E, in ICTLEP, *Proceedings IV.*

16. *Holloway v. Arthur Anderson Company,* 566 F2d 659 (9th Cir. 1977).

17. *Sommers v. Budget Marketing, Inc.,* 667 F2d 748 (8th Cir. 1982).

18. *Ulane v. Eastern Airlines, Inc.,* 742 F2d 1081 (7th Cir. 1984).

19. Sister Mary Elizabeth, SSE, *Legal Aspects of Transsexualism* (ISBN: 0-9625976-0-0) (International Foundation for Gender Education, 1990). Sister Mary may be contacted at E-mail mary.elizabeth@aegis.com.

20. As an example, after three years of lobbying, I saw the Houston, Texas, Code of Ordinances, Section 28-42.4, be legislatively repealed on August 12, 1980. The ordinance prohibited a person from appearing in public dressed with the intent to disguise his or her sex as that of the opposite sex. During those three years of lobbying and being subject daily to arrest, my spouse had the additional burden of having to come home from her job not knowing if I had been arrested that day.

21. Sharon Stuart, "The International Bill of Gender Rights" (ICTLEP). The JoAnn Roberts document can be found on-line at www.3dcom.com/pw/bgr.html.

22. FTM International, Inc., 1360 Mission Street, Ste. 200, San Francisco, CA 94103. Web site http://www.ftm-intl.org, E-mail TSTGMen@aol.com, tel. 415-553-5987.

23. The National Center for Lesbian Rights and ICTLEP published a joint statement against the continuation of the gender dysphoria diagnosis of the *DSM.* For the text, go to www.abmall.com/ictlep or ICTLEP, *Proceedings V* (1997): A1–2.

24. The American Boyz, Inc., 212A S. Bridge Street, PMB 131, Elkton, MD, 21921. Web site www.netgsi.com/~listwrangler, E-mail transman@netgsi.com.

25. See note 10.

26. The National Gay and Lesbian Task Force has a Web site at www.ngltf.org. For a photo of that historic gathering, send me an E-mail at prfrye@aol.com.

27. The National Lesbian and Gay Law Association sponsors the annual Lavender Law Conference and has a Web site at www.nlgla.org.

28. It's Time America can be contacted through its national director, Jessica Xavier, at thexgrrrl@aol.com.

29. Transgendered Officers Protect and Serve can be found through its founder, Tonye Barretto-Neto, at tbhawk@aol.com.

30. Cheryl Chase is the executive director of the Intersex Society of North America at www.isna.org.

31. See note 5.

32. The Sexual Orientation and Gender Identification Legal Issues Section of the State Bar of Texas can be found at www.texasbar.com.

33. Elvia R. Arriola, "The Penalties for Puppy Love: Institutionalized Violence Against Lesbian, Gay, Bisexual and Transgendered Youth," *Journal of Gender, Race and Justice* (University of Iowa College of Law) 1, no. 2 (1998).

34. See note 4.

23. ORGANIZATIONAL TALES: INTERPRETING THE NGLTF STORY

1. I would like to acknowledge Ruth Eisenberg, Nan Hunter, and Jim Oleson for helpful readings of an earlier draft of this essay. Jason Gagnon provided inestimable research assistance by organizing and sorting through my own extensive files on NGLTF. A grant from the Schlesinger Library of Radcliffe College allowed me to spend time examining the papers of Charlotte Bunch. Finally, to all the staff and board members of NGLTF, past and present, with whom I have worked, I can only express the deepest thanks for making my time with the Task Force intensely passionate, if not always pleasurable!

2. The social science literature on organizations is vast. For a recent discussion, see S. Andrews, C. Basler, and X. Collier, "Organizational Structures, Cultures, and Identities: Overlaps and Divergences," *Research in the Sociology of Organizations* 16 (1999): 213–35. For a recent analysis of the gay and lesbian movement, see Mary Bernstein, "Celebration and Suppression: The Strategic Uses of Identity by the Lesbian and Gay Movement," *American Journal of Sociology* 103 (1997): 531–65. Nancy E. Stoller has published an insightful comparative study of AIDS organizations, with particular attention to how social identity shapes the culture of an organization, and how organizational culture, in turn, shapes the mission, goals, and day-to-day practices of a group. See *Lessons from the Damned: Queers, Whores, and Junkies Respond to AIDS* (New York: Routledge, 1998).

3. The information for this history of the Task Force comes less from research in the traditional sense than from direct participation, with the implications this participation had for observation and for access to documents. In particular, I was a board member of NGLTF from November 1988 to October 1993, and a staff member from June 1995 to May 1997. In addition, to aid in strategic planning for the organization, I spent a week in the spring of 1989 combing through NGLTF's office files to write a brief history. Later, in October 1992, I examined the papers of Charlotte Bunch, who served on NGTF's board in the 1970s; her papers are at the Schlesinger Library of Radcliffe College. Aspects of the Task Force's history are touched upon in many of the chapters in this volume, as well as in the following books: Howard Brown, *Familiar Faces, Hidden Lives: The Story of Homosexual Men in America Today* (New York: Harcourt Brace Jovanovich, 1976); Toby Marotta, *The Politics of Homosexuality* (Boston: Houghton Mifflin, 1981); Eric Marcus, *Making History: The Struggle for Gay and Lesbian Equal Rights, 1945–1990, an Oral History* (New York: HarperCollins, 1992); Martin Duberman, *Cures: A Gay Man's Odyssey* (New York: Dutton, 1991) and *Midlife Queer: Autobiography of a Decade* (New York: Scribner, 1996); Urvashi Vaid, *Virtual Equality: The Mainstreaming of Gay and Lesbian Liberation* (New York: Doubleday Anchor, 1995); John-Manuel Andriote, *Victory Deferred: How AIDS Changed Gay Life in America* (Chicago: University of Chicago Press, 1999); and Dudley Clendinen and Adam Nagourney, *Out for Good: The Struggle to Build a Gay Rights*

Movement in America (New York: Simon and Schuster, 1999). Of these, Vaid and Clendinen/Nagourney provided the most sustained discussions. Finally, for researchers interested in pursuing in depth the history of NGLTF, the organization's papers have been deposited in the Human Sexuality Collection at Cornell University.

4. For Brown's coming out, see *New York Times,* 10/3/73, 1.

5. Voeller wrote an account of the founding of the National Gay Task Force and his experience as executive director. See Bruce Voeller, "My Days on the Task Force," *Christopher Street,* 10/79, 55–65.

6. See the interview with O'Leary in Marcus, *Making History,*. 261–73.

7. See the interview with Brydon in Marcus, *Making History,* 305–13.

8. For the work of the antiviolence project, see Gregory M. Herek and Kevin T. Berrill, eds., *Hate Crimes: Confronting Violence Against Lesbians and Gay Men* (Newbury Park, Calif.: Sage Publications, 1992).

9. For a discussion of Vaid's years at NGLTF, as well as analysis of the movement's politics in this period, see Vaid, *Virtual Equality.*

JOHN-MANUEL ANDRIOTE is the author of *Victory Deferred: How AIDS Changed Gay Life in America* (University of Chicago Press, 1999). His articles have appeared in a variety of publications ranging from *The Advocate* to *The Washington Post*. A freelance writer and speaker, Andriote holds a master's degree in journalism from Northwestern University and lives in Washington, D.C.

CHARLOTTE BUNCH is the founder and executive director of the Center for Women's Global Leadership at Douglass College, Rutgers University. An activist, author, and organizer for three decades, she was a founder of Washington, D.C., Women's Liberation, The Furies Collective, and *Quest: A Feminist Quarterly*. She served on the Board of Directors of the National Gay and Lesbian Task Force from 1974 to 1982. Bunch was the first open lesbian inducted into the National Women's Hall of Fame, 1996. She has edited seven anthologies and authored two books: *Passionate Politics: Feminist Theory in Action* (1987) and *Demanding Accountability: The Global Campaign and Vienna Tribunal for Women's Human Rights* (1994).

THOMAS J. BURROWS served as special assistant to NGTF co-executive director Lucia Valeska from 1979 until 1981. He represented NGTF at the White House Conference on Families and the First Amendment Congress. He was liaison to the gay and lesbian community for the Manhattan Borough President from 1981 to 1985 and was a member of the original steering committee that established the NYC Lesbian and Gay Community Services Center. After law school, he joined the New York City Law Department, Family Court Division. He lives in West Hollywood with his partner of twenty years, Randy Gardull, and is a juvenile court referee in the Los Angeles County Superior Court.

DAVID L. CHAMBERS became a certified, self-avowed homosexual less than a decade ago, after thirty years in a suffocatingly stuffy closet. He is a professor of law at the University of Michigan, where he teaches family law. In the last decade, he has written a good deal about the legal consequences of marriage and the legal position of same-sex couples. He is a past president of the Society of American Law Teachers and a current member of the Executive Committee of the Association of American Law Schools.

CATHY J. COHEN is an associate professor of political science and African and African-American Studies at Yale University. She also serves as the codirector with Rogers Smith of the Center for the Study of Race, Inequality, and Politics at Yale. Cohen is the author of *The Boundaries of Blackness: AIDS and the Breakdown of Black Politics* (University of Chicago Press, 1999) and coeditor with Kathleen Jones and Joan Tronto of *Women Transforming Politics: An Alternative Reader* (NYU, 1997).

JOHN D'EMILIO teaches gay and lesbian studies and history at the University of Illinois at Chicago. He is the author of *Sexual Politics, Sexual Communities: The Making of a Homosexual Minority in the United States, 1940–1970* (2nd ed., 1998); *Making Trouble: Essays on Gay History, Politics, and the University* (1992); and, with Estelle Freedman, *Intimate Matters: A History of Sexuality in America* (2nd ed., 1997). He is currently writing a biography of Bayard Rustin, an American pacifist and civil rights leader. From 1995 to 1997, D'Emilio served as the founding director of the Policy Institute of the National Gay and Lesbian Task Force.

CHAI R. FELDBLUM is a professor of law and director of the Federal Legislation Clinic at Georgetown University Law Center in Washington, D.C. At the clinic, she created the term *legislative lawyer* to describe a lawyer who combines an understanding of law and politics to draft and negotiate legislation. She has been actively involved in federal legislative issues affecting the GLBT community since 1990, including challenging the military's ban on service by gay men, lesbians, and bisexuals, opposing antigay and anti-AIDS amendments, supporting hate crimes legislation, and serving as the lead drafter of the Employment Non-Discrimination Act. She serves as a legislative consultant to the National Gay and Lesbian Task Force in Washington, D.C.

BARNEY FRANK is now serving his tenth term as a member of the House of Representatives for Massachusetts. He previously taught at Harvard, Boston University, and the University of Massachusetts and served in state and local government. In 1972, as a member of the Massachusetts House of Representatives, he introduced gay rights legislation for the first time in the history of Massachusetts. In 1987, he became the first member of Congress to voluntarily acknowledge that he was gay. In 1992, he published a book on the role of the Democratic Party, entitled *Speaking Frankly*.

PHYLLIS RANDOLPH FRYE spearheaded a successful effort to overturn the Houston, Texas, cross-dressing law. In 1979, 1981, 1983, and 1985 she was elected, as an out transgender delegate, to the Texas Democratic Party Convention and was also instrumental in persuading the party to adopt a gay rights plank in 1983. She also served, as an out transgender woman, as an elected director and later a vice president of the Houston League of Women Voters. In 1998 she was also appointed by the State Bar president to the Committee for Legal Matters Concerning the Indigent in Criminal Matters. In 1999, she was honored with the highest award given by the transgender community to one of its own—the Virginia Prince Lifetime Contribution Award from the International Foundation for Gender Education. She now practices law part-time and teaches consumer rights at the Thurgood Marshall School of Law. On the Internet, she is known as the Phyllabuster. Her Web address is http://members.aol.com/prfrye.

CLAUDIA HINOJOSA was cofounder in 1978 of the Grupo Lambda, one of the first visible lesbian/gay groups in Mexico City and in Latin America. She was one of the first public voices of the lesbian feminist movement in Mexico. Her early activism led her to many years of journalism and independent scholarship. She is currently a consultant from Mexico with the Center for Women's Global Leadership at Rutgers University on a project on the politics of language and translation in cross-cultural exchanges and on organizing for women's human rights. She is also a closet musician and the mother of one son.

LEONARD P. HIRSCH is a graduate of Pomona College and received his Ph.D. in political science from Northwestern University. He is international liaison at the Smithsonian Institution. He has been president of Federal GLOBE (Gay, Lesbian, Bisexual Employees of the Federal Government), a not-for-profit educational and support group for federal employees. Hirsch is head of the Smithsonian Institution Lesbian and Gay Issues Committee and is active in the Lesbian and Gay Caucus of the American Political Science Association. He is past president of the Network of Gay and Lesbian Alumni/ae Associations.

FRANKLIN E. KAMENY founded the local gay movement in Washington, D.C., in 1961, and with it created gay activism and militancy nationally. He initiated picketing and public demonstrating by gays in 1965; coined the slogan "Gay Is Good" in 1968; and has worked extensively for some forty years in the area of government versus gays. He initiated in 1963 and with others pursued efforts that succeeded in 1973 in reversing the American Psychiatric Association's sickness theory of homosexuality. In 1971 he was the first openly gay person to run for federal public office (for Congress from D.C.) and the second openly gay person to run for any political office anywhere. In 1975, he became the first openly gay appointee to D.C. government (Human Rights Commissioner). He remains active in local D.C. gay-related politics and functions as an informal gay movement "walking history book."

N'TANYA LEE is a coordinator of PACE's Lesbian/Gay People of Color Curriculum Project.

ARTHUR S. LEONARD is a professor of law at New York Law School. He edits the monthly newsletter *Lesbian/Gay Law Notes* and also writes for *POZ* magazine and *Lesbian & Gay New York,* a community newspaper. He is a graduate of Cornell University and Harvard Law School. In 1977, he started the organization that is now the Lesbian & Gay Law Association of Greater New York.

TIM McFEELEY, a lawyer, writer, and consultant, was the executive director of the Human Rights Campaign Fund from July 1989 to January 1995. During his tenure McFeeley directed HRCF's efforts in three federal election cycles and several legislative debates, including the debate over the military's policy of excluding gay and lesbian Americans from service. He currently divides his time between Washington, D.C., and Provincetown, Massachusetts.

DON MURPHY, a public-school teacher and member of PACE, is active in the black community and education struggles in New York City.

LISA NORTH is a lesbian mother, elementary-school teacher, and a member of PACE.

JEAN O'LEARY has had national leadership roles in the gay and lesbian community for almost thirty years. She served as executive director of the National Gay Task Force (1975–80) and National Gay Rights Advocates (1981–89). She organized the first meeting of gays in the White House during the Carter presidency, is a member of the Executive Committee of the Democratic National Committee, and with Rob Eichberg was a founder of National Coming Out Day in 1989. She is the owner of TransWorld Imaging, Inc., a computer supply business in southern California, where she lives with her partner, Lisa Phelps, and their daughter, Victoria Phelps.

MARJ PLUMB is a health-care policy consultant who specializes in women's and lesbian/gay health policy. She has served in senior management positions with the Gay and Lesbian Medical Association, the New York City Department of Health, and the National Gay and Lesbian Task Force. She was a founding member of the Washington, D.C.–based Lesbian Health Advocacy Network and was executive director of the San Francisco–based Lyon-Martin Women's Health Services. She is the author of several articles and publications on lesbian health, including a recently published article on the history of the lesbian health advocacy movement in the *Journal of the American Medical Women's Association* (January 1999).

NANCY D. POLIKOFF is professor of law at American University Washington College of Law. Previously, she supervised family law programs at the Women's Legal Defense Fund, and before that she practiced law as part of a feminist law collective. For more than twenty years, she has been writing about and litigating cases involving lesbian and gay families. She was successful counsel in the case that established joint adoption for lesbian and gay couples in the District of Columbia, and in a Maryland case overturning restrictions on a gay, non-custodial father's visitation rights. She has a seventeen-year-old daughter, Lainey.

CRAIG A. RIMMERMAN is professor of political science at Hobart and William Smith Colleges, where he has taught since 1986. He teaches courses in American politics, including the presidency, environmental and urban policy, and gay and lesbian politics. Rimmerman is the author of *Presidency by Plebiscite: The Reagan-Bush Era in Institutional Perspective* (Westview, 1993), *The New Citizenship: Unconventional Politics, Activism and Service* (Westview, 1997), editor of *Gay Rights, Military Wrongs: Political Perspectives on Lesbians and Gays in the Military* (Garland, 1996), coeditor (with Kenneth Wald and Clyde Wilcox) of *The Politics of Gay Rights* (University of Chicago Press, 2000), and is currently writing a book examining the contemporary lesbian and gay movement.

JOE ROLLINS completed his Ph.D. in 1998 at the University of California, Santa Barbara. His research emphasizes public policy and law surrounding AIDS and state funding for the arts. He is currently assistant professor of political science at Queens College, where he teaches courses on American government, politics and sexuality, and art and the First Amendment. His current projects are two: exploring the construction of sexuality in AIDS-related litigation and a public opinion survey of gay/lesbian Middle America.

NADINE SMITH is cochair of the Federation of Statewide LGBT Organizations. She was cochair of the 1993 March on Washington for Lesbian, Gay and Bi Equal Rights and Liberation and is currently the executive director of the statewide advocacy organization Equality Florida. She also serves on the national board for Equal Partners in Faith. She was the campaign manager for Citizens for a Fair Tampa, a successful effort to prevent the repeal of the city's human rights ordinance (which includes sexual orientation) in March 1995. As the first openly lesbian African-American to run for City Council in Tampa, she garnered 42 percent of the vote in the 1991 campaign, building coalitions between lesbians/gays, African-Americans, environmentalists, students, and progressive communities. She has been the youngest member of the Democratic National Committee and served as cochair of the 1992 lesbian/gay caucus.

RICHARD TAFEL is executive director of the Log Cabin Republicans, a grassroots Republican gay and lesbian organization. From 1991 to 1993, Tafel served as a political appointee under Massachusetts governor William Weld, working on issues including medicaid and public health reform. Tafel graduated from the Harvard Divinity School in 1987, earning a master of divinity degree, and was ordained by the American Baptist Church in 1988. He earned his BA in philosophy and speech communications in 1984 from East Strouds-burg University in Pennsylvania.

WILLIAM B. TURNER received his Ph.D. in history from Vanderbilt University and teaches United States history at St. Cloud State University in Minnesota. He has published on lesbian/gay civil rights and immigration policy in the *Journal of Policy History* (spring 1995) and is currently working on a book about lesbian/gay civil rights and federal policy from 1976 to 1996. He served for four and one-half years as the cochair of the Lesbian and Gay Coalition for Justice, Tennessee's LGBT civil rights organization.

JULIET UCELLI is a public-school social worker and a member of PACE.

URVASHI VAID is director of the Policy Institute of the National Gay and Lesbian Task Force, a think tank dedicated to research, policy analysis, strategy development, and coalition building to advance the equality of gay, lesbian, bisexual, and transgendered people. She is author of *Virtual Equality: The Mainstreaming of Gay and Lesbian Liberation,* which received the American Library Association's 1996 Gay Nonfiction Book Award. She served as executive director of the National Gay and Lesbian Task Force from 1989 to 1992, and as the organization's public information director from 1986 to 1989. Vaid is a graduate of Vassar College and Northeastern University School of Law.

DAVID M. WERTHEIMER, M.S.W., M.Div., was executive director of the New York City Gay and Lesbian Anti-Violence Project from 1985 to 1989. He served on the New York State Governor's Task Force on Bias-Related Violence and as a New York City human rights commissioner. He lives in Seattle, Washington, where he is service and systems integration administrator for the King County Department of Community and Human Services. He a member of the adjunct faculty in the Graduate Program in Psychology at Antioch University/Seattle.